OBJECTS IN THE REARVIEW MIRROR

A Social History of Coeducation under the Dome

Deborah A. Dell, ND 1976

monte ceceri

Grateful acknowledgment is made to the following individuals and organizations for permission to reprint previously published material, including photographs and images:

Photography used in cover illustration:
Notre Dame © T. D. Paulius and car mirror © FreeImages.com/orange430
(https://www.freeimages.com/photo/view-outside-1524750)
Artwork and references from *The Observer* (April 13, 2022)
Photographs from September 3 and 5, 1972
(https://www.newspapers.com/clip/100714379/the-south-bend-tribune and
https://www.newspapers.com/clip/100714474/the-south-bend-tribune)
© *South Bend Tribune*—USA TODAY NETWORK (July 11, 2022)
Photograph per PARS International Corp License
Agreement #REF 000102721 from *The Miami Herald* (March 9, 2022)
Artwork and illustrations © Barbara Montgomery O'Connell (December 2, 2021)
"W Is for Women" from *L Is for Leprechaun* © Barbara
Gowan and Jane Pitz (January 6, 2022)
Artwork previously printed in *Notre Dame Magazine* © Jennifer Downey
and © Gary Hovland (November 30, 2021)
Photograph © Ann Patnaude, McDonald Studio (January 27, 2022)
Photography © Edward J. Brower (December 6, 2021)
Award © gankogroup (https://www.vecteezy.com/free-vector/award),
rocks glass © Mona Adel (https://www.vecteezy.com/free-vector/scotch), and
Maraschino cherry © Hemaraj Laten (https://www.vecteezy.com/free-photos)
Diploma © Mary Gober (https://www.freeimages.com/photo/diploma-1240401)
978-1-949512-07-6 (cloth) • 978-1-949512-06-9 (paperback)

Monte Ceceri Publishers
P. O. Box 60623
Savannah, GA 31420
www.montececeri.com

In thanksgiving to Reverend Theodore M. Hesburgh, CSC,
for his vision and commitment to the University of
Notre Dame and its coeducation transformation.

To the esteemed Notre Dame administrators and teachers
who supported this book but passed before its publication:

Emil T. Hofman
Chuck Lennon
Sister John Mariam Jones, SC
Sister Jean Lenz, OSF
Reverend Matthew Miceli, CSC
Reverend "Moose" Mulcahy, CSC
Reverend Thomas Tallarida, CSC
Reverend Edmund Joyce, CSC

And to the Notre Dame daughters and sons who shared
their experiences and insights for this social history.

Contents

Note on Language

Viewpoints and perspectives conveyed in source materials or by contributors are presented as originally created or expressed. Some content in this book may contain attitudes, language, or cultural depictions that are no longer fashionable and may cause offense today.

The author and the publisher are committed to improving diversity and inclusion. Part of the mission of this book is to depict aspects of this social history as they existed and how they have — and have not — changed over the past half-century.

Foreword

The doors of the University of Notre Dame du Lac officially opened to women in the fall of 1972. Some alumni felt coeducation was long overdue; most said it was not yet time. However, in the world of higher education, places like Harvard, Princeton, and Yale were admitting women, and the time was right for Notre Dame to embrace this fundamental shift in the culture of America. Somewhere along the way, the inspiration came to make this change, and I have no doubt it came from the Holy Spirit. Then, once we made the decision, I believe our blessed Mother herself guided us in doing the right things to welcome, to instruct, and to teach women.

Coeducation had a powerful effect on the university and its family, and thank goodness, the presence of women created a more normal, healthier campus. Now I have nothing against men — being one of them — but Notre Dame is better all-around because half of our student body is now women. The university no longer draws on only half of the talent of the human race; we now draw on one hundred percent, resulting in a more academically competitive Notre Dame.

It all began more than a generation ago. The first 365 coeds, who moved into two converted dormitories in the heart of the campus, were a combination of daughters of alumni, transfer students (most from Saint Mary's), and young women who just wanted to be a part of this new tradition. All were bright and eager to begin the journey together. Of this elite group, 125 were freshmen who would experience college and Notre Dame for the very first time.

But no pioneer's journey escapes the struggles of forging a new trail. There were tears and laughter. There were challenges and achievements. Bonds formed that would last a lifetime. I like to think I had a small hand in this because of my advocacy for single-sex dorms. I truly believe women need the time and space to relate to women. Even though the University only modestly improved the dorms prior to their arrival, these women had their own space to grow up together academically, spiritually, and socially. To this day, this experience still differentiates Notre Dame from other universities.

In the end, the members of the class of 1976, who experienced the first four years of coeducation, will be remembered for their place in Notre Dame history. These ladies will always hold a special place in my heart. It is their journey chronicled through the reflections on coeducation in this book. Join them as they reflect on this "maiden voyage" and its impact on their lives.

I add my special blessing to all Notre Dame women:

> May our blessed Mother Mary bless all of you good alumnae with her wonderful child Jesus.

Ever Devotedly in Notre Dame,

Rev. Theodore M. Hesburgh, CSC
President Emeritus
February 7, 2007

Preface

"The key to unlocking the door to our future," the 1972 *Time Passages: Commemorative Yearbook* notes, "opens with a journey into the past."[1] My past — and the pasts of many of my colleagues, mentors, and institutions of which I have been a part — shaped the roads I have traveled. On these journeys, each of us as travelers has left our marks as well. My fellow alumnae and I changed the complexion of the University of Notre Dame du Lac forever. Whether we entered as freshmen or transfer students, we altered the history and journey of this previously all-male stronghold. Framed against the larger social history of the Catholic Church making one of its few gender concessions at this most macho institution, I joined other young, intelligent, primarily Catholic girls (for most of us were still teens) who applied to Notre Dame. Upon acceptance, we became foot soldiers in the fight for female equality in the midst of second wave feminism.

During the social upheaval of the late 1960s and early 1970s, as the Gloria Steinems and Germaine Greers of the world earned book deals and attended fabulous parties in the name of the feminist movement, a group of strong-willed young women in the fall of 1972 sat in hastily converted dorms near South Bend, Indiana, wondering, "Now what?" We soon found ourselves in a challenging atmosphere of heavy academics, relationships, drinking, drugs, sex — and football — that colored our collegiate lives. Not fully aware of it at the time, this experience would steer me in several directions as well as shape significant aspects of my identity.

Years later, after completing two advanced degrees and as my career prospered, something always drew me back to this starting point. Like a car wheel pulling to one side, I knew I wanted to better understand how Notre Dame shaped my post-collegiate life. How did my experience differ from that of the other 364 female trailblazers? What was the significance of this time, individually and collectively, then and now, on our lives? Over the two-decade time span that has encapsulated this project, the words of Meat Loaf (aka Michael Lee Aday, a 1970s musician) continually reverberated in my mind, playing on a loop through a mental radio. In my initial reflections, and as my feelings intensified about the objectification of women in those early years, I first thought "it was long ago, and it was far away." But Meat Loaf's song "Objects in the Rear View Mirror May Appear Closer Than They Are" captures the essence of our Notre Dame lives "being just a highway" and our souls solely the cars.[2]

I am not alone in this conclusion; others have long recognized that—at such formative institutions—we are more passengers than drivers. As Notre Dame professor, historian, and author James O'Rourke has phrased it:

> Young men and women change more between the ages of 18 and 22 than during any other four-year period of their lives. And, since Notre Dame is primarily a residential, undergraduate institution populated with men and women in that age group, whatever success or fulfillment they may eventually find in life must be due in large measure to what they learn, feel, and experience at ND.[3]

So in the fall of 2000, I began to research Notre Dame's coeducation journey. I had just published *ThinkPad: A Different Shade of Blue*, the story of IBM's early notebook brand, and I knew that I wanted to write about another shade of blue—or, rather, blue and gold. I turned to the Notre Dame Alumni Association (NDAA) for help in contacting my female classmates—the only direct route in these years before Facebook, LinkedIn, and other easily navigable social media. After Reverend Matthew Miceli, CSC, vouched for my integrity, and Reverend Theodore M. Hesburgh, CSC, supported the project, the NDAA's Chuck Lennon and Janet Meade provided a computer printout of the names and addresses. Using this information, I sent paper surveys to the 185 female graduates of Notre Dame's class of 1976.

I received eighty-seven responses—not a bad return on an unsolicited survey (see "The Survey" in the appendix). I then interviewed many respondents by phone, and my Notre Dame connections multiplied. Approximately a year later—and a quarter of a century after our 1976 graduation—I attended our 2001 silver reunion to map out my objectives and confirm initial findings for this social history.

This time together not only strengthened the original bonds among friends but also provided an avenue for more research. I conducted interviews and a focus group with faces I recognized and some I didn't, all etched through their own journeys. At the memorial Mass for those deceased, my fellow classmates and I embraced each other and sang "Notre Dame, Our Mother," the alma mater, and the solemnity of the gathering strengthened my conviction that we did, indeed, have a story to tell. At the end of the service, roommates and friends met inside a white tent behind the Morris Inn, the sole hotel on Notre Dame's pastoral campus, where we consumed top-shelf liquor, champagne, and reserve wines—so different from our days as students drinking beer from cans or sampling "purple passion" (wine and hard liquor known by some as "wapatula") served in garbage cans that only sometimes were lined with plastic trash bags. At the reunion, stories flowed as freely as the liquid libations, and we reveled in how we survived Notre Dame and how each of us had navigated the intervening years.

This project expanded because of these interactions (deepening but also prolonging this road trip). Interviewees suggested the inclusion of male as well as female perspectives, a significant departure from my initial approach and in stark contrast to most books about coeducation. As I extended the scope of this social history, I sent electronic surveys to male members of my class, the displaced residents of Badin and Walsh halls, and the female pioneers from the class of 1977. This broader set of reflections enriched my own memories and perspectives.

In the fall of 2001, I assembled the surveys, notes, and interview tapes, and I set myself up in a comfortable efficiency in South Bend's Residence Inn, a short drive to the Notre Dame library and its archives. I stocked my makeshift office with all my favorites—coffee, chocolate, and wine—and I asked the hotel staff to bring me a computer table. I did everything but write. A more pressing history took precedence: I could not avert my gaze from the news coverage of the September 11 attacks and the bombing in Afghanistan that emerged in the aftermath.

Since I wasn't writing, I muted the television and played the recordings of my interviews. Father Hesburgh's words filled the room: He stressed that whenever he faced a major decision, he put his faith in Our Lady, the patroness of Notre Dame. How had I missed that? Of course! I needed help—in whatever form that might take. I turned off the television completely and turned to the Lady of the Dome. An outline for the story started to flow, and my path on this highway (soul traveling speedily as the car) opened wide ahead.

As I passed the mile markers toward my destination now known as *Objects in the Rearview Mirror*, I realized that this book could not and does not represent the view of every graduate, student, or administrator. Over the years, I have collected many personal stories from Notre Dame alums, faculty, and decision-makers as told against the emotional backdrop of this collegiate transformation and from their own perspectives and memories. I also have incorporated parallels to the coeducation experiences of other notable universities such as Yale and Princeton. Woven in between, as side trips on a larger journey, are my own reflections—some that resemble those of others, some that are mine alone. Thus, what has transpired is a multifaceted retrospective, a nonlinear, topical view of coeducation á la Notre Dame, rather than a strict chronology.

As it is wont to do, life happens, and what was supposed to be an excursion turned into a (seemingly endless) trek. I encountered numerous delays, but looking back these unintended breaks were the exact rest stops needed to chart a better course. Through my roles as class president (2005–2016) and as a director on the Notre Dame Alumni Association Board (2008–2011), I gained a more realistic view of the university. I met second-generation daughters (2006–2016) such as Emily Weisbecker Farley, who reinforced that college is, and should be, a time for self-discovery. Emily joined me on the road, and through our partnership, we highlighted the elements that have remained virtually unchanged, those that have changed dramatically, and those still in need of revision.

History again altered my path, though this time in ways more conducive to reflection and writing. During the coronavirus pandemic and following the passing of my parents and brother and my retirement from IBM, I found the time to refocus and committed to completing this book in 2022 — the year of Notre Dame's fiftieth anniversary of coeducation.

Life today bears remarkable similarities and some striking differences with the reflections in the mirrors of our past. With my last looks at these *Objects in the Rearview Mirror*, my reflections — and those of the other contributors to this social history — have helped me to understand how the shadow of the Golden Dome draws people closer to who they once were and, more importantly, to who they became under its golden glow.

Debi Dell, ND 1976
July 2022

Choosing the Destination

University of Notre Dame Golden Dome
Art by Barbara O'Connell (2011)

The history of the University of Notre Dame influenced its transition from a premier Catholic, single-sex institution to a coeducational university. The decision to admit female undergraduates affected not just women but also the male students and all elements of campus life. The first female pioneers, whether first-year or transfer students, brought new perspectives to Notre Dame. While these women shaped the university in both obvious and unsuspecting ways, the university shaped them. As Father Robert Griffin, CSC (1925–1999), wrote in an essay for *Notre Dame Magazine*: "If you want to belong, you have to learn the myth. You have to wrap your heart and mind in it. You have to believe the meanest rocks of the place to tell a story."[1]

In the Rearview

"It is odd how the past lies hidden in the present," so mused author and Notre Dame philosophy professor Ralph McInerny (1929–2010) in one of his Father Dowling mysteries.[1] For some women, the desire to attend the University of Notre Dame emerged from their childhood and early experiences: Some spent time on campus as children of professors, administrators, or alumni. A few lived in the communal world of Vetville, Notre Dame's married student housing in the 1950s and early 1960s. Others just wanted to be part of the changing collegiate landscape.

◇◇◇

My journey to Notre Dame began with my father. After serving in the Korean War, my father graduated with a bachelor's degree in business administration from Loras College in Dubuque, Iowa. He aspired to become a lawyer, and the University of Notre Dame accepted him into its law school in 1958. So off we drove — my parents, my two brothers, and a four-year-old me — to South Bend, Indiana. We spent our first year in a trailer park near the airport, and then we moved to Vetville.

A city within the campus, Vetville emerged when the federal government transferred thirty-nine prisoner-of-war barracks from Weingarten, Missouri, to university property in 1946. The university cleared the site and installed water and sewage at a cost of forty thousand dollars. They subdivided each of the already constructed eighty-foot-long buildings into three rental units. Each of the

Trailer before moving to Vetville (1958)

resulting 117 units had a small sitting area adjacent to an eat-in kitchen, where moms washed dishes (and often babies) in a big ceramic sink below a kitchen

Vetville Community (circa late 1940s)
Photo by Chuck F. Lennon, used with permission[2]

window. A black iron heater warmed the two bedrooms, bath, and storage closet. Residents sometimes shared telephones by drilling holes through adjoining walls.

The brainchild of Theodore M. Hesburgh, CSC, the fifteenth president of Notre Dame, this community addressed the unique demands of married students, many of whom were returning veterans. According to Hesburgh's autobiography, *God, Country, Notre Dame*, these veterans "were the first married students ever to come to Notre Dame in any substantial numbers, and there were no precedents for ministering to their needs. They also had to contend with some formidable practical problems. The worst was housing."[3]

Hesburgh, as Vetville's first chaplain, oversaw the neighborhood's spiritual needs and the day-to-day challenges facing its young families. A village of mostly Catholic families, its population growth of 106 babies in its first year

With Fathers Hesburgh and Ladewski

surprised no one. While the husbands attended classes, the wives generally stayed home, tending to their own children or assisting other wives with theirs. In later years, Hesburgh often expressed delight when children of Vetville returned as students—many having listed Notre Dame as their birthplace on admissions applications.

The administration, aware of the limited incomes of most Vetville residents, offered low-cost or free activities for the community. It hosted family picnics and organized holiday events such as Christmas parties and Easter egg hunts. The adults gathered for Saturday night dances in the village's recreation center. These

Roman Ladewski, CSC

activities fostered lifelong friendships and future Vetville reunions.

Adding to this sense of community and offering much-needed breaks from the daily routine, another Vetville chaplain, Roman Ladewski, CSC, taught the women how to play bridge while their children attended school. Since this game was an inexpensive form of entertainment, the wives capitalized on these lessons and hosted card parties. My parents, not too interested in the community dances, often played bridge or euchre, a favorite Midwest card game, on Saturday nights. Fellow law student David Link and his wife frequently came to our home to play cards. Link later served as dean of Notre Dame Law School, and Dad kept abreast of changes at the school through Link's Christmas letters.

During these Saturday evenings, we kids watched the black-and-white television and stayed up late eating popcorn and drinking root beer Kool-Aid. Neighbors knew when we had company, since the sounds and smells permeated the paper-thin walls.

The next day was always reserved for family, especially since Indiana's blue laws prohibited stores from opening on Sundays. My family went to Mass and enjoyed a traditional pot roast dinner. Before bedtime, we watched *The Ed Sullivan Show, Bonanza,* or *Walt Disney Presents*—with us children acting as the remote control, turning the dial as instructed.

> Reverend David T. Link (1936–2021) earned his BS and JD from Notre Dame in 1958 and 1961, respectively. He became a member of ND's law school faculty in 1970. As its dean from 1975 to 1999, he worked to increase the number of female law students. During one of the longest tenures among American law school deans, Link coined the phrase "a different kind of lawyer"—one who wields the law to better the world. After his wife's death, he entered the Sacred Heart School of Theology and was ordained in 2011 at the age of seventy-one.[4]

Over Monday morning coffee, the wives discussed the bridge games, campus life, children, and articles found in Vetville's community newspaper, the *Vet Gazette* (founded in 1947 as the *Vetville News* and later became *The Villager,* the *Vetville Herald,* and the *Villette*). They looked forward to Hesburgh's "The Word," a weekly column covering topics from birth control to women's participation in intellectual events. In one issue of the paper, he encouraged the Vetville wives to stay abreast of the world around them:

I think that interest stems from a desire to keep from going intellectually stagnant. It's especially easy for you wives to get into a rut soon after you are married, to let the hubby do all the thinking, to merely string along with the opinions he formulates.[5]

Given the Cold War and ever-present threats of communism and nuclear attack, the women also reviewed carbon copies of emergency preparation guidelines, including how to assist in childbirth. They periodically checked the expiration dates on supplies stored in their husbands' military duffel bags, and they communally shared tasks such as picking up children from school, helping those who were pregnant, and sheltering together in the law school basement if a tornado was imminent.

Children in Vetville ranged from infancy through school age. Like many small children who challenged their mothers to keep track of them, my youngest brother, Doug, was quite a handful and always into

mischief. My father, along with other Vetville men, asked the administration to add a community playground to the empty field across the access road. The university provided the land and the equipment—a slide, swings, and a jungle gym—but it required the families to build the safety features. The parents helped to answer that call. Having worked construction in his hometown of Dubuque, my father spearheaded the group that enclosed the site with a wooden fence, complete with a flip

Doug in front of playground (1961)

latch on the gate out of reach of little "Dougs." My mother painted it. After ten years of marriage, she finally got her white picket fence.

With the playground complete, parents no longer worried their children might play in the road. Of course, few residents owned cars, so the risk of injury was low even if (and when) we escaped. Since the playground was behind our unit, my parents kept it neat and secure. My mom often walked across the road to wipe down the slide after little ones left marks from leaky diapers.

The jungle gym became my own "schoolhouse," where I taught prayers and the alphabet to Doug and his playmates, or the "hospital," where I ministered to their cuts and bruises. My pretend vocations reflected the most prevalent occupations for my gender at the time—mother, teacher, nurse. Were I a

With Barbie (1962)

child today where the sky's the limit in role-playing, I would most likely sit on the gym's highest wooden bench pretending to be a judge or even the president.

Beyond the playground, my mother shared special times with my brothers and me. After an Indiana snowfall and when temperatures permitted, she would bundle us into snowsuits, and off we went. Like the ducklings on Saint Mary's Lake, we trailed Mom into the open field past the playground and our building. On knolls topped with evergreens and new powder, we traced her footsteps as she made hearts in the snow. I can still hear her laughter as she chased us in circles or showed us how to make snow angels. We inevitably grew tired, cold, and wet, but we went home immensely happy. On

Doug's birthday

those winter treks, I had an unobstructed view of the landmark Golden Dome shimmering against an atypical brilliant blue winter sky, creating an emotional, everlasting connection with that sight.

In the fall of 1959, I went to kindergarten at Saint Mary's Academy, a part of Saint Mary's College, a women's college located less than a mile from the University of Notre Dame on what was then US 31. Under the watchful eyes of the Sisters of the Holy Cross, CSC, I enjoyed going to school. I particularly loved my first teacher, Sister M. Teresa. Her traditional white cornice reminded me of the halo of an angel. With her help, I excelled in school and childishly expected to stay with her forever. I proudly told anyone who listened that I was a Saint Mary's graduate, albeit only kindergarten.

Unfortunately, my parents could not afford to keep me at Saint Mary's since it charged tuition for grades 1–8 higher than the parochial schools. Instead, they enrolled me in Saint Joseph's Catholic Grade School. I celebrated my First Communion in the school's church after practicing with Necco candies to ensure I would not chew the Host. I still cringe when I look at the commemorative photo remembering how embarrassed I was to be one of the tallest girls in my class.

My shaky self-image improved as academic success bolstered my confidence. This did, however, have a downside. My increased sociability caused me to talk in class, landing me with a once-in-a-lifetime punishment. Sister Angela, my second-grade teacher, required me to print "I will not talk in class" twenty-five times on the chalkboard—not an easy task for a second grader. Staying after school to complete my task made my father late for his own class. After he drove me home, I hid in my bedroom closet until Mom found me just in time for dinner.

This humiliation laid the groundwork for perfect conduct through high school. I knew I needed to behave so my parents could focus on our future. My father left early in the morning each day and returned home late at night as he balanced the demands of school, home, and part-time jobs. While my mother, a licensed cosmetologist, stayed home with my younger brothers, she occasionally cut and styled hair for other Vetville wives. Many evenings, my parents worked together to make ten-cent sandwiches to sell at the law school basement commissary. I did not understand why the ham, turkey, roast beef—even bologna—sandwiches stacked on our off-white Formica table were off-limits; they were so much better than our standard PB&J fare.

My father's ND years coincided with Hesburgh's efforts to make Notre Dame a great Catholic university and to develop its law school from an easygoing men's club into a demanding scholastic legal institution. Dean Joseph O'Meara tightened entrance prerequisites, curriculum requirements, and exams; he set new standards for faculty performance. O'Meara often said, "Every law school needs an S.O.B....and, around here, I'm it."[6]

I saw my father struggle with the challenging law school curriculum as my mother typed his papers late into the night. Despite his determination, my father flunked out after his second term. In the spirit of the Notre Dame family, O'Meara arranged tutors for Dad's most problematic courses and later approved his readmission. In reflection and perhaps some foreshadowing, this was just the first time ND went the "extra mile" for my family.

I now wonder if Hesburgh's awarding honorary diplomas to my mother and the wives of Dad's all-male classmates in 1962 not only acknowledged the women's contributions to their husbands' success but also provided a glimpse into Hesburgh's vision of ND's future.

Dad's parking decal

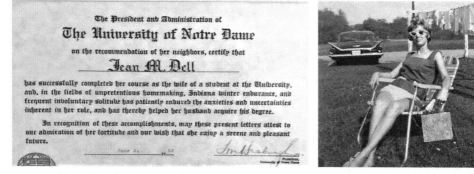

Jean M. Dell's honorary diploma, awarded prior to the move to Florida (1962)

The most powerful memory influencing my feeling about Notre Dame occurred as my father approached his graduation. One fall Saturday in 1961, I watched my parents head to the football stadium with the president of Palm Beach's largest bank, also an ND graduate, and a senior partner from a West Palm Beach, Florida, law firm. These men introduced my parents to a side of Notre Dame we could never have afforded. They described how moving to Florida would provide a path to a better life — and better weather.

An 8 mm home movie recorded us kids waving to the adults as they walked toward the "House that Rockne Built." Though the movie has no audio, my brain overlays the sound of the nation's oldest collegiate marching band playing Notre Dame's fight song, "Victory March." Heard for the first time in front of the Main Building in 1909, the music soon became a favorite for Catholic schools around the country. Given the widespread recognition of the tune, stories abounded about soldiers singing and humming it during World War II and in Vietnamese prison camps, which forbade the singing of our national anthem. One ex-POW reflected that "it was the one song we all knew."[7] Whenever I heard that song wafting across campus, my desire to be a part of the ND tradition grew. I promised myself that I would someday attend a football game wearing a yellow mum corsage like the one my mother wore so proudly that eventful Saturday.

Grandma Ethel visits Vetville

I sometimes find it difficult to believe how vividly I recall memories of my early life within sight of the Golden Dome. The caring atmosphere provided by my parents, neighbors, and the religious leaders at both Notre Dame and Saint Mary's fostered my interest in belonging to this strong Catholic community. These people and places became part of me and influenced my direction and dreams. In time, my desire grew from just attending a football game to becoming a student at Notre Dame.

That Notre Dame was an all-male institution was not within my childhood purview and was never discussed — even by my parents or grandparents. My paternal grandpa was a self-educated man who never finished grade school yet read the classics and talked knowledgeably about law, philosophy, and religion. When I visited him in Iowa, in his wooden shack with its black-bellied wood stove, he puffed on hand-rolled cigarettes or enjoyed his occasional chew. While teaching me to play (and cheat at) cards, he stressed the importance of good grades and going to Notre Dame, but he failed to mention that ND only accepted men. When I later learned of his escapades as a bootlegger and gambler with the likes of Al

Capone, his maniacal focus on education seemed quite a contradiction to his own life.

We took many trips to Dubuque during dad's law school years, but my memories are most vivid about those days spent on Notre Dame's campus. Midway through our stay in Vetville, Hesburgh announced an ambitious construction project to build one of the nation's largest university libraries, along with a score of academic buildings and dormitories. He envisioned the library as the academic heart of Notre Dame. Along with the Main Building, the Basilica of the Sacred Heart, and the Grotto, it is now one of the iconic structures on campus. The Memorial Library (renamed Hesburgh Library in 1987) and its *Word of Life* mural, commonly referred to as *Touchdown Jesus*, are symbols of excellence and the pursuit of truth.

This expansion required razing Vetville, thus ending affordable campus housing for many families. In its sixteen-year run, Vetville housed more than seven hundred families. The late Chuck Lennon, the longtime director of the Notre Dame Alumni Association and with whom I worked as an alumni regional director (from 2008–2011), was the last to move his family into Vetville in 1961. Chuck, then a low-paid baseball coach and new family man, pleaded — and won — his case to live in Vetville, despite the moratorium on adding new residents. Years later, he demonstrated his love for this close-knit community by periodically displaying photos of it at the Notre Dame Eck Visitors Center.

Doug and Dad before the move to Florida (1962)

In June 1962, my family left Vetville the day before contractors demolished our building to make way for the library parking lot. My mother packed our belongings and cleaned the house, leaving the doomed building in better condition than when we arrived. After attaching a U-Haul to the family Buick, my father locked the door for the last time. We piled into the car and headed around the corner toward Notre Dame Avenue. Driving away from campus on that tree-lined street, I leaned over Dad's shoulder and saw the reflection of the statue of Father Sorin, the founder of Notre Dame, and the Golden Dome looming high above. I just knew this would not be the last time that I would see those objects in the rearview mirror.

Studying the Map

As the ancient Chinese philosopher Lao-tzu notes in the *Tao Te Ching*, "A thousand-mile journey/Begins with a single step."[1] The University of Notre Dame's mission of educating young adults began one hundred thirty years before female undergraduates officially took their first steps onto the campus. As students, these women soon discovered the heritage, traditions, and even myths relevant to their experiences as daughters of Notre Dame.

◇◇◇

The Congregation of Holy Cross founded l'Université de Notre Dame du Lac in 1842 and has remained its most prominent influence. A year earlier, Edward Sorin, CSC, a twenty-eight-year-old French Holy Cross priest, arrived in America to teach in a small wilderness school near Vincennes, Indiana. However, he envisioned a college that not only educated Catholic scholars but also prepared Catholic men for life. Sorin persistently promoted this idea to Vincennes' Bishop Célestin Guynemer de la Hailandière. To quiet these constant requests, Hailandière eventually awarded Sorin an abandoned 524-acre mission near South Bend, Indiana. Father Stephen Badin, the first priest ordained in the United States, had purchased this acreage in 1832 and then transferred its ownership to the bishop in 1835. The property, a Native American mission known as Sainte Marie des Lacs, consisted of three shabby log buildings near two lakes.

As a condition of this grant, the bishop challenged Father Sorin to establish a college and orphanage within two years. He and four Holy Cross brothers accepted the challenge. They arrived at the property with few possessions and limited funds. Sorin described their November 1842 arrival to Basil Moreau, CSC, founder of the Holy Cross order:

> [W]e came to Notre Dame, where I write you these lines. Everything was frozen, yet it all appeared beautiful. The lake particularly, with its mantle of snow, resplendently white, was

to us a symbol of the stainless purity of Our Lady....Like little children, in spite of the cold, we ran from one end to the other perfectly enchanted by the beauty of our new home.[2]

Other religious brothers arrived in February 1843 in time to complete a larger, sturdier log chapel in which to worship and live. On March 19, 1843, the feast of Saint Joseph, this first Notre Dame "family" celebrated Mass in this building, still used today for special occasions.

The four brothers accompanying Sorin were Irish, providing one explanation for Notre Dame's christening as the home of the "Fighting Irish" — as these men fought the severe Indiana environment. The preponderance of ND students, faculty, and administration of Irish-Catholic descent also supported this moniker. According to Reverend Charles M. Carey, CSC, "it began as a slur — a term of opprobrium. But we took it up and made it a badge of honor — a symbol of fidelity and courage to everyone who suffers from discrimination; to everyone who has an uphill fight for the elemental decencies, and the basic Christian principles woven into the texture of our nation."[4]

Additional reinforcements, including four sisters, came in July 1843.[3] Adhering to acceptable women's roles and becoming the bedrock of day-to-day living, the sisters cooked, washed, sewed, and nurtured both the students and resident orphans. They performed manual labor and milked dairy cows to support the school financially. The sisters lived in the chapel's loft among its bugs and cobwebs. Sorin viewed these accommodations as comfortable — perhaps foreshadowing hall life and its ever-present roaches one hundred and thirty years later.

On January 15, 1844, the Indiana state legislature granted the school a university charter, fulfilling the Bishop of Vincennes' original commission. To recognize his accomplishment and expand the school, Sorin received a grant of an additional 375 acres in 1846. Initially, Notre Dame included training for religious novitiates, preparatory and grade schools, and a manual labor program. During its first decade, it primarily provided a liberal arts education.

To grow its student population, the university advertised in the *South Bend Free Press*, citing a beautiful location accessible from several major cities via stagecoach. These notices described its buildings, including a gymnasium, and emphasized its on-site sisters and physicians. They also avowed Notre Dame's intentions to guard student morals by enforcing Catholic doctrine while allowing non-Catholic students to pursue their religious convictions without obstruction — principles unchanged today.

Despite the school's proximity to South Bend, Sorin wanted Notre Dame recognized as a standalone entity on America's map. He secured a postal station in January 1851 and served as its first postmaster. The post office provided income while the postal riders increased national awareness of the school. Through revenues from its postal service, dairy, and farm, the university broadened its programming, increased its student base, and acquired more land.

In addition to its growing revenue stream, the administration welcomed gifts, including a bell for the church. Such donations not only supported the university but also helped others. In 1855, Sorin was able to give fifty acres and five thousand dollars to the Holy Cross Sisters to establish Saint Mary's Academy (later Saint Mary's College).[5] As part of this grant, Sorin stipulated that the sisters must continue as nurses and caretakers for ND's all-male population, including the "minims," grade-school-age boarders.[6]

With the ever-increasing number of graduates, by 1868 Auguste Lemonnier, CSC, then-vice president of the university, recognized the need for a formal alumni organization. Neal Gillespie, CSC, the school's first graduate, became its first elected president. The 1872–1873 Notre Dame Alumni Association catalog defined its members as the president and the vice president of the university, all graduates, all who held honorary Notre Dame degrees, and all professors. According to its constitution and bylaws, the organization was "to preserve and strengthen the common tie that binds us to each other and our Alma Mater, by means of annual reunions and literary correspondence."[8] In its first thirty-five years, Notre Dame's alumni base expanded into almost every state, with Illinois and Indiana contributing the greatest numbers.

> Notre Dame expanded its curriculum to include mathematics (1859), physics and geology (1863), and science (1865). In 1869, it added the first Catholic law school in America. It also became the first Catholic American university with schools of engineering (1873) and architecture (1898). Its Manual Labor School, the first Catholic trade school in the United States, altered its training in 1890 so that its participants, mostly orphans, were on a "forty-four-hour week," working in a variety of trades as apprentices and spending four hours a day as students. Notre Dame also created a graduate program in 1918 and its College of Business Administration in 1921.[7]

The university worked to ensure consistent messaging with its many factions and broadened its communications efforts. The *Scholastic Year*, launched in September 1867, moved from a weekly chronicle of events to a monthly publication of articles. Now known as *Scholastic*, it is ND's oldest continuous collegiate publication. For more than a century, the university also published the religious-themed *Ave Maria* magazine to a national readership. While alumni received various publications and reports through the years, today's quarterly *Notre Dame Magazine* provides news about specific classes and colleges to the extended ND community.

In addition to an alumni association and a broad set of communication vehicles, Lemonnier, the little-known fourth Notre Dame president (1872–1874), implemented a "circulating library." Established in 1874, this repository housed thousands of books, manuscripts, and memoirs documenting Catholic history in America. Lemonnier also initiated the Notre Dame Archives, cited as one of the nation's foremost archival repositories for the study of American Catholicism. Now housed in the university's library that sits on the land previously occupied by Vetville, its content has been instrumental in researching this social history.

Many books documented the significant challenges that Notre Dame faced beyond funding and the often-brutal Indiana weather. On April 23, 1879, a fire, the eighth in the school's history, destroyed the Main Building and several other structures. Sorin, then sixty-five, reflected:

> The fire was my fault. I came here as a young man and founded a university which I named after the Mother of God. Now she had to burn it to the ground to show me that I dreamed too small a dream. Tomorrow we will begin again and build it bigger, and when it is built, we will put a gold dome on top with a golden statue of the Mother of God so that everyone who comes this way will know to whom we owe whatever great future this place has.[9]

It took only four months to construct the present Main Building, a brick edifice with a traditional French entrance on the second level and a rotunda rising through five floors to a gilded dome. Its topper, however, did not arrive for another three years. In October 1882, Saint Mary's College donated a statue commemorating the Immaculate Conception, a replica of one erected by Pius IX in Rome's Piazza di Spagna, for the top of the Main Building.

This gift from the university's female collegiate counterpart became the heart of the campus, which is laid out in a cross. The statue of Mary atop the Golden Dome stands at the foot of the cross. The South Quad forms the horizontal bar, and the

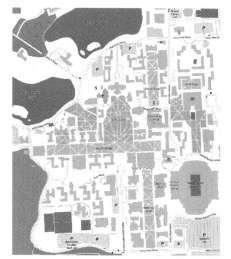

Campus layout (2016)
OpenSourceMaps, CC BY-SA 2.0

God Quad from the Administration Building to the campus entrance forms its vertical bar. Despite an ever-increasing number of buildings, the Golden Dome remains the most recognized symbol of Notre Dame. It represents not only ND's religious mission but also its corporate and brand identity.

The university became quite adept at addressing change. It was one of the first US colleges to install electric lighting in 1855. While most students slept in open dormitories and studied in public areas, a small number slept in designated sleeping rooms in the Main Building. When officials realized these students performed better academically, they built a residence hall. A *Catholic World* statement marked this decision as the beginning of the fusion of tradition and the demands of the present.[10] During his May 27, 1888, golden jubilee as a priest, Sorin blessed the cornerstone of Notre Dame's first and oldest dormitory, Sorin Hall. The building contained the law school lecture hall, a chapel, and fifty small, single rooms designed to encourage study and discourage after-hours visitation. Eventually, though, no room proved too small to share.

In 1896, Notre Dame completed a replica of the grotto at Lourdes near Sorin Hall and the Main Building. This sanctuary offered a pastoral refuge for meditation and prayer. Visitors lit candles for deceased relatives and classmates, special intentions, and (most likely) athletic and scholastic success. A frequently visited landmark, Notre Dame's Grotto of Our Lady of Lourdes links memories of the past, moments in the present, and dreams for the future.

The nineteenth-century administration not only established beautiful surroundings and a strong curriculum, it also fostered many important elements of student life and culture that still shape Notre Dame student experiences. Over the years, administrators consciously and purposefully organized free-time activities for its growing student body. In 1846, the Notre Dame community heard its first band play, often from rafts floating on Saint Mary's Lake. After performing at the November 11, 1849, dedication of the new church, the band established its place as the soul of campus activities and soon began playing at student events, including the emerging sport of football. In September 1876, Notre Dame students watched the school's first football match. Ben Heeb of Dubuque, Iowa, and Jim Hagerty of Saint Louis, Missouri, led forty-two men on two intramural teams. In response to the growing national interest in collegiate football, Notre Dame established its first official team in 1887. The university soon had to deal with its student body's sometimes unmanageable postgame behavior.

The constant presence of the priests and brothers, coupled with such informal reprimands as dunkings in the lakes, dampened overenthusiastic behaviors. Residential life guidelines prohibited fraternities and hazing new undergraduates. Senior students smoked with parental permission, but the university discouraged the drinking of alcohol in any form. The local paper advertised the prosecution of anyone found guilty of selling or giving liquor to students. These publications also warned local females to cease prowling the campus or risk seeing their names in print. A "black book" from the late 1870s contained handwritten records of students expelled for such infractions as drinking, leaving campus without permission, or skipping class: "J. L. Breunau was a good sort of a poor fellow, but when he got a chance, he soaked himself in whiskey."[11]

After the turn of the century, Notre Dame expanded its football program, which proved more popular than baseball. From 1918 through 1931, under the direction of Knute Rockne, Notre Dame acquired a reputation as America's most successful football team. Rockne's winning percentage over thirteen seasons was .881, a record that stands even today as one of the highest among major college coaches who coached at least ten years. *New York Post* and *New York Daily News* sportswriter Frank Wallace (ND 1923) wrote about Rockne's success with the "Fighting Irish," a name previously known only to vociferous fans. In 1927, Notre Dame's athletic teams formally adopted the moniker after University President Matthew Walsh, CSC, gave his blessing to its use.

Despite the Great Depression, a growing nationwide admiration for Rockne and his teams provided new revenue streams. Given its growing athletic accomplishments and press coverage, the university saw the need to replace the bleachers of Cartier Field with a stadium. During halftime at the stadium's dedication game in 1930, the alma mater, "Notre Dame, Our Mother" debuted. Composed by band director Joseph Casasanta (ND 1923), with lyrics by University President Charles O'Donnell, CSC (ND 1906), the song also played at the 1931 premiere of Universal Pictures' *The Spirit of Notre Dame* at South Bend's Palace Theatre. Regrettably, Rockne never saw the film as he died in a plane crash on March 31, 1931, while on his way to Hollywood to consult on the picture.

Biographies and testimonials to Rockne's character and football genius guaranteed his immortality as the most famous American college football coach. The 1940 film *Knute Rockne, All American*, with Ronald Reagan playing the ill-fated football star George Gipp, perpetuates Rockne's legacy. Even today, incoming students learn about Rockne through showings of the film at freshman orientation, and they experience his legacy inside the Rockne Gymnasium and ND Stadium.

During this time, the University of Notre Dame du Lac represented more than a male bastion only focused on football and athletic success. Between 1900 and 1933, Notre Dame added fifteen buildings to accommodate its tripling student population and faculty. This dramatic growth fueled the administration's desire for a new, more relevant coat of arms. Until 1931, the school's coat of arms was almost indistinguishable from that of the Congregation of the Holy Cross. The resulting design symbolized Notre Dame du Lac as an institution of learning and highlighted its ties to the Congregation of Holy Cross and its two lakes. Incorporating the recognizable blue and gold colors of Our Lady — Notre Dame — its Latin motto translates into "Life, Sweetness, Hope."

The update to Notre Dame's coat of arms heralded a new era in which the university focused on becoming an academic powerhouse under the leadership of Reverend Theodore M. Hesburgh, CSC. Prior to becoming Notre Dame's president, Father Hesburgh spent several years within the Notre Dame community. He initially enrolled in Holy Cross Seminary in the fall of 1934. His teachers soon sent the young seminarian to the Pontifical Gregorian University in Rome, Italy, where he graduated with a bachelor's degree in philosophy in 1940. After the outbreak of World War II, Hesburgh returned to the United States and studied theology at Holy Cross College. He became a Congregation of Holy Cross priest (*Congregatio a Sancta Cruce* in Latin, abbreviated as CSC) in June 1943. He joined Notre Dame's faculty as an instructor in the Department of Religion in 1945. In 1948, he rose to head of the Theology Department, followed quickly by his appointment to executive vice president in 1949. After spending three years in this "training" position, Hesburgh succeeded John J. Cavanaugh, CSC, as president and remained in this role until his retirement in 1987.

Theodore Martin Hesburgh, CSC (1917–2015), was Notre Dame's most well-known president. In addition to his roles as an educator and author, Father Ted was a social activist involved with many American civic and governmental commissions, papal assignments, and international humanitarian projects. Father Ted received numerous honors and service awards, most notably the US Presidential Medal of Freedom and the Congressional Gold Medal in 1964 and 2000, respectively. Until his death, he held the world's record for the individual with the most honorary degrees, receiving more than one hundred fifty in his lifetime.[12]

Hesburgh envisioned transforming Notre Dame into a first-rate undergraduate college, upgrading its graduate school, and creating an ideal: a catholic (i.e., wide-reaching) Catholic university.[13] Reflecting this goal, when asked by a photographer to pose hiking a football, the thirty-five-year-old new president said no. He wanted any spotlights focused on Notre Dame to illuminate more than just football.

Making Hesburgh's goal a reality required revolutionary changes: more relevant rules and regulations, a predominantly lay board of trustees, higher academic standards, and a diverse student population. Known as Father Ted by the community, he shared the administrative mantle with Edmund P. Joyce, CSC, his chief financial officer. Together they increased the university's resources and its international reputation. They maintained relative calm while maneuvering through army recruiters and Vietnam War protests, the civil rights movement and acceptance of African American athletes, student unrest at peer universities, and the sexual revolution of the 1960s.

Wanting to challenge his students academically, Father Ted advocated increasing research funding and adding well-known scholars to the faculty. The administration enforced stricter rules than most private colleges, including six-day-a-week class schedules, mandatory weekly Mass, and a prohibition against female visitors in the dorms. The university adopted a written honor code in 1964, an action that was not popular among the students or in line with the times, which, as Bob Dylan sang, were already "a-changin.'"[14]

On Hesburgh's recommendation, Notre Dame switched to a board of trustees comprised entirely of laymen in 1967, becoming one of the first Catholic universities governed by a lay board. This decision bothered many alumni who viewed the action as a threat to the school's Catholic nature. Father Ted believed that this action would enable Notre Dame to discover new avenues for growth — such as, in time, enrolling female undergraduates.

◇◇◇

REARVIEW REFLECTION When I first fell in love with Notre Dame as a child, I never anticipated the impact of Vetville's first chaplain on Notre Dame as a whole and on me personally. With the help of Reverend Matthew Miceli, CSC, rector of Cavanaugh Hall and officiant at my 1978 wedding, I interviewed Hesburgh, Joyce, and numerous administrators for this project. Father Ted's graciousness and love for ND was evident every time we met.

Father Ted in his office (2006)

For my first interview, I spent more than an hour with Father Ted — with the Golden Dome of Sacred Heart Basilica and its spire visible through his office's picture window in the Hesburgh Memorial Library. No question was off-limits. At the end of our time together, Hesburgh had a task for me. He wanted me to ask my father about his thoughts on coeducation at Notre Dame. I told Hesburgh that I already knew my father was proud of my acceptance; nonetheless, he asked me to humor him and pose the question.

When I called my parents that evening, I gushed about the interview. As the call wound down, I told my dad that Hesburgh wanted me to ask him a question. My father, an appellate court judge, seldom gave his opinion on anything potentially controversial, but I asked the question anyway. After a pause so significant I thought the connection had dropped, my father said he initially believed the admittance of undergraduate women was a huge mistake. Though happy I graduated from ND, for many years he wished the school had remained an all-male institution because he feared the loss of its traditions. However, by 2000, he saw the value and wisdom of the decision. I hung up flabbergasted! Hesburgh knew I needed this alum's perspective before moving forward with this story.

Years later, after our 2006 Reunion Mass, a small group of classmates, including Shelley Muller Simon and I, breakfasted with Hesburgh and Miceli at Sorin's restaurant in the Morris Inn.

> ◇ *Shelley Muller Simon, ND 1976:* "'You'd better hurry...' Father Hesburgh spoke those words when I asked if he would write the foreword for this book on coeducation; it sent a chill down my back. It summed up my feelings at the conclusion of our 2006 reunion weekend where Father Ted, the hero of our generation, had concelebrated our class Mass. He filled his homily with his poignant memories of the special class of men and women he created by taking a bold stand for the University of Notre Dame du Lac — embarking on coeducation."

Sitting next to Father Ted, it was as if no time had passed since our October 2000 discussion. He again stressed that, no matter how long it took, I should not abandon this book. He reminded me, when things got tough and the words did not flow, not only to ask Our Lady for help but also to pray (much like I had done in 2001, sitting in a South Bend hotel attempting to work on this book during the events of September 11):

> Come, Holy Spirit, fill the hearts of your faithful
> And kindle in them the fire of your love
> Send forth your Spirit and they shall be created
> And You shall renew the face of the earth

Neither my classmates nor I had traveled this road alone.

Paving the Way

Most public universities and some private colleges shed their all-male approach and embraced the admission of women long before the University of Notre Dame. In fact, by the mid-nineteenth century, women and society at large had chipped away at the notion of colleges educating only males — as well as at laws that specifically excluded women from higher education and most professions. Some of these reforms began with first wave feminism, spearheaded by Lucretia Mott, Sojourner Truth, Susan B. Anthony, Elizabeth Cady Stanton, and Alice Paul. The twentieth century brought changes as well. While some women had always worked outside the home, more did so during the World Wars — in larger numbers and across racial and socioeconomic classes. Second wave feminists such as Simone de Beauvoir, Betty Friedan, and Gloria Steinem carried the torch forward during the postwar era as a new hope emerged. ("After all," as Steinem wrote in her 2015 memoir, *My Life on the Road*, "hope is a form of planning."[1]) By the 1970s, many young women had learned that their fearless grandmothers and mothers never returned to their prewar subservient domestic roles, and thanks to such role models and the expansion of coeducation, women had more college options than prior generations. Such societal shifts paved the way for females to seek admission as undergraduates at Notre Dame.

◇◇◇

The acceptance of coeducation is closely tied to the advancement of women's rights and opportunities in American society. Before 1848, laws excluded women from higher education and most professions. The United States, following the British common law principle of coverture, declared that in marriage "husband and wife are one... [and] the one is the husband."[2] When a woman married, she lost control over her finances, and her wages went directly to the husband; if her marriage dissolved, the children automatically went to the husband. A woman could not own property in her name, and most states prohibited a woman from signing contracts, serving on juries, and voting.

Before the twentieth century, society strictly defined a woman's role and generally limited her skills to the home. Men often placed women figuratively on pedestals and treated them as helpless creatures, incapable of performing any serious function in a "man's world" as "women knew their place." A proper woman married, raised a family, and pleased her husband. If unmarried by the age of twenty-two, she received a label of "spinster" or "old maid." If college-educated, a woman filled an "acceptable" role such as teacher, nurse, or secretary.

Despite the prevailing attitudes and prejudices, some institutions viewed coeducation as an emerging virtue within the American higher educational system. Oberlin Collegiate Institute in Oberlin, Ohio, opened in 1833 as the first coeducational college in the United States. It admitted twenty-nine men and fifteen women to its preparatory department, initially awarding women with diplomas from its "Ladies Course." In 1837, the institution fully integrated women into its bachelor's degree program. For the first time in the United States, four women earned bachelor's degrees from a coeducational college in 1841.[3]

In American colloquialism, "coed" or "co-ed" references mixed-gender situations. As an adjective, "coed" describes the integration of the sexes; as a noun, it refers to a female student in a mixed-gender school. The use of the term is often viewed as unprofessional and sexist since, technically, both male and female (and gender-nonconforming) students at coeducational institutions are "coeds." Today, most organizations use the gender-neutral term "student" or, when gender is relevant, an appropriate adjective such as "female student" or "nonbinary student."

Still, legislation lagged in recognizing the rights of women. The ratification of the Fourteenth Amendment in 1868 extended the Constitution's equal rights and due process protections to all citizens, regardless of race or gender, but the Fifteenth Amendment extended the right to vote only to *male* citizens. Women's rights advocates saw these amendments as an opening to push for universal "suffrage" (from the Latin *suffrāgium*, meaning the right or privilege to vote). In 1869, Elizabeth Cady Stanton and Susan B. Anthony founded the National Woman Suffrage Association to fight for an amendment to the US Constitution.

Mirroring this drive for women's equality, legislators and administrators across the country also debated the effects of mixed-sex education. Supporters argued its emotional, academic, and institutional benefits, asserting the female presence offered a calming, even "civilizing," influence on the males. Some educators also predicted greater success for females by sharing the classroom with men. Those opposed to coeducation, particularly Catholics, objected on religious and moral grounds. They stressed that placing eighteen-year-old boys and girls in close proximity increased the likelihood of sexual activity.

For the remainder of the nineteenth century, public universities paved the way for coeducation, acknowledging its benefits not only to students but also for enrollment. While most private postsecondary institutions were still slow to admit females, Wheaton College in Illinois graduated its first female student in 1862, while Cornell University in New York and the University of Michigan admitted female students in 1870. By the end of the century, coeducation had achieved broad acceptance as a standard American educational practice.

There were some exceptions, however. Florida, for example, passed the Buckman Act in 1905, which mandated the consolidation of Florida's six higher education institutions into three: the University of Florida for white men, the Florida Female College (now Florida State University) for white women, and The State Normal School for Colored Students (the future Florida A&M University) for African American men and women. It would take more than four decades before these institutions admitted students of both sexes (and even longer to desegregate). In the postwar period, few returning veterans and college students wanted a single-sex education, and Florida repealed the law in 1947.[4] (In other states, many single-sex institutions also altered their policies and admitted small numbers of the opposite sex with little fanfare, as Chicago's DePaul University did in 1948.)

While women slowly increased their presence at the collegiate level at the turn of the twentieth century, suffrage efforts also gained momentum and resulted in the establishment of the National Woman's Party (NWP) in 1916. When the United States entered World War I, women—especially college-educated women—were highly visible in providing war relief services and industry support. Such contributions shifted the opinions of many American males on the subject of women's equality. Midway through the war, President Woodrow Wilson—previously vocal on his resistance to women's suffrage—acknowledged:

> [D]emocracy means that women shall play their part in affairs alongside men and upon an equal footing with them.... [S]hall we admit them only to a partnership of sacrifice and suffering and toil and not to a partnership of privilege and right?[5]

On May 21, 1919, the House of Representatives passed an amendment giving women the right to vote, and the Senate passed it two weeks later. The Nineteenth Amendment to the Constitution, ratified on August 26, 1920, stated that the right "to vote shall not be denied or abridged by the United States or by any State on account of sex." The ratified amendment, nicknamed "The Susan B. Anthony Amendment," had an impact that went far beyond the ballot box. Women found new opportunities opening up to them in many aspects of American life: employment, education, sex education, and birth control. As the number of women in the workforce increased, individual states began to grant women the right to keep their wages and to own property. Women not only improved their lives but also

36

shaped the government—through voting and, eventually, running for office. And yet, twenty percent of working women, more than half of whom labored in the textile and garment production industrial sector, still worked for menial wages.

Society was definitely changing, and women were finally receiving long over-due recognition in a variety of professions. Their presence not only increased in advertising, ads also reflected and supported issues of equality. In the arts, Zona Gale received a Pulitzer Prize for drama in 1921, followed by Edna St. Vincent Millay for poetry in 1923. That same year, with inequities still persisting in many fields, the National Woman's Party proposed a Constitutional amendment prohibiting all discrimination based on sex. After numerous revisions, the Equal Rights Amendment finally cleared Congress in 1973 but failed ratification by three-quarters of the states. As of this writing, more than a century after the original version of the amendment was proposed, Congress has not passed a resolution to restart the ratification process.

Timex presents equal time for women.

Men don't have to wind watches anymore. Why should women?

The Ladies Electric TIMEX. There's no other watch quite like it in the world.

1972 Timex ad

Even with all these advances in women's rights, many private universities and colleges continued to adhere to their traditions of single-sex education. However, a social revolution, especially among college-age youths, swept the nation in the 1950s and 1960s. Disparate groups advocated for nuclear disarmament, environmental reforms, freedom from sexually repressive norms, and the decriminalization of marijuana and hallucinogenic drugs. The fights for civil and workers' rights, women's empowerment, and gender equity in education forced colleges, especially Catholic and Ivy League institutions, to reevaluate admission policies and coeducation. All-male institutions investigated "coordinated" activities with nearby women's colleges, de facto integration with sister colleges, and the admission of women. Many universities commissioned studies on all aspects of coeducation and examined gender equity in course offerings, athletic opportunities, and facilities.

One of the most high-profile schools to explore such possibilities was Yale University. Even though female graduate students had attended Yale since the late 1800s and the school had appointed its first woman instructor in the Department of the History of Art to teach its male undergraduates in 1943, female undergraduates had yet to attend. In his 1956 annual report, Arthur Howe, Jr., dean of admissions at Yale, characterized all-male schools as outmoded and harmful, both academically and socially. He cited studies that showed a drop in same-sex school applications as many students felt coed colleges offered a more natural, realistic, and progressive learning environment.[6]

Yet, not until 1965 did Yale broaden its admissions beyond male prep school students. It recruited more African American students, more scholarship students, and a wider geographic spread to avoid "inbreeding" and excessive parochialism. More than one hundred years after Oberlin College opened as a coeducational institution, Yale and its alumni still debated the pros and cons of any form of coeducation. In contrast, Harvard University and Columbia University were practically coed in the 1960s, after tightly incorporating Radcliffe College and Barnard College, respectively.

In 1966, after evaluating the Harvard–Radcliffe model, Yale proposed to Vassar College that it move its facilities to New Haven. Vassar rejected the proposal. In November 1968, Yale's president, Kingman Brewster Jr. announced — after engaging hundreds of women from other colleges at "Coed Week" — that the university would admit five hundred female undergraduates for the 1969–1970 academic year, finally aligning itself with other coed US colleges.[7]

Brewster's plan for the soon-to-arrive females originally included off-campus housing for two hundred fifty transfer students and a single residence hall for two hundred fifty incoming freshmen. Yale's newly formed Office on the Coeducation of Women agreed to place the freshmen together in Vanderbilt Hall but wanted the female transfers housed across the other eleven colleges. This approach effectively established some of the first coeducational residence halls in the United States.[8]

Brewster's announcement caught most "Yalies" — as well as members of fellow Ivy League school Princeton — by surprise. In reaction, Princeton's president, Robert F. Goheen, told *The Daily Princetonian* that it was inevitable that Princeton would educate women. Following Yale's announcement, Princeton publicized plans to admit ninety female transfers and forty first-year women in 1969. Things did not go smoothly. In 1970, more than one hundred male Princeton students petitioned for the removal of women from campus after observing them lifting weights in the gym and seeking membership in Princeton's storied eating clubs. However, the university continued with its plans. By 1983, its undergraduate female population was 37 percent, finally reaching an equal gender distribution in 2020.[9]

Undergraduate Women Admitted to All-Male Universities	
1969	Princeton
	Yale
1970	Colgate
	Johns Hopkins
	Rutgers
	University of Virginia
	Wesleyan University
1971	Brown
	Lehigh
1972	Duke
	Notre Dame
	Dartmouth
1975	Harvard (with Radcliffe)
1976	US Military Academy
1983	Columbia

Both Yale and Princeton suffered the growing pains typical of coeducational conversions at many single-sex schools. For example, when Yale exceeded its original target of five hundred women by eighty-eight, it experienced a housing crunch and additional pressure from male students and alumni. Media coverage of the schools' decisions to admit women often stereotyped the Yale and Princeton women, sometimes as "superwomen." Such perceptions contributed to women suffering boorish behavior, discrimination, and alienation from male classmates. Some professors disapproved of women in their classes, even citing discredited studies that women were physically incapable of higher education. Others found it uncomfortable even to acknowledge the women's presence and ignored them. Gaining access to an institution did not guarantee the acceptance of women as equals, the attainment of positions of power, or protection from sexual harassment.

Parallel with these secular university transformations, Catholic secondary and postsecondary schools also began to address single-sex education as inherently unequal. Several private universities followed Yale and Princeton, accepting coeducation and admitting women between 1970 and 1972. Some took this action strictly in anticipation of Title IX of the Education Amendments Act of 1972. Passed by Congress, this legislation heightened public awareness of equity issues related to gender and drove institutional changes:

Coeducation at Catholic Universities	
1909	Marquette
1948	Gonzaga
1961	Santa Clara University
1968	Villanova
1969	Georgetown
1970	Boston College
1972	University of Notre Dame
	University of San Diego
1973	Loyola Marymount
1974	Fordham

> No person in the United States shall, on the basis of sex, be excluded from participation in, be denied the benefits of, or be subjected to discrimination under any education program or activity receiving Federal financial assistance.[10]

Title IX prohibited sex discrimination, including sexual harassment and sexual violence, in all university programs and activities, including, but not limited to, admissions, recruiting, financial aid, academics, services, discipline, grading, athletics, housing, and employment. Eventually, institutions receiving federal funds accepted that Title IX gave female athletes the right to equal opportunity in sports. Despite the disproportionate spending on men's sports, Title IX slowly forced major changes in programming, scholarships, and facilities.

At Notre Dame, Hesburgh envisioned the university following the path of the Ivy League colleges, particularly Princeton with its strong undergraduate and graduate schools. Visualizing a "Catholic Princeton," he asked Dr. Goheen how ND could grow its own reputation for academic prowess. The Princeton president replied, "First, fire the football coach," implying football overshadowed the educational mission of the university.[11]

Notre Dame also wanted to join those renowned all-male Catholic universities that had embraced coeducation and admitted female undergraduates. According to Hesburgh:

> Tradition is a mighty and beautiful thing. The tradition of the Dome, as great as it is, is short because the Dome neglected, throughout the years, to educate the other half of society. Women complement men and men complement women, and together they form one. Women and men are equal in society, why should they not be equal in education at Notre Dame?[12]

Soon, the words of Father Andrew M. Greeley, a noted sociologist and journalist, captured the effect of the university's coeducation change: "As Notre Dame goes, so very likely will go all of the Catholic higher education in this country."[13]

◇◇◇

REARVIEW REFLECTION Like me, many of Notre Dame's first freshman women entered this world in 1954. As young girls, we benefited from the 1963 publication of Betty Friedan's *The Feminine Mystique* and from the National Organization for Women's (NOW) push for the Equal Rights Amendment, both of which challenged traditional female roles. We had the rights to own property, to vote, and to manage our finances. In time, we saw women such as Chris Evert Lloyd, also born in 1954, become the first woman in tennis to earn more than one million dollars.

Still, the advancement of women's rights and opportunities did not eliminate the debate about coeducation. Accepting arguments by curriculum experts advocating separate vocational courses for girls and boys, many of us attended Catholic secondary schools that remained single-sex institutions well into the 1960s. Unfortunately, our experiences as students in same-sex high schools sometimes fostered the potential for greater intolerance and misunderstandings when we arrived at coeducational colleges and universities.

Until 1969, girls and boys in my co-institutional high school occupied separate buildings, coming together only at lunchtime. The administration, controlled by priests, discouraged us from taking courses such as physics and calculus or starting girls' sports teams. The nuns controlled us girls, checking for makeup or uniform skirts worn above the knee. Just before my sophomore year, the school decided to integrate. Thereafter, the sexes came together in everything except physical education classes. Coeducation awakened a spirit of equality and camaraderie that crossed gender lines. This integration prepared me for my move into a coeducational university... or so I thought.

Merging Lanes

As the poet Johann Wolfgang Von Goethe said in conversation with fellow writer Johann Peter Eckermann, "It is not enough to take steps which may sometimes lead to an aim; each step must be in the right direction."[1] Father Hesburgh saw coeducation as a goal worthy of the university's namesake. Initially, Notre Dame explored merging with nearby Saint Mary's College and evaluated the impact on admissions, academics, and alumni attitudes. When the merger failed, Notre Dame chose to admit undergraduate women into its own student body.

◇◇◇

The University of Notre Dame student body actually included women even before the coeducation decision—just not as undergraduates. Since its 1918 inception, the ND Graduate School quietly accepted women. These women, nearly all members of religious orders, neither challenged nor changed ND's traditions or culture, and none lived on campus during the academic year. In 1965, to provide residential space for its growing population of female graduate students without displacing any male undergraduates, the university built Lewis Hall behind the Administration Building. Anne Lenhard Benington, a 1965 lay alumna of Notre Dame's since-terminated graduate program in education, recalled, "The women on campus who were not nuns definitely felt that they stood out.... You were sort of an anomaly.... [Gender inequity] was just a fact of life."[2]

Many articles tell the story of the women who entered Notre Dame in 1972, but they seldom mention the proto-pioneers—the handful of laywomen who earned graduate degrees during summer sessions or through independent study. As the conventional-minded priests wrestled with the changing role of women in American society, approximately forty-eight hundred women graduated from Notre Dame between 1918 and 1971, representing about 8 percent of all degrees awarded during that period. This presence bolstered Hesburgh's confidence in ND's ability to accept coeducation and women at the undergraduate level.

As early as 1961, long before merger discussions began with nearby Saint Mary's College (SMC), Notre Dame explored the possibility of relocating Barat College in Lake Forest, Illinois, or Rosary College in River Forest, Illinois, to its campus. Neither school expressed interest in moving, so Hesburgh continued to encourage activities that drew SMC women to Notre Dame's campus. He even turned a blind eye as SMC women sometimes sat in on ND undergraduate classes.

Notre Dame actually started down the road to coeducation by accident when, in 1964, six male students enrolled in a chemistry class at Saint Mary's. Recognizing the value of such interaction, ND and SMC initiated what the institutions called a Co-Exchange Program, allowing a preset number of students to attend courses at either campus in 1965. Saint Mary's students took language or science classes at Notre Dame, and Notre Dame students enrolled primarily in education courses at SMC. If courses occurred before or after lunch, students had the option to eat in the campus cafeterias where their courses were held.

Saint Mary's College (SMC) is a private Catholic women's liberal arts college in Notre Dame, Indiana. Founded in 1844 by the Sisters of the Holy Cross, Saint Mary's was the first women's college in the Great Lakes region. Today, it offers five bachelor's degrees and more than thirty majors. SMC has master's degree programs in data science, speech language pathology, and autism studies. Its master's programs and doctorate in nursing practice are coeducational.[4]

In the program's first year, Assistant Dean of Arts and Letters Robert Waddick authorized forty-four SMC women to register for classes at ND and fifty-two ND men to register at SMC.[3] Since this was not a move to "coeducation," the administration coined the term "co-exchange." This program broadened academic options and increased the female presence on ND's campus. The schools exchanged no funds, even though ND tuition rates per credit hour were more than double SMC's. Even when the cost reached a million dollars, no accounting occurred — suggesting that the presence of women on the ND campus had a value of its own.

Initially, only juniors and seniors participated in the program, but it was expanded to freshmen and sophomores in 1969. However, even when participation tripled, the program failed to foster the desired integrated feel. Hesburgh recognized that it would take years for women to assimilate with such a limited-scope program. He privately acknowledged that an all-male educational experience would soon be archaic, as financial, demographic, and cultural factors propelled men's colleges to admit women.

While the two institutions struggled to integrate their student bodies without disadvantaging either school, students discovered their own ways to interact. Women and men served together on the staff for the student newspaper, *The*

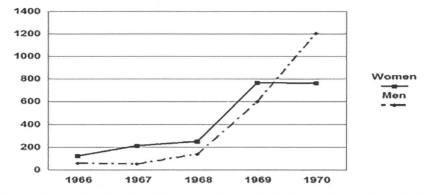

Rising enrollments from the Notre Dame–Saint Mary's Co-Exchange Program begun in 1965

Observer, and the monthly *Scholastic* news magazine that were available on both campuses. Barriers eroded as men and women attended Mass together, met at local bars, and visited dorm rooms. Both sexes enjoyed jointly sponsored concerts, cultural events, and the combined male–female student section at football games. Women appeared in ND classrooms, dining halls, the Rockne Memorial pool, and (eventually) on its golf course. Yet ND still had a long way to go — as demonstrated by the 1968 opening of its multimillion-dollar Athletic and Convocation Center (ACC) without women's locker rooms.

A 1968 study of sixty-two hundred ND undergraduates indicated that "more than half came from all-male Catholic high schools" with limited daily exposure to girls.[5] Increasingly, boys wanted to attend a coed college for a less artificial and more contemporary learning and social environment. According to the Dean of Arts and Letters Charles Sheedy, CSC, students viewed certain traditional collegiate features as anachronistic:

> Replacing the old and cherished notion of an isolated, leisurely, elitist learning is the higher education of involvement, an outgrowth of social consciousness, the concern for the equality of opportunity, and the breakdown of class separatism....In this environment of diversity, the integration of the sexes is a normal and expected aspect, replacing separatism.[6]

A follow-up 1969 ND study indicated that nearly one-third of accepted applicants did not enroll due to its single-sex status. It also reported that 72 percent of enrolled students considered transferring to a coeducational school.[7] Such indicators reinforced the changing culture and financial implications facing the administration. Vice President of Student Affairs Thomas Blantz, CSC, recognized that it would take time for Notre Dame to benefit from coeducation. In a 2013 article and his recent history of Notre Dame, he highlights the main reasons why the university went coed:

> They included attracting better students and faculty by recruiting from the other half of the human race; changes in Catholic high schools as single-sex parish schools merged into coed central schools; and financial pressures closing many small Catholic women's colleges that couldn't attract funding without graduate research, leaving those women in need of new options.[8]

In April 1970, the administration contacted Lewis B. Mayhew and Rosemary Park, noted administrators in the California university system, to evaluate the possibility of a future collaboration between Notre Dame and Saint Mary's. Their report, issued in December 1970, indicated that a merger was highly feasible, especially when considering coeducation beyond academics and inclusive of social and residential life.

In January 1971, Notre Dame and Saint Mary's released a joint report recommending SMC join ND as a separate entity within the university. Based on plans to eventually merge, the report recommended the integration of registrars, admissions offices, psychological services, and security staffs. It proposed that Saint Mary's take the official name of Saint Mary's College in the University of Notre Dame and to primarily provide educational programs for women. This approach mimicked similar actions by Radcliffe College with Harvard University, Barnard College with Columbia, and Pembroke College with Brown University.

Criticism of the report was immediate across both campuses. Sheedy identified obstacles to the merger as the "pretentiousness" of Notre Dame's attitude and the "defensiveness" of Saint Mary's. He saw the best plan as a "solid, self-possessed and competent women's college" at SMC and both men and women at ND, concluding that "Notre Dame will be co-ed [sic]...but not until all of us realize that it is a fact of life."[9]

A survey of SMC women at the time indicated that they already considered themselves an integral part of ND. Of the one hundred fifty respondents, 94 percent were dissatisfied with the level of coeducation, and 28 percent wanted a merger that achieved a greater exchange of women and men in classrooms, a more varied curriculum, and women living at ND and men living at SMC.[10] To address the lopsided male–female ratio, 66 percent wanted the merger as well as increased admission rates for women until a one-to-one ratio was reached. None wished SMC to retain its separate identity if it drove ND to go coed independently.[11]

As discussions continued, 857 Saint Mary's women enrolled in Notre Dame courses in the spring of 1971. That fall, without a formal agreement in place, Notre Dame agreed to grant Mary Davey a bachelor's degree in business administration, with a specialization in marketing, and officially accepted Mary Ann Proctor as an undergraduate architecture student. Mary Ann paid her fees to Notre Dame, lived on campus, and enjoyed all the benefits afforded to a Notre Dame student.[12] Headlines in *The Observer* announced, "No Longer Notre Dameless" and "Put the Dame in Notre Dame."

As the joint committee continued to study the integration of faculty, curricula, and buildings, Sheedy noted that both schools were delaying commitment to any plan. Each operated with their own methodologies and knew, for example, how to handle registrations; however, neither knew how to oversee registrations for a combined institution. When asked about the discussions, Hesburgh acknowledged Saint Mary's concern about Notre Dame "gobbling them up" and stressed the need for better collaboration.[13]

On March 21, 1971, the schools officially approved the unification plan. Two months later, on May 14, 1971, trustees for both institutions ratified the proposal. They issued *The Joint Policy Statement on Unification*, which stated:

> [T]he ultimate goal of this unification is a single institution with one student body of men and women, one faculty, one president and administration and one board of trustees....Unification of all academic departments at ND and SMC should be accomplished by the start of 1972–73....The academic year 1974–75 is the target date for the completion of unification, but it is hoped that it might be accomplished even before that time.[14]

However, in October 1971, the Sisters of the Holy Cross refused to give or lend SMC buildings to Notre Dame and insisted on leasing them. Budget conflicts plagued the merger finalization, and in November, the merger collapsed. Financial arrangements, the method for policy decisions, and the freedom of the institutions to rearrange academic units and facilities on the SMC campus contributed to the merger's demise. Mother Olivette Whalen and Edmund Stephan, chairs of the Saint Mary's and Notre Dame boards of trustees, respectively, announced the indefinite suspension of unification negotiations in a joint statement of their own. Hesburgh put this decision into perspective years later:

> I got together with the nuns at Saint Mary's, and we agreed in principle that we would merge. But, as conversations went on, as soon as we got close to closing the deal, the nuns said they needed more money, more buildings, or that they didn't want to lose their name.[15]

> One day, I compared the merger discussions to a marriage. I told the sisters that I had the impression that they wanted to be married but, one, didn't want to take our name and, two, didn't want to work with us. They agreed I was right. So, we agreed to

disagree and went our separate ways. I told them that we [Notre Dame] would move forward with coeducation but would do it in a way that did not hurt Saint Mary's.[16]

In response to the decision, SMC students boycotted classes and blamed Sister Alma Peters, the acting Saint Mary's College president, for the merger collapse. Its student government tried to pressure SMC's trustees to reverse their decision, which also caused a major setback in the relationship between SMC and ND student bodies. When the combined faculties of the Education, Speech, and Drama departments split and returned to their own campuses, students lost the benefits of a growing *esprit de corps* and the sharing of resources.

On December 1, 1971, Hesburgh announced Notre Dame's plans to admit 325 women (125 freshmen, 200 transfers) into its male student population of 6,357 for the 1972–1973 academic year. Despite the initial ratio of almost twenty men to each woman, Hesburgh believed the constant presence of women would temper the boys' club atmosphere. He often expressed disgust with male reactions and crude behaviors when women walked across campus as "feeding time at the zoo — all those whoops and hollers!"[17] He believed integrating women into the fabric of Notre Dame was critical to the personal growth of its students. Per Father Blantz:

> If Notre Dame men really came to grips with the question of communication between themselves and the women on campus, establishing favorable conditions while minimizing obstacles, they would necessarily touch a human problem. In other words, the context for considering friendship between men and women will become the larger matter of what is at stake between persons, whether male or female, Black or white, American or Vietnamese.[18]

Other administrators shared Hesburgh's view on the value of coeducation to collegiate life. Dick Conklin, Notre Dame's public information director, saw the direction of society, especially with regard to women's equality, and pointed out:

> If Notre Dame is serious about the business of higher education, it had better educate the other half of the human race. And if it wants to teach future leaders of society, it should open its classrooms to the sex which will increasingly influence major American institutions.[19]

Jane Pitz, the assistant rector of Walsh Hall, summarized the value of coeducation best — saying, "It is not that women need Notre Dame, but that ND needs women."[20]

Even male students shared their expectations of what coeducation meant to ND.

◇ *Dale Planicka, ND 1974:* "I went to an all-boys high school as did many ND students; few came from public schools. In my first two years, conversations often turned to the merger with Saint Mary's. Some guys asked why we needed women on campus as many guys had 'hometown honeys' (HTHs), gals from home brought to campus for special events. These girls stayed at Saint Mary's when they visited because no female accommodations existed on campus.

"It was an environment where everyone on the floor shared one sports coat; we had few reasons to dress up. This limited exposure to women resulted in a warped attitude—we referred to women as 'cattle' or 'objects.' However, these attitudes were not necessarily bred at Notre Dame but brought to ND. Many males were not ready for the changing role of women—on campus or in the days to come. Despite Saint Mary's, women were 'inaccessible.' In cases where they were 'accessible,' the Catholic guilt complex often tainted meaningful relationships. It was the worst of times! I rejoiced when the announcement canceled the merger and indicated a true movement by ND toward coeducation. We needed something new! We needed normalcy."

With the decision made, Notre Dame now had less than nine months to prepare for the fall arrival of its first female undergraduates. Hesburgh understood that a successful transition required not only acceptance by ND's administration, faculty, students, and alumni but also a smooth entry path for the new female undergraduates. The administration formed The Advisory Committee on Coeducation to determine how to introduce coeducation. The resulting report became known as the *Malits Report,* after Sister Elena Malits, CSC, the committee chair. The committee's goals included an increase in female faculty and administrators, avoidance of an oversolicitous attitude toward the women or a neglect of their concerns, periodic evaluation of coeducation and documentation of lessons learned, and ongoing relations with SMC. Specific recommendations covered residence halls, counseling, and administration.

Sister John Mariam
Jones, SC (1997)

Before the committee even finalized its report, Notre Dame hired two women: Mrs. Susan Roberts as a consultant to the Office of the Provost and Sister John Miriam Jones, SC, as assistant to the provost. Hesburgh directly recruited Jones, an ND graduate who completed her doctorate in microbiology at the university in 1970. As the first high-ranking woman in ND's administration, Jones largely oversaw the transition to coeducation. She also coordinated affirmative action activities and faculty appointments, addressed the needs of students with disabilities, and served as liaison to ROTC programs.

Jones often recalled how she looked into her own rearview mirror when she left campus after graduation and wondered if ND would ever truly integrate women. If it did, she hoped to play an integral part in the transition.[21] When asked about her return to ND in August 1972, she reflected:

> It is time women become part of Notre Dame because women are now moving into the framework of society....We went up to the wire on the merger. When that came unglued, the university decided to admit women in 1972. Since Saint Mary's women had already started developing majors at ND, some immediately transferred. Since they had enough credits, we had women ready to graduate in 1973.[22]

◇◇◇

REARVIEW REFLECTION For me, the ND–SMC merger promised the best of both worlds—a Notre Dame degree and a life within a proven Catholic women's residential college. It resolved my roadblock to attending ND, as I could not have passed for a male. Altering one's outward appearance may have worked for Joan of Arc, but I was certain I would not escape detection. After the merger fell through, I, along with other female applicants, received postcards asking our preference for consideration by ND, SMC, or both. When I saw Notre Dame's 1971 advertisement in *Parade Magazine*—asking, "Is Notre Dame a place for women?"[23]—I knew yes was the only answer for me. With my heart already committed to Notre Dame, I did not apply to Saint Mary's...or anywhere else.

University of Notre Dame advertisement
The Observer, March 10, 1976

48

The Seventies Model

"She is a pioneer capable of choosing her own path," author Avijeet Das has been noted as saying. "She is a trailblazer capable of achieving new horizons. Just give her some time and see her bedazzle the world."[1] For generations, a macho image, forged in a tough academic environment heavily influenced by Catholicism and athletics—especially football—described the typical Notre Dame male. However, no single description applied to every woman entering in the fall of 1972. Each brought her own perspectives and goals to Notre Dame and to her role as a trailblazer of this rough, uncharted terrain.

◇◇◇

While the merger negotiations proceeded, future freshmen were in high school investigating their college options. Since 72 percent of non-Catholic male-only institutions accepted women by 1960, and most of the remaining schools switched to coeducational status in the late 1960s and throughout the 1970s, women had broader collegiate possibilities.[2] Women applying to newly coeducational universities, especially Notre Dame, were objects of interest to many. Numerous articles and surveys—then and now—have captured some of the reasons why the original 365 female undergraduates, and some of their fellow male classmates, applied to ND.

The Challenges and Promises of Coeducation

◇ *Janet Krier Breen, Saint Mary's transfer, ND 1975:* "When a guidance counselor used the word 'pioneer,' I became intrigued with going to Notre Dame. Since the fourth grade, I devoured tales about women of courage—pioneers [such as] Abigail Adams, Laura Ingalls Wilder, Jane Hull, and many others. I did not have it in me to wear the same muslin dress for six months while riding in a wagon across the Great Plains. However, the challenge

49

of being one of the women who helped ND achieve coeducation could be my contribution to the societal changes of the 1970s."

◇ *Cathy Donahue, ND 1976:* "It was a cold, rainy spring day on campus. When I entered the admissions office, I felt like I was the first woman they had ever encountered. I am not sure they knew what to do with me. After my interview, my mother and I went to dinner for my birthday. Mom made a pretense of going to the bathroom while actually arranging for a cake. As she walked back to the table, she heard two priests talking about Notre Dame. She stopped and told them that she had a daughter who had just met with ND admissions. The priests introduced themselves as Father Hesburgh and Father Joyce! She explained that I was trying to decide whether Notre Dame was the right school for me. They offered to talk with me and joined us for cake. We talked about coeducation and its challenges as well as the long-term advantages of a Notre Dame education. Their passion for the university convinced me to give Notre Dame a chance."[4]

◇ *Dan Reagan, ND 1976:* "I had already wanted to apply, but I would say that the fact that Notre Dame was now going to be coed to me was a great thing and made me want to be accepted that much more....I think it was a really healthy thing and we were happy to hear [about it]."[5]

World events in the early 1970s reinforced the transformation that was about to occur at Notre Dame. The CBS sitcom *All in the Family*, a satire about an unenlightened (and bigoted) Archie Bunker barking barbed insensitivities at his "dingbat" wife and feminist daughter, held the number one Nielsen ranking for five years.[3] Bernice Gera, at forty, won her appeal before a New York state court to become the first woman to umpire a professional baseball game. Andy Warhol produced and directed the 1971 comedy film *Women in Revolt.* The FBI recruited women as special agents for the first time in its forty-eight-year history. Sally J. Priesand, twenty-five, was ordained the first woman rabbi in the United States and only the second in the history of Judaism.

The Appeal of a Strong Catholic University and Community

◇ *Jeanine Sterling, ND 1976:* "Notre Dame became my home long before I was college-age. My father returned to ND after the Korean War (with a wife and two babies). We lived in Vetville from the time I was two years old until I was seven when Vetville was torn down."

◇ *Donna Crowley Campbell, ND 1976:* "I knew I wanted a Catholic university, and ND was the premier one. Notre Dame is one of the leading universities in the country and perhaps the best-known Catholic university. Her past reputation is due to her football prowess, but I believe that her scholastic reputation has grown parallel to and surpassed her athletic competence."[6]

◇ *Nick Fedorenko, ND 1976:* "I wanted to go to a school recognized as a winner. ND is a winner at academics, sports, and my Catholic faith."

◇ *Susan Prendergast, ND 1976:* "I think there is a feeling of community, of togetherness, at Notre Dame not felt at many schools. It is an elusive feeling, hard to capture or describe, yet it exists…an invisible bond composed part by religion and tradition."[7]

◇ *Maggie Waltman Smith, ND 1976:* "My older sister transferred to ND in the fall of 1972 when the Saint Mary's merger fell through. I was a freshman at another college, and when I visited her on campus, I was struck by everyone's friendliness. While she was at a class on Friday afternoon, I walked down the sidewalk on South Quad from Badin Hall, and so many students said 'hello.' I'll never forget how different that was from my experience where I attended. I told my mom during Thanksgiving of my freshman year that I would not be staying at my original school."

◇ *Roxanne Jabbra Gunther, ND 1976:* "My father was my motivation for attending Notre Dame. He was the first Lebanese immigrant in Minnesota to attend college anywhere. Coach Bernie Bierman, Pac-10 rival of Knute Rockne and Notre Dame, recruited my father, skilled in high school football and track, to play for the University of Minnesota. He always talked about the thrill of playing at the Notre Dame stadium.

"After his death in 1970, my junior year of high school, I was determined to attend Notre Dame, a college about which I knew nothing. As his daughter, I wanted to do this for him, making a choice that would have fulfilled his dreams. I wrote for an application and found out that Notre Dame was not coed. Given the merger discussions, I applied to Saint Mary's College across the highway. I enrolled at Saint Mary's in the fall of 1971. The breakdown of the merger in the spring of 1972 disappointed many Saint Mary's students and presented a huge problem for those of us focused on Notre Dame for our careers. Although a fine arts major at Saint Mary's, I took architecture classes at Notre Dame. I'm not sure how many women transferred with me; however, since the architecture program is five years, my graduation coincided with the first freshman women's graduating class."

An Outstanding Academic Reputation

◇ *Kathy Cekanski-Farrand, the first Badin Hall rector, ND 1973:* "They [the new coeds] are here for a countless number of reasons, but primarily to obtain a fine education. They, just like the Notre Dame men, are searching — searching for academic pursuits while seeking values, goals, and a fresh and more meaningful outlook on life. Again just like Notre Dame men they have much to contribute and give of themselves."[8]

◇ *Rosemary Tirinnanzi Lesser, ND 1976:* "ND's preprofessional program provided a solid foundation for building a career."

◇ *Ann Pytynia, ND 1976:* "The decision to attend ND was a mixed bag for me. Neither of my parents went to high school, so they questioned the value of a college education — kind of the reverse elitism we see today. Although a push-pull for me, I chose ND because of the strength of its programming."

◇ *Nancy Brenner Sinnott, ND 1976:* "I came to Notre Dame to prepare for life and a career."

The Breadth and Depth of Its Athletic Prowess

◇ *Shelley Muller Simon, ND 1976:* "One of my earliest memories of ND was seeing the Golden Dome gleaming in the sunlight from the toll road between Pennsylvania and our home in Indiana, indicating we only had one hour left in the car. When I was older, my father and I attended a football game there together. And, as a varsity cheerleader in high school, I was thrilled to lead cheers in the Joyce ACC for our boys' basketball team. Little did I know I would be doing the same for the Irish! I found the perfect combination of engineering, architecture, sports, and faith when ND went coed."

Connections to the University

◇ *Laura Dodge-Ghara, ND 1976:* "I knew Notre Dame was a prestigious university as my father, Dr. David L. Dodge, taught sociology there. Although I planned to study journalism, I realized ND did not offer that major at the time. I decided to follow in my father's footsteps and to pursue sociology. It was the 1970s, and there seemed to be a higher calling to the 'helping professions.' I've never regretted my decisions to go to ND or to have a career in social work."

◇ *Christine Carroll Lang, ND 1976:* "After graduating from Palos Verdes High School in Southern California, I attended Whitman College for my freshman year of college. Over spring break, I visited my boyfriend, Mark Arminio, who entered ND in the fall of 1972. I fell in love with the campus. I interviewed with admissions to transfer and was accepted for sophomore year."

Serendipity and Fate

◇ *Beverly Cesen Winterscheid, ND 1976:* "I was eight years old and on the typical 1960s family vacation driving across the country. Four hours after leaving Cleveland, Ohio, driving on the Indiana Turnpike, we approached South Bend. My dad, an avid football fan, caught a glimpse of the Golden Dome on the horizon. Suggesting a quick detour, my mom nodded her approval, and we were on our way.

"I was so excited to see an actual campus and started daydreaming about living on my own and going to college. On that drive up Notre Dame Avenue, I saw the Golden Dome straight ahead. That memory has stayed with me.

"I did not go to a Catholic high school, my name was not Mary, and my dad was not a graduate of Notre Dame; I even applied to two other schools. I guess I may have been a 'diversity' candidate in the ND admissions pool of women applicants. In March 1972, a skinny envelope arrived in the mail, and my heart sank immediately.

"I listlessly opened the envelope to read the dreaded decision—but discovered I was on the wait-list. Slightly disappointed, I realized I better get a move on and decide between the College of William and Mary in Virginia and a school in Ohio. Then on May 1, I got the fat acceptance envelope from Notre

Dame that changed my future! I would return to that beautiful memory from so long ago."

◇ *Darlene Palma Connelly, ND 1977:* "For years, I questioned whether or not prayers alone were responsible for my acceptance. After some time on campus, I learned the 'dirty little secret' of the time — CSC priests could tip admissions in your favor. Not until 1987 did I confirm my suspicions after enjoying dinner with Tom Chambers, CSC. Just before dessert, I asked if he was the reason for my acceptance. He looked surprised at the question, but, as a priest, he gave me a simple, honest yes.

"Bingo! Now I could fill in the missing number on my ND admissions game card — his mother lived in the same apartment building as my best friend's parents. Father knew we both applied, and just that simply, I was soon sharing a dorm room with my best friend."

No matter the reasons or who influenced their decisions to apply, these women were extremely talented and dedicated. According to Emil T. Hofman, Notre Dame chose the girls on the same scale as boys: high school grades, class rank, activities, scholastic achievement test scores, citizenship, and personal recommendations.[9] Counselors also looked for "allocentrism," a quality of deep caring for others as well as for oneself.

In reality, Notre Dame accepted 125 freshman women from a pool of 1,134 female applicants.[10] This 11 percent acceptance rate reflected a more stringent selection process than the 30 percent acceptance rate for the fifteen hundred men selected from an applicant pool of five thousand. According to numerous sources, including the first report on academic life after the women arrived, eighty-seven percent of the females in the freshman class were in the top tenth of their high school class, one in four was among the top five students, and one out of four served as a class officer or on the student council. Their test scores were higher than the already elevated Notre Dame average. Most of the women came from Catholic families. They were active in high school and participated in community projects. Many played at least one sport — such as field hockey or powder-puff football, a gentler version of touch or tag football. One actually was the 1971 first runner-up to Miss Teenage America.

Dean of Freshman Year of Studies Emil T. Hofman (often known as "Emil T.") described this first class of undergraduate women thusly:

We brought in about 1,600 in the freshman class of which 125 were women.... The saying was these 125 women were not in addition to the men but in place of the men. Many of the men were at the low end of the acceptance curve. Women at the high

1972–1973 Enrollment		
Undergraduates (full-time)	n	(%)
Women	365*	(5.7%)
Men	6,367	(94.3%)
Total	6,732	(100.0%)
Male–Female Ratio	17:1	
Graduate Students		
Women	247	(13.3%)
Men	1,606	(86.7%)
Total	1,853	(100.0%)

*Increased from the announced 325 women

end of the acceptance curve replaced these candidates. So, the saying around campus was that we replaced dumb guys with smart broads.[11]

The 125 freshman women shared the changing ND landscape with 240 female transfer students, up from the planned two hundred. The University accepted 40 percent of the 588 who applied as transfers, with 211 transferring from Saint Mary's College.

The August 1972 *Notre Dame Magazine* chronicled the results from the first survey of these women conducted by Richard Conklin, Notre Dame's public information director. Ninety-six females received questionnaires; eighty-five, representing twenty states, returned surveys, including forty-two first-year students, thirty-three Saint Mary's transfers, and ten transfers from other colleges and universities. One-third had alumni, faculty, or university administrators as parents. After the survey, Conklin expressed his view that the women were remarkably like the males who inhabited this undergraduate domain alone for one hundred thirty years. His "Alice in Irishland" article documented participant views on numerous topics of interest, including careers, religion, and the changing role of women in society.[12]

The 1970s were a time of career consciousness, and the first female undergraduates at Notre Dame eyed male-dominated fields such as medicine, engineering, law, and upper corporate management.

> ◊ *Ann Pytynia, ND 1976:* "I grew up in Michigan City, Indiana, a
> short drive from ND. In high school, we talked periodically about
> Notre Dame allowing women to attend. I distinctly remember
> some (in theory) ND–SMC recruiters coming to my high school
> to answer questions about attending college under the Dome,

but they were clearly SMC women. At one point they said, 'The thing about going to ND — it's just so hard. There is a chemistry professor who gives weekly quizzes, and people stay up all night studying.' I never took Emil T.'s class, but knowing there was someone like Emil T. at ND just solidified my desire to go there."

◇ *Darlene Palma Connelly, ND 1977:* "My best friend in high school and I wanted to be doctors; her hero was Dr. Tom Dooley, an ND student in the 1940s. One morning when we met at our lockers, she excitedly announced Notre Dame was accepting women and 'we' were going. My response was less than enthusiastic as I believed she was referring to Notre Dame College in Cleveland, run by the same nuns who ran our high school. She quickly set me straight. We did apply, and we each got a fat envelope from the University of Notre Dame du Lac in the spring of 1973."

The survey also addressed the subject of religion. During the 1970s, religion was openly debated — even on a Catholic university campus — as young people questioned its value and validity.

◇ *Kathleen Gallogly, ND 1976:* "There appears to be a shift in the attitudes of young people today, particularly in the area of religion. Many have converted from apathy to active participation and interest, bringing new life into the traditional Church atmosphere."[13]

Respondents did not shy away from addressing the changing role of women. While most did not overtly identify with the women's liberation movement, they did indicate staunch support for liberation from the kitchen and bedroom.

◇ *Shelley Muller Simon, ND 1976:* "As a career-minded feminist entering Notre Dame in the fall of 1972, I believed I could do almost anything. I wanted to develop my own sense of self by becoming independent in my thinking and my living. I did not want to be judged by my gender or background; rather, I sought equal treatment and respect for all, based on each person's strengths."

◇ *Martha Vasquez, Saint Mary's transfer:* "ND is a school of the past which is rapidly moving with the present to maintain its identity in the future....The newly coed Notre Dame is a miniature of the world....Women have begun to assume new roles and accept new responsibilities. Out the window go the clean, white, hand-embroidered handkerchiefs, and on the ground they'll stay forever....[I]t's ridiculous to expect women to remain glued to their kitchen sinks and smile about it."[14]

After that article, Conklin found himself an "instant expert" about the emerging coeducation trend on America's previously all-male collegiate campuses. Eventually, the Washington-based newsletter *Women Today* picked up the article. Despite the article's nonscientific approach, leading universities such as Yale, Bryn Mawr, and Wellesley expressed a high level of interest in the women's musings. Ironically, these requests for the survey responses came from institutions that knew more about coeducation than ND. Conklin saw this as a reaction to the fact that the "role of women in society is definitely changing, and there is a nation-wide sensitivity to this. Institutions of higher education are very serious in this sensitivity."[15]

Time Magazine, Newsweek, and even *Parade Magazine* reported on Notre Dame's efforts to recruit women. Emil T. recalled media challenges in those first years. He expressed chagrin over the reporting of an ND coed who gave birth that first semester, driving the university to establish ways to deal with inappropriate media coverage.[17]

> According to Matt Storin, Notre Dame's chief communications executive before his retirement in 2014: "The media love to love Notre Dame and they love to hate Notre Dame, because either option draws eyeballs to the page or viewers to the screen....They [the media] don't understand our caring faculty and staff, our residential system, commitment to the Catholic faith, the dedication and inspiration of our Holy Cross priests, and the prayerful and bonding experiences of a dorm Mass—or how these experiences don't fade easily into postgraduate indifference."[16]

The *South Bend Tribune* periodically checked on the progress of coeducation starting with its January 21, 1973, article by Richard Conklin, "Coeducation at Notre Dame—How Are the Girls Getting Along?"[18] The story recounted the failed merger, the successful Co-Exchange Program, and positive comments that overshadowed the challenges. It cited concerns about the perceived diminishing admissions of men and the potential lack of affinity and university support after graduation by alumnae. Over time, alumnae donations and support laid this particular concern to rest.

The first Notre Dame female undergraduates remained in the limelight for years. But, unlike athletes, many were unprepared for the constant scrutiny.

> ◇ *Janet Krier Breen, ND 1975:* "I remember my driver's ed teacher cautioning, 'Be respectful of how you use your brights. When you are alone in the dark, use them to illuminate the unknown expanse of the road ahead. Always turn off your brights in

populated areas and everyday driving conditions. Otherwise, you will annoy other drivers.'

"A few hundred female undergraduates needed such driver's ed advice. They used their 'brights' to be admitted to ND in the early 1970s. They used their 'brights' to deal with unforeseen obstacles. Most instinctively 'turned off their brights' to blend into mainstream traffic and let their talents speak for themselves. They earned the respect of the other 'drivers' by being courteous, trustworthy, and team players. The Notre Dame experience prepared us for any type of scrutiny under bright lights."

◇◇◇

REARVIEW REFLECTION Many of the first undergraduate women at Notre Dame keenly felt and grappled with the changing expectations for women in American society. As girls born in the 1950s, many of us played hide-and-seek or ran through sprinklers with or without bathing suit tops. We took our lunches to school in brown paper bags or in lunch boxes with thermoses filled with chocolate milk. We wore Keds or P. F. Flyers with ugly gym uniforms. We acted in plays and sang in choirs. When sent to the principal's office, we feared what awaited us after school; our parents and grandparents were more frightening than any peer pressure to misbehave. After school and when homework was done, we lay on our backs in freshly mowed grass and talked with friends about the boys from whom we didn't want to get "cooties" (although we really did!), the cloud that looked like an angel, or anything else on our minds. Some of us rode bikes or played tag, dodgeball, and red rover. Before dinner, we watched *The Mickey Mouse Club* or *Dark Shadows* on the family television.

While our mothers dressed us in crinoline slips, Mary Jane shoes, and white anklets, we dressed our Barbies in outfits reflecting our dreams to become schoolteachers, doctors, or even astronauts. We imagined ourselves as brides and mothers while baking cookies in Easy-Bake ovens.

Our goals and aspirations grew from time with family, role models, and friends. In my September 1971 early decision plan admission application to the combined University of Notre Dame–Saint Mary's College freshman class, I described my Vetville upbringing and captured its spirit as my primary reason for applying to the proposed merged institution:

> The University of Notre Dame–Saint Mary's is my first choice as the school I would like to attend. I went to Saint Mary's grade school when I was little and while my father was attending Notre Dame. I always remember the friendliness of the people on campus and in the town of South Bend. The spirit of the people is what really amazed me, even when I was small. Everyone

seemed to care about one another, and to me that would be the ideal situation in which to learn.

When the merger fell through, I asked for consideration by Notre Dame. Although my high school prepared me to pursue a bachelor's degree at a prestigious university, I had no specific career plans. I knew I wanted to combine a career with the traditional roles of wife and mother but was at a crossroads in my thinking on many current issues. However, I was sure of one thing: "The part of women's liberation with which I agree is the philosophy of being a movement for human equality. . . . [A]ll individuals should have the right to strive for self-fulfillment in whatever way they can."[19] Fifty years later, I only wish our culture had made more progress regarding women and equality for all.

On April 3, 1972, I received my acceptance letter from John Goldrick, the director of admissions. With the words, "I am pleased to inform you that you have been accepted for admission to the 1972 Freshman Class of the University of Notre Dame," I achieved my childhood goal. I would soon travel a long, winding road with a small, determined group of future daughters of Notre Dame!

Caution: Road Work Ahead

John Heywood, a sixteenth-century English dramatist, offered encouragement to those facing difficult tasks: "a hard beginning makth a good ending."[1] Such encouragement would have been helpful to the Notre Dame administration, faculty, and student body, all of whom had a great deal of work ahead of them to integrate the incoming women into the university. Although many women saw their acceptance as the realization of childhood dreams and others envisioned new freedoms and friends, few considered how coeducation at Notre Dame would affect those already on campus as well as the incoming students of both genders. In many ways, it was a hard beginning for most of those involved.

◇◇◇

On February 8, 1972, Vice President of Student Affairs Thomas Blantz, CSC, designated Badin and Walsh halls as the first two female undergraduate residences. Badin Hall, built in 1897 as Saint Joseph's Industrial School, was renamed in 1917 to honor Stephen Badin, the first Catholic priest ordained in the United States and the original owner of the acreage for Notre Dame's initial land grant. Walsh Hall, constructed in 1909 and named for Reverend Thomas Walsh, Notre Dame's sixth president, featured closets and private bathrooms. Both halls offered a variety of rooming options, including singles (private rooms), doubles, and quads (a central room flanked by two bedrooms). Viewing Badin and Walsh as having adequate facilities, including lounges for social activities, the administration expected any necessary renovations to occur at a reasonable cost and on an expedited schedule.

The administration selected these halls in part because of their proximity to each other and their central location on the South Quad. Since these two halls housed approximately 330 residents, they easily accommodated the original plan of 325 women students to be accepted. Blantz also preferred not to house the women in a single dorm as such a decision would result in a single female rector and hall president.

Blantz informed the displaced male residents that they could relocate to the other eighteen dorms or move off campus. After the students, especially those from Badin and Walsh, had notified their rectors whether they planned to move off campus, the administration knew the number of males remaining on campus. All residence halls then received allocations to accommodate the displaced residents and incoming male freshmen.

After moving women into Walsh Hall in 1972, Father Blantz originally planned to turn its basement into a women's social center. However, this designated space did not appear until 2004. Notre Dame's Gender Relations Center (GRC) was the first office of its kind within collegiate student affairs nationwide. The GRC implemented programs discussing healthy relationships, gender, and sexuality consistent with the university's Catholic character.[2]

Unfortunately, given the university's incredibly short learning curve, it did not address the cultural and emotional needs of upperclassmen who did not want women at ND or who were affected by the dorm decision. Some of the Badin residents tried to resist the inevitable, an interesting dichotomy given that Hesburgh, a former Badin resident himself, drove the coeducation decision. The Badin Hall Council sent a letter to *The Observer*, stating:

> We, the residents of Badin Hall, regret the decision to convert Badin to a female dorm. We regret it because it destroys the community that we have striven to build in this hall and because it prevents the University from creating a genuine co-ed dorm. But we realize that some halls must be chosen for female housing. We ask that the University justify its decision to pick Badin and if this decision must stand, we also ask that other members of the Notre Dame community also sacrifice for co-education. We further ask that some elements of our community be preserved by allowing us to move, in sections, to other halls and by guaranteeing that sections in other halls would be available for that purpose. We also ask that we never be displaced again, in the spirit of fairness to those who have already made this sacrifice.[3]

The Badin Hall president also questioned how this dorm met the criteria detailed in the announcement, since resident complaints included insufficient storage and lounges. He challenged the reasoning behind having both dorms on the South Quad instead of selecting one dorm on the North Quad.

The rectors of both halls weighed in on the decision. Father Leonard Biallis, Badin's rector, asked the men to accept the women as ND students without discrimination or bitterness. He viewed the change as "cutting the umbilical cord of

"Orphans in the Storm"
The Observer, February 11, 1972

the past to move on to more mature relationships...[and] only the first step in a series which will hopefully culminate in a resurrection to a truly adult, Christian university."[4]

Father Daniel O'Neill, the Walsh Hall rector, reasoned:

> [I]f Walsh is as great a hall as it is supposed to be, they will accept this as men...the girls must be placed in the best possible spot...I only hope that we can live the semester out with the same spirit we shared and then turn the hall over with graciousness.[5]

Overall, the Walsh Hall residents were less vocal in expressing their disappointment but still emotional about changing their college home.

> ◇ *Randy Sarton, ND 1974:* "From the time I was in fourth grade, I wanted to go to Notre Dame. I grew up in Chicago and only attended Catholic schools, so ND was the only college in which I was interested. My guidance counselor encouraged me to apply elsewhere, but there was no other choice for me.
>
> "My brother lived in Walsh Hall and definitely influenced my dorm preference. When I arrived as a freshman, ND had a stay hall policy, which meant I would stay in the same dorm for all four years. Such a system fostered strong friendships and built one's sense of belonging versus the previous policy where each hall housed the same class (e.g., all freshmen). Since Walsh was one of the oldest dormitories, I felt privileged to live there. As freshmen, most of us were scared when we arrived on campus. The juniors and seniors helped us to acclimate to the college environment.

"The night before the official announcement, Father Dan O'Neill called us to a meeting in the basement. We thought we were in trouble because of the previous weekend parties. When O'Neill announced our dorm was one of the two dorms assigned to the incoming coeds, we were speechless! Although we were all pro-coeducation, we had not realized that it might hit so close to home — especially our campus home. No one felt worse about this decision than Father O'Neill, but he called upon us to accept the decision graciously.

"We were never officially told why they chose Walsh. Maybe, it was because it was centrally located. Maybe, it was our reputation as a party hall, and this was a way to break up the party group. We only knew we had to find a new place to live.

"After my friends and I transferred to our new hall, we never really felt accepted by its existing residents. Even the hall rector seemed to focus on us more closely than the guys who were there before us."

Eventually, support for coeducation came from some within the male community.

◇ *Frank Devine, ND 1975:* "[T]he brilliance of what [Father] Hesburgh did was gently change the culture....You probably won't hear this from any of the women who felt a little awkward or alienated...but in fact, we were ready for coeducation by the time it came."[6]

Sister John, one of the few female administrators, summarized the environment, reflecting that Notre Dame "was a very macho place. Maleness was the hallmark. It's understandable that the change was a little traumatic for some graduates and students. We had some emotion, some resistance."[7]

The existing Badin and Walsh hall governments reassigned their soon-to-be former residents to other halls. Those halls continued their standard room selection process based on a lottery, grade point, or class, and allowed the displaced students to select rooms equally with residents. Returning students from abroad and transfers added to the already complicated process.

The Observer covered the impact on the displaced Walsh and Badin residents and the changes meant to welcome the women. However, the reporting of what the incoming male freshmen of the class of 1976 were about to face was minimal. These males confronted greater-than-expected residential hardships as a shortage of rooms and beds arose not only due to the incoming women but also due to the decreased numbers of upperclassmen moving off campus. Vice President of Student Activities Robert Ackerman noted that ND students defied the national trend of moving off campus, indicating a general satisfaction with community life. However, he expected the resulting overcrowding situation to test the community's spirit.

To resolve the anticipated overcrowding, the administration considered but discarded housing students in mobile homes or the LaSalle Hotel in downtown South Bend. With the first picks and access to the best accommodations, upperclassmen felt less impact from the rooming dilemma. However, the male freshmen in the fall of 1972 were relegated to the back seat, driving them into less-than-desirable spaces. They lived in hall lounges, basements, and study rooms — lodging viewed acceptable by the administration. As James Riehle, CSC, the dean of students in charge of student housing, explained, only fifty students lived in "cramped housing." He defined "cramped housing" as three-room suites housing six freshmen and two-room suites accommodating four freshmen, compared to previous years housing four and three students, respectively. As beds became available, Riehle guaranteed relocation priority to those in cramped rooms, followed by residents of the converted lounge, study, and basement rooms.[8]

> ◇ *Dan Adler, ND 1976:* "Freshman year, I was in a forced triple in Breen-Phillips. Sophomore year, I was kicked out to make way for more girls. A girl from my hometown got my room."

> ◇ *George Bienfang, ND 1976:* "They told us the three-room quads in Morrissey were originally built as doubles, and they were putting four students in space originally designed for six. In 1975, I did some research in the university archives for the hall's fiftieth birthday. I learned those three-room-quads were originally singles — not doubles — and the university assigned four students in a space originally designed for three."

Even as the administration worked out the final details, change was already underway. Completion of the roughly one hundred forty thousand dollars in renovations caused Badin and Walsh halls to lose some endearing — and some not so endearing — characteristics. Badin lost its Vintage Cinema and metal "closet" lockers forever. The bowling alley in the basement and the bat nest on the fourth floor of Walsh were soon history. The cockroaches survived, and the mice still found holes in the walls. Urinals remained for some time after the women arrived.

Badin and Walsh received half curtains, new sinks, medicine cabinets with mirrors, five-foot-wide wooden clothes cupboards, and chests of drawers. Full-length mirrors and frosted glass in the restrooms addressed perceived basic needs of the soon-to-arrive women. Card-locked doors, fire doors, new fire escapes, and floodlights improved safety and security in the areas surrounding these dorms.

Basements now contained kitchens equipped with new pots, pans, and dishes. The university installed washers, dryers, and ironing boards in lieu of the traditional laundry service covered by room and board charges. For decades, Saint Michael's Laundry had supported the laundry needs of male students. Accompanying their room assignments, the men received a five-digit laundry number that remained with them through graduation. Except for a few enlightened males who took home economics in high school, mothers or grandmothers indelibly marked or stitched numbered tags into all clothing coming to campus. The female students never experienced the ritual of dropping off a numbered laundry bag and then picking up clean clothing in bundles wrapped in brown paper and tied with string. According to Sister Jean Lenz:

Classic ND laundry bag (circa 1972)

> Until undergraduate women were admitted to the university, there was only Saint Michael's general campus laundry, designed primarily to handle clothing for the male population. Women's residence halls added brand-new laundry facilities to campus, which quickly caught the attention of the men who lived in the vicinity.[9]

In a 1972 article by Jerry Lutkus, Sister John conveyed her satisfaction with the initial renovations:

> "The girls…pick up the Notre Dame flavor fast. They are not over feminized and both [dorms] are available for a woman's personal touch." [She] also commented on this generation's move toward simplicity in their style of living. She claimed that Notre Dame is a leader in that move.[10]

◇◇◇

REARVIEW REFLECTION The conversion of the male halls symbolized the first of many challenges facing Notre Dame's student body during the initial five years of coeducation. We, along with the administration, soon learned that retrofitted dorms alone were insufficient to ensure the quality of campus life.

> ◇ *Janet Krier Breen, ND 1975:* "When I took driver's ed, I remember the instructor telling us the merge lane was a place to be cautious. The mainstream traffic had the right of way. Entering traffic had to slow down, be patient, and consider the rights of

the traffic already there. To cram oneself into the merge lane could cause considerable trauma to all parties.

"Entering as a female undergraduate at traditionally all-male Notre Dame in the fall of 1972 was comparable to driving an eighteen-wheeler off the merge lane into rush hour traffic on the Indiana Toll Road. Taking it slow and observing the rights of existing traffic would have been a reasonable approach to this monumental change.

"What difference would more time have made on ND's history before embarking on coeducation? The university could have built new residential halls for female students, ensuring the stay-hall system so important to a decade of male students. The university could have admitted more females in its first year without creating a view of them as taking spots from male applicants. The first female students, pitifully few in number, took seats away from male applicants, and their presence caused men to be booted out of their stay-hall family. If this was not already a 'traffic accident' in the making, the females entered with higher academic and SAT standards than their male counterparts. Rumors abounded that the girls were smarter than the boys, adding to the angst of those early years.

"For change to occur, someone has to be first. How does that saying go? 'If it doesn't kill you, it will make you stronger.' The women soon came to understand the meaning behind those words."

"Why sure, coeducation is just around the corner!"
The Observer, October 21, 1971

Packing Our Gear

While Notre Dame and its men awaited the start of coeducation, the soon-to-arrive freshman women took senior exams and prepared for high school graduation, many as valedictorians. They could have easily sung along with Meat Loaf: "It was always summer, and the future called / We were ready for adventures, and we wanted them all."[1] But for some of Notre Dame's first female undergraduates, their Catholic education and strict upbringing resulted in emotional baggage, often weighing more than the physical items they packed.

◇◇◇

REARVIEW REFLECTION When my April 1972 acceptance letter arrived, my father immediately shared the news with my grandfather, who was always our cheerleader when it came to education. My father's April 14 letter (though spelling my nickname his own way) captured his confidence in Notre Dame:

> Debbie has probably already told you, but I will tell you again. She was one of 125 girls out of the entire United States to be accepted as a student at Notre Dame. She will start there in the fall. We are all very happy for her. As you know, it is really a great place and gives a person a start in life he or she couldn't get anywhere else. We are planning to come home this summer, but have not decided when. With Debbie going to Notre Dame, we will, undoubtedly, have to make more trips North.

On June 9, 1972, I received my invitation from Dean of Freshman Year of Studies Emil T. Hofman to take the freshman year guidance tests. Examinations took place during the summer or at the start of freshman orientation. The department administered placement and education credit exams to satisfy ND's foreign languages and mathematics requirements. With the fall term less than three months away, the letter also informed me that: "However, at this date, we cannot designate the dormitory to which you will be assigned [in the fall]."

My parents decided I should register for the first test slot—July 7. After dropping my mother and siblings off in Dubuque to visit relatives, Dad and I drove to Notre Dame. Dad taught me how to communicate with truckers on his CB (citizens band) radio and purchased a license for me. I could never remember my official call sign, but my handle was "Double D." A year later, when I finally got a car in my sophomore year, Dad installed a CB radio, using the car's antenna rather than the normal trunk top mount. This setup allowed me to listen to conversations without others knowing I had a CB to call for assistance. One afternoon, I heard men discussing my appearance and making plans to force me to pull over. I drove to a nearby fire station and waited for the situation to pass.

> Citizens band radios gained popularity in America in the 1970s. Known as CBs, they allowed short-distance, two-way voice communications. After the 1973 oil crisis, drivers used CBs to locate service stations, to notify other drivers of speed traps, and to organize convoys to protest 1974's fifty-five miles per hour national speed limit. The Federal Communications Commission (FCC) required a call sign and a twenty-dollar license to use the assigned radio frequency. People often ignored the license requirement and invented their own nicknames (known as "handles").

While on this trip, I came to appreciate country music. I listened to Dad sing "Chantilly Lace," my parents' song, with his quirky smile and a twinkle in his eyes. I knew that he missed my mother, his regular travel partner, especially when I failed to put the right amount of cream in his coffee or to anticipate his cravings for cookies. We listened to updates on the break-in at the Watergate Office Building and the return of seventy thousand troops from Vietnam. My memories of these historic events are faint compared to the intensity of my feelings as we headed down Notre Dame Avenue toward the Golden Dome. For the first time since driving away in 1962, I felt I was returning home. This emotion, common to most alumni, was a strange sensation for a teenager without a campus visit in a decade.

Upon arrival, I met Beverly Cesen. Realistically, our assignment to the same dorm room during our placement exams was probably due to the limited number of women on campus, possibly coupled with some Irish luck. However, I prefer to believe that Student Housing gave some thought to this process. I wondered if its employees considered our similar educational backgrounds and the resulting potential for similar interests. I thought perhaps it was because our June birthdays were within four days of each other, making us both Geminis. Whatever the reason, we forged an immediate connection that first night in Walsh Hall.

◇ *Beverly Cesen Winterscheid, ND 1976:* "I'm one of those people who do not do well with ambiguity. However, when I met Debi during the summer testing weekend, my nervousness disappeared; we almost immediately made plans to request each other as roommates in the fall. We had a good time getting to know each other, balancing our nervousness over taking the placement tests with laughter from sharing our lives up to that point. But no one is truly ready to leave home for the first time and to create a new 'home' with a few strangers in a dorm room.

"Debi and I could not have been more different. She was from south Florida, a debutante, her dad was an ND grad, an attorney, and a judge, and she loved all things Elvis, especially his music. I was the daughter of a city employee and teacher, a second-generation American who grew up in a midwestern industrial city, and a wannabe hippie. After all, it was the early seventies! But we had the most important things in common. We both wanted to 'break out' of our families and begin living our independent lives. We wanted to stretch our wings to see how far we could fly on our own. Most importantly, we shared some basic human values that our families instilled in us. Those values were (and are) the bond that saw us through the good times and the bad."

After deciding that we would indeed enjoy rooming together, Beverly and I discovered that we were tentatively assigned to Badin Hall, a dorm with mostly single rooms. We immediately requested Student Housing to reassign us to Walsh. After they agreed to our request and given the restrictions on the use of hall elevators, we chose the second floor overlooking the main campus. With no doubles available, our only option was a quad containing a middle room with a bedroom on either side. We selected the bedroom with the least offensive color: an intense yellow (the other bedroom was a green reminiscent of mold). The small bedrooms held bunk beds, a sink, and one closet.

Before leaving ND that weekend, we agreed to write each other and to limit phone calls to avoid long-distance charges. We eventually decided to decorate our new room in pink and aqua, colors popular in the mid-seventies, to overshadow the walls. We eliminated duplicate stereos, hot rollers, hair dryers, and typewriters. Sometimes our families even engaged in our preparations: Beverly's grandmother gave us a pink rug and aqua-flowered curtains for the communal area. We hoped our other quad mates would find these items acceptable, especially if their decorating funds were as limited as ours.

Besides planning my first room away from home, I looked forward to a wardrobe that did not include a school uniform. Although my mother had the best of intentions, she had never attended college, so her shopping list reflected that of the wife of a young professional. We filled my pink trunk with skirts, blouses, and blazers. I practiced wearing high-heeled shoes and stockings. Mom convinced me that this was a typical wardrobe for a female freshman.

Shortly after arriving at ND, I realized I lacked the true college staples—jeans, T-shirts, sweatshirts, and socks. After years of living in Florida, we also forgot winter coats, boots, and gloves. My attire was a major disconnect from the norms of my new world. Although the 1970s was a decade of acceptance, I was out of sync with this Indiana campus and garnered undue attention.

College students' clothes are even more casual today, with professional attire primarily reserved for interviews, presentations, and formal events. Their footwear includes running shoes, flip-flops, and sandals. While dorm rooms still require bed linens, hygiene products, and small appliances, poster putty has replaced nails for hanging pictures, while cell phones address the functions of many items brought in the seventies—an alarm clock, a music or television source, a camera, and even a flashlight. Despite the myriad social media choices today, message boards sometimes still hang on doors.

I wasn't the only female student whose clothing choices attracted attention. Some male students actually preferred the more conservative, professional look, and they let other women know. One anonymous female student (ND 1976) recalled: "One guy I dated suggested I dress more like a girl he knew at Saint Mary's. She only wore heels and did not own a pair of jeans. Good grief! This was 1972!"

That summer's planning included more than room decor and clothing—I also received lots of advice. My parents emphasized that I should just do my best, and everything would fall into place. Other women also received guidance before arriving on campus, as I learned from my alumnae surveys. Some advice was highly practical such as to call home if trouble arose. Others received more philosophical guidance, stressing that once you have started on an "inner journey" of self-reflection, it never ends, and everyone faces the start of that journey at some point.

◇ *Christie Gallagher Sever, ND 1976, citing a 1933 memorial service program for former president Calvin Coolidge:* "Nothing in the world can take the place of persistence. Talent will not; nothing is more common than unsuccessful men with talent. Genius will not; unrewarded genius is almost a proverb. Education will not; the world is full of educated derelicts. Persistence and determination alone are omnipotent. The slogan 'press on' has solved and always will solve the problems of the human race."[2]

◇ *Ann Pytynia, ND 1976:* "I remember one of my high school teachers, a nun in her eighties, was working on her second or third doctorate while teaching freshman biology. [She] showed me that you should never stop learning, never stop trying to learn new things, and it is never 'too late' to do anything."

Many of us also received some curious advice in the mail from male members of the ND class of 1974. I saved all those mimeographed and handwritten letters, and they still make me smile and reflect today:

"I don't want you to think this is some upperclassman who is trying to put some moves on the so-called helpless frosh chicks. If you are uncertain, bring a friend or five, and we'll all chat over beers or Cokes."

"Once you arrive on campus and get settled, I would love to help you get familiar with Notre Dame. Just give me a call, and we will set up a time to get together. I have plenty of reference materials in my room."

As each letter arrived, my parents cautioned me to be wary of men potentially playing games. Still, I looked forward to meeting the guys who came forward early because I believed their offers of assistance were genuine. When I finally did meet one of the letter writers, I learned once again that my parents knew best. This first dorm meeting ended abruptly after the guy demonstrated his control box for the room's lights, music, and drapes!

Reading the Signs

Freshman Orientation 1972
Art by Barbara O'Connell (2011)

A champion of coeducation, Father Hesburgh long recognized that "[w]omen who came [to Notre Dame] have a great story to tell, they are pioneers. If they could get through those few years here, they can make it in any man's world anywhere!"[1] However, the chaos of hastily adding women to the Notre Dame community was evident everywhere. The first undergraduate women experienced the awkward fits and starts of getting to know roommates, classmates, and professors.

Dangerous Curves Ahead

Move-in day and freshman orientation finally arrived. Three hundred six-ty-five women — both freshmen and transfers — arrived at the University of Notre Dame eager to become part of this Catholic, historically male bastion. For these pioneers, the collegiate journey of self-discovery had begun. But both genders had serious adjustments to make: The men, too, were facing "dangerous curves ahead." As Margaret Mead noted in her 1964 *Continuities in Cultural Evolution*, it takes the "conscious" effort of committed individuals "to bring about change," and "the whole context is relevant to the initiation and outcome" of such innovations.[1]

◇◇◇

REARVIEW REFLECTION In the fall of 1972, my dad and I returned to ND after a three-day drive from Florida. Shimmering like a mirage, Our Lady stood bold and bright through the car's windshield, no longer a reflection in the rearview mirror.

Although Notre Dame's security normally restricted vehicle access, it allowed cars on campus long enough to drop off our belongings at our residence halls. With the exception of my wardrobe, I brought personal items in line with the university's directions to other freshmen and my discussions with Beverly. On this hot and muggy Saturday, September 2, 1972, we unloaded the car between periodic rain showers. My father could have moved my belongings into the dorm on his own — he was only forty-one — but former residents of these newly designated female halls offered to help. Admittedly, I enjoyed watching as former Walsh and nearby Sorin hall residents graciously assisted us.

As the first to arrive in our room, I placed my trunk in the bedroom that Beverly and I had selected during freshman placement testing. Unlike today's students who receive information about their future roommates, we knew nothing about the other quad members. We made our plans in a vacuum, which led to some minor residential challenges that first semester. If I could live that day over, I might anticipate the "dangerous curves" involved in such close quarters and not

Campus entrance (1972)   Walsh Hall (1972)

presume to select that bedroom, move my desk into the communal area, or put the room's telephone number on adhesive tape in our window. However, as an eighteen-year-old, I followed my parents' example of just getting things done — an early error in judgment.

While I moved into Walsh, some classmates took the required placement exams. These students had arrived earlier in the week, so they had a slight head start on learning the campus and its day-to-day routine. Some even caused a stir just by being female and new.

> ◇ *Jo Lund Chamberlin, ND 1976:* "In the fall of 1972, I arrived on campus a few days early to complete placement tests. Since the tests started at 8:00 a.m., I stumbled out of bed by seven and dressed in the standard college student uniform of bell-bottom jeans, sandals, T-shirt, and a small strand of 'love beads.' It would be a long day of tests, and I knew I needed a good breakfast to make it through the morning.
>
> "As I stepped through the large wooden doors into the noisy hubbub of the South Dining Hall, the room instantly fell quiet. What was up? Was it time for morning prayers? Did I miss an announcement? All faces turned my way. When I turned to look behind me for whatever had caught everyone's attention, it suddenly broke across my half-asleep brain that I was the cause for the pause!
>
> "At that moment, an upperclassman came through the door, looked at me, looked at the rest of the room, and approached me saying something like, 'Hi! I'm _____. This is probably confusing to you, so let me show you how things work around here.' The noise started again at the tables behind me.
>
> "He walked me through the food line, showing me where to find the trays, utensils, juice, cereal, etc. He informed me that he was a senior and a resident assistant at one of the South Quad

dorms. He walked me to a table, wished me good luck on my tests, and disappeared to the other end of the room. I wish I could remember his name. I believe he did more to advance the cause of coeducation in those few minutes than anyone else during my time on campus!"

Those first few days away from home and adjusting to living with strangers challenged every student, both male and female.

◇ *Anonymous male, ND 1976:* "When my parents dropped me off at the dorm and unloaded my gear, I was one of several hundred anonymous men streaming onto campus. We came from diverse backgrounds blessed with different gifts. Whether through academics, athletics, or both, we had experienced success in our respective schools—such achievements soon to be but distant, pleasant memories.

"I soon climbed the steps to an old brick building that was not what I had envisioned. When I finally located my third-floor room, a high school classmate greeted me and introduced one of his friends who would also share our quad; the fourth roommate turned up several days later. As we surveyed the three spartanly decorated rooms, we quickly decided to use the middle room for a lounge and the wings for our bunk beds and desks. After unpacking and waving goodbye to my parents, I ventured to the basketball courts for a little personal adjustment time.

"In no time at all, disaster stories associated with the arrival of women filtered across campus. Although many of us believed some administrator had forgotten the housing needs of the men displaced by the women, the acceptance rate of male freshmen was higher than expected that year. The result was chaotic—study areas converted to rooms, quads became six-man suites, triples became quads, etc. However, many believed it was a small price to pay when you could look forward to enjoying the feminine charms of your new classmates!"

The formal freshman orientation program started the evening before my roommate Beverly had even arrived. Dean of Freshman Year of Studies Emil T. Hofman warmly greeted my father and me at the welcome reception for freshmen and parents in the Athletic and Convocation Center (ACC). During Dr. Hofman's presentation, he encouraged us to pick up the freshman orientation booklet, *A Willingness to Experience,* from our respective hall rectors. This booklet discussed academics, social activities, and campus organizations. Hofman's team had improved our booklet over prior versions, adding advertisements and details about the area relevant to the new coeds. Before leaving the session, I grabbed a copy of the year's schedule and a much-needed campus map.

After my father left for his hotel, I found my way to my first college party at Sorin Hall, the men's dorm next to Walsh. I met a great group of men who happily offered advice to a naïve freshman. I particularly took to heart a suggestion from one senior, whom I later nicknamed "Teddy Bear Man" after he delivered a red rose and teddy bear to my room. He advised me to get to know my male classmates before writing them off, either as friends or prospective dates. He stressed that every guy deserved at least one date and that taking this approach would help to improve the image of women on campus. He claimed guys loathed the perceived "choosy" and "elitist" attitude of Saint Mary's "SMC chicks" (pronounced "smick chicks"). Although I did not date before coming to Notre Dame, I had numer-

EZ Haul ad in orientation issue
The Observer, September 1, 1973

ous male friends in high school, so his advice seemed logical. Unfortunately, Teddy Bear Man failed to mention that men might also develop negative stereotypes of such "available" Notre Dame women.

Beverly arrived the next day, and we unloaded her belongings aided by Dave Gray, a junior from Bloomfield Hills, Michigan. We listened attentively as this former Walsh resident described the pitfalls of our new home. He warned us about the oversized cockroaches — as lifelong residents, they were there before we arrived and would remain long after we graduated.

Beverly and I quickly discovered the inadequacy of the room's closet as we both had an overabundance of new clothes. Beverly took the bedroom closet, and I filled the freestanding open-front wardrobe. No matter where we placed these

Dave Gray, Jim Roe, and Ray DeCarlo help Beverly Cesen on move-in day
South Bend Tribune, September 3, 1972
© *South Bend Tribune* – USA TODAY NETWORK

Below: Beverly moves into Walsh Hall

wardrobes in the shared area, they were eyesores and not worth the space they occupied given how little they held.

We attended the freshman Mass at the Grotto. Despite the blur of weekend events, one moment from the Mass particularly stood out for me and some of the other "first daughters." During Father Hesburgh's homily, he looked up at the statue of Mary on the famed Golden Dome and said, "I just apologize that it's taken so many years to welcome your daughters."

> ◇ *Betsy Kall Brosnan, ND 1976:* "My most vivid memory of Notre Dame's Grotto is also my first memory of the Grotto from the fall of 1972. I still remember as if it [were] yesterday the way the Grotto looked on that beautiful fall day. During freshman orientation weekend, Father Hesburgh celebrated Mass at the Grotto for the new women students. Even though I had attended Catholic schools from first grade through twelfth grade, and attended the many, many Masses that went with the Catholic education, I had never attended Mass outside. To look up through the trees that grew on top of and on the sides of the Grotto at the beautiful blue sky was amazing to me. To this day when I visit the Grotto, I look up to the sky and remember that first time I visited there. That was the best introduction to Notre Dame my family and I could have been given. It seemed so natural that Father Hesburgh be there to welcome us to Notre Dame. And what a beautiful place to do it from!"[2]

After Mass, Campus Ministry welcomed us with a picnic on the Main Quad (often called the "God Quad"). The welcome sign proclaiming "We're Glad You're Here" remains an integral artifact in the pictorial history of ND.

◇ *Bob Quakenbush, ND 1976:* "Many believe Notre Dame moved so quickly into coeducation that the university was not fully prepared. Just like most entering freshmen, it faced a steep learning curve. The university tried anything and everything to make the young women feel welcome, including a "We're Glad You're Here" banner on the South Quad as a backdrop for our first outdoor picnic as freshmen."

The Observer, September 15, 1972
Photo by Jim Hunt

On that first official day of coeducation, a university official stated that he could not think of a place on campus where women would not be welcomed. Even the ND marching band opened its doors to the women.[3] Hesburgh regaled us with stories about his own days as a student and his classmates' reactions to women crossing the quads. He emphasized how our presence was critical to ND becoming a great university. He encouraged us to rely on our rectors and their staffs whenever we felt confused. His comments touched my heart and soul for the first of many times.

That night, Saint Mary's held a "Tennis Court Match," a mixer for ND and SMC freshmen. I did not attend, but I doubt that I missed much as some classmates remembered the event as a bomb.

◇ *Anonymous female, ND 1976:* "They herded everyone onto the tennis courts and closed the gates. Kids who went have never forgotten it. The men expressed very unusual attitudes. The guys asked if you were from Saint Mary's; if you said, 'No, I'm from Notre Dame,' there was a definite withdrawal. Sometimes the reaction was, 'Okay, so you're not a dope like these Saint Mary's girls.' I always found that strange since most transfers were from Saint Mary's. Which school we attended caused the men to react differently to us."

◇ *Jeanine Sterling, ND 1976:* "The mixers were ridiculous—like something out of the early 1960s. Many of the SMC girls were unfriendly and rude. Some actually mocked us. The guys acted like they'd never seen a female before. My roomie and I left as soon as we could. It was *not* an impressive welcome to ND's first female undergrads."

Talented rectors, assistant rectors, and resident assistants acted as role models and sounding boards, making their selection crucial. The university selected two ND graduate women for Badin and Walsh halls, the first rectors not members of a religious order:

• Kathy Cekanski, a third-year law student, was Badin's rector.

• Joanne Szafran, a graduate student in history with experience as a residence hall director at Saint Mary's, was Walsh's rector.

Assistant rectors also guided residents:

• Susan Bennett, a PhD student in psychology, was paired with Cekanski as Badin's assistant rector.

• Jane E. Pitz, Walsh's assistant rector, graduated from the University of Notre Dame with an MFA in visual arts. Today, she lives and works in South Bend, Indiana, and remains in touch with the first pioneers.

Monday was Labor Day, and we were on our own; I did not realize how truly "on my own" I was until much later. Since attendance at scheduled events was optional, Beverly and I spent the day getting to know our roommates and meeting other Walsh residents. That night, we attended more informal mixers in the male residence halls. Relishing my new freedom, I drank too much — no one had ever explained to me the consequences of mixing beer, vodka, and bourbon. I possessed the academic intelligence for admittance to Notre Dame but proved unable to avoid a major hangover. To this day, I wonder how I navigated my way back to Walsh, given that I could not find my way around campus when sober! I vomited in the bushes as I passed Sacred Heart, reminding me of Sundays in Vetville when I got sick from smelling the incense at High Mass. My guardian angel, or perhaps the Lady atop the Dome, worked overtime that night, watching over me as I stumbled back to Walsh.

Luckily for me, no cameras caught my first night of foolishness. Little did I know that immediately following any coeducation announcement at a major college or university, the media scrutinized the incoming females. When Notre Dame achieved the long-awaited and singularly crucial step of "going coed," it received more national press coverage than any of the other Ivy League schools when they took the same step.[5] Even popular ABC News Radio broadcaster Paul Harvey mused that, someday, "the Four Horsemen would have to be called the Four Horsepersons."[6]

> Paul Harvey Aurandt (1918–2009), better known as Paul Harvey, was an American radio broadcaster for ABC News Radio. He broadcasted *News and Comment* and his famous *The Rest of the Story*. Premiering in May 1976, *The Rest of the Story* grew to six broadcasts a week, continuing until Harvey's death in 2009.[4]

◇ *Dan Reagan, ND 1976, former associate vice president of University Relations:* "[Coeducation] was written about...and televised and spoken about not only within Notre Dame circles, but it also reached the national level....I think CBS was on campus for a few days right at the beginning....It had an air about it that this was important, that this was a pretty monumental change for the University."[7]

When ND's first female undergraduates arrived, cameras popped out from behind bushes and buildings. They photographed us walking to class, to the dining hall, to just about anywhere. A deluge of microphones descended on us, and a corps of reporters often misquoted us.

◇ *Jane Pitz, assistant rector, Walsh Hall:* During that year "[I] felt the whole world was watching, 'waiting for women to jump into some main stream. All we could see was a puddle.'"[8]

First snowfall (October 1972)   The women added drapes (1972)

◇ *Kathy Gwynn, ND 1976:* "The whole thing of coeducation hit me on registration day while I was walking back from Stepan toward Walsh....I turned around to find three cameramen from CBS following me around. They explained that they had followed me through the entire registration process. I was completely unaware of them....They interviewed me and one of their first questions was, 'Did you come to Notre Dame because of the guys?'"[9]

The news crews wanted a certain slant for their stories, and the actuality of hall life rarely fit with their perceptions. According to Christie Gallagher Sever (ND 1976), a team set up light stands in her and her roommates' room and told them to do what they normally did, so the young women continued playing poker. That footage never aired. The crew left to find a room with more "girly" girls.

◇ *Becky Banasiak Code, ND 1976:* "Coeducation at Notre Dame was certainly getting its share of media coverage. Most of the women grew tired of the scrutiny of living in the first co-ed class fishbowl. Still, we were excited when we heard that a major TV network was coming to our dorm to film a story for a national broadcast. My two roommates and I cleaned up our room in anticipation but did nothing extra to project any particular image to the camera. Ours was a typical dorm room filled with books on the shelves, posters on the walls, candles on the dressers, and family pictures on the desks. I had a Mickey Mouse bedspread on my bed in the top bunk. The rest of the furnishings, however, were standard university issue. Although I was involved in athletics, I did not have many sports-related articles hanging up except for maybe a small basketball hoop over the wastebasket. Overall, we had a rather gender-neutral room.

"Our room was on the first floor. The film crew billowed in a bustle of glaring lights, clattering equipment, and swarming energy. A quick glance into our suite was all they needed before moving down the hall to the next room and the next and the next. It was obvious they were searching for something, some preconceived idea of what the form of coeducation at Notre Dame should look like. I forget whose room they finally settled on, the one that made them say, 'Aha! This is it.' We finally saw the holy grail of their quest when their program aired on TV: a room with pink frilly curtains and matching bedspreads, sugar and spice, and everything nice, that's what this room was made of. So much for unbiased reporting! One of the first lessons in mass communications I learned at Notre Dame.

"The ND women's experience with the press was not much different than the first class of women accepted to Yale; the media had already classified them as 'super women' given the limited number accepted against many applicants. This image contributed to initial feelings of uneasiness in the early days of coeducation. The women soon tired of the interviews and surveys, and they resented being singled out as an oddity versus being accepted as a Yale student."[10]

On Tuesday, September 5, 1972, for the first time in the University of Notre Dame's one hundred thirty-year history, female undergraduates stood in line with men to register for classes. The *South Bend Tribune* photographed my quad mate, Mary Beth Miracky, as she registered. Although not as famous as Neil Armstrong's "That's one small step for man, one giant leap for mankind" as he planted the American flag on the moon, it represented a momentous occasion for 365 women and a small step forward in the advancement of women in general.

For those on campus who missed the national coverage, the student paper, *The Observer*, also reported on the registration process:

Mrs. Richard C. Kaczmarek helps Brian Pearsall and Mary Beth Miracky register
South Bend Tribune, September 5, 1972
© *South Bend Tribune* – USA TODAY NETWORK

The process of change at Notre Dame has now reached that point where male and female undergraduates will have the opportunity to fully share an educational community as coequals. This new community that can now be developed has been under preparation for a long time and a great many details have received attention. What remains is for each of us, individually in a creative way, to realize the personal growth that this new community makes possible.[11]

Coverage of ND continued, and on September 7, 1972, CBS News commentator Walter Cronkite shared reporter Ike Pappas' interviews with several ND women on the evening news.

◇ *Diana Wilson Ostermann, ND 1976:* "Regarding the media on campus, I vaguely remember a reporter getting in my face with a microphone and asking in a harsh, demanding voice, 'How does it feel to crack an all-male institution?' I answered that was not why I chose Notre Dame; I listed its academic strength, enrollment size, distance from my Illinois home, etc. Notre Dame's turning coed just meant I now had access to a school that met my criteria. Unfortunately, the only quote on CBS that made the cut was my reference to how 'guys looked at us like cattle.'"

A broadcast journalist for three-quarters of a century, Walter Leland Cronkite Jr. (1916–2009) served as anchor of the *CBS Evening News* from 1962 until he retired in 1981. He was the first to inform the nation of JFK's assassination, and during the 1960s and 1970s, opinion polls cited him as "the most trusted man in America." Known as "Uncle Walter," he is remembered for his catchphrase with which he signed off his broadcasts: "And that's the way it is."[12]

The male perspective added balance to Cronkite's story. While some male students expressed unhappiness over the crowded dorm situation, others offered counterpoints on Notre Dame's gradual inclusion of women:

◇ *Bill Etter, ND 1972:* "[T]his is a good thing for the Notre Dame male. He's condescending enough in some ways and competing with women and knowing that women are just as good as he is or just as equal in the classroom is going to be stimulating."[13]

◇ *Mike Creaney, ND 1973:* "Tradition doesn't end with the beginning of women. I think we are just adding another chapter in the long legend of Notre Dame."[14]

That evening, many of us gathered to watch the news in the basement of Walsh. Afterward, Beverly and I returned to our room for the first of many late-night talks. We toasted the effectiveness of our pre-arrival planning with rum and Cokes. As we mapped out the next day's activities, we failed to truly recognize the historical significance and personal impact of our decision to attend Notre Dame.

The Week Before Classes

Ron Skrabacz, ND 1976

'Twas the week before classes, in Seventy-Two,
Not a future was certain, not even a clue.
The freshmen just hung by their dorm rooms and prayed,
In hopes that a friend or two soon would be made.

The brave ones were venturous exploring South Bend,
While dozens more searched for a dance to attend.
And a few with exhaustion, and some with the blues,
Had just settled down for an afternoon snooze.

When out on the quad rose a loud orchestration,
We sprang from our rooms thinking, "What in tarnation?"
Away down the hallways we flew with a buzz,
Tore open the front doors to see what it was.

The sun on the crest of the famed Golden Dome,
Gave assurance that N.D. was proudly our home.
When what to our wondering eyes should we scan,
But America's oldest — and best — marching band,

With a little pep rally amidst all the fuss,
We knew in a moment it must be for us.
More vocal than ever the cheerleaders came,
And they called out traditions of old Notre Dame:

"There's hall life! And football! In P.E. there's swimmin'!
There's Hesburgh! And Heismans! And now we've got women!
At the top of the list! At the top of them all!
That's where we are! Who we are! Fall after fall!"

Then all heard the stir the Irish football team made,
When they met with the leprechaun, clad in green suede.
So up to the stage hopped the cheerleading crew
With the gridiron boys, and Parseghian too!

And then, in a twinkling, we heard Ara state
The passing and running, of course, would be great.
As he drew back his head, and was furling his brow,
Bold and gutsy, Parseghian came with a vow.

He would guess that for sure, from our first year to fourth,
At least one would be filled with a championship berth.
A number of times he had knocked on that door,
And he spoke like a legend who'd been there before.

The crowd—how they listened! His message, how stirring!
His focus was winning, with defense and scoring!
His uplifting speech left us beaming with pride,
And we cheered for our coach as he stepped to the side.

Then one final speaker was last, but not least,
And we stood there in awe of this iconic priest.
He had a strong face, and a slew of credentials,
With a gait when he walked, that was most presidential.

He was humble yet bold, a crusader for freedom,
And we laughed when he said one of us might succeed him.
A wink of his eye over what he had said
Soon gave us to know we would love Father Ted.

He spoke a few words, about faith and good deeds,
And filled all our hearts with the challenge to lead.
Then saying a little about highs and lows,
And trusting in God, from the platform he rose.

He sprang to his feet, to the crowd gave a blessing,
And away he departed with issues more pressing.
But we heard him exclaim, to our new coed mix:
"Best of luck to you all—Class of Seventy-Six!"

Travel Guides

In his novel *The Witch of Portobello*, author Paulo Coelho points out a universal aspect of experience (whether by road or by water): "When we venture into that unfamiliar sea, we trust blindly in those who guide us, believing that they know more than we do."[1] Countless resources on the Notre Dame campus helped students—both male and female—settle into university life. Brochures and ads for student insurance and refrigerator rentals inundated the mailboxes of incoming freshmen. Unsolicited communications from upperclassmen provided suggestions for an easier transition to college.

But not all of these resources understood the new women on campus. Student government and the Ombudsman Service offered ways to integrate into campus life, but these organizations did not initially make any significant overtures to the women. Periodicals and *The Observer* still saw their primary audience as straight males, although some advertising promoted products using overt sexuality—not equality.

◇◇◇

One of the first resources intended to help freshmen was a directory of their male and female classmates, nicknamed the "Dog Book." Unlike Facebook with its updatable photos and profiles, this static guidebook contained only names, hometowns, and photos (if provided). With it, students familiarized themselves with the fresh faces on campus. They used it to recall the names of those met in classes, at parties, or in bars, often preventing unexpected surprises when freshman dates arrived for the first time. Both males and females sometimes perused the book as a welcome break from studying.

> ◇ *Sally Naxera Benson, ND 1976:* "I initially thought it [the "Dog Book"] was a good reference. Coming from a small, rural community where my graduating class was a whopping eighty-eight students, it helped me to navigate my new university experience

88

by referencing the book from time to time. I later learned it became a vehicle of ridicule for some, especially women."

◇ *Ray Pikna, ND 1976:* "Upon returning to our freshman room, my new friends and I went through the 'Dog Book.' This pictorial directory allowed us to memorize the names of all 125 of our women classmates so we could meet them or impress the other guys with the women we knew. Let's not kid ourselves. The 'Dog Book' wasn't just used to put a name with a face. Both men and women used the 'Dog Book' to check out members of the opposite sex, and it wasn't uncommon for upperclassmen to borrow ours."

◇ *Frank Fransioli, ND 1976:* "I remember the book but not how it was distributed or by whom. I remember looking at it after there was a glitch in the campus phone system, a massive sort of 'party line.' I used it to match faces to the voices of the people I'd met 'online.' I regret I did not realize other schools had similar books and to see the potential of this paper-based 'face book.'"

◇ *Darlene Palma Connelly, ND 1977:* "Members of the class of '77 responded to the form they received about the '1973 Freshman Register' (aka, the 'Dog Book') by either sending a picture or accepting placement in the 'No Picture Available' section. With or without pictures, the identifying information listed your nickname (if you shared it), hometown, intended ND major, and extracurricular interests. Only one person who either saw a prior version or knew something the rest of us missed sent quite a unique picture with his entry."

The "Dog Book" was the only pictorial directory on campus in the 1970s. On February 4, 2004, Harvard sophomore Mark Zuckerberg launched Facebook (now Meta). He built a website as a social media platform to connect his fellow students. The original name evolved from "face book" directories given to American college students.

"Dog Book" photo
(1973–1974)

89

Some women, like Jeanine Sterling, knew exactly what role the "Dog Book" played on campus:

> ◇ *Jeanine Sterling, ND 1976:* "When I received the mailer about contributing my photo to the 'Dog Book,' I knew exactly what it was going to be used for and immediately pitched it into the trash. I knew about this nasty little piece of work because, when I was younger, I had read a series of teen-oriented books from the 1950s and early 1960s. I couldn't believe this was a thing at Notre Dame in 1972."

The first ever publication of the "Dog Book" anticipated women entering Notre Dame as full-time undergraduates in the fall of 1971 as part of the proposed ND–SMC merger. It displayed photos of both ND and SMC freshmen and included a welcome letter from John Barkett, the 1971–1972 ND student body president. He described the changing makeup of the freshman class and the world of Notre Dame. His words foreshadowed coeducation's impact:

> No class in Irish history will experience the changing Notre Dame more than yours. For 1971–1972 is the start of coeducation at Notre Dame and Saint Mary's and, before you graduate, there will be one thousand more women and less men at the new Notre Dame.[2]

Succeeding Barkett as student president in 1972–1973, "King" Robert Calhoun Kersten's bizarre "Dear Rabble" letter in the "Dog Book" welcomed ND's first women with a message that exemplified some of the sexist attitudes found on the male-dominated campus.[3] The 1973–1974 version of the directory improved, with welcome letters from both the chairman of Saint Mary's student board of governance and Dennis Etienne, Kersten's successor. Etienne counseled the incoming class of 1977 freshmen on both campuses:

> You will get out of Notre Dame what you put into it. And your years at Notre Dame will be as fulfilling as you are willing to invest yourself in the University—its people and growth. At times, this investment will demand sacrifices of you and cause you anguish....Notre Dame's most valuable asset, contrary to popular opinion, is not the football field but the people of the University—people who are willing to invest themselves—people who are committed to the success of Notre Dame as an institution dedicated to the education of Christian scholars—people who are not only willing to speak out but who are also willing to listen.[4]

For freshmen entering in 1974, the "Dog Book" opened with a cosigned welcome letter by ND and SMC student body officials, a rare example of joint communications. This progress was lost when only male ND student body representatives signed the 1975 welcome letter — although its message addressed both communities and encouraged freshmen to embrace

> the traditions of Notre Dame and Saint Mary's, a national championship football team, a recognized athletic program, dedicated action on behalf of the campus community and the South Bend area...and many worthwhile and challenging student activities.[5]

Another resource on campus for the broader community was *The Observer*, the daily newspaper serving Notre Dame, Saint Mary's, and Holy Cross College. Founded by students in 1966, it was the primary source of news and campus information. The paper operated without faculty advisers or close oversight by the administration.[6] As an Associated Press (AP) newspaper, *The Observer* also printed wire stories of national and world news.

The Observer memorialized the university's coeducation journey from the decision to merge–not to merge, to admitting and increasing the number of women at ND, to the impact of their presence. It spent a great deal of ink describing the residential hall controversies, alcohol policies, and drug regulations. Changes in ND and SMC communities and personnel reflected the noteworthy adjustments of a university in transition.

The Observer's letters to the editor expressed student opinions on parietals, alcohol abuse, and off-campus living, especially security issues, that proved to be unsettling reading. While the holy grail of male athletics — football — caught more than its fair share of reporting, major coverage of women's sports did not surface until October 1974. Brief and infrequent articles covered Saint Mary's College and South Bend activities. Despite a robust concert schedule, students seldom read in-depth interviews with the performers, many of whom later joined The Rock and Roll Hall of Fame.

Several publications documented the campus atmosphere and attitudes encountered by the women. *Notre Dame Magazine* published its first issue in February 1972. Its articles covered the abandoned ND–SMC merger, with students predicting the demise of "the girls' school" across the road. The magazine, the brainchild of Ron Parent (ND 1974, MA), combined *Notre Dame Alumnus* and the university's quarterly *Insight* into a single publication. It paved a new path in academic publishing:

> The magazine is an extension of the classroom....Our primary area is alumni and we cover all kinds of different subjects, thoughts and ideas to give them something to think about and discuss.[7]

Newsweek cited *Notre Dame Magazine* "for excellence in relating an institution to public affairs" after just eighteen issues and ranked it in the top tenth of alumni magazines; 87 percent of surveyed alumni agreed, rating the publication as "excellent" or "good."[8] Then, as it does now, essays covered thought-provoking issues facing the ND community such as abortion, euthanasia, contraception, and the convergence of technology, humanity, and God.[9] According to editor Kerry Temple (ND 1974):

> [*Notre Dame Magazine*] replicates in print the full Notre Dame experience...a magazine that helps nurture Notre Dame's aspirations toward intellectual leadership by addressing the vital issues of the day while telling Notre Dame stories of service and academic achievement, stories of its people, stories of the heart and mind and soul.[10]

Additional publications addressed the diverse interests of the ND extended family. *Scholastic*, a monthly magazine, offered students a valuable motto to guide their lives: *Disce quasi semper victurus, vive quasi cras moriturus*, which translates to "Study like you will live forever; live like you will die tomorrow."[11] Students particularly enjoyed *Scholastic*'s annual football review, and its coverage of a wide range of topics encouraged on-campus debates. According to its 1976 editor, John Phelan:

> Although we are financially dependent on the University we do not have to fear reprisals if we criticize the administration as long as we run an interesting and respectable magazine....We are not flaming radicals."[12]

The *Scholastic* team also provided production consulting and facilities for other publications. *The Technical Review, The Business Review,* and *The Science Quarterly* delivered information on engineering, business administration, and science, respectively. The *Juggler*, established in 1919, was the second oldest publication at Notre Dame. Published semiannually, it showcased student art and literature.

Beyond such periodicals, the "Dog Book," and *The Observer,* some halls also produced dorm papers. Taking both serious and humorous looks at residential life, these publications provided dorm-specific information and stories. The first such paper, Morrissey's mimeographed *Bullsheet*, appeared weekly starting in 1969. Others included the *Keenan Rag*, which used a Xerox offset copying process to include photos, and the monthly *The Fisher Nothing*. Not until 1975 did a women's dorm publish its own paper, Walsh Hall's biweekly, one-page paper, *The Solicito*, followed by *The Farley's Follies* and Breen-Phillips' *Provocative Press*.

While campus publications reported on the changes taking place at Notre Dame, organizations such as the student government actually had to manage and oversee these changes. The "boys' club" needed to evolve before women could experience any level of normalcy across all elements of their college years.

As a service organization, the Notre Dame Student Government listened and responded to the students, while its nonpolitical arm, the Student Union Board, ran concerts and social activities. For the first two years of coeducation, the student government made few changes to its programming. When Pat McLaughlin became student body president for 1974–1975, he promised to reform the school's judicial code and improve relationships with the university's board of trustees. The board commissioned the tripartite (student, faculty, administration) Committee on Undergraduate Life (COUL) to investigate academics, residential life, coeducation, finances, and student affairs. Yet few substantive changes resulted.

In March 1975, 57 percent of ND students elected Ed Byrne and Tom "Fitz" Fitzgerald as student body president and vice president, respectively, for the 1975–1976 academic year. These two enlisted friends in every dorm, including the women's halls, to support their candidacy. Their platform, using the initial COUL report as its organizing principle, centered on improved communication, governance, and coordination within the Student Union Board, the Student Life Council, the Hall Presidents Council, the Academic Council, the Ombudsman Service, and the dorm-based judicial boards.

Byrne and Fitz's first test dealt more with national politics than campus life. The week following their election, President Gerald Ford visited campus. McLaughlin as student body president, Byrne as his incoming replacement, and students from the Academic and College councils were invited to the session with Ford. Neither McLaughlin nor Byrne felt these invitees represented the student body, so they decided not to attend. This caused the national media to portray them as part of a group of students planning to walk out of the event in protest of Ford's acceptance of an honorary degree and his "new isolationism" policies.

After the AP wire stories hit, Byrne reversed course and attended the session to raise student concerns about foreign policy. Afterward, the Notre Dame community sent Ford a letter. According to Ed Byrne, he and more than a dozen student leaders asked Ford to listen to the "tide of history" the president had acknowledged "on our campus and thousands of others." President Ford, in his April 11, 1975, reply, wrote words relevant to students' future roles. As Byrne tells it, the president emphasized that "ideals developed in the academic community and tempered through daily, practical experience can indeed properly become goals toward which an individual, and a nation, direct its best efforts."

Years later, Byrne had an opportunity to ask Ford if he remembered Saint Patrick's Day in "1976" at ND. Ford corrected Byrne immediately, noting that, when president, he was on campus in 1975. Then Ford smiled, Byrne remembers him saying, "You know, that was the most enjoyable day of my presidency." For an offensive lineman from the University of Michigan, Ford said genuinely wonderful things about Notre Dame.

The media continued to pay a great deal of attention to Notre Dame, even after the novelty of coeducation died down. One area that received much attention in the summer of 1975 was drinking on campus. One magazine — sometimes seen in the male dorms — sporadically published lists of hard-drinking colleges, though by this time ND's reputation was beginning to change. As Byrne recalls it, *Playboy* removed the university from this roster and declared ND students "professionals" and not the "amateurs" found on other campuses.

Thus, it was ironic when Keith Hewitt of the National Institute for Alcoholism and Alcohol Abuse approached Byrne about holding a nationwide conference on alcohol use on college campuses. Byrne agreed to host the inaugural University 50 + 12 Seminar with fifty public and twelve private universities in attendance. Classmate Diana Merten (now Bourke) led the November 1975 gathering. Byrne recalls that Diana talked about how:

> There is no institution in our society that has taken it upon itself to introduce young people to alcohol. Most families do not do it. Students are forced to drink behind closed doors or to sneak it out.... All this does is form a real mystique about drinking.

This historic gathering had long-term impacts. Following the event, Diana worked on the Whole College Catalog's publication, *Drinking: A Guide to Alcohol Abuse Prevention*.

> ◇ *Ed Byrne, ND 1976:* "Decades after the first 50 + 12 Seminar, I attended a conference sponsored by ski areas trying to get a handle on student drinking during spring break in Colorado. As its leader and I discussed their mission and ND's small part in its [the 50 + 12 Seminar] creation, I mentioned attending the original seminar. He gasped, 'You were *there*?' He pointed to it as the beginning of their efforts to promote responsible drinking. He seemed to look at me with newfound respect, although maybe he just could not believe how ancient I must be."

Concerned about the phenomenon of underage students making the trek to Michigan where the legal drinking age was eighteen, the student government decided to challenge Indiana's legal drinking age of twenty-one and its related tight alcohol policies. Student fatalities happened far too often as students traveled back and forth to bars north of the state line. Tom Black, Darlene Palma (now Connelly), and others on the student government team took on

Darlene Palma
The Observer, January 19, 1976

the challenge of convincing the state legislature to lower the drinking age to nineteen. The lobbying efforts of these students came within a handful of votes of success.

The student government also, at times, challenged Notre Dame's administration. Before Christmas break in 1975, Michael Gassman, an Academic Council representative, announced that the proposed 1976–1977 academic calendar required class attendance on the Friday after Thanksgiving. This spurred students who were unhappy with this illogical and unenforceable change to create a new form of protest. Under ND's Vietnam War-era student protest rules of not interfering with classes nor exceeding fifteen minutes, these protest organizers decided to use the short skit format of the popular *Laugh-In* television show.

Comedians Dan Rowan and Dick Martin hosted *Rowan and Martin's Laugh-In*, an NBC television comedy that ran from 1968 to 1973. Its title derived from the 1960s hippie culture and the "love-ins" and "sit-ins" common to the civil rights and anti-war protests of the time. Catchphrases from the program included: "I'll drink to that," "You bet your sweet bippy," "Sock it to me," "Verrry interesting," and "Want a Walnetto?"

◇ *Bob Quakenbush, ND 1976:* "When the university introduced an academic calendar requiring classes on the Friday following Thanksgiving, the almost universal reaction was 'No Way!' Byrne assembled student leaders to plan our *Laugh-In* response. Ed bought five laugh boxes that emitted loud, infectious sounds. At about 12:55 p.m. on the day of the protest, the sound of laughter echoed across the God Quad. Soon approximately twenty-five hundred students gathered at the Administration Building's stairs.

"For this campaign, I created a tagline: 'Would you rather call home now? Or would you rather call home next Thanksgiving?' We plastered hand-lettered posters campus-wide asking students to encourage their parents to write letters expressing their displeasure. We asked the letters to be sent to our office so we could determine the level of support before delivering them to the administration.

"When we heard Hesburgh was speaking in one of the dorms following the announcement, a large group crashed the event. As executive coordinator of the Hall Presidents Council, I drew the short straw to voice our concerns to Father Ted that night. I decided to try an emotional 'rearview mirror' analogy, pointing out that I, and others at ND, had sisters at Saint Mary's. I asked Father Ted how he thought our parents were going to feel when they picked up our sisters for Thanksgiving weekend, only to see us in their rearview mirrors on Notre Dame Avenue, sadly waving goodbye as they drove away. The tension broke, and eventually saner heads prevailed. Within a month, the Academic Council quietly reversed their decision."

Besides presidential visits, conferences, and the academic calendar, the Notre Dame Student Government also investigated student concerns. VP Fitz designed a food-based co-op for off-campus students, staff, and faculty. The membership drive failed to attract enough interest for either the co-op or even a buyers' club. However, Fitz leveraged the approach to establish a travel bureau that provided reduced airline fares to students.

Students in the '60s and '70s had limited methods for easily making signs or copies of flyers. Before Chester Carlson invented the copier, documents were replicated by hand, photography, carbon copies, or mimeograph. In fact, carbon paper remained useful until the advent of word processors in the late 1970s. Today, most email programs allow an author to send a carbon copy, or cc, to additional recipients.

John Lonsberg and Mary Ellen Keenan analyzed the judicial board system that existed in some halls. Through their efforts, every hall eventually had a board to address situations not settled by hall staffs and the dean of students. These judicial boards ensured more consistent handling of alcohol and parietal violations for both men and women.

By mid-January 1976, the Student Life Council successfully implemented twenty-six of the original thirty-nine initiatives developed by COUL. Accomplishments included the extension of services to off-campus students, improved infirmary and placement offices, long-range housing plans, and a study on creating and maintaining social spaces — the lack of which heightened the tensions of those early years of coeducation.

As graduation approached for the first class of freshman women, the committee chairs delivered their reports to Notre Dame's Board of Trustees. Ed Byrne recalled that the paper, subtitled "A Case for Giving More Responsibility to Students," reflected a dichotomy between preparing students "in the classroom and on the practice field," yet the controlled, unrealistic, and in loco parentis environment was not representative of real-life situations, making the application of personal values sometimes difficult.

While the student government sought to improve campus life and to bring the realities of life inside the Notre Dame bubble, students found additional resources to turn to for assistance. One little-known resource was the Ombudsman Service. Originating in 1967, this office sporadically supported the Notre Dame community as a source of information. In the fall of 1972, the first female undergraduates benefited from Student Body President Kersten's appointment of Bill McLean as the Ombudsman Service's director. Under McLean, the Ombudsman Service became an effective, reliable arm of student government, quickly outgrowing its single desk, phone, and borrowed telephone directories. He grew this office to more than 120 male and female volunteers. McLean's unbridled energy in answering questions about campus life made a difference in that first year of coeducation, and he quickly earned the nickname "The Wizard of OM." His leadership and commitment were evident as McLean addressed many common issues and answered questions in his "Action Express" *Observer* column. Ever proactive, he even instituted a "Quickie Bus" shuttle service to discourage students from walking to the Michigan bars to drink, thus reducing the number of accidents.

In May 2022, William "Bill" M. McLean died from complications from blood and bone cancers after a nine-year-long battle. Born in 1953, Bill was a member of the Notre Dame class of 1975 and earned a master's degree and an MBA from DePaul. Bill taught for more than three decades and was widely admired and respected by his students.

McLean officially retained the role for the next two years. He stayed well beyond his own 1975 graduation, helping his successors, Matt Cockrell (ND 1976) and the first female ombudsperson, Bridget O'Donnell (ND 1977). O'Donnell expanded the role's responsibilities to ensure that student body elections came off without a hitch. Its reach had almost no bounds, and no issue was too big or too small for this dedicated team of volunteers.

> ◇ *Bridget O'Donnell Provenzano, ND 1977*: "For Christmas 1976, Father Griffin requested Christmas lights for a large fir tree outside LaFortune Student Center. The Ombudsman Service got the call to make Father's Christmas wish come true. We raised the necessary funds, and then another Ombudsman volunteer and I raided the South Bend Sears store, buying every string of lights. I contacted facilities for a bucket truck so we could string the lights. Magic fell that night when we turned on the tree. Father Griff got his Christmas wish!"

◇◇◇

REARVIEW REFLECTION Personally, I regret not getting more involved at ND from the start. When I received the letter requesting my senior picture for inclusion in the "Dog Book," I ignored it. By not responding, I failed to participate in this initial coeducation artifact. I envy today's freshmen who no longer need a "Dog Book," given the myriad social media avenues available to them. The "Dog Book" was just one tangible example of how the male-dominated student government operated before we arrived in September 1972. After ND undergraduate women joined the student-run organizations and clubs, these collegiate mainstays took on new dimensions. And, as participants, we developed not only lifelong contacts but also skills to work within and with diverse teams.

Filling Stations

In their first semester at Notre Dame, students often missed things previously taken for granted, such as home-cooked meals. Although the dining halls served food, they were, more importantly, places to gather. They offered opportunities to see or be seen within Notre Dame's new coeducational context. For some, they also provided venues in which to let off steam while adjusting to new roommates and responsibilities. How the men decompressed from such pressures was shocking—food fight! Pearl Bailey, in her collection of short essays titled *Hurry Up, America, and Spit*, points out that "[w]e look into mirrors but we only see the effects of our times on us—not our effects on others."[1] Looking into the mirror fifty years later offers an opportunity to see how the Notre Dame dining hall experience affected some of its new women.

◇◇◇

The cafeterias offered front-row seats to observe and participate in a core collegiate activity—eating. The South Dining Hall, the older of two eateries, opened in 1927. Its Gothic architecture was reminiscent of a medieval guildhall, and its pleasant environment included polished wood paneling, lofty ceilings, and murals by recognized artists. The contemporary North Dining Hall, built in 1955, offered the same menu as its counterpart. It welcomed students with *The Last Supper*, an original wood relief carved by famed sculptor Ivan Mestrovic. Given that women in the ND–SMC Co-Exchange Program ate in both locales with little fanfare, the administration anticipated no problems related to mealtimes.

The men, however, despite expressed sentiments of wanting more women on campus, made mealtimes challenging. From day one, an unnatural coolness permeated the air as ND's first female undergraduates entered the cafeterias. Notwithstanding the Co-Exchange Program, women were not highly visible in this setting in the past, and their presence made some men uncomfortable. The men viewed the women as novelties and as "objects" of discussion over plates of food. How the males expressed this interest varied by table and ranged from silence to cheers to jeers.

> ◇ *Bob Quakenbush, ND 1976:* "I distinctly remember an amusing attempt to be 'welcoming' that happened more than once in the North Dining Hall. While Notre Dame is French for Our Lady, 'dame' was also slang in the mid-twentieth century for an attractive woman. So, imagine when some clever soul thought it 'welcoming' to play Rodgers and Hammerstein's 'There Is Nothing Like a Dame' from the 1949 musical *South Pacific* at full volume over the public address system. I'm fairly certain the men thought it was funny, but, looking back, I wonder what the women thought. Perhaps by admitting women, Notre Dame was simply doing its best to help the male students. Consider the last three lines of the song: 'There ain't a thing that's wrong with any man here / That can't be cured by putting him near / A girly, womanly, female, feminine dame!'"[2]

> ◇ *Tim Demarais, ND 1974:* "I felt sorry for the women. The dining hall was like going to the zoo [with men] staring at the women as if they were some exotic, often beautiful, animals."

Historically, male students at Notre Dame dressed in coats and ties, were served by student waiters, and dined family style. Mirroring the changing times, by the 1970s they came dressed as they wanted. Most women, however, worried about what they wore and how they looked. They seldom wore pajamas or sweaty workout clothes; some even wore nicer clothes than those worn to class.

> ◇ *Janet Krier Breen, ND 1975:* "We looked forward to dinner as a welcome respite from a busy day and a chance to gather the dorm buddies together. We even discussed appropriate attire. Male students appeared straight from a workout—all smelly and wearing dirty sweats. Gross! We agreed casual but clean was most fitting for dinner."

"Hey look—freshmen!"
The Observer, September 18, 1972

Students, especially freshmen, often sought the comfort found in "packs." Cliques sometimes evolved as individuals ate with the same friends and sat in the same section of the same dining hall day after day. How ironic that the first female undergraduates, who wanted to integrate Notre Dame, often sat with those similar in gender or from the same dorm and class year. Such behavior likely discouraged social advances from more timid individuals, adding to the stereotype of Notre Dame women as unapproachable.

> ◇ *Becky Banasiak Code, ND 1976:* "The South Dining Hall was wide open and provided more opportunities for meeting new people. Yet people tended to eat in the same section, so you tended to see the same people at all your meals."

Not just students ate in the cafeterias. University Food Services provided a program for faculty and administrators to eat with the students — ten luncheons for ten dollars or ten evening meals for fifteen dollars.[3] Participating professors announced their plans to be at a certain dining hall location at the conclusion of their classes. Students, who normally sat with friends, took these opportunities to meet informally with faculty members, sharing ideas and sometimes seeking advice or asking questions inappropriate during lectures.

> ◇ *Maggie Waltman Smith, ND 1976:* "As a transfer student in the fall of 1974, I had the option of purchasing a university meal plan that included weekday lunches. I think I did that for one semester but came to prefer the atmosphere at the public cafeteria off the South Dining Hall lobby. Commonly referred to as the 'pay cafe,' it served patrons who were a mix of off-campus students, grad students, and university faculty. It was a wonderful place to spend time between classes, to eavesdrop on conversations among professors — and to get a bottomless cup of coffee for a quarter."

The fascination with "people-watching" in the dining halls was not restricted to men staring at women. Students of both sexes frequently gawked at notable ND sports figures such as Joe Montana, Dave Casper, Willie Townsend, Ross Browner, and Adrian Dantley. One group of attractive, smartly dressed female students became known as the "Dining Hall Delights." When these individuals walked by with their trays, conversations stopped as both males and females stared in admiration.

On many evenings, guys waited for women to pass through the lines and then rated them by holding up cards numbered one to ten. Although initially targeting women, this practice was also occasionally directed at men. These "rating sessions" typically lasted twenty minutes or less, and those not on the judging panel participated by applauding and cheering. When this offensive ritual became an almost nightly event, the dining hall staff confronted the organizers. The young men justified their actions by explaining that everyone recognized these events as practical jokes since they included arbitrary ratings, joker-type cards, and at times other males.

◇ *Jeanine Sterling, ND 1976:* "Fortunately, I never saw the rating card abuse. What I do remember is the repeated, excruciating experience of getting up in the middle of a meal to get another glass of milk, walking down the main aisle to reach the beverage–salad station, and having every boy along the way stop talking and stare at me as I filled my glass and walked back to my seat in dead silence. I felt like an exhibit at the zoo. I was all of eighteen years old and had no idea how to respond."

> Notre Dame did not own the market on the immature behavior indicative of the culture and times: Many coed colleges experienced similar improprieties. "Better Dead Than Coed" banners fluttered across Dartmouth's Fraternity Row, even though the college admitted women several years prior to its class of 1979. The guys also held up signs from dorm balconies, grading girls who walked to dinner on a scale of one to ten.[4]

◇ *Anonymous male, ND 1976:* "At the time, I didn't think much of it [the rating game], other than a bunch of clowns trying to get the girls' attention. I rarely wondered if it was hurtful, though undoubtedly it was to some. It is too bad no one in authority asked the women how they felt, although they may have had mixed emotions—the traditional gender roles conflicting with the nascent feminist views of that era. I suspect their views became stronger over time. Political correctness today demands that we condemn the behavior, but perhaps it was nothing more than a prelude to a primitive mating dance.

"Eventually, some behaviors stopped as the campus normalized with the arrival of more women and the graduation of men from the previous all-male classes. Perhaps the men also realized that their behavior was offensive or considered how their mothers or sisters might have felt if subjected to such treatment. Nevertheless, the emphasis on looks seemed commonplace among young men and women adapting to their raging hormones. Hopefully, such practices have evolved since our time at ND, but the hypocrisy in our society is still evident as we fawn over the 'beautiful people' or so-called 'reality show' celebrities."

Although the staff continually discouraged such rating games, the antics continued well into 1975 when Dean John Macheca officially banned the activity.[5]

◇ *Brian O'Herlihy, ND 1976:* "Having attended public school, it was not unusual for me to be in a class with women, but for most of the boys in the class, it was strange and, I suspect, threatening as they had attended all-male Catholic high schools. This may explain some of the growing pains in those early years of coeducation. I cannot imagine the humiliation of entering the dining hall to tables full of men holding placards rating each woman's appearance. While I was not one of those holding the placards, I did join many others encouraging what clearly was inappropriate and juvenile behavior. Years later, I remember what we did to the female members of that first coed class, and I am embarrassed by what I did and what I did not do at the time. I cannot imagine that any of us who have had daughters or nieces attend Notre Dame over the years would have wanted them to endure the same treatment these brave women endured. I thank them for the important contribution they made in bringing a vibrant and healthy coeducational environment to Notre Dame."[6]

Another new tradition quickly emerged as ND women experienced "dining hall dates." Though some made fun of this practice as a pitiful excuse for a one-on-one meeting, it offered a level of normalcy reminiscent of high school. This practice joined the rating ritual and other more established, unsettling dining customs. Sports teams humiliated new members by having them climb on chairs in the center of South Dining Hall dressed in frilly pink dresses or wearing giant diapers. Upperclassmen encouraged male freshmen to eat their food directly off their trays—no dishes, no utensils, no hands. Everyone eventually experienced a food fight, especially on days before and after major sports events, or such practices as "Viking Night."

Reflecting some college antics, *National Lampoon's Animal House*, a 1978 American comedy film, made "food fight" a recognizable collegiate reference. The movie contains a crass, childish-yet-hilarious food fight scene. John Belushi's "Bluto" character instigates a food fight to stop some guys from chasing him around the cafeteria.

◇ *Ann Pytynia, ND 1976:* "*Ding ding ding!* The sound of utensils banging against glasses signaled the beginning of a food fight. Chaos always ensued, and it was a good idea to get out as fast as you could. I recall only getting hit once by a piece of fried chicken, so I was one of the lucky ones."

◇ *Maryanne Reis Rogers, ND 1976:* "One evening, Shelley Muller [now Simon] and I headed to our normal North Dining Hall destination. I went through the serving area first and entered the dining room where the boys flashed signs with numbers. As a math major, I tried to interpret the meaning of the numbers. As the numbers appeared random, I concluded these men had no number sense.

"A male math major sensed my confusion and rushed over saying, 'Maryanne, I thought someone would have told you. Tonight is Viking Night. The guys waited for some unsuspecting women to enter the dining area. Those numbers are your ratings. The goal is to gross out any coed who enters the cafeteria and drive her away.'

"The boys had garbed themselves in Viking attire complete with horned Viking helmets and scanty cavemen-like clothing. Many ate with their hands; some just slurped food with their mouths — grunting, burping, and farting as they satisfied their 'manly' hunger. Their eating got grosser and louder, and one guy inhaled Jell-O through his nose. Although outraged, we tried to ignore this bizarre behavior, determined to stay no matter what. After the Jell-O incident, we had enough and got up to leave. The boys stood, jeered, and cheered to celebrate driving us out.

"We left the dining hall defeated and discouraged. Yet, in hindsight, this experience provided some surprising results. It prepared me for my future as the mother of three boys with Viking-like tendencies, and I believe that I successfully taught them appropriate, civilized, gentlemanly behavior.

"We harbored some resentment toward the males from that night, but we put it all in the rearview mirror. However, at a 2006 graduation party of a friend's son, I actually met 'Shrek,' the friend's brother-in-law — a 1977 ND graduate. As we reminisced about ND, I discovered Shrek's claim to fame was reintroducing Viking Night to the North Dining Hall. Small world!"

When the males were not "serving up" the food, the cafeteria primarily provided sustenance — and food fight ammunition — in the form of meat and starches; a large salad bowl at the end of the serving line offered one of the few healthy alternatives. Students looked for ways to customize the standard fare by putting vanilla ice cream in machine-dispensed Coca-Cola or adding broccoli, cauliflower, or turkey to salads. Luckily, when a mouse jumped out of the bowl of iceberg lettuce, no one added it to their meal. Special meals included shrimp during Lent and a monthly steak night. Guys wanting even more meat traveled to Saint Mary's for its Saturday steak nights. Some ND women, resenting SMC restricting this meal to ND males, gave their ND steak tickets to male friends to stem the rush across the highway.

It was not unusual for students to stash portable food items in pockets and take them back to the dorm for study breaks and late-night snacks.

◇ *Ron Skrabacz, ND 1976:* "We soon realized the dining hall could supplement our ever-active lifestyles and the burning of calories from sports, walking, and/or running to our classes, or just staying busy.

"If you ask my Alumni Hall friends about my greatest claim to fame at ND, they might say walking out of the South Dining Hall with thirty-six boxes of cereal (the small breakfast size) at one time under my khaki poncho. A true snacking coup — hopefully, the statute of limitations has expired, and the university can't void my alumnus status or back bill me at today's rates."

The cafeteria, a daily bottomless pit of experiences, was truly a pathological place. Conversations often centered on not only the latest rating targets but also the varied eating habits on display. While athletes carried trays with huge quantities of food, the women often put little on their plates. Few went back for seconds as they were loath to become the target of the men's cafeteria games.

Some students ironically compensated for their high-caloric intake by drinking Tab or Fresca in lieu of regular soda. Others exercised to burn off the calories accrued from eating enormous quantities of food. Several potentially anorexic females, including one girl so thin her elbows looked like sharpened weapons and her legs like toothpicks, seemed to struggle to carry their trays. Others, hiding eating disorders, seldom went to the dining hall at all, practicing

Anorexia nervosa, a serious psychological illness related to eating, is linked to perfectionism, phobias, and obsessive-compulsive disorder. Approximately 9 percent of those affected with it die, and 95 percent with the disease are female.[7] In the 1970s, the disease reached epidemic proportions as, according to the American Psychiatric Association, one in two hundred fifty young women suffered from it. In 1978, the psychologist Hilde Bruch claimed anorexia nervosa was a pervasive problem in many American colleges and universities.[8]

what is now viewed as a form of "social isolation." The administration's ignorance of eating disorders on campus was typical of the times. General awareness of such issues did not surface within the American culture until well after the first female pioneers graduated.

◇◇◇

REARVIEW REFLECTION My own cafeteria experiences were a mix of the good and the bad. At one point, I was struggling with how to handle an uncomfortable situation with a male classmate during dinner, and I received assistance from a surprising source: a female professor who often ate with the women students.

My roommate Beverly was taking a class from Dr. Carole Moore, one of ND's few female professors. After listening to my tirades about how one male's behavior unnerved me, Beverly mentioned to Moore how this guy approached us almost nightly in the dining hall. "Bug Eyes" never looked at my face, so he had no idea how I reacted to his presence. Moore said she had a solution and proposed we meet for dinner. She suggested another three or four girls join us, ensuring a full table.

One night soon after, Beverly, Dr. Moore, three dorm mates, and I went to dinner and sat in our regular section. As expected, Bug Eyes soon approached us. He did his normal thing and talked to my breasts. The difference on this night, however, was how I and the others reacted—Moore had instructed us to stare at his crotch. Sitting at the table, our eyes hit the intended target. He stammered, blushed, and then went quiet. Eventually, he looked at my face! I learned an effective technique that night and used it later in work-related situations. Still, the incident stayed with me and even resurfaced after many decades at an alumni event.

> ◇ *Stephen Klug, ND 1976:* "Debi and I reconnected at the 2005 Alumni Leadership Conference. As we made plans to attend the evening's cocktail party, we reviewed the attendee list for class of '76 members. She freaked when she saw one particular name. After explaining her interactions with this guy, I found it difficult to believe his approach around women would not have changed. Imagine my surprise when almost thirty years after graduation, this guy still had the same 'affliction.'"

Not all of my dining hall experiences were negative. Some, such as the ubiquitous food fight, were simply odd. My first food fight involved fried chicken, mashed potatoes, and a slew of easily thrown foods. The perpetrators who started the fight quickly escaped by crawling into the large metal carts where we placed our trays after meals. I hid under a large wooden table, watching the chaos as strange thoughts ran through my head. I struggled to understand such childishness and waste. I worried about the food permanently ruining my tweed skirt and staining my white blouse. I wondered if SMC women experienced such bizarre antics. I found the situation unbelievable.

Embarrassingly, before the 1973 Orange Bowl game, a *Miami Herald* article on coeducation quoted me as calling this my most memorable first semester experience.[9] Thankfully, food fights are long a thing of the past — my past. Most likely, today's students are only familiar with the concept through movies and conversations with their "elders."

For many, dining provided much more than simple nourishment and social interaction. I was one of these individuals. I ate and drank for comfort. Gaining weight from less-than-healthy eating habits, I quickly learned about the "freshman fifteen." The food showed up not only on my clothes after a food fight but also on my hips! I soon outgrew my new clothes as I ate unlimited quantities of starches and sugars.

I supplemented my regular three meals a day and unlimited Coca-Cola with late-night pizzas. I enjoyed beer while playing pinball at off-campus bars. I even convinced a friend who worked at the ice cream counter at The Huddle in the LaFortune Student Center to deliver hot fudge pecan ice cream sundaes to my room after his shifts.

My eating habits were terrible, and on top of that, I loved participating in specialty food eating contests.

With Marta Suarez-Murias
and the late Diana Lewis,
Dome in the background
Miami Herald
January 2, 1973
Photo by Mike O'Bryon

One Friday night, Beverly ate forty-one fried popcorn shrimp without getting sick. Given my sweet tooth, I preferred a twelve-pack of Fudgsicles that particular night.

Sometimes I avoided the noise and antics of the dining hall by using the kitchen in Walsh. Cooking soon became my favorite hobby. I made late breakfasts or celebratory meals, sometimes for one, other times for friends. I baked chocolate chip cookies and shared them in class. They became conversational icebreakers and resulted in creative poems and invitations.

Once, when some obnoxious males made pig noises as heavier-set women passed by with their cafeteria trays, I made a special batch of "chocolate" cookies for them. My use of Ex-Lax was my personal strike against such sexism.

107

Watch Out for Falling Jocks

The new women students encountered overwhelming male resistance at every turn at Notre Dame, but particularly in the athletic realm. Since athletics influenced much of the Notre Dame life, many women wanted to participate in all its forms. The benefits of athletic activity to all students were made apparent in John F. Kennedy's position from six decades ago: "Physical fitness is not only one of the most important keys to a healthy body, it is the basis of dynamic and creative intellectual activity."[1] But athletics don't just support intellectual development; success on the playing field also depends on the mental resources brought to the game. One of Arnold Palmer's best-known comments on golf is that "[s]uccess in this game depends less on strength of body than strength of mind and character."[2] The first women in sports at Notre Dame became quite aware of this reciprocal relationship between inner and outer strength.

◇◇◇

The primary locations for sports-related activities were the Rockne Memorial building (the "Rock") and the Athletic and Convocation Center (the "ACC"). The Rock opened in 1937 as a recreational facility for students, faculty, and staff. Available seven days a week, it housed a swimming pool, weight rooms, and handball, basketball, squash, and racquetball courts. The ACC, now the Edmund P. Joyce Athletic and Convocation Center, opened in 1968. Renovations to accommodate the female undergraduates included new lockers and changed designations and signs on several restrooms. Those females wanting to participate in athletics acknowledged these limited accommodations as indicative of the need for radical change (most glaringly apparent on the men-only Burke Memorial Golf Course).

In 1972, Notre Dame's Physical Education Department accepted the Malits Coeducation Committee's recommendation to require physical education classes for women as they had for men. This decision resulted in all rotations (i.e., specified time periods by sport) going coed except for soccer, the only contact sport offered in rotation and available only to the men. However, not until 1974 did the university add a female physical education instructor, Astrid Hotvedt.

◇ *Jeanine Sterling, ND 1976:* "ND's phys ed requirement was painful. Title IX wasn't around during my public high school years, so we only had girls' basketball and cheerleading. I wasn't tall enough for B-ball, loved cheerleading, but was ready to move on and try something different in college. Yet my choices at ND were laughable. Gymnastics was scaled to guys — the guys had to lift me up to be able to reach the parallel bars. Ice-skating was fun but not much exercise. I envy all the choices that later female students had and have."

◇ *Denise Crowley Brenner, ND 1976:* "I felt that many of ND's professors were extremely prejudiced about women. I remember the PE instructor gave us specific exercises that would be good for us when we had babies."

◇ *Ann Pytynia, ND 1976:* "ND did seem quite unprepared for women. I remember a friend who told me her swimming instructor had no idea what to say when she said she had to miss a class because she had her period."

A 2012 *Wall Street Journal* article on student swim tests across the United States noted one exception to ND's requirement: Edward A. "Monk" Malloy, CSC, ND president from 1987 to 2005. A varsity athlete, he "was exempt during basketball season," and his chemical engineering labs "kept him out of the pool" for the rest of his undergraduate days. He told the newspaper, "I had thoughts that maybe (my diploma) would be blank," and Malloy "never did learn to swim."[3]

A 2014 "survey indicated that 74 percent of students wanted the phys ed requirement" to continue. However, in 2015, the university replaced it with a program of study that included seminars and group discussions on "physical and mental wellness, spirituality, culture, [and] academic success."[4]

◇ *Anonymous female, ND 1976:* "Three of us women got together in the same racquetball court. However, because the rules required four per court, they [the schedulers] put a guy with a broken foot with us, implying that a male needed to be 'handicapped' to compete fairly against women."

In contrast, some women enjoyed the opportunity to try different sports they may not have been exposed to in the past.

◇ *Darlene Palma Connelly, ND 1977:* "PE at ND was nothing like the PE classes at my all-girls high school with its limited sports resources. Thus, ND's PE requirement seemed like a cafeteria of sports fare. As a lifeguard for several years, passing the swimming requirement was a no-brainer. All other PE rotations were failures. None more so than the abysmal ice-skating rotation; I was unable to ice-skate in a forward motion. Go figure. I could only skate backward—and s-l-o-w-l-y. The instructors, mostly grad student TAs, took pity. In lieu of forcing me to meet the required competencies, they promised a passing grade if I made every 8:00 a.m. class during that rotation. I did, and I managed not to break any bones."

The swimming requirement was something all students, both male and female, faced. With rare exceptions, swimming was mandatory for freshmen. The swimming test surfaced during World War II when the US Navy trained recruits on ND's campus. As military personnel often died from drowning, this requirement made sense for recruits — not so much for freshmen on an Indiana campus.

The passion to participate in sports extended beyond the required physical education. An interhall athletics program gave young men a chance to continue playing their favorite high school sport at a competitive level. Those just wanting to stay active tossed a football, baseball, or a Frisbee around the quads whenever weather permitted. Notre Dame soon discovered these same sports-related passions in its female students.

"Because of the weather in South Bend, all freshmen must pass a swim test."
The Observer, September 25, 1972

◇ *Ann Hawkins, ND 1976:* "I was on the National Ski Patrol and enjoyed helping others and noted this spirit at ND. I wanted to ski professionally. In 1972, as an athlete, I could only pick my sports as tennis or skiing. I played tennis for two years and skied for four. I became a feminist as opposed to a traditionalist from attending ND."

◇ *Rosemary Tirannanzi Lesser, ND 1976:* "I joined the crew team in my sophomore year at the urging of my roommate. It was the year that I was in the best shape ever."

It only took slightly more than three weeks for women to stake a claim to one of ND's long-standing athletic traditions. A short blurb in the Friday, September 22, 1972, *Observer* announced the university's first women's athletic competition — an interhall football game — between Badin and Walsh.[5]

The sands of time have relegated that "first of its kind" battle into an idyllic Sunday afternoon outing with personal black-and-white photographs serving as the only remaining artifacts. Nearly fifty years later, most women vaguely remembered the game while others wondered whether they played.

Despite the historical significance of this game to ND's coeducation transformation, no *Observer* article covered how the players performed or even which hall won: Legend maintains Walsh beat Badin, 16–6. In those early days, coverage of women's athletics in *The Observer* ranged from sketchy at best to nonexistent at worst. Yet increasing such coverage was key to building awareness of and support for women's athletics.

A few weeks after the Badin–Walsh game, *The Observer* announced a freshman swim meet — open to men *and* women — scheduled for October 11, 1972. Apparently, the novelty of women on campus found *The Observer* wanting for proper pronouns, as the announcement reflected, "A contestant may swim only for the hall in which he (or her) [*sic*] resides."[6] Tim Neuville (ND 1975) gave women top billing for the first time:

Badin Hall sets weekend activities

Flicks, fun, and football are all part of the activities planned this weekend by the women of Badin Hall.

The famous Badin Vintage Cinema will return for a two-night stand Friday and Saturday with the Movie "Citizen Kane," to be shown in the chapel at 7:00 p.m. and 10:00 p.m. Prices remain unaffected by inflation—still seventy-five cents per person. If the showing is a success, the Badin Vintage may return permanently.

Also on Friday evening from 9:00 p.m. till 2:00 p.m., Badin will host a party for the former residents of the hall, to be held on fourth floor.

Sunday will feature the first Badin-Walsh interhall football game. Kickoff is slated from 2:30 and will be on the field next to the University Club.

Badin–Walsh interhall football game
Photo courtesy of Wendy Duffey

> The annual freshman swimming meet highlighted intramural activities...with a new note. ND girls were involved for the first time this year....In the girls meet, Walsh swept all points in the 28–0 shutout win over Badin, as only two girls, R. [Rita] Fritz and K. [Kathleen] Gallogly competed. Both were stars, with Fritz winning three events and Gallogly taking two firsts and a second.[7]

A women's sporting event had finally hit the journalistic trifecta: advance notification, postgame coverage with results, and participants' names.

After that, the stream of publicity slowly but steadily increased. During that first year, *The Observer* published no more than sixteen articles related to women's athletics, most about Saint Mary's sports. By the end of the 1975–1976 academic year, more than seventy *Observer* articles appeared, with many written by Eileen O'Grady (ND 1977). In her 2020 interview with Ron Skrabacz (ND 1976), O'Grady reflected on her male friends' reactions to her reporting:

◇ *Eileen O'Grady Daday, ND 1977:* "Friends I knew — guys — would hand it back to me after it came out and, with a red pen, would have it all marked up. They were like chiding me for not getting some reference right in football terms or something. That was annoying — but at least they were reading it!

"That's really what opened my eyes to women's sports at ND. It was out there and was not getting any recognition. I did discover at some point, maybe my junior year, a niche for me to start writing about women's sports."

The ever-present maleness of Notre Dame was evident not only in the men's reactions to women participating in sports but also in the vast varsity athletic programs available to the men. Football and basketball — as well as baseball, fencing, golf, tennis, and track-and-field — provided opportunities for male athletes to compete if recruited or after successfully trying out. Early on, fencing, sailing, skiing, and diving allowed female athletes to join their ranks.

However, Title IX of the Education Amendments Act of 1972 started the ball rolling. Enacted by Congress and signed into law by President Richard Nixon, it prohibited sex discrimination in any educational program or activity receiving federal financial aid. Less than three months old at the start of the 1972–1973 academic year, Title IX assured women athletes that they would receive the same opportunities as men. When applied to athletic programs, it guaranteed: effective accommodation of student interests and abilities (participation); financial assistance (scholarships); and other program components.[8] Components included a "laundry list" of benefits and treatment of student athletes: equipment, scheduling, travel and per diem allowances, tutoring, coaching, locker rooms, medical and training facilities, publicity, and recruitment. Yet some resistance to women's full participation in campus athletics continued.

◇ *Shelley Muller Simon, ND 1976:* "Sporting events — football, basketball, hockey, baseball, and rugby — definitely played a role in my college experience. An electrifying atmosphere surrounded all athletic events. Freshman year a group of us became 'bat girls' for the baseball team. Earlier in the year, we called the Athletics Department and tried to become football managers (the answer was no), and when we offered up our six-foot-tall female classmate to try out for the Irish Guard, the answer was 'Hell no!'"

By the time Congress passed the final revision of Title IX on July 21, 1975, ND had three years of coeducation under its belt and women making inroads in its athletic landscape. The final provisions specifically prohibited sex discrimination in athletics and allowed three years for educational institutions to fulfill Title IX requirements. Attempts by some institutions to curtail its enforcement continued into 1978. However, in 1979, the Department of Health, Education, and Welfare (HEW) issued a final interpretation of Title IX's effect on intercollegiate athletics. HEW mandated educational institutions to provide equal opportunity in athletic programs to men and women.[9]

Joining in the spring games and cheering on from the sidelines
Photos courtesy of Pat Gleason and Ed Brower

◇◇◇

REARVIEW REFLECTION Before Notre Dame, I never enjoyed or even cared about sports—not even Notre Dame football. My dad religiously listened to ND games on the radio on Saturdays and then watched Sunday replays on the television. We attended early Mass to ensure that he did not miss Lindsey Nelson, an American sportscaster, reviewing the Irish plays. During those play-by-plays, my mom grilled hot dogs, and we kids sang the "Victory March" after each touchdown.

My distaste for sports actually affected my education. Phys ed was the only high school course in which I received a B. I used every excuse I could think of to avoid gym class. I attributed my grade to successful exams on sports rules rather than any athletic ability. At freshman orientation, I dispiritedly learned that ND required two semesters of phys ed to obtain a bachelor's degree. Adding insult to injury, most rotations were coed, a departure from my high school's separate gym classes.

Dreading the required swimming rotation, I learned that demonstrating competency in freestyle and the backstroke satisfied the requirement. I foolishly thought, since I swam when I water-skied, I would easily pass. This was not the case, and I failed the competency test. I went with other women to purchase our requisite swimsuits at the ND bookstore — one-piece, dark blue suits with no bust support. Fortunately, the males also now had to purchase suits; before our arrival, they swam nude.

The Rock housed the indoor swimming pool. To my surprise, its locker rooms had open showers; I expected separate stalls like in my Catholic high school locker room. I found this arrangement uncomfortable, so I usually changed in the dorm and then walked across the South Quad in a maxi-styled cover-up. While this approach worked early on, it proved foolhardy in the frigid winter months.

The class confirmed an existing sexist attitude among the males and the instructor. To pass, we had to float for a specified time. Imagine my chagrin when I stopped floating and realized I was the only one in the pool. My male classmates cheered as I exited the pool, trying to cover what my bathing suit failed to hide.

I thought my humiliation was short-lived given that my next rotation was golf. How difficult could swinging a club and hitting a little white ball be? Lacking coordination and a good, unobstructed swing, I left that rotation determined never to golf again.

I chose skating as my final rotation, hoping to emulate the grace of Olympic female skaters. I initially thought finding something to wear in the cold rink would be my biggest problem since I had no jeans or sweaters. Gilbert's Campus Shop, the only campus retail store besides the bookstore, did not carry women's clothes that first year, so I headed to downtown South Bend to buy jeans. I quickly learned that clothes were not the issue: My biggest hurdles were a lack of athleticism and balance.

However, this rotation reinforced the value of friends. Assisted by Walsh resident Diana Wilson and after lots of practice, I finally skated — if you call my awkward movements "skating." My last day of class, I focused on skating unassisted around the rink, stopping, and going backward. Unfortunately, I hit the wall, fell on a skate blade, and tore a hole in my jeans. Luckily, the instructor took pity and passed me! I sewed a "Behind the Irish" patch over the tear as a reminder of this epic effort.

License to Drive

The university had no women's sports teams, facilities, or coaches in the fall of 1972. Young girls had no legendary female Notre Dame athletes to admire or emulate — to ignite their passions. The female sports landscape was as barren as the Indiana frontier territory Sorin found in 1842. Fortunately, many strong women shared the same dogged determination as ND's founder and — assisted by Title IX legislation propelling women's athletics to the forefront — they soon drove changes in ND's athletic landscape. They learned from their own experience as women athletes what Oprah Winfrey expressed in her wise comment that "you also have to know what sparks the light in you so that you, in your own way, can illuminate the world."[1]

◇◇◇

Notre Dame athletics for men ran the gamut from basketball hoops behind the dorms and hall competitions to intramural sports, club sports, and varsity games. Despite the breadth of those programs, little thought was given to establishing a women's athletic program during the merger discussions or subsequent coeducation decision. Yet the year before coeducation officially began at ND, six Saint Mary's women joined ND's previously all-male fencing team, one of the first Notre Dame varsity sports programs to welcome women.

Still, in the fall of 1972, cheerleading was the only recognized program for women in the Notre Dame sports arena. Although the cheering squad had won first place in the nation from the National Cheering Foundation in the previous year, Notre Dame's cheerleaders received minimal help from the university. To raise money to cover expenses, squad members initially sold "rumper stickers" for fifty cents. The bookstore soon horned in on that market, selling "cheap imitations" for fifteen cents. After the students filed complaints with the Athletics Department, the university eventually provided funding, coaching, and insurance for the group.

◇ *Sally Naxera Benson, ND 1976:* "My selection as a Fighting Irish cheerleader was one of the great honors of my life. That year, George McLaughlin, my eventual cheer partner and also a senior, and I joined two other classmates (Mary Ann Grabavoy, ND 1976, and Amy McDonald, SMC 1976) on the squad for our senior year. Shelley Muller Simon (ND 1976), a cheer-leader in our sophomore and junior years, chose not to participate as she was accelerating her five-year architec-ture curriculum to graduate with the ND class of 1976. Pat Murphy (ND 1976) was our leprechaun junior and senior years.

"The cheerleading team, consisting of six men and six women, participated in hours of required rehearsal in dance, gymnastics, and partner stunts. Everyone contributed to the choreography, with Mary Ann adding many new routines given her profes-sional dance experience. The entire squad cheered at the football games, but we often split the basketball games as it was difficult to attend so many and keep up with our academic load.

"As a 'club' sport, our budget barely covered the cost of uni-forms. Thankfully, through the Linebacker Club's sponsorship and private plane, we often 'hitched' rides to away games. To fund our travel expenses, we sold 'I'm Behind the Irish' rump-er stickers—adhesives were two dollars each and sew-on fabric ones were five dollars. If we 'installed' the adhesive stickers, we added a surcharge! We often received twenty dollars from an alumnus for an installed sticker and photo op!

"Our first game was at Boston College, nationally televised and Dan Devine's inaugural game as head coach. It was also the first time the Irish played BC in football, setting up a rivalry that became known as the 'Holy War.' After getting to Boston on the Linebacker's plane, the squad attended a dinner rally and auction sponsored by the Notre Dame Club of Boston. One of us won a signed football, and the club allowed us to re-raffle it. When several male cheerleaders conducted an auction to get me to sing with the orchestra, I couldn't say no to a two-hun-dred-dollar bid—but I had a few words with the guys for putting me on the spot!

"Ever wonder where traditions begin? One football cheering tradition began at 6,621 feet above sea level. On October 18, 1975, we were guests of the Air Force in Falcon Stadium, Colorado Springs. Ranked number fifteen and a three-touchdown favorite, we trailed most of the game. To make matters worse, every time the cadets scored, their all-male cheerleaders (the Air Force did not have female cheerleaders until 1980) counted off their score with flourished push-ups; enthusiastic cadets in the stands followed suit.

"Beginning the fourth quarter, the score was Air Force 30–Notre Dame 10. But then momentum shifted with a Notre Dame score with just ten minutes and twenty-six seconds remaining. With AF 30–ND 17, the Irish faithful echoed our competitor's humiliating push-ups with some of our own along the goal line! With five minutes and twenty-nine seconds on the clock, we scored again and pumped out twenty-four gratifying push-ups. Finally, with three minutes and twenty-three seconds left, our quarterback Joe Montana pitched the ball to star Al Hunter, who ran a thrilling forty-three yards to set up our winning touchdown. I have never since completed thirty-one pride-filled pushups, but I will remember those thirty-one for as long as I live."

Cheerleading would not remain the only official athletic program for women. Joining

Before 1966, the longest race for women sanctioned by the Amateur Athletic Union (AAU) was one and a half miles. However, on April 17, 1972, eight women officially competed in the Boston Athletic Association's Boston Marathon, with Nina Kuscik becoming its first official female champion with a time of 3:10:26. This occurred one year after the AAU permitted women to enter its marathons. Prior to formal acceptance as competitors, women took extraordinary measures to participate. Roberta "Bobbi" Gibb ran the full Boston Marathon in 1966 without an official race number; she also ran in 1967 and 1968. Joining her in 1967 was Katherine Switzer, who did not identify herself as a female on the race application. After issuing Switzer a bib number, marathon officials tried unsuccessfully to remove her once she was identified as a female entrant. She was disqualified from the race and then expelled from the Athletic Federation, preventing her from competing in other races. In the past fifty years since such historic first efforts, women have made significant strides across numerous athletic platforms; more than twelve thousand women competed in the 2022 Boston Marathon.[2]

women across the country who were looking for ways to participate in athletic competitions formerly available only to men, ND women came to understand the university's existing "Interest Group to Club to Varsity process" in 1973. This approach provided a road map for developing a broad women's athletic program. This three-stage process progressed from the formation of an interest group, followed by advancement to a club sport, and finally recognition as a varsity sport. Each stage had its own timetables and obstacles.

Initially, a team registered as an interest group and operated on its own for at least the first year. Its organizer usually recruited players and volunteer coaches, arranged practices, scheduled competitions, and coordinated transportation. Combined with fundraising for uniforms and equipment, the group needed a committed organizer to thrive.

When Knute Rockne started boxing as a training regime for his football players in 1920, he never expected the practice to eventually become an ND tradition. Notre Dame's Bengal Bouts emerged in 1932 under director and coach Dominic "Nappy" Napolitano (ND 1932). For more than fifty years, Nappy encouraged his fighters to provide service to others. The Bouts' motto, "Strong bodies fight that weak bodies may be nourished," exemplified this purpose. In 1997, Baraka Bouts, ND's Women's Boxing Club, was founded to bring women together in that same spirit of service and athleticism. Both groups raise funds for the Holy Cross missions.[4]

If the group survived its first year, the university might grant club status and provide a seven-hundred-fifty-dollar budget (nine hundred dollars by 1975–1976).[3] As a club, the players and the program had to show steady improvement. Competitive success was key to the coveted promotion to a varsity sport. With varsity status, the team's budget jumped to eight thousand to ten thousand dollars, with paid part-time coaches and traveling expenses to state, regional, and national tournaments. Jumping through all the required hoops usually took three to five years for men's sports. It proved much longer for most women's sports.

To increase the focus on women's athletics, *Observer* reporter Eileen O'Grady (ND 1977) continued to spread the word about women's sports. Her efforts eventually gained her the byline "Women's Sports Editor." Since the male writers were not always willing to cover these stories, O'Grady's increasing involvement created one spindle in the three-legged stool necessary to make women's sports a reality—gaining attention. The women also needed to increase student interest (both male and female) and gain greater support from the administration.

Unfortunately, the initial number of 365 undergraduate women created a major roadblock for justifying equal sports opportunities—no matter the level of play.

The number was too small to guarantee a steady flow of female athletes and too limited to field entire teams. Dominic Napolitano, the head of Notre Dame's Non-Varsity Sports Program, commented that women were not beating down the doors of the ACC despite unrestricted access. This perception blurred reality. Women not only wanted to compete within the athletic arena, but like their male counterparts, they were willing to sacrifice to find time for daily practices and competitions.

Director of Athletics Edward "Moose" Krause expressed both optimism and the desire to do things right for the women's athletics program. He felt that the program had started well and the university had allowed women to participate in any sport they wanted. However, he emphasized the criticality of timing: "It would be a sad mistake if we start a varsity program immediately, and then have the interest die down....On a club basis, there is always the opportunity to step to a higher level."[5] While Krause was right to proceed with caution, he underestimated the tenacity of ND's female athletes.

> ◇ *Becky Banasiak Code, ND 1976:* "ND was not prepared in terms
> of providing women with the same athletic opportunities as the
> men. In basketball and field hockey, we had no paid coaches,
> scholarships, or training tables. These things didn't happen until
> way after I graduated."

Several athletically inclined women, including class of 1976 members Mary Clemency, Betsy Fallon, and Becky Banasiak and class of 1977 members Jane Lammers, Ellen Hughes, Barb Breesmen, Bonita Bradshaw, Anne Dilenschneider, Mary Fitzsimons, Mary Spalding, Patty Coogan, Judy Shiely, Donna Losurdo, Maureen Maloney, and Jody Gormley, accepted the challenge to establish early programs and teams. They, along with numerous other committed individuals such as Cindy Rebholz, Kathy Valdiserri, Marilyn Crimmins, Meme Hanson, Nancy Cueroni, Annie Hawkins, Christie Gallagher, and Mary Ryan, laid the groundwork for women's athletics. With the additional 417 women who arrived in the fall of 1973,[6] female athletes soon emerged "in numbers too big to ignore."[7] In 1973, women's athletic interest groups included tennis and golf, joined in 1974 by basketball, field hockey, and track.

The women gradually received assistance from staff members, coaches, and male students, both on and off the field of play. As the sole female physical education instructor and volunteer coach for women's field hockey, Astrid Hotvedt assisted Napolitano in developing women's club teams. Together, their advocacy and combined knowledge paid dividends.

Bookstore Basketball, a hallowed tradition on campus, saw the entry of a women's team in 1973, and eventually the Office of Non-Varsity Sports instituted a program for interhall competitions for women, which gained momentum as the number of female dorms increased. Two student assistants in the non-varsity office, Betsy Bernard and Sue O'Brien, codirected the women's interhall program, which eventually expanded to include football, basketball, softball, volleyball, tennis, and racquetball. The core women who comprised the Farley Hall basketball team — including Mary Clemency, Patty Coogan, and Judy Shiely — formed the nucleus of the intercollegiate club basketball team in 1974, coached by assistant rector Jeanne Earley and later on Lewis Hall rector Sally Duffy. Ellen Freeman (ND 1976) spoke with *The Observer* about this growth in 1974: With five dorms competing, the "competition is more serious and the rivalry between dorms is growing.... The women involved regard it as a skill. We go out there to perform as well as we can to win."[8] Many women, such as Patricia Gallagher Shields, learned important life lessons from participating in these intrahall sports.

> ◇ *Patricia Gallagher Shields, ND 1976:* "I played dorm basketball but, outside of height, didn't have much talent. Probably one of the most gratifying (and perhaps backward) compliments came from Bonita Bradshaw ('77) on my team. She told me something like, 'I got to give it to you, you've got hustle.' Now, as a coach, I apply that to my players — I don't care how good or not, but if you've got hustle, you're okay in my book."

In 1973, Joni Evan Barnett became Yale's director of its recreational and instructional programs. From 1973–1979, a decade after accepting female undergraduates, thirteen women's sports attained varsity status: tennis, field hockey, squash, basketball, crew, fencing, swimming, lacrosse, volleyball, cross-country, track-and-field, and softball.[10]

During the early 1970s, Tom Kelly of ND's Intramural Sports office described the pace of the women's sports programs development:

The number of women at Notre Dame is increasing every year...and women's sports are evolving from the intramural level to the club level, etc. We'd like to get a few women's clubs started slowly and successfully — not use a shotgun approach and have half of them fall on their faces.[9]

In January 1973, Betsy Fallon of ND and other tennis players challenged Saint Mary's to an informal tennis match, which SMC won. The next year, Fallon — joined by Jane Lammers, Carole Simmons, Ellen Callahan, Sharon Sullivan, and Ann Gardner from the class of 1977 — proved that ND women supported a tennis team as an interest group, and tennis became an official club in the spring of 1974. Professor Carole Moore served as volunteer coach. The first team included thirteen female players, with Andrea Smith as team manager and John Donahue (ND 1977) and Tom Haywood as assistant coaches.[11]

◊ *Janet Krier Breen, ND 1975:* "Who has the balls? Women entering college in the early 1970s did not have much experience participating in group sports. Schools were not yet legally required to spend time and money on women's sports. Three cheers for the female student-athletes and their coaches who started the first women's sports teams at Notre Dame. I had the opportunity to play a minor role on the first women's tennis team for a while. Our first-string players (bless them) were dedicated to establishing a legitimate team. Our coach was a faculty volunteer; our assistant coaches were volunteers from the men's team. We had no uniforms.

"No one ever came to watch our matches even though admission was free! I should not say that no one came. In the last match of the year, there was a lone male pre-med student strolling behind the fence and watching us play. I won

The Observer, March 10, 1976

my singles match that day and was packing up to leave when he came inside the fence. He picked up a tennis ball, wrote the score of my match on it. His words echo to this day: 'Keep this memento. You guys are pioneers.'"

September 1974 saw the organizational meeting for basketball as a club sport, thanks to the efforts of Mary Clemency, Sally Smith, Patty Coogan, and Jeanne Earley.[12] Basketball, golf, crew, field hockey, track, and cross-country all achieved club level in 1975, with skiing and sailing under the umbrella of the coed clubs; grants-in-aid up to nine hundred dollars for some sports also became available that year. University policy stated that these clubs would receive the same non-varsity office support as comparable men's clubs. However, making the jump from club sport to varsity sport was still out of reach for these teams.

◊ *Anonymous female, ND 1976:* "We applied for varsity status for tennis and fencing. We thought we had approval until articles showed up in *The Observer* referencing something called 'interim status,' i.e., somewhere between a varsity sport and a club sport. In general, the coverage in *The Observer* on women's sports was inaccurate, short, and limited. The basketball games between

Notre Dame and SMC got the best coverage but probably for the wrong reasons!

"The women's tennis team formed at the beginning of our sophomore year after some brave players tried out for the men's team and did not make it. The rules stated that we had to be a club sport for three years. We actually petitioned a year early and received a no — no special exceptions. To become varsity, the team had to be successful as a club; the tennis team went five and two that first year of competition.

"Our original request for varsity status did not even request scholarships, just money for a coach and travel. Up to this point, most players subsidized their participation themselves. Varsity would mean money for tennis balls and practice time in the ACC. The hours assigned for the women's team to practice — something like two hours every three weeks from January to the end of March — were ridiculous. These pioneers were not doing it to get a varsity letter but to leave a legacy.

"No one will really know if the initial reservations in establishing female varsity sports were financial, discriminatory, or just too soon for a school that had just accepted women. Across the nation, many women were just beginning to realize what sports were truly available to them. Most, as children, were not encouraged in this area."

Numerous ND women's athletic interest groups and clubs strove to achieve varsity status. With sports as varied as basketball, tennis, crew, golf, and fencing, their approaches differed. There was just one thing left to do — organize. These women shared the same athletic desire as the men who came before them, but these were not just any women. These Notre Dame women — many with the Fighting Irish DNA of fathers, grandfathers, uncles, and brothers (such as Lammers, whose father earned a monogram at Notre Dame in baseball in 1944) — were determined to "win overall."

The sports arena was opening up for women. Chris Evert Lloyd became the Associated Press Female Athlete of the Year four times (1974, 1975, 1977, and 1980). Tennis was in Evert's blood; her father, Jimmy Evert, honed his skills on wooden courts in his Chicago hometown. He later received a tennis scholarship to Notre Dame, where he was captain and number one in singles.[13]

In the spring of 1974, Jane Lammers and Ellen Hughes, members of the class of 1977 and cocaptains on their tennis and golf teams, respectively, recognized the need for women athletes to approach the university with a unified voice. To promote women's athletics at all levels, they founded the Women's Athletic

Association (WAA), an organization comprised of captains and cocaptains of the women's teams.

The association elected Lammers (tennis/crew) as WAA president, Maureen "Moe" Maloney (field hockey/basketball) as vice president, and Hughes (golf) as secretary; Astrid Hotvedt became the WAA faculty adviser.[14] They developed a game plan to work constructively with the Athletics Department.

After the group secured more than four hundred signatures on a petition stating the university should offer varsity teams for women, these three students met with athletes in all dorms to secure a unified support of a proposal. Soon the WAA had its first high-profile meeting on April 21, 1975, when the organization met with the Athletics Department to review its proposal to promote women's basketball, fencing, golf, and tennis to varsity status. In attendance were Dominick Napolitano, director of non-varsity athletics; "Moose" Krause and Colonel John Stephens, director and assistant director of athletics; Sister John Miriam Jones, assistant provost; and Father Edmund Joyce, executive vice president in charge of athletics. Despite high expectations among the WAA faithful, Joyce put a damper on the proceedings when he proclaimed, "There will be no varsity sports for women at the present time." He cited his primary reasons as the financial impact on athletic funds and the teams' failure to complete the standard process.[16] Following this disappointing meeting, Dr. Carole Moore, a staunch advocate for women in both academics and athletics, stressed the importance of a well-developed women's sports programs:

> The Monogram Club is comprised of former Notre Dame student-athletes, support staff members, an on-campus staff, and a board of directors. The club traces its roots to 1896 when Frank Hering, the first full-time Irish football coach, envisioned a varsity club to promote sportsmanship and camaraderie for the fewer than one hundred student-athletes who competed in school-sponsored sports: football, basketball, baseball, and track.[15]

> Women in general have waited too long as it is for participation and they aren't anxious to wait any longer....The athletic hierarchy was made aware of the day-to-day problems of becoming a club....And it seemed that by the end of the meeting the men were made more aware of the practicasl [sic] problems we face....[T]o expand and bring more women in for the enjoyment of sports and also as a recruiting ground for club and varsity sports...athletics are important to every female's development and it is important to bring as many women as possible into sports to have the experience not encouraged in the lower levels of schooling.[17]

(L–R) Kathy Cordes, Ed "Moose" Krause, Jane Lammers, and Mary Schukis

Astrid Hotvedt, Tom Fallon, Kathy Cordes
Photos courtesy of Jane Lammers

Some WAA women, grateful for the meeting, acknowledged the progress made in increasing the administration's awareness. According to Jane Lammers, WAA president, "the meeting was a step in the right direction. 'All those concerned in women's athletics were gathered in one room talking about the problems.'"[18] And WAA adviser Astrid Hotvedt noted, "We're pleased that the administration acknowledged the WAA in discussing the (varsity status) plans. We appreciate the consideration and detailed discussion towards women's sports taken by the administration."[19]

In the spring of 1976, another WAA proposal for varsity status for women's basketball, fencing, golf, tennis, and crew was presented in a room under the Golden Dome, with standing room only and a crowd overflowing into the hallway. This meeting resulted in a June decision to elevate fencing and tennis to varsity status. That summer, the first woman to coach a varsity team at Notre Dame also was hired from a pool of more than two hundred applicants.[20] Coach Kathy Cordes wasted no time in beefing up the schedule, arranging for Father Keller to serve as team chaplain, securing a tennis leprechaun logo for the flashy green warm-ups, and even obtaining green shamrock patches to be sewn onto the players' tennis panties. Coaches Mike DeCicco and Tom Coye took similar steps for the varsity fencers. Those women returning for the 1976–1977 academic year were ecstatic by the news. After slightly more than two years, the WAA won its first varsity teams, and women athletes continue to reap the benefits of this pioneer group. These two varsity sports resulted in the first groups of female varsity monogram recipients: tennis players Jane Lammers and Mary Shukis and fencers Christina Marciniak, Kathy Valdiserri, and Catherine Buzard.[21]

However, this success came after the first class of ND freshman women had graduated. Betsy Fallon explained how the delay affected her:

◇ *Betsy Fallon, ND 1976:* "I wanted to play sports on the same level as my friends played at other colleges. ND was totally unprepared for women's needs and desires for athletics. I worked to start the tennis team. We funded ourselves and had many struggles to get access to courts and funds. I never got a varsity letter, but they went varsity right after I graduated. I got over the fact that I was not really coached or helped in tennis by playing and starting the team. It bugs me when histories and stories about our start are wrong, though."

Another student spoke more generally about what female student-athletes faced in the early days of coeducation at Notre Dame:

◇ *Anonymous female, ND 1976:* "As in many areas of our early campus life, some women still harbor some bitterness toward the 'maleness' of Notre Dame. Such feelings stymie the 'feel-good'-ness of the pioneers' initial effort and dedication. It's like American history; no one wants to know about all the negatives. We must trumpet their accomplishments, both in competition and in trailblazing. Pioneers always have it rough (we *know* that), but people want to know how they overcame the often debilitating and emotional obstacles! We know they did because of the fantastic success of our women's teams today. The women athletes today and going forward need to know that, as Isaac Newton said in 1675: 'If I have seen further it is by standing on ye shoulders of Giants.'"[22]

In her 1976 interview with the *South Bend Tribune*, Sister John recalled how a "jock" image was attached to some female athletes. Yet their tenacity drove the formation of many club sports and an expanded intramural program for women.

The first group of women monogram winners of 1977 at the Penn State game (2006)

(L–R)
Jane Lammers
Christine Marciniak
ND Pres. Rev. John I. Jenkins
Mary Shukis Beyler
Kathy Valdiserri
Cathy Buzard
Julie Doyle

Doyle, the first woman president of the Monogram Club and a volleyball star at Notre Dame, presented the flag

Ann "Muffet" McGraw served as head coach for women's basketball at Notre Dame from 1987 to 2020, compiling a 905–272 record. She led her team to nine Final Fours, seven championship game appearances, and two national championships (2001, 2018). In December 2021, Notre Dame recognized this three-time consensus national coach of the year. McGraw joined former players as the seventh woman to earn the distinction of the university's Ring of Honor: Ruth Riley-Hunter, Skylar Diggins-Smith, Niele Ivey, Beth "Morgan" Cunningham, Kayla McBride, and Natalie Achonwa.[23]

In two separate articles, *The Observer* captured the spirit of the changes to ND's athletic landscape, per the words of Carole Moore:

> Men are going to have to sacrifice, but that kind of cooperation is vital if we are to be a community that looks out for each other's best interests. I want us to remember why we play sports, for the satisfaction, beauty, and discipline of participating in them.[24]

> Possibly the incorporation of women into the collegiate athletic structure will help us return to a more balanced sense of what athletic participation should be—the development of grace, discipline and character.[25]

◇◇◇

REARVIEW REFLECTION As with any sports commentary, the replays highlight the struggle, competition, and marks left by the players (see "Athletic Replays" in the appendix). Ron Skrabacz gathered the information for this chapter by interviewing players and contributors from those early years of women's sports, including Sally Naxera Benson, Mary Clemency, Kathleen Cordes, Eileen Daday, Anne Dilenschneider, Laura Dodge-Ghara, Betsy Fallon, Jody Gormley,

Men from the ND class of 1976 celebrate the success of ND women's basketball

(Kneeling)
Ed Byrne

(L–R)
Lionel Phillips
Muffett McGraw
Ron Skrabacz
Tom Klein
John Carrico
Mark Nishan
Bob Quakenbush

Jane Lammers, and Sheila O'Brien. Their insights, as well as those of many other individuals, added depth to the story of women's sports at ND. Their efforts laid the groundwork for women's athletics, including ND's national championships in basketball, soccer, and fencing.

> ◇ *Jane Lammers, ND 1977:* "The women of the early years, especially members of the classes of 1976 and 1977, enjoyed dealing with the sports challenges we faced and, in particular, building teams. Who wants everything done for them? Not ND women! We saw it as an adventure that mattered. We established an incredibly strong foundation for the women who followed and the thirteen world-class teams of today."

Shattered Glass

The athletic arena was not the only area where Notre Dame's hastily conceived coeducation plans put the women on an inevitable collision course with the male population. This momentous cultural shift fed both male student resentment and awkwardness by male professors. Sexism overshadowed the dining halls, athletics, and the classrooms. But as Helen Keller reminds us, "Life is either a daring adventure or nothing," and "No pessimist ever discovered the secret of the stars or sailed to an uncharted land."[1] Women survived shattered egos and damaged self-images by relying on the qualities that brought them to Notre Dame—intelligence, perseverance, and a touch of humor.

◇◇◇

As the women adjusted to new living and learning environments, they came to understand just how much the university and its male-dominated culture had to learn. One column in an April 1973 *Observer* noted that "girls must feel like the woman on the dome—isolated, protected, gold-plated coeds who are all too aware of their 'visibility on campus.'"[2]

> ◇ *Mary E. "Libby" Ford, ND 1975:* "When 240 of us 'upperclassmen' arrived in the fall of 1972, the university was not physically ready for 365 women to live on campus. There were no women's restrooms in the science and math buildings where I had most of my classes. I either hiked over to a 'ladies' room' in one of the Arts and Letters buildings—a definite challenge with back-to-back classes—or begged a restroom key from one of the secretaries in the building. Eventually, every building had at least one bathroom available for women."

> ◇ *Anonymous female, ND 1976:* "ND had not figured out how to handle women on campus. They still bussed in girls on the weekends. We still had urinals in the bathroom."

◇ *Marianne Ridge O'Connor, ND 1976:* "Facilities had not been adapted—in particular, phys ed equipment. The difference in laundry services, intramural teams, etc., was obvious…we look back now and laugh."

◇ *Marylu Iredale Ernzen, ND 1976:* "In the major areas, ND was prepared for females. They tried hard to make us feel welcomed. So what if the bathrooms were sometimes labeled 'Men'—that was part of the experience!"

Hesburgh tried to lead by example. To connect with his "trailblazers" and acknowledge their challenges, he attended a town hall in Badin, his former dormitory. During this October visit, the residents "presented him with a miniature paper 'Badin Woman' t-shirt [sic], a large Snoopy 'welcome' card, and a steel-wire floral arrangement," alongside a decorated sheet cake declaring, "Welcome Back to Badin, Fr. Ted!" This caused him to grin and comment: "I've gone to a lot of halls, but I've never gotten anything like this before.…It just proves girls are different."[3]

But day-to-day residential and facilities challenges paled in comparison to the difficulties these women faced in the classroom. For many women, their ND classroom experience began with summer placement testing, which offered a typical standardized testing environment. However, given their small numbers, those who took the tests in the fall experienced an atmosphere anything but welcoming.

◇ *Jeanine Sterling, ND 1976:* "Nothing prepared me for Notre Dame. I was unprepared on about every level you can imagine—intellectually, emotionally—for my personal ND experience. It was as if someone took a baseball bat and hit me on the side of my head. I was reeling through most of my four years. I will never forget how strange the whole social experience was.

"The boys did not know what to do with us! So many of them had gone to all-boys high schools and only viewed females as potential dates—rarely as potential friends. Coming from a coed public school where relationships were more normal, I just had no patience for the ND games. When I took the freshman placement exams, I first realized what I was getting into. I walked into the testing classroom—and all talking abruptly stopped. Every pair of male eyes followed me to my desk before conversations resumed.

"At lunchtime, one of the guys asked if I wanted to grab a bite to eat. As we walked through a 'gauntlet' of guys, I glanced back—and the boy walking beside me had raised his fist in a salute to the others behind my back! I was furious. For the first time in my life, I felt like an object. I did not know how to deal with that. I did not talk with anyone about it. I was just angry and disillusioned."

The women could not ignore the roadblocks—real or imagined—in the classroom. With only 365 women across all four classes, the imbalance in the overall classroom makeup sometimes intensified tensions, especially during discussions. Such conflicts often fed the men's perceptions of the women as extremely competitive and too intellectual.

◇ *Paul Shay, ND 1976:* "I came to ND from an urban public high school active in the anti-war effort. Senior year, we consolidated the city's 'white' and 'black' high schools into a massive ill-designed campus. The move created diverse groups so different from our first three years. And, in the end, some of my best friends were girls.

"As such, I arrived on campus excited about having female classmates but dismayed by the small number. I was also chagrined that so many classmates thought the women represented the 'end of Notre Dame as we know it,' as if we knew anything. I cringed every time a professor asked a fellow female freshman to give 'the woman's point of view'—even though it often let my hungover head off the hook with respect to 'all-male' thoughts on whatever the subject.

"On my first date as we walked the quad, I learned my female classmates shared the same concerns about fitting in and succeeding in a tough academic environment. Over time, I also learned we manly men were largely woeful with respect to asking women out.

"I cannot begin to say thanks to the women of ND for choosing to follow a path like mine. I also offer a belated apology for not standing by their side in those early days."

Broad acceptance of ND's new students took time and challenged personal levels of comfort and self-esteem. A 1972 depiction of typical seating arrangements in a Notre Dame classroom, created and shared by classmate Kim Kittrell (ND 1976), illustrated how the women viewed their position in the classroom—a single X set apart in a sea of Y chromosomes. Often arriving early to class, the women sat in the rows where they expected the males to sit or sometimes brazenly sat next to a male. Some purposely sat with no one on either side and waited to see if anyone sat next to them. For those who found other women in their classes, they often sat together. When late for class, the women dreaded the male eyes that followed them to their seats, although a small number may have wondered if the men looked twice. The first seat by the door remained their last resort for perceived anonymity. Some felt this spotlight keenly.

> ◇ *Anonymous female, ND 1976:* "Because our numbers were small, it made it difficult to break the rules or cut corners. Absence from class was noticeable. And if a guy wanted to chat and a girl even looked at him, the professor was on you in seconds."

> ◇ *Susan Newbould Andrews, ND 1976:* "Notre Dame seemed prepared for women, but I am not sure male students were. I didn't think much about being in the minority until I would go to class and be one of three women in a class of twenty-five or more."

Some women came from all-girls high schools and had just as much trouble adjusting to coeducation as many of the male students did.

> ◇ *Mary Dondanville, ND 1976:* "It was weird at first because I came from an all-girls high school. Just to be thrown back into a class with guys would have been difficult; I hadn't been in that kind of situation since grade school.
>
> "I was overwhelmed when I walked into my freshman chemistry class. First, it was the largest class that I ever had in my life, four hundred-plus students and maybe fifteen women. I think when I first walked in, I only saw three or four women, and I really wanted to walk out the door. But since it was a lecture class, it didn't require you to participate in any class discussions, unlike my philosophy class where I was the only girl with eighteen or nineteen guys."

When the males entered the classroom, they rarely voluntarily sat in the same row as a woman. Fearing the woman might question their intentions, the men hardly acknowledged her. Most failed to recognize that the woman probably wanted to engage in conversation since she seldom spoke first. In smaller classes, every guy knew the names of the few women. Unfortunately, the reverse was not true, perpetuating a misconception that the women were aloof or uninterested.

> ◇ *Anonymous male, ND 1976:* "The men seldom mingled with the women. Most were ignorant to what many of the women were trying to do. The women did not understand why the men did not want to sit with them."

> ◇ *Susan Davis Flanagan, ND 1976:* "I remember being in classes with so few girls, and there would be an empty seat by me. Some guy would come in late, and rather than sit in the close seat by me, he would climb over ten guys to get a seat way in the

back! I think the guys were intimidated that there were so few girls. They figured we had guys falling all over us, so why even bother?"

While the classroom created some uneasiness among its audience, it was a logical place to meet individuals with common interests. Whatever the subject, for some it offered an icebreaker — a starting place for normal conversation. For others, they relished the new experience of sharing the classroom with the opposite sex.

> ◇ *Darlene Palma Connelly, ND 1977:* "Having come from an all-girls Catholic high school where we only had nuns and laywomen in the classroom, I found being in the minority and so close to guys in daily life as curious and as fascinating as they found us. I found hearing guys' perspectives in class refreshing. Apparently, while we sat in classrooms dominated by male professors, they had similar thoughts when a girl spoke."

Even love was not out of the question in this setting. One student shared his hope to find love in the classroom but only found disappointment:

> ◇ *Anonymous male, ND 1976:* "By mid-September, I was smitten with a young woman in my chemistry lab. We only had the lab once a week, and my dream girl always walked in with a friend and sat in the same place.
>
> So, I arrived early one day and planted myself squarely where I expected them to sit. They did sit in the same row — but several seats away. Not discouraged by this minor setback, I struck up a conversation and learned that my dream girl was not only beautiful but also my intellectual equal.
>
> "I plotted to catch this goddess apart from her friend so I could ask her out. When I finally found the courage, I rushed through my lab project to walk out when they did. As they left the building, I bounded down the steps after them. After a little small talk, I asked my dream girl out. I was crushed when she said, 'Sorry, I'm busy this weekend.'
>
> "After a few weeks of calling her, she finally drove the dagger into my heart and told me she was dating a senior. I was just as dense as her friend; neither of us could take a hint."

Timing classroom arrivals and departures and selecting seats were not the women's only challenges as they worked toward academic success. Although women (mostly members of religious orders) took graduate classes and SMC undergraduates had participated in the Co-Exchange Program, before 1972 both students and professors were confused about how to act in the newly "integrated" classrooms.

> ◇ *Pat Novitzki, ND 1976:* "I always found it interesting to hear the stories of how the women felt in a sea of men. During summer school, I suffered a similar experience when I walked into class to find only female graduate students and nuns. After that class, I had a much better understanding of what the women were facing."

Professors either welcomed the women's contributions, challenged their presence, or unfairly judged them as curve-breakers. Carole Moore, a history professor, noted that the competition for grades and dormitories often pitted the men and women against each other.[4]

> ◇ *Anonymous female, ND 1976:* "Some professors were unprepared to deal with females. One professor frequently referred to me as 'Mr.' I was the only female in the class; it should not have been too hard to get it right."

> ◇ *Anonymous female, ND 1976:* "When I walked into calculus class on the first day of freshman year, I got a standing ovation. The teacher said, 'Well, now the class is integrated.' A calculus pun to be sure, but I didn't appreciate it."

> ◇ *Diana Wilson Ostermann, ND 1976:* "Not everyone wanted the university to go coed; some professors clearly resented female students in the classroom. I experienced one such professor for statistics, a class where I was one of two female students. Early in the semester, I raised my hand to ask a question. The professor called on me, and I stated my question. I am not known for being cryptic, so I know that I clearly stated what I needed to be clarified. He responded in a voice dripping with ridicule, 'This woman wants to know...' and gave a ludicrous version of my question. The class laughed uproariously. I waited

ND female experiences were similar to those of women attending other recently integrated male institutions. In her book, *Babes in Boyland*, author Gina Barreca gives a typical example:

"Every time I raised my hand to answer a question, I was asked my opinion *as a woman.* It frustrated and angered me, because I wanted to be treated as an individual and not as a representative of a group....It occurred to me that nothing was neuter or neutral. I saw that her responses were determined in part by the fact of my gender—as well as by other factors such as my class and ethnicity."[5]

133

for the laughter to subside and stated in a loud voice, 'That was *not* my question! What I want to know is...' Unbelievably, the professor did it again, evoking more laughter. Determined not to leave class without my answer, when the hilarity abated, I stated again, 'That was *still* not my question! My question is...' Finally, he gave me the answer. I never asked another question in that class; if I did not understand something, I asked a classmate."

◇ *Jill Donnelly, ND 1976:* "In my economics class, I had gotten an A on every exam, but my midterm grade was a B-.... The professor said it was because I had poor attendance, but I always sat in the front row and had never missed a class. He refused to change the grade."[6]

Unfortunately, these experiences were common. As with other recently integrated institutions, half of the women in those first few years of coeducation at ND experienced a class in which the professor caused them discomfort.[7]

◇ *Shelley Muller Simon, ND 1976:* "As I stood in the Architecture building in front of a panel of three male professors critiquing my drawings, I was interrupted when one of them cleared his throat, saying 'Miss Muller, before you begin, I feel compelled to tell you your slip is showing.'"

According to Sister John, some professors tried too hard to include the women. They ended up spotlighting them by asking for the female perspective, even in courses like statistics, accounting, or economics.[8] Sometimes the request for a woman's viewpoint was mocking, sexist, or irrelevant. Being treated as representatives of their gender, rather than as individuals, frustrated many women. Such attention also caused resentment among some male students and made fitting in even more difficult.

◇ *Jeanine Sterling, ND 1976:* "That experience, that feeling, was reinforced repeatedly during my first years at ND—by other male students and even some male teachers. I remember sitting in a class on the first day of each semester and praying another female would walk in and not leave me to be the sole representative of the female viewpoint for the next four months. I was so uncomfortable not being treated as just Jeanine."

◇ *Diana Wilson Ostermann, ND 1976:* "As the only female in my business ethics class, the professor early on asked me for the women's point of view. I answered I could not speak for all of womankind, I was only able to share my opinion."

The women were often disappointed in the lack of forward-thinking by some professors. They questioned how such attitudes could still exist in the 1970s. Still, these situations forced the women to learn to stand up for themselves — not only to survive but also to thrive.

◇ *Betsy Kall Brosnan, ND 1976:* "I was the only girl in freshman French class, and the teacher one day was particularly hard on me, making fun of my enunciation. The entire class felt bad for me. The next day walking to class, he was right in front of me. I could have cowered behind him but, instead, I passed him saying, '*Bonjour.*' He apologized to me in front of the class that day, and all was great after that. I learned to stand up for myself that day."

◇◇◇

REARVIEW REFLECTION My own collegiate classroom experience was quite different from high school, where religious and lay teachers, both male and female, respected my opinion. I never felt isolated, singled out, or a failure. In contrast, the scrutiny I underwent as a female minority in the ND classroom bothered me. I never asked questions or volunteered to answer any. I was subdued in discussions compared to my lively participation in high school. I feared my contributions might suggest that I lacked the academic credentials to attend ND.

One professor, an ND graduate, persistently asked me to sit in the front row of his sociology class. I was one of two women in this class, and he relentlessly interrogated me on the day's material. His focus made me so uncomfortable that, in a departure from the norm, some males sat near me in a show of support.

I finally decided to "address" the situation. I rarely hid my femininity, but this day, I flaunted it. I donned jewelry, lace stockings, and heels. I unzipped the front of my diagonally striped, black-and-white dress to a revealing position. I curled my hair and put on makeup, which I usually reserved for dates. After carefully studying the class content for the day, I was ready.

I arrived early, sat in the front row, and crossed my legs. The professor did a double take as he walked to the chalkboard. I was more active in class than usual, raising my hand to answer more than my fair share of questions about India's culture. Distracted, he tripped over his words while discussing Hinduism's veneration of cows: Instead of saying "herd of cattle," he said "head of curls." After class, my "circle of protectors" congratulated me on my novel, ironically feminine, approach in addressing the professor's targeted attacks. From then on, my participation was strictly voluntary. He never asked me to sit in the front row again — although I often did!

Moving Violations

The steeplechase jockey and crime writer Dick Francis has offered an original perspective on the changes everyone endures in life. In his biography of jockey Lester Piggot, Francis makes the point that "[e]veryone journeys through character as well as time. The person one becomes depends on the person one has been."[1] This insight may apply to institutions as well to individuals — as for the first time, Notre Dame, a Catholic university with a formerly male student body, faced the problem of providing physical security for female students while offering equity in its residential life. Since many of its newly arrived women students came from sheltered, structured, and often Catholic homes and schools, few anticipated that the university's policies would cause significant angst. However, the newfound freedom of college had some unexpected results and definitely influenced the individuals whom the undergraduates became. Both women and men found their way to challenge some Notre Dame guidelines.

◇◇◇

The Notre Dame Security Police Department (formerly Campus Security) was an authorized State of Indiana police agency and, over time, grew from a handful of retired police officers to an impressive, uniformed force equipped with firearms, communications devices, squad cars, and motorbikes. Sworn police officers and unsworn security officers, all male, patrolled campus and responded to emergencies. They secured the entrances and issued citations to those individuals ignoring posted parking designations. Not until the spring of 1973 did the university add female officers to its previously all-male security force: The first two were Micky Hess and Doris Stombaugh. The criteria for these positions stated the department wanted "girls with a college education in social work, sociology, or criminology."[2]

The department also managed the campus lost and found, a singular location for misplaced or stolen items. As far back as 1922, after someone stole University President John O'Hara's two-wheeler, security campaigned for all students to register their bicycles after arriving on campus. For a nominal fee — one dollar in the 1970s — registered bicycles also received guaranteed winter storage. A computerized system tracked registered property descriptions, serial numbers, ID numbers, makes, and owners. Security even considered purchasing etching pencils to label valuables with the owner's social security number, a practice viewed as unwise today. The dual flaw in either approach: students had to participate and had to know the serial numbers of their items.

Despite the changing makeup of Notre Dame's student body, a subtle attitude existed that coeducation required few changes to security. Arthur Pears, director of security, acknowledged that the "only change made [to security] is that instead of having male hall monitors in each of the dorms, we have female hall monitors in each of the women's halls."[3]

The use of in-hall security descended from the decades-old fire watch program. These monitors existed in the men's dorms until the installation of fire sprinklers and smoke detectors in 1980. However, the women's dorms employed married women with high school educations to watch over the residents' comings and goings well into the twenty-first century.

At the onset of coeducation, hall staffs in nearby male residence halls volunteered to assist as the women settled into their dorms. These men received safety training and were on call to assist with emergencies. Given the success of this approach, the administration eventually added a standardized safety session to freshman orientation in all dormitories. The initially informal partnerships between male and female dorms morphed from safety and assistance to cohosting activities.

Following the April 16, 2007, shooting massacre at Virginia Tech, Notre Dame (like many other educational institutions) announced an innovative communications strategy. Students who provided their personal cell phone numbers to the university would receive text messages in the event of an emergency. The service was implemented across campus in 2008.[4]

In 2019, the university announced its new "Irish1Card" policy permitting access to individual halls only by residents and essential staff. This replaced the previous policy that had granted students access to all halls during select hours.[5]

Regardless of whether a dorm housed males or females, all halls had phones at their main entrances so that residents could gain access during lockdown hours. Whereas the female halls were always locked, the male halls opened their doors at 11:00 a.m. However, this approach was not viewed as adequate when it came to the physical security for the women.

The university also increased physical security measures in Walsh and Badin, installing an electronic key card system (much like those in today's hotels), locks, and alarms on the halls' doors. Only two men's dorms, Dillon and Alumni, had this level of security due to their proximity to the campus entrance. Many of the women considered the card system—affectionately called "Detex"—helpful,[6] and four months later surveys showed that "77 percent of the students polled said they would turn to security for help if they were victimized by crime."[7]

Following a rash of burglaries in the spring of 1973 in the ACC and Alumni, Fisher, and Cavanaugh halls, security recommended a "closed-dorm system" across campus.[8] With many students leaving their rooms unlocked, security wanted a consistent policy to function as a crime deterrent. Although the recommendation to lock all doors and post guards at all main entrances failed to gain traction, vigilance improved in most residence halls.

These burglaries did drive a renewed focus on increasing campus lighting. Still, Father James L. Riehle, the dean of students, argued that adding an extensive lighting system on campus

> probably wouldn't make much of a difference. The parking lots are the best lighted areas on campus, yet more vandalism occurs there than anywhere else. Secondly, we do not want to brighten up the campus at the expense of destroying its present pastoral beauty.[11]

Despite poor lighting in many remote corners of the grounds, at the time, few females recalled feeling uneasy walking on campus; however, Campus Security went ahead and introduced an on-demand walking escort. The service responded to requests from groups of three or more girls with fifteen minutes notice since, according to Pears, "It would be practically impossible to get an escort for every girl."[12] Few actually used this service given the lack of campus phones and the perceived slow response times to requests.[13] Security also escorted Saint Mary's students as far as the Notre Dame bus stops. When these students missed the last campus shuttles, SMC security officers picked the girls up and safely returned them to their halls.[14]

At Yale, the 1969 admittance of female undergraduates forced its residence halls to go coed. Although deans in the dorms followed Yale's parietals and cohabitation policies, each hall enforced the policies differently. Most ignored violations given the number of women visiting on the weekends; coeducation simply extended cohabitation during the week.[9]

Parietals and single-sex dormitories were not unique to Notre Dame. Villanova, a Catholic university outside of Philadelphia, also had both. Eventually, a few of its dorms went coed by floor, but parietals still separated the sexes during certain hours. Parietals drove many students, especially upperclassmen, to move off campus or to coed university-owned apartments.[10]

Reported crimes against women were rare. Officers made evening rounds primarily to assist students in need or to serve as deterrents to college pranks. Students making out by the lakes or brave enough to skinny-dip in Saint Joe's Lake tried to avoid these patrols.

Security did not get actively involved in the enforcement of dormitory regulations. Incoming freshmen received letters welcoming them to their dormitories and informing them of the residential rules and regulations. One regulation defined visitation hours for the opposite sex, known as "parietals."

Student Body President John Barkett, in his February 1972 letter anticipating "Women at Notre Dame," urged the administration to consider how best to set parietals for the women's dorms. Provost James Burtchaell, CSC, responded that women's residences could tighten their parietals hours over those used in the male dormitories, but they could not expand them.[15]

The male undergraduate halls allowed such visitations from nine in the morning to midnight on weeknights and until two in the morning on Fridays and Saturdays. Hall rectors Kathy Cekanski and Joanne Szafran, in partnership with Sister John, established the same parietals as the men's dorms. They also developed additional guidelines to encourage a feeling of family within their halls.

Ordained in 1960, James T. Burtchaell III, CSC (ND 1956), was a popular spiritual director on campus. Burtchael earned a doctorate in divinity at Cambridge before returning to Notre Dame in 1966. He served as chair of the Theology Department for two years before his appointment as provost, the university's chief academic officer. After stepping down from this position in 1977, he returned to teaching. Following allegations of improper behavior, Burtchael resigned from the faculty. He was relieved of his sacramental responsibilities in 1991.[16]

The student life guide, *du Lac*, documented the university's and board of trustees' rationale for parietals, which was based on the principle of in loco parentis. They believed that parietals nurtured Christian ideals and gave students a sense of responsibility by helping them develop character and become more humane. In reality, parietals and the university sexuality code sought to prevent premarital sex on campus. Transfer students familiar with less strict hall policies at other universities faced major adjustments. If unable to adapt, many either moved off campus or left Notre Dame.

While not specifically prohibiting sex, the sexuality code stated that the genuine expression of love through sex required the total commitment of two persons in marriage. Dean John Macheca threatened to prosecute anyone caught in a premarital sexual union. Two well-publicized cases, which combined the sexual prohibition with the ironclad parietals restrictions, involved a Dillon Hall male undergraduate and a Lewis Hall female graduate student. In both cases, the students were severely sanctioned.

Macheca and the Student Leadership Council (SLC) continued to work to clarify the longstanding unwritten rule against premarital sex. In October 1974, Pat McLaughlin, the student body president, asked the SLC's Rules Committee to determine whether the sexuality code simply stated Church doctrine on human sexuality or existed as a rule for student behavior. The committee agreed that, if a rule, it needed to protect student privacy, apply equitably to all cases, and establish consistency in any resulting punishments. Brian Hegarty (ND 1976) lobbied for counseling and education, not punishment for violators. In response, Hesburgh admitted, "Any student or adult who wants to get into trouble, alcoholic, sexual, or otherwise, can easily enough do so — with or without parietals."[17]

"Thank God it's only two in the afternoon"
The Observer, April 16, 1975

Stories about students who barely avoided parietal violations or who used parietals as a reason to terminate an uncomfortable encounter abounded on campus.

◇ *Diana Wilson Ostermann, ND 1976:* "My freshman year I dated a guy in Fisher Hall. By the end of the first semester, I was spending many nights in his second-floor room. Unlike the female residence halls, maids arrived first thing in the morning to vacuum and clean the guys' rooms. For me not to get caught violating parietals, my boyfriend always checked the hall to see if it was empty, and then I quickly headed to the stairs and out the first-floor door. One winter morning, bundled up in a jacket, big hood pulled up, and a scarf around my neck, I hurried down the hallway. I yanked open the stairwell door and came face-to-face with one of the cleaning ladies. I quickly stepped around her and raced down the stairs. There was no way for her to know who I was visiting, and she could not tell what I looked like. I think the cleaning ladies sided with the students and did not report such incidents as I never heard anything about it."

Sometimes, enforcement of parietal rules led to humorous situations.

◇ *Anonymous female, ND 1976:* "During my freshman year, a student in the dorm complained people would knock on her door at night, trying to throw a man out of her room. However, it was just her voice that they heard. She had a cold that had given her a deep voice. It was pretty funny! A sense of humor certainly helps in life!"

For many, parietal rules did indeed prevent sex.

◇ *Anonymous male, ND 1976:* "While upperclassmen definitely had more sex, freshman and sophomore interactions normally did not progress that far. Generally, parietals were a major deterrent. You met a girl at a party at eleven, danced for a while, and maybe made out a little. By the time you were ready to hook up, it was past one, and parietals were at two. If you did break parietals, you kept her there all night. She could not even go to the bathroom. Worse, you had to talk to her in the morning. It was easier to get something to eat before heading to bed!"

◇◇◇

REARVIEW REFLECTION As a freshman, I felt that the hall staff exercised reasonable-yet-vigilant efforts to replace "parentals" with parietals. I did not anticipate parietals to be an issue, given dating itself was a new experience. On one hand, I had roommates, a natural deterrent to the opposite sex staying after hours. On the other hand, as a good Catholic girl with only basic sexual knowledge, I assumed breaking parietals meant having intercourse. I was not ready for that.

However, my attitude on parietals soon changed. I quickly realized that there were many ways to spend intimate time with a man without having intercourse. Overcompensating for not dating in high school and following Teddy Bear Man's advice, I accepted dates for lunch, dinner, movies, studying at the library, and late-night pizza. However, one guy from Sorin, "Movie Man," captured my untouched heart. He convinced me to let him stay overnight right before Thanksgiving.

My first overnight with Movie Man introduced me to deep kissing and cuddling while clothed. We talked about current films and how they compared to romantic classics such as *Gone with the Wind*, *The Sound of Music*, and *Doctor Zhivago*. He later gave me the theater one-sheets for these movies as a reminder of our evening—I still have the *Gone with the Wind* poster. Unfortunately, the night ended abruptly when my father called from the lobby at six in the morning.

My brother had an admissions interview to join ND's class of 1977. The timing allowed my father to accompany him and then drive us home for Thanksgiving. With my dad's call announcing his early arrival, a recently learned four-letter word escaped my lips. As my date left by one exit, I shakily faced my father at the main lobby door. I cannot remember which was my biggest fear: getting caught breaking parietals, incurring Dad's wrath over my new "vocabulary," or disappointing my date with my cuddling-only rule. My answer: all of the above!

As late as November 1985, the punishments for parietal violations sparked campus-wide debates. Students felt that overly severe punishment was harmful to the campus community and violated the intent of residence hall regulations. Columns, letters, and two ads funded by the Hall Presidents Council in *The Observer* hoped to influence changes on the punishments levied. Students did not question the university's right to implement parietals but challenged the disciplinary actions levied for violations.[18]

Over Thanksgiving break, I nervously discussed parietals (and breaking them) with my mom. I expected a narrow-minded viewpoint from her since she had started dating my dad at sixteen and married him at nineteen. Through such "adult" conversations, I came to appreciate my mom, her friendship, and her compassion. She always came through for me, both while I was at Notre Dame and also later in life. Though she was appalled by the thought of sharing a bed before marriage, she discussed the topic without judgment. However, she was either unable or unwilling to answer my more "technical" questions about sex. Mom stressed the importance of straightforward conversations about what was in- or out-of-bounds with potential sleepovers. I eventually learned that, while such discussions sometimes worked, some nights inevitably ended in disappointment. Before returning to campus, we shopped for peignoir sets — her sign of unspoken support for clothed sleepovers.

November 1972 was not my only parietal violation. When guys stayed over, I foolishly believed they liked cuddling and sharing private time as much as I did. With little experience in understanding their feelings and minimal knowledge of the male sex drive, I often missed the obvious. Wanting to know if they "saw" me, I asked, "What are you thinking?" or "May I ask you a question?" or "What color are my eyes?" I had many questions, some as silly as how they made it through the night without using the bathroom.

Eventually, Joanne, Walsh's rector, called me into her office to discuss my reported parietal violations. She was not judgmental, but she did encourage me to reflect on whether staying at ND was worth obeying this rule. She made good points about courtesy to other residents and the unfulfilled expectations of those staying overnight; many things mentioned in *du Lac*. I stopped breaking parietals after that...until, that is, I moved to Breen-Phillips Hall and a new rector for my sophomore year (1973–1974).

Remaining wary about parietals, I decided to try something different. One spring evening, I took the plunge and went swimming with my date in the lake heated by the campus power plant. This romantic evening turned into just another encounter that shattered my self-image. At an extremely intimate moment, the boor actually said that he preferred girls who looked like my roommate — slight and short. As I angrily left the water, I just missed the late-night patrol. Serendipity — I smiled as I watched from the bushes as the boor received a written warning for swimming nude in the lake.

In September 1973, my father allowed my freshman brother and me to bring a new car to campus. Since freshmen could not register cars in their first semester, I purchased the required parking pass from the Notre Dame Police Department. My brother oversaw its servicing and gas, and I dealt with its handwashing — my father's conditions for having the car. One Saturday, as I carried water from Breen-Phillips Hall to our parking space, I found our car without its hubcaps — a special chrome set for our 1973 Buick Skylark. I dropped my bucket and ran to my brother's Cavanaugh Hall room. Bursting in, I screamed out about the stolen hubcaps. He asked why I was so upset, to which I responded, "Well, we can't drive it without the hubcaps — the wheels will fall off!" Besides experiencing the vandalism rampant in the parking lots, I realized that I had a lot to learn about both cars and men.

Deer in the Headlights

Tech entrepreneur and Oracle cofounder Larry Ellison has said that sometimes running a company results in paralysis: "You get frozen like a deer in the headlights. All you can do is all you can do."[1] Adjusting to Notre Dame in those first few months often resulted in startled expressions — like those of a deer staring into headlights. Sharing small spaces with strangers, eating in the dining halls with raucous boys, attending class as possibly the only female in the room, and unraveling the complexity of course material were all unfamiliar. Survival required understanding not only the language and the environment of the university but also human behaviors — including one's own.

◇◇◇

REARVIEW REFLECTION Days started and ended in the dorm or, for some, in off-campus housing, often with roommates who were study partners, sounding boards, and fellow partygoers. Students learned each other's personalities and habits, sometimes meshing, sometimes not. Janet Krier Breen described this experience with an apt metaphor:

> ◇ *Janet Krier Breen, ND 1975:* "A commercial in the 1960s encouraged you to 'See the USA in Your Chevrolet.' The father [of the family portrayed in the ad] appeared relaxed, confident, so proud, and in control behind the wheel. The mother's smile beamed with sheer radiance as she gazed upon the beautiful scenery. The kids sat quietly, obediently, and wide-eyed from the pleasure of going for the ride.
>
> "The ad never gave us a glimpse of traveling through unfamiliar territory, in tight living quarters, with people who do not normally associate under such conditions. We never saw its occupants suffer from car sickness as the wheels continued turning. There was no rest stop for miles! The family had to learn

patience and to compromise. Perhaps they even developed deeper affections for one another.

"The early days of coeducation at Notre Dame often felt like such a road trip. With the decision made, the trip began. Once invited on the trip, we gratefully settled into our positions. We did not always get along, but we helped each other. We grew to enjoy and understand each other more deeply."

Of course, the father in the driver's seat at ND was Father Hesburgh, and he was often there to help diminish our confusion and anxiety as key passengers on this eventful ride.

For most freshmen, that first semester was a whirlwind of emotions. After having my own room at home, I struggled with having roommates. As only one member of our quad, I did not decide when to stop the music or turn off the lights in the communal area. I had no control and no experience in negotiating such a situation.

After seeing an advertisement for an October Grassroots concert in downtown South Bend, I decided to try and improve my quad mates' opinions of me.[2] In high school, I attended The Association's concert, and the band invited me to join them on their tour bus—until they discovered I was fifteen. I naïvely thought if I got the Grassroots to come to our room, my roommates might see value in the outgoing side of my nature. Although not as well-known as Chicago, The Guess Who, or Blood, Sweat and Tears, the Grassroots had several hit songs. What a coup if I got them to Walsh Hall!

Since first-semester freshmen were not allowed cars, I took the bus to the Morris Civic Center. Not a sellout, the event emptied quickly. As I approached the stage, a band member asked why I was hanging around since there was no meet and greet after the event. I responded with the first thing that popped into my head: As a sorority pledge, I needed the band's autographs. He invited me backstage, and my plan was in motion. Once backstage, he introduced me to the band and informed them of my quest. As they signed their autographs, a cute blond guy walked up and asked me where I went to school. I replied, "Notre Dame," and proudly threw out my chest. "Oh really?" he responded. "Notre Dame does not have fraternities or sororities." Busted! Before leaving with my autographs, I invited them to stop by the dorm that evening and gave them my telephone number. Unfortunately, when they called, my roommate viewed it as a prank and hung up on them.

As I left the concert, I discovered that buses did not run after 10:00 p.m., so I started walking. Eventually, a yellow Volkswagen Beetle stopped, and the driver offered me a ride. Though he looked like a typical "hippie" of that time—long hair, T-shirt, scruffy jeans—his car was clean. I accepted his offer; after all, it was a college town, and we seldom heard stories of assault...and I did not want to walk the three miles to campus in heels.

Jack Kerouac and the Beat generation of the 1950s and 1960s romanticized hitchhiking — the asking of individuals, usually strangers, for rides. Still in vogue in the 1970s, students without cars hitchhiked to off-campus venues and restaurants. Laws started to surface against it, and law enforcement warned of "sex maniacs" or "vicious murderers." As parents trained their teenagers not to get into cars with strangers, the days of thumbing for a ride eventually disappeared.

Hitchhiking like this was not unusual in South Bend.

◇ *Maggie Waltman Smith, ND 1976:* "Living off campus as a female transfer, none of the four of us in our apartment had a car. We were forced to walk or hitchhike to class or anywhere else. Hitching a ride up Notre Dame Avenue to class in broad daylight wasn't so bad. Most of the traffic was headed to or from campus. But the mall was quite a bit farther away and in an unknown part of South Bend. I think I did that only once, and I'm sure I didn't tell my parents about it!"

The "hippie" driver and I had a pleasant conversation on the short drive to campus. He went directly to the main gate, and the guard allowed him to deliver me to my dorm. As I exited his car, he asked for a date. I politely declined and thanked him for the ride.

Living in the Notre Dame bubble provided an unrealistic sense of security. After our room received phone calls from a "heavy breather," I soon understood that "protection" did not extend to off-campus situations. I regretted giving my name to that Volkswagen owner and allowing him, a stranger, to drive me to Walsh. I thought the timing of the calls was a coincidence until, a week later, I saw him outside Walsh, looking shabbier in the daylight. Since I was late for class, I blew off his offer to grab a Coke. In retrospect, I should have asked him about the calls. Eventually, after our blowing a whistle into the phone's receiver several times, the calls stopped.

Obscene, harassing telephone calls increased across the ND community in the spring of 1973. To address such calls, the Bell System installed a tracking device on the central switchboard. Instructions in *The Observer* informed students to leave the phone off the hook and to call security from another phone.[3]

After that ill-fated encounter, my roommates did not see me as someone whose adventure positively added to the room dynamics — only as a victim of obscene calls.

I continued to suffer a roller coaster of emotions, like many freshmen, as I struggled to fit in. When Badin and Walsh halls jointly requested that the Student Life Council (SLC) add one female member with full voting privileges for the year,

I ran for the position. This position opened because Dennis Etienne advanced to the vice presidency, and the SLC permitted a woman to fill Etienne's open seat. I ran against six candidates in the primary: Kris Anhut, Wendy Duffey, Maureen Lathers, Candy Kelly, Diane McDonnell, and Janet Waltman. *The Observer* captured McDonnell's thoughts about this special election: "After over a hundred years of wholly male thinking, I think it's necessary to have a woman's voice in student government."[4] With less than half of the 365 women voting in the primary, Lathers, McDonnell, and Waltman advanced to a runoff. Lathers, a transfer from the coeducational University of Michigan, won. She soon encouraged the SLC to view this seat for a female representative as *temporary* and to add female dorm representatives in the future:

> The seat was created to allow woman students representation and to allow them to work with faculty and administration, and it shouldn't be regarded as a token seat.[5]

> I feel I know what real coeducation is like ... after my last year at a coeducational school [Michigan State].[6]

Notre Dame women now had their first female student representative to work with the faculty and administration. Still, I can't help but wonder whether if I — and other women — had pushed for additional pivotal organization roles earlier, the administration might have understood our challenges sooner.

The hitchhiking experience and election loss caused me to further question if Notre Dame was right for me. Following the election, I called my parents and asked to come home. I surprised them with this request, given my optimistic outlook about the election during our previous Sunday call. Now, I was defeated, lonely, and nervous about my upcoming midterms and the increasingly chilly weather — it had snowed already! Even though my parents were empathic to my election loss, they explained that coming home was not an option — Dells do not quit! Concerned, my dad called my godfather in Dubuque (more than six hours away with the recently legislated fifty-five-mile-per-hour speed limit) and asked if he would drive over and bring me to my grandparents for a much-needed break.

My grandparents were vested in my success at ND. My maternal grandmother, who owned her own beauty shop, did my hair and cooked my favorite meals. My paternal grandmother bought me a winter coat and boots since I had neither. While shopping, I learned that grandma knew about my illegal use of a number given by a classmate to make long-distance calls. She agreed to pay my outstanding charges if I promised to be more suspicious of anything "free." My grandpa reminded me about my father's academic challenges at ND. I returned to campus armed with homemade chocolate chip cookies, a couple of dollars, and a much-needed coat.

Even still, I could not wait for Christmas and the parties surrounding my Palm Beach Junior League debut. The debutante cotillion was my parents' idea, so I told only my roommates. I worried that my classmates might criticize my participation in such a sexist event, especially during this volatile time related to women's rights. Even though several male friends would be in Florida for the New Year's Orange Bowl, I invited no one from ND as my escort as I feared their rejection.

A little hungover from preholiday partying, I waited for the commuter flight to Chicago O'Hare. I was excited to give my father his Christmas present — a portrait taken at McDonald Studio in South Bend for the debutante publicity. After a woman asked whether I thought my wrapped package would fit in the small overhead bin, we struck up a conversation. When she learned that I was a freshman at ND, not SMC, she asked many questions. I loved expressing my opinions one-on-one, so I shared my experiences and disappointments from that first semester. I talked about residential life, the dining hall, the attitudes of my professors, and anything else that came to mind. It was cathartic and improved my disposition (well, at least until grades arrived).

McDonald Studio
(Fall 1972)

Reprinted with permission

As we headed outside to climb the plane's portable stairs, I noticed a distinguished priest in front of me. He turned around, told me he overheard my conversation, and asked my name and dorm. He said he was sorry to hear of my challenges over the past few months. Before starting up the steps, he invited me to talk with him after Christmas. As I asked the location of his office, I looked down and spotted a brass tag on his large leather case: Reverend Theodore M. Hesburgh, CSC. He kindly responded, "The Main Building." I wanted to crawl under a rock; instead, we shook hands.

I would later learn that Hesburgh preferred the hours of two to three in the morning to get his real work done, yet he remained available to any venturesome student who climbed the Administration Building's fire escape and tapped on his window for a late-night chat. Unfortunately, I chose not to visit him upon my return — I was too embarrassed. However, four years later, when my parents and I proceeded through the receiving line at the graduation reception for ND's first class of freshman women, I experienced his graciousness yet again. Hesburgh embraced me and said, "Debi, I am so glad that you made it!" After moving into the crowd, my father asked how Hesburgh knew my name.

Many stories, then and now, about Hesburgh's legacy of kindness and insight exist. His compassion spanned generations — from his days as a Vetville chaplain, as a young university president handling 1960s protests, and as a champion for coeducation.

◇ *Laura Dodge-Ghara, ND 1976:* "One Sunday, my rector, Kathy Cekanski, and I went to Mass at Sacred Heart Cathedral as Father Hesburgh was officiating. After Mass, we waited in line to greet him, after which he invited us to breakfast in Corby Hall. Upon entering the dining room, many older priests stopped eating and stared at us with their mouths agape. Hesburgh told us to pay them no mind and promptly sat us at a vacant table. When he returned with our fare, we were surprised to receive black coffee and burnt toast. We drank, ate, and visited as if this were an everyday occurrence. All the while, the other priests kept staring. As Father escorted us to the exit, we learned we were the first coeds to get inside the priests' residence."

◇ *Sally Naxera Benson, ND 1976:* "My most moving memories were a POW memorial Mass with Father Hesburgh at the [Athletic and Convocation Center] and a candlelit Mass at the Grotto. Awesome to share faith and break bread with friends! I grew up in a non-Catholic Missouri town. Sharing faith was great!"

◇ *James A. "Mickey" Rowley, ND 1976:* "I joined the Knights of Columbus, an all-male fraternal organization, at my father's urging. I was quite impressed to learn that Notre Dame's chapter...[was] the only chapter in the world...[that] admitted women. I learned that Father Hesburgh insisted that all campus opportunities be open to both men and women with no exceptions."

◇ *Paul Graf, ND 1976:* "As a sophomore in early '74, a friend and I were walking past the Dome when Father Ted came out of his office in the Administration Building. He stopped us and asked if we knew about the 'Wizard.' A little hammered, we blathered, 'No, Father, what's that?' He told us to look up at the spire of Sacred Heart and its two clocks, which were the Wizard's eyes! We told him we saw it, but I had to go back several nights later to really 'get' it! Father Ted was a giant among men—never too busy for us."

◇ *Dr. Brian Kirkland, ND 1974:* "I first met Father Ted at the foot of the steps of the Administration Building in 1970 when he welcomed me to ND, a ritual he extended to countless freshmen during his tenure. During my four years and for decades thereafter, I saw his tireless crusade for equality, justice, and peace.

"I was overjoyed when women first matriculated in 1972. The coeducational transformation marked a major inflection point in the fulfillment of the university's motto: *Vita Dulcedo Spes* (Life, Sweetness, Hope).

"When I was extremely ill from a life-threatening disease, my partner arranged a meeting with Father Ted. During an inspirational moment discussing times when he was unable to find a solution despite his earthly abilities, he gestured at the Golden Dome through his office window, saying, 'I gave it to Her, and She gave it to her Son.' Although my trek to wellness was arduous, I am fully recovered. I am eternally grateful to Our Lady of the Lake, speaking through Hesburgh. 'And our hearts forever, love thee, Notre Dame.'"

Father Theodore M. Hesburgh
Photo by Ed Brower

As available as Hesburgh made himself and as often as the light shone through his window, he had his naysayers. Some said the difference between God and Hesburgh was that God was everywhere — Hesburgh was everywhere but on campus. But wherever he was, his students knew the depth of his love, both for them and for ND.

◇ *Frank Fransioli, ND 1976:* "After a day of classes at the Architecture Studio at 76 Via Monterone [in Rome], I was heading back to the Hotel Paradiso, our coed dorm in the center of the Eternal City. In a pool of light ahead, I noticed a dark figure approaching. As the distance closed, I saw it was a priest, a common sight in Rome. We had almost passed each other when our eyes met. Recognizing Father Hesburgh, I introduced myself as a Notre Dame student in Rome's architecture program.

"Hesburgh informed me that he was late for a meeting at the Architecture Studio. Realizing I did not know the names of the streets that I walked daily, I suggested I just accompany him to his destination, and we set out at a deliberate pace. The details of our conversation have faded, but I remember it as pleasant and warm. After thanking me for my help, he disappeared into the old palazzo and headed upstairs, his footsteps fading on the marble stairs.

"As our spiritual leader and moral compass, we knew him as a counselor to presidents and popes. Few of us can say we showed Father Ted the way … even if just along the streets of Rome."

Sharing the Road

LaFortune Student Center
Art by Barbara O'Connell (2011)

"The mystique of Notre Dame reaches far beyond the football field. It extends into its classrooms, residence halls, chapels, social circles and more."[1] As with the world outside the Notre Dame bubble, tolerance for women or other minority groups varied across the community. However, these years on campus provided students with opportunities to learn from and relate to each other on varying levels. Such interactions prepared them not only for daily encounters but also for future personal and professional relationships.

No Vacancy

"Great things happen when there is time to mold our ideas into better ones, and that only happens when we give the process of finding solutions more of our time."[1] This wise advice applies to many situations in life, but it particularly applies to Notre Dame's housing situation, which was an early casualty of coeducation. The university continued its policy of making room for women by converting male dormitories into female ones well beyond that first year. For every "Congratulations, you've been accepted to Notre Dame" letter received by a woman, a resident of a to-be-converted dorm received an "eviction notice." The policy pitted a growing number of disgruntled, disillusioned men against the women. Whether a student was fortunate enough to stay in the same dorm for all four years, accepted the challenge of moving to a different hall, or moved off campus either by force or choice, residential decisions affected almost every dimension of collegiate life. In particular, the on- versus off-campus decision forced many, including women, to ask, "Should I stay, or should I go?"

◇◇◇

In the 1970s, the Notre Dame campus consisted of three named quadrangles or quads: the South, North, and "God." In addition to four dorms, the "God Quad" included the Main Building, Sacred Heart Church (now Basilica), and the Grotto. Although most activities were accessible from any quad, some dorms were more coveted than others due to their location. Students considered family history and proximity to specific buildings or facilities when requesting their new "home."

Art courtesy of Jane Pitz

Residence Life and Housing used a computer program to achieve geographic diversity across the dorms. This process was meant to broaden one's horizons beyond the familiar elements of one's hometown or state. Using a geographic mix—instead of personality or interest tests—also introduced an element of "Irish luck" to the probability of room harmony. Room assignments could just as easily lead to lifelong friends, room-mates of convenience, or roommates from hell.

The controversy associated with the conversion of male dorms to female residence halls sprang from a nexus of hall traditions. Before 1965, the university designated residential halls by graduating class: Notre Dame students moved from hall to hall each year and stayed to-gether by class year. Then, in 1965, Emil T. Hofman and Professor John Houck,

"There's more than one way to make a hall livable"
The Observer, February 11, 1972

Farley Hall fellows, tested the concept of a stay-hall system. In their model, every dorm housed a representative percentage of each undergraduate class rather than a single class year. By 1969, the stay-hall system became university policy, and each hall received quotas of freshmen. This new assignment system made assimilation of the newbies easier.[2]

As the stay-hall system solidified, the halls functioned as unofficial fraternities and, later, sororities. Each hall had its own mascot, identity, pranks, and inter- and intrahall competitions. As Fred Baranowski, president of Holy Cross Hall from 1972–1973, explained:

> The hall...is quickly becoming the center of student life at Notre Dame. Each hall develops its own personality which acts as a unifying factor among its students....[T]he hall operates as a closely-knit group, so ideas tend to be executed more effectively.[3]

After the random first-year assignments, students decided whether to remain with their current roommates or change living arrangements. The factors for se-lecting rooms—such as grade point average or class year—varied by hall. For instance, Dillon Hall used an "Adjusted Average System," with room selections based not only on grade point average but also on length of time in and contribu-tions to hall life and the university.

For some, the annual room selection process was awful:

> ◇ *Anonymous, ND 1976:* "Room pick time was horrendous. Some-one always seemed to get hurt. It was difficult to say, 'I want to

live by myself,' 'I want to live with this other person,' or 'I just don't want to live with you anymore.'"

◇ *Anonymous, ND 1976:* "It [room pick] was a terrible time of year and needed to change. It was easy to lose contact with people if you lived on different floors or in different dorms, much less on different quads."

The foundation of the stay-hall system shook as the number of women increased, and halls illuminated virtual "no vacancy" signs. The shifting population not only affected men displaced from their dorms but also forced a lottery system on the unaffected dorms. In addition to the freshman quota for each hall, the remaining all-male dorms now also received a quota of displaced residents from Badin and Walsh in 1972, Breen-Phillips and Farley in 1973, and Lyons in 1974. Male students often bemoaned the changes to campus and dorm life.

◇ *Joe Henderlong, ND 1975*: "I recall the rector meeting with us to explain the choice of Farley Hall and Breen-Phillips as the first two North Quad dorms to go coed in the fall of 1973. With this advance notice, some took matters into their own hands and found housing off campus. However, most assumed they would be placed in another dorm, only to find out they were not successful in the ensuing lottery.

"Although the university's vision was good, the delivery left much to be desired and contributed to hard feelings by many males for years after."

This changing and challenging residential landscape caused hard feelings. Some men resented losing their halls, traditions, and roommates. Some even reacted with destructive behaviors and attitudes.

◇ *Anonymous male, ND 1976:* "Some unintended consequences followed the announcement of another dorm conversion. Since everyone knew the selected dorms were to be remodeled, some students did things they would not normally have done had they remained in the same dorm for four years. In one dorm, students moved lockers into the halls and spray-painted them; their outlines remained on the walls after the lockers were returned to their rooms. Hallway carpets soaked with water became 'slip and slides.' The women can thank us for the extensive repairs required from our mischief."

◇ *Anonymous male, ND 1976:* "As our freshman year drew to a close in 1973, the school needed more room for women. They took our beloved Farley Hall, trampled on its male traditions, and gave it to the women. Our close-knit bunch, forever known as 'The Farley Ten,' scattered throughout campus and South Bend like orphans. Notre Dame and its men would never be the same."

The resistance on the part of some male students left a bad taste in the mouths of many women.

◇ *Jeanine Sterling, ND 1976:* "The day that ND announced that B-P [Breen-Phillips] and Farley would be the next two women's dorms, I was walking across North Quad and saw a sheet hanging outside one of the Breen-Phillips windows. On it was painted 'B-P Goes TWAT.' Yet another warm and welcoming message from our fellow male students."

any female wishing to move in now and try farley on for size... please apply within for co-occupancy information

The Observer,
January 19, 1973

In actuality, the women faced their own residential challenges. The small number of women in each class year led to imbalances within their halls. With the class of 1977 expecting three hundred fifty freshman women along with roughly seventy transfers—more than doubling the number of women on campus—the university asked sixty Badin and eighty Walsh residents to voluntarily move to North Quad's soon-to-be converted Breen-Phillips and Farley halls. Mirroring the experiences of the displaced men, these women were denied the benefit of the stay-hall system.

Sister John encouraged the women to accept yet another challenge and assist with balancing the hall populations and preventing segregation of the newest arrivals: "We are asking some of you to move, to volunteer to help in the new beginnings on the North Quad. We need people to be the nucleus of those halls."[4] Anticipating that some people would be negative about the changes, Sister John continued: "We can't get growth on demand....[I]t takes patience, waiting, and giving....[I]t's a real adventure leaving what is secure and moving into the unknown."[5] Many women answered this challenge and moved across campus.

This approach illustrated the similarities in residential life for both men and women. For example, all students residing on campus signed housing contracts. Despite the changing times, these contracts granted the university far-reaching rights. Rectors, assistant rectors, and resident assistants (RAs) enforced these policies as they supervised hall life.

The University reserves the right to: make whatever reassignment or adjustment in accommodations deems necessary; to inspect rooms for cleanliness or to make repairs; and to enter rooms without a search warrant...for the purpose of maintaining security, discipline and the orderly operation of an educational institution.[6]

Whereas priests were central figures as rectors and confessors in the male halls, the female rectors arranged their own ministry programs. Rectors such as Sister Jean invited priests to celebrate the Eucharist and the Sacrament of Penance, often with late-night Masses and special liturgies. Women even attended Sunday night Mass in pajamas and curlers without embarrassment or judgment.

Under the watchful eyes of rectors, hall governments established activities for their residents. They invited faculty and administration to share their perspectives during hall coffee hours. Other activities included intra- and interhall sports, football weekend barbecues, hall formals, and Mardi Gras.

As time passed, the men came to appreciate certain benefits found only in the women's residence: The laundry provided ways to avoid jean shrinkage, and the kitchens offered facilities for private dinners, birthday parties, and special events.

To improve residential life, Notre Dame updated its tradition of bachelor "don" male faculty living in the dorms. Modernized as a faculty-in-residence program in 2013, live-in faculty act as mentors and role models with no administrative or disciplinary duties.[7]

◇ *Tom Young, ND 1976:* "Male dorms did not have kitchens, but I offered to make an old-fashioned Italian meal using the kitchen in Walsh Hall. Discovering that the available pans were inadequate, I borrowed pots and pans — although about three sizes too big — from the South Dining Hall.

"When I went grocery shopping to buy the ingredients, I was appalled that no store near campus sold ricotta cheese for the lasagna. After assembling the lasagna in the borrowed oversized pan, I placed it in the oven, only to discover that the oven door did not close all the way. Luckily, having bought aluminum foil for the garlic bread, I used the leftover foil to bridge the gap. About a dozen women and men enjoyed this 'home-cooked' Italian meal, even with my substitution — which I will not share — for the ricotta."

Still, the women found some gender inequities hard to accept. The university asked the women to make their own beds while providing maid services to the men; it provided women with sheets every two weeks, although many brought their own. For the 1973–1974 academic year, Jerome Wilson, CSC, vice president for Business Affairs, terminated the bed-making services for the men due to cost. The maintenance department allowed the affected thirty-five or so maids to apply for janitorial positions, provided they were under the age of sixty-five and viewed as fit enough. This approach mirrored policies at Purdue and Penn State that allowed women to work in more physical, higher paid, traditionally male positions.[8]

Another double standard allowed the men to move off campus after freshman year, while women had to live on campus until their senior year, unless their families resided in South Bend. Although most women did not want to live off campus, those interested in doing so found this policy inequitable. Reporter Marlene Zloza pointed out that even the 1972–1973 student manual supported the women's argument, since it did not specify male-only eligibility:

> Single, undergraduate students over 21 years of age may reside anywhere in the South Bend area. Single, undergraduate students under 21 years of age must living [sic] in housing approved by the Dean of Students.[9]

Discussions about allowing the women to participate in a lottery to live off campus achieved no traction primarily due to the university's concerns over security and safety issues.[10] This policy of keeping women on campus also limited the number of women admitted due to a room shortage. Judy Snyder, president of the Women's Rights Association and third-year law student, captured the dissonance:

> I consider it a denial of their [women's] rights as individuals and citizens and discriminatory in regard to men, who can live off-campus....Also, the administration is limiting the number of women that [sic] can come here, restricting total enrollment by not letting those who want to move off and accepting more to live on campus....I think they have an obligation to women students and I hope they will realize this themselves and cease this disservice and manipulation.[11]

In the spring of 1973, ND students expressed a preference for on-campus housing, contrary to the national trend of living off campus. Student Affairs operated under the assumption that a bed existed for every student who *wanted* one. However, as more male-dorm conversions occurred, the housing situation worsened. Displaced males faced three options: abiding by lottery results, living in overcrowded rooms and converted study halls, or moving off campus.

The debate between the merits of residence hall versus off-campus life never stopped. Campus life offered a student community and a greater sense of security, while South Bend suffered from a high crime rate. Off-campus life permitted greater social freedom — no parietals — and created opportunities for personal growth. Students learned to prepare their own meals, make their own beds, clean their own spaces, and pay bills. Yet many men viewed off-campus living as a harsh alternative, given its safety and affordability issues.

◇ *Stephen Klug, ND 1976:* "My senior year, six friends and I left Grace Hall and moved off campus. We found a duplex a few blocks from The Library (the bar, not the renowned *Touchdown Jesus* Memorial Library) on the edge of an 'iffy' neighborhood.

"Security immediately became an issue. We caught someone attempting to steal a stereo during our move-in weekend. After this experience, we took extra precautions to secure our valuables, especially televisions and stereos, including the adoption of a German shepherd from the local animal shelter. We also arranged to store our belongings in the garage of a Notre Dame professor on football weekends and before breaks.

"Learning to live on our own, cooking, cleaning (yeah, right), doing laundry at the laundromat, and fending for ourselves was a new experience without mom, Notre Dame food, or maid service."

The selection processes to determine which male students moved off campus varied. When selection by grade point average failed to win approval, Associate Vice President of Student Affairs James Flanigan, CSC, suggested that students not contributing to hall life or not living in harmony with others should move off campus. Dean James Riehle, CSC, who was in charge of student housing, counseled that viewing "off-campus living as a 'penal colony'" only inflamed the situation.[12]

Without other options, the off-campus lottery for men continued. In February 1974, James Shilts, CSC, director of off-campus housing, tried to help those forced off campus. He developed a list of properties—rooms, houses, apartments—by size, location, price, and pros and cons for each. Shilts discouraged oral rental agreements, stressing that leases guaranteed stable rent and set expectations on both sides.[13]

For the 1974–1975 academic year, the women continued to strongly voice their displeasure with the housing restrictions. Some male hall rectors such as David Schlaver, CSC, wanted the women treated like part of the ND community—not like guests.

◇ *Cathy Donahue, ND 1976:* "As in the ban on women living off campus, there was sometimes too much of a sense of 'By golly, we let you in. We want people to see you'—a feeling that we were somehow on display."

Even as more women arrived each year, many opposed converting another male residence hall.[14] As a viable alternative, the administration decided that incoming female transfer students should live off campus. Their acceptance letters instructed them to find off-campus housing.

◇ *Maggie Waltman Smith, ND 1976:* "I lived off campus after I transferred to ND as a junior. With not enough space in the female dorms, it was a stipulation in my acceptance letter. I met two strangers in the parking lot at Notre Dame Avenue Apartments with the same dilemma. We signed a contract that day. Serendipity!

"We became close to the guys in the apartment across the hall; one of them walked me down the aisle. The mix of genders and class levels living in close proximity is something I felt was unique to the off-campus environment...perhaps even more so at ND since the university is so dorm-centric (and unisex)."

In February 1975, policy makers shelved the planned Grace Hall conversion, eliminated the lottery, and approved women moving off campus.[15]

◇ *Darlene Palma Connelly, ND 1977:* "'Should I stay, or should I go?' Moving off campus senior year was an easy decision for me, except for leaving my best friend and roommate to fend for herself with the B-P lottery. Directors of Student Housing—Father 'Moose' Mulcahy, CSC, and later Father Tom Tallarida, CSC—gave me a student-aid job in the off-campus housing office, a great vantage point for finding suitable housing. To help other students with their rental decisions, I read the South Bend police blotter to pinpoint troubled areas. I also inspected rentals before we approved them as acceptable options. I found a spacious two-bedroom in a duplex downtown, away from other student housing and the crime. I had my first taste of what the future held juggling multiple roles and responsibilities—one of my best decisions as an undergraduate."

Whether male or female, off-campus residents did not have the same campus privileges as dorm residents. Since they did not pay room and board, some

Reverend Thomas C. Tallarida, CSC (1923–2013) graduated in 1942 from Aquinas Institute in Rochester, New York. In 1947, he graduated from ND and was ordained a priest in the Congregation of the Holy Cross in 1951. After earning a master's degree in religious studies and several pastoral assignments, Tallarida returned to ND in 1970. He served as rector of Zahm Hall, director of off-campus housing, and director of the foreign students' program. His students knew him as a friend, another father, or a brother.

Father Tallarida

activities required them to pay a fee. As a senior, Kathleen Dickinson Villano (ND 1977) wrote a letter to Hesburgh because, as an off-campus resident, she had to

Father Ted (1997)
Photo by Darlene
Palma Connelly

pay ten dollars to attend a student picnic. Father Ted responded with a gracious note and two five-dollar bills. Thirty-five years later, during a dinner recognizing Hesburgh, Villano not only returned the ten dollars but also handed him a check for $132.68 for the Thanking Father Ted Foundation — "the current value of the $10 at 6 percent compounded interest."[16]

Even female graduate students could not avoid the disparate treatment of males and females or the on-versus off-campus dilemma. They reacted negatively when the university announced their move from Lewis Hall into Badin Hall for one year. Given the magnitude of their own upheaval, some males expressed little patience for the female graduate objections:

> The grad students will remain on campus — perhaps forcing under-grads [sic] to move off. They're simply moving to smaller singles. Badin Hall, like Lewis, has a kitchen and a rec room. It's also well-situated; the bookstore, south cafeteria, and the Rock being a short walk away. We believe grad students should have to make a few accommodations too. We are ALL members of the Notre Dame student body, and the under-grads' [sic] tuitions and fees are worth just as much as those of our counterparts.[17]

Across the nation and at Notre Dame, the number of female graduate students was increasing. The university decided to build new town houses to house 144 of its 460 graduate women. This alleviated some residential constraints starting in the fall of 1976.[18] At that time, 90 percent of the women resided on campus and occupied six halls; those off campus remained at a percentage about half that of the men.

Even with the addition of town houses for female graduate students, the university still needed a solution to the quagmire of limited dorm rooms and increasing female admissions. Coed dormitories offered an obvious alternative and elicited many studies and a wealth of student and alumni input over the years, probably garnering a *Guinness Book of Record* for never-ending studies. Before squelching the conversion of Grace Hall to another women's dormitory, discussions turned to conducting a coed experiment for juniors and seniors in the hall.[19] Another proposal suggested allowing residence halls either to opt to remain single-sex dormitories and maintain the stay-hall practice or to become coed. Rector reactions ranged from a willingness to explore the possibilities to outright, vocal rejection.

The proposed timeline for adding a coed dorm alternative was the 1978–1979 academic year, but—once again—the university postponed such plans. Even talk show hosts like Phil Donahue (ND 1957) explored the coed dorm debate and how the changes brought about by the sexual revolution. Ultimately, Notre Dame kept its traditional approach to residential hall life and its sex code policy, traditions holding firm fifty years later.[20]

Hall Life through the Years

Above: Beverly practices Breen-Phillips Hall sports (1973)

Above right: Santa visits Lyons Hall (1974)

Alumni "Dawgs"

Recycling in the 1970s

Above: One way to store the beer

Above left: Janet grades papers (1975)

◇◇◇

REARVIEW REFLECTION After moving to North Quad in the fall of 1973, Beverly and I met not only freshmen but also many transfers. It felt strange giving advice to them with only one year of college experience. To help these new residents fit in better than I did as a freshman, I became a hall clerk for Breen-Phillips. I learned a great deal from time spent with the rector, other hall clerks, and Sister Jean Lenz, the Farley Hall rector. Some men came to know the wisdom and wit of the women's rectors like Sister Jean.

⬦ *Bob Quakenbush, ND 1976:* "When the Woolworth store in downtown closed, they sold everything, including the fixtures. Two Farley girls returned to campus with their new prized possession, a full-size male mannequin. They decided to prank their rector, Sister Jean, but needed a pair of men's pajamas to pull it off. They asked me if I had a pair they could borrow. Although I doubt whether I ever wore them at ND, I delivered a pair of neatly folded blue pajamas with the understanding that they never

2020 Housing Quadrangles

- East: Dunne, *Flaherty*, *John Family Hall*
- God: *Lewis*, Saint Edward's, Sorin, *Walsh*
- North: *Farley*, *Breen-Phillips*, *Cavanaugh*, Keenan, Stanford, Zahm
- Mod: Knott, *Pasquerilla East*, *Pasquerilla West*, Siegfried
- South: Alumni, *Badin*, Carroll, Dillon, Fisher, *Howard*, *Lyons*, Morrissey, Pangborn
- West: Baumer, Duncan, Keough, *McGlinn*, O'Neill Family, *Ryan*, *Welsh Family*

Holy Cross Hall was demolished in 1990. The two male towers, Grace and Flanner halls, were converted to administrative buildings in 1996 and 1997, respectively.

Italics = women's residence hall

reveal the pajamas belonged to me. They dressed the mannequin, gained access to Sister Jean's room, and put the mannequin in her bed! But the prank backfired—on me! Sister Jean, known for her sense of humor, took it in stride and apparently took delight in telling people how Bob Quakenbush's pajamas ended up in her bed. How did she find out who owned the pajamas? Simple. I forgot my mom had sewn laundry tags with my name and laundry number onto both the pajama top and bottom!"

In an October 2000 interview with Sister Jean, she explained how women's halls in close proximity (Walsh and Badin, Farley and Breen-Phillips) built lifelong bonds and a sense of security. Sister Jean loved her role as mentor and friend to ND women:

> Eighty-five percent of my rectoring time was spent talking to students about roommate problems, romances, and friendships. I gave great doses of conversational energy to stressful relationships involving parents, professors, and on occasion an administrator or two....They let me confront them with strong words and congratulate them with deep joy....They let me worry about them. Best of all, they let me believe in them."[21]

10-4 Good Buddy

"At a cultural level, there is a lot of lip service about friendship being wonderful and important, but not a lot of social support for protecting what's precious about it," writers and friends Aminatou Sow and Ann Friedman note in their book *Big Friendship*.[1] In college—especially during these early years of coeducation—authentic female friendships were essential. Like truckers, who recognize the importance of staying connected with their buddies on the road and have developed their own language to ensure safe travels, the ND buddy system included those dorm mates and friends who provided unwavering support and love despite one's unflattering traits and worst habits. A landmark study titled "Behavioral Responses to Stress" by Laura Cousins Klein and Shelley Taylor (2000) has suggested that women respond to stress with a cascade of brain chemicals that causes them to maintain friendships with other women—a "tend-and-befriend" pattern.[2] Perhaps this response explains why most women at ND maintained their friendships despite hall changes and the university's challenging environment.

◇◇◇

REARVIEW REFLECTION When Beverly and I chose Walsh over Badin Hall, we knew neither Badin's traditions nor its history as home to ND notables such as Austin Carr (ND 1971, first overall pick in the 1971 NBA draft), Terry Hanratty (ND 1969, former ND quarterback who played in the NFL in the 1960s and 1970s), or Hesburgh himself (who occupied room 417 in 1945). Likewise, we did not comprehend the value of the stay-hall system. We believed that sharing a quad in Walsh, versus single rooms in Badin, would provide an easier transition to college life. So, we began our adventure as "roomies" with a common purpose—making our first dorm room habitable. Other women that first year took similar approaches.

> ◇ *Shelley Muller Simon, ND 1976:* "My freshman roommate, Donna Crowley, came to campus over the summer [of 1972] with her twin sister, Denise. She chose our room color (a 'lovely peach'

from ND's palette of peach, yellow, or green) and purchased matching curtains and bedspreads. I remember thinking it was not exactly 'my style,' but you could always count on Donna to get things done, efficiently, economically, and fairly.

"Our room was on the fourth floor of Walsh Hall; if I removed the screen from the double-hung window and opened it, we could straddle the sill and get a glimpse of the Golden Dome. If we stretched our necks outside the window on a football Saturday, we could search the quad for the twins' father in his yellow slicker and rain hat worn faithfully to the games held in inclement weather.

"The twins became the first of my 'Chicago connection' of Notre Dame friends. Next came Mimi Philbin, who lived in a single room on the third floor. The four of us quickly became close friends, and as a bonus, I met two wonderful families. The Crowleys and the Philbins were strong Catholic families, providing me with a model for the family I wanted. Family became one theme of my freshman year. Many referred to 'The Notre Dame Family,' and I quickly realized that the caring attitudes of many professors and administrators made us feel part of a large, ever-growing family. As in any family, the personalities, conflicts, and misunderstandings could cause some tension and anxiety but ultimately led to personal growth and understanding."

The quad experience showed me how privileged I was before Notre Dame. I loved the privacy of having my own room and controlling the optics. I seldom spent the night at others' homes; slumber parties were usually at my house. Foolishly, I believed that dorm life would be just one big slumber party for the next four years.

I forged a small group of friends that first semester. We looked forward to celebrating one roommate's December 8 birthday after Thanksgiving break. Each of us brought something from home: Beverly shared her Grandma Mary's *potica* (a Slovenian coffee cake), and I contributed lobster, frozen after our family's August trip to the Florida Keys. We gathered in Walsh's basement, listened to guitar music, sang Christmas carols, and

The first known use of the phrase "slumber party" was in 1925. The term usually refers to an overnight gathering of teenage girls, an adolescent rite of passage. Sleepovers are widely represented in pop culture. The 1971 musical and 1978 film *Grease* captured well this phenomenon. The Library of Congress acknowledged the film in 2020 as "culturally, historically, or aesthetically significant" and selected it for preservation in the US National Film Registry.[3]

Post-Thanksgiving (Walsh, 1972): Beverly with Dave Gray; Sharon Zelinski and Randy Sarton

enjoyed a smorgasbord of sensory and culinary delights before heading into marathon studying for finals.

Soon after, though, Beverly and I determined we needed to change rooms to improve our grades. We swapped rooms with two girls living in a double who wanted to move into our quad. After Christmas break, we moved from room 209 to room 219. Beyond increasing our privacy, the long "bowling alley" room had a great window ledge to straddle in the spring.

I appreciated the quiet of our new room as I worked to understand an experience from Christmas break that bothered me (and does to this day). Before heading home to Florida, a classmate from Walsh Hall asked to stay with me when Notre Dame played Nebraska in the 1973 Orange Bowl. Hoping a new friendship would develop from our time together, I agreed. However, I soon realized that she only wanted a free place to stay. I felt used and snubbed when she did not invite me to join her at numerous pregame events. She was also inconsiderate, causing my parents to stay up well into the early-morning hours on several nights awaiting her return. Before I left for the second semester, I wanted to understand how I had misread her intentions. I talked to my mother, who firmly reminded me, "You are truly blessed if you can count your true friends on one hand." Returning to a new space with a familiar roommate softened that visitor's blow to my ego. I looked forward to better times.

Notre Dame Magazine, Autumn 2004
Art courtesy of Gary Hovland

First semester grades were a shock. Both Beverly and I had underestimated the effort

Roomies forever: Off campus (1976) and celebrating on a birthday cruise (2019)

needed to balance academics, quad living, and social activities. We set a schedule in our "new" double that worked for us. We both had biology at eight in the morning, and neither of us enjoyed getting up that early. We took turns going to the lecture, improved our note-taking, and taped the session for the one lucky enough to stay in bed. We both got more sleep, and the recorded lectures were a terrific way to prep for exams. In the evenings, we splurged on pizza delivered from nearby pizzerias. To keep the smell of our large pepperoni and extra cheese pie from drifting into the hallway, we placed towels across the doorjamb and closed the overhead transom.

We explored new interests and relationships, giving us time apart from each other and reducing stress in our day-to-day living. Beverly became a disc jockey on the classical music radio station and signed up for piano lessons. She convinced me to give both a try; I did but not for long. I made a mistake by not sticking with the piano lessons, given that they only cost fifty dollars for the semester.

No relationship is without conflict, but we managed it well. Beverly tolerated my singing along with Elvis Presley with headphones on while typing papers. She suffered my periodic need to move the furniture into the hall to clean the room. I tried to curb the "green-eyed monster" as Beverly's grades improved at a pace much faster than mine. We made minor tweaks to our living and studying habits as needed. We strengthened our connection, going from "roomies" to friends. As one ND graduate put it:

> In fact, the most tangible gift the university gave me is not a man at all; it's my very best friend.... [O]ur lives have mirrored each other, intertwined in the most intimate of friendships. It is this friendship—with a woman—that is my most precious degree.[4]

The move to a double helped to restore some of my self-confidence, and I again invited some friends home. Walsh resident and friend Sharon Zelinski (now Haverstock) came to Florida as my houseguest for spring break 1973. This trip home was better than the one at Christmas—no embarrassing airport conversations with Father Ted within earshot!

Sharon and I enjoyed the sun and surf of Fort Lauderdale Beach. The sun burned her feet so badly she wore flip-flops on our return flight. While her sunburn and pain faded, a different pain followed me back to campus.

Sharon and I scheduled haircuts at my favorite Palm Beach salon with my stylist, Todd. Before fall term, he had convinced me to cut and layer my long, straight hair into the Farrah Fawcett curls then in vogue—the same "dolled-up" style I used to stop my sociology professor from calling on me incessantly. I had no plan to change that style. However, after seeing the chic short cut he styled on Sharon, I said what many women later regret: "Todd, do whatever you think best."

Farrah Leni Fawcett (1947–2009) appeared in 1960s and 1970s ads and television series, displaying her iconic hairstyle. She rose to fame after playing a private investigator in the television series *Charlie's Angels* (1976–1977), a role transcending gender norms at the time. Her 1976 red swimsuit poster sold six million copies in its first year of print, exhibited on dorm walls worldwide.[5]

Sharon went to the nearby ice cream parlor to grab something to hold us until dinner. Since we had partied hard the preceding evening, I nodded off in Todd's chair. When Sharon returned with milkshakes, Todd had finished. As he turned me around to appraise the "new me" in the mirror, I saw shock register on Sharon's face. I soon understood why—my hair was no longer than one inch anywhere on my head. Horrified as I was, reality truly hit when my mom and grandmother, both skilled hairdressers, teared up after seeing Todd's handiwork.

The situation worsened when my father came home that evening. He threatened to sue the salon, even though he did not believe in frivolous litigation. His reaction convinced me that this was indeed a terrible look. In tears, I told my parents that returning to school like this was not an option. I was serious, and they knew it. Luckily, with her cosmetology license in hand, Mom headed to the nearest beauty supply store and bought an expensive wig made from real hair. As I boarded the plane to return to campus, I worried about my classmates' reactions if they ever learned about this deception.

When Beverly walked into our room that first night, she immediately complimented my hair. Imagine her surprise when I pulled off the wig and threw it at her! She screamed as she caught a handful of hair and saw my shorn head. I wore the wig everywhere for weeks, and to my knowledge, no one ever suspected the truth.

This incident taught me a great deal about keeping confidences. Neither Beverly nor Sharon ever divulged my vain secret. Remembering Mom's guidance about loyal friends, I now knew that I had two at Notre Dame.

Our second-semester change to a double room improved my study habits, resulting in a slightly better grade point average at the end of my freshman year.

However, it was not enough to qualify me for priority selection of a decent dorm room, a feat I did not achieve until junior year. Since residence hall policy, class year, and grade point average drove selection in the hall lottery, my annual hall changes put me in the middle of the residential life quagmire.

With the conversion of Farley and Breen-Phillips (B-P) halls to address the almost doubling of women in the second year of coeducation, Beverly and I accepted the challenge to move to B-P on the North Quad. Located directly across from Cavanaugh Hall where Beverly's boyfriend and my brother lived, B-P was a prime location for us. It provided easy access to the student parking lot; now sophomores, we both had cars. B-P's location also placed us near our colleges—the School of Arts and Letters for Beverly and Hayes-Healy School of Business for me. Even in winter, we frequently walked from our dorm to nearby LaFortune for her favorite choco-mint shake and my beloved hot fudge butter pecan sundae.

Our first-floor room, number 121, offered an excellent view of the North Quad but with higher noise levels than our second-floor Walsh accommodations. Our efficient use of this space, larger than our Walsh "bowling alley," compensated for this inconvenience. We used our bunk beds as sofas and placed our desks near the door. The freestanding closets shielded us from open doorways or the light of late-night studying. For entertainment, we enjoyed our stereo and black-and-white television, while satisfying late-night cravings with "pizza"— English muffins topped with cheese, pepperoni, and sauce—made in our toaster oven. We often left the door open for floor mates to drop in.

More than residence hall members stopped by room 121. We never gave a thought to our predecessors on campus or from our assigned rooms, but soon Notre Dame's past got too close for comfort. One Saturday night, I awoke to see a large dark figure looming in the mid-

> In 2019, ND was nineteenth on a list of most haunted US colleges (down from twelfth in 2012).[6] Suspected hauntings on campus include:
>
> • ND founder Father Sorin, who died on Halloween in 1893, walking the halls of the Main Building.
>
> • ND football great George Gipp of the 1920s is said to frequent Washington Hall after dying of pneumonia, following a night outside on its steps. Gipp is most known for his request to Rockne: "[W]in just one for the Gipper."
>
> • Saint Liam Hall, aka the student health center rumored to be named for an award-winning horse, supposedly has deceased nuns making after-hours rounds.

dle of our room. Since Beverly and I agreed to tolerate overnight male visitors so long as we did not disturb the other roomie or get caught breaking parietals, I assumed it was Beverly's boyfriend. Yet something about the large shadow made me nervous, so I quickly turned my back and pulled the covers over my head. The next morning, I asked Beverly about her guest. She looked at me quizzically and turned the question back on me. She, too, had witnessed the "visitor" and, like me, said nothing. We nervously laughed and wondered who or what had visited us.

This "visitation" occurred the same semester that one of my classes explored satanism, seances, and the black mass; it also coincided with the release of *The Exorcist*. A group of us went to see the film in its full glory — or is that *gory?* — on the big screen in downtown South Bend. As we walked back from student parking past the North Dining Hall, we heard howling and strange noises. Normally, we paused here to inhale the scent of baked goods after our off-campus activities. However, this night, no one wanted to loiter long enough to knock on the back door to try and score some munchies. Food was the last thing on our minds. I privately wondered if the mysterious figure who visited our room had returned.

Somewhat more secure in my new hall and my role as one of its clerks, I hoped to leave any negative perceptions of me behind in Walsh. Memories, however, proved to be long for some Walsh women who moved to B-P. Many remembered me as one of the first women to receive red roses and a teddy bear during freshman orientation, my very feminine style of dress, and someone who seemed to have a constant stream of male visitors. Others commented on the constant flow of Valentine's Day yellow roses. Friend Laura Dodge-Ghara once labeled my rooms as "funeral parlors" due to all the flowers. I was not the only coed to receive such attention, but it still drew hurtful remarks wherever I lived. If only the guys had known that I preferred chocolate.

Robert Carrier invented the Slip 'N Slide, a toy manufactured by Wham-O. First sold in 1961, it is a plastic sheet with wetting tubes. The wet surface becomes very slippery, allowing the user to slide down the sheet.[7]

One day in the spring of 1974, I went to lunch in the North Dining Hall with two fellow B-P residents, one of whom was Janet Krier (now Breen). Our spirits reflected the weather on this rainy, chilly day. We sat with some guys from the class of '74, including Dale Planicka, a contributor to this book project. He teased us about going outside and "melting" in the rain. With that, the women rose from the table and stepped outside.

The flooded North Quad taunted us to challenge any preconceived notions others may have had of us — me as prissy, Janet as athletic, and our friend as intellectual. We romped, splashed, and rolled across the grass and in the mud as if it were our personal Slip 'N Slide. Dale and other males eventually joined us, and we made a fun-filled memory out of a less-than-stellar day. Several men expressed surprise that we could actually "let our hair down." As we frolicked about, past monikers melted away, and we became known as the "Mud Queens." I felt sorry for the groundskeepers and especially the housekeeper who dealt with the mud

The "Mud Queens" frolic in the flooded
North Quad (Breen-Phillips, 1974)

Joe Winterscheid and Beverly at
the Spring Formal (Lyons, 1975)

in the shower. Only later did I realize this stunt reflected an emerging level of self-confidence.

Timing is everything in life, and that definitely includes the college experience—whether it be acceptance to and staying at Notre Dame, taking a leap of faith in the pursuit of the unfamiliar, or just embracing the day-to-day. We shared a specific time in Notre Dame's history that influenced us and our relationships in so many ways.

> ◊ *Ron Skrabacz, ND 1976:* "Our lives, for most of us, were only touched peripherally by the Vietnam War. Unless someone in our class had a relative who was killed or wounded, we were not directly impacted since we did not have to serve. Our birth year was the first for the all-volunteer army. From a life perspective for me, not having to go to Nam was a stroke of good fortune—I was born at the right time. From an ND perspective, the other stroke of good fortune was living in Alumni Hall for all four years. Without either of these strokes of luck, my life path could have been tremendously altered. As they say, timing is everything."

Because I lived in three residence halls in four years, I came to understand the disruption that males faced with each dorm conversion. Our junior year, Beverly and I, along with the other Mud Queens, moved to the newly converted Lyons Hall on the South Quad. One anonymous female student (ND 1976) recalled the atmosphere in Lyons in that third year of coeducation: "Not having upperclassmen in the dorms really affected the character of the dorm. By the time we arrived in

Lyons (fall 1974), it was the most all-together women's dorm, because it achieved the best balance across the classes."

Janet, as a senior, asked me to share her excellent fourth-floor pick, room 409. My time with Janet proved to be a true turning point for me as a Notre Dame student. With her tutoring, I experienced a level of academic success that had previously eluded me. After we graduated, we shared an apartment in Chicago, and she was the one who encouraged me to pursue a master's degree. My hand grasped that of my third ND friend.

In Lyons, Beverly achieved a great room pick and selected a single. Still, our friendship remained solid, and we actually attended the Junior Class Semi-Formal dance together. For this traditionally popular campus event, classmates discarded jeans and sweat suits and dressed for the evening. As the only formal event both Beverly and I attended, I still smile when I remember her bursting into my room looking for a slip to wear under her formal. As she usually wore casual "hippie" attire, my plethora of "dress-up" clothes came in handy. Beverly eventually married her date, and I sometimes take credit — especially after a glass of wine — for helping her show him her elegant side.

For the 1975–1976 academic year, living off campus became an option for the women, and I considered following Beverly off campus. My father quickly squelched that idea, citing my improved grades and focus. In reality, hall life benefits outweighed any negatives like parietals, and a move off campus would have put me in a house with multiple roommates. I finally obtained a single in the basement of Lyons, and I looked forward to decorating room 014.

Senior year brought a new maturity in both female and male relationships, and I hoped those within my circle felt this change. That year, I reached beyond the comfort of roommates and cemented a lifelong friendship with Diana Wilson (now Ostermann). Diana helped me find constructive ways to fill any remaining emotional voids. She became the fourth friend of the five whom my mom said I would come to cherish.

Notre Dame women were appearing in all corners of campus. Their presence resulted in new traditions. While the "ghosts of our campus past" reflected the objectification of female undergraduates, the "ghosts of our campus present" allowed us to enjoy our time together and to shape the "ghost of campus future." Despite marriages, divorces, children, and careers, we continue to find time to be together. We laugh over such unflattering memories as the wig story and our crazy years under the Dome. Through reflections from other insightful alumnae, I have come to understand the many similarities and differences in our experiences and have achieved a better knowledge of those figures in the rearview mirror.

Mixed Signals

"[T]he day will come," Susan B. Anthony said in 1897, "when man will recognize woman as his peer, not only at the fireside, but in the councils of the nation. Then, and not until then, will there be the perfect comradeship, the ideal union between the sexes, that shall result in the highest development of the race."[1] Despite the years since Anthony had envisioned women's full equality in the United States, many Notre Dame men in 1972 failed to recognize women as peers and continued to question the female presence in the university's hallowed halls. Unfortunately, the administration as a whole — even some of its more enlightened men — failed to anticipate Notre Dame's own "battle of the sexes."

◇◇◇

Merriam-Webster's Dictionary defines "battle of the sexes" as "a struggle for power between women and men."[2] Notre Dame's decisions to initially admit only 365 women and to convert male residence halls provided fertile ground for such a conflict. The administration underestimated what was truly needed to sensitize its male community to undergraduate women.

The inordinately lopsided male-to-female ratio — almost twenty to one in the fall of 1972 — exacerbated social challenges as students struggled to fit into this semi-adult world. Disruption to campus harmony seemed inevitable when this previously all-male school admitted women with above-average qualifications. Even universities applying the same standards to applicants of both sexes experienced some impact from perceptions of women as better qualified. Diana Wilson Ostermann offered one explanation on the impact of this disparity on social relationships:

"What exactly is a 'woman'?"
The Observer, September 26, 1974

Partying with Diana Wilson
and Steve Klug (1976)

Enjoying a night of "home" cooking
with Janet Krier and Mike Schafer

◇ *Diana Wilson Ostermann, ND 1976:* "It is no secret given the few openings for freshman women that the administration took the top female applicants, instead of 'first come, first served.' The acceptance bar for women was significantly higher than for males. Of course, there were some highly intelligent male students, but they mixed with others further down the IQ scale. That first year, some women found some males not on their same intellectual level. While acceptable for platonic friendships, some women had specific expectations for the long-term. Not only did the male–female ratio work against the men but the intellect disparity caused them to feel they did not measure up in the eyes of ND women. A lot of rejection and misunderstandings existed early on."

Though the ND experience felt unique to those on campus at the time, it mirrored the struggles of other previously all-male institutions — just substitute "Notre Dame" for "Yale" or "Princeton" in many references. Yale University first admitted women in the fall of 1969 with an initial ratio of eight men to one woman. Although subsequent incoming classes improved the overall acceptance of women, Assistant Dean of Students Robert Ackerman wrote that Yale's class of 1972 handbook still encouraged male students to:

> Treat Yale as you would a good woman. Take advantage of her many gifts, nourish yourself with the fruits of her wisdom, curse her if you will, and congratulate yourself for the possession of her. But treat her with respect. When you leave her, as you ultimately must, profit from the education she has given you.[3]

Such objectification identified females not as individuals but as members of a category known as "girls," and the 1970s sexual revolution did not eliminate all gender role expectations. A prevalent misconception in recently coed colleges was that every woman desired a "Mrs. degree" and not a diploma. Some men, perhaps fearing rejection, assumed the women were already taken. Many men opted to date women from nearby female colleges. When asked about future life partners, one male Yale student commented that men generally preferred dating women with whom they were not in constant contact:

> What happens when you go to an all-men's school is you forget how really good girls can be. You get entangled in a weekend-to-weekend existence, and you become a product of it. You lose sight of the single fact that girls are people, just like you and me. Instead they become things to play with on allotted days.[4]

Double standards—such as the stereotype of girls solely as sex partners, not peers, and trashing a girl's reputation for "sleeping around" while simultaneously praising guys who "conquered" women—persisted. According to J. Barry O'Neil, "wiser females educate the unsuspecting freshman girls that the men at Notre Dame have but one intention—sex."[5]

Other stereotypes also arose from interactions with women from nearby women's colleges. Father Robert "Griff" Griffin, appreciated by the ND community for his satirical-yet-compassionate insights, tried to debunk some female stereotypes:

A "Mrs. degree" is a sexist term suggesting that young women attend college to pursue spouses rather than their own academic and professional goals. In the early days of coeducation, for some women, college was a means to interact with men preparing for successful careers. Women seeking their "Mrs." seldom used their college degrees, if they even graduated at all. A term of courtesy for married women common in the twentieth century, "Mrs." began to fade during second wave feminism (though it did not disappear) toward the more neutral "Ms."[6]

> So now, when the autumn comes again, the women will be among us, not as painted dolls with sawdust for a heart who arrive for a weekend with a trunk full of toggery from Saks, Fifth Avenue; sophisticates of the tables down at Maury's or the Winter Carnival at Dartmouth, who find football childish and Mardi Gras jejune...not as Hometown Honeys, shy and breathless with love...not as the young lovelies from the ladies' colleges who arrive on Friday and leave on Sunday, sadder but wiser girls, swearing never to return again, at least not before next weekend...not as commuters who arrive each morning from across the Dixie to spend their day among us [the men of Notre Dame] like roses visiting a briar patch.[7]

To be fair, Notre Dame men did not escape stereotyping either. Articles in university publications such as *The Observer, Scholastic*, and *Notre Dame Magazine* described the then-male student as Catholic, white, overachieving, law-abiding, physically fit, and clannish. Most wanted to make a difference as professionals, community members, and family men. Even the 1974 American Council on Education issued a composite of the Notre Dame male as white, Catholic, and (compared to national averages) with above-average grades and fathers educated beyond high school.[8]

Robert "Griff" Griffin, a Baptist convert to Catholicism, graduated from Notre Dame in 1949 and was ordained a priest of the Congregation of Holy Cross in 1954. Beginning in 1974, he served as the first university chaplain until health problems forced his retirement. Griffin presided at a popular "Urchin Mass" and hosted a Saturday morning children's radio program on the student radio station, WSND-FM. Griffin's columns in *The Observer*, especially his "Letters to a Lonely God," touched on sensitive topics for college students.[9]

In anticipation of coeducation, Griff asked Saint Mary's and Notre Dame students — male and female — to discover the best parts of themselves as people and to ignore stereotypes. However, in his pleas for understanding between the sexes, Griff's description of Notre Dame's males unknowingly perpetuated the stereotypes:

> Come September, and the ladies will be among us: [The men will be] fighting their way through the food lines to episodes with dysentery; dribbling basketballs, possibly in the topless tradition of the courts behind the bookstore; sharing their weekends with the dudes in the Brooks 'Brothers' suits — from the schools of the Eastern Establishment.[10]

Hesburgh joined Griff in his entreaty for widespread understanding and acceptance. He urged faculty and students to use the time between the coeducation announcement and the arrival of ND women to reflect on the significance of this change:

> I'm simply saying that there are many dimensions to be explored, many aspects to be thoughtfully considered if the Notre Dame community takes seriously the change which is about to occur.... This means that all of us connected with this traditionally male University are going to have to take a long, hard, and perhaps critical look at our assumptions and presuppositions.... We'll never quite be the same again, but hopefully, better — vive la difference [sic].[11]

The Notre Dame and Saint Mary's counseling centers eventually recognized the need for honest dialogue between the sexes. They attempted to answer the age-old questions — "What is man?" and "What is woman?" — through sponsored male–female communication groups. Students attended sessions in the Bulla Shed, a nearby residence left to the university. The priests made it a welcoming spot for informal, outside gatherings by planting gardens and vineyards. Father Tom Stella, director of Bulla Shed, Chris Gallagher, and Kevin McCormich organized bimonthly luncheons as opportunities

Crossing the Line

The Observer, April 5, 1974

to exchange ideas across the ND–SMC community. At its first gathering of approximately sixty students, Hesburgh acknowledged the need for more social spaces and encouraged hall rectors to create them. In the pages of *The Observer,* Trish Moore, a junior government major, minced few words to this end:

> [T]he students can and must be the moving force. We will loudly proclaim the need for more informal gathering places to foster a social and cultural atmosphere which is non-existent on this campus....Innovations should begin within the individual halls as they are the core of student life on campus. Hall funds should be allocated and utilized towards the creation and funding of informal co-ed activities, rather than for the traditional purposes of purchasing pool tables and color T.V.'s [*sic*]. A second suggestion is for the creation of student art shows and concerts...to fill the great cultural void on this campus.[12]

Hall rector Kathy Cekanski suggested:

> [T]he best way of trying to contribute to making this place a better one is to strive for greater interaction — between roommates, residences and staff, guys and gals, students and faculty and administration. Only in this way can a 'community' grow and develop.[13]

Everyone dealt with the opposite sex differently — some more successfully than others. Although the campus offered various clubs, special interest groups, hall events, and even classes as places to meet and connect, students wanted more social activities and better facilities.

Yale attempted to normalize its social environment in two ways that Notre Dame did not. First, Yale established coed living by assigning women to its previously all-male residential halls (called "colleges"). Such day-to-day living arrangements with members of the opposite sex broke down some social shields. On the other hand, with only thirty women in each college, women sometimes found it challenging to find compatible roommates. Notre Dame did not (and most likely will not) integrate males and females into the same undergraduate residence halls due to its Catholic character. Yale also added a noncredit course on human sexuality in its first year of coeducation, 1969–1970, to improve the understanding between the sexes and dispel stereotypes.[14] ND eventually offered seminars and classes dealing with sex, family, marriage, and stereotypes, but it did not do so right away.

Cattle for the Cows

Dear Cattlemen:

Next year when you begin your annual "drive,' (otherwise known as "Here come the Busses!"),could you please either include some MEN in your herd, or bus us women out? Thank you for your inattention.

Sincerely,
Those at home on the range

The Observer, February 7, 1974

Like Yale men who dated women from nearby colleges, ND males continued to bring women to campus through the first three years of coeducation. The females, resenting the men's "flesh on the hoof" attitudes, referred to this practice as "catcalling," "cattle shows," and "meat markets." In reaction, one *Observer* letter entitled "To Greener Pastures" urged, "when you begin your annual 'drive' (otherwise known as "Here come the Busses!"), could you please either include some MEN in your herd, or bus us women out? Thank you for your inattention."[15]

Tit-for-tat responses flooded *The Observer.* J. Barry O'Neil expressed his displeasure:

> It is extremely disheartening to see that many students would rather intensify the competition between males and females rather than attempt to initiate a spirit of cooperation. Perhaps the recognizable similarity in the words co-education and co-operation is not quite accidental. The crux of the problem which exists here at Notre Dame was expressed by the fact that the authors of many of these letters had requested that their names be withheld....Rarely does one find another person who is willing to expose his-her thoughts and emotions without fear of becoming vulnerable to others....As long as individuals refuse to express their feelings to one another in a frank and open manner, the present social atmosphere will prevail...but if these masks cannot be successfully stripped away, no possible progress can be made toward alleviating the perverted social atmosphere which now exists.[16]

◇ *Diana Wilson Ostermann, ND 1976:* "After my sophomore year abroad, I returned to find a battle of the sexes going on. Nasty letters to the editor appeared in *The Observer*, including one describing a woman by using the chemical abbreviation WO. After seemingly much rejection, many males just stopped trying to date; campus was not a healthy environment. It required those students burned by their freshman year experiences to graduate for the male–female relations to normalize."

◇ *Christie Gallagher Sever, ND 1976:* "I recall *The Observer* running a series of letters to the editor documenting the gender war in my sophomore year. I suppose it demonstrates an inherent human distaste for change."[17]

Weekly parties in the male residence halls offered opportunities to dispel negative attitudes. These settings allowed groups of women to decide when to arrive and leave. Unfortunately, even this tactic fed additional stereotyping and resentment. Several anonymous women described these events:

(L–R) Phil Volpe, Father Ted, Mike Carini, John Tartaglione

◇ *Anonymous female, ND 1976:* "The guys' dorms had weekend parties. Oftentimes, freshman women stopped by a party, had a beer, and then left. As a girl, if you had a male friend whose section was throwing a party, he begged you to bring your friends. Unfortunately, once you got there, he expected you to stay — no matter how few women were there or if you felt uncomfortable."

◇ *Anonymous female, ND 1976:* "Parties tended to be superficial. Many males were not used to females in the classroom, much less a social environment. It was easy for the women to take advantage, sometimes dumping a date or girlfriends for a better opportunity. Lots of games — most without any rules!"

Male students also recognized the awkwardness of these interactions.

◇ *Ray Pikna, ND 1976:* "As an introvert, I was uncomfortable at parties. Alcohol was ever-present, the music was loud, and conversations were difficult. The few women who showed up traveled in groups and were invariably outnumbered by the men. Not until years later did I realize some women felt as I did about the social craziness."

◇ *Jack Bergen, ND 1977:* "I attended more dances sponsored by female dorms than my dorm mates. As few students actually dated, it was an opportunity to invite the opposite sex who were 'just friends' as your date. I was not especially great looking and definitely not a good dancer. Maybe word got around that I wouldn't 'try anything' after the dance. As I look back, either the girls knew something I didn't or maybe that should have been a clue as to what the future would bring."

Within this challenging, extremely limited social environment, odd traditions should have surprised no one. While food fights were a pre-coeducation tradition, the individual rating system in the dining halls was a new behavior primarily directed at the women. And, even with women on campus, another sexist tradition continued as ND males still traveled to Saint Mary's for panty raids after football victories or due to spring fever.

◇ *Mary Sheeran, SMC 1976:* "Another memorable moment…was waking up in the middle of the night to hear hundreds of men yelling 'We want panties!' I thought, is this the 1950s? I was appalled—women urging them on, no one stopping them, as they broke into the dorm, breaking fire locks and destroying private property.… [I]t did not serve either Notre Dame for shrugging its shoulders or Saint Mary's for not fighting back or calling out the behaviors of those inside the dorm. It was another time.…I am glad that the college (and ND) has changed for the better."[18]

◇ *Ray Pikna, ND 1976:* "Were they [panty raids] immature? Yes. Was it funny? Sometimes. Most men would yell to the women and ask for a 'trophy;' they did not break in or steal clothing. Some women wrote their phone numbers in their panties; others would throw old bloomers into the crowd—XX-large. The women who tossed the panties seemed to be having as much fun as the guys."

The university officially banned panty raids in the fall of 1974. Yet the ban had its challengers throughout the first five years of coeducation.

◇ *Anonymous male, ND 1976:* "Our junior year, the university prohibited panty raids, and violators faced disciplinary action. Viewing the ban as an unconstitutional violation of our right to free association, a group of us planned a raid in search of souvenirs from the lasses at Saint Mary's. As we walked toward SMC, a security car rounded the corner and caught us in its headlights. We dove to the ground, but too late—busted!

"Fortunately, inspiration struck. I told one guy, who was asthmatic, to toss his inhaler away from where he was standing. I told the group to appear to be looking for something. I then walked over to the officer. I explained that our friend had lost his inhaler earlier in the day, and we were helping him to find it. After 'finding' the inhaler, my friend exclaimed, 'I've got it!' The officer was skeptical, but the story was plausible. We managed to hold our laughter until we had crossed back to ND's side of the road."

Before panty raids disappeared, a new fad emerged—streaking. Supposedly one night, Farley Hall rector Sister Jean met a group of naked men at the doors yelling, "You're not coming in here like that!"—causing the men to target another hall.[19] On March 27, 1974, two male streakers even bared their buns in Emil T. Hofman's chemistry class.[20]

Eventually, the women turned the tables on the men. On September 20, 1973, in a highly publicized "Battle of the Sexes" tennis match, top women's player Billie Jean King, age twenty-nine, beat Bobby Riggs, age fifty-five, a former number one-ranked men's player. Riggs (1918–1995), a self-proclaimed chauvinist, said that women were inferior and could not handle the pressure of the game. He boasted that, even at his age, he could beat any female player. King decided to take him on and redeemed the name of women's tennis, muffling Riggs' nonstop mouth with a decisive 6–4, 6–3, 6–3 victory.[24] King's win resonated strongly with ND's female trailblazers who spontaneously stormed the quads in celebration. Flipping the panty raid tradition on its head, men heard female voices shouting, "Jock raid!" throughout the night.[25]

> The first documented "panty raid" by male students occurred in February 1949 at Augustana College in Rock Island, Illinois. Men entered the Woman's Building to wreak havoc and steal undergarments (and some of the women appreciated the fun, despite a newspaper article deeming them "hysterical").[21]
>
> Panty raids, whether seen as humorous or offensive, sometimes were considered "tradition," as with Notre Dame's "annual panty raid on St. Mary's."[22]
>
> While such raids gained popularity, both when colleges admitted women for the first time and as protests against curfews and other restrictions, the ritual began to fade with the emergence of coed dormitories and more relaxed sexual mores. Police cracked down, and women pushed back.[23]

◇ *Ann Pytynia, ND 1976:* "When Billie Jean King won, it prompted a round of males streaking around Badin Hall. A friend and I

"Streaking," people running naked in public, was a 1970s fad, especially on college campuses. Notre Dame even had a "Streakers Olympics" in the spring of 1972. According to the March 6, 1974, issue of *The Observer*, such frolicking took a political turn with a massive "impeachment" streak to "force President Nixon out from behind the towel."[26]

The fad "busted out all over," as women joined the naked antics and administrators spoke out against the "craze."[27] Previously termed "indecent exposure," streaking showed up in many aspects of life: stand-up comedian Bob Hope included it in his shtick; the National Safety Council issued an advisory on how to streak;[28] and *Time*'s March 18, 1974, issue explored the fad.[29] Americans saw streakers bicycling, roller-skating, horseback riding, and pogo-sticking—even skydiving. Ray Stevens' song, "The Streak," hit number one that year.[30]

were looking out the windows when a male Domer raced by *au naturel*. I remember her saying, 'Did we see anything?'"

◇ *Shelley Muller Simon, ND 1976:* "After the victory, the women took to the quads in celebration. We ran through the men's dorms yelling, 'Who's the King? Billie Jean! Who's the King? Billie Jean!'"

◇ *Anonymous male, ND 1976:* "One guy got a call from his sister at Saint Mary's to warn him that a jock raid was coming. We banded together with other male dorms and waited for the women on the road between the lakes. We formed a human chain and forced them to retreat or end up in the water. For those who fell into the lake, we generously offered to take them back to the dorm to dry off. Did the strategy work? Yes, to stop the invading force; to meet the women, not so much."

◇◇◇

REARVIEW REFLECTION The night of this epic tennis match, music blared across campus. Men played The Rolling Stones' "Under My Thumb"[31] while women blasted Helen Reddy's (1941–2020) "I Am Woman,"[32] the women's movement national anthem. After winning the best female pop vocal performance Grammy for the song, Reddy thanked "God, because *she* makes everything possible" in her acceptance speech.[33]

Yet the celebration of King's victory and the banning of panty raids were only symbolic victories of women making progress in worlds dominated by men. The media continued to feed stereotypes and seldom debunked prevailing attitudes: Women did not belong in the same venues as men, and males were superior and dominant. Even 1970s movies underlined the need for attitude readjustments.

⋄ *Darlene Palma Connelly, ND 1977:* "Early in the fall of 1974, the Student Union sponsored a showing of the 1970 movie *Little Big Man* starring Dustin Hoffman. I vividly recall feeling like 'an object' (a term unknown to me then) when the predominately male audience wildly clapped and *roared* with derision at a punch line dealing with sex and white women. Herd mentality took on a new meaning."

To maintain a positive attitude, sometimes our fight against the constant objectification of women needed a lighter touch. After an upsetting encounter when a tightly knit group of upperclassmen ogled me in the North Dining Hall, I decided to gauge their awareness of their comments and actions. I knew that they had scheduled an annual get-together to celebrate spring in the raunchiest of ways. Helped by Dale Planicka, I posted the following ad in *The Observer,* February 1, 1974): "To the boys whose minds are in the gutter: Grovel in Dirt Week!" Overhearing them asking each other what 'grovel' meant, I submitted an additional ad *The Observer*: "DIRT WEEK: To grovel-v., to wallow. DIRT WEEK: it is bustin' out all over."[34]

They never knew I posted these ads. For several days, I overheard them as they laughed and complimented each other on their notoriety. The subtlety of my jab was unfortunately lost on them!

Slippery When Wet

Country singer, songwriter, and actor Tim McGraw has been frequently quoted as saying, "We all take different paths in life, but no matter where we go, we take a little of each other everywhere."[1] In less-than-optimal conditions, roads often prove slippery to navigate. The same holds true for relationships. As Notre Dame's all-male campus transitioned to a coed environment, a universal desire to connect continued across the student body. Unfortunately, for some the lopsided male–female ratio, youth, and lack of sexual experience often got in the way, leaving many lonely hearts.

◇◇◇

The campus makeup was significantly more homogeneous in the early 1970s than it is today. Primarily white male students,surrounded by those similar in economic class, academic achievement, and religion seemed to increase the likelihood for friendships and effortless communication. The introduction of undergraduate women threatened the existing social mores and culture.

> ◇ *Shelley Muller Simon, ND 1976:* "For many of us, Notre Dame relationships came to define our college experience more than any other aspect. It was a new chapter in our lives and, for many, the beginning of a new legacy. Some of us made the best of it, while others struggled to define themselves individually. Society and the Notre Dame community seemed determined to define and analyze us [the women] as a group."

> ◇ *Jack Bergen, ND 1977:* "Campus was a microcosm of society. The conservative values learned from our Depression-era parents were strongly embedded into our psyche. Most of us went to Mass and were faithful Catholics. Priests and nuns watched over us like hawks to ensure we followed parietals. Opposite-sex relationships were difficult given the male–female ratio, but even

more difficult because of a dearth of social activities. Dating usually consisted of movie night in the engineering auditorium or a racquetball match at the Rock."

However, despite such initial tensions, university administrators such as Burtchaell expressed high hopes for good relationships between men and women: Coeducation will "provide day to day companionship for men and women students. Friendships will be more frequent, more realistic, and more humanized."[2] And Sister Jean recalled:

> I remember the first time I heard a senior from Grace Hall stand up in the midst of a large gathering of students and say that one of the best things that happened to him at Notre Dame was that he developed good friendships with women—and everyone applauded loudly.[3]

Even Hesburgh lived to see progress in this arena and happily reflected on the radical difference from those early days: "If a girl walked between Cavanaugh and Zahm in the early years, it was like feeding time at the Bronx Zoo in the monkey cage. Now, there's a totally different attitude, no more whistling and calling."[4]

Typical of colleges everywhere, relationships on campus ran the gamut from getting to know someone to marriage. Notre Dame students experienced being single, one-night stands, dating, and various levels of commitments. Some guys had long-term or long-distance relationships with "hometown-honeys" (HTHs) or with women at other schools. This was not generally true for the women, although a few did have HTHs or boyfriends in the military, even in the waning years of the Vietnam War.

> ◇ *Anonymous female, ND 1976:* "I came to ND with little dating experience and just assumed the point of dating was to find someone with whom to spend the rest of your life. For most of freshman year, I dated a senior whose best friend was involved in a long-distance relationship with a woman at another college. As their graduation approached, I asked him about his intentions regarding his girlfriend. He was rather pragmatic about it, telling me that a long-distance relationship allowed him to focus on his studies during the week and to get laid on the weekends. After graduation, he planned to start his career and leave that relationship behind. I thought that was terrible!
>
> "However, by the time I was a junior, I found myself in somewhat similar circumstances. I was dating someone whose company I enjoyed, and yes, sex was involved. It was a comfortable

relationship, but I had no plans to spend the rest of my life with him. When he proposed, I turned him down."

Most students wanted friends as much as they wanted dates. Still, the sudden thrust into the freedom of the collegiate environment amid a definite gender imbalance created unique approaches to meeting the opposite sex.

◇ *Anonymous male, ND 1976:* "One of the funniest tactics used to meet women became the talk of the women's dorms. One enterprising classmate, who carried his books in a strap, swung them into the books cradled in the arms of a comely coed. This fellow was bright, talented, and on the pudgy side, with less fashion sense than me. Seemingly ignoring her shocked look as her books went flying, he scurried over to pick them up. He put her books under his left arm, then extended his right hand and said, 'Hi! I'm _____.' Although his unorthodox approach reflected poorly on men everywhere, he deserved an A for effort. While most of us were figuring out how to meet women, he plowed ahead with all the finesse of a bull in a china shop."

Misunderstandings and competition between and among the sexes were inevitable. When upperclassmen arrived as freshmen, there were no ND women to date. These men later often encouraged in-coming males to get as many women's phone numbers as possible to improve their dating odds. Stories of women having multiple dates in one evening were pervasive. Since every no could damage a male ego and potentially harm a female's reputation, women often accepted a multitude of engagements. Given this and the limited number of women, many men believed every woman had dates on Friday and Saturday nights. Yet, on many weekends, plenty of women sat in their dorms, studying or gathering with female friends.

◇ *Anonymous female, ND 1976:* "When we first arrived [at Notre Dame], men actively competed for dates with the limited number of females. I remember having three dates in one evening — early, lat-er, and even later — just because I received so many invitations and did not want to disappoint anyone."

◇ *Ann Pytynia, ND 1976:* "Women routinely spent weekends in the dorms just hanging out with friends. Most men on campus did not ask women out because they assumed that they were already in a relationship. We were OK with this. We were busy and constantly studying."

Women did try to debunk the "every woman is dating someone" misconception. One Walsh Hall resident and female member of the class of '76 created a dating service to show disillusioned male friends that dating opportunities exist-ed. She walked male friends through Walsh on weekend nights so the men could see for themselves that not all women had dates. Any follow-up was left to the individuals.

Yet, even as upperclassmen graduated, memories of those early days lingered.

◇ *Ray Pikna, ND 1976:* "Most women in those first few years end-ed up dating upperclassmen. So, when we became upperclass-men, we had little interest in asking classmates out who rejected us as underclassmen—why get kicked in the teeth twice? We opted instead to ask out the younger women. There were not only more of them, but we also had no prior bad experiences to discourage us from asking them out."

◇ *Anonymous female, ND 1977:* "While at Notre Dame, I learned about drinking, music, and sports. From living and learning to-gether, I came to understand numerous types of 'adult' relation-ships. For women, ND was a 'target rich environment.' I dated a lot during college. These opportunities arose from more than just the ratio of men to women. I had a wide circle of contacts in a variety of majors. I interacted with others, including women from Saint Mary's, and through student government. I met many guys in casual group settings. Although I do not recall exclusive-ly dating anyone, I dated several interesting people.

"Our backgrounds played into these collegiate relationships. For me, perhaps my Midwest origin helped as we were always a friendly lot. Maybe it was my Catholic upbringing to treat every-one with dignity and respect. I was taught to look people in the eye and see them as individuals as we are all children of God.

"For many of us, people came, and people went. Some left without notice; others seared your brain or heart with their ab-sence. They left snippets of themselves as they moved through our lives. 'You will think of me on your wedding day.' Thanks, Joe, for breaking my heart freshman year. I have thought of you but not on my wedding day. 'If you are still a virgin, I am not going to be the guy who takes that from you.' Thank you, John. 'You can't always get what you want/But…sometimes…/You get what you need.' True that, Terry, quoting Mick Jagger."[5]

Despite many accounts of warm, positive, and supportive friendships between men and women, the kind of relationship that received the most attention was the dating relationship. *The Observer* dedicated many pages and editorials to male–female relationships (or lack thereof) and gender frustrations. In a letter to the editor, class of 1976 members Tom Young, Paul Shay, Rick Supik, Augie Grace, Jim Augustine, Mike Disbro, and Brian Sontchi accurately described the Notre Dame dating environment. They encouraged guys to act like men and women to give the men a fair chance — at least one date, emphasizing such behaviors would help to reduce campus tensions.[6]

◇ *Tom Young, ND 1976:* "My ND education began in 1971 in the last all-male undergraduate applicant pool, the Notre Dame class of 1975. While campus changed slightly in 1972, the visibility of the pioneer women, while making a mark, was limited. I took a leave of absence after sophomore year in which I had shared classes with some female transfers. By my return in the fall of 1974, Notre Dame had changed noticeably having admitted two additional coed classes.

"I experienced coeducation before and after the women arrived. While there were still growing pains and acceptance issues on both sides of the new dynamic, things seemed to be improving. However, some male students, not to mention faculty, still seemed resistant to the presence of women. Interestingly, my sister began her education at Dartmouth in 1972 under the same conditions as the female ND class of 1976. The assimilation process (or lack thereof) was similar at both institutions. After discussions with my sister, I wanted to address it with the general Notre Dame student body.

"A group of friends, affectionately known as 'F-Troop,' submitted a signed letter to *The Observer* that delineated some of the differences and feelings. After its publication, we learned that people see or read what they want to see or read. The women commented they were grateful that we called out the males on their boorish behavior — not exactly what we wrote. The men thought we had recommended that the women should treat them better because they were here first — also not exactly what we wrote. We asked the guys to stop ogling women and to talk to them. We recommended actions related to role reversal. We asked the women to put themselves out there and ask a guy to lunch. We did notice a slightly lighter atmosphere for a few weeks."

Despite such advice, some ND males still found it difficult to view women as capable, strong individuals.

◇ *Diana Wilson Ostermann, ND 1976:* "One year, I dated the president of the then-male Howard Hall whose responsibilities included placing the customarily twelve-foot Christmas tree on the roof of the hall's main entrance. When the Howard volunteers failed to show up to get the tree, he and I went alone. We drove to the woods north of campus and hiked until we found a stand of evergreens. We cut down a lovely tree more than twelve feet tall. We worked well in tandem as we dragged it to the car, tying it to the car roof. Arriving back at Howard, some residents helped place the tree on the roof [of the hall]. When asked who went with him to get it, my boyfriend said my name; they asked who else helped. They were surprised the two of us managed a tree that size, and I saw new respect reflected in their eyes."

Over time, such perceptions dissipated, and the tensions eased. As the day-to-day interactions between the sexes normalized, more genuine friendships resulted.

◇ *Cathy Donahue, ND 1976:* "Most of my friends at ND were men, and I think that affected my life since — most of my friends today are still men."

◇ *Betsy Kall Brosnan, ND 1976:* "While at ND, I discovered that males and females can share the same type of relationships that exist among males or females — that of true friendship. Many people go through life not knowing that a deep friendship can exist between a man and a woman."

◇ *Jerry Lutkus, ND 1974:* "Many students coming after us will leave behind a solid base of true, realistic, and human relationships between men and women. It is this kind of base that the students coming after us will build upon. It is these kinds of relationships, minus the base animal manifestations of many people here today, that are essential for coeducation to work at ND."

◇ *Stephen Klug, ND 1976:* "I met Debi our freshman year, and we became friends. We never dated but shared many business classes, occasional beers, and a few parties. Senior year, she offered to cook dinner for my six roommates and me in our off-campus housing. She insisted on doing all the shopping and prepared a spaghetti dinner.

"Graduation came, and we went our separate ways. The luck of the Irish brought us together at the April 2005 Alumni Leadership Conference, me representing the South Jersey Alumni Club and Debi as incoming class president. We connected with other '76 alumni, and we talked about old times. At one point, Debi asked if I remembered the dinner that she made for me. I smiled as I remembered the smell of the homemade sauce and what a fun evening it was. She started talking about the shopping and prep work for the dinner: the size of the turkey, how many potatoes, and what kind of stuffing. As she mesmerized the 2005 group by her Betty Crocker-like recollections, she urged me to share how good that Thanksgiving was.

"Hmm…all four years, I went home for Thanksgiving, so I was not sure what to say. My roommates and I never ate her turkey dinner, but the way she told the story you wished you were there. Not wanting to embarrass her nor wanting to lie, I simply stated I had one of the best Thanksgiving dinners ever that year. Later, when we were alone at the bar, I mentioned I loved the story and just wished I had been there. I reminded her that 'ours' was a spaghetti dinner. She thought about it, smiled, and then laughed. She has yet to reveal who ate that turkey dinner!"

◇ *Maggie Waltman Smith, ND 1976:* "I got to be friends with a male transfer student, Tom Cassidy, who lived across the hall from me and my two female transfer apartment mates in the fall of 1974. I had just returned from a semester on the Rome program, and he was just back from a study abroad program in Paris. I had to explain to my mom during Junior Parents Weekend why he had jumped off South Bend's Twyckenham Bridge (probably on some drunken dare), and she undoubtedly wondered about my judgment in friends. But when I got married in 1977, I had no doubt who was going to give me away…since my dad had died during senior year. We remained close friends until [Tom] died unexpectedly in February 2022. I will remember him—and his love for Notre Dame—forever."

Nancy Brenner and Joe Sinnott, May 17, 1976

Under the Dome, while some found lifelong friends of the opposite sex, others heard wedding bells. The October 19, 1972, *Observer* reported the first noteworthy marriage after coeducation—between one of the original eight women added to the famed "Band of the Fighting Irish" and the band president."[7] From 1950 until 1972, marriages between Saint Mary's women and Notre Dame men steadily increased, with one in four SMC graduates exchanging vows with ND men. By the end of the 1970s, the number of SMC–ND marriages

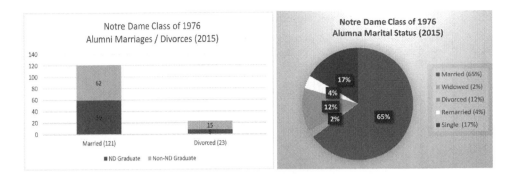

Notre Dame Class of 1976
Alumni Marriages / Divorces (2015)

Married (121) — Divorced (23)

■ ND Graduate   ■ Non-ND Graduate

Notre Dame Class of 1976
Alumna Marital Status (2015)

■ Married (65%)
■ Widowed (2%)
■ Divorced (12%)
■ Remarried (4%)
■ Single (17%)

dropped to one in ten, then leveled off in the 1980s, and precipitously declined in the 1990s.[8]

The 2000–2001 survey for this social history and the 2015 Alumni Directory indicated that fifty-nine, or 31 percent of the class of 1976's 186 women, married classmates or members of other ND classes.

Respondents shared insights into their marriages, whether to ND graduates or others, and their partner-ships and living styles.

◇ *Shelley Muller Simon, ND 1976:* "The first Saturday night at Notre Dame, the old Walsh Hall residents hosted a party for the new Walsh Hall residents. Although a few of us went to the party, we left early due to overcrowding. A few days later, a senior girl who lived down the hall told me that I had a phone call in her room. I thought this was odd, but I vaguely remembered the [caller] from the party. He asked me to go to the concert that Friday night. I said yes, even though I thought he wanted to go out with the good-looking girl with whom I went to the party.

"On September 15, 1972, the same senior informed me that my date was in her room waiting for me. Walking down the hallway, I hoped I recognized him and that he would not be surprised I was the one he invited. As I entered her room, she told me to look behind the door, where my date sat in a crouching position. From his expression, I knew he was tipsy, so we were not off to a great start.

Roughly 12 percent of the ND marriages ended in divorce, compared to an estimated 28 percent of US Catholic adults (as reported by the Center for Applied Research in the Apostolate at Georgetown University).[9]

"We walked to the Seals and Crofts concert at Stepan Center with a few other couples. Even though it was not 'love at first sight,' it was a memorable first date. We both dated others throughout our time at Notre Dame, but we eventually married.

193

We had two children, including a daughter who became a second-generation alumna."

◇ *Sharon Zelinski Haverstock, ND 1976:* "I enjoyed a serious committed relationship through all four years. I married him right after school, and we divorced eleven years later. I somewhat regret not experiencing other male relationships, which would have given me a greater understanding of myself and my partner. I also missed out on even greater female friendships by not being available to develop them."

◇ *Ann Pytynia, ND 1976:* "My husband and I share things equally. There are work tasks we both enjoy [or] don't enjoy, and it ends up working out equally. We do things independently of each other on occasion, and that just strengthens our bond and gives us more to share with each other."

◇ *Anonymous female, ND 1976:* "In 2000, I married my Notre Dame boyfriend. After no contact for twenty-five years, I found him again."

◇◇◇

REARVIEW REFLECTION I never expected to find my soul or life mate at ND; the ideal union remained elusive for my four years at Notre Dame. Amid the turmoil around me, I tried not only to understand my male peers but also to answer the question, "Who am I anyway?"

I had little experience with dating before I arrived at Notre Dame, not atypical for some of my fellow undergraduate colleagues who had attended same-sex high schools. Those first few days on campus, several Sorin Hall upperclassmen encouraged the freshman women to accept any invitation and to get to know a guy before dismissing him. Naïvely, I honestly believed that accepting every invitation was better than rejecting one. Since I had little to no experience in refusing a date, I often had several dates in one night. I do not remember ever canceling a date for a "better" one, but I do remember worrying about making it back to the dorm on time for the next engagement. Worse yet, if I was having fun, I hated cutting the date short. In trying not to make anyone unhappy, I made few—including myself—happy.

I actually found it easier to develop friendships with men from Sorin, Alumni, Keenan/Stanford, Cavanaugh, Fisher, Grace, and Flanner halls and the towers. These friends taught me to play bridge, poker, and euchre and suffered through my favorites of Scrabble, Boggle, and little-known Score Four. Open dialogue and humor usually prevented any confusion as to whether these were friend sessions or dates.

> ◇ *Darlene Palma Connelly, ND 1977*: "Our class president demonstrated how politically savvy he was when he added two women to his winning election ticket. As a class officer, I often worked with him in my room. However, what do you do when, as a male friend, he gets that look in his eye and the ever-helpful parietals are hours away? You try to break the spell without damaging the relationship.
>
> "Food was always a great distraction. The Huddle was out of the question, as we had class business to finish. As I looked in my mini-fridge, I spotted a pomegranate. After cutting it in half, I pulled it apart, seed by seed. The spell was broken, and our friendship remained intact. We do not ever recall talking about that night in all the years we have remained friends. All I know is a golden pomegranate Christmas ornament arrived years later without a note. Just his return address!"

Many wonderful male friends encouraged me to stay when I wanted to leave Notre Dame; I still have every letter of encouragement that they sent. They offered advice on dealing with the few males with perverted or stunted views of women, a valuable skill in the male-dominated tech world. They supported me as I ineptly handled ever-changing relationships.

I had my share of missteps. My unintentional flirting contributed to a few misunderstandings. I cringe even fifty years later whenever I recall how I winked for emphasis, ran my finger around the top of a beer bottle, or touched a hand or leg to make a point — no wonder some men were confused.

Confusion abounded each and every semester. My first semester, I invited a male classmate to my room to study. When the quad proved too busy to concentrate, we moved to Walsh's chapel. I rebuffed him after he tried to kiss me. He took revenge by telling others that I liked making out in chapels. It was my first exposure to true cruelty and put me on guard early on.

In the fall of my sophomore year, a friend majoring in psychology stopped by my room unannounced. He expressed concern that I had yet to experience sex to its fullest. After suggesting I was "frigid," he offered counseling and his hands-on services to solve the "problem" of my virginity. I tried gently to tell him I was not frigid but just did not find him attractive in that way. We somehow remained friends for many years after graduation.

Resolving the virginity question was not just an issue for women. One male friend suggested I help him lose his virginity. This soon-to-graduate senior hand-delivered a letter with a bottle of Mateus. His letter described his admiration for me and how, unless I helped him, he would graduate a virgin. A friend since my freshman year, he hoped the longevity of our relationship would justify remedying his (and my) situation. That relationship did not survive the resulting conversation; a Mateus bottle always reminds me of him.

The Mateus brand of wine began worldwide production at the end of World War II. This rosé appealed to the developing North American wine market and was a part of social life on campus.[10] A line in the lyrics of the 1973 Elton John song "Social Disease" even mentions the wine,[11] and the cover of Graham Nash's 1973 album *Wild Tales* also depicts a Mateus bottle. In 1978's *Animal House*, a bottle of the wine serves as a candleholder in the home of Professor Dave Jennings (played by Donald Sutherland).

During spring break, my mom, B-P friend and dorm mate Janet, and I drank coffee, ate coconut cream pie, and talked well past two in the morning discussing Notre Dame and relationships. Janet surmised that my academic difficulties were, most likely, due to the number of men I had dated that semester. My diary did not support the number she spouted. She described my typical night as an early dinner date, followed by studying or some event with another date, and ending with a third, late-night walk around the lake. Suddenly, we heard a familiar creaking of knees. My father, whom I assumed was asleep in the other room, walked into the kitchen. I had so much to explain, I never finished my pie!

As a junior, I spent time with a classmate who transferred into our class. We never connected on any level, so I tried to set him up with my roommate. Instead of grasping this opportunity, he stormed off. To this day, he fails to acknowledge me whenever our paths cross at reunions or on campus.

Senior year, I primarily spent time with friends—afraid to "cross the line" with graduation looming and an uncertain future. However, the heart wants what the heart wants. I eventually realized that intimacy deepened, not endangered, a relationship. The totality of my experiences provided insights into myself and the publicized, often discussed obsession with sex common to those early days. Although many dates stand out in my memory as I reflect on all four years, only one individual affected each and every relationship in my life, starting in the fall of my sophomore year.

After a summer of tanning and waterskiing when not working in my dad's law office, I returned sophomore year ready to tackle both academics and relationships. As I waited in line to register for classes, an attractive, suntanned senior in a pressed white shirt stood in front of me. I thought that if I turned my registration card just so, he could read my name and dorm room—that is, if my own tan, my white hip-huggers and crop top, and my pageboy hair (grown out from my haircut fiasco) caught his interest.

Two weeks passed with no contact. Then on Saturday, September 13, 1973, the day of the away football game against Purdue, I saw him again. With no interest in the game, I headed out to hand-wash my car. Helped by a freshman dorm mate, we set about our task on a day hot enough for a Florida chick yet cool enough for carrying buckets of water to the parking lot. Suddenly, an old car pulled up, and two athletic males jumped out. I recognized one as "Registration Guy," but it was his friend with the bluest eyes, "True Blue," who caused butterflies.

Unlike his buddy, who made me think of candlelight and piano solos, my attraction to True Blue was pure magnetism — until he asked what we were doing.

Duh, I thought, wasn't it obvious?

"You're doing it all wrong," he said.

Reacting to the chauvinistic comment, I retorted, "If you know a better way, grab a sponge," but no help was forthcoming.

Before they walked away, Registration Guy asked for my number. After completing our task, my friend and I returned to my room just as the phone rang. Answering, I heard this vacuum cleaner-like laugh before Registration Guy invited us to meet them in the North Dining Hall and then go out to celebrate the team's victory. Although I wasn't sure who was pairing with whom, eventually Registration Guy took my hand as we walked over to the hangout known as Senior Bar. Later that evening, as I sat on his lap, he leaned back, and his hair slid into an electrical outlet. As sparks flew, another vacuum-cleaner laugh rang out as True Blue said that he, too, wanted sparks to fly.

Shortly after that, Registration Guy and I went to his room. He lived in a single, so no necktie on the doorknob was necessary. After a little French kissing, he suggested we do more. When I explained my position on the subject, we continued to snuggle on his bed. He eventually pushed my head down his chest toward his stomach. I had no idea what he wanted but knew things were heading in the wrong direction. I said I wanted to leave and was told, "Go ahead!" I walked back to my dorm alone.

Collegiate life has its own language, both verbal and nonverbal. Decades ago, a necktie or a sock placed on a dorm room doorknob meant "Do not enter." Today, text messages, dead bolts, code words on dry-erase boards, and Mardi Gras beads provide such warnings.

The next weekend, True Blue called and asked me out. After checking with my friend and considering her cautionary comments, I accepted. I soon spent nights in his Flanner Hall room staring at the Dome through the window, as Merrilee Rush's song "Angel of the Morning" played in my head. Our relationship ranged from dating to hating and from fighting to making up until he graduated in May 1974. We dated sporadically until I graduated in 1976 and moved to Chicago to see if our connection had a future. It did not. In October 1978, he married someone

Sharing my wedding day with forever roomie, Beverly (1978)

else. One month after his wedding, afraid that I was soon to become a "spinster," I married someone from work.

Upon reflection, I realize my feelings for True Blue prevented me from opening up to other outstanding men. Still, I count him as that fifth true, lifelong friend that I can count on one hand. Of all my ND friends, True Blue helped me when Hurricane Wilma destroyed my Florida home in 2005. Since 2008, he has checked on my Notre Dame home during the winter. More importantly, regardless of weather or work commitments, he traveled to Dubuque, Iowa, for the funerals of my mother (2010), my father (2012), and my brother Doug (2015). He is — and will always be — True Blue!

Divided Highway

In the chapter titled "Economy" in his well-known philosophical work *Walden*, Henry David Thoreau makes the point that "[i]t is never too late to give up our prejudices."[1] Over time, the increasing number of women on the Notre Dame campus slightly eased some of the day-to-day tensions between men and women. However, it did little to lessen the friction between the women of Notre Dame and Saint Mary's. A cultural chasm emerged—a divided highway of sorts. Even though many ND transfers from SMC remained connected with their friends there, some friction was palpable—especially when stereotypes came into play.

◇◇◇

Despite the belief that the tension between Notre Dame and Saint Mary's resulted from the failed merger, the strain actually dates back to a nineteenth-century request by Saint Mary's to allow its women to play golf on the ND golf course. Father Charles Leo O'Donnell, Notre Dame's twelfth president, denied the request:

> The reason for this decision seems to be, in a general way, the same reason which Rome so often gives—*Non Expedit* [it is not beneficial]. The real reason, which I do not mind giving you unofficially and confidentially, is that you have never allowed our boys to go boating on your lake.[2]

US institutions with exclusively, or almost exclusively, student populations of women peaked at 281 in the 1960s and dropped to roughly thirty-five in 2021. By 1970, many of the 137 four-year Catholic women's colleges in the United States suffered from reputations for weak academic programs. While some reinforced conservative attitudes on the "woman's place," others emphasized vocational training in traditional, low-paying occupations such as nursing, library science, and domestic sciences like home economics.[3]

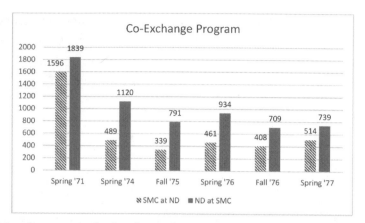

Co-Exchange Program

Saint Mary's proactively fought such perceptions through its strong alumnae base and programs with Notre Dame. The Co-Exchange Program and nonacademic activities connected the ND–SMC student bodies, but the arrival of ND's female undergraduates initially lessened such opportunities.

The schools jointly announced the failed merger in November 1971, and Notre Dame quickly revealed its plans to admit women on December 1. Merger discussions unofficially resurfaced on February 7, 1972, only to collapse twenty-two days later. In response, the SMC administration dealt with student strikes, protest meetings, window banners, threats not to pay tuition, transfer requests, and the resignation of one trustee. According to Maria Gallagher, there was a change, "a new, growing spirit of awareness," after some SMC women lamented the previous year, "What are we going to do without Notre Dame?" Yet by the fall of 1972, they declared, "Look at all we can do without Notre Dame!"[4] That fall, even the SMC freshmen did not cross the road for traditional icebreakers on the ND campus.

> ◇ *Mary Meruisse Richardson, SMC 1975:* "Mostly I remember the anger, disappointment and frustration when the merger didn't go through....I remember the song, 'There's a Riot Going On' wafting out from dorm windows. I felt betrayed because I had accepted to come [to Saint Mary's] expecting the merger to go through and then it didn't. When the merger fell apart, many of my friends transferred to ND. It split up our class and that was hard."[5]

Hesburgh reassured SMC women of their continued involvement with ND:

> Geography, history, programs, activities, [and] human relationships have always made Saint Mary's women part of Notre Dame life. That's not going to be changed by the fact of women undergraduates at the University. I would hope that foolish myths

creating rivalries never get started, and that friendships among women living on both sides of the highway will flourish.[6]

Interestingly, as Notre Dame planned for its own women, it failed to take advantage of its historic relationship with Saint Mary's. Instead, it hired John Miriam Jones, SC, a member of the Sisters of Charity, in lieu of involving Saint Mary's Sisters of the Holy Cross. The university failed to expand the Co-Exchange Program to bring more women to campus, even as nonresidents. After women enrolled at Notre Dame, the Co-Exchange Program initially excluded the ND females. In fact, the number of women visible on ND's campus and the number of men at Saint Mary's decreased in the first five years of co-education, reducing opportunities to interact through shared classes.

The 211 women who transferred from Saint Mary's in 1972 made up the majority of ND transfers that year. For these women, maintaining friendships with their friends at SMC proved difficult due to the physical separation and a lack of social opportunities between the two schools. Some subtle jealousy initially caused rifts between these two groups, as not all women who applied to ND were accepted. On ND's campus, the transfers stayed connected with fellow transferees, often limiting the time available to spend with the first-year females.

> Today, only two academic areas — religious studies at Saint Mary's and theology at Notre Dame — are formally deemed cooperative departments. Nevertheless, all faculty have full library privileges at both schools, and some collaborate on research projects. Unlike credits from other schools, Notre Dame and Saint Mary's accept each other's credits and are included in grade point averages.

◇ Mary E. "Libby" Ford, ND 1975: "After twelve years of Catholic school, the last four spent at an all-girls high school, I was as unprepared for the chaos of Notre Dame's first several years as a coed university as Notre Dame itself. Growing up an introverted Catholic girl, I was scared to leave home [to be] a newly minted Saint Mary's freshman. Despite this fear, I entered Saint Mary's, 'just across the highway' from my father's Notre Dame, in the fall of 1971.

"At that time, Notre Dame and Saint Mary's had plans to merge, so my first-year classes as a Saint Mary's biology major were at Notre Dame. As a science major, I typically was the only girl/woman in my regular-size classes and one of a handful in the auditorium-size classes such as 'Emil T's' general chemistry. Every morning, I commuted by bus across the highway to attend class. Usually, I traveled back to Saint Mary's for lunch, since Saint Mary's students could not eat in the ND dining halls without paying, returning to ND for afternoon classes. During that transition year, Notre Dame failed to set aside any dedicated space for us 'bussed-in women' to hang out between classes.

"When the merger failed, Notre Dame announced its own co-education plans. As the university focused on admitting freshman women and growing the female presence on campus, it accepted a number of transfer students. My parents felt strongly [that] 'a degree from Notre Dame will mean a lot more than one from Saint Mary's,' so I applied to and was subsequently admitted to ND."

Despite new classes of students arriving each year, some word-of-mouth labels persisted. Scuttlebutt maintained that SMC women only wanted to find husbands and obtain "Mrs. degrees." Statements in *The Observer* called out this fallacy: "Notre Dame men who strike out with their female peers can easily find a Smick Chick.' We ride the 'Sluttle'" to cross the road.[7] Conversely, SMC women heard that ND girls focused strictly on academics with little interest in anything fun or feminine.

Some men used such perceptions as excuses for why they were not dating or in relationships with women from either school. It was easier for the guys to say, "She's just interested in an Mrs., and I am not," or "She's only interested in pursuing an academic degree, and I want a woman who shares my interests." Either way, some guys secretly blamed the women for not making them feel better about themselves or for not providing the social interactions they expected from coeducation.

Fueled by the rumors and myths perpetuated by ND males, women on both sides of the highway interacted with some suspicion. A mutual standoffishness arose as hostilities and jealousy grew, most without merit.

◇ *Mary Clemency, ND 1976:* "According to an article in the *Chicago Tribune*, there was some animosity. I took education classes there [at Saint Mary's] and never encountered any problems. However, sometimes, when a guy went out with a girl from here and then she found out he was also going out with a SMC girl, there were bad feelings. The reverse was probably true as well."

◇ *Anonymous female, ND 1976:* "Freshman year, we were sitting around talking when this freshman girl from across the hall said she hated SMC girls. In fact, she had never met an SMC girl. She said it was based on what the guys told her."

◇ *Anonymous female, ND 1976:* "Not that many girls were interested in doing anything with our SMC counterparts. We were

ND students. We would not go out of our way to do something with IUSB [Indiana University South Bend]. No prejudice—just didn't want to get involved."

As young adults, it is often easier to stereotype someone than to see the whole person. Maryanne Ries (now Rogers), an SMC transfer and 1976 classmate, investigated SMC stereotypes for a class paper. She described four labels applied to SMC women, although no individual fit into just one category:

- **Socialites**—primarily from all-girl private schools who dated males from nearby boys' schools. These women enjoyed a plethora of dates often resulting from their "Dog Book" ratings based on appearance.
- **Unsocialites**—"dorm dwellers" who usually found studying seven nights a week or "homeheaders" from closely-knit families who suffered from homesickness.
- **Flower Children**—liberal, freethinkers who rebelled against the capitalist-motivated society despite coming from wealthy backgrounds.
- **Poohbahs**—competitive women, actively involved in everything, friends with professors and administrators.[8]

Another stereotype emerged as feminists started to surface on the SMC campus. These young women openly disavowed events such as the Miss Universe pageant, questioning the purpose behind this parade of flesh. Many experienced job discrimination during summer employment searches. These and other dynamics—such as the attitude of some ND males—fostered the desire to prevent such treatment of women in the future.

ND women also suffered from stereotyping based on perceptions of their primary interest:

- **Intellectuals**—academics
- **Jocks**—athletics and sports
- **Dining Hall Delights**—appearance
- **Potheads**—drugs
- **Flirts**—seeking "Mrs. degrees"

If any woman on either side of the road was pursuing a "Mrs. degree," it was seldom, if ever, acknowledged or discussed openly.

◇ *Ann Pytynia, ND 1976:* "I *never* heard of anyone who was in it for a 'Mrs. degree.' Everyone worked hard and had their ultimate goal to achieve their bachelor's degree and beyond. No one was looking at marriage as the ultimate goal of going to ND—contrary to *The Observer* and *Notre Dame Magazine* articles (grrr!)."

In November 1972, "King" Kersten tried to reduce the tension between the campuses. He named Steve Paspek—"Steve from Cleve," as he was known on campus—as ND's representative to SMC. Kersten appointed Paspek to this position, hoping his presence might induce more SMC girls to visit Notre Dame. Kersten observed Paspek's ability to converse with women without trepidation and was convinced he was the right man for the job.[9]

Tensions, however, continued. In April 1973, *The Observer* printed "A Campus Cookbook" containing the recipe for a "Canned Merger." Ingredients included: "two tons of beef (or bull), several chickens, some hot potatoes, [and] sour grapes." The instructions summarized the administrations' attitudes to "[s]immer in lukewarm water for five years, and then throw everything out."[10]

In the fall of that year, Sister John and the administration established an organization dubbed SMAND (Saint Mary's and Notre Dame) with the mission of uniting the women of both institutions.[11] SMAND sought to propagate an understanding of each school's history and traditions and to resolve any ill will or competitive feelings. Ten representatives, one from each female residence hall, planned activities to break down perceived barriers and to encourage friendships among the women.

Given the Catholic nature of both schools, SMAND also recognized that volunteer organizations were excellent points of intersection. For example, students traveling together in foreign exchange programs showed how friendships could be maintained upon return to their respective campuses. In April 1974, Barbara McKiernan, student body president of Saint Mary's College, commented:

> There is one thing among many that I see, however, as a way to bring the situation [ND–SMC relations] to better ends. That is keeping an open and honest communication going between the women of Notre Dame and the women of St. Mary's College. There is a wealth of knowledge and experience to be learned by both groups and to deny each other those benefits is not only wrong but wasteful. St. Mary's women really do experience different educational pressures and social pressures than Notre Dame women, and vice-versa.[12]

SMAND established a special Women's Council in September 1974. Focused on women's studies and career opportunities, its organizers stressed that the council was not a separate or militant feminist group but rather an open, responsive way for women to meet other women with shared interests. Sister John hoped that, with each new class of freshmen, the need for such focused efforts would dissipate.

However, SMAND's impact was minimal, as demonstrated in the November 1974 price increase for ND basketball tickets. No SMC representative participated in the ticket negotiations between Pat McLaughlin, the student body president, and Father Edmund Joyce, the university's executive vice president. The result was that SMC students paid twenty-eight dollars for bleacher seats, ten dollars more than ND students. ND students only protested the fact that their own ticket prices were doubling, not the impact on SMC students. This decision reinforced the myopic view of ND student leadership and one of the many inequities between the two campuses.

The SMAND committee did influence freshman orientation programs, Co-Ex meal plans, clubs, women's sports, and intramural competitions. In 1975, the ND Athletic Department and the universities' boards of directors agreed to continue sharing certain female club sports with SMC students. Financially, ND donated seven hundred dollars to each club's treasury, with SMC contributing proportionately based on participation. Notre Dame provided sailing and crew equipment, and both the ND and SMC fencing teams used the ACC. As the number of women athletes increased, both institutions developed new sports programs. Over time, Saint Mary's developed a sports program for its new gym, while Notre Dame attempted to improve offerings for its own female contingent.[13]

In February 1975, the SMAND council announced plans to study the schools' relationship. A twelve-women panel garnered input on perceived difficulties and potential resolutions from several focus groups of thirty to forty women each. In September 1975, the group recommended merging SMAND and the Co-Exchange Program; two administrators, two faculty members, and five students from each school comprised the core team of this newly merged committee. Co-Exchange Program Commissioner Joe Corpora explained that this new committee would serve as a catalyst for encouraging people to work together and make suggestions to other commissions on both campuses. Corpora also noted that, since his freshman year in 1972, the division *between* the two schools had continued and that something needed to be done.[14] As its first order of business, the commission reopened ND's freshman colloquium course, which had been closed to SMC freshmen since 1972.

Reverend Joe Corpora, CSC, serves as the assistant director of Pastoral Care Outreach in Campus Ministry and as the director of University–School Partnerships in the Alliance for Catholic Education. He graduated from Notre Dame in 1976, entered Moreau Seminary in 1977, and was ordained a priest in 1984. In Campus Ministry, he serves as chaplain to Latino and LGBT students. In 2016, Pope Francis appointed Father Joe to serve the Church as a Missionary of Mercy.

As late as the 1976–1977 academic year, communication problems persisted between the schools. The Advisory Committee on Coeducation once again recommended that SMC women continue to be present in ND classes and social situations and that joint social opportunities be provided for ND and SMC students, both males and females.[15]

While ND and SMC students struggled to improve their relationships, the university acknowledged a need to strengthen acceptance of ND women by its male alumni base, many of whom had married Saint Mary's women. In the spring of 1973, the university selected "Coeducation at Notre Dame" as the topic for Universal Notre Dame (UND) Night, time set aside for clubs and groups of Notre Dame alumni to hear directly from university administrators. More than thirty faculty and staff members planned to speak at the 1973 UND nights, including Sister John, Jane Pitz, and Kathleen Cekanski. When distance allowed, male students often accompanied the speakers. For the first time, local alumni clubs across the country invited female undergraduates to discuss and present their views of the coeducation experience.[16]

◇◇◇

REARVIEW REFLECTION Lives intersect at seemingly unlikely points. Thanks to my childhood days in Vetville, I wanted to go to Notre Dame. How ironic that my best friend from childhood in Florida grew up in an ND legacy family with a Notre Dame alumnus father, alumni uncles, a Saint Mary's alumna mother, and alumnae aunts. Although we often talked about Notre Dame, we did not expect coeducation to happen in time for us. When we discussed attending Saint Mary's together, we foresaw the best of two worlds: the comfort and safety of a women's college with the academic excellence of Notre Dame through its Co-Exchange Program. The merger announcement made us more confident of our chances for a shared collegiate experience and a great education.

We wrote our admissions essays together. When I received my acceptance letter from Notre Dame, I could not wait to share my news with her and to plan for the fall. To my surprise, my friend chose Saint Mary's. The summer of 1972 passed with minimal contact, but I still optimistically believed that we would reconnect in South Bend. Having weathered the ups and downs of adolescence and micromanaging parents for so many years, I could not imagine life at Notre Dame without her. After all, the schools were almost as close as our Florida homes.

Graduating from Saint Mary's (May 1960)

However, once we arrived, I found that the distance might as well have been a thousand miles.

My friend and I did not see each other during freshman orientation or at the SMC mixer. Besides, crossing the road held little appeal for me as the male dorms offered numerous welcome events. After hearing about the stereotyping of ND and SMC women, I realized that the distance between Saint Mary's and ND was not just physical. Any hopes of spending time with my friend quickly faded.

We finally reconnected over Christmas 1974 when she hosted a party for ND and SMC students before the 1975 Orange Bowl. After that reunion, we stayed connected, occasionally getting together. While our paths diverged after our 1976 graduations, we return to that intersection of our youth whenever we can.

If I felt any tension in this ND–SMC area, it came into my life by way of alumni rather than through student connections. In the early 1970s, several Notre Dame alumni coached and taught at my high school, Cardinal Newman, and they often shared their insights into collegiate life. So, when Angelo Schiralli, the president of the ND Club of the Palm Beaches and a member of ND's 1966 national championship football team, invited me to speak at the club's 1973 UND dinner, I was honored.

The March 1, 2013, edition of *The Observer*, as part of a five-part series called "Her Loyal Daughters," documented the ongoing ND–SMC discord. Its writers asked all students to unite to:

• "[D]rive the administration to reform the freshman orientation experience and set a more positive tone for gender relations";

• "[B]uild a sense of sisterhood" among all female students;

• "[E]mbrace coeducation" as "a community of men and women, studying together, learning with and from each other";

• And "make this road…into a two-way street."[17]

I had recently been home for spring break, but my dad, one of the founders of the Palm Beach club, happily agreed to fly me home. I wanted this opportunity to talk about Notre Dame; I felt I owed Father Ted a more balanced picture of coeducation. Still, I was nervous about facing an audience of ND men, many of whom were married to SMC women. Not all ND alumni wanted women on campus, and not all Saint Mary's alumnae wanted to hear about our first year.

I *hated* prepared speeches and preferred to speak extemporaneously. So, following the main speaker from the university, I stepped up to the lectern and candidly explained how the university had failed to prepare for its new female students. I described the dorms with their urinals, the dining hall food fights, and the professors' need to ask the "woman's viewpoint" in almost every class. I balanced these observations against the backdrop of that wonderful feeling of walking around campus knowing things were changing dramatically. The audience laughed at the more lighthearted comments and listened intently to my more serious points.

Then I made my biggest mistake—I opened the floor for questions. After several softballs from a few men, one woman derisively said, "You did not discuss the relationship between Saint Mary's *women* and Notre Dame *girls*. You must be aware there is a women's college nearby."

I was shocked. An adult woman, married to a successful ND graduate and friend of my parents, was trying to intimidate me—a young girl of eighteen. Thankfully, I had given some thought to the ND–SMC relationship and had consciously decided not to mention it. I responded thoughtfully, taking deep breaths between each point:

> Of course, I know Saint Mary's is nearby—after all, I graduated from its kindergarten in 1960. However, I am more focused on adjusting to being away from home for the first time than any perceived rivalry.
>
> And, as some of you know, my best friend from here is at Saint Mary's, so, again, I haven't experienced any problems between the two groups of women.
>
> Finally, you will never insult me by calling me a "girl" because that is exactly what I am—a Notre Dame girl trying to find herself at a great university during a wonderful time of her life.
>
> I grew up in West Palm and just completed the first winter of my adult life. Believe me, it was a different experience than when my mom walked us through the fields near ND and gave us hot chocolate afterward.
>
> I am sure there is tension between the two campuses, but someone must look for it to find it. I just haven't had the time—nor inclination—to look.

I guess my answer was acceptable as the club invited me back the following year!

Gaining Speed

"I will not follow where the path may lead, but I will go where there is no path, and I will leave a trail" is a statement often credited to Emerson but has never been located in his works. Found instead in the writings of poet Muriel Strode, it is an appropriate characterization of the efforts of numerous groups to incorporate their identities into the University of Notre Dame.[1] Hesburgh's dream of a catholic (i.e., "universal") university gained traction in the 1970s as African Americans, Hispanics, Native Americans, gays and lesbians, and others sought equality on campus. Their legacy at Notre Dame mirrored that of its first women — all were pioneers, academically, socially, and culturally. They had few guides to help them survive, let alone thrive and succeed. With the university expanding its admission objectives, the women accompanied growing numbers of other minorities as these groups influenced not just sports but also student government and class activities.

◇◇◇

Well before the 1954 *Brown v. Board of Education of Topeka* Supreme Court decision and the civil rights movement of the 1960s, Frazier Thompson (ND 1947) became the first Black American to graduate from Notre Dame. However, unlike the decision to admit 365 women to the university by filling two residential halls that first year, adding minorities to ND's student population was a slower and more sporadic process. In the 1966–1967 academic year, only twelve minority students — all African American — entered as undergraduates. By the 1967–1968 academic year, forty-six African Americans and thirty-one other minorities across all classes accounted for 1.24 percent of the 6,237 undergraduate students. The 132 graduate and five law students in populations of 1,106 and 259, respectively, brought the year's total percentage of minority students to 2.81 percent.[2]

In 1970, Notre Dame broke its own forty-five-year ban on postseason football appearances and used the resulting funds to increase student aid and to grow

Shortly after Martin Luther King Jr.'s 1968 death, third-grade teacher Jane Elliott made prejudice brutally real for her class. After (controversially) segregating her students by eye color, she told her brown-eyed students that they were superior in intelligence and should not play with their blue-eyed classmates; she sat the blue-eyed students in the back of the room.

Within minutes, some of the brown-eyed students began to victimize their blue-eyed classmates. The reverse occurred when she reversed the exercise.

ABC News documented the (problematic) exercise in its 1970 film *The Eye of the Storm*. By the 1990s, Elliott offered diversity workshops and similar exercises for college students. She believes the exercises prove that racism is a learned response—that racism, discrimination, and prejudice are not biologically rooted or "givens." Elliott's exercises on racism have caused some participants to get up and leave. Her response: "You just exercised a freedom that none of these people of color have....When [they] get tired of racism, they can't just walk out."[6]

the number of minorities in its student body. Receipts from the 1969 Cotton Bowl provided $40,600 in aid, renewable for four years, to forty-one ethnic minorities. The next year, David Krashna became the first Black student body president, the only one until Corey Robinson in 2016.[3]

For the 1972–1973 academic year, minorities represented 3.75 percent of the university's student population. Undergraduates included 137 African Americans, 19 American Indians, 17 Asian Americans (termed "Orientals" in early 1970s reports), and 99 Spanish Americans—or 4.06 percent of the undergraduate population—while 2.4 percent of the 1,870 graduate and law students included 17 African Americans, 17 Asian Americans, and 11 Spanish Americans. During a September 1972 session with sixty Badin Hall women, an African American sophomore questioned Hesburgh, the US Civil Rights Commission chairman, about this level of minority representation and recruitment. He responded: "We've told the admission office...that we want to keep increasing the number (of minority women) every year. This year we fell low on men, but there was a run on chicanos [sic]. Every chicano [sic] we offered a scholarship to took it,"[4] adding that "[s]everal black [sic] male prospective students...turned down ND scholarships to attend other universities."[5]

Unfortunately, as Hesburgh indicated, progress was not steady. The October 17, 1972, *Observer* reported that the freshman class had a slight reduction in the number of African American freshmen over previous years. Although the number of applications from and acceptances of African Americans was as high for 1972–1973, fewer actually enrolled. The class of 1976 welcomed

With Ed Byrne and Augie Grace (2006) and with Shelley Muller Simon and Lionel Phillips (2011)

twenty-seven African Americans, twenty-five men and two women; one of the women died tragically the second semester of that first year.[7]

The university offered African American students the choice of living in a cluster of Black students or living in the general student population; they could also formally request an African American roommate. These were major departures from the standard residential policies.

> ◇ *Lionel Phillips, ND 1976:* "A freshman in the class of 1971 came home for break in April 1972 with an application, which I completed and sent back with him. In May, I received my acceptance. Although I had planned to play sports at another school, my mother told me I would be a fool to turn down the University of Notre Dame. Of course, my mother was right.
>
> "In August 1972, I boarded a Greyhound bus in downtown Saint Louis, Missouri, and headed into the unknown. I had never visited Notre Dame before stepping off that bus in front of the Athletic and Convocation Center. That bus carried about seventy-five incoming freshmen, all of whom seemed better prepared for this new experience. Their conversations referenced sites on campus and the names of existing and incoming athletes, things about which I knew nothing. I was in awe and, frankly, a little afraid.
>
> "During my first days at Notre Dame, I roomed with three great individuals, all of whom were white. We lived in a dormitory suite designed for three. After a week in these overcrowded conditions, a knock at our door changed my living arrangements.
>
> "In 1972, only one dorm had a designated Black community, Dillon Hall; other dorms had pockets of Black students, including Cavanaugh, Grace, and Fisher where most Black athletes lived. The university had reserved a section on the third floor

211

of Dillon exclusively for Black students, often referred to as the 'Black Concentration.' That knock on the door provided me with an opportunity for a single room on the third floor; it took me about ten minutes to relocate. Unlike most freshmen, I spent my first year living in solitude and comfort. My neighbors were all intelligent and Afrocentric young men, with one common belief— they hated being at Notre Dame. By year-end, all except me graduated, transferred, or moved off campus. My original roommates moved into vacated rooms for our sophomore year and still brag about living in the Black Concentration."

Augie Grace was also one of the twenty-seven Black students admitted at the onset of coeducation. Similar to Lionel, he was encouraged to apply to Notre Dame:

◇ *Augie Grace, ND 1976:* "The civil rights movement of the 1960s provided the opportunity to attend college to many African American students. Although many incoming freshmen had families who had attended college, this was not true for most African American students. In general, African American students had no 'compass' to guide our collegiate journey.

"I mostly applied to colleges around Boston. One day after basketball practice, I ran into Tom Young. Tom shared his first-semester experiences at Notre Dame and encouraged me to apply. I think most minority students probably attended ND because of conversations with an influential teacher or friend. Convinced ND was right for me, I applied. One evening while working at the Hot Shoppe's restaurant, ND Admissions Director Dan Saracino called and told me that my acceptance letter was in the mail. My high school classmates did not believe me about the call, and I started to question if it had been a prank. I overcame my skepticism when my admission letter arrived, and I quickly accepted the offer to become a member of the ND class of 1976.

"My experiences as a minority student were at times similar and at other times different than my minority classmates. With my father serving in the military for most of my childhood and then settling into a Boston suburb with a small Black population, I was mindful of isolated instances of racism. Notre Dame's campus environment did not shock me nearly as much as other minority students. I soon learned of instances during freshman orientation where some classmates and their parents, upon learning their roommate was Black, demanded a change in room assignments. During move-in, African American classmates were sometimes mistaken for the dormitory housing staff and asked to carry luggage. Fortunately, I did not experience these awful situations.

"As Black freshmen, we indicated our residence hall preferences. One choice was Dillon Hall in an area set aside for Black students, an attempt by the university to help us feel more comfortable; however, I chose Cavanaugh Hall where Tom Young was a resident. My first week, I noticed other African American students eating together, and I joined them. Later, I wanted to meet as many classmates as possible, so I began eating with roommates and fellow Cavanaugh residents.

"In most classes and activities, I was the only Black participant. I worked as a student manager for various athletic teams to connect more closely with the Black athletes. Junior and senior years, I became class president for the class of 1976, allowing me to make an impact on campus life and the university.

"Although our numbers were small, contributions of my Black classmates like Chuck Wilson at the Student Union and Elton Johnson who served as the chairman of the Hall Presidents Council helped to shape a better Notre Dame. Our experiences, like those of the first women, were difficult on occasion, but these challenges made us stronger people and leaders."

Just as the acceptance of women caused angst among some students, so did the addition of minorities. In 1972, Assistant Admissions Director Dan Saracino told *The Observer* that he wished to "dispel the image that some white racist students have of blacks [sic]":

> They seem to think that "minority student" means "inferior student."…We take pride in the fact that over 30 percent of the minority students in this year's freshman class are Notre Dame scholars while only 15 percent of the entire freshman class have been accorded that honor.[8]

The Admissions Office increased its focus on enrolling students from other minority groups. Saracino pointed out that the overall numbers of minorities increased in 1972, with "twice as many Chicanos and Indians [sic]…enrolled in this year's freshman class as in 1971."[9] However, Saracino attributed the year's decline in Black enrollment to the fact that every college and university in the country was seeking academically qualified African American students. Aside from the higher collegiate competition for these students, Saracino also blamed the decrease in African American enrollment on the federal government withholding sixty thousand dollars in National Educational Opportunity Grants. By the time the university received its full funding, it was too late to enroll students needing scholarships. A decrease in both athletic grants-in-aid and ROTC scholarships further contributed to a decline.

Saracino recognized the need for a coordinated effort to contact qualified African American students. In 1972, the Admissions Office established a committee of seven Black students to contact each high school senior who applied to Notre Dame. Saracino himself talked to African American women such as Gail Antoinette King at Saint Mary's during the first years of coeducation.

> ◇ *Gail Antoinette King, ND 1975:* "When Dan Saracino, then an assistant director in the admissions office, asked me if I would consider transferring from Saint Mary's to Notre Dame for the start of my sophomore year, I knew it was an opportunity that I could not pass up. . . . If Black students are comfortable in colleges today, it is because students like me were uncomfortable yesterday. Somebody had to be first, to pave the way, to open the door for others."[10]

Admissions counselors and minority students made special trips to cities with high concentrations of minorities, such as Detroit, Chicago, and Philadelphia. Notre Dame also worked with the National Scholarship Service and Fund for Negro Students (NSSFNS), recognizing that NSSFNS served as a "guidance counselor" for Blacks attending high schools with counseling services of dubious merit.[11] The university used all these approaches to introduce applicants to life as a minority student at Notre Dame.

In 1972, no one campus agency addressed the welfare of all minority students, although an African American woman on the Freshman Year of Studies staff tended to all freshmen. As minorities grew in number, *The Observer* documented the challenges facing African Americans as Notre Dame's second largest minority group, behind the women. When the women arrived, the Student Life Council added a temporary seat for a woman representative. Despite a presence on campus for more than a decade longer, African American students had no such representation.

African American students saw some changes in February 1973. The administration appointed Granville Cleveland, who would become an assistant librarian for the law school, as acting director of Black Student Affairs.[12] The African American faculty and staff also established an organization, the Society of UJAMMA, to combat bad publicity and misconceptions about the Black community.[13] Its chairman, Dr. Alech Che-Mponda, an assistant professor of government and international relations with a PhD from Howard University, joined ND that semester to teach Black studies and a Swahili language course.[14] Although minority students were always part of ND's history—the first minority student was Native American—UJAMMA recognized that they became lost in the crowds moving across the quads. However, as the minority population had increased nearly four times over the past decade, so had the severity of their academic and social problems.

Black representatives presented their concerns to the Hall Presidents Council, with Hesburgh in attendance. They complained about Campus Security's frequent and humiliating requests to see the IDs of African American students. They requested more Protestant services for non-Catholic students. Finally, they recommended that all students be required to take a minority experience course. The requests for additional Protestant services and increasing the sensitivity of the university's security force were accepted as actionable. However, the administration and the HPC felt requiring a minority experience course restricted the academic choices of all students.[16]

The council also discussed the need for a "Black House" off campus, an idea brought forward by some African American students. Although the Cultural Arts Center served as an academic and educational center for all, the primary users were those living off campus. Its Black Studies Program newsletters touted social activities such as bringing African American women to campus in the spring, not as a "cattle exposition" but to increase interest in Notre Dame by Black women. Both the Black Studies Program and UJAMMA used the center's small library to house program materials, hold meetings, and offer informal counseling. Its Minorities Counseling Center, separate from the university's Psychological Services, offered financial, academic, vocational, and emotional support for all minorities. It offered information on graduate school scholarships and handled inquiries from industries seeking to employ minorities.

Many viewers credited *The Flip Wilson Show* as the first TV show starring an African American person to achieve fame with a white audience. According to the Nielsen TV ratings, it was the second-most watched show in the United States during the 1970–1971 and 1971–1972 seasons.[15] Wilson's character, Geraldine, popularized the phrase, "The Devil made me do it!" Beverly Johnson made history in August 1974 as the first African American model to appear on the cover of *Vogue* magazine in the United States, and American tennis player Arthur Ashe became the first Black man to win Wimbledon in July 1975. Cicely Tyson and Maya Angelou starred in the TV miniseries *Roots.* Premiering in January 1977 and based on Alex Haley's novel of the same name, *Roots* tells the story of an African boy sold into slavery in America and the lives of the subsequent generations of his family. More than half of the US population in 1977 watched the show.

Closed temporarily in 1974, the counseling center reopened in 1975 with an expanded mission: to connect with the larger South Bend community, mentor its African American children, and recruit more African Americans to Notre Dame.

The fall of 1973 saw the addition of a Black Student Affairs director, Cassell Lawson, and the appointment of Joe Moskowitz as the Student Union's Minority Social Commissioner. A Black Student Convention brought forward many of the previously rejected recommendations: a list of community resources, a Black student directory, a monthly activities calendar, and a course evaluation system where seniors could provide their views of professors and course materials. The event ended with a social gathering of more than two hundred African American participants from ND and SMC.[17]

In October 1973, the Black Studies Program allowed students to gain a second cognate interdisciplinary major, along with a major in another field such as behavioral sciences or humanities — a departure from the rules prohibiting double majors. The new major was recommended for students planning to work in urban areas or in professions whose clientele might be substantially African American, Puerto Rican, or other minorities. Complementing this program, the New Frontier Scholastic Society sponsored forums on the Black experience in America. Held at the Black Cultural Arts Center, these forums discussed political, economic, and cultural topics related to increasing Black people's contributions to the sociopolitical environment.[18]

> Combining rock, rhythm and blues, jazz, and soul, funk music was an African American musical form associated with "Black Pride" and the civil rights movement. Its most famous artists were James Brown (1933–2006), Sly and the Family Stone (active 1966–1983), and Curtis Mayfield (1942–1999). The Motown sound out of Detroit soon followed. As the "Godfather of Soul" once said: "[I]f people [want] to know who James Brown is, all they have to do is listen to my music."[19]

In March 1974, the New Frontier Scholastic Society, the Society of UJAMMA, the Black Graduate Student Union, the Black American Law Students Association (BALSA), and the Minority Social Commission sponsored a Black Arts Festival. Its theme, "Black Perspectives in Transition," highlighted some tools and ways to stimulate social change through Black expressions in drama, art, and music.

Despite some positive changes, African American students at ND continued to feel isolated even as the administration recognized the need for the Black population to feel connected.

> ◇ *Lionel Phillips, ND 1976:* "We chose to be separated — it was never forced on us. In the dining halls, we sat together at unofficially 'designated' Black tables. We rehashed daily happenings

and roasted each other —a practice commonly called 'Joning.' We enjoyed a sense of security and kinship as we talked about life, nothing serious — not racism, politics, or academics. We were no different than those sitting at the 'white tables.'

"We also met on the third floor of the LaFortune Center at the Black Cultural Arts Center. Opened from 11:00 a.m. until 4:00 p.m. every weekday, we used it for parties on weekends and to host such individuals as political activist Angela Davis and poet Nikki Giovanni. We were immensely proud and not afraid to collectively stand up to and against injustices, including racism.

"If you worked hard at Notre Dame, you did well. However, that did not prevent me from witnessing treatment that, at times, felt unfair. In the first semester of my senior year, I experienced what many of the first women went through—a professor who had a habit of calling on me first to give my opinion on assigned readings. After about a month, a classmate confronted the professor and asked if he was intentionally targeting me. The practice stopped immediately. However, my final semester, the same professor offered me a B- on a group project in which every other team member received an A. Adding insult to injury, no one in the class received less than a B, exempting all but me from the final exam. When the professor announced to the class [that] he needed to meet with me to schedule the final exam, I dramatically walked out, stating I was not taking one. I somehow received a B, and it remains one ND experience that prepared me for postgraduate life. I learned what it took to be successful in life, to be confident in my skills, and to stand up for myself.

"Our close-knit group included the Black student athletes. Although some of us went to high school with white students, for the most part the classroom was the only thing we shared; this trend continued at Notre Dame. Most Black students in the 1970s were first-generation college attendees who struggled to find a social life. After classes and on weekends, we were all about the Motown sound and *Soul Train* dancers. We made our own fun: playing bid whist, partying with South Bend's Black community, importing girls from nearby colleges, and taking road trips. As a result, I had limited interactions with the ND women. I did not identify with them, nor them with me, through no fault of either party. The lack of a meaningful social life at Notre Dame was (and is) the major reason that many Blacks seldom returned to campus. In 1985, the university acknowledged that fact and created the Black Alumni of Notre Dame affinity group, which has drawn Black alums closer to each other and Notre Dame."

Other minority students experienced similar discomfort on the predominantly white campus. Peter Conrad Rodríguez described his first day at ND:

◇ *Peter Conrad Rodríguez, ND 1976:* "Before my departure from San Juan, Puerto Rico, to the United States in August 1972, my father warned me about a bad 'disease' that I would most likely face in Indiana. I asked him what the disease was, and he answered, 'I want you to experience it first.' I asked him, 'What if I catch it, Dad?' — to which he replied emphatically he would kick my butt.

"On my first day at Notre Dame, I ventured to dinner alone. As I was leaving the dorm, I heard music at the end of the hallway. As I was about to knock on the doorframe, the room's occupants — three Black seniors — saw me reflected in their mirror and called me by name. These guys were listening to Earl Klug, Bobby Benson, and Gillespie, and I was introduced to — and fell in love with — jazz.

"We left together for the cafeteria. They took me to a buffet line with collard greens, corn bread, pinto beans, and a style of fried chicken I had never tasted. It was a feast that tasted like my home in Puerto Rico.

"When I arrived back at my room, my three roommates asked me why I was sitting with Black folks for dinner. However, they did not say Black — they used the 'N-word.' My response was threefold. First, I told them I did not like that 'N-word' I had first read in *Huckleberry Finn* and *Tom Sawyer*; it had a bad connotation then, and it still had a bad connotation. Second, the Blacks ate my kind of food and listened to my type of music. Third, and most important, it was none of their business with whom I ate. They backed off and agreed with me.

"Despite Hesburgh, our university president, replacing the assassinated Reverend Martin Luther King as chairman of the civil rights movement, his message had not reached everyone on campus. I had found what my dad called the 'disease.'"

Such experiences captured the isolation felt by minority groups on campus. Just as the number of women faculty was lacking, minority students had few minority staff and faculty with whom to identify.[20] A lack of support at the administrative and faculty levels continued despite the *Malits Report* recommendation of adding an associate provost or vice president of special projects to address the needs of

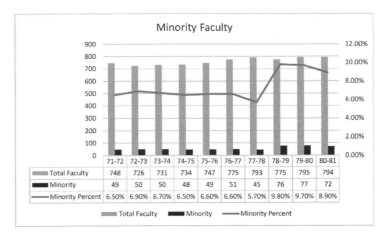

	71-72	72-73	73-74	74-75	75-76	76-77	77-78	78-79	79-80	80-81
Total Faculty	748	726	731	734	747	775	793	775	795	794
Minority	49	50	50	48	49	51	45	76	77	72
Minority Percent	6.50%	6.90%	6.70%	6.50%	6.60%	6.60%	5.70%	9.80%	9.70%	8.90%

all minority groups, including women. Although none of the four colleges made any special accommodations to address minority needs, the administration encouraged each to assist the women and minorities with their educational and career objectives.

Not until September 1975 did the university direct all departments to utilize women and minority faculty to recruit applicants for faculty and staff positions. It encouraged the appointment, promotion, and inclusion on committees of women and minorities. This directive also recommended the promotion of minorities and women to responsible faculty positions as vacancies occurred.[21]

This guidance coincided with the 1975 admission of 107 new minority students, of which 27 were women, in the freshman class of 1,636 total—almost tripling the number of minorities enrolled in the 1969–1970 academic year. These first-year students included 53 African Americans, 40 Spanish Americans, 13 Asian Americans, and 1 Native American; an additional seven students were readmitted as part of this class. All but seven applicants finished in the top 20 percent of their high school class, with more

> Adam S. Arnold Jr. came to Notre Dame in 1957. He was its first African American faculty member and the first African American to receive tenure.[22]

than half finishing in the top 5 percent. They came from thirty-one states, the District of Columbia, Puerto Rico, and Spain. For the 1975–1976 academic year, minorities were 6 percent of the student population.[23]

Notre Dame also concentrated on strengthening its international presence. The fall of 1975 saw 308 students from 62 countries. For the first time, enrolling international students—194 graduate and 114 undergraduate students—preferred Arts and Letters to Engineering. These students received support from the International Student Association (ISA), the only official student organization representing the international student community at ND and SMC. It assisted the foreign students and coordinated events and activities. Within ISA, three national associations — Indian, Chinese, and Pan-American — maintained their individual identities and budgets while participating in activities for all international students.[24]

The first class of ND freshman women graduated in 1976, the year of the nation's bicentennial. Racial equality and designations were emotional issues that year, both on and off campus. The Reverend Jesse L. Jackson expressed his views on these concerns in a 1976 *Time* letter, responding to a previously published article in the magazine on "why Jimmy Carter appeals to black voters":

> In that article you quoted me and identified me as a "black leader." I consider this journalistic racism. No one refers to George Wallace as a "white Governor" or Gerald Ford as a "white President." If a label must be attached to my leadership, as a minister of the gospel I prefer "moral leader." Moral leadership, which essentially deals with ideas and values, is a universal category. Black is not.[25]

Vernon Jordan Jr., executive director of the National Urban League, addressed the graduating class and their guests at the 1976 commencement. Although some attendees walked out during his speech, his words rang with an element of truth:

> In this Bicentennial year, the jury is still out on whether our nation shall inherit the mantle of glory or the shroud of shame. Our progress toward equality has been halting, characterized by brief spurts of forward motion followed by long arid stretches of retreat and withdrawal.[27]

The student population is changing in many ways. Notre Dame's freshman applicant pool is increasingly more diverse in terms of racial, economic, ethnic, and global characteristics. In 2021, roughly 39 percent of its incoming class were "U.S. students of color or international students, up from 30 percent in 2014."[26]

While this progress has indeed been halting at times, Notre Dame continues to strive toward fully equality.

> ◇ *Joe Sinnott, ND 1976:* "I was a first-generation college student, as my parents lacked the financial resources to attend any college, let alone one with the stature of ND. While there, I met students of different nationalities, backgrounds, and sexual orientation. Today, these groups are an integral part of the student body. ND is closer to the identity Father Ted sought, starting with the admission of women."

REARVIEW REFLECTION The integrated environment of my high school offered classes, activities, and friendships with the opposite sex and with individuals from different ethnic and cultural backgrounds. One student in my advanced courses was an African American woman who became one of my best friends. She even taught me how to drive a manual stick shift in the school parking lot. As a result, I was shocked and horrified when the Breakers Hotel in Palm Beach banned her from the pool during my sixteenth birthday party in 1970; the hotel's management restricted us to the beach and my parents' cabana.

I did not understand such attitudes. As part of the changing culture of South Florida, we came to know individuals for who they were — not based on color, religion, or sexual preference. The sea of virtually all-white male students truly shocked me those first days on campus. I was not alone in this reaction.

In 1987, Hesburgh instructed the Notre Dame Alumni Association to create the Black Alumni of Notre Dame to help with recruiting and retaining African American students and to build a community of Black graduates. Since then, the NDAA has established groups for Native Americans, Hispanics, Asian Americans and Pacific Islanders, women, seniors, and young alumni to enhance their engagement with the university through shared interests and unique experiences.[28]

◇ *A. Michele Parnell Garrett, ND 1976:* "My parents acted as role models for me, as they were always open to people of all races and cultures and celebrated diversity. Studying abroad, living in France, and becoming trilingual — French, Spanish, and English — has been a great asset in understanding other cultures."

Still, I wish I had been more aware of the struggles of other minority groups during my time at ND. Some say misery loves company; others find it helpful to know they are not the only ones who struggle. Minority groups felt "different" from the majority of white males who, at times, acted like they owned the place and treated all others as temporary visitors.

It was not until I managed professionals that I grasped the benefits of how diversity improves a team's chance of success. Then, when I joined the ND Alumni Association Board in 2008, I realized the full effect of the small numbers of women and minorities within the ND "family" network and its programs. Unfortunately, despite the increasing diversity of student population today, if minority students were not present in the 1970s, they cannot be connected now. Hopefully, anyone disenfranchised by an ND experience will give the extended, more diversified ND family a second chance.

The Open Road

In the film *Furious 7*, Dominic Toretto, a character played by actor Vin Diesel, is known for his philosophy of the road: "They say the open road helps you think about where you've been, where you're going."[1] But it was difficult to share such thoughts in the mid-1970s, when topics such as sexual orientation or gender identity seldom surfaced in classes or *The Observer*. Few students—whether male or female—openly discussed questions of sexual or gender identity as they engaged in their own self-discovery.

◇◇◇

Editions of *The Observer* from September 1972 to May 1976 presented little on the topic of sexual orientation or homosexuality. The only reference to such issues during our first two years was a November 2, 1972, letter to the editor inviting both ND and SMC students to contact an informal group through a post office box.[2] This group's information occasionally surfaced in *The Observer*'s ad section. Given the limited information in print, alumni have shared some of their experiences as part of this social history as they have looked back on their ND pasts and paths. For example, Tom Bower described what Notre Dame was like as a young gay man prior to the official start of coeducation:

> ◇ *Tom Bower, ND 1970:* "Notre Dame was a sparkling, intellectually exciting place full of great discussions flowing from Vatican II—but still with more of a sense of 'awakening' than being 'fully awake.' Life as a not-out gay person on campus before the time of liberation—1969—was good, but strange. Personally, I did not know what gay was; the name that dare not speak itself was well hidden when I was there. This was typical of the times and of my fellow students: A Catholic all-male college on the edge of nowhere was certainly not sought out by early gay activists. The advantage of going to ND for one who had no interest in women,

given so few women relative to men, was easy cover for invisible gay activities like dinner, movies, or theater events with another male. It also provided cover from inquiring aunts who asked whom I was dating.

"As an art and art history student, I shared classes with Saint Mary's women, so the arrival of women as classmates seemed a natural progression of the increasingly open attitude toward coeducation. The admission of women students was a hard-fought effort, but it happened. Maybe now, a half-century later, LGBT rights will gain traction in spite of leadership's foot dragging."

Tomasi Hubbard also explored ND's "gay underground" during the late '60s and early '70s:

◇ *Tomasi Hubbard, ND 1972:* "In 1971, 'One Who Cares' wrote several anonymous letters to *The Observer* wondering what a gay student should do at ND.[3] His editorials created a minor sensation on campus. My experiences were similar yet different from 'One Who Cares.' After graduating from high school in New Orleans and starting to come out in 1968, I had no idea what to do or where to go at ND. There were no openly gay people, no support organizations, and no places to meet on campus. South Bend was also an unknown.

"During a late-night bull session in my sophomore year, a dorm mate blurted out [that] there was a gay bar in South Bend, the Jolly Spot. When my SMC girlfriend (having a steady girlfriend helped to dispel any notion that I was coming out) went home

In response to the "lavender scare" during the McCarthy era and the Stonewall riots in 1969, the gay rights movement gained new momentum, including more visibility on TV. However, not all portrayals were progressive. Percy Dovetonsils, a character on *The Ernie Kovacs Show*, utilized stereotypes common during the 1950s and 1960s; on other programs, homosexuality, same-sex marriage, and transgender health care were sometimes exploited as sources of humor (for example, in episodes of *The Steve Allen Show*, *The Jack Benny Show*, and even *Leave It to Beaver*) or seen as something "unhealthy" or "dangerous" (in some medical dramas and police procedurals). On the other hand, sitcoms such as *Bewitched*, *All in the Family*, and *Alice* offered early advocacy and anticipated cultural and legal changes—including "The Puppy Episode" on *Ellen* in 1997 and the US Supreme Court's 2015 *Obergefell* case that legalized same-sex marriage in the United States.[4]

to Cleveland, I summoned the courage to cross [the Jolly Spot's] threshold. Lesbian couples, mostly stereotypical 'butches' and 'femmes,' occupied the sleazy bar in front, and the back half contained a semicircular organ bar where Harry Glick played show tunes while drag queens and gay men warbled along. I freaked out and went back into the closet for six months. The bar was torn down in 1971 as part of South Bend's urban renewal.

"I eventually found the gay underground on campus, a clique with about seven members who met off campus. We came to know several gay CSC priests, one of whom advised us to shut up or we might never graduate. During the summers and after graduation, I stayed in touch with several of my friends — no different from any other college student. The difference: We experienced the new, nascent gay lifestyle in big coastal cities unlike the closeted, 'Boys in the Band' world of South Bend and the uptight hyper-macho campus. Given our experiences, many of us felt the best view of the Golden Dome was in the rearview mirror."

Summarizing ND's lack of support for LGBTQ students during this period, Jack Bergen reflected:

◇ *Jack Bergen, ND 1977:* "Notre Dame in the 1970s was a very homogenous place, with little diversity as we now know it. The typical student was white, male, from a traditional Catholic family, and most often the product of Catholic school education; even with the introduction of women and students of color, the ND student body was overwhelmingly the same. As a result, few students were exposed to individuals who looked, thought, or acted different than themselves — and certainly even less to anyone suspected of being 'homosexual.' The 'gay revolution' started by the Stonewall riots in 1969 had not reached mainstream America and was not openly evident on the Notre Dame campus.

"Given homosexuality was forbidden by the Catholic Church during this era, ND had no support or tolerance for anyone suspected of being gay. Neither the Church nor ND needed young adults with raging hormones under their care to act on those desires; they had other demons to face."

If gay men were rare on campus during the 1970s, lesbian women were even rarer. One transfer from Saint Mary's struggled with her sexuality and her faith while at ND:

◇ *Mary E. "Libby" Ford, ND 1975:* "I never thought about my sexuality. I dated males in high school, primarily because it was expected. Despite the unbalanced ratio of women to men, Notre Dame guys were not beating down my door for a date, but I did not particularly miss dating. I recognize now that I was lonely and not forming the deep bonds for which ND was known. I spent time with people I liked (men and women) more as a 'friend of a friend' than because I was close to any dorm mates or classmates. When I came out to someone I considered a good friend several years after graduation, she cautioned me not to tell two other close classmates and soon dropped all contact with me. I regret I have no ongoing friendships with fellow Domers from that era.

"I spent my collegiate summers working at Girl Scout camps. At the camp between my senior year and graduate school, I fell in love — with a woman. Suddenly, a lot of things in my life made more sense. However, at the same time, after sixteen years of Catholic education, I returned to ND as a graduate student, trying to deny this new realization. I never thought to seek out other 'gays' or 'lesbians,' because not only was I not ready to accept myself but also I was convinced there were no other gays or lesbians on campus. I did not think there were any sympathetic ears that would listen as I struggled to come to terms with what felt like my 'God-given' lesbian self and the strong Catholic messages that sex was only allowed between a married man and woman to create a new life. Frankly, without 'compartmentalizing' those feelings I did not want or understand, I probably would have been mentally paralyzed and unable to finish my master's.

"Despite having no one with whom I could share these new realizations, I found myself growing more comfortable with being a Catholic woman. I loved attending the less formal Sunday Masses in the Walsh chapel, and I often volunteered to distribute Communion, something forbidden in the Catholic Church of the 1950s and 1960s. I left Notre Dame as a devout Catholic but not one who blindly adheres to all Catholic doctrine. I learned to question and, even at times, reject Catholic doctrine and yet remain a 'good Catholic.' Notre Dame taught me the value of finding the 'real' message and disregarding much of the historic trappings and absolutes with which I was raised. This knowledge led me to a catholic (small 'c') church, where I and several thousand other excommunicated Catholics (1) feel called to recognize women as belonging on the altar, (2) believe that Communion is a banquet to which everyone is invited, and (3) offers a welcoming place for LGBT+ individuals."

Discussions about LGBTQ issues at ND increased in the 1974–1975 academic year. In October 1974, the director of the professional program in the Department of Theology, Oliver Williams, CSC, organized a two-day workshop on homosexuality. Williams' objective for the workshop's roughly fifty attendees was to make future priests more sensitive to the needs of young gay people. He believed that the Church was largely responsible for young gay people feeling so paranoid about their place in society. He strongly felt a Catholic university should discuss such sensitive, complicated issues. The lectures covered the ethics of homosexuality, New Testament scriptural aspects, and discussions on the life in society. Father Oliver Williams hoped these sessions would "enable these organizations to come above ground and be more open in their activities."[5]

LGBTQ+ is an initialism for lesbian, gay, bisexual, transgender, and queer or questioning, terms used to describe a person's sexual orientation or gender identity. Gender identity is an individual's "internal, personal sense of being a man or a woman (or as someone outside of that gender binary). Sexual orientation describes a person's...physical, romantic and/or emotional attraction to another person (for example: straight, gay, lesbian, and bisexual). Transgender people may be straight, lesbian, gay, or bisexual."[6]

That same fall, several students and faculty organized a group for gay men and women, although its membership was primarily male. The Gay Students of Notre Dame established a forum in which members could share ideas, experiences, and activities. The organizers focused on medical, religious, and legal concerns; family acceptance; and relationship issues. They gathered in homes and apartments off campus to ensure anonymity. The organizers emphasized that the group was "not designed to determine the direction of a person's life; rather, it 'exists for those members of this university who wish to explore aspects of their own selves and help others do the same.'"[7] They did not try to change campus attitudes.

In January 1975, three *Observer* articles by Andy Praschak further examined homosexuality at ND.[8] Despite its veiled existence, The Gay Students of Notre Dame, also known as The Gay Student Alliance, hoped those reading this series would recognize its members as humans. One anonymous student wrote in a letter to the editor:

It is always taken as a milestone when bigotry and indifference are overcome and replaced with compassion and understanding. This was recently done in the series 'Homosexuality' by Andy Praschak....The series of articles proved for the most part interesting because it chose not to be overtly partisan but acted as a sounding board to show an element of society that exists today but has always been ignored in the past in hopes that it would disappear....While to many of the student body the topic of the series may not seem worthy of being printed in the newspaper I can bet you that more newspapers were taken home and read than usual. I know that they were read because there were numerous discussions throughout the campus concerning the articles. It was very helpful for those of us who are caught up in an identity crisis.[9]

In the series, Dr. Sheridan McCabe, director of the Notre Dame Counseling Center, stressed that no gay person had approached the center complaining of persecution on campus. Referencing Dr. Charles Kinsey's 1949 report stating that approximately 5 percent of America's male population were practicing homosexuals, Dr. Charles Arens, acting director of ND's Psychological Services Center, placed the potential number of gay people on campus at around four hundred — slightly more than the number of female students in coeducation's first year. He also noted that same-sex attraction was no longer considered an illness by the American Psychiatric Association but, rather, an alternate lifestyle.[10]

Well-respected university chaplain Father Griffin described the school's atmosphere as less open than that of other schools, due in part to the religious conservatism of the Midwest. He also acknowledged homosexuality as a complex, human condition about which students needed to learn more. He acknowledged the difficulty of speaking publicly on this topic, concluding:

gay rapping

Editor:

We are a group of gay Notre Dame students, who are interested in gathering together, to discuss our mutual experiences and problems. We are aware of the great difficulty that oftentimes faces an individual, when he begins to confront his own sexuality, and his overall identity. Considering the prevalent social taboos that presently exist at Notre Dame, we feel that it would be beneficial, if we joined together and exchanged ideas and views, in private atmosphere. Within the confines of this group, we hope to offer acceptance and encouragement, to all who are interested. It should be stressed that we are a private group, and have no intention of becoming involved in any sort of public movement. We recognize the dangers of notoriety, and we choose to find strength within ourselves, rather than to try to force our views and life-style upon society.

signature withheld on request
Any person within the N.D.-S.M.C. community interested in participating in group discussions or meetings, may write to:

GAY AWARENESS (G.A.)
care of The Observer
Post Office Box Q
Notre Dame, Indiana 46556

Any information received will be kept strictly confidential.

The Observer, March 12, 1975

> You must be careful not to make any irresponsible statements about the nature of a sexual problem that I and others can never fully understand....At the same time, I want to be sensitive to the gay person who is working out sexual problems for which there are not a lot of established guidelines.[11]

Father Griffin's comments had an impact, as David Pais recalled:

⬦ *David Pais, ND 1972:* "The first time I remember a mention of 'homosexuality' at Notre Dame was an article in *The Observer*.

227

I think it was in Father Griffin's weekly column. The gist of it, if I remember correctly, was someone went to Griff for support counseling because he was gay. Griff wrote a beautiful, supportive, caring response."

The university faced a long road to understanding and accepting members of this community. In March 1975, a student submitted a prayer for homosexuals for inclusion in *The Notre Dame Prayerbook*. The latter's editors decided not to publish the submission, but they did have it published in *The Observer*.[12] With interest on the topic gaining speed, Campus Ministry hosted a "Christian and Gay" panel in April. At the discussion's conclusion, Dr. Morton Kelsey, an education professor, encouraged attitude changes toward homosexuality, stating: "As I understand Jesus Christ, it was his acceptance of people that brought them to a life of love."[13]

While the topic did not go dormant during the 1975–1976 academic year, *The Observer*'s coverage of LGBTQ issues on campus was minimal. It did, however, print reactions to a September 8, 1975, cover article on homosexuality in *Time* magazine. *Time*'s seven-page article surveyed the political and social activities of the gay community, emphasizing cultural changes since its own groundbreaking 1969 story on the beginnings of the gay movement. Several members of The Gay Students of Notre Dame, now in its second year of operation, saw the article's conclusions as absurd. In response to *Time*'s statement that passing civil rights for gay people would undermine the accepted family structure, one member of the ND group responded that "psycho-social evidence consistently reveals that human sexuality preference [begins] possibly by the age of five, probably by the age of six, but definitely by the age of seven. We cannot 'create' more gay people; we may, however, help those who already experience a homosexual preference to find themselves."[14] Don Reimer, the author of *The Observer* article, added that "The Gay Students of Notre Dame indicated that this quest for personal identity was precisely the function of their organization" and invited those who wished to receive further information to write to a post office box.[15]

In March 1976, Cliff Dearagon shared his campus experience as a gay person in *The Observer*.[16] For the next month, letters to the editor presented arguments

My Lord and Brother,
I am going to accept my own personal sexual orientation.
This is the way I am--so be it!
As a member of a despised monority
I am tempted to despise and deny myself.
Help me to think as positively as possible about myself
And about my future as a sexual being.
In a mainly heterosexual world I will often be lonely and out of it.
Don't let me accept isolation and defeat but teach me to look for friendship and support
where and when I need it.
Your love is unfailing;
be my Teacher and Guide as I search for love
and for appropriate expressions of my own sexuality.
You alone, Lord Jesus,
are the Way, the Truth and the Life.

The Observer, March 12, 1975

against same-sex attraction, some even responding in the context of Pope Paul VI's *Humanae Vitae*, the 1968 encyclical on contraception and other human rights topics.[17]

Even with the increasing coverage and discussion of LGBTQ issues on campus, ND was still far from being an open, inclusive place for members of that community.

> ◇ *Jack Bergen, ND 1977:* "Life for someone gay at ND was difficult. Imagine trying to date someone of the same sex, nevertheless be in a 'relationship' with them. If one were to enjoy the company of their own sex, it was often done off campus and away from other students; any community and support structure was hidden. You had to be underground and invisible. If you were outed, you would be scorned by your dorm mates and sometimes considered a pariah by some on campus.
>
> "Many at ND who later came out as gay did not have a clue. Being brought up in a typical Catholic family, you went to a good college, got married, and had kids. Nowhere along this journey was there a gay role model for a same-sex attraction. On campus, the few students who displayed 'flamboyant' behavior were often theater or architecture majors. Their behavior was written off as 'one of them.' To this day, the Film, Television, and Theatre Department remains one of the most inclusive and welcoming places on campus."

Still, as time passed, LGBTQ students on campus found ways to explore their identities.

> ◇ *Mike Gorman, ND 1981:* "As a young student (1976–1981), Notre Dame was a positive and also difficult place for a young, exploring gay man. My collegiate seminar professor, who happened to be the assistant dean of the College of Arts and Letters, was influential in assisting me with accepting my sexual orientation and Catholicism. She was a wonderful human being who guided me in my discovery of myself through the reading of the 'great books' — Notre Dame liked to use that term. I cannot thank Notre Dame enough for removing a great deal of guilt from my life. At the same time, you still had to hide; it made life easier. This is why I spent my senior year in Japan as part of my five-year program. Living in Japan allowed me to be on my own without 'in loco parentis.' ND having the program in Japan was another way the university assisted my gay development.

"Some of my best friends came from my years at Notre Dame and include both straight roommates and gay friends. I look back on my experience with pride and a feeling of enjoyment. I would definitely go back and do it again."

ARC ND—or the Alumni Rainbow Community of Notre Dame—is an Alumni Association group for ND LGBTQ alumni and allies. Officially launched in January 2022, ARC ND replaces GALA-ND/SMC, an unofficial gay and lesbian alumni group that was formed in 1996.[18]

The debate on same-sex attraction is still raging, not only at Notre Dame but also other universities. At a March 1998 session in ND's Center for Continuing Education, Hesburgh expressed his opinions on human rights as related to race, religion, and sexual orientation: "I don't think anyone ought to be discriminated against if it's not under your control. I happen to believe (sexual orientation) is more biological, but we don't know enough about that yet."[19] (For a brief history at ND, see the "The Open Road" in the appendix.).

◇◇◇

REARVIEW REFLECTION I learned two important lessons in college: never be afraid to say "I don't know" or "I need help." Both came into play as I worked on this book and contemplated diversity on campus during the 1970s. I never considered what individuals with a same-sex orientation faced within the Notre Dame culture. The one time I saw two guys kissing during a party in one of the male dorms, I naïvely thought they were just horsing around. Since I never consciously acknowledged color, ethnicity, religious, or economic differences when I was younger, I knew little of their impact on our ND experience. It was only through reaching out to the ND community for help that I could include this topic as part of a memoir on those transformative years.

As a young college student, I never suspected that the emerging social discussion on sexual orientation would touch my family. My younger sister, Gina, joined our family when I was a thirteen-year-old eighth grader. From the day Mom told us about "the birds and the bees," I prayed the rosary every night for a baby sister. I was so excited about the prospect of a sister that I paid little attention to the technical details shared that day.

My prayers were answered, and Gina arrived; Mom even let me name her. I loved her from the day she was born, but it took many years for me to understand her. No matter how hard I tried, she refused to play with dolls, wear dresses, or sit quietly when I read to her. However, she and our brother Doug developed a special relationship despite the ten years between them. Doug taught her how to play basketball and ride a bicycle. He helped her with tennis and encouraged her love of popcorn and 7-Eleven Slurpees.

We did grow closer as we grew older. I visited her at Penn State and met her future partner; at the time, I thought they were simply good friends and roommates. Not until they had a baby did I comprehend that they are a couple. Unlike my own marriage, their relationship is strong, and they have many shared interests.

Although we have talked every day since the loss of our parents and Doug, it took writing this chapter for me to ask Gina about her sexual orientation. After sending a draft to her, I could not wait to hear her thoughts, especially since she has a PhD in psychology. As we talked about the material, I realized that we had never openly discussed this part of her life. During our conversation, I asked Gina if she ever told our mom that she is gay. A long silence on the phone made me think I had offended her. When her response finally came, it made my heart ache: "No, I was afraid she would love me less." I asked her if that was why she had kept her commitment ceremony from the family and, in particular, from me. Sadly, she answered yes.

When I first began this social history, I expected that recalling experiences at Notre Dame would provide me with insights into many of my life decisions. Never did I expect this chapter to add understanding and depth to my relationship with Gina—my sister, my best friend.

Taking the Scenic Route

University of Notre Dame Stadium
Art by Barbara O'Connell (2011)

"[T]here are great complementary energies in all of us, whatever our ages," wrote Sister Jean Lenz in her memoir of Notre Dame, "and...as long as we live, we have deep powers to influence each other as men and women."[1] Sharing interests in a variety of venues alleviated some pressures of collegiate life and blurred the problems resulting from a lopsided male–female ratio. Through athletic and social events, students discovered and forged friendships and relationships. Special interests and volunteer activities also brought together those with similar service and career aspirations.

Sun in Our Eyes

"If you could find a way to bottle the Notre Dame spirit," so said Notre Dame and Washington Redskins (now Washington Commanders) football great Joe Theismann, "you could light up the universe."[1] Despite the less-than-optimal conditions for women on or off the field, most looked forward to Notre Dame's crown jewel — the first home football game of the season. Football Saturdays were (and are) a spirit-filled tradition, embraced by students, alumni, and parents alike. As the university community increasingly included women and minorities, the ND mystique continued to be palpable — though changing — during these multigenerational gatherings of people who love ND and those who came just for the game. Students, worried all week about academics, could take a break from studying and meet alumni and hear stories linking their Notre Dame pasts to their professional futures. For the women, these Saturdays also offered firsthand experience in dealing with prevailing alumni views of coeducation.

◇◇◇

In the fall of 1972, the Irish played one away game before the first home game against Purdue University. The pregame activities heightened the students' spirits, as captured by Sister Jean:

> The sporting events are hardly the only things that take place on campus during a game day. A weekend *Program of Events* guides fans to the right time and place for a glee club concert, a drama production, a Folk Choir program, or possibly an Emil T. Hofman Lecture.[2]

Most football weekends started on Thursday nights, with local bars promising cheap drinks and even cheaper beer. On campus, the Alumni Club, commonly known as Senior Bar, hosted an unofficial pep rally that included characters such as the "Knaked Klunker." After taking over the 1916 structure previously

235

occupied by the Faculty Club, the bar opened in January 1969 with seniors as "employees." It continued operating in that format until it closed in 1982.[3]

Freshmen were not yet legally old enough to buy liquor in Indiana, but nothing prevented them from standing outside the 1916 structure and enjoying the alcohol-induced antics. Males and females alike benefited from the alumni who walked through the crowd and shared their beers or boilermakers honoring Purdue's moniker.

Male residence halls came alive with student-painted banners and sheets; the women's dorms soon joined in this long-standing tradition as well. Varying in size, the messages captured game-related taunts. Visiting alumni and parents with younger teenagers probably had to answer questions about some of the signs' meanings. Jo Lund Chamberlain recalled one of the more memorable ones.

◇ *Jo Lund Chamberlain, ND 1976:* "'Toto, I don't think we're in Kansas anymore.' Our sophomore year, we played against the University of Southern California (USC) the week before we played the Naval Academy. Following tradition, many dorm rooms hung bedsheets with painted messages as banners to support our team. Before the USC game, many signs caused more snickers and whispers than usual. Rumors abounded that Father Hesburgh had walked the campus with a grim face and demanded the removal of the signs before Saturday. The only one I specifically remember said, 'Break the Trojans, bring on the Seamen.'

"Well, I did not understand all the fuss. What did these signs say that caused such a stir? Finally, my resident assistant, Maryann, sat me and another girl down and explained the alternate meaning of 'Trojan.' At that time, I understood about condoms and their intended purposes; I even knew people sometimes called it a 'rubber.' I was, however, unfamiliar with the brand name."

The "Knaked Klunker" performed at Senior Bar but was most visible in the stadium. In October 1973, Father Terry Lally, the assistant dean of students, requested Ed "Knaked Klunker" Klunk to stop performing his third-quarter striptease. Responding to alumni comments that the act was in bad taste, Lally stressed that attendees came to see the game, the band, and the cheerleaders...and not Klunker's act. Klunker ended this short-lived tradition and his seven-game streak, stating in *The Observer,* "I think the university has been stripped of one of its bare essentials."[4]

To get into the spirit, students watched the ND film favorite, *Knute Rockne, All American*, in Washington Hall. Campus lore claimed that the ghost of George Gipp, a key player for Rockne, lived in that very building and made his presence known on football weekends. Today's players recall his story each time they dress in the locker room where a bronze plaque memorializes Rockne's words to "Win one for the Gipper."[5]

Before the school's official pep rally on Friday, Emil T. Hofman hosted a barbecue as an introduction to the weekend's traditions. He encouraged freshmen to have a good time, while reminding them that Monday would arrive whether they wanted it to or not. He subtly suggested, "Don't drink too much!"

The pep rally for this first home game started with the Notre Dame Marching Band playing the "Victory March" at 6:45 p.m. in Stepan Center. Students followed the band from the main steps of the Administration Building to Stepan Center, escorting the players, the cheerleaders, the leprechaun, and a group of burly nonathletes known affectionately as the "Meat Squad." In all the craziness, most students paid little attention to the sidewalks. Some missed the metal wires meant to keep participants off the grass and fell flat—even before consuming any alcohol.

Stepan Center
Art by Barbara O'Connell (2016)

Jammed into Stepan, everyone listened as Coach Ara Parseghian, accompanied by cocaptains Greg Marx and John Dampeer, pumped up the crowd. The women danced the Irish jig, while adding the words "and daughters march" to the fight song. In the years since, ND women have championed a formal change to the song to reflect the total student population beginning with that the first football weekend in 1972:

> What though the odds be great or small
> Old Notre Dame will win overall
> While her loyal sons *[and daughters march]* ~~are marching~~
> On~~ward~~ to victory!

After fifty years, that dream became reality at Notre Dame's celebration of coeducation in June 2022.

On Saturday, students woke to Rockne's voice booming his "Gipper" speech from numerous dorm windows. Halls unlocked their doors early to allow alumni to see their old rooms and share stories of living there. The women's dorms became stops for former male residents who wanted to see how the females had changed their rooms.

◇ *Marylu Iredale Ernzen, ND 1976:* "One of the last football Saturdays of my freshman year, there was a knock on the door of my single room in Walsh around 11:00 a.m. When I opened it, I saw three guys standing there. They scanned my room with its rocking chair and teddy bear. I naïvely asked who they were. One answered, 'It was our room last year.' When I asked which one of them had the room, they replied in unison, 'All of us — it was a triple.' I felt dumb — sensitivity was the lesson there!"

◇ *Jeanine Sterling, ND 1976:* "The morning of our first football Saturday brought a whole new round of scrutiny. My roommate and I bounded out of Badin's side door on our way to breakfast at South Dining Hall. Two steps out the door, we realized we were surrounded by older alumni and their wives who had stationed themselves right outside our entrance to see 'the girls' emerge. I remember none saying anything particularly welcoming. We bolted through the crowd and wondered yet again what in the heck had we gotten ourselves into."

◇ *Melanie Connell, ND 1976:* "I lived in Badin my freshman year. What I remember clearest about those first games was the total lack of privacy on the mornings of the games. When the door unlocked before 9:00 a.m., alums who had lived in Badin started coming in to show their families where they lived while at ND. Woe to you if the alum lived in your room! Too many times to count, the alum just walked into the room without knocking! We learned that either we got dressed early or we locked the door so at least they didn't surprise us."

The ND Fighting Irish Leprechaun is a five-foot-tall, redheaded, bearded student in a cutaway green suit and Irish country hat who is chosen annually at student tryouts. The leprechaun brandishes a shillelagh and interacts with the spectators. Iconography of the leprechaun caricature shows him with his fists balled up, ready to battle anyone in his way. Once depicted with a bottle of whiskey by his foot and smoking a pipe, alcohol and cancer awareness led to the removal of both. The first leprechaun took to the football field in 1961 to bring good luck to the team after several dismal seasons, becoming a registered university trademark in 1965.

Walking to breakfast, students enjoyed whiffs of aromatic smoke from sausages, hot dogs, and hamburgers grilling at almost every sidewalk intersection. *The*

Observer published a list of authorized hall-sponsored stands that funded social activities and charitable projects throughout the academic year. The Knights of Columbus Hall also sold steak sandwiches for those with more discerning taste (and fatter wallets), and its queue often intersected the line of shoppers waiting to enter the bookstore.

Students and fans alike spent a good portion of the day wandering around the bookstore while enjoying the sounds of bagpipes wafting across campus. Upon entry, they quickly cleared every shelf and rack, buying T-shirts, jerseys, and any other ND-monogrammed items. Unlike the variety of retail choices today, the university-operated Hammes Bookstore was the only option available. Romy and Dorothy Hammes underwrote its construction at the center of campus, where it remained until 1999. This building, costing two hundred fifty thousand dollars and dedicated on September 23, 1955, contained general merchandise on the first floor — including, in the fall of 1972, recently added feminine hygiene products, Midol, and pantyhose — with student textbooks on the second level. Originally, it also held ten bowling lanes and Gilbert's men's store.[6] Although it was easier to access during the week, everyone usually found a reason to spend time in the bookstore on football weekends.

After grabbing something to eat and making the requisite bookstore purchases, many headed to the Grotto. Walking by Corby Hall (the priests' residence near Sacred Heart) and heading down the path toward the lake and its ever-present swans and ducks, most took pictures of the Father Corby statue with his raised right hand. Although meant as a reminder of Corby blessing the Union troops before the Battle of Gettysburg, it was better known by its nickname "Fair Catch Corby."

Eventually, the music in the dorms stopped (along with the various alum visitations), and game attendees hurried to their seats to see the Irish Guard and band enter the stadium. Those not attending the game reveled in the peace that enveloped the empty campus — all the hubbub now ensconced in the stadium. These students used this time to catch up on their studies, enjoy other pastimes, or just relax.

> ◇ *Roxanne Jabba Gunther, ND 1976:* "Four of us architecture students decided to play golf, two boys, two girls. As we were putting on a green near the road where cars parked for the game, two men came up to the fence and watched us. They eventually asked when we were going to the game; we replied that we were not going. They were obviously alumni because that set them off. One man said, in his day and age, everyone had to attend the games and students would not consider missing a home game. The other said, and I quote, 'I guess that's what happens when you let women in.'"

Molly Kinder, a 2001 ND grad, served as the first female member of the Irish Guard before the university removed the height requirement. Eliminating the height requirement in 2014 allowed more females to participate, since only two women had previously qualified. Experience as a musician or manager in the marching band replaced the open tryouts for the positions. Band Director Kenneth Dye wanted to "make the Guard an integral part of the band" and establish the guard as "a leadership position" for seniors, similar to the drum major.[9]

Not all guard members and alumni welcomed these changes. They expressed concern in letters to the university and to Dye: "With three to four years of experience, the traditional Irish Guard performed with military precision....With the height requirement, stature, and posture, it presented a most imposing sight. To create resume builders for a small number of Band members hardly justifies the destruction of a Notre Dame football tradition."[10]

On this particular September Saturday, as the Notre Dame band entered its 127th year, eight new female members marched with the previously all-male ensemble. These women underwent the same rigorous audition process as the men. In all the publicity surrounding this historic change, the 117 male members made it clear that they held no resentment toward their new female colleagues. Yet *The Observer* still posed the question: "A new addition to Irish tradition...but how will they look in uniforms?"[7] Band President Jerry Baker recalled that the women marching with the band "do just as well, if not better, than some of the guys."[8] The band, ironically with only a few music majors, represented all colleges and fields of study at Notre Dame, Saint Mary's College, and Holy Cross College. It performed the "Victory March" and a program of selected songs during halftime. Its presence could be seen and heard all weekend: From Friday's pep rally and performing on the steps of both the Administration Building and the Architecture Building (renamed "Bond Hall" in 1997) to marching into the stadium on Saturday, the band, often accompanied by cheerleaders and the leprechaun, marched more than five miles by the end of every home football game.

The marching band entered the stadium led by the Irish Guard and the drum major—another tradition integral to the pageantry of Notre Dame football. H. Lee Hope, band director from 1942–1951, formed the Irish Guard precision marchers in 1949. He established a six-foot-two height requirement and auditions for these coveted positions.[11] In 1970, the university certified the plaid worn by the guard and the marching band as an original Irish design.[12]

Most freshmen took advantage of the university's gift of football tickets to its undergraduates. According to Don Bouffard, director of ticket sales: "Since the university gives it (the studetnt [sic] ticket) as a gift, we don't think the students should abuse the privilege."[13] Despite a policy prohibiting resale above face value, students sometimes scalped their tickets, with high-value games bringing in twenty-five to fifty dollars per ticket—a great deal of money in the 1970s. Enforcing this prohibition against scalping proved difficult, and the university eventually changed its once strict secondary market policy.

On September 30, 1972, game attendees—including those freshmen walking past the sideline planters filled with yellow mums and entering the stadium for the very first time—found themselves under slightly cloudy skies with an ideal football temperature of seventy-seven degrees, waiting for the 1:30 p.m. kickoff. The 59,075 in attendance sat on the stadium's original wooden bleachers. High on the top of the stadium's north side, flags of the game's competitors blew in the wind and drew all eyes toward *Touchdown Jesus*, the mural gracing the front of Memorial Library (renamed the Hesburgh Library in 1987). As fans stood, they removed their caps and sang "God Bless America" and the national anthem, with hats and hands over hearts. The student section stood for most of the game, joining the cheerleaders in firing up the crowd, cheering as Eric Penick ran more than one hundred yards against Purdue and booing the competition—not a tradition supported by everyone in the stands. After a touchdown, students lifted other students (mostly

Notre Dame Stadium opened in 1930 with fifty-four thousand seats, expandable to sixty-one thousand with temporary bleachers. In 1966, its capacity increased to 59,075 by reducing seat width from 18 inches to 17 inches; 1997 renovations increased capacity to more than eighty thousand. The 2017 renovation, known as Campus Crossroads, attached academic-related buildings to three sides of the stadium and reduced seating to 77,622.[14]

Inside the stadium, the field aligns north–south, providing fans with a view of the library's *Touchdown Jesus* mural. The stadium's playing surface changed to artificial turf in 2014 after 84 seasons on natural grass. Each end of the field includes nine lines, totaling eighteen, positioned at a forty-two-degree angle equating to 1842, the year Father Sorin founded the university. The lines slant toward the Golden Dome and the Basilica of the Sacred Heart.[15]

241

females) off their feet, with screams of "Pass them up!" Those balanced on hands in the air "surfed" across the crowd, while others near the top of the stadium shouted out threats of "Over the wall!"

Historically, the press recognized ND's student body as the "twelfth player" on the field; their excessive noise made the stadium one of the toughest places for a visiting team to play. Friends met under the bleachers at halftime and learned that nothing tastes better than a cold Coke and a hot dog. At the end of every third quarter, Sergeant Tim McCarthy (1931–2020), an Indiana State Trooper, would come across the public address system with a measured, "May I have your attention, please."[16] He gave safety advice—laden with a heavy dose of humor—for those anticipating a drive home: "You won't be taken to the cleaners if your driving is spotless," "Driving half lit is not very bright," or "If you drive like lightning, you might crash like thunder!"[17] Fans laughed and looked forward to his message at every home game.

> ◇ *Darlene Palma Connelly, ND 1977:* "My father died in 2019 before the football season began. A Morris Inn menu from the ND versus Navy game of November 3, 1973, my freshman year was among his papers and went unnoticed until I sat down to see if he kept anything related to ND. Aside from a few of my letters, the only piece of ND memorabilia in his mountains of paper was that menu, a reminder of our weekend.
>
> "He rooted for ND during that game and until the day he died. ND's record in 2019 was 11–2. Without taking any credit away from the team and its coaches, I am confident my dad's cheering from the heavens played a minor role."

In the 1970s, games started earlier in the day, allowing fans to go to dinner, attend Mass, or nap before the postgame events. Bands usually performed in

Stepan Center or in the ACC where tickets cost three dollars or an extravagant five dollars and fifty cents for floor seats. At that first concert in the fall of 1972, attendees listened to Chicago's newest release, "Saturday in the Park," and earlier hits such as "25 or 6 to 4," "Color My World," and "Does Anybody Really Know What Time It Is?" Afterward, some went to see the ND interlocking logo recreated in mums at the entrance of campus; others ended the night with ice cream and a walk around Saint Joe's Lake.

> ◇ *Stephen Klug, ND 1976:* "I never attended a Notre Dame game, so my first home game weekend was quite memorable. My

hometown honey (HTH) flew in for the weekend, and I snuck her into my Grace Hall room. Little did I know that Grace became coed for every home game! The upperclassmen arranged one bathroom on each floor for female visitors, with guards standing by in the mornings.

"With housing covered, I got a student ticket for my girlfriend from a dorm mate and borrowed a student ID required with the football ticket and for entry into the dining hall. The student ID was a temporary ID (no photo) that a friend got when he lost his ID. Many of us used that ID throughout the fall.

"Sitting in the stadium for the first time, I joined in the passing up of students with each score. Just before the end of the third quarter, I heard my first 'traffic announcement.' This unforgettable weekend ended with a fantastic concert."

◇ *Pat Sarb, ND 1976:* "My high school sweetheart, Lynda, my wife since 1974, drove to campus for the first 1972 home game in her 1964 Ford Galaxy. Two Walsh Hall friends and fellow 1976 classmates invited Lynda to stay with them that weekend. Although disappointed I did not make the game-day 'dress' squad, I happily arranged for Lynda and me to sit together in the stadium. My beautiful girlfriend in her hot pants and tight blouse not only garnered male students' attention but also showed the females on campus that I was taken!

"That Sunday we went to Mass in the basilica. My mom's brother and his wife, who lived near campus, just happened to sit behind us. They called my parents to tell them they saw me in church and met my girlfriend. Later that week, my dad ran into Lynda's mom and shared the 'exciting' news. Since our parents did not know about Lynda's ND trip, two newly independent college freshmen got in trouble for going to Mass on a football weekend."

◇◇◇

REARVIEW REFLECTION For me, this first home game connected my past — as a child from Vetville who dreamed of attending ND — to my present as a student going to a football game.

In truth, I enjoyed the peripheral activities more than standing in the stadium. I attended the pep rally the night before the game with my roommate Beverly, and then we went to watch the fireworks together. My parents never took me to see such displays, so this first experience is a vivid memory. My chills had nothing to do with the sixty-degree temperature.

Room 409, Lyons Hall (1974–1975)

Afterward, campus lamplights illuminated our path back to Walsh. We veered off course to catch a glimpse of some one hundred students in the stadium — including SMC and ND women — repainting the team's gold helmets for Saturday's game. Volunteers applied different blends of gold dust, lacquer, and lacquer thinner depending on the weather. The helmets — like the student body — were ready for the game.

For future games, I often gave my ID and student tickets to male friends with visiting girlfriends. I preferred the buzz of tailgates and pre-kickoff quad activities and then later listening to the roar of the crowd from my favorite spots on campus — the Grotto, the view from Saint Joe's Lake, or in Father Miceli's Cavanaugh room, drinking his grappa and watching the game on his black-and-white television.

Only one other football weekend as a student stands out in my memory. A special guy at the time invited me to meet his parents at a pregame tailgate — again, a game against Purdue. He warned me that jeans would be inappropriate and strongly suggested a skirt in a color to complement a yellow mum corsage. Such advice surprised me for a "tailgate" invitation, but it reminded me of the prevailing sexist male attitudes.

Given the tight restrictions for driving on campus during football weekends, my next shock was him parking his car behind my dorm when he picked me up at my room. We took Highway 31 (now 933) to the Ramada Inn, one of the few hotels in South Bend considered acceptable in the 1970s. The "tailgate" was held in a ballroom, complete with a hosted buffet and open bar. A little intimidated, I drew on my experiences with similar gatherings from my life back home and tried to relax. Always a (soon-to-be) project manager at heart, I expressed concern to my date as game time approached; he told me not to worry "my pretty little head." Shortly thereafter, everyone headed to their cars. A police escort ensured that we arrived at the stadium just in time for kickoff.

Unfortunately, I failed the parental approval test. I never heard from him again, except for the flowers that arrived the following Tuesday with a card, "Thanks for the memories."

That same season, I answered a knock on my door in Lyons Hall to find several men standing outside in the hallway. One stated that my room was his when he was a student in the early '70s. I invited him in, along with his friends, so he could see how my roommate and I had decorated his former abode. He was pleased to see that we left in place the wall constructed to subdivide the sitting and sleeping areas.

In the years since I graduated from college, returning to Notre Dame and attending the football games created wonderful memories. Most of these were with classmates, but some were with family. In 2008, as my mom battled terminal cancer, she asked to see my second home in South Bend. While Dad attended the game with friends, Mom and I sat on my patio where we could hear the roar of the crowd and the band playing in the distance. She laughed as I picked dandelions, remarking, "Only at Notre Dame could such a miracle happen." It was her way of acknowledging I never liked gardening or sitting outside.

Mom passed in May 2010. Thinking that a football game in comfortable surroundings might

Mom and Dad at Notre Dame

help Dad as he processed his grief, my Development Office contact Tom Molnar arranged press box tickets for us. Throughout the game, Dad tried to act happy, but his smile was forced. As I wheeled him to the elevator after the game, he mumbled, "Debi, this was nice, but I missed sitting in the stands. The band didn't sound the same through the glass. Next time, let's just sit with everyone else."

There was not a next time for Dad. On New Year's Eve 2011, I sat with my father when he was in the hospital, and we watched college football on TV in the room. With his death imminent, I asked him if he could let me know that he was okay after he passed. My dad never put much stock in such conversations. Most likely his response came from watching the games.

He indulged me, merely saying, "Little girl, you will know that I am okay if Notre Dame goes 10–2 this coming season. If ND goes 11–1, I am with your mother, and we both are okay. And, if I think you are doing the job I expect of you, Notre Dame will go 12–0." My father passed away in February 2012. Notre Dame went 12–0 that fall. My mistake lay in forgetting to ask Dad about the bowl game. We played Alabama for the BCS National Championship in Miami, Florida, losing 42–14. I will never know what message he sent with that loss!

Did You See That?

Notre Dame and Saint Mary's students generally put aside their differences when the Irish faced any formidable athletic team—because, as contemporary romance writer Emma Chase points out, "the greatest part of a road trip isn't arriving at your destination. It's all the wild stuff that happens along the way."[1] For sports enthusiasts, the first five years of coeducation (1972–1977) were a sports fan's paradise filled with great moments. The shared excitement of cheering for the Fighting Irish and its varsity sports generated many opportunities for connections to flourish.

◇◇◇

As a Catholic university, Notre Dame students often came together on Sundays in chapels across campus. However, those assemblies paled in comparison to the student congregations on Saturday afternoons inside Notre Dame Stadium. Football devotees took welcome breaks from the academic grind to enthusiastically support their classmates on the field of play.

Students were in the presence of greatness every time they entered the stadium. Ara Parseghian, head coach of the Fighting Irish, was beginning his ninth season with one national championship and two near misses under his belt. His teams never lost more than two games in his first eight seasons, compiling a record of 66–12–4. After a disappointing 8–3 season in 1972, punctuated by a 40–6 loss to Nebraska in the Orange Bowl, everyone waited for Ara's magic to return.

The 1973 season opened with a 44–0 win at home against Northwestern, and the eighth-ranked Irish never looked back. The team put away Purdue, Michigan State, Rice, and Army to build a 5–0 record, yet it was still only ranked eighth as seven undefeated teams remained ahead of ND in the AP poll. The Irish faced the number-six Southern California Trojans as its next opponent.

In 1966, the year of ND's last national championship, the Irish handed the Trojans an embarrassing 51–0 defeat at the Los Angeles Coliseum. Following the game, John McKay, USC's head coach, is rumored to have vowed never to lose to ND again, and for the next six seasons, he went 4–0–2 against ND. Now, on an overcast and rainy October 27, 1973, afternoon, Southern Cal took on Notre Dame at ND's stadium—the forty-fifth meeting between the two storied programs—with a Trojan twenty-three-game undefeated streak (21–0–2) on the line.

Photos in this chapter courtesy of Pat Gleason and Ed Brower

The week leading up to the game was like none other. There was a quickness to everyone's step and a defiant look in people's eyes that screamed, "Beat the Trojans!" This wasn't just the football team squaring off against USC; this was something much bigger. Every student shared a common purpose—to smite this mighty foe. Every dorm hung banners from its windows, and even the most casual fans suddenly became ardent football fanatics.

After an early Irish lead, Southern Cal jumped ahead 7–3, with a one-yard touchdown run by ND archnemesis Anthony Davis. By halftime, the Irish reclaimed the lead 13–7. An eighty-five-yard touchdown run by tailback Eric Penick gave the Irish a 20–7 lead four minutes into the third quarter.

Fan participation, "the twelfth man on the field," was a foregone conclusion. During the action, as the rain steadily poured down, the ND student body—in unison—called on the one person most likely to forestall a likely quagmire: "Ara, stop the rain! Ara, stop the rain!" Almost miraculously, the rain stopped. After the game, the Notre Dame team acknowledged the boisterous support of 59,075 fans in the 23–14 defeat of USC:

> ◊ *Tom Clements, quarterback, ND 1975:* "They helped us a lot [and]…we felt as if we were playing for them as much as for anyone else."[2]

> ◊ *Eric Penick, tailback, ND 1975:* "The crowd made a 100 per cent difference….I love to play before our crowd, they make the biggest difference in the world."[3]

In *The Observer*'s lead article on the Monday after the game, even the USC head coach recognized the impact of ND's unified support:

> [A]s McKay faced his visitors, it was he who broke the spell of muffled silence. He broke it by humming a tune which had vibrated back and forth across Notre Dame Stadium many times during the afternoon: the Notre Dame Victory March. "There is," he told his surprised listeners, "nothing else to hum."[4]

With this win, the Irish moved up to number five in the AP poll, finishing the season with wins over Navy, Pittsburgh, Air Force, and Miami (Florida). With a 10-0 record and a number-three ranking, ND accepted an invitation to the Sugar Bowl in New Orleans. Only top-ranked Alabama (11-0) stood in the way of an undefeated season and a national championship.

On New Year's Eve, the Irish faced the Crimson Tide — an epic battle between coaching legends Ara Parseghian and Paul "Bear" Bryant. While number-one Alabama outscored its opposition 301-44 in eleven regular-season games, number-three Notre Dame was just as impressive with a 358-66 scoring edge in its ten games. Some dubbed the contest the "Game of the Century."

The 1973 Sugar Bowl lead changed hands six times. Compliments of Al Hunter's ninety-three-yard kickoff return, the largest lead was Notre Dame's 14-7 advantage during the second quarter, which Alabama reduced to 14-10 by halftime. During the game, the two teams combined for 738 total yards of offense, thirteen punts, two missed extra points (one for each side), and six turnovers (three for each side). Notre Dame prevailed, beating Alabama 24-23.

The Associated Press poll gave the number-one spot and the national championship to the undefeated Irish. It was the first time Notre Dame won

> Ara Raoul Parseghian (1923–2017), an American football player and coach, led Notre Dame to national championships in 1966 and 1973. He joins Knute Rockne and Frank Leahy as part of ND's "Holy Trinity" of head coaches. In 1980, Parseghian was inducted into the College Football Hall of Fame with a career coaching record of 170-58-6.
>
> Parseghian retired from coaching in 1974 and was an analyst and commentator on college football games for ABC and CBS. He dedicated himself to medical causes after his daughter's multiple sclerosis diagnosis and three of his grandchildren died from a rare genetic disease.[5]

eleven games in a single season, and this was its ninth national championship, the second under Parseghian. Shortly after the Sugar Bowl, Pat Sarb, a defensive back on this 1973 championship team, helped to seed the next great ND football team.

> ◇ *Pat Sarb, ND 1976:* "While still celebrating the '73 national championship, Ara and his staff had an extremely successful January 1974 recruiting weekend. Many visiting recruits signed letters of intent, including Joe Montana, Gary Forystek, and Terry Eurick. As members of Ara's last recruited class, they quickly became the nucleus of ND's 1977 national championship team.
>
> "As a scholarship player, I hosted Michigan high school standouts Terry Eurick and Terry Murphy that weekend. I took them

to an Alumni Hall gathering and introduced them to 'typical' students. The two Terrys sat with my fiancée, Lynda, and me at the UCLA game, along with some fifty thousand other fans who claim they were there! They later said [that] spending time in Alumni Hall and seeing ND beat the Bruins greatly influenced their decisions to come to ND."

The Irish launched the 1974 campaign sporting a number-two ranking but quickly moved up to number one after an opening victory against Georgia Tech. With seven straight wins after a loss to Purdue, fifth-ranked ND headed to Los Angeles to face six-ranked USC. Twenty-nine minutes into the game, the Irish built up a 24–0 lead over the Trojans. What followed was a gut punch best described by a *New York Times* article the next day:

> Scoring for the first time in the last 10 seconds of the first half, the Trojans went on to score 35 points in the third quarter and 14 more in the first two minutes of the fourth. In a span of 17 playing minutes, U.S.C. scored eight touchdowns against a team that was ranked No. 1 nationally in defense, and had yielded just nine touchdowns in 10 previous games.[6]

The loss dropped the Irish to number nine, with two losses and no chance of repeating its stint as national champions. The week following the disappointing loss to USC, students received a second gut punch even more debilitating than the first. After eleven seasons as head coach and the second-winningest coach in ND history up to that time, Ara Parseghian was stepping down. The Notre Dame family was losing its favorite relative.

Even an invitation to the Orange Bowl against number-two Alabama (11–0) was small consolation for what might have been. Notre Dame defeated Alabama 13–11 on January 1, 1975 — the second loss to ND in two years for "Bear" Bryant — shattering Alabama's championship hopes and ending the "Era of Ara." Parseghian walked away with a record of 95–17–4 and two national championships; he joined Rockne and Frank Leahy as the only ND coaches with multiple national titles.

Dan Devine replaced Parseghian, bringing experience and know-how to the collegiate level, but he lacked Ara's charisma. Devine's first season saw the Irish finish with a record of 8–3, the same as Ara's record in 1972. As seniors, the class of 1976 watched as sophomore Joe Montana rallied the Irish from a 30–10 deficit against Air Force to a 31–30 win with three fourth-quarter touchdowns. Devine later gained notoriety in the 1993 film *Rudy* as the Notre Dame coach who allowed Daniel "Rudy" Ruettiger to take the field in the waning seconds of the last home game of 1975 against Georgia Tech. Ruettiger, a member of the class of 1976, became famous for taking advantage of the moment and sacking the Yellow Jackets' quarterback.

Football was a key dimension to campus life and often at the core of social activities. Notre Dame's football record in the first five seasons of coeducation was 46–11: in the fall of 1972 (8–3), 1973 (11–0), 1974 (10–2), 1975 (8–3), and 1976 (9–3). Students also celebrated a national championship in that time frame. Those games provided some of the most unifying moments for the early coeducational pioneers and helped them to understand the ND mystique.

Compared to the reverence afforded football, basketball was a pleasant diversion for Irish fans. Basketball coach Digger Phelps, however, was determined to move the needle on the fan-o-meter from tepid to passionate. Digger's flamboyance in coaching, communicating, and clothing made him — and the Irish — hard to ignore.

Phelps led his first team (1971–1972) to a 6–20 season. The next season, Phelps achieved an 18–12 record and an invitation to the National Invitation Tournament at Madison Square Garden. Unfortunately, the Virginia Tech Hokies ended Notre Dame's bid with a one-point victory of 91–90 in overtime.

Undaunted, Digger's team had raised expectations for his third season. The 1973–1974 team, captained by Gary Novak and John Shumate, opened with twelve straight victories. The tenth victory in that streak, however, forever placed Notre Dame and Digger Phelps at the center of the college basketball map. Many of Notre Dame's first women witnessed it in person.

> Born on July 4, 1941, Richard Frederick "Digger" Phelps is a former American college basketball coach, most notably of the Notre Dame Fighting Irish. From 1993 to 2014, he served as an ESPN analyst. His nickname "Digger" came from his father, a mortician in Beacon, New York. During his twenty seasons at Notre Dame (1971–1991), Phelps' teams went 393–197 (.666), with fourteen seasons of twenty wins or more.[7]

January 19, 1974...for a ND basketball fan that date conjures up the frenzy of the final three minutes and twenty-two seconds of what some consider the greatest basketball game in Notre Dame history. It also brings to mind the number eighty-eight — as in the eighty-eight-game winning streak the UCLA Bruins brought into the ACC that surreal afternoon.

The UCLA Bruins had won every basketball game since January 23, 1971 — a span covering seventy-six regular-season games and twelve NCAA tournament contests. The Bruins won the NCAA national championship seven seasons in a row and were ranked number one coming into this first of two 1974 confrontations with second-ranked Notre Dame. No stranger to facing teams on a roll, the Irish was the team that last defeated the Bruins before its eighty-eight-game streak began. Notre Dame legend Austin Carr scored forty-six points in that battle, leading the Irish to an 89–82 triumph over UCLA and snapping a modest nineteen-game Bruins winning streak.

The stage was set for a battle between two undefeated top-ranked teams and two coaching opposites — UCLA's John Wooden, the sixty-three-year-old veteran with a calm demeanor, and Digger Phelps, the thirty-two-year-old budding showman. If the hype fazed the UCLA players, they never showed it; they closed the first half with a 43–34 lead and a 70 percent shooting effort. In the second half, Digger played his five "speed" guys — Gary Brokaw, Dwight Clay, Ray Martin, John Shumate, and Adrian Dantley — anticipating that UCLA's 70 percent shooting pace would return to earth. The Irish barely made a dent in the deficit throughout the second half, and the Bruins had a 70–59 advantage with three minutes and thirty-two seconds on the clock. Ten seconds later, Digger called a time-out to gather his team and separate the wheat from the chaff, telling his players: "If you don't think we can win, get out of here. Go shower right now."[8]

Only a Hollywood scriptwriter could have imagined what happened next. For the Irish to win, UCLA had to miss — and did — its last six shots and turn the ball over four times. Two fortuitous referee calls also went ND's way: one for traveling and an offensive foul on an easy layup. Notre Dame had to play flawlessly, which it did. Six-for-six from the field along with zero turnovers and no fouls — too unbelievable even for a blockbuster film.

Digger and Ara

A clutch shot from the corner by "The Iceman," aka Dwight Clay, is the most iconic image — from the most iconic game — in ND men's basketball. When asked about the game's impact on the students at that time, Digger later reflected that the "TVS Television Network, the brainchild of Eddie Einhorn, in its 'game of the week' concept captured the four thousand students [who] poured onto the court after the final buzzer. Once again, the student body became an important 'member' of the team and was instrumental to the team's success going forward."[9]

> ◇ *Mark Nishan, ND 1976:* "Fate sometimes places unsuspecting people in the right place at the right time to witness epic moments. As sophomores, Alumni Hall brother Tom Klein and I ended up in the upper bleachers of the ACC, slightly behind the basket, for the UCLA game. The Bruins and Bill Walton controlled the game until the last few minutes. We decided to stay to the end, giving us a 'front-row' view to history.

"As Notre Dame mounted its comeback, our poor seating at the ND end ironically put us in the perfect position to witness 'The Iceman' Clay's shot that put ND ahead. We were beside ourselves — hugging any girl in reach, getting hoarse, and just going crazy. Unfortunately, we were too far up to storm the court after ND's victory. At that moment, I thought life could not get any better…but it did. Such experiences built lifelong friendships that still sustain us fifty years later."

In the January 22 AP poll, Notre Dame and UCLA traded places — the Irish now ranked number one while the Bruins slipped to number two. Coupled with its football national championship just three weeks earlier, banners appeared across campus that read "God Made ND #1." For one brief shining moment — a week actually — the Irish sat atop the college sports world.

But as with many things in life, the students quickly learned the Lord giveth, and the Lord taketh away. The Irish finished the season 26–3 with a number-five ranking. During the next two seasons, the Irish never rose higher than that position despite records of 20–9 and 23–6. Digger's teams defeated top-ranked teams six more times before he retired — but none had the impact of that UCLA victory. Digger acknowledged this in a January 19, 2019, interview with the *Sporting News*:

> That game, for me, did more for college basketball.…This game to me had more drama than any other game as you look at that time and that moment for college basketball. This was the moment. I think that UCLA game was the first time the nation saw people storming the court.[10]

From the fall of 1972 through May 1977, the Irish basketball team won 110 games while losing only 38. But basketball games offered something more than just wins. Given the creative flair of

Dave Kelly as the Pink Panther

one student, Dave Kelly, students enjoyed the antics of a new mascot — the "Pink Panther" — at the games. Working with female classmates and the cheerleaders, Kelly enhanced the appeal of the games while demonstrating the value of such joint male–female activities, even if the joint activities were limited to fan participation.

When not attending football or basketball games, Notre Dame men frequently enjoyed interhall hockey late at night in the ACC. From a varsity perspective, the varsity ice hockey team opened its 1972–1973 season with a loss to the Bowling Green Falcons but soon delivered a home record of 12–3–0. After losing two December contests on the road to eventual national champion Wisconsin, the Irish returned the favor in late February with a pair of victories, 8–5 and 4–3, at home. That two-game series introduced an athletic controversy that continues to this day — seeing a sea of competitors' colors overshadowing ND's own. As nearly one thousand red-clad Wisconsin fans invaded the ACC to try to wipe out Notre Dame's home advantage, the red sea only served to rile up the Irish players and fans.

Such emotional outpourings, coupled with a great cast of characters, made following the ice hockey team so exciting. Notre Dame finished the season 23–14–1 overall, with a WCHA record of 19–9–0 — good for second place. The team's Rookie of the Year Award went to class of 1976 freshman Pat Novitzki, who became a team captain during his senior year. Yet over the next three seasons, the team never quite reached that same level of success. Still, many students continued to attend ND varsity and interhall ice hockey games.

> ◇ *Pat Novitzki, ND 1976:* "The 1972–'73 team was one of ND's best; we had great leadership and chemistry under Coach Lefty Smith. With a strong group of returning lettermen, only two spots were available on the twenty-man roster. I made the team as a penalty killer — right spot at the right time. Going into our sophomore campaign, we were rated number one. Given the Sugar Bowl win and a number-one ranking in football, followed closely by the UCLA win and a short-lived number-one ranking in basketball, it was a wonderful time to be a Notre Dame sports fan. Yet my most cherished memories reflect the camaraderie shared with teammates and ND '76 classmates Jimmy Augustine, Tim Byers, Dave Howe, Rick Martinello, Tom McCurdy, Mark Olive, and Tom Wurst and team manager Bob Keys."

Probably one of the least heralded championship sports at Notre Dame, fencing was and is one of its most successful programs. The Irish fencers boasted an impressive match record of 223–52 (.811) from 1934 through 1961. However, when Michael DeCicco became head coach in 1962, his teams compiled a stellar mark of 175–19 (.902) through its 1972 spring season. During the next four years, students saw the men's team attain an impressive record of 86–6 (.935). The team achieved a 26–0 mark during the 1976 season and finished third in the NCAA championship tournament in the 1975 and 1976 seasons. By the time the ND class of 1976 graduated, the team had won forty-four dual meets in a row. The following year, the women's fencing team gained varsity status in the 1976–1977 academic year, the same year that the men won their first national title.

Notable fencers included class of 1976 members Sam Difiglio and Mike Sazdanoff. Difiglio, a saber specialist and three-time monogram recipient, went 130–23 (.850) in his career, earning NCAA All-American honors in 1974 and 1975 and the Walter Langford Memorial Award recognizing sportsmanship, leadership, and teamwork in 1976. Sazdanoff ended his saber career with two monograms and a mark of 63–35 (.643).

◇ *Sam Difiglio, ND 1976:* "I spent my freshman year at Holy Cross Junior College practicing, but not competing, with the Irish fencing team. I transferred my sophomore year, fencing for ND in 1974, 1975, and 1976. With one more year of eligibility in 1977, Coach DeCicco offered me a half-scholarship to get my MBA and stay with his team. In retrospect, I wish I would have taken him up on it. The ND fencing team won the NCAA men's championship in 1977—had I stayed, I would have earned a national championship ring. Oh, the choices we make..."

Ultimately, for many ND students, sporting events were as much about the experience and the camaraderie as anything else. Recalling these events are highlights at any ND gathering.

◇ *Darlene Palma Connelly, ND 1977:* "Sporting events of any kind did not exist in my 'out in the boonies' all-girls high school. Arriving at Notre Dame in the fall of 1973, I expected I'd be going to Irish football games, even though I barely understood anything other than the purpose of the goal line and was not certain what the uprights were all about. Football tickets were free, but not so for other team sports. Had it not been for the women in the class of '76 who left South Quad to help with settling the wilderness of North Quad, I never would have attended either a basketball or a hockey game. Those wonderful women on the first floor of B-P convinced me to buy basketball tickets so that one of the taller women in the group could meet a basketball player she could look up to. They offered a different rationale when it came to ice hockey. While today I only occasionally follow Irish football and the women's basketball team—and still know little more about either game than I did forty-nine years ago—I shudder to think I almost missed out on the full Notre Dame experience."

◇◇◇

REARVIEW REFLECTION Winning was contagious, and as students we viewed "win overall" as more than just a lyric in the fight song. While football and basketball victories and seasons were well documented in the press, the background stories were often lost in the years before social media and the pervasive use of the internet. We missed out on capturing oral social histories as told by Ara Parseghian, Digger Phelps, Mike DeCicco, and countless others. We wanted the details behind Hesburgh and Joyce's decision to establish the first program in the country to ensure that our student-athletes graduated. Today, such personalized accounts are often captured through interviews with notables in the ND Monogram Club's newsletters. Members of the ND family, both males and females, not only revisit such narratives but also revel in the growing success of the university's women's athletic teams.

Pit Stops

"Life is a journey with problems to solve and lessons to learn," Mumbai author and lifestyle coach Divya Trivedi has commented, "but it is important to experience the joy."[1] In addition to attending athletic events, students went to hall parties and local bars for study breaks and, sometimes, to escape mystifying relationships. Just like pit stops for long-haul truckers, students paused at these venues for refueling or attitude adjustments. However, most "drivers" knew that too much time in a pit stop or too many libations when drowning their sorrows might affect the outcome of the "trip."

◇◇◇

Despite Indiana's legal drinking age of twenty-one, Notre Dame and Saint Mary's students of all ages found ways and locations to drink, both on and off campus. They chose from a variety of pit stops to escape the academic rat race, places both within walking distance and those requiring transportation to reach them: from residence hall parties or the one on-campus "watering" hole to favorite hangouts in Michigan just across the state line, where the drinking age was eighteen.

When the first women arrived in 1972, the university allowed parties in dorm rooms, a departure from other Indiana colleges that banned all undergraduate possession or use of alcohol. Notre Dame, with its city designation and own security force, permitted its undergraduates — regardless of age — to drink within its boundaries.

> ◇ *Jerry Welch, ND 1976:* "ND students studied hard but then partied even harder on the weekends."

> ◇ *Becky Banasiak Code, ND 1976:* "If you weren't into drinking, there weren't many social outlets on campus."

However, the university's alcohol policy changed several times during the first five years of coeducation, and students needed to stay abreast of it. Prior to September 1973, the rules allowed moderate drinking and parties in private rooms if they did not attract undue attention. That fall, however, Dean of Students John Macheca and the Student Life Council (SLC) issued new policies on drinking in public places. The guidelines, established by the Office of Student Affairs and approved by the SLC, prohibited drinking not only in residential hall communal areas but also in peripheral campus areas such as the stadium parking lots. Students viewed these restrictions as impacting their already limited social options; the administration felt this approach curbed social distractions and reinforced the university's mission of academic excellence. One anonymous student offered a perspective on this new policy:

◇ Anonymous, ND 1976: "Although the intent of the [alcohol] policy was to limit social distraction, those of us who didn't drink were forced to leave our rooms and study elsewhere when the music and noise from alcohol-fueled parties resonated in the halls and neighboring rooms. Driving the parties away from common areas with proper supervision actually placed our studying at risk."

In 1935, Indiana passed a liquor control act that only allowed retail whiskey sales in drugstores, the selling of beer and wine in restaurants, and a drinking age of twenty-one. The state prohibited all liquor sales on Sundays, holidays, and Election Day. Over time, package liquor stores sold warm beer (1953) and then cold beer (1963). In 1971, wine sales were permitted on Sundays, but not until 1973 could commercial establishments and clubs sell alcoholic drinks. The state lifted its ban on Christmas Day sales in 2015. In February 2018, Indiana finally allowed Sunday carryout sales from grocery, convenience, and liquor stores between noon and 8:00 p.m.[2]

This change still allowed gatherings for holidays, special events, or celebrations where the consumption of alcohol was not the primary objective. Each hall had its own interpretation of the guidelines, causing some dorms to develop well-deserved reputations as party centers. Such get-togethers required rector approval of all details: food, beverages, the number of invitees, and the date and time. When students held parties without preapproval, rectors notified the dean.

Obtaining alcoholic beverages and transporting massive quantities to the halls required creativity. Students covertly brought in beer (especially the ever-popular Coors beer, only available from Colorado in the 1970s), liquor, and wine. Entrance gate security seldom found the bootleg booze buried under groceries or blankets. Kegs were tougher, but they always showed up when needed.

During the actual events, resident assistants (RAs) periodically checked with the party's student sponsor. Working together, the sponsor and hall staff strove to meet the spirit and letter of the guidelines, disbanding gatherings when problems arose such as loud noise, too many attendees, or excessive consumption of beer or "wapatula" — a combination of grain alcohol or vodka, Tom Collins mix, fruit punch, and sliced fruit, often served from a large garbage can. Tom Young and his friends threw many such parties and recalled one particular "social experiment":

◊ *Tom Young, ND 1976:* "Our group took on the self-proclaimed moniker of 'F-Troop' as a tribute to the old TV show about a group of misfit Civil War soldiers. As such, we brought much mayhem to Cavanaugh Hall, long known as the nerd dorm. Occasionally, our antics drew the attention of the inimitable Father Matthew 'Black Matt' Miceli, the strong disciplinarian rector known campus wide. He was actually a caring priest who just needed someone to tease him to make him remove his pipe and evoke that 'penguin' laugh of his. We threw some well-attended and — by Miceli's standards — raucous parties, ending up on the same 'double secret probation' that *Animal House* residents suffered under Dean Wormer. Yet we still scheduled a big spring blowout. Concerned our housing privileges were in danger of revocation, especially as the room lottery approached, we conducted a 'social experiment' party.

"Instead of beer, we provided a potent punch — without either potency or punch. We told our guests that the fruit punch was spiked with vodka. As some partygoers started acting inebriated, our social experiment proved successful! When attendees discovered that we never added any alcohol, one irate partygoer argued in very slurred speech that, based on his buzz, it was impossible that he only drank fruit punch all night."

The drinking of alcohol was not just reserved to the residence halls. Students also availed themselves of the free food and drinks at alumni tailgates before football games. Given the policy change restricting drinking in the parking lots, students requested clarification from the administration to avoid sanctions. According to Dean of Students John Macheca, "Drinking in the parking lot is not a problem because no one is infringing on someone else, whereas, big parties in dorms can infringe on other's rights."[3] In this, Macheca justified the position as reflecting ND's interest in educating students both socially and academically and helping them to learn and mature.

Additional policy changes occurred when several legal cases — such as the April 1974 *Brattain v. Herron* decision of the Indiana Court of Appeals — emphasized the

"Where have all the drunkards gone? Gone from campus every one..."
The Observer, September 15, 1971

liability of institutions and individuals in providing and sanctioning the use of alcohol by minors.[4]

In the wake of such cases, the Indiana Alcoholic Beverage Commission (ABC) cracked down on beer and liquor promotions as well as advertising on state college campuses. Students received warnings about using fake identification when acquiring or consuming alcohol. Only those twenty-one or older drank without fear of reprisals. When these students held parties, they carded partygoers at the door in an attempt to avoid problems.

Based on the potential ramifications, the university realigned its alcohol policies to adhere to Indiana state laws. In a two-page statement to rectors and hall staffs, Macheca emphasized that the university's responsibilities included not only respect for the law but also the need to confront those who violated the rules. This directive reversed the previous year's guidelines that had allowed underage drinking in moderation. It outlawed parties for minors and outlined enforcement procedures, including a fifty-dollar fine for serious violations.

Senior Bar, circa 1974
Art by Barbara O'Connell (2011)

In the 1970s, only one establishment at Notre Dame sold liquor libations. Senior Bar, with its sign emblazoned "ND Alumni–Senior Club," occupied a 1916 two-story house sporting a slanted roof over the front entrance.[5] The building, previously known as Andre House, served multiple purposes before beginning its life as the Alumni Club and later Senior Bar: monastery, convent, faculty housing, and faculty club.[6] It was truly a place where "if the walls could talk, they'd tell a hell of a story." Seniors and girls from all classes partied within the sparsely furnished rooms. With the popularity of streaking and stripping, students sometimes strutted their stuff on the porch roof. Alumni willingly purchased a keg of beer or bought "drinks for the house." Discussions with alumni always proved enlightening for current students, especially as the former automatically labeled all the females present as Saint Mary's girls.

Because Senior Bar was on university property, underage drinking was not viewed as a problem until 1974 when Indiana tightened its legislation on alcohol consumption and expanded liability exposure. After that, as a student-operated establishment with alumni oversight, senior class officers and their "employees" checked IDs at the doors or at least had a process to do so. Students managed, bartended, and cleaned—the latter often depending on personal standards.

◇ *Phil Potter, ND 1975:* "Shortly after turning twenty-one, I started bartending and 'carding' at The Library bar on Notre Dame Avenue. However, as a senior, I wanted to work at Senior Bar, a grand, old two-story house flanked with tall, golden oaks. In those days, the owner of the house, the Notre Dame Alumni Association, left senior management alone in running the establishment. The old house was not too efficient in serving thirsty seniors, often reeking of stale beer, but it was *our* house. Football weekends saw classic coed celebrations often pushing the limits of its 2:00 a.m. closure. The 'Old Lady' is long gone, replaced by an efficient, soulless single-story building. A watercolor of the 'Grand Dame' in my family room keeps the crowds, music, and distinctive beer odor alive in my mind!"

Senior Bar antics (1976)

TONITE at the
SENIOR BAR
Especially for the Girls:
ICE CREAM NITE!
All Ice Cream Drinks 50¢
including:
- ★ Chocolate Dreams ★ Grasshoppers
- ★ Brandy Alexanders ★ Creamsicles
- ★ Golden Cadillacs ★ Pink Squirrels
- ★ Chocolate Soldiers ★ Velvet Hammers
   & many more!

21 ID Required.

We'll be open before and after Saturday's basketball game to celebrate the NCAA bid

Senior Bar hosted a variety of events for students. Wednesdays through Saturdays, it offered beer and drink specials priced just to cover expenses. The bar also sold affordable passes to students and alumni for repeat admission. Camaraderie abounded as students drank, conversed, shot pool, and played air hockey while listening to music. They spilled out onto the front lawn or enjoyed burgers cooked on open barbecue pits in the backyard.

◇ *Sally Naxera Benson, ND 1976:* "Wednesday nights at Senior Bar were special as we went out on a school night! I remember the guys always watching *Charlie's Angels* on TV and the whoops and hollers when Farrah Fawcett flipped her hair in slow motion. No one focused on the sexism of that moment — we simply enjoyed the fun and silliness of sharing the time together."

◇ *Darlene Palma Connelly, ND 1977:* "I knew little about football or ND's rivalry with Southern Cal. I soon learned Southern Cal was a fierce opponent, and nothing is sweeter than beating them. I remember three things from my first USC game, October 27, 1973: (1) We won, (2) I ended up at Senior Bar drinking as a freshman without a fake ID, and (3) I will never touch another tequila sunrise."

◇ *Shelley Muller Simon, ND 1976:* "I went to Senior Bar all four years and participated in annual canoe races, where canoes sat on the ground with cases of beer stacked in the middle. Participants perched uncomfortably on the side and raced to finish drinking the beer first. The rules stated you could go to the bathroom, but an escort ensured you did not throw up. I was a proud member of the championship team in the first all-female division."

Returning graduates can only relive those days in their memories. In 1982, the university razed Senior Bar, replacing it with a one-story brick establishment, Legends. In 2003, the latter became a restaurant and pub open to the public.

When wanting something different, students walked to an area known in the early 1970s as "Five Points" that was just 1.2 miles from campus. There, students

Five Points, circa 1974
Art by Barbara O'Connell (2011)

gathered at Corby's, Nickie's, or Bridget Maguire's Filling Station, moving from bar to bar through an unwritten progression somewhat linked to class year. The weather never deterred students from frequenting these nearby drinking establishments, complete with sticky floors, smoky hazes, overwhelming smells, and dubious restrooms. Students often met interesting locals while letting off steam and without worrying about others' opinions. Everyone went just a little crazy in these spaces, crammed during peak hours with sweaty bodies, as ND students escaped academic pressures and the long Indiana winters.

Senior "Death March" (1976)

To get into the bars, underage students either obtained fake identification cards or borrowed driver's licenses from older classmates, as bar owners and bouncers cursorily checked IDs. While minors using fake IDs faced minimal fines, owners could encounter significant penalties, a possible shutdown, or the loss of liquor and business permits. Owner liability diminished when bars began requiring patrons to produce three pieces of identification. Still, women were seldom rejected at any bar. In fact, Bridget's, a friendlier, less raunchy location, accepted residence hall Detex cards as IDs.

Nickie's offered decent burgers to absorb its ridiculously low-priced alcohol. Its lax approach to carding resulted in the arrest and booking of twenty-six students in April 1973. In a show of solidarity, approximately forty male and female students, along with Notre Dame and SMC hall representatives, joined together to raise bail money while waiting for the police to clear the streets.[7]

> ◇ *Joe Pusateri, ND 1976:* "I had a fake ID made by using an ND ID from the previous semester. I presented it to the bouncer at Nickie's, and he said, 'This is the *best* fake ID that I've ever seen!'...And he still let me in."

> ◇ *Shelley Muller Simon, ND 1976:* "My boyfriend played rugby and introduced me to the sport and all of its 'pageantry.' Rugby players loved to drink and to sing X-rated songs after their games. After one game with his family in town, he transported his father and me to a rugby party at Nickie's. I stood at the bar getting to know his father, pretending we did not hear his son singing raunchy songs with a beer balanced on his head."

Seniors and athletes hung out at Corby's. "Boots" Lange and fellow Corby's bartenders wore black shirts with "Corby's" emblazoned on the front. Its depraved décor included the Satin Doll and Wizard pinball machines and the dirtiest windows. At peak hours, individuals urinated in the sink, the toilet bowl, the toilet tank, and the ever-overflowing trash cans.

In October 1973, despite Corby's horrendous appearance, its regulars got "Busched" when Technisonic Film Studios and Gardner Advertising of Saint Louis, Missouri, chose South Bend along with Flint, Michigan, and Columbus, Ohio, as significant markets for their Busch Bavarian Beer. Corby's owner Joe Mell delighted in the day's turnout, the film's large crew of extras, and Busch sales taking the lead from Stroh's by nearly a two-to-one margin.

⬦ *David Szymanski, ND 1976:* "I recall seeing the parking sign outside Corby Hall [the priests' residence on campus] that read 'Corby Car' and thought it was a shuttle to the bar."

⬦ *Darlene Palma Connelly, ND 1977:* "Visiting Corby's in daylight was surreal. One afternoon, a day student whom I was dating suggested we play pinball at Corby's. Corby's physical flaws were painfully obvious in the absence of bodies, loud music, and beer. I was tempted to [retreat] back out the door, but the pinball machines beckoned—I swear I heard The Who singing "Pinball Wizard." Taking turns, we played one machine as if it were a priceless musical instrument. With no one bumping into me or spilling beer down my back, I took my score higher and higher, with extra plays on a single quarter. Definitely the best time I ever had at Corby's."

In 1988, students heading to Florida for spring break pulled into "Pit Stops" in Indiana, Tennessee, and Georgia. Anheuser-Busch created the idea, with state tourism and highway departments cosponsoring it.[8] At these Pit Stops, travelers were handed brochures about highway safety and responsible drinking, blood alcohol charts, and refreshments. According to Students Against Drunk Driving founder Bob Anastas, students are "very aware of what can happen to them....But they have to be reminded...that if you party, if you go off the deep end, death is lurking for you. These Pit Stops are the constant reminder they need."[9]

The Library on Notre Dame Avenue offered an alternative to the Five Points establishments. Originally called Frankie's, the venue's rebranding allowed students to tell parents about time spent at "the library." In 1977, the bar again changed ownership and its name. Surrounding homeowners objected to its continued presence and worked diligently to shut it down. The bar closed before the 1980–1981 academic year and eventually fell into disrepair. Today, it is a vacant lot filled only with memories.

◇ *Joseph Rominski, ND 1976:* "I was a bouncer at The Library. My folks were so proud of me when I told them I got a job at 'the library,' until I took them there after a game."

The more adventurous traveled farther from campus and even Five Points to The Linebacker. Nicknamed the 'Backer, its reputation as a place to experience groping, unpleasant body odor, and questionable cleanliness seldom deterred its regular patrons from indulging in its cheap offerings and loud music. It is the only remaining site from the 1970s for late-night bacchanals.

Students with cars or those willing to bum rides headed to Sweeney's with its *Cheers*-like atmosphere in South Bend. Frank O'Malley, one of Notre Dame's legendary professors, often drank with his students and discussed philosophy there. A classier and higher-end tavern, Sweeney's possessed a pool table and a bar that ran the length of the place. It sold the coolest white football jerseys with "Sweeney's" printed on the front in dark green lettering above a green shamrock. Sweeney's closed in 1976, departing along with ND's first class of coeds.

> *Cheers*, a television series on NBC, ran from 1982 to 1993. Set in Boston, Massachusetts, it focused on locals drinking and socializing at a bar named Cheers Beacon Hill. Its theme song, cowritten and performed by Gary Portnoy, added the show's catchphrase, "Where Everybody Knows Your Name" to American pop culture.

Another *Cheers*-like locale, Fat Wally's on State Road 23, touted the best burgers. During the 1970s, the waitress uniforms drew overly enthusiastic males more often than the burgers did.

◇ *Maggie Waltman Smith, ND 1976:* "I worked at Fat Wally's senior year. I hated waiting tables on quarter mixed drink night (Mondays). The only thing worse was waiting tables on dime beer night (Tuesdays). I subbed one Tuesday and said, 'Never again.'

"When I started working at Fat Wally's, the waitresses wore short, tight uniforms. Another student from IUSB [Indiana University South Bend] started about the same time as I did. After our first week, we went to the manager's office and informed him that we would not wear the uniforms. The next day, we were in jeans—my first experience as a feminist."

◇ *Thomas G. Ryan, ND 1976:* "The newly commissioned ensigns and second lieutenants from Navy ROTC used Fat Wally's for our post-commissioning 'wetting down' the night before graduation.

All that I remember is that we closed it after consuming copious amounts of adult beverages."

When students wanted something other than raucous bars and greasy fare, two nearby restaurants fit the bill: Louie's and Rocco's. Many strolled to Louie's, a pizza joint less than a half mile from campus, and never worried about walking back to campus after its 2:00 a.m. weekday and 3:00 a.m. weekend closings. Students filled booths and tables, and owner Louis Rappelli often personally served the and pizzas and beer. Music played on the jukebox—five tunes for a quarter—while candles burned in Mateus bottles. After Louie's was remodeled in the summer of 1973, the restaurant increased seating to two hundred people and sported a bar, a small dance floor, and a game room. Louie hoped the renovations would keep students "in South Bend rather than fleeing to Michigan on the weekends."[10] Louie seldom carded as he possessed a sixth sense when it came to visits from the ABC. However, after the South Bend Vice Squad raided his establishment in September 1974, Louie sold the restaurant, which became Club 23.

◇ *David A. Martin, ND 1976:* "Freshman year, Louie's served me a pitcher of beer with my pizza *if* it was a weekday night. One night, the pitcher was filled with Pepsi—Louie apologized and said he knew the ABC was in town."

Another family style pizzeria, Rocco's, opened in 1951. The restaurant originally sat only twelve, with the family cooking and serving the guests. A visit to Rocco's remains essential for any return trip to Notre Dame.

◇ *Dan Adler, ND 1976:* "In 1975, friends and I went to Rocco's. At some point, we started singing. The little old Italian hostess came over and said, 'There's no singing in the restaurant.' When I returned in 2003 with my kids, a former roomie, and his family, the same hostess was there. I said to her, 'I'm sure that you won't remember this, but in 1975 I was here with some friends, and we started singing. You told us there was no singing in the restaurant.' She looked at me, gave a little smile, and said, 'I do remember that. But I didn't say no singing in the restaurant. I said *you* can't sing, so you can't sing in the restaurant.' Then she led us to our table. We talked, played cribbage, and ate pizza that couldn't be beat."

Despite all the places close to campus, students often made their way to Michigan to drink. After Michigan lowered its drinking age to eighteen in 1972, groups of ND and SMC students crossed the state line to drink legally. One of the most popular venues was Kubiak's Tavern. Founded in 1933 and located a mere thirty feet from the border of Indiana, Kubiak's still operates today.

Students waited in line to enjoy Kubiak's jukebox and bumper pool table. Old-timers shared stories about the free movies shown on the side of the building like a drive-in theater. Each night, Kubiak's owners closed the bar's doors when it reached its maximum capacity of three hundred patrons, and students waiting outside often climbed through the bathroom windows. Within the walls of this Polish tavern, with its exuberant polka music and cheaply priced pitchers of beer and pizza, no one cared whether a woman was from ND or SMC.

Kubiak's (Photo courtesy of Ed Brower)

◇ *Shelley Muller Simon, ND 1976:* "As a freshman, I dated a junior and loved going to Kubiak's with ten of his closest friends. I danced all night, rotating partners with each song! I remember the old women doing the two-step with each other and thinking how weird it was. Ironically, now as an 'old' woman, I enjoy dancing with women (not the two-step, though) because they are usually more fun and better dancers!"

◇ *David A. Martin, ND 1976:* "Freshman year I went to Kubiak's with a junior who had a car. Going to Kubiak's at night was always scary. I figured every car coming south on US 31, with its four lanes and no center divider, had a drunk teenage driver."

◇ *Nancy Brenner Sinnott, ND 1976:* "I still have the pitcher I 'borrowed' from Kubiak's! They checked for students trying to take them, so it was a contest to see who could apprehend one!"

A drive-in theater usually had a large movie screen, a projection booth, a concession stand, and a gravel or asphalt parking lot. Some included playgrounds and picnic tables. Moviegoers watched films through their windshields while listening to the movie's sound through individual speakers hung on the car's side window. Attendance started to decline in the late 1960s as home entertainment options improved with color, cable, and video. The energy crisis resulted in a reduced use of cars, and the adoption of daylight saving time caused the movies to start later. As higher taxes on the land came into play, drive-ins increasingly struggled to remain profitable.[11]

Shula's 31 Bowling Alley offered a more comprehensive food and drink menu than Kubiak's. Rumors abounded that Tommy James of Tommy James and the Shondells frequented the place. An American rock band formed in Niles, Michigan, in 1964, Tommy James and the Shondells had charted two number-one singles: "Hanky-Panky" in 1966 and "Crimson and Clover" in 1969. To this day, the band's music reminds many 1970s ND students of music and bowling—when the only thing that mattered was how one bowled!

◇ *Anonymous, ND 1977:* "Only in Indiana during the winter would you even think about bowling. But that's what some of us did on a regular basis. Another innovative 'Moose' Mulcahy, CSC, idea—bringing guys and gals together in nonthreatening social settings. Contrary to the notion that 'the only thing that mattered was how you bowled,' we had a blast drinking beer and throwing gutter balls. After almost fifty years, one special memory includes Moose giving me a pair of bowling shoes and a bowling ball [that was] a little lighter than those typically found at Shula's, with a nice blue Naugahyde bag. I kept that gift for many years, but I finally had to let go of [it]—but not the memory!"

After a late night of drinking, dancing, bowling, or even studying, students often satisfied cravings at a twenty-four-hour diner. Officially named The White House Restaurant but more lovingly called Fat Shirley's, it offered strong coffee, fatty bacon, fried eggs, home-style potatoes, and buttery white toast. As cigarette smoke and the smell of grease permeated the air, patrons straddled vintage vinyl counter stools and talked about Notre Dame football and local politics. A cash-only establishment, students usually paid with a five-dollar bill, with change leftover.

The Observer,
March 1, 1976

◇ *Richard Steiner, ND 1976:* "We capped off many nights of studying at Shirley's. The night before an exam in our solid-state physics course, one guy brought his textbook. An older town resident kept looking at the book title. Suddenly, his 'idea bulb' lit up, and he proclaimed, 'I get it! Solid state. Without tubes!' Kudos to him for recognizing the onset of transistorized TVs and radios as electronics without vacuum tubes."

◇◇◇

REARVIEW REFLECTION While researching these gathering spots, my mind filled not with thoughts of the often-dilapidated buildings and horrendous odors but of the freedom enjoyed in these locales. Although there were sometimes questionable behaviors exhibited by members of both sexes, we shared a kinship in knowing others faced the same collegiate struggles we did.

Dad prior to and at Senior Bar (1973)

I took my first drink during freshman orientation and quickly learned the dangers of mixing liquor and beer. As a female, I easily got into most bars, with or without an ID. However, to stay on the legal side of the road, my crew and I often found transportation or hitchhiked to Michigan with its legal drinking age of eighteen. By the time Michigan's legislature increased the drinking age to nineteen on December 3, 1978, and to twenty-one just eighteen days later on December 21, 1978, I was a married woman living in Chicago.

When I think about all the time spent drinking, my favorite memory involves my dad and Senior Bar. This particular day started out sunny as we toured campus and inspected the renovations of the law school. However, by the time we made it to the bar, the plummeting temperatures drove my father to borrow a winter parka, and at Senior Bar it seemed that his cigarette muted the taste of his favorite beer...Schlitz! Photos from this time together remind me that we all sport multiple looks and have many dimensions to our personalities.

Turning the Dial

Assorted styles of music played not only in the pit stops students frequented but also across campus. Students listened to music while studying, relaxing, dating, or sharing special moments. Sometimes, by just "turning the dial," they could focus on academic goals or intimacy needs. Nearly three centuries earlier, William Congreve's much quoted passage from *The Mourning Bride* (1697) still applies: "Music has charms to soothe a savage breast, / To soften rocks, or bend a knotted oak."[1]

◇◇◇

The early 1970s were as chaotic as the 1960s, as protests against the Vietnam War and demonstrations for various equality struggles continued. New movements rejected earlier elements such as communal living and Lyndon B. Johnson's Great Society, while a New Right defended political conservatism and traditional family roles.[2] Following Watergate and Richard Nixon's resignation, students wanted less political turmoil and easier lifestyles. The music described not only the times but, often, the feelings within hearts.

> "The '60s are over," a slogan one only began to hear in 1972 or so, mobilized all those eager to believe that idealism had become passé, and once they were mobilized, it had. In popular music, embracing the '70s meant both an elitist withdrawal from the messy concert and counterculture scene and a profiteering pursuit of the lowest common denominator in FM radio and album rock.[3]

Students enjoyed a broad range of musical styles: hard and soft rock, country, jazz, and rhythm and blues. The deaths of Jimi Hendrix, Janis Joplin, and Jim Morrison — all at the age of twenty-seven — reminded students to live life. With the emergence of disco and other genres later in the decade, adults, particularly parents, felt that these new musical forms signaled civilization's decline, similar to the thinking surrounding the dawn of rock and roll in the 1950s. Watching reruns of Elvis Presley's 1956 appearance on *The Ed Sullivan Show* and listening as grandparents denounced his music and style reminded students to keep their minds open during such periods of social change.

Fabulous tunes by Chicago, The Rolling Stones, and many others constantly blared from large speakers perched on windowsills. This music frequently acted as a magnet, drawing students to weekend parties. Tom Young and his friends set a "weekend mood" through their music selections:

> ◊ *Tom Young, ND 1976:* "Our junior year, part of 'F-Troop' had a corner quad in Cavanaugh facing the North Quad. Every Friday, once a quorum of the group finished classes, we cranked up the stereo and officially started the weekend by playing an instrumental called 'Mae' by Herb Alpert and the Tijuana Brass. The song had a hot and sexy sound, and—when wafting over the quad—it elicited that great end-of-the-week-ready-for-anything feeling."

The technology of how students listened to music evolved greatly during this time. Through the 1960s, AM and FM radio were the mainstream. Car stereos became common, first adding FM radio, followed by eight-track and cassette tapes. Vinyl records replaced the shellac format. Stereo systems combined multiple formats into one box—phonograph, cassette and eight-track players, a recording microphone, and floor-standing speakers. All of these formats, techniques, and styles are now considered 1970s "retro."

Appreciation for a diverse set of artists grew from exposure not only to party music but also to roommates' and friends' preferences. Luckily, when roommates could not agree on the music, headphones—like those worn by pilots—often helped to restore domestic harmony. For many students, music they heard at ND served as a touchstone—both at the time and across the years—connecting them with others:

> ◊ *Ann Pytynia, ND 1976:* "I will forever associate the music of Cat Stevens with those ND years. My ND boyfriend introduced me to Cat, and his words and music will be forever nostalgic for me. A few years ago, I experienced a time where I could not get Cat Stevens' work out of my head. After 'just checking' on my ND boyfriend after so many years, I discovered he passed away a few months prior. Coincidence?"

> ◊ *Darlene Palma Connelly, ND 1977:* "For a brief time, I dated an upperclassman who was in the five-year engineering program.

He lived off campus and played music I had never heard before. The one album I vividly recall was Harry Nilsson's *A Little Touch of Schmilsson in the Night.* Two of the songs, 'It Had to Be You' and 'Makin' Whoopee,' sum things up, but maybe not as you expect. I went to his house on his birthday with a cake to surprise him. At this point in the relationship, I wasn't sure if 'It Had to Be [Him],' but, although we had no plans to celebrate, I thought baking a cake seemed the right thing to do. He was not there when I arrived, and his housemates were acting a little more than squirrelly. My 'boyfriend' finally arrived, and we did the birthday song and cake thing. Noticing something odd in his behavior, I left. Not long thereafter, I discovered he was, tongue in cheek, 'making whoopee' with a gal from Farley."

Even when certain music was not a part of campus life, it had the power to evoke that specific time

◊ *Joe Henderlong, ND 1975:* "I find that I can listen to music (such as the soundtrack to *Grease*), and even though it may not have been a mainstay during our years at ND, I imagine embracing it and singing it during the times together at ND. Sometimes, you just know those things in life that were meant to be shared with the people who meant something to you in life.

"Distance may keep people apart, but true connections with each other keep them together."

Music was not just enjoyed on radios and stereos. Over time, touring bands transitioned from playing small clubs and theaters to playing to thousands in sports arenas and outdoor stadiums. For college students, this trend drove a robust concert schedule. Big-name bands no longer traveled by bus but flew in private jets; they most likely found the small South Bend airport disappointing upon their arrival.

Ticket prices to attend the concerts of both legendary and emerging rock performers seemed extravagant at the time. During those years, the most expensive seats cost ten dollars for Elvis Presley; seven-and-a-half dollars for Elton John, Chicago, the Carpenters, The Jackson 5, and Rod Stewart; and seven dollars for Alice Cooper, The Beach Boys, and The Doobie Brothers. Ticket prices for more than sixty concerts from 1972–1976 ranged from three-and-a-half dollars to six-and-a-half dollars for performers such as Aerosmith, America, the Eagles, The Guess Who, Helen Reddy, Queen, Santana, Seals and Crofts, and even lesser-known musicians like Bruce Springsteen. *The Observer* announced upcoming concerts, a prelude to many date invitations. Students attended concerts on campus at the Athletic and Convocation Center and Stepan Center. Many traveled to downtown South Bend to attend the more than thirty concerts held at the Morris Civic Auditorium, listening to the music with a special someone or in groups, on weekends, and occasionally on school nights.

◇ *Christie Gallagher Sever, ND 1976:* "Loved the Seals and Crofts concert. Afterward, the two of them invited anyone interested to a Q and A in the pit at Grace Hall. I also stood in line overnight to get front-row seats to the Elton John concert."

◇ *Sally Naxera Benson, ND 1976:* "I was fortunate to attend many concerts on campus; mostly on dates, but some in groups. My most memorable was Sha Na Na in September of '74. You see, the lucky gal crowned 'Dancing Queen' by Bowser on stage was yours truly! My friends and I had great seats near the front. We had visited a local resale shop for 1950s style clothing; so, I went rocking a swing skirt, a sweater, bobby socks, and a ponytail! In the middle of the concert, the band chose three girls from the crowd for the dance contest. Bowser asked each her name, age, and high school. When the third gal haughtily announced she was from Purdue (we'd just suffered a painful loss to them that afternoon), the crowd booed her off the

Athletic and Convocation Center
Art by Barbara O'Connell (2011)

stage. I seized the moment and took her place. Of course, when they asked me the same questions, my enthusiastic response was "Sally, twenty, *Notre Dame!*" Guessing from the immediate shift from boos to cheers, my win had more to do with Notre Dame pride than my dancing prowess."

◇ *Joe Sinnott, ND 1976:* "First date with Nancy [Sinnott] was to The Beach Boys freshman year. It must have gone all right as we have been married since the day after graduation. Other favorite concerts included James Taylor, Rare Earth, Seals and Crofts, Yes, and Gordon Lightfoot."

◊ *Rosemary Tirinnanzi Lesser, ND 1976:* "My most vivid memory was the Carpenters' concert the night of our victory over USC in 1974. Although I loved the Carpenters (yes, I admit it), they were not the right musical mood for that particular event."

Some classmates worked as ushers and even got up close and personal with band members.

◊ *Maggie Waltman Smith, ND 1976:* "One of my roommates and I worked as ushers at the ACC. We received six dollars per event but got to watch concerts, basketball games, and hockey games for free. We enjoyed the job for two years as it was not difficult, especially hockey games, which were not well attended."

◊ *Peter M. Roddy, ND 1976:* "My favorite concert was The Beach Boys. A few of us knocked down the set, working for fifty dollars and backstage passes for access to washtubs of Heineken in the band's locker/dressing room. I had a request to come out to sign an autograph for an SMC student in the front row as, at the time, I was the spitting image of Mike Love. Long story short — I did so. After the pack out (that stuff was heavy!), we retired to a booth at the Ramada Inn bar. Sometime later, The Beach Boys moved into the booth behind us. Mike Love looked at me, and we each shrugged with a WTF expression. I should have invited my groupie back to my room, but I think she would have figured out that Mike didn't live in Dillon."

◊ *Mark Gibson, ND 1976:* "I was working The Beach Boys concert, and during the rehearsal, Carl Wilson asked me what song would resonate with our school. I said, 'Well tomorrow is the Notre Dame–USC game. You should sing "Be True to Your School."' They started playing it, with Al Jardine on lead guitar and Mike Love on vocals, but quickly realized they needed more practice."

Beyond the rock and pop concerts, cultural events such as the Midwest Blues Festival, the ND JAZZ Festival, and the Sophomore Literary Festival allowed students to discover new interests. Both the ND and SMC campuses hosted the Chicago, Milwaukee, and Indianapolis symphonies and the Julliard string quartet. The Notre Dame Glee Club, the Notre Dame Jazz Band, the Notre Dame Band, and Saint Mary's Choir all displayed the talents of male and female students.

Ballets and plays added to the options available for personal cultural development. Sometimes the activities brought students into contact with future stars.

> ◇ *Richard Steiner, ND 1976:* "Chekhov's *Three Sisters* (I think) was a professional play at Saint Mary's. Near the end, one of the actors has a sad soliloquy, something about hearing a bird in the distance. At that moment, the sound of a jet flying overhead cracked up the cast. That actor was an unknown at the time—Kevin Klein [*sic*]. I may still have the program."

When nothing was available locally, the city of Chicago was just ninety miles away by car or the South Shore train.

> ◇ *Dan Jarvie, ND 1976:* "I drove to Chicago in a blinding blizzard in '75 to hear the Chicago Symphony perform Beethoven's Seventh. Got stuck in Michigan City on the way home. Believe it or not, I learned to love classical [music] while in the navy."

Movies offered reasonably priced social alternatives to the more expensive concerts and events. The Student Union showed films in the Engineering Auditorium, but more recent releases cold be found at South Bend's Morris Civic Auditorium or the downtown movie theater. Professor Paul Rathburn of the English Department actually started the first film festival by renting films with his own money and showing them in his classes. After three years of his own programming, he persuaded the Knights of Columbus to advertise the films and raise money for needy organizations. In 1974, he got the Cultural Arts Commission to take over the film festivals and broaden the offerings, including shows featuring Shakespearean actors such as Richard Burton and film stars like Clint Eastwood and Barbara Streisand. Rathburn also developed a radio program with the campus station WSND, presenting short commentaries before playing records of famous Shakespeare performances.

> ◇ *Darlene Palma Connelly, ND 1977:* "Date invitations made it less likely for a group of the coeds to get tickets together for different events, but that was not the case when it came to seeing movies sponsored by the Student Union. At one dollar a ticket, we saw everything. I remember seeing *A Clockwork Orange* in Washington Hall. I recall how its violence disturbed me. I am not sure I saw the end of that movie, even though I never left my seat. I am sure I never watched it again."

> ◇ *Frank Fransioli, ND 1976:* "I remember going downtown to the Morris Civic Auditorium to see *The Exorcist*, a frightening tale of good versus evil pitting the devil himself against our own 'Men in Black.' Although I saw the film at a matinée and [the

movie] was set far away in Georgetown, walking across campus at night seemed just a little bit creepy for the next couple of weeks. Nineteen-year-old Mike Oldfield's theme, 'Tubular Bells,' became an instant hit and the breakthrough album for Richard Branson's Virgin Records."

◇ *Jeanine Sterling, ND 1976:* "Jason Miller was nominated for an Oscar for his role in *The Exorcist.* He was a lifelong fan of The Irish—he even played Ara Parseghian in the film *Rudy.* I love this ndnation.com post about Jason Miller's 1974 campus visit: 'With a group of freshmen, we walked to the Morris Civic to see *The Exorcist,* walked back to campus—still a little "on edge" from the movie. Got back to the dorm, and in one of the dorm rooms was Jason Miller—there for the Sophomore Literary Festival. The sophomores hosting him invited us in, and he told stories about *The Exorcist.* Let's just say the room was a little "smokie [*sic*]." Jason Miller was there for his play *The Championship Season,* and for those that haven't seen *The Exorcist,* he was the priest in the movie. I can still remember how that freaked us out after just seeing the movie.'"[4]

◇◇◇

REARVIEW REFLECTION In high school, my first concert—Neil Diamond—and first play—*A Midsummer Night's Dream*—prompted a lifelong appreciation of music and the performing arts. Notre Dame's proximity to Chicago also exposed me to opera and ballet, including seeing the famous ballet star, Rudolf Nureyev.

In college, concerts provided opportunities to spend time with dates without the need for constant conversation. I enjoyed pop and singer-songwriter musicians such as the Carpenters, The Association, Van Morrison, and Joni Mitchell. I broadened my musical tastes to include Chicago, America, and Fleetwood Mac. Before graduation, I saw Elvis Presley—twice. Unfortunately, I never met my idol. The closest I came was in association with the girl I tutored. Her mother, a maid at the hotel where Elvis stayed, received a car from him before he left town.

Once, I went outside my comfort zone and accepted an invitation to see The J. Geils Band. I liked my date, but I detested the music and acted like a total witch as a result. Anyone asking my date about that night probably heard him describe me as "possessed." Our friendship survived my childish behavior—but just barely!

The tables turned when I invited True Blue to see Crosby and Nash, with Linda Ronstadt as the opening act. I was always trying to impress him, so I went downtown and bought a blue velvet dress—Bobby Vinton's "Blue Velvet" was my favorite get-ready-for-a-date song. I made dinner reservations for us at the Morris Inn and asked him to come by my Breen-Phillips room for a drink before dinner. He showed up late, and we barely made it to the concert. With the exception of hall formals, this was the first — and only — time I asked a Notre Dame guy on a date.

Two-Way Street

Primatologist Jane Goodall points out that "[w]hat you do makes a difference, and you have to decide what kind of difference you want to make."[1] As an alternative to the social scene, service projects helped students interact with the other sex, while putting the focus on someone else and not each other. The university required community involvement for admittance and encouraged participation in volunteer and community projects once there. Before, during, and after college, dedicated Domers exemplified the meaning of "two-way street."

◇◇◇

Notre Dame provided not only a source of academic enlightenment but also opportunities for students to grow their faith and demonstrate their Christian values. Starting in the late 1960s, providing service—giving back—to those less fortunate was deemed integral to the personal development of ND's students. According to John Jenkins, CSC, the university's president and an ND classmate: "Genuine service and a commitment to community make demands on us and require sacrifice, yet they provide a joy greater than any other. One must experience that to believe it, and I hope our students experience it."[2]

The majority of residence halls established community service directors to assist students in finding the volunteer activities best suited to their interests and abilities. All directors met regularly and determined which community projects to undertake. Projects originated through Campus Ministry and included activities such as renovating a home for the elderly, assisting in blood drives, collecting money for the American Cancer Society, and organizing clothing drives for tornado and flood victims.

The Neighborhood Study Help Program involved more than four hundred ND and SMC students, who concentrated on tutoring children in reading, math, and other subjects,[3] while those working for the ND–SMC Council for the Retarded[4] primarily volunteered on Saturday mornings at Logan Center and assisted with field trips for the organization's participants. The Indiana Public Interest Research

Group (INPIRG) worked with other higher education institutions as well as legislators to preserve the environment, protect consumers, and hold the government accountable on topics of public interest. Students for World Concern kept its volunteers outwardly focused beyond the campus domain.

Every year during the 1970s, approximately 20 percent of the graduating senior class in the College of Arts and Letters made a one- to two-year commitment in areas related to public and private education, family and children services, after-school programs, developing countries, and nongovernmental organizations. Postgraduate service provided life-changing experiences and transferable skills. Such service continued to build a sense of community among both participants and recipients and bridged divides of culture and class. For some, this time at Notre Dame even led them "into a life of service," as Jane Pitz, assistant rector of Walsh Hall, has explained. "[S]omeone or something at ND put them on such paths."[5] (See also the "Women of Impact" in the appendix.)

Students leveraged their skills and commitment to humanitarian work in organizations such as the Peace Corps, VISTA (Volunteers in Service to America), and other related programs. As early as 1961, ND linked itself with the then-newly formed Peace Corps. Shortly after President Kennedy created the Peace Corps, he asked Father Hesburgh to develop an approach to prepare its members. In less than four months, fifty-two young Americans, including eight ND and two SMC graduates, arrived at Notre Dame to prepare for a Peace Corps mission to Chile.

> Peace Corps volunteers, US citizens who typically have college degrees, work abroad for two years. They support governments, schools, and nonprofit and nongovernmental organizations in education, youth development, community health, business, technology, agriculture, and the environment. Since its inception, "more than 235,000 Americans...have served in 141 countries." In 2020, the global coronavirus pandemic necessitated evacuation of all volunteers from all posts.[6]
>
> VISTA, or Volunteers in Service to America, emerged as part of President Lyndon B. Johnson's Great Society and the Economic Opportunity Act of 1964 and is the "domestic equivalent of the Peace Corps." Volunteers serve in communities throughout the United States, focusing on enriching educational programs and vocational training for the nation's underprivileged classes.[7]

◇ *Mike McCauley, ND 1970:* "The PC [Peace Corps] certainly was not a 'religious' experience, but I did use it to develop a deeper appreciation for others and a sense that all people are unified in a search for meaning in life."[8]

◇ *Ann Pytynia, ND 1976:* "I have so many former coworkers who did this and [who] have amazing stories and memories. I have no idea why this did not appeal to me at the time. I missed out on so much."

The giving nature of students was visible in many ways. Alan Patrick Sondej (ND 1974), known to many simply as "Al," stood every day, rain or shine, in front of Notre Dame's North Dining Hall at lunch and its South Dining Hall at dinner throughout those first few years of coeducation. As cofounder of the Notre Dame–Saint Mary's World Hunger Coalition, he—along with Greg Gramelspacher, who manned Saint Mary's LeMans Hall—collected donations for the

Alan Sondej collecting donations
Photo by Pat Gleason and Ed Brower

group's Third World Relief Fund. The coalition's goals included raising awareness in the Notre Dame–South Bend community about key spiritual, moral, and social issues related to the world food crisis and developing creative responses to these problems. Through educational discussions about these topics, many gained real compassion for the people and issues involved, including the crises in India and Africa and the ethics of unequal access to food and energy in modern society.[9]

Al encouraged students to acknowledge their obligation to contribute not only to campus life but also beyond our ivy-covered walls. As the primary organizer of the Third World Relief Fund, Al donated this money to several relief agencies, including Catholic Relief Services, CARE, Church World Services, and UNICEF. He clearly and often stated, "The money will be used for the development of social equality in a finite world."[10] It was (and is) impressive to see students care for someone they'll never see.

HELP THE HUNGRY ...

tonight and Thursday night sign your pledge form in the dining hall . . .

12 meatless Tues. & Fri. suppers and/or 6 fasts from Wed. suppers (50¢ rebate for fast from each Wed. supper)

PROCEEDS TO THE HUNGRY IN BANGLADESH AND SO. BEND

NOTRE DAME WORLD HUNGER COALITION

In addition to his humanitarian efforts, Al had other interests. Often dressed like a 1930s gangster, he was a look-alike for Arnold Schwarzenegger, and in his junior year (1972–1973), he provided bodyguard services for "King" Kersten, the student body president. He also lived in the ND firehouse and volunteered as a campus firefighter. His room was spartan, with his workout equipment the only memorable decoration.

After Al graduated with a sociology degree in May 1974, he remained on campus for several years. Those who attended ND in the first five years of coeducation remembered him as "the big guy who collected money for the hungry outside the dining hall."[11]

> ◇ *Greg Szatko, ND 1974:* "Al and I always had a laughing contest. We both had the loudest, craziest laughs back then. One time, while he collected money for the homeless by North Dining Hall, we stood outside catching up. A classmate stopped and told us a joke. We both laughed so hard, students heard us inside the cafeteria. Our loud laughs brought attention to what Al was doing, so students came out and put more money in his milk jug."

> ◇ *Mary Beth Gillespie Cernanec, ND 1976:* "Notre Dame is where I learned that it was OK to be different and who you want to be — who can forget the strength of character of Al Sondej!"

> ◇ *Susan Davis Flanagan, ND 1976:* "I remember Al collecting money in all sorts of weather — nothing deterred him. In a way, he is part of the mystique of Notre Dame. Where else could someone be remembered and appreciated so many years later?"

Al wanted to collect as much money as possible: In 1973 alone, he raised more than twenty-five hundred dollars during Lent.[12] He ended his years of collection ten times that level, at approximately twenty-five thousand dollars.[13] In the spring of 1975, Hesburgh recognized Al's impact on the ND community and encouraged him to go even bigger. Hesburgh sent him to places such as Bangladesh and Guatemala to aid hunger relief efforts and bring home the lessons of what he saw.[14] Through these journeys, Al shifted his focus to larger, more difficult challenges. His reflections on his Bangladesh trip in the September 18, 1975, *Observer* brought tears to many eyes. He framed his article as a letter to Father Hesburgh:

> You knew what you were talking about when you said that you thought it would be a good idea for me to see the faces of the hungry, the sick, the homeless, the illiterate, and the poor....I originally did not think that this trip would affect me that much, but...nothing has affected me more. Last year I earned $35 a week, but after seeing 1-5th [*sic*] of Bangladesh's 75 million people each making only $18 a year, I know that I will never be poor. The filth, the stench, the garbage, the [muck] that the people of poverty eat in, work in, sleep in, and die in is something that could never be imagined. And what is really horrible is that these conditions affect most of mankind, and will continue to do so until people change their basic attitudes and behavior.[15]

After returning from his trip, Al collected funds outside the dining hall for another year. He knew that some questioned his motives for continuing this practice, and he addressed those concerns in *The Observer*:

It is with these thoughts in mind that I have decided to panhandle at Notre Dame for the last year. If I objectively state what a penny and dime could buy, smile warmly and sensitively at those who don't contribute, thank those who do, and above all, realize that I am dealing with people and not dollar signs, I think that there should not be too much of a sense of obligation or guilt created among the students.... And most of all, I would not panhandle if I did not think that the students would experience at least some of the Joy and Happiness in Giving.[16]

A letter from Hesburgh to Tom O'Neil, *The Observer*'s editor, acknowledging Sondej's last day of collection

At the end of Al's 1976 stint on the ND campus, many administrators commented on his contributions. According to an article in *The Observer* by Peter Arndt, Robert Griffin, CSC, described Al as "the most effective teacher on campus," even though (as Arndt notes) he "was not a paid member of the faculty staff, and yet he's taught so many. He has taught the difference a life can make."[17] William Toohey, CSC, director of Campus Ministry, added:

At first, you feel an immediate impulse to say, "Thank God, he's going; now we won't be bothered any more by having to give money every time we enter the dining hall." But then you realize how false this reaction would be; and you acknowledge how important it has been to have him standing before us, bombarding our consciences.[18]

After leaving ND, Al interned with the Overseas Development Council and traveled across the country speaking about world hunger, organizing students into advocacy groups, and collecting money. In 1977, he continued his graduate education at the University of Maryland while working with the Vatican on ways to solve the global hunger problem. Loving his time as an ND volunteer fireman, he also worked as a live-in volunteer firefighter at the Hyattsville Volunteer Fire Department in Prince Georges County, Maryland.

On January 27, 1988, after nearly eleven years, Al worked his last night with the fire department before heading overseas to teach sustainable agriculture techniques—another volunteer position. During this last shift, he and his crew responded to a house fire. As he searched for a woman reportedly trapped inside, flames overtook Al. He suffered burns over sixty percent of his body, and only his incredible physical condition enabled him to escape the house. On March 16, Alan P. Sondej succumbed to complications from his injuries.[19]

Alan Sondej and Ed Scales on a Notre Dame fire truck (1974)

In 1990, Sondej received the Dr. Thomas A. Dooley Award for his contributions to ND and the underprivileged in so many communities. His classmates established a fund in his name at Notre Dame through the Center for Social Concerns. The National Fallen Firefighters Foundation also founded the Alan Patrick Sondej Memorial Scholarship Fund for Families of Fallen Fighters, recognizing Al's bravery and spirit.[20]

◇ *Ed Scales, ND 1974:* "When I lived in Los Angeles from 1976 to 1980, Al stopped and stayed with me for almost a week. He had just returned from a trip to several impoverished countries that Father Hesburgh had sponsored for him, and he really needed the R & R. During his visit, I tried to give him some much-needed clothes. On the day he left, he graciously thanked me for the items, but he told me that he could not accept anything, given the poverty he had just seen on his trip. Typical Al—he did not want anyone to think he might be profiting from his collection efforts.

"When Al died while serving with the Hyattsville Maryland Volunteer Fire Department, he was taking agricultural classes at the University of Maryland. He wanted to learn the latest techniques so he could pass them on to farmers in [other] countries. I doubt we will ever know all the people and lives Al touched. I hope we can keep his legacy alive through the Alan P. Sondej Memorial Fund managed by the Center for Social Concerns."

◇ *Ron Skrabacz, ND 1976:* "The Al Sondej story is unique and very much a part of our four years at Notre Dame. If you compare it to sports—look at how much is written about male and female athletes at ND. These students are recognized for their commitment, often practicing day in and day out. They're visible to the student population at large and, in many cases, are campus icons, at least during their years of play. A few, especially football and basketball players, bring in revenue to the university. They were, and still are, important to the collegiate experience.

"Al fit the description above: (1) did his thing every day, (2) was visible to the entire student body, (3) was a campus icon, and (4) brought in revenue—in his case, for an even greater good than the university! During his years on campus, Al was known by almost everyone. If they didn't know him by name, mention 'the guy with the milk carton collecting for food for the hungry,' and they knew exactly who he was—bringing to mind a vivid image of his blond hair and muscular body. How many students, outside of our athletes, can make that claim? The fact [that] he gave his life as he lived it (in service to others) makes his story relevant to each of us."

◇◇◇

REARVIEW REFLECTION Throughout grade school and high school, I loved volunteering—from watching over the kindergarten kids at lunch to creating programs for the ever-increasing migrant population in South Florida. On my September 1971 admissions application, I indicated an interest in future service for the Peace Corps. It was not until after I arrived on campus that I discovered Notre Dame's unique connection to this organization.

Application for Admission

1972 Freshman Class, University of Notre Dame/Saint Mary's College

At the present time my vocation is still a mystery although I have been thinking about it the last two years. I have a strong inclination towards teaching children of kindergarten or first grade. I had experience with these age groups when I was in grade school and really enjoyed the times I was with them. After college I would like to spend two or three years abroad with either the Peace Corps or the U.S.O. Marriage is not in my plans of the future.

Unfortunately, I lost the drive to serve in my first three semesters at Notre Dame. I did not rediscover the joy of visiting seniors and tutoring children until the second semester of sophomore year. I first volunteered with the Community Service Organization, whose mission advanced meaningful, effective social service experiences.

I enjoyed working with the elderly, so I visited a local nursing home. I met Ethel, a cantankerous woman with whom I had interesting discussions. Given that I lost my paternal grandmother—also named Ethel—just before sophomore year started, I considered this a sign. It took months to crack this Ethel's crusty veneer, but we eventually found things in common: her love of crocheting, Notre Dame, and sweets. I brought her homemade cookies and a woolen throw my grandmother Ethel gave me before college. When I left for home that summer, we embraced and promised to stay in touch. I called her several times but never connected; the home said she was unavailable. When I returned in the fall of 1974, I called the center to set up a visit. The staff informed me that "she had expired." From this callous statement, I pictured a parking meter whose time ran out and for which there was no reprieve. I pray her "court" appearance went well.

I met Al Sondej upon my return to the South Quad—Lyons Hall and the South Dining Hall—in the fall of 1974. When Al collected money, he smiled at everyone. His smile melted one's heart…and eventually drew money from one's pocket, wallet, or purse. Until I spent time with him, I believed he was just one of the "Dirt," a group of males who were mostly athletes and partyers. Although he frequented the local bars, I never saw him take a drink; he once told me that he just

enjoyed watching people. When I finally talked to him beyond his post outside the dining hall or at a bar, I realized that he was so much more than merely good-looking.

In time, Al became a good friend. He offered valuable insights about campus life and other guidance; in fact, he tried hard—and often—to educate me on the male perspective of dating and relationships. Unfortunately, I did not listen. During my last two years at ND, he provided his broad shoulders to cry on and words of encouragement after several of my less-than-stellar dates and male encounters.

Al in Lyons Hall (1976)

Al wore the same clothes every day, and I thought I could perhaps help him. I worked part-time at Gilbert's Campus Shop and received a discount on clothes sold there. As his birthday approached, I bought him some new clothes. I also planned a surprise birthday party, asking "Dirt" members and his 1974 classmates to return for this celebration. I worked with "Big Jerk," an off-campus cohort of the "Dirt," collecting money to cover

Diana Wilson with Al (1975)

food, drinks, and a donation to Al's cause. "Big Jerk" later absconded with three hundred fifty dollars, which in 1975 was quite a financial setback for me.

The good news: We surprised Al, and everyone had a fun time. The bad news: I did not understand the real Al Sondej. On the Monday after his party, he stood in front of the dining hall in his usual white shirt, black pants, and tennis shoes; his new clothes were nowhere in sight. I asked him whether he did not like the clothes or if they did not fit. He responded that the clothes were fine, but he had returned them, adding the money to his ever-present plastic milk jug. My face was bright red with embarrassment. I should have realized that raising funds for his cause was far more important to him than new clothes. In that moment, I felt like a poor friend and realized that I still had a lot to learn about —and from— Al!

Emerging from the Fog

The Grotto
Art by Barbara O'Connell (2011)

"There's power in allowing yourself to be known and heard," former First Lady Michelle Obama emphasizes in her memoir *Becoming*, "in owning your unique story, in using your authentic voice."[1] No one can anticipate or prepare for every twist and turn of a journey. The women who attended Notre Dame during those first five years of coeducation gained knowledge from their academic studies to address their professional ambitions and more. They learned about themselves, each other, and the opposite sex. Still, they needed more female role models, a broader range of athletic programs, and improved physical and mental health resources and career services. The original pioneers pursued such changes within the university and eventually left no "mean stone of the place" untouched.

(No) Passing Zone

"As a rule," Nobel Prize-winner Albert Schweitzer wrote in his *Memoirs of Childhood and Youth*, "there are in everyone all sorts of good ideas, ready like tinder. But much of this tinder catches fire, or catches it successfully, only when it meets some flame or spark from outside...and light[s] a new flame within us."[1] Notre Dame's academic programs and faculty not only increased student knowledge but also heightened students' reasoning abilities. The courses and professors encouraged many to pursue a lifetime of learning and personal development. They also offered opportunities to move away from the narrow-mindedness of a mostly white, middle-class, Catholic upbringing, to explore and embrace new ideas and work with diverse teams.

◇◇◇

The University of Notre Dame du Lac established its academic reputation and distinctive learning atmosphere in the nineteenth century. Its reputation grew as it added leaders in emerging fields and established dedicated centers for biological research, medieval studies, and civil rights. Today, Notre Dame is a private, coeducational, national Catholic research university. Its programming encompasses four undergraduate colleges: Arts and Letters, Science, Engineering, and the Mendoza College of Business. Its School of Architecture, Law School, Graduate School, and ten major research institutes complete its academic offerings.

During the 1930s, the university strengthened its biology, philosophy, physics, and mathematics curricula. When Belgian-born Father Julius Aloysius "Arthur" Nieuwland joined the ever-growing faculty of distinguished European scholars, he taught botany and organic chemistry. ND's Chemistry Department gained prominence after Nieuwland discovered the basic formula for synthetic rubber. Through this effort, the DuPont Corporation eventually invented neoprene, from which—by the time the patent expired just before World War II—the university received almost two million dollars in royalties.[2]

The Bacteriology Department pioneered the technique to raise germ-free mice and guinea pigs for experimental research—with the offspring of one of these eventually going to the moon. Such efforts led the fight to eliminate the *Aedes aegypti* mosquito, the lead carrier of yellow fever. In the early 1970s, the department's undergraduate program was one of the nation's best. According to Jewish author Norman Mailer, if his son were ready for college (ten at the time of the quote), he might try to talk him into Notre Dame: "It's a great college.... What you get from the students is a lively Catholicism plus a lively agnosticism. I can use the word 'soul' there, and they don't snicker."[3]

A key academic tradition, the Freshman Year of Studies (FYS), required a core curriculum for all undergraduate students regardless of their intended major. Established in 1962, it assisted with the transition from high school to college. FYS provided a uniform foundation for intellectual and personal development by prescribing liberal arts requirements for all first-year students. This program was one reason Notre Dame's retention rate between freshman and sophomore year was one of the highest in the country in the 1970s; fewer than one percent of all freshmen suffered academic dismissal in each of coeducation's first four years.[4]

Women attended Notre Dame for the same reasons as the men: to obtain a college education and graduate with a degree in their chosen field. As the women's numbers increased, they became more adept at handling the gender ratios and sexist attitudes. Most enjoyed great success, but even those who had a shaky start eventually made it through their chosen curriculum.

> ◇ *Christine Gallagher Sever, ND 1976:* "You were aware of the disparity of numbers of each gender in each class, but once you got over that, your focus was learning the material and doing well on the tests and the papers."

> ◇ *Maureen Creighton Downs, ND 1976:* "If you were the only girl in class, you were pretty much guaranteed that you were called on every day. So, you were always visible. And when you were visible, you had the opportunity to shine or to be an abysmal failure. You had to bring your A game every day."

Notre Dame's 365 women, across all classes, had an overall grade point average of 3.12 in the first term of coeducation, compared with the university average of 2.94. Where one out of every five males received deficiency slips, only one in seven women received them.[5]

Making the dean's list required a 3.25 minimum grade point average (GPA) until the fall of 1974–1975, when the requirement changed to a 3.40 or better. This higher requirement resulted in 30 percent of students attaining this honor, declining from the previous year's 37 percent.[6] From the spring of 1975 through the

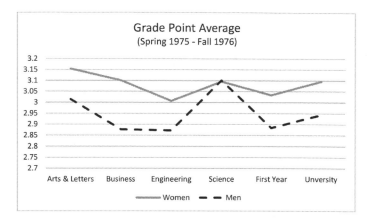

Grade Point Average
(Spring 1975 - Fall 1976)

Legend: Women, Men

Categories: Arts & Letters, Business, Engineering, Science, First Year, University

fall of 1976, the GPA difference continued, with women maintaining a slight lead. According to Emil T. Hofman, the dean of FYS:

> Around 1974–1975, the American Council on Education defined Notre Dame as a "private university-selective." I showed them our records since coeducation [was] part of a request for reclassification to "private university-highly selective," the same category as the Ivies, Stanford, and Duke. Hesburgh always talked about coeducation making ND a more gracious place. I believe coeducation raised the university's *academic* standards.[7]

Male students did appreciate what women brought to the ND classrooms:

> ◇ *Phil Potter, ND 1975:* "Some would mark the beginning of co-education in the fall of 1972 as a momentous event. However, as an incoming sophomore who attended a large public coed high school, I viewed that fall as the world finally returning to its axis. Gone was the social nuclear winter of freshman year with the first signs of a new social life on campus. Like the first buds of spring, the spattering of women in our classes indicated the arrival of a new social spring. Sure, there were naysayers who preached 'better dead than coed,' but they were rare, a dying species. Life finally began to reflect the outside world and only improved each succeeding year. Regarding the argument that women ruined the grade curve, given my meager grade levels, that argument was a non sequitur!"

> ◇ *Anonymous male, ND 1976:* "I never really thought ill about the women at ND because I always found girls who were high achievers in academics and/or athletics very, shall we say, exciting! Especially if they didn't flaunt it and were just being

themselves. It didn't bother me that most of the women in our class were smarter than me. I was always impressed by them. I was just too shy to talk to any of them."

Naturally, course quality and difficulty level varied as did the professors' skills and commitment levels. Classes came in a mixture of formats and sizes. Professors used overhead projectors, still wrote on chalkboards although dry-erase boards existed, and sometimes played videotapes or 8 mm films. They handed out mimeographed tests with blue-covered booklets for handwritten essays. Many students typed papers on standard typewriters, although a lucky few had electric Smith Coronas in impenetrable cases. Project teams used black carbon paper when they needed more than one copy of their output. Ballpoint pens, new to the scene, replaced cartridge or fountain pens. Most students did math longhand or sometimes used slide rules. Handheld calculators were too expensive for most; the 1975 price of a $195 calculator was equivalent to $985 in 2020.

Such advances in technology not only changed the way students studied but also resulted in new courses — such as programming for the masses. Ray Pikna described one of the first computer classes:

◇ *Ray Pikna, ND 1976:* "Like all first-year engineering students, I had to learn to program. After learning the basics, we had to type a program on punch cards that we fed into a computer. This yielded a printout that hopefully showed the correct answer to the problem. With more students than machines, usually you dropped your deck off and picked up the deck and printout the next day.

"One evening as I waited for my cards and printout, a professor waltzed in, peremptorily removed all decks in the feeder, inserted his cards, and left. Such action required a response! I quickly created cards for an endless loop, nervously looked around as I went to the feeder, removed most of his cards, and interspersed my newly created cards throughout his deck. I waited to see the fruits of my labors. Perforated paper soon began spewing out of the printer. Success! Not waiting around for the professor to return, I left and picked up my printout the next day."

Shelley Muller Simon also struggled with the back-and-forth process of printing out these punch cards and then troubleshooting:

◇ *Shelley Muller Simon, ND 1976:* "Freshman year, I learned to use a slide rule and to write computer programs in FORTRAN. After typing a punch card for each step in the program I wrote, I went to feed my stack of cards into the giant computer. After waiting in a long line, my cards were inevitably rejected. At that point,

I traversed the cold, dark hallways of the engineering building to find the closet of the old, bearded computer guru with his long, yellowish-brown fingernails. He flipped through my stack of cards one at a time until he discovered my (stupid) mistake. He pointed a dingy fingernail at my error and grunted. No conversation — I had to figure it out myself. I then retyped the offending card and returned to the line to wait to feed the entire stack into the computer again. The number of times I repeated this process was too numerous to count!"

Professors such as the "computer guru" were becoming more visible on campus. Despite Notre Dame's history of having a primarily religious faculty, by the mid-1970s priests made up less than 10 percent of the 745 faculty members. More liberal priests encouraged discussions on Church reform, existentialism, and even the Immaculate Conception. Although Catholic faculty outnumbered other denominations by more than two to one, the administration still fielded questions on a perceived loss of its Catholicity. As the distinction between Catholic and Christian blurred, Hesburgh often stressed that a Catholic university must continue to emphasize moral leadership, spirituality, and a commitment to justice.[8] Mary Brown Hollock attested that these qualities were exactly what Notre Dame emphasized:

◇ *Mary Brown Hollock, ND 1976:* "The education that I received at ND was character-based, which eventually made itself known in career development ways. It was not outstanding in and of itself. But over time, as I grew into it, I realized how fortunate I was to have been exposed to something so special."

Despite Notre Dame's improving image and academic rankings, attracting top scholars proved difficult. According to the American Association of University Professors (AAUP), in 1974 the average pay increase for faculty members at Notre Dame was in the bottom tenth of schools reporting increases in faculty salaries. This survey, a follow-up to one the AAUP had conducted three years earlier, showed little progress: At that time, all reporting institutions indicated an average 5.5 percent increase versus ND's 3.2 percent.[9] Even with Notre Dame's moratorium on building during those first years of coeducation, the university undertook a campaign to endow three to four faculty chairs a year at roughly eight hundred thousand dollars each. The administration strengthened its faculty pool by hiring PhDs right out of doctoral programs and from places such as Harvard, Yale, and Stanford.

Notwithstanding the low salary and pressures to conduct or publish research, most professors demonstrated interest not only in teaching but also in ensuring that their students understood subject matter. Professors made themselves

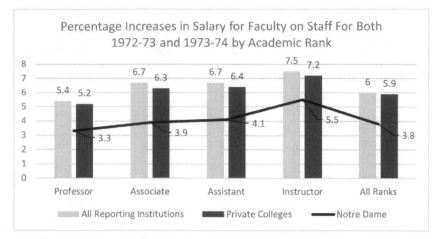

Percentage Increases in Salary for Faculty on Staff For Both 1972-73 and 1973-74 by Academic Rank

	Professor	Associate	Assistant	Instructor	All Ranks
All Reporting Institutions	5.4	6.7	6.7	7.5	6
Private Colleges	5.2	6.3	6.4	7.2	5.9
Notre Dame	3.3	3.9	4.1	5.5	3.8

available through office hours, appointments, and luncheon or dinner gatherings. Some students, when registering for classes, investigated faculty credentials, reputations, and the quality of their courses before enrolling.

Beverly Cesen Winterscheid recalled the positive impact that one professor had on her, not only at ND but also in her career:

◇ *Beverly Cesen Winterscheid, ND 1976:* "As a junior, I took an elective in the General Program of Liberal Studies. This course involved a lot of books to read, lots of discussions, and a *lot* of papers to write. My grades on these papers started out as a B-, improved to a B, and then stalled at a B+. About two-thirds into the term, I scheduled an appointment with the professor. I wanted to discuss my frustration with my grades and to inquire into what he looked for in an A paper. What he told me has stuck with me to this day. He said, 'When you think you've done the best job that you could possibly do, pushing your ideas as far as they can go, put the paper away for a day, sleep on it, and pick it up the next day. Go through your paper one more time, pushing your ideas even further still, then hand it in.'

"His advice served me well as I pursued my PhD and later as a business executive. And yes, I got an A in his course when all was said and done!"

Like all students, Angela Lamm Zarnoti had both good and bad professors, but she learned that her own efforts and ability were what truly mattered:

◇ *Angela Lamm Zarnoti, ND 1976:* "Some courses were a total waste of time and money. Many were fabulous. Several professors stand out for their incredible passion for their discipline.

The overall lasting effect from the academic experience has been the knowledge of my own problem-solving and coping abilities. Knowing I was able to go into new situations and classes and do well has given me tremendous confidence and comfort through the years."

Darlene Palma Connelly learned her greatest lesson through failure — and from a wonderful professor:

◇ *Darlene Palma Connelly, ND 1977:* "One of my more difficult first-semester courses was calculus. Its professor, Father Burke, did everything possible to help struggling students, so I met with him before the final. As we discussed my study habits and other courses, it came out [that] the calc exam was my last exam. When Burke heard my mother had arrived to take me home as soon as it was over, he said, 'Darlene, I do not think there is anything you can do to pass this course. I suggest you forgo further prep and enjoy this beautiful spring weather with your mother.'

"When I got to the exam, I reviewed the 'hieroglyphics,' put my name on the blue book, and handed it in blank. If I could rewind the tape to that moment, I would add, 'Thank you, Father Burke. I learned more from you and failing this class than at any other point in my life.'"

The women soon recognized which professors had less-than-welcoming attitudes or displayed sexist attitudes. Janet Krier Breen had one professor with an "interesting" approach to giving advice and guidance to his female students:

◇ *Janet Krier Breen, ND 1975:* "I remember going into my first classes in the College of Business at Notre Dame full of excitement to participate as an equal with my fellow male students. I did not expect special treatment, and I knew there would be few females in my classes. I found it disturbing, however, that many male students were unsupportive, even negative; it was always difficult to get invited to participate in a study group. The males who did speak to me usually wanted to ask me out, rarely to study together.

"The administration and faculty made little effort to guide us. They surely knew that the first female students needed academic advice and/or a job placement support network. I finally invented one for myself by obtaining a teacher assistant position with one of the few female faculty members. I sometimes felt that she needed a friend in the business building even more than I did!

"Ultimately, the 'sensitivity training' award went to a Marketing Department professor. After witnessing that I did most of the work for a group presentation, he gave me a C while the three males received As. When I asked why, he replied, 'Get used to it if you want to work in a man's field.' Apparently, this was his way of giving guidance to his female students."

Jerry Lutkus felt that some professors were uncomfortable with or not fully prepared for coeducation:

◇ *Jerry Lutkus, ND 1974:* "Even on the faculty level, coeducation has had difficulty making progress. That includes Physiology professors who lecture and make comments about the female anatomy, but relegate discussions about the male parts to a simple mimeograph handout and no lecture…and further to profs who pass women for their skirts or figures, and finally to other professors who again view the women as an opportunity to make education at Notre Dame a realistic and human endeavor."[10]

Libby Ford recalled well-intentioned, if slightly inappropriate, questions from male faculty:

◇ *Mary E. "Libby" Ford, ND 1975:* "It was clear to me the university expended minimal effort to prepare the professors for women in their classrooms; although well-intentioned, some of the situations were comical. Although chemistry and calculus were fact-based classes, I laughed (to myself) when a science professor asked for 'the female perspective' on a biological principle."

Several professors were understanding of the women's challenges as minorities in the classroom. Some even sought guidance on how to work in this new environment. When asked by a male professor what to call his female students, Sister Jean told him to call them by their first names.

Yet setbacks in simple things — such as the informal, all-male study groups and academic buildings without female restrooms — were beyond a professor's control. Notre Dame women became classroom "crash test dummies," either when their biological differences became obvious or they hit a wall after trying to move through barriers. They learned to deal with the stereotypes associated with being intelligent, focused females and with the male-to-female ratios in the collegiate and professional worlds of the 1970s. The competitive, challenging times at ND prepared many for equally competitive, challenging careers.

◇ *Susan Schneider-Criezis, ND 1976:* "The courses were rigorous, tough, and the professors were harder on female students. One professor stated in class that girls did not belong in architecture and were only in class to meet husbands. He also graded women lower. I was determined to prove him wrong.

"Being at Notre Dame and being in a major with few women (as well as eventually a male-dominated career) made me 'tough.' I had to put up with a lot, work hard, and defend myself. I felt [that] if I could deal with ND, then I could handle any professional experiences that might come my way. I had to develop a lot of self-confidence to survive ND, and it made my professional life easier."

As dean of the Freshman Year of Studies, Emil T. Hofman made himself available for one-on-one discussions. He helped freshmen integrate into campus life and influenced thousands of students in his more than four decades of service to the university. His first- and second-semester general chemistry classes achieved particular notoriety—even infamy—as Hofman instilled dread among his students with weekly Friday morning quizzes. These quizzes even inspired a tongue-in-cheek poem published in *The Observer* in 1975.

Starting every class with an "Our Father," Hofman appeared standoffish and set in his ways. But he designed innovative lectures, developed programs to train high school science teachers, and established "Emil's Army" that took groups of former students to Haiti for service projects.[11] Despite his wry sense of humor, those lucky enough to know him found a heart bigger than The Grinch's on Christmas morning.

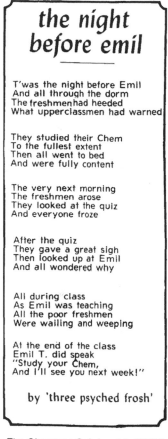

the night before emil

T'was the night before Emil
And all through the dorm
The freshmen had heeded
What upperclassmen had warned

They studied their Chem
To the fullest extent
Then all went to bed
And were fully content

The very next morning
The freshmen arose
They looked at the quiz
And everyone froze

After the quiz
They gave a great sigh
Then looked up at Emil
And all wondered why

All during class
As Emil was teaching
All the poor freshmen
Were wailing and weeping

At the end of the class
Emil T. did speak
"Study your Chem,
And I'll see you next week!"

by 'three psyched frosh'

The Observer, October 16, 1975[12]

◇ *Becky Banasiak Code, ND 1976:* "Dr. Emil T. Hofman [from chemistry] organized bus trips for freshmen to Chicago museums or the Indiana dunes. He cared about your personal life, not just your academic [life]. He believed that we must lead balanced lives to develop our personalities and not just our careers. He also believed that we needed to look out for others and not go through life with blinders on—to make sure others are made to feel included and given opportunities."

For some, the struggles with Hofman's chemistry class led them to new paths.

◇ *Shelley Muller Simon, ND 1976:* "To graduate with an engineering degree, passing grades in chemistry and chem lab were required. Rumors about the infamous Emil T. chemistry class ran rampant: He invented Friday seven-point quizzes because he saw too many students at the bars on Thursday nights. Rumors also flew that Emil wore a toupee because, while he was developing the formula for Prell shampoo, an unsuccessful trial batch blew up and singed his hair off—permanently. I soon discovered the course's rigor lived up to the academic-based rumors; I received an F in chemistry and a D in chem lab! Despite review sessions and study tapes, I developed a mental block to these courses. Second semester, I dropped engineering and focused on architecture; I registered for a summer design studio to validate my decision.

"During the summer of '73 design studio, I crossed paths with Emil as I walked across campus. My first thought was to act invisible, but—too late—we made eye contact. He asked if I had time to talk, and we proceeded to his office. I quickly learned he knew that I had not returned to his class second semester. I was surprised this legendary professor was so aware of one student in a class of four hundred, but I should not have been. We talked about his class, study techniques, and life in general. He then asked about my future plans, and I explained my focus on architecture. He looked me in the eye and said, matter-of-factly, 'I believe my class has created some of the greatest lawyers and architects in the country.'"

Over time, professors, even those resistant to coeducation, recognized the value of women in their classes. In a survey taken at the end of the 1975–1976 academic year, the majority of male faculty noted how women either stabilized or strengthened the university's overall academic quality. The classroom atmosphere and discussions became more serious and more competitive. The stereotypical image and expectations of females gave way as the men recognized the abilities of the individual women. Some faculty commented that women brought new aspects to Notre Dame traditions without compromising the old. Before coeducation, cynicism and a lack of civility existed in most classrooms. As the number and influence of women increased, classes became more diverse, more open-minded, and more Christian, with the women often helping their male counterparts.

◇ *Diana Wilson Ostermann, ND 1976:* "I was dating a football player. One evening as I was studying for an exam, he called and asked if I could help him with a paper. I told him I could edit whatever he wrote, but I couldn't do more than that. When he arrived at my room, he had the book for the paper with him but had not read it. I told him to flip through the book, pull out quotes at the beginning, middle, and end, and then describe what the quotes meant to him. As promised, I edited his grammar and punctuation, and I reworded an awkward sentence or two. To our surprise, he got an A! He must have found the quotes significant to the story."

◇ *Anonymous male, ND 1976:* "Women brought maturity and compassion to ND. When I took Russian, a difficult language, a female classmate tutored me and got me through it. It was the nicest thing anyone did for me at ND."

◇◇◇

REARVIEW REFLECTION During my first semester at ND, I enjoyed my new-found freedoms but had a less-than-auspicious academic start—with a first-semester cumulative average of 2.1 and my first C and two Ds. This outcome resulted in a meeting with Emil T. I still remember the queasy feeling in the pit of my stomach before that conversation. After our discussion and a supportive letter from my father, I tried to buckle down (life is but a car, after all).[13]

> Dear Debbie:
>
> I have enclosed a copy of your report for the first semester.
>
> Mom and I are pleased with your first semester grades and we are very pleased with your A and B. Don't be discouraged because your grades are not on a par with high school. The first semester is always difficult because of the need to adjust to new methods of teaching and because you must develop completely new study habits.
>
> I believe that the change in your room will be helpful to you, and if you maintain a continuous review I am sure you will experience a substantial improvement in your grades this semester.
>
> I know you are doing your best and as I told you at the beginning, as long as you do that, I am satisfied with whatever grades you produce. We all love you and we miss you already and we are waiting for the Spring break.
>
> Love,
> Dad

Moving to a double room for the second semester helped my study habits. My semester average improved to 2.7, due in part to dropping intermediate French and approaching the early morning biology lecture differently.

To avoid the language requirement, I switched from the College of Arts and Letters and to the College of Business Administration in my sophomore year. This was a big mistake, as I traded one problematic course for three—accounting, economics, and statistics. I compounded this decision to switch majors with three more mistakes: not joining any study groups, taking few notes, and creatively interpreting management and marketing materials on exams. My grades plummeted to a 1.5 that fall, followed by a 1.95 in the spring of 1974. With two semesters on academic probation, I faced dismissal, my parents' ire, and a one-way ticket home.

I knew about my dismissal before leaving campus for the summer and realized that I needed to take immediate action and negotiate my return for junior year. I met with Emil T., and we discussed my past efforts to improve my grades during the second semester of my freshman year. He agreed to support my request for reconsideration but informed me that he was not the lone decision-maker. I also needed to convince Vincent Raymond and Frank Yeandel, the associate dean and assistant dean of the College of Business Administration, respectively.

Vincent R. Raymond earned an MBA from Harvard in 1951. He joined the Notre Dame faculty in 1957 and taught courses in management. He also helped to establish ND's freshman-year program "before becoming assistant dean of the College of Business [Administration] in 1966 and associate dean in 1973. He retired on May 21, 2000."[14]

Francis A. Yeandel, a retired US Air Force colonel, was a professor and assistant dean in ND's College of Business Administration for more than twenty years. "From 1963 to '66, Yeandel taught ROTC at Notre Dame," and from 1969 through his retirement in 1989, he taught management classes at both ND and Saint Mary's College.[15]

I next met with Associate Dean Raymond, an imposing figure not used to women in the Business Administration College. Luckily, he believed in the importance of one's sophomore year:

> The sophomore year is a crossroads.... The whole issue of "What am I going to be" comes out at this time. [I'd] like to show them that they need to devote more time to becoming a well-rounded person and less time worrying about which course is going to help them get which job.[16]

He agreed to my request after obtaining my commitment to achieve no less than a 2.5 going forward. He also suggested that I increase my course load to eighteen credit hours to quickly improve my cumulative GPA. Looking back on my past academic struggles, I wonder if this was a gutsy suggestion or a vote of confidence.

With both Hofman's and Raymond's support of my improvement plan, my meeting with Assistant Dean Yeandel went smoothly. Afterward, I prepared my arguments for my father. He eventually ruled in my favor and allowed me to return to ND. Through these meetings, I realized that I had both the logical arguments and negotiation skills for a successful career.

I embraced my second chance and learned the importance of taking — and giving — second chances. My semester averages increased from 2.5 to 3.083, then 3.3, and finally 3.7. I remain grateful to my "Three ND Wise Men" for their guidance and later support of my application (and acceptance) in my senior year to ND's dual-degree juris doctorate–MBA program.

While I did not enter this combined program, I did pursue several advanced degrees after graduation — similar to more than half of my fellow trailblazers. I attribute my motivation for continuing my education to the men who believed in me more than I believed in myself. I eventually used my own academic failure in future Women in Technology presentations to encourage female high school students and show them that anything is possible with the right "GPS" (guidance, perseverance, study)!

Some of the trailblazers on graduation day (1976): Karla Grazier, Betsy Kall Brosnan, Mary Kay Rochford Demetrio, Mary Anne Kennedy Reilly Roeder, Shelley Muller Simon, Donna Crowley Campbell, Denise Crowley Brenner, and Michelle Berberet Maher

Photo courtesy of Shelley Muller Simon

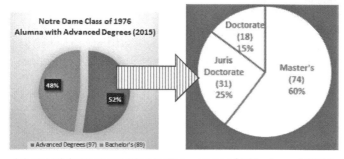

Advanced degrees reported by the women of ND's class of 1976 in *University of Notre Dame Alumni Directories* (1981–2015)

Riding Shotgun

"For what is done or learned by one class of women," wrote Elizabeth Blackwell, the first woman to earn an MD in the United States, "becomes, by virtue of their common womanhood, the property of all women."[1] Living this creed, she passed along the benefits of her education to other women, founding the New York Infirmary for Women and Children and training other women to become physicians. Perhaps she realized that driving in the fog is always easier with someone in the passenger seat—an extra set of eyes focused on the road ahead. When the University of Notre Dame embarked upon its coeducational path, it added Sister John Miriam Jones, Joanne Szafran, Susan Bennett, Jane Pitz, and Kathleen Cekanski-Farrand to advise and support the women. Yet in the university's main arena—the classroom—women students found few female role models. Although Notre Dame—"Our Lady"—presided on top of the Dome on the university campus, some women wondered if she was a beacon or a token.

◇◇◇

When Hesburgh became university president in 1952, there were no registered female undergraduates and no women on the faculty.[2] While Title VII of the Civil Rights Act of 1964 prohibited employment discrimination based on race, color, religion, national origin, or sex, it exempted academic personnel and government employees, unless they qualified as federal contractors. Despite Hesburgh's active involvement in the civil rights movement, Notre Dame's efforts to integrate women started slowly and encountered opposition from both faculty and alumni. Not until eight years later did the Equal Employment Opportunity Act repeal the academic personnel exemptions, increasing the likelihood of women professors.

After the failure of the merger with Saint Mary's, the university needed to add women to its administration. On February 15, 1972, John Barkett, in his role as student body president, offered suggestions in a paper titled "Women at Notre Dame." He recommended that the university actively recruit more female professors and counselors, while acknowledging that the administration faced a significant challenge as few qualified women worked in higher education. In March 1972, Father Burtchaell, then provost, praised Barkett for his forward-thinking efforts to improve ND's future coeducational environment.[3]

Later that year, the university's Advisory Committee on Coeducation reached the same conclusion as Barkett in its published *Malits Report*:

> It is the strong conviction of this committee that Notre Dame's decision to admit undergraduate women necessitates employing professional women in increasing numbers on every level and in each department of the University....For the welfare of all its students and in order to uphold the University's tradition of excellence in education and social relevancy, the committee recommends that ND significantly increase the number of qualified women on the faculty and include them in all administrative ranks.[4]

Barkett had also recommended establishing a "Co-Education Office to be headed by a woman"; however, Burtchaell opposed having a special dean for women.[5] Perhaps if the administration had accepted this recommendation, even if only temporarily, preparations might have extended beyond dorm renovations and into the classrooms and curricula. Although the hiring of Sister John as assistant to the provost in September 1972 addressed some of Barkett's and the *Malits Report*'s recommendations, she arrived late in the planning cycle.

The absence of women administrators was not just a problem for Notre Dame. In 1969, the Carnegie Commission on Higher Education evaluated the number of qualified women versus qualified men in faculty roles. For example, only about 5 percent of Yale's 839 faculty members were women, including only two tenured professors, seventeen assistant professors, and eleven lecturers.[6] The Carnegie Commission's analysis of institutions with this low percentage of women faculty—similar to Notre Dame's at the time—predicted that, in twenty years, a 20 percent hiring rate would increase representation of women in the faculty pool to 11 percent; at 30 percent, the female presence would increase to 14 percent; and if every other hire were a woman, this would mean that only 22 percent of faculty were women.[7] So, if a raison d'être for coeducation was creating a more normalized educational environment and an equitable extension of ND-related opportunities, this rationale also applied to its female professionals. The university needed these women to achieve its objectives, and women needed motivation to come to Notre Dame.

With this information and the 1972 *Malits Report* as a starting point, the university established the Academic Affirmative Action Committee just before the female undergraduates arrived. This committee not only drove appointments of

	1972–73	1973–74	1974–75	1975–76	1976–77
Teaching and Research Faculty	25	44	39	44	51
Special Professional Faculty	6	7	6	6	10
Special Research Faculty	0	0	0	0	0
Library Faculty	17	21	19	15	15
Total Women Faculty	48	72	64	65	76
Total Faculty	728	731	733	747	758
% of Total	6.6 %	9.8 %	8.7 %	8.7 %	10.0 %
% Without Library Faculty	4.4 %	7.0 %	6.1 %	6.7 %	8.0 %

Female composition of the Notre Dame faculty during the early years of coeducation

minorities and women but also set goals and timetables for achieving better numbers. However, with the dearth of qualified females and the competition to recruit within the collegiate sector, Notre Dame saw no significant increase in its female ranks between 1972 and 1975.

After the 1972–1973 academic year, the female composition of the faculty was only 6.6 percent (4.4 percent when excluding library faculty). The university had no female full professors, only three associate professors, nine assistant professors, eleven instructors, six professional specialists, and eighteen librarians.

Even when Dr. Josephine Ford of the Theology Department became the first Notre Dame woman professor to gain tenure, James Cooney, executive director of the Notre Dame Alumni Association, recognized that adding female professors needed to become a priority for the university. Sister John Miriam Jones described the issue as "a long road to hoe, but one that we have to be very serious about attacking."[8]

In 1975, Notre Dame established an affirmative action plan, becoming one of only thirty universities with such plans in place. Hesburgh noted that the progress in hiring women professors lagged behind the female student population. In the first five years of coeducation, the percentage of female teaching and research faculty grew in both numbers and percentage of the total Notre Dame faculty, climbing from 4.4 percent to 8.0 percent, excluding library faculty.[9] While the female student population grew from 365 to 1,350, a 270 percent increase, the number of faculty women went from 48 to 76, a 58 percent increase.[10] Despite this minor improvement, the university continued to fall slightly behind its 1975–1979 hiring goals, in part due to a freeze on faculty size and a shortage of degree-qualified women.[11] A few administrators, who translated "goals" as quotas, were recalcitrant and resisted any aggressive attempts to improving faculty diversity.[12]

Sister John's concern about the number of professional women on campus was universal. In a 1976 South Bend Tribune interview, she expressed concern about not only the number of female faculty members but also the number of females in contact (administrative) positions. She had the foresight to identify another pitfall in the numbers game: the ability to retain female professionals. The average turnover rate (e.g., attrition) was 10 percent for men and 26 percent for women.

Sister John suggested that the university look beyond the obvious departmental and personal reasons for the departures.[13]

Several university reports identified sexism and some "old-school" attitudes as one explanation for the disparity between male and female retention. An oft-cited example was a 1973 incident in which campus security tagged one female science writer's car in the professional staff parking lot because the officers believed she was a secretary. With female faculty and professionals still a rare phenomenon, the university's Athletic Department also did not provide her with football ticket applications purportedly because its leaders thought women in general were not interested in athletics, even as fans. This was a big mistake — as this ND employee was a graduate of Michigan State, a school known for its devoted sports fans.[14] On a positive note, she reported that she was pleased that more females were joining the tenure track.[15] She reflected, "Women are struggling to obtain new niches, the world is ready for women in new ways, and Notre Dame is rethinking the position of women."[16]

In a 1973 faculty address, Hesburgh said he was committed to affirmative action, and an *Observer* article covering this speech, Valerie Zurblis referenced the increasing number of females students (then 1,350) compared to that of women professors ("from 41 to 61" in the past year).[17] Hesburgh told the faculty:

> We're totally committed to this plan....Many people make the decisions to find and appoint qualified people for the faculty. It has to be something we're all committed to....I pray that all of us may meet this challenge and fulfill the promise of this place.[18]

In addition to reported instances of overt sexism, allegations of unequal pay, discrimination, and difficulty with the bureaucracy did not help to reduce the gap between male and female faculty. Some found the administration "patriarchal" and believed there was discrimination within the university's hiring, promotion, and tenure decisions. Testing the validity of this assumption, a group of female professors took legal action and filed a sex-discrimination case against ND. The parties settled out of court in 1981.[19]

By the end of the first decade of coeducation, women held 16.2 percent of the 951 Notre Dame faculty positions.[20] Today, as the university approaches fifty years of coeducation, only 27 percent of full-time tenured or tenure-track faculty is female.[21]

In general, with many women faculty, the male administrators, hall staffs, and faculty required sensitivity training before the female students arrived, a practice not yet common in work environments. Although several male professors and advisers were caring and made themselves available to the women, they sometimes did not understand the kind of guidance the women needed or wanted.

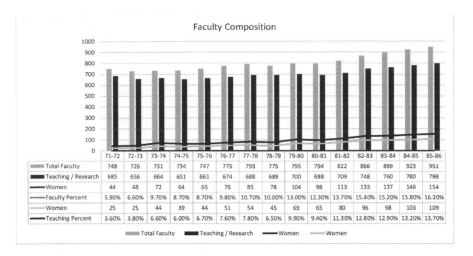

Faculty Composition

	71-72	72-73	73-74	74-75	75-76	76-77	77-78	78-79	79-80	80-81	81-82	82-83	83-84	84-85	85-86
Total Faculty	748	726	731	734	747	775	793	775	795	794	822	866	899	923	951
Teaching / Research	685	656	664	651	661	674	688	689	700	688	709	748	760	780	798
Women	44	48	72	64	65	76	85	78	104	98	113	133	137	146	154
Faculty Percent	5.90%	6.60%	9.70%	8.70%	8.70%	9.80%	10.70%	10.00%	13.00%	12.30%	13.70%	15.40%	15.20%	15.80%	16.20%
Women	25	25	44	39	44	51	54	45	69	65	80	96	98	103	109
Teaching Percent	3.60%	3.80%	6.60%	6.00%	6.70%	7.60%	7.80%	6.50%	9.90%	9.40%	11.30%	12.80%	12.90%	13.20%	13.70%

Total Faculty   Teaching / Research   Women   Women

◇ *Mary E. "Libby" Ford, ND 1975:* "My assigned adviser, a biology professor, did not want my schedule overloaded with math and science courses. Since my Advanced Placement [exam] in English prevented me from taking a freshman literature class, my adviser recommended advanced poetry writing. I hated poetry! But as a 'good Catholic girl' who never questioned authority, I agreed. When I arrived for my first class, I found it populated by senior English majors, who were surprised (and annoyed) by my presence in this sought-after class. I felt out of place but viewed it as something I just had to tolerate given my adviser's recommendation."

Not surprisingly, the women during those early years looked to and appreciated their female rectors and Sister John.

◇ *Kathleen Gwynn, ND 1976:* "There were several strong women: Sister John Miriam, Sister Jean Lenz, Dean Isabel Charles, and Jane Pitz. They were successful, dedicated, compassionate, accomplished, and—above all—human and kind."

◇ *Susan Newbould Andrews, ND 1976:* "Thanks to Jane Pitz, I overcame my homesickness and elected to remain at Notre Dame. She understood how I felt and helped me put those feelings in perspective: 'Life goes on' [for my family] with me away from home. I did not realize at the time that I was part of history in the making—the early years of women at ND. I'm glad I stayed at ND—it helped me grow up in a lot of ways. I still write to her once a year during the Christmas season."

◇ *Donna Crowley Campbell, ND 1976:* "Sister Jean Lenz was someone whom I admired. Her faith and kindness to all is something I strive to emulate."

Still, students struggled to find female and nonreligious faculty members to serve as role models or mentors. Many wished they had examples of professional women whose track records offered career paths to follow:

◇ *Shelley Muller Simon, ND 1976:* "Although I have some negative memories, most of my professors were supportive and accomplished. Only 5 percent of architects at the time were women, and so the lack of female role models prepared me for the real world."

Some questioned whether the female teachers and administrators were genuinely interested in helping the new women.

◇ *Jeanine Sterling, ND 1976:* "I had three female teachers during my four years at Notre Dame: Sheila Brennan, a philosophy professor; a graduate student TA [teaching assistant]; and TA Señora Daher, the wife of a grad student. Señora Daher was the closest...female role model at ND whom I encountered. I stayed away from the women in authority—Sister John, our rector, etc. I assumed they were more interested in rule compliance and not convinced they had my best interests at heart."

Others acknowledged some influence on their future career choices, less by female faculty members and more by the administrators and rectors at the time.

Toward the end of the twentieth century, career development—especially for members of minority and underrepresented groups—grew in importance. This included a need for new role models and opportunities for networking as well as more formal methods of mentoring. Mentoring is "a process for the informal transmission of knowledge, social capital, and psychosocial support perceived by the recipient as relevant to work, career, or professional development,"[22] and it helps individuals break through "glass ceilings" to reach their own goals and create a more equitable society. A term not necessarily known or used during the early years of coeducation, today mentoring and other career placement services have become mainstream.

◇ *Darlene Palma Connelly, ND 1977:* "If I had any female professors during my brief stint in premed or later as a psychology major, they were not memorable. Other than Sister John, I knew only two possible role models: the rector of my dorm, Kathy Cekanski, and the TA for my freshman seminar.

College	Majors			Women Faculty		Men Faculty	
	Men	Women	Total	Number	Ratio	Number	Ratio
Arts and Letters	1,239	594	1,883	39	1:48	296	1:6
Business Administration	1,205	244	1,449	2	1:725	55	1:26
Engineering	787	91	888	2	1:444	92	1:10
Science	731	207	938	5	1:188	152	1:6

Gender composition of Notre Dame majors and faculty during the early years of coeducation

"As I reflect on the road that led me to law school, perhaps their presence unconsciously influenced my career choice. Since Kathy was in the field of law, perhaps she affected my answer to the inevitable question, 'What am I gonna do after graduation?'"

This was particularly true in the College of Arts and Letters, where a high percentage of women undergraduates studied during those formative years. The Malits Committee anticipated this trend: It recommended hiring an additional assistant dean of Arts and Letters, preferably a woman, to assist the women and act as an accessible, sensitive academic counselor for both men and women.

In the fall of 1973, the university appointed Sister Isabel Charles, OP, as assistant dean in the College of Arts and Letters. She later made history in 1976 when she became the first woman dean at Notre Dame. Sister Charles recalled, "When the search committee approached me about actually taking the job, I was quite surprised in the sense that I really did not think Notre Dame was quite ready."[23] Upon her appointment as dean, she assumed leadership of the school's largest undergraduate sector, which comprised some 280 faculty and 1,700 students, and achieved mutual respect with its department chairmen, all men. She also shared her plans to increase the number of female faculty members, then totaling twenty-six, given the steady increase in the college's enrollment since 1972.

Female faculty, like their contemporaries outside of academia, balanced personal and professional challenges along with managing childcare and household duties. A professor's work extended beyond the classroom and, like today, included serving on college or university-wide committees, engaging in academic research, and publishing articles and books. Many women faculty found the burden of "breaking into" the previously all-male Notre Dame faculty isolating and frustrating. Since the social environment embraced couples and families and acknowledged males as the head of the household, single women and male spouses of female faculty had a challenging time inside the Notre Dame bubble. Luckily, most female faculty decided the challenges were worth it. They saw the students as cooperative and academically superior to those at other institutions and wanted to contribute to the normalization of this previously male-dominant university.[24]

◇ *Anonymous female, ND 1976:* "I remember that there was one female faculty member in the English Department my freshman year. When I returned from my sophomore year abroad, she was no longer there—probably because she made a lot of waves as she was very much a feminist. It was strange that she was always asking me for the female point of view, since I was the only woman in her class. You think she would have known that being singled out did not allow us to fit in—it highlighted the fact that we were different. I also felt that she expected my comments to be more enlightened."

As women in administrative and faculty positions increased nationwide, colleges and universities reevaluated their curricula, particularly regarding the evolving role of women in society. Three years after Yale went coed, it added ten women's studies courses to its curriculum.[25] Initially, no such structured women's studies program existed at Notre Dame, but women did attend women-oriented conferences, courses, and topic-specific lectures.

In the fall of 1972, Carole Moore, a history professor, taught "History of American Women" (later renamed "Women and American History"), the first course recognized as a prelude to a women's studies program. Many of Moore's students used her course to examine their own attitudes and lifestyles. Moore purported that this was a tremendous advantage to coeducation at Notre Dame. Her course opened the doors for offerings such as "Images of Woman," proposed for the fall of 1973. The professors who developed this, Elisabeth Schussler Fiorenza and Mary Lynn Broe, described the course objective as asking (and answering) the question, "Does the image of women reflect her real situation and her own reaction to it, or is it an imitation and justification of accepted and defined cultural values of the time?"[27] They were adamant that this was not a "jock course" and that active participation included the completion of three projects, ranging from research papers to meeting with women in the South Bend area to discuss image- and role-related issues. In the spring of 1973, they invited students to meet with them to help shape the course content and ensure an interdisciplinary approach, as "our women here [at Notre Dame] are scattered in every field of education."[28] In addition to these offerings, a special directed reading program called "Images of Woman in America," taught by

> In 2019, Provost Thomas Burish (ND 1972) tapped Elly Brenner (ND 1998) to establish a "centralized, University-wide advisory service for all [undergraduates]." Advisers were "embedded into the degree-granting colleges" to address the needs of those who knew where they wanted to go as well as those who had never taken liberal studies courses in their lives.[26]

Professor Madonna Kolbenschlag, centered on a study of female stereotypes in American public mythology and media.

The students who took these courses soon asked for an expanded cluster of women's studies courses and a slate of electives cross-listed by department. By 1974, four departments—Theology, History, the General Program, and English—offered classes related to women's studies. Even the College if Business Administration recognized this developing area and offered a business lecture, "Toward the Development of Assertive Women," by Suzanne Areson.[29]

Sister John also believed in continuing education for all women on campus. She planned a lecture series and a nationwide two-day conference, "This Person Called Woman," centered on the human qualities of womanhood. Speakers addressed questions such as "What does it mean to experience God as a woman?" and "What are the demands it takes to balance women's roles in these difficult transition years?" When discussing the conference's objectives, Sister John said, "God has been defined by man often. So many things are expressed by men and not asked by women."[30]

In February 1976, Notre Dame offered a series of presentations by its women faculty. During this opportunity to learn more about the challenges facing women, Professor Carole Moore stressed to the predominantly female audience:

> Choice is the basis of the feminist movement....Feminists do not say we should cease to be mothers, cease to be wives, or cease to be in love....We can't expect to be handed these things just because we're women....A new order must be forged in which human qualities are emphasized.[32]

Despite such offerings and their high enrollments, the university did not establish a women's studies program until 1988.[33] Some professors and administrators claimed that there was no need for a specific women's studies program. They recommended that courses examine the contributions of both men and women in lieu of separating the viewpoints. According to Dr. Eunice Roberts, a special programs consultant for women's programs at SMC, "The more the sexes are separated, the less chance you will have of getting them together in society."[34]

In 1988, Notre Dame established its interdisciplinary Gender Studies Program, which integrates learning and research with social change. Today, more than eighty students pursue gender studies majors, supplementary majors, and minors at the undergraduate and graduate levels. The university acknowledged the program as a minor in 2002 and added a graduate-level minor in 2008 and a primary major in 2013. The program's on-campus network regularly cosponsors events with other programs, centers, and institutes.[31]

As Notre Dame began its fifth academic year as a coeducational institution, the *South Bend Tribune* interviewed two female administrators. In an October 1976 article, June McCauslin discussed her career. She started as a secretary in 1960 and, eleven years later, became the director of Financial Aid and Scholarships at ND. As one of the few strictly administrative appointments, McCauslin demonstrated women's ability to progress in a primarily male business environment. Joining her for the interview, Elisabeth Schussler Fiorenza, then an associate professor in the Theology Department, arrived at Notre Dame in 1970 with her husband. At the time of the *Tribune* interview, she taught a three-day schedule, while her husband, also a professor, taught two days. Professor Fiorenza drew on her own life experiences when counseling women who wanted to be both professionals and wives and mothers.[35]

◇◇◇

REARVIEW REFLECTION Although I relished my math courses in high school, that interest and aptitude dissipated after a tough time with freshman calculus. At ND, I gravitated toward the softer skills of writing and speaking, which steered me in the direction of a management major. Still, I dreaded the required finance courses necessary for a business degree. Luckily, my junior year roommate, Janet, was a finance major and earned a teaching assistant (TA) position with Sophie Korczyk, one of the female faculty members in the College of Business Administration. I struggled with Sophie's course but, with Janet as her TA, I received directed tutoring and coaching.

Despite average performance in the course, Janet vouched for me, and I became Sophie's TA in my senior year. The TA role forced me to develop an understanding of finance versus merely a test-taking mentality. It also allowed me to observe firsthand the plight of a female professor at ND. Sophie and I often discussed women in business, and she provided formidable insight on working in a man's business world.

Years later, after I joined IBM, I realized that sharing our own collegiate experiences and academic challenges could translate into potentially valuable insights for others. Initially, the other first female undergraduates and I benefited from the wisdom imparted by the Saint Mary's transfers. As juniors and seniors, we later helped the "new kids on the block" and imparted our insights on student life, courses, professors, and the best place to hide during a food fight. Although not a term used widely in the 1970s, this kind of "mentoring" carried over into our professional lives.

I expected such help from the Notre Dame family to continue after graduation. While it did when I worked for Commonwealth Edison, it did not in my early years at IBM. As a member of IBM's personal computer team, I worked with two ND graduates — a male and a female transfer student. The male was an old-school sexist who saw women as good administrators but poor executive material. The female was the antithesis of other IBM females I knew, who were generous with their mentoring and encouragement. She seldom helped others break through the glass ceiling, even ND alumnae. Working with these two temporarily crushed my trust in the ND family, and it took fifteen years before I glued back together the pieces of that shattered belief.

In retrospect, she unknowingly did help me. Because of her, I made a point of mentoring young women as they joined IBM's personal computer, mobile, and project management teams. From my return from the academic abyss and after finding the right mentor, my experiences provided great career discussion materials for high school girls considering college majors and careers in technology.

Potholes

Novelist Nora Roberts shares a vivid and pragmatic view of reality in her observation, "Potholes and bumps? Welcome to the world. Every road has them. They're there to be navigated, avoided, driven over or through to the other side."[1] At Notre Dame, the pressures to succeed, to be the best, and to fit in were (and are) tremendous for students of all genders. Many at ND struggled to balance residential, academic, and social experiences. Some, when feeling overwhelmed, turned to alcohol and drugs, and these students soon learned that even minimal use required continual watchfulness so as not to impact grades and, more importantly, relationships.

◇◇◇

Throughout its history, the university, like its students, searched for the proper relationship with alcohol. Mirroring trends in the United States as a whole, ND policy swung from total abstinence to limited engagement (where blue laws prohibited sales on Sundays) and then to allowing anyone of legal age to buy alcohol almost anytime, anywhere. Although Sorin initially banned hard liquor but not the consumption of beer, the university banned all alcohol in 1881.[2] Not until the late 1960s did the administration soften its ban for those of legal age and ignore underage violations.

Students in the 1970s faced the return of stronger restrictions on drinking as Indiana law revised its stance on institutional liability for underage consumption, exposing the university to significant risk. From the 1980s through 2002, the university's policy focused on containment and the prohibition of kegs. Today's ND rules ban hard liquor in all undergraduate halls (even during alumni reunions and for those long past the legal age), though the university permits beer and alcohol for in-hall dances. Undergraduates of legal age — twenty-one — may host tailgates in a designated parking lot as long as they have preregistered the event.[3] As *Notre Dame Magazine* explained in 1997:

For many students, attending college presents their first opportunity to experiment with alcohol and drugs.

In 1999, a study by the Harvard School of Public Health found that binge drinking was more prevalent at schools in the Northeast and North Central regions of the country, at "very competitive" institutions, and those in rural or small-town areas.[5] Institutions with major football and tailgating traditions also increase drinking on campus.

Many of these characteristics clearly describe ND.

A 2008 article by Christine M. Dietz, a Saint Mary's alumna, highlighted that the "culture of alcohol" on college campuses is influenced by "a number of elements," including:

- Drinking games and events
- Greek life
- Athletic events
- Students' new autonomy
- Perceived peer approval
- Attempts to appear older or more mature
- Pushback against perceived hypocritical rules
- Higher levels of tolerance because of age
- The "work hard–play hard" myth[6]

Notre Dame was a dry campus for many years through the 1960s. Alcohol abuse was a problem then, just as it was in the '70s and early '80s when our policies were far more lenient. It's still a problem today under more restrictive rules. A dry-campus policy is not likely to change how students drink, but where.[4]

Alcohol fueled the social scene across and around campus. It helped to remove inhibitions and paved the way for conversations, good times, and occasional pranks. One student recalled a prank played on a heavy-drinking dorm mate:

◇ *Anonymous male, ND 1976:* "One guy in our dorm always came back wasted after a night of hard drinking. He lived in a single with a daybed that pulled out to the width of the room. One night while he was out, we took the door to his room off the hinges and slid in a Coke machine, preventing him from opening his bed. We plugged in the Coke machine and put the door back on. [...]

"When he finally staggered into his room, a string of expletives announced his discovery of the Coke machine, after which he promptly passed out on the couch. The final straw occurred the next morning, when one of my friends woke him up and asked if he could get a Coke."

As the university took steps to restrict undergraduate alcohol use, nearby bars became the center of social life for many students. The owners supplied alcohol despite rowdy patrons and the legal hassles that could come from violating liquor and business licenses as well as Indiana drinking age laws. Proprietors of establishments such as Corby's, Nickie's, and The Library managed the crowds and dealt with damages to flooring, pool tables, and bar counters due to spilled wine and alcohol, cigarettes, and general abuse by overzealous drinkers. Theft of glassware and pitchers drove the use of paper and plastic cups.

Unfortunately, for some, drinking ruined more than property; it also harmed self-images, academic success, and relationships. The consequences became more serious if consumption rose to the level of binge drinking (defined as four drinks for women or five drinks for men in a single sitting within a two-week period).[7] A host of nightmare situations often resulted from repeated binge drinking: academic underachievement and dismissal, vandalism, indecent public behavior, fights, sexual assault (including date rape), and accidental death.[8]

Despite the risks, many students turned to alcohol to ease the social awkwardness of the newly coeducational environment:

> ◇ *Shelley Muller Simon, ND 1976:* "The sheer ratio of males to females made for an uncomfortable situation at times. Whether because of a lack of girls to date, whether the guys were too shy to ask the girls out, or whether the girls were without dates on the weekends, somehow the presence of alcohol made it easier to cope. Almost everybody drank on occasion — some more than others."

Others used drinking as a way to relate to and fit in, while some turned to alcohol to shore up their courage:

> ◇ *Patricia Gallagher Shields, ND 1976:* "I remember the beginning of sophomore year and seeing one of the girls I knew in a beer-chugging contest with a group of guys. And I thought, 'What a terrible way to be accepted.'"

> ◇ *Jack Bergen, ND 1977:* "I witnessed too much drinking (myself included) as the men tried to work up the courage to ask a girl out. Several of my dorm mates came from traditional single-sex Catholic high schools and had not learned about social interaction with females. Many of us were socially awkward, eighteen-year-old Catholic boys thrust into this environment of having to date girls for the first time outside of a prom."

Articles on the extent of alcoholism and alcohol abuse at ND appeared in *The Observer*. The administration voiced concerns about the excessive consumption of alcohol. While ND's Center for Continuing Education indicated that one out of every ten to fifteen drinkers in the United States was an alcoholic, Rosemary Lough, director of the Alcoholism Council of Saint Joseph County, believed that at least one out of ten drinkers in a student population like Notre Dame's was in the earlier stages of alcoholism.[9] Dr. Sheridan McCabe, director of ND's counseling center, spoke of alcohol abuse rather than alcoholism:

> What we are talking about here are students who take alcohol on a regular basis to the point where they are stuporous or beyond that point.... We are talking about the students who get bombed every weekend, who drink without caution to the point of loss of control. In some cases this means two or three drinks in other instances, it means half a fifth.[10]

In 1956, the American Medical Association (AMA) identified alcoholism as a disease that alters the part of the "brain that controls a person's motivation and ability to make healthy choices."[11] Since the end of the 1970s, many health professionals and organizations have discouraged using the term "alcoholism" — due to both its inexact definition and its tendency to stigmatize those who are struggling with alcohol dependence. Instead, alcoholism is known today as "alcohol use disorder" (or AUD), which can range from mild to severe.[12]

McCabe did not, however, push a "crackdown" policy, indicating that alcohol was fine when consumed in moderation. Instead, he advocated for more outlets and activities through which students could change their attitudes toward drinking:

> [T]here should be some more appropriate way to release tension than by getting drunk every weekend. We need some consciousness raising so that students can examine what they are doing to themselves and look for alternatives — while simultaneously having a good time![13]

Lough also suggested that students be aware of the warning signs of problematic alcohol consumption, applicable to both males and females, and describing these with memorable monikers:

- The High Tolerance drinker who continues drinking long after friends have stopped.

- The Blackout drinker who fails to remember what he or she did during all or part of the time spent drinking.

- The Focal Point drinker who uses any reason to drink — after passing a test, after failing one, or if a professor never even shows up to give the test.

- The Jekyll-Hyde drinker who undergoes a radical personality change during or after drinking.

By recognizing these signs, friends helped to prevent destruction not only of property but also lives.[14]

◇ *Anonymous, ND 1976:* "I have friends who had things shaved — eyebrows, heads, stuff like that. Some friends even peed on one guy who had passed out. I could tell you many stories related to drinking, but mostly just people breaking things, doing stupid stuff, [having sex with] a girl they would not normally hang out with."

Alcohol was not the only drug used on ND's campus. While a US government study reported that alcoholism was the number-one drug problem affecting nine million Americans and costing about fifteen billion dollars a year,[15] the National Commission on Marijuana and Drug Abuse announced that twenty-four million Americans (15 percent) experimented with marijuana — though only one-third used it regularly.[16] In 1972, a Gallup Poll revealed that half of college students had tried marijuana, while 18 percent had experimented with mind-expanding drugs — a sharp increase compared to the rates of 5 percent and 1 percent, respectively, just five years earlier.[17] Ray Pikna recalled how casually marijuana was treated at ND:

◇ *Ray Pikna, ND 1976:* "I met a few guys playing basketball during my first few weeks on campus but didn't know any of them well. One of the older guys struck me as a stereotypical hippie. As the TV lounge filled up rapidly for the national premiere of *Goldfinger* on a September night that will forever remain etched in my memory, this guy and I ended up sitting on the same couch. He lit up a joint, took a hit, bumped his elbow into mine, and offered the joint to me. I had never smoked and had no intention of starting, but how could I extricate myself from this situation without offending him or violating my principles? Should I partake to keep the peace? Would I be laughed at by my peers if I refused? I blurted out, 'You know, I've read stories about that!' He looked at me strangely at first, but when I grinned, he started to laugh, then passed the joint in the other direction. Crisis averted, and (thankfully) he never offered me a joint again."

The university recognized the combination of alcohol and drugs as a growing problem. According to McCabe, "for every student who is abusing drugs like 'downers' and so forth there are many, many more who are abusing alcohol in a way detrimental to their well being and to their participation as students on campus."[18] Dean John Macheca, supporting this observation, emphasized that drugs represented a lifestyle issue requiring a dedicated focus if administrators were to rid the campus of the problem. He also clarified the Student Life Council's drug regulations, which deemed the use of marijuana as unacceptable and regarded providing drugs to others or possessing or using "any narcotic or hallucinogenic" as serious violations. He also "warned students not to bring quantities of drugs" to campus. By providing fair warning about the consequences of drug violations, Macheca believed all students understood the university's position.[19]

However, this was not the case, as questions of enforcement still arose. In October 1973, Macheca and other university personnel conducted raids on three residence halls: Saint Ed's, Dillon, and Grace. According to *The Observer*, the involved students ran the gamut from users to dealers of both marijuana and LSD.[20] The resulting punishments ranged from probation to suspension to expulsion. Student reactions varied, and some even questioned the school's right to enter rooms. Vice President for Student Affairs Philip Faccenda attempted to calm concerns over privacy violations by stressing that the university would only enter a room when there was a reason to believe that a rule violation was in process. Since rooming contracts provided for "access for cause," he further defined "reason" as "covering only those situations" where a witness or a university official "saw, heard or smelled a violation."[21]

Despite the potential consequences, students smoked marijuana. In lieu of lighting up, parties often included "grassy" brownies that prevented aromas from entering the hallways. However, some students did not appreciate pot's presence on campus, while others tried to avoid discussions of drug use.

> ◇ *Anonymous male, ND 1976:* "I always thought it strange that people smoked weed and yet complained when others smoked cigarettes."

> ◇ *Anonymous female, ND 1976:* "I worried about my roommate, who appeared to use both marijuana and some stimulants. These activities did not appear to affect her coursework, and since I had no direct knowledge of the usage, I stayed away from discussions on the topic. I just knew her essays were always quite 'creative.'"

> ◇ *Ann Pytynia, ND 1976:* "There was substance use and abuse on campus. Lots of alcohol everywhere we turned. Pot, speed, and mushrooms were visible like there was no tomorrow. Still, tame compared to today. For me, such usage was a huge adjustment from high school. I always thought that the great amount of

contraband during those days was somehow tied to how well-off ND students were. Many had the money to spend on these things."

Counseling services existed to help students address concerns over the potential abuse of alcohol and drugs. The first student health service appeared at Amherst College in 1861, and a half-century later "Princeton University established the first mental health service in 1910," addressing issues such as academic performance and personality development.[22] Counseling services and psychological support were generally not part of the student support system until the 1960s and 1970s. During this period, collegiate institutions encouraged students to engage in physical activities to complement their academic pursuits and left counseling primarily to the clergy.[23]

In the 1971–1972 academic year, Notre Dame's Psychological Services, whose only mission at the time was crisis intervention, consisted of three male psychologists and one female psychiatrist. Despite pre-coeducation experiences with graduate women and the Co-Exchange Program with Saint Mary's, the fall 1972 arrival of women on campus brought no changes to this department. In 1975–1976 alone, 421 Notre Dame students sought help: 353 males (6.5 percent of the male students) and 68 females (5 percent of the female students).[24] The use of these services by Notre Dame women conflicted with data from other universities, indicating that women used such services more than men. Staffing levels only changed after the 1976–1977 "Report of the Committee to Evaluate Coeducation." Notre Dame's Psychological Services added a female therapist, a female counselor, and a male psychiatrist acting as a consultant.

Students struggled not only with the day-to-day but also with what lay ahead. The need to succeed academically, athletically, and socially caused varying levels of frustration and stress. Irresponsible drinking, use of drugs, and promiscuity at times obscured such anxieties. ND's Psychological Services helped students with all these topics and many more. Several anonymous students turned to this resource to work through deeper issues:

> ◇ *Anonymous male, ND 1976:* "I counseled briefly with the male head of ND Psych Services regarding same-sex relationship problems that I was having at the time. They told me that I was not gay; that my same-sex relationships were 'just a phase.' They were not correct. I hope, for the sake of current gay students, that ND–SMC has become less homophobic by now and realizes that some people are gay and deserve support systems (like counselors and social clubs) for their special needs. There are very few, if any, places after college to meet and socialize with gay people who are as highly educated, have as high ethical standards, and

have similar backgrounds to the people with whom I went to college. I thought I was the only gay person at ND–SMC; I certainly felt like the only one. College would have been a good place to start some friendships."

◇ *Anonymous, ND 1976:* "I used the on-site psychological service, and it started a long-term therapeutic process dealing with many aspects of my life, particularly the impact of my father and the Catholic Church on my development."

◇ *Anonymous, ND 1976:* "Junior year, I had a period of depression for which I should have been treated."

Notre Dame Magazine, Spring 2014
Art courtesy of Gary Hovland

Besides Psychological Services, Notre Dame's Counseling Center also offered a professional staff and graduate students to advise undergraduates in areas of personal development. Both ND's and Saint Mary's counseling centers targeted issues arising from relationships within the ND–SMC community. In the spring of 1975, the two centers established eight-week discussion groups with equal numbers of men and women. The unbalanced male-to-female ratio on campus magnified social disparities within the community. Discussions covered problems with building relationships, the games men and women play in dating and courtship, and the significance of changing gender roles. Early on, conversations focused on the women's impact on Notre Dame, but seldom did they explore the impact of Notre Dame on the women—a topic that was raised in later surveys, articles, and panels.

◇ *Betsy Kall Brosnan, ND 1976:* "I am concerned with the fact that with all the avenues open to women, they put too much pressure upon themselves to perform. Some of us wanted it all—career, marriage, and family—and yet were unable to define our priorities and perspectives. We needed to realize that we all have limits; we needed to define our goals and be able to accept life as it comes, even if that means we can't be 'perfect' in all of our chosen careers."

Some students worried that these professionals did not understand their needs and would not protect their privacy. To fill the void and combat such concerns, some residence halls provided outreach programs as an extension of the Counseling Center. Hall section leaders participated in a leadership-training program offered by the Center to support their efforts.

Students also sought out friends, resident assistants, and rectors as sounding boards. Rectors, especially ones such as Sister Jean or Father Miceli, filled many roles in their interactions with students, even becoming lifelong friends who attended or officiated at weddings, baptisms, and funerals. Erin Hoffman Harding (ND 1997), in her role as Notre Dame vice president for Student Affairs, defined the rector's role "as pastors of this community...forging bonds, fostering faith, or knowing what to do when a student opened up about divorce or violated the alcohol policy or parietals...even calling the plumber when needed."[25]

Many students found professors who went beyond just teaching a particular subject and wanted to educate the entire person. Such approaches mirrored Hesburgh's actions when he started a "Marriage and the Family" course in Vetville after realizing that the vets and their wives needed a combination of theory and practice in communicating and operating as a unit. A similar course, "Sex and Marriage" taught by Father Joseph Hoffman, gave students a safe space for relationship discussions.

Given the weak economy facing college graduates in the mid-1970s, the ND Counseling Center also offered life-planning workshops. Separate from the Placement Center, which focused on job placement, these sessions taught life skills and how to set personal and career goals. The programs addressed anxiety management, assertiveness training, job interview techniques, life planning, and marriage. In the fall of 1976, the center documented 567 hours of student contact, with seventy-five students (sixteen women and fifty-nine men, or roughly 1 percent of each group).[26]

Unfortunately — and sadly — failure to resolve or address personal and psychological issues sometimes resulted in depression, despair, and (in rare cases) the loss of life of fellow students.

◇ *Janet Krier Breen, ND 1975:*

"Despair is staring at the springs under the upper bunk.
Despair is being awake but unable to blink.
Despair is knowing your arms and legs won't move.
Despair is counting the days until graduation,
Without a clue about what comes next."

◇ *Ray Pikna, ND 1976:* "When I returned my sophomore year, I was shocked to find out that one of our classmates had committed suicide during the summer. He had been a 'big man on campus' in high school. Had he failed to adapt to the anonymity of being just another student on campus? What despair could have driven a young man with so much promise to take his own life? We had never been close, but how could I have missed the warning signals? I still don't have the answers, and I never will."

◇ *Anonymous, ND 1976:* "The suicide of a colleague taught me that life is fragile, and we take good mental health for granted. I have learned not to take myself too seriously and to try to really listen to other people. I learned to ask myself, 'When I'm on my deathbed, will I wish that I had worked more?' It also made me realize that a person should not be damned for their physical impairments. I cannot believe that God damns a person for their mental impairments, which I believe my colleague had. I can't believe she's in hell for taking her own life."

According to Notre Dame's University Counseling Center and Campus Ministry statistics, only thirteen documented suicides occurred in Notre Dame's population from 1849 to 1994,[27] yet the need for such services continues. Rob Danzman, a licensed clinical mental health counselor, notes that:

> The American College Health Association's 2018 Annual Survey found that 60% of students experienced debilitating anxiety, 40% of students were too depressed to go to class or hang with friends and 55% felt hopeless in the last year. Nearly 20% considered suicide and about 1,100 commit suicide each year. Only 10–15% of these students seek help at campus counseling services.[28]

Tragic cases occur, like those reported in articles in the *South Bend Tribune* and the *Chicago Tribune*: A senior at Notre Dame's Mendoza College of Business died in March 2015, less than a week after overdosing on lethal drugs in a suicide attempt,[29] and a nineteen-year-old freshman at neighboring Saint Mary's College battled depression and died of an apparent suicide nine days after telling Notre Dame police she was sexually attacked by a football player in a dorm room in 2017.[30]

◇◇◇

REARVIEW REFLECTION In high school, the "cool kids" drank, smoked pot, and took drugs. I did not run in those circles; I got my high from classes, clubs, and waterskiing. At Notre Dame, however, alcohol became my "drug" of choice, although I did try pot several times. I had little interest in stimulants or hallucinatory drugs, but I now realize that my diet pills fell in the former category. Because a doctor prescribed them, I never considered them a violation of ND's drug policy.

In some ways, I was a "pusher" because I encouraged others to get prescriptions for such pills. One of my deepest regrets is strongly urging a male friend to obtain them, since his weight affected his looks and ability to date. I foolishly thought that, if he lost weight, other females would "see" him and his wonderful personality. He came back to school our junior year in great shape. That summer, he had used marijuana and hard drugs, not prescription diet pills, to lose weight. His addiction eventually overwhelmed him, and he overdosed after graduation. I think of him often and hope my prodding did not create his demons.

In addition to the diet pills, I abused alcohol during my first two years at ND. The combination of my weight, academic failures, and lack of experience in this new setting made me feel insecure, which in turn drove me to many nights of drinking. The more I drank, the less I studied; the more I went out, the more weight I gained. My usage never prevented me from attending class, but I often lacked focus, especially in morning sessions. The more I drifted from my core values, the more I wanted to leave Notre Dame. It was all one vicious cycle.

Junior year was a turning point for me. Early one Sunday morning, I stopped by Beverly's room and overheard her weekly phone call with her mother. I froze in my tracks as I listened to her describe my previous night's alcohol consumption. Even worse, she told her mother how bloated the drinking made me, comparing me to Jo Anne Worley, the busty, dark-haired actress on the popular television show *Rowan and Martin's Laugh-In*. Beverly's comments were the unintentional slap in the face I needed. I was mortified by her description of me and vowed to change my ways.

If I had any doubt that I needed to control my drinking, a priest who became a lifelong friend and mentor helped me to find my way. I eventually realized that I turned to alcohol because I was never really sure whether guys were actually interested in me or just wanted a date with one of the few women on campus. I came to college with little faith in male–female relationships after a boy I asked to my high school Sadie Hawkins Day dance did not show up. My dad sheltered me from any reoccurrence of this pain by limiting my dating to homecoming (I was on the court) and senior prom. Not wanting others to experience the pain of that Sadie Hawkins fiasco, coupled with Teddy Bear Man's advice to give each guy a chance, I rejected few invitations. Like everyone, I just wanted to find someone who recognized my frailties but loved me anyway.

Father Joseph Hoffman helped me to understand these issues when I took his "Sex and Marriage" course. In class, he told a story about a high school student who observed a classmate taking all his books home on a Friday. The first student realized something was off, and he befriended the other student; he kept him from committing suicide. Hoffman emphasized that I would not be at Notre Dame if I did not have something to offer to others. He encouraged me to look at how I spent my time and to reset my priorities. Through this course and countless

Robert "Bob" Rieman, a twenty-year-old government major and Stanford Hall resident, died when his bicycle swerved into a tanker truck. Rieman was active in campus activities, including with the Logan Center, tutoring programs, and the Ombudsman Service.[31]

conversations after, I came to trust Hoffman with my most personal issues.

In time, I began volunteering at a nursing home and as a tutor. Life seemed less confusing as I returned to familiar activities I had done in high school. I befriended guys instead of dating them. When one Keenan-Stanford friend, Bob Reiman, died in an auto accident, his parents told me they found my signed picture in his wallet. Their comments came at a pivotal time for me and reinforced not only the value of male friendships over dates but also that I had value.

Driving Defensively

"Owning our story can be hard," Brené Brown, a research professor of social work at the University of Houston, encourages women, "but not nearly as difficult as spending our lives running from it."[1] Some women at Notre Dame experienced firsthand the administration's failure to adequately address alcohol and drug use. In addition to being ill-equipped to initially handle such issues, the university's medical and counseling facilities also struggled to respond knowledgeably and openly to questions about gender and sexuality. This failure became deeply traumatic for some when sexual tensions resulted in violations of personal space, varying degrees of sexual assault, and rape.

◇◇◇

When the university announced that it was going coed, it took some steps to ensure the health of its students. In the spring of 1972, Notre Dame renovated the second floor of its infirmary in anticipation of female patients in the fall. These changes enlarged the infirmary's footprint and segregated the sleeping sections by sex. The changes were made in response to studies by the Advisory Committee for Coeducation that found women used infirmary services twice as often as men.[2]

The infirmary staff consisted of a full-time physician, a part-time orthopedic surgeon, a consulting psychiatrist, and nineteen registered nurses. Even though infirmary hours were from 7:00 a.m. to 10:30 p.m., its physicians generally left at 3:30 p.m. to fulfill other responsibilities. And despite Student Body President John Barkett's recommendation in his "Women at Notre Dame" paper to add a gynecologist to ND's medical services, Provost Burtchaell rejected the suggestion for financial reasons, saying "the University does not have the money for specialists."[3] Instead, the infirmary's diagnosticians referred females to local gynecologists and those physicians offering preferential appointments.

During the 1970s, birth control and the right to abortion were hot topics across America and on college campuses. In an October 1972 meeting with the Badin

On January 22, 1973, the Supreme Court issued a 7–2 landmark decision in *Roe v. Wade* that held that the Due Process Clause of the Fourteenth Amendment provided a fundamental "right to privacy," generally protecting a pregnant woman's right to an abortion. That decision struck down many federal and state abortion laws and fueled a fifty-year debate. On June 24, 2022, the Court overturned *Roe* in *Dobbs v. Jackson Women's Health Organization*, with Justice Samuel Alito writing in the majority opinion that the right to abortion is not "deeply rooted in the Nation's history and tradition" nor considered a right when the Due Process Clause was ratified in 1868.[6] Many legal and reproductive scholars have taken issue with these conclusions in *Dobbs*, not necessarily because of the originalist approach used by the majority but because the decision appears to cherry-pick the data: In the seventeenth and eighteenth centuries, "legal authorities Edward Coke, Matthew Hale and William Blackstone had all advocated for or condoned abortion," and it was widespread through the mid-nineteenth century particularly before "quickening," or "when the mother realizes that the fetus moves in her womb, approximately the fourth month of pregnancy."[7] Historians Leslie J. Reagan and Mary Ziegler have also documented abortion's legal, medical, and social history in the United States.[8]

Hall women, Hesburgh vetoed the proposed birth control campus center advocated in *The Observer*.[4] He stated that such a center, similar to Planned Parenthood, implied condoning immorality. He stressed that adults on campus could advise and refer students to suitable agencies if the need arose.[5] Bottom line, gynecological health care and gender-specific health information for ND women were almost nonexistent on campus.

◇ *Anonymous female, ND 1976*: "I went to the infirmary and asked for a pap smear because the one at home had come back inconclusive. Even though overdue for this important follow-up, I did not receive the test. The nurse dismissed my concerns."

◇ *Anonymous female, ND 1976*: "My second year, I really wanted to talk to a female doctor. Let's just say that I was in a 'crabby' situation caused by an infestation in the dorm restrooms. No one talked about such things, and I had experienced nothing like it. The cure was simple. I also learned to stand up when using public restrooms, something my mother tried to teach me whenever we traveled."

◇ *Anonymous female, ND 1976*: "I went to a female physician [in South Bend] who was terrible. She said I was in the second stage of syphilis based on a rash on my abdomen. I said, 'Lady, what about the first stage and the contact?'"

◇ *Susan Davis Flanagan, ND 1976:* "I do remember the infirmary was definitely not ready for girls and female problems. As I recall, it had a waiting room where we all sat, and most people were sneezing, coughing, etc. The nurse would come out and ask about your problem and symptoms in front of everyone. For most people, it was fever, cough, sore throat, and no one was embarrassed to discuss those symptoms. However, I had a lump on my breast and came to have it checked. When they got to me, I had to say it aloud in front of a roomful of guys. The nurse stopped in her tracks and had no idea what to say or do. Every guy in the place instantly stopped coughing. I just recall a dead silence, with no one quite knowing how to handle this, and I was terribly embarrassed."

Not all experiences at the infirmary or with South Bend doctors were negative.

◇ *Laura Dodge-Ghara, ND 1976:* "Shortly before first-semester final exams, I went to the infirmary accompanied by a couple of friends. In addition to other symptoms, I had a high fever and could not sleep. The infirmary kept me overnight. The staff continually checked on me, and I'll never forget their kindness. One nurse divulged I was the first female to stay overnight."

In 2007, ND's University Health Services, University Counseling Center, and Office of Alcohol and Drug Education moved into an eight-million-dollar renovated infirmary building, renamed Saint Liam Hall. The remodel replaced the aging mechanicals of the building while maintaining its original slate roof. A new vestibule on the east side welcomed students to the improved facilities, complete with state-of-the-art medical equipment and patient and examining rooms.[9]

On July 10, 1973, just before a new class of women arrived, the infirmary addressed some of the women's privacy concerns and expanded its first floor to include two additional screening rooms. The first female doctor, Dr. Helen M. Calvin, also joined the staff. In an initial interview with *The Observer*, Dr. Calvin expressed her belief that women have more compassion in certain areas as a result of "women just being women." However, she stressed that her role did not include gynecological counseling — in particular, in matters of birth control.[10] Notre Dame women went elsewhere for such medical attention and guidance.

A large-scale influenza outbreak hit Notre Dame in January 1975. To manage the epidemic, Sister Miriam Dolores Hartrich, the infirmary's administrator, gave priority to the seriously ill and the twenty-five students staying overnight to see the doctor. Despite the federal government encouraging a massive immunization program during the extensive 1975 and 1976 flu seasons, Notre Dame deemed the flu shot nonmandatory.[11] Although another physician joined the infirmary's staff in July 1975, the university took no additional precautions to protect the health of its student body.

From July 1975 to June 1976, 41 percent of the women and 46 percent of the men visited the infirmary. In a survey for the 1976–1977 academic year, more than 70 percent of males ranked the infirmary's services as "good" or "excellent," while less than 50 percent of females gave it such high ratings.[12] The men's positive views most likely reflected the differences in the medical treatment provided to male athletes. The standard student insurance, which covered most injuries sustained during hall competitions, may have skewed the survey results given how many more men participated in sports than did the early female athletes, who were offered limited sports opportunities. For participants in club-level athletics — of which there were few for women — university insurance covered expenses not covered by the student insurance, while coverage at the varsity level depended on the sport.

ND's decision to offer sex-specific medical services for women was much like the chicken-and-the-egg question: Which came first? With perceptions that the care provided often was terrible and inconvenient, the women did not use these university resources unless they had no other option. Since few came forward to request services related to gynecology, infirmary administrators saw no need to add that specialty. A January 15, 1976, *Observer* article compared ND's health services with those at other coed universities. One senior woman summarized the situation: "Notre Dame has certainly ignored the needs of its newly-admitted women when it comes to health care services. There is just a total lack of understanding when it comes to certain matters, especially when it concerns the 'taboo' matter of sexuality."[13] A part-time gynecologist (a male) finally joined the staff in the fall of 1976, after the 365 pioneers had graduated.

In the late 1960s and 1970s, discussions of male and female anatomy, the reproductive system, and sex were fairly open — but generally not in Catholic schools or in strict, conservative homes. The ND infirmary was ill-equipped to answer students' questions related to their bodies and physical relationships, and the university remained unprepared to address health or sexuality education. This conservative approach also caused the administration to miss events never anticipated. As Emil T. Hofman reflected:

> We were shocked to learn that one of our first women students was pregnant and did not realize it. When she went into labor, it was something that we had never encountered and had not anticipated. I think we did a fairly good job of keeping the situation relatively private, but the stories eventually came out and were, of course, exaggerated.[14]

Given the lack of information from official sources, women sought information beyond biology and other science classes in books such as the classic guide to women's health, *Our Bodies, Ourselves*. The authors, the Boston Women's Health Book Collective that was founded in 1969, clarified the book's purpose:

> Learning to understand, accept, and be responsible for our physical selves, we are freed of some of these preoccupations and can start to use our untapped energies. Our image of ourselves is on a firmer base, we can be better friends and better lovers, better *people*, more self-confident, more autonomous, stronger, and more whole.[15]

On October 23, 1972, William H. Masters and Virginia E. Johnson gave a lecture on "Sex as a Natural Function" in Washington Hall. From 1957 until the 1990s, Masters and Johnson pioneered research into human sexual response and the diagnosis and treatment of sexual disorders and dysfunctions. They jointly wrote two classic texts in the field, *Human Sexual Response* and *Human Sexual Inadequacy*, published in 1966 and 1970, respectively. During the lecture, Masters talked about religion as one of the greatest obstacles to normal sexual life in America. Johnson defined sex as

In 1972, the first X-rated cartoon, *Fritz the Cat*, achieved notoriety on college campuses and brought heightened awareness of physical needs. That same year, the pornographic movie *Deep Throat* launched a new era in the genre. ("Deep Throat" also was the pseudonym *Washington Post* reporters Carl Bernstein and Bob Woodward gave to their informant in the Watergate scandal. The public came to know this "Deep Throat" in Bernstein and Woodward's 1974 book, *All the President's Men*. Mark Felt, an associate director with the FBI, revealed his identity as their source in 2005. He died in 2008.)

> Social controls developed for natural function, but through misunderstanding and hopefully not maliciousness, the assigned controls to sexuality did not represent the naturalness of the function.... [T]he common assumption that sexuality can be exposed to artificial controls and still remain healthy, creative, and a birthright is a myth....Sexual functioning is the most effective means of communication between a man and a woman. Communication is the exchange of vulnerability....Sex is with someone, not at the expense of someone.[16]

Rejecting traditional values and presenting sex as an effective communications tool on a Catholic campus with parietals caused quite a conundrum for both the administration and the students!

Sexual assault, which includes sexual contact, behaviors, or acts that occur without explicit consent "is a public health and public safety problem with far-reaching implications." It can "cause immediate, as well as long-term, physical and mental health consequences," and it significantly increases the risk of suicide.[17] In 1975, an article in *The Observer* warned the women of Notre Dame campus: "Since 1960, the incidence of reported rape on college campuses has increased 160 per cent and 65 per cent of all rape victims are university coeds."[18]

Today, it is estimated that 19–27 percent of women and 6–8 percent of men on college campuses experience sexual assault, although these numbers likely underreport the true scope of the issue due to methodological challenges in research studies and persistent social stigmas about sexual assault and those who are affected by it. Victim costs related to sexual assault can exceed one hundred billion dollars per year.[19]

Over the past several decades, reported rape on college campuses has increased, in part due to legal changes and increased awareness, but sexual violence on campus remains a pervasive issue.[20]

By the fifth year of coeducation, administrators identified the need for comprehensive programs about sexuality and responsible sexual behavior. They acknowledged that a lack of awareness and understanding about these topics influenced the total development of men and women and sometimes even proved detrimental to individual health, well-being, and relationships. The university developed a multidimensional approach that included the existing University Health Services, University Counseling Center, Campus Ministry, and the Theology, Sociology, and Anthropology departments. The program encompassed education, issue resolution, and new courses on the practical elements of human relations and sexuality. The university balanced the program's content with its commitment to Catholic tradition, rules governing visitation, and its strongly articulated belief that intercourse was solely for married couples. In the first two semesters the program was offered, approximately "100 Notre Dame women and 325 men were enrolled" in the program's various courses.[21]

Despite this multidimensional approach to sexuality and sexual behavior, students still heard little about the intersection of alcohol, drugs, and sex and sexual assault in those first five years of coeducation. Notre Dame failed to drive awareness of and establish policies related to violations of personal space, varying degrees of sexual assault, and rape, as well as how these intersected with substance use. Numerous research papers reported (then and now) that a significant number of college sexual assaults involved the perpetrators, victims, or both having consumed alcohol in alcohol-related settings (e.g., parties, bars).[22]

Although girls and women in their late teens and early twenties—the age range for most college students—experience the greatest risk of "date rape," a term coined by Susan Brownmiller, few students at the time were familiar with this danger.[23] Early on, date rape primarily referred to women as the victims in situations where pleasantness turned to unpleasantness and more. The term has since changes and covers rape that takes place within any romantic or sexual relationship between individuals. Acquaintance rape involves victims and perpetrators who are in non-romantic, nonsexual relationships, such as coworkers or neighbors. Today's Notre Dame students receive information about the ways spiked drinks or "date-rape drugs" create situations of vulnerability and how excessive drinking can lead to inappropriate and even dangerous situations for young women as well as men.

Such crime on campus—or at least the reporting of it—was rare. But assaults occurred and were reported outside the boundaries of campus. In the early 1970s, South Bend experienced high crime rates, and in 1973, the city's Women's Committee on Sex Offenses established its Sex Offense Staff (SOS) and an SOS hotline in response to concern over rising sexual crime statistics. In the first eight months of 1974, SOS handled forty-five rape reports, with victims ranging in age from three to eighty-three.[24]

To enlighten female students about this issue, SOS offered seminars about rape at both Notre Dame and Saint Mary's College. Female ND security officers also presented a program entitled "Ladies Take Warning" in each female residence hall. In addition to performing the same duties as the male ND security officers, these officers also interviewed female assault victims. Director of Security Arthur Pears stated:

> When you've got girls that we have on campus, we feel we should have a girl so that they can talk girl-to-girl....We try to have women officers interview them (the assault victims). A girl can talk to a girl more easily than a man and often with a result of getting more information. Incidents come up weekly where we have women patrolmen take over an investigation.[25]

During the 1974–1975 academic year, the university received numerous reports of violent assault against women and at least twenty cases of indecent exposure, yet no *Observer* articles on male assaults appeared in the first four years of co-education. *The Observer* put headlights on the problem, reporting the string of assaults:

> • *October 1974:* Women off campus reported a man exposing himself using a ladder to reach the second floor of the buildings. A

331

female student showering in the ACC encountered three males; she recommended adding a key card system. Security rejected the idea based on cost.

- *November 1974:* The university asked the victim of a rape near the Administration Building to keep quiet to avoid panic. A sophomore female walking to Lyons Hall was also assaulted by five males.

- *January 1975:* Three off-campus women suffered a break-in and attempted assault. Although they reported that the perpetrator had exposed himself throughout the first semester, the police did nothing until the break-in. Officers identified the man through student ID pictures, but the university referred prosecution to the South Bend police. After his arrest, he made bail and, while on probation, attended classes.

- *March 1975:* A freshman woman was attacked between the Administration Building and Sacred Heart Basilica but escaped the two men wielding "cutting weapons"; passersby ignored her requests for help. A driver also assaulted a woman hitchhiking to campus.[26]

Despite these stories, Dean Macheca again dismissed the need for increased security lighting across campus due to expense and how this would mar the beauty of the surroundings. However, short-term plans did include better lighting in a few targeted areas around Lyons and Lewis Halls.[27]

Campus Security and SOS encouraged students to report any sexually deviant behavior or assaults as soon as possible. Confidentiality practices protected the involved parties, and it remained up to the victims whether to make the reports public. Reasons for not reporting such incidents included wanting to forget the incident, reluctance to get the perpetrator in trouble, uncertainty as to whether what happened constituted an offense, or blaming themselves for what happened. Also, many students were not sure whether reporting an assault would solve anything and did not want to go through the university process as a result.[28]

The university leveraged *The Observer* and hall presentations to encourage safe practices. Methods involved carrying whistles and using keys as weapons when walking alone or to and from the student parking lot at night. Other suggestions included checking back seats before entering cars, trying to convince the attacker to leave, and fighting back, especially after taking self-defense courses.

Subtler forms of sexual harassment existed on campus beyond overt sexual assault. Patterned after the 1964 Civil Rights Act, Title IX of the Education Amendments of 1972 addressed both. The US Supreme Court guidance regarding actionable sexual harassment in Title IX applied when an institution knew of sexual harassment, was deliberately indifferent to that sexual harassment, and whose sexual harassment was "so severe, pervasive, and objectively offensive it effectively" barred the victim access to an educational opportunity or benefit. Title IX did not, and could not, mandate that institutions respond to every offensive comment or action.[29] Thus, things such as the ratings game in the dining halls, catcalls, and the stereotyping of women in *The Observer* were not legally sexual harassment nor punishable by the university. However, these actions contributed to a "hostile environment" — although not a "hostile work environment."

> By 1976, America's three service academies allowed female students into their elite, male-dominated world. Yet women cadets faced sexual assault and discrimination in the academy culture. Finally, in 2003, the Air Force Academy chiseled off the words "Bring Me Men" from its entrance arch.[30]

Even when professors with ulterior motives approached students, no clear path existed for reporting questionable behavior. One anonymous student had such an encounter with a professor:

◇ *Anonymous female, ND 1976:* "Freshman year, I remained after class to discuss my grade on a paper. [As I leaned] over the professor's desk to point out certain passages, he responded [that] I could definitely improve my grade. He turned my face toward his and tried to kiss me. I do not remember what I said, but I got out of there fast!"

ND's slow response to issues such as sexual assault and sexual harassment was similar to that of most universities. When Princeton established its Women's Center in 1971, the facility received no funding until 1977. It hired its first full-time director in 1987. Boston College opened a Women's Resource Center in 1973, staffed with a graduate student working part-time; a permanent director was not appointed until 2002. Despite Yale University setting up its Women's Center in 1970, sexual assaults and harassment of women went unaddressed until the administration established sexual harassment grievance procedures. It held its first Rape Awareness Week in January 1986.[31]

The Campus Security Act of 1990 required schools to compile and provide statistics on alleged crimes reported to campus security and staff, issue timely warnings when a violent assault occurred, and report statistics on nearby properties or those used for school activities. In April 1996, ND sponsored a workshop called "Sexual Harassment II: Popular Culture, Policies, and Power," which explored teacher and student relationships, living in a hostile environment, and sexual harassment.

Not until second-generation ND graduate Emily Weisbecker Farley wrote her play, *Loyal Daughters and Sons*, did a work openly discuss sexuality and sexual assault on campus.[32] Emily's project captured one of the major differences between student generations — the candor with which they shared their stories. As Emily explained:

> ◊ *Emily Weisbecker Farley, ND 2007:* "People wanted and needed to talk about it. They were looking for the right kind of venues where they could bring it up. Some did not feel they could talk about what happened to them, even with their friends or their parents. And just telling their stories was healing to them."

During the four full-house showings in the Decio Theater in 2006, the play revealed the stories of fifty-five women and men as they disclosed experiences of love, relationships, sex, faith, and violence and shared views on Notre Dame's policies and culture. They included personal confessions such as:

- As a [male] high school student, I was raped by an older man.
- As a freshman, I was sexually assaulted at an off-campus dance.
- As a freshman, I was raped by a male acquaintance in Walsh's basement bathroom.
- As a [male] freshman, I was raped by a girl when I was too drunk to protest.
- As a sophomore, I was raped by a friend of a friend on spring break.
- As a sophomore, I fell asleep studying with a friend at my off-campus apartment and woke up with him on top of me.
- As a junior while abroad in Australia, I was anally raped in my dorm.
- As a junior while abroad in Africa, I was raped by my interpreter.
- As an undergrad, I was raped at knifepoint near the tennis courts.
- As an undergrad, I went to the hospital after a date-rape drug stopped my breathing.
- As a [male] undergrad, I experienced an attempted rape by another male.[33]

("A Brief History of Sexual Assault" in the appendix documents the university's public and ongoing conversation about sexual assault as well as its related initiatives.)

REARVIEW REFLECTION I grew up in a stilted sexual environment, where sex was never discussed and modesty was always practiced. I never saw my parents naked or in the bathroom. I showered in private stalls after high school gym. Imagine my surprise as dorm mates dressed in front of each other, and I saw for the very first time the open showers in the Rockne Memorial. When I spent three days in the infirmary with strep throat, the male doctors who were typical of the times did not shock me; however, the open-backed gowns did!

I did not rely on the infirmary for (nor expect it to address) sexual or reproductive health concerns; I learned about these subjects in less-formal settings. My roommates and I sometimes discussed the famous *Our Bodies, Ourselves* book during our Sunday evening popcorn gab sessions. I always acted nonchalant during these sessions, but inside, I was mortified by my lack of knowledge. I quickly learned that my rudimentary understanding only scratched the surface of this vast-yet-intimate subject. I knew little about topics such as menstrual options, French kissing, birth control, or same-sex attraction. Despite similar Catholic backgrounds, the spectrum of my quad mates' knowledge and experience surprised me. Beverly recognized my naïveté and gave me a copy of the book and a box of tampons. Not ready for either, I threw them into the trash.

My knowledge expanded through trial and error. I also learned a great deal from the discussion groups and papers required for Father Hoffman's course, "Sex and Marriage." No topic was off-limits as we explored sexuality in different relationships. In addition to his giving me one of my first As in college, Father Hoffman and I became friends. For years afterward, he was a cherished friend, counselor, and cheerleader; I still miss his letters.

Even as I learned more about sexuality, I knew nothing about sexual harassment or assault did not. That experience with my sociology professor was indeed sexual harassment, but no one referred to incidents like this in such terms in the early 1970s. When a female management major and I attended a conference in

UNIVERSITY OF PORTLAND
PORTLAND, OREGON 97203

April 27, 1976

Department of Theology

Dear Debbie,

This was my lucky day, April 28! I got you on the phone. I am glad that you chose to answer your phone, although I have shared your attitude at times, that of not picking the darn thing up.

And indeed I discovered a new Deborah. Serious-minded without being bookish, at home with herself when no one is around, and content to develop new hobbies. Altho I have wanted to write and ask about your final year under the Dome, I should have told you at the outset that I am an excellent but seldom-heard-from correspondent. I have been fortunate enough to keep up my letters to my mother who now lives off campus, having retired from Lewis Hall when that place was turned over to undergrads.

Saint Louis at the request of our professor, I was still too naïve to correctly assess the situation. We took my classmate's car and roomed together, sharing our notes from the lectures. The second evening, she returned to our room following dinner due to a sensitive stomach, and our professor invited me to have a drink with him. After I said yes, he suggested we go to his room, saying that it sent the wrong message sharing drinks in the hotel bar. I was not concerned; in my mind, this was no different from drinking in male dorm rooms. Also, since I babysat for his children, I was comfortable in his presence outside the classroom. As we enjoyed our wine, we discussed the day's topics and the keynote speaker's address. But then, he tried to kiss me, and I abruptly left. We never spoke of it, but I also never babysat for his family again.

Despite such situations with professors, my campus bubble seemed impenetrable by anything truly dangerous. I never feared sexual assault during my many evenings of partying, barhopping, or returning to campus in the early morning hours. However, all that changed over Easter weekend in 1974. On Friday night, a guy from my criminology class called and suggested we have a drink. Although he always made me nervous, I gave him the benefit of the doubt and accepted his invitation. I soon came to regret not listening to my gut.

He came to my room with Tanqueray gin, tonic, and lime in hand. As I made our drinks, we talked about our recent field trip to the Indiana State Prison in Michigan City. As we sat on our makeshift "sofas"—the room's bunk beds lowered to the floor and placed at a right angle—he asked if I had ever seen handcuffs. After I foolishly replied no, he pulled out a pair and demonstrated how they worked. He put one end on my right wrist and the other on the metal bar running across the head of the bed. I laughed at his silliness until I saw his predatory expression.

I tried to cajole him into removing them, but he refused. He warned me that fighting or screaming was futile; he knew that the security guard had just completed her tour of the first floor and had three more floors to patrol, providing him a window of about forty-five minutes. Realizing that the hall was virtually empty, I panicked and screamed.

Suddenly, there was a knock on the door. Thankfully, my assailant had failed to lock the door, and three male friends entered. They filled the room with their presence and their athletic physiques. Relief flooded through me. Taking in the scene—and misunderstanding it entirely—one of the guys apologized for interrupting, and they turned to leave. I screamed that I needed help, but all four males just laughed. Thinking I was kidding, the three men left, taking with them my hopes of getting out of this unscathed.

"Handcuff Guy" smiled and moved to lock the door. Before he reached it, though, it burst open—my male friends had returned. Evidently, they had finally caught on to the reality of my situation. One picked up my aggressor by his shirt and asked him if he had the key for the handcuffs. After freeing me, my friends escorted Handcuff Guy out. When they returned a brief time later, they offered to shadow me for the remainder of the weekend.

Over the years, I learned that several friends and classmates had experienced different outcomes in similar situations. I was one of the lucky ones.

Roadside Assistance

"You may not control all the events that happen to you," poet and civil rights activist Maya Angelou notes in her autobiography, *I Know Why the Caged Bird Sings*, "but you can decide not to be reduced by them."[1] By the time Notre Dame undergraduates mastered collegiate life — if they ever did at all — they were often in their last years. With graduation looming, seniors focused on their next steps and the world beyond Notre Dame. They considered whether they wanted to pursue financial goals or advanced degrees or give back via professions such as teaching, religious life, or service. During this process, some discovered the inadequacy of the placement and career resources on campus.

◇◇◇

During the merger discussions, the Notre Dame Placement Bureau offered its services to Saint Mary's students. Once Notre Dame admitted its own women, the bureau added two female counselors: Karen Bergwall assisted students majoring in Arts and Letters, and Paula Dawning managed student workshops. While they supported both male and female students, these women understood the emerging career interests of women.[2] Unfortunately, few students knew about these individuals or what guidance they had to offer, as *The Observer* published little on career counseling.

For the 1972–1973 academic year, the Placement Bureau primarily addressed the needs of seniors and provided limited career counseling to the other classes. In actuality, the Freshman Year of Studies program handled the first step of placement by administering academic and career-interest inventories as well as guidance tests before or at the beginning of the first semester. The freshman exam results covered three areas: a "Subject Matter Achievement Test," a "Psychological Survey," and a "Student Activities Report." According to Peter Grande, the assistant dean of the Freshman Year of Studies, the Psychological Survey included "a very mild personality test. It is not a clinical examination that attempts to identify abnormal behavior. It merely indicates academic attitudes and motivations."[3]

One anonymous male described these freshman exams as useful, even if later help from the Placement Bureau was not:

◇ *Anonymous male, ND 1976:* "I recall the ND tests basically duplicated the several Advanced Placement (AP) tests that I took in high school. I placed out of French (the advantage of six years of elementary school in France), Spanish, and first semester calc. Notre Dame allowed me to skip one year of one language; ironically, it did not matter, since I took Russian for fun our senior year.

"I may have spoken with someone in the placement office a few times, but I can unequivocally say that the career that I've enjoyed was the direct result of the contacts I made at ND, not the placement office."

Some tests applied to both sexes, while others specifically targeted women and compared results to national norms. These guidance tests focused special attention on the traditional careers and concerns of women as viewed by a male-dominated administration. The Freshman Learning Resource Center supplemented the discussions of results with literature and videotapes prepared by various ND colleges and departments.

◇ *Joe Sinnott, ND 1976:* "The test results reflected the times. I just came across a 1966 game for girls with the title 'What Shall I Be?' The only choices in the game were nurse, fashion model, teacher, actress, ballerina, and yes, flight attendant. I understand there is also a boys' edition of the game, only the choices include doctor, lawyer, banker, professional athlete, etc. And for some, they look back fondly [at what they] considered the good old days."

◇ *Rosemary Tirinnanzi Lesser, ND 1976:* "How coincidental: My personality test also matched me up to be an airline stewardess. I suspect the algorithm had a limited number of matches."

◇ *Anonymous, ND 1976:* "My career guidance test informed me that I would make a good forest ranger. My introversion and preference to work alone must have really stood out."

Of course, most students make career decisions over time, not in a single moment or via a standardized test. Young men and women needed assistance to understand their personal values, gather and evaluate information, assess risks, and make and implement decisions.[4] Unfortunately, the road toward graduation failed to include any formal, periodic assessments. It wasn't until the spring of

1974 that the Freshman Year office finally recognized the need for personalized career counseling.

> ◇ *Ann Pytynia, ND 1976:* "Notre Dame was not prepared to assist female students psychologically when it came to academic advice. Women want to talk things out, so we needed more outreach programs to discuss careers and majors. We knew that we could not have our entire life plans set by the age of nineteen. I wish someone would have taken me aside and spoken to me about career options."

> ◇ *Darlene Palma Connelly, ND 1977:* "In the summer of 1974, my parents received a form letter addressed to me from Reverend Joseph L. Walter, CSC, Chairman, Department of Professional Studies. Aside from the fact that the letter got my gender wrong and used the male pronoun, it had my cumulative GPA average correct, reflecting that I had flunked calculus and received a D in chemistry. There was no mistake [that] it was [addressed personally] to my situation. After pointedly noting that the average GPA for ND students accepted into the health professions was higher, it suggested that I talk to my parents and consider whether to continue in my pursuit of a health profession. He suggested that I consider 'courses not quite as demanding as medicine [such as] dentistry, osteopathy, optometry, podiatry, public health and hospital administration.'
>
> "Thanks, Father. I wonder if others received similar guidance suggesting they consider health professions other than medicine."

> ◇ *Maggie Waltman Smith, ND 1976:* "By senior year, I desperately wanted to take a class in marketing. Since I was in the College of Arts and Letters, I had to get special permission from the dean of the College of Business to enroll in 'Marketing Communications 315.' I guess that was my 'career counseling.' Ironically, despite taking only that one business class in college, my entire professional career ended up being in advertising, business communications, and product marketing."

Once the need for career counseling became apparent, the Freshman Year office and the Placement Bureau, in cooperation with local professional women, scheduled seminars for ND's freshman women. The series showcased professional opportunities from female viewpoints and covered business (marketing, accounting, finance, management, governmental relations), arts and letters (education, government, social work, law, journalism), and science (medicine, dentistry, veterinary medicine, psychology). The sessions coincided with freshmen selecting their intended course of study for the following year. Emil T. Hofman, dean of Freshman Year of Studies, emphasized that the "seminars will be important and valuable to the Notre Dame freshmen [sic] women. They are needed to allow women a chance to hear from professional career women themselves."[5] Although not available to the first female undergraduates, such seminars eventually became part of the ND landscape.

The Placement Bureau focused on assisting graduating seniors. It had strict policies regarding its postcollege job interview process. It had strict policies regarding its interview process. Students, in September of their senior year, received a placement manual containing the rules and regulations for the bureau's facilities

> The Meruelo Family Center for Career Development supports ND undergraduate and graduate students in all stages of career development. Students prepare for career readiness and success through strategic partnerships, personalized services, and innovative programs.[6]

and information about how to schedule interviews. Students who registered for interviews had to arrive on time and dress professionally: suits and ties for men, dresses for women, and no tennis shoes allowed. Students provided résumés before interviews and, afterward, sent thank-you notes. Given the few employment opportunities available at the time due to the poor economy, interviewing companies held all the cards.

> ◇ Diana Wilson Ostermann, ND 1976: "With a depressed economy in 1976 and companies limiting their hiring, the ND administration restricted students to three interviews. If you wanted an interview with a top company, you slept on the steps of the Administration Building the night before sign-ups to get one of the 'good' slots when you reached the front of the line. During one such sign-up period, I used one of my three allotted interviews for an interview with Lady Arrow Shirts.
>
> "The day of the interview, I entered the room, and a male interviewer greeted me. Once seated, he told me that he could not interview me since they only hired males for sales positions. In consolation, he offered me the use of their offices to job hunt for positions with other companies. How could a women's clothing company tell a woman [who had] the intelligence and determination not only to enter Notre Dame as one of its first freshman females but also to graduate with high marks in a marketing major that the company only permitted men to sell their women's clothing? I asked the reason for this policy. He said that the

job was very physical, requiring sales reps to push around heavy racks of clothing. I asked if the racks had wheels on them. He laughed and said of course. I told him that, if the company had a physical test to determine if a person could do the job, I was sure — given my height and athletic ability at the time — I could pass it. He merely repeated that it was company policy not to hire women for that position.

"I was so angry ND allowed this sexist company on campus that I complained to the administration. I demanded of the person in charge of on-campus interviewing that the university bar Lady Arrow Shirts from campus for a period of time; I regret not demanding they be barred until they hired women! My demand fell on deaf ears, and the university took no action."

The 1975 and 1976 classes graduated during a slow economy. After college, some graduates pursued advanced degrees to prepare for their professional lives. Others, despite strong academic achievements, graduated with no job.

◇ *Joe Henderlong, ND 1975:* "We were at the end of the antiestablishment movement, and many of us had older siblings to attest to the negative results of free love, sex, and destiny (LSD). We had everything before us, yet we had nothing before us, due in part to what the older generation tore down. However, we were intelligent and filled with dreams to contribute to our world.

"Some students left to make it a better place and others to optimize their God-given talents. Yet the class of 1975 found the economy in a recession and job placement slow in coming. Still, we surged forward, knowing our stay at ND induced a formula that would produce positive results if we did not forget the road we traveled."

◇ *Janet Krier Breen, ND 1975:* "Every student entering Notre Dame believes that an ND degree will add to his or her life. Some strive for a great education. Others crave a rewarding career. Still others dream of meeting that perfect mate who will share their culture and values. A few just want to prove to their parents they can graduate.

"I wanted all of these things, the whole package. That is why I wanted to be one of the first women at Notre Dame.

"Yet, in the spring of 1975, all I had to show for my efforts at ND was a pile of job search rejections and memories of a relationship that almost became a marriage but did not. Debi understood what was happening, and she took me to the infirmary where they treated me for exhaustion. She also took me to Senior Bar, where every job rejection was worth a free beer — many, many free beers. The economy was terrible in 1975! She also tried to help me mend my broken heart. Friends were on duty 24-7 when the Placement [Bureau] and Counseling Center were not."

◇◇◇

REARVIEW REFLECTION My results on the Strong Vocational Interest Blank for Women, the career interest and aptitude assessment I took the summer before I entered ND, reflected my eighteen years in Catholic schools and a very structured, traditional home. It indicated that my primary interests were stereotypical for females in the 1970s, including teaching, office work, and homemaking. On the Occupational Scale, I placed high in teaching, banking, dietetics, and law. Ironically, my lowest personal interest — athletics — appeared to hold the highest occupational potential for me, either as a phys ed teacher or YWCA staff member. No wonder I was confused; despite my academic prowess in high school, these tests indicated that I had limited potential for any nontraditional career — nontraditional for a woman at the time, that is — except for law. Had I received any one-on-one career counseling instead of interpreting the results myself, I probably would have realized earlier that nothing was out of my reach.

I found the personality test portion of the freshman exams particularly confusing. One question on the Psychological Survey asked, "Are you gay?" As an innocent, soon-to-be freshman in July 1972, I thought that the question referred to my state of mind and that "gay" meant "happy." Since I was in a testing situation and not happy about it, I answered no. I was quite embarrassed when I later learned the societal definition of "gay."

My Subject Matter Achievement Test results placed me in advanced French. Although I excelled at writing and reading this language, speaking it was another matter…and since the professor demanded we speak French in class, my first semester grade reflected my lack of oral proficiency. I dropped French and switched from the College of Arts and Letters to the College of Business Administration. No one questioned my reasons, and I failed to realize that this decision would be life-altering.

As I approached graduation, I was aware that the economy was weak and employment opportunities were at a premium. The Placement Bureau held mock interviews and other events to facilitate employment after graduation.[7] In anticipation of pursuing a career, I attended a Management Club seminar titled "Interview Management for Women." Moderated by Sophie Korczyk, the finance instructor for whom I was a teaching assistant, the seminar focused on job search concerns, problems encountered by female job applicants, and effective management of the interview and selection processes. Other presentations included "Legal Aspects of the Job Search" by Kathy Cekanski, deputy city attorney for South Bend; "Interviewing Psychology for Women" by Mary Clare McCabe, director of Student Development; and "What Employers Look for When Interviewing Women" by Barbara Estes, manager of human resources for the Bendix Corporation. I left the seminar realizing that, as women, we would most likely have a more challenging time convincing interviewers (most of whom would be males) of our qualifications. Interviewing would require us to project self-confidence and a certain bravado.

The second semester of our senior year brought an influx of interviewers to campus. Spring can be beautiful at Notre Dame, and this was true the day of my interview with Chicago's electric company, Commonwealth Edison. The Placement Bureau's guidelines prohibited last-minute cancellations, so I hoped that the interview would go quickly and I would be able to join my friends on the quad. I dressed in skirt and a halter top under a blazer, with no stockings. I assumed the interviewer would take one look at me, ask a few basic questions, and terminate the interview. I was dead wrong!

My résumé included my dorm address for future correspondence; amazingly, one of the two interviewers previously lived in my room in Lyons. We talked about the differences between his time at ND and my own experiences as a female student. Because I did not care about the outcome of this meeting, I was relaxed and projected self-confidence. I candidly shared the highs and lows of my time at Notre Dame without reservation. We discussed the value of ND connections, and he offered to discuss any job offers I received. We ran over our allotted hour, after which both men asked to see the changes in Lyons. After our meeting, I wrote a heartfelt thank-you letter to both representatives for the engaging meeting. I never did make it outside that day.

Even while scheduling job interviews, I recognized that I had neglected to prepare adequately for my next step. To increase my chances of having some path after graduation and given my improved grades, I applied for Notre Dame's combined JD–MBA program. When my admissions letter and the Commonwealth Edison job offer arrived almost simultaneously, I requested a year's deferment at ND while I figured out what I genuinely wanted.

On my first day in Edison's Executive Training Program, the former Lyons resident greeted me. I learned the value of having a senior executive mentor and realized that ND had prepared me for the male-dominated world of business. After a year in my own apartment and earning a paycheck (albeit small), returning to academia full-time held no interest for me. I never sought guidance from my past champions—Emil T. Hofman, Associate Dean Raymond, Assistant Dean Yeandel—nor did I investigate ways to fund a return to Notre Dame through scholarships or grants. Fortunately, my position at Edison, its tuition reimbursement program, and the support of my mentor all enabled me to complete a master's degree in business administration at Loyola University of Chicago. In retrospect, I should have negotiated a return to ND with Edison and developed my career as an executive, promising to return for a specific period following the program. Alas, it was a life lesson learned too late!

Under the Dome Light

As members of the university family, students came to understand and embrace its code of "God, Country, Notre Dame." That phrase encapsulated the spirituality, patriotism, and mystique of living under the Dome, all eventually influenced by its female undergraduates. Even when students and others strayed while at ND, most returned to their core values and these guiding principles. As architecture student Howard Roark says in Ayn Rand's novel *The Fountainhead*, "I came here to learn about building. When I was given a project, its only value to me was to learn to solve it as I would solve a real one in the future." When the dean asks him, "My dear fellow, who will let you?" Roark replies, "That's not the point. The point is, who will stop me?"[1]

◇◇◇

The University of Notre Dame du Lac offered a smorgasbord of ways for men and women to live their faith. Students attended Mass and retreats or went to the Grotto. In the 1970s, Mass occurred more than twenty-five times each weekday and increased to forty on Sundays during the academic year. These celebrations addressed audiences in English, Latin, and Spanish as well as in the different ways Catholics celebrate Mass. While the traditional High Mass in the Basilica on Sundays at 10:45 a.m. featured incense, hymns played on the organ, and a formal, solemn procession, the 12:15 p.m. service embraced informality by encouraging participants to introduce themselves before Mass and join hands during the "Our Father."[2]

Homilies in the residential hall chapels covered issues and questions common to college students. During Communion at Father Griffin's Urchin Mass, men and women took the Host into their hands and drank wine from chrome trays filled with little shot glasses. This practice evoked the ire of some organizations and the more traditional Catholics outside the Notre Dame bubble.

Recalling the religious atmosphere and community at ND were important elements in the lives of most students — and remained so even after graduation.

◇ *Anonymous, ND 1976:* "I loved the Catholicity of Notre Dame, going to the Grotto to pray alone, with a date, with friends—you were never embarrassed to do that. Each dorm had its own chapel and almost every Mass was packed....I loved the emphasis on others, on service projects, a true living out of your faith. It was a wonderful place to be and to be educated."

◇ *Donna Crowley Campbell, ND 1976:* "Visits to the Grotto offered me a place of contemplation that I found immediately upon my arrival. I could go to the Grotto for comfort through prayer. I could go there in happy and sad times. The peace found in prayer there was always special. My experiences at the Grotto strengthened my faith and the realization that God is always there for me. The ability to celebrate Mass in my hall at night with other students was also important to me. The ability to live and practice my faith daily is a value I cherished then and now."

As dorms and buildings increased on campus, so did the number of Masses. In 2002, the university offered roughly 125 Masses per week during the academic year, increasing to more than 176 in recent years. From 1986–2005, Father Edward "Monk" Malloy and Father E. William Beauchamp offered short, pointed homilies at the 11:30 a.m. Mass in Sacred Heart. In the 2007–2008 academic year, the university also offered more traditional practices, including the Tridentine Mass in Latin using the 1962 Roman Missal of Pope Saint John XXIII.[3]

◇ *Jack Bergen, ND 1977:* "I witnessed a remarkably close dorm community where everyone came together at Mass on Sunday nights to end the long week and weekend, as we reflected and reenergized. I loved the peacefulness of Mass in the nontraditional settings like the Alumni Hall basement rec room and Father Griffin's Mass where we sat on the floor while we held a Host and a shot glass of wine."

The place had a way of lifting spirits when personal and national tragedies struck.

◇ *Tom Young, ND 1976:* "I often stopped by the Grotto, but my most memorable and important visit was the night of January 27, 1973. That evening, my mother, who was fighting breast cancer, somehow tracked me down at an off-campus house....Despite my desire to remain by her side [during her illness], she insisted I [stay at] ND for spring semester. We had a nice, albeit brief, conversation, after which I told her I loved her and said good night. When I got back to campus, I went to the Grotto to light a candle and pray; I only asked God to take away her pain. I know God, through his own Mother, answered my prayer. The next morning, my father called to tell me my mom had passed. I am so grateful for that last call."

Since 1975, the ND Office of Campus Ministry issued several versions of *Day by Day: The Notre Dame Prayerbook for Students*. In 2010, it offered a new option to inspire students, faculty, and alumni: *The Notre Dame Book of Prayer*, which contains traditional and contemporary prayers centered around twelve recognizable campus landmarks.[5]

Through Campus Ministry, students received not only spiritual guidance but also access to reconciliation, preparation for confirmation and marriage rites, and the Rite of Christian Initiation of Adults. The university also published an updated version of its *Day by Day: The Notre Dame Prayerbook for Students* in the fall of 1975.[4] For those who preferred individual prayer and meditation, the book's reflections used contemporary language to encourage students to focus on world concerns, stewardship of resources, and poverty.

◇ *Denise Wilt Miller, ND 1976:* "As a non-Catholic who attended ND, I had a vastly different experience. At ND, people who saw the world differently surrounded me; I had to learn to function in that environment. I then spent a year in Japan where no one was even Christian. Again, I had to learn to be surrounded by people who viewed the world differently and learn that my point of view and values were still valid."

◇ *Anonymous, ND 1977:* "Every time I visit ND for a reunion, football game, or class, I leave feeling that every child should have the opportunity to go to college there. The campus is beautiful, the education is excellent, the profs, students, and staff have good morals and are genuinely good people, and religion is important and can be expressed (rather than suppressed, as is often the case in our secular world). How many colleges can boast that visits to the church and grotto are a must for any visit! I always come home and feel I am a better person."

Because it was a Catholic university, anyone applying to Notre Dame knew of its faith-based connections. On the other hand, it sometimes required spending time on campus to recognize Notre Dame's long association with the US military. One early example included the blessing of troops before the Battle of Gettysburg by Father William Corby. In 1880, Corby, as university president, revived military training for students to provide exercise and discipline. Known as the Hoynes Light Guards—after William Hoynes, the professor who sponsored it—cadets practiced marksmanship at a firing range between Corby Hall and Old College and received academic credit for their training. Under University President Father John Cavanaugh, the course became required for most students in 1917. The university sought to make this military training program part of the government's Student Army Training Corps (SATC) program, a precursor to the Reserve Officers' Training Corps (ROTC). Despite initially deeming the program subpar, the government eventually accepted seven hundred students into the program in late 1918, and "[m]ore than 2,200 Notre Dame students and alumni served in the armed forces during World War I."[6]

University architects Francis Kervick and Vincent Fagan designed the east transept door of Sacred Heart Basilica to commemorate the forty-six Notre Dame men who died in the Great War. The archway is inscribed with the words, "Our Gallant Dead / God, Country, Notre Dame / in Glory Everlasting," and displays a carved panel with two eagles supporting a shield that bears the university seal and carrying a ribbon with the inscription in their claws. "A light fixture made from an army helmet hangs just inside the doorway. Rev. Charles L. O'Donnell, C.S.C., university president from 1928 to 1934, wore that helmet as a World War I army chaplain."[7] Father Matthew Walsh, also a former army chaplain and university president from 1922 to 1928, dedicated this landmark at an outdoor Memorial Day Mass on May 26, 1924, linking faith and military service in his remarks:

> The real purpose of a memorial, from the Catholic point of view, is to inspire a prayer for those we desire to remember....No one who knows Notre Dame need be told of the spirit of loyalty and faith that has animated this university from its beginning. We should imitate our dead in that they have shown us the lesson of patriotism. If only the people of America would follow their example there would be no discrimination because of race or creed.[8]

Notre Dame suffered a significant reduction in enrollment during the 1930s and the 1940s, thanks to the Great Depression and the enlistment of droves of college-age men during World War II. According to Hesburgh, Notre Dame was almost out of business when the US Navy stepped in and kept the university afloat. Given the limited space available to house and train war-bound men, the navy worked with the university to transform the campus into a virtual military base. Approximately twelve thousand naval officers trained on the campus' version of a military base. In gratitude, Hesburgh established Vetville for returning military men with families. To specifically acknowledge the navy's role, he included the

Naval Academy in Notre Dame's football series for as long as the navy wanted.[9] The only time these two institutions put the football series on hold was in 2020 due to the COVID pandemic.[10]

Air Force and Army ROTC programs joined the Navy on campus in 1947 and 1951, respectively, making ND one of only a dozen schools hosting all three military branches. The university posted ROTC students, one from each military branch, at the World War I Memorial door of the Basilica for Memorial Day Mass. This tradition disappeared once the academic year ended before Memorial Day.

In the late 1960s, while approximately sixteen hundred students at Notre Dame proudly wore military uniforms,[11] other students attempted to burn down the ROTC building in protest of the Vietnam War. ROTC participation dipped in the mid-1970s due to such anti-war sentiments.[13] According to a 1973 *New York Times* survey, the "number of cadets in all three programs [nationally] has plunged from 212,400 in 1968 to about 75,000 this year."[14]

Women and the Armed Forces

- 1970: Air Force ROTC admits women.

- 1972: Army and Navy ROTC accept women on a test basis.

- 1973: The draft ends. The US Army begins to include women in its ranks, and the US Navy admits eight women to pilot training.

- 1975: The Stratton Amendment mandates that the academies admit women on the same basis as men, and it is later modified to make women eligible for both appointment and admissions to the service academies.

- July 1976: A total of 119 women enter the US Military Academy at West Point; 81 enter the US Naval Academy at Annapolis; and 157 enter the US Air Force Academy at Colorado Springs. Opportunities for women within US Army ranks increase from 19,000 in 1972 to 160,800 in 1976.[12]

◇ *Ann Pytynia, ND 1976:* "My ND boyfriend and I were good friends with a classmate who was a former medic in Vietnam. We listened to his stories about his time as a medic and as the only person left alive in his squadron, because even the Vietcong knew the value of a medic. Ultimately, the Vietcong shot him and left him for dead. When [members of] the Vietcong smashed in his face to see if he was dead, he moaned. Hearing the moan, another US soldier shot and killed [them]. Luckily, few members of our class have such memories. What he saw—there are no words."

The ROTC program was visible on campus during the first five years of coeducation. In October 1972, two freshman women — Mary Ann Palinski, a biology major, and Rosemary Tirinnanzi Lesser, a science major in the preprofessional program — joined the Air Force Reserve Officer Training Corps (AFROTC), another first associated with coeducation.[15]

⋄ *Rosemary Tirinnanzi Lesser, ND 1976:* "As our packed Chevy Caprice drove toward Notre Dame in August 1972, I worried how my family was going to afford this college. Having never set foot on the campus, I based my dreams of Notre Dame on the thick catalogs that described colleges across the country. I had spent my sixteen years of life in an air force military family, moving around the country and Germany with my dad's assignments. We never visited [any] new assignment until we moved there, so my arrival at ND stayed true to the pattern. I soon arrived at Walsh Hall and met my roommate, a junior transfer from SMC.

"Just as my family gathered information about a new town in person, I headed to freshman orientation at the ACC. Dozens of organizations informed us about their activities. Worried about funding my ND education, the Air Force ROTC booth immediately caught my attention when I saw its poster: 'Scholarships available.' Without a second thought, I signed up for AFROTC, a solution linking the air force world I had known my entire life *and* how to pay for ND.

"When I joined AFROTC, my freshman physical education requirement was replaced by our training. As we marched — or, rather, sprinted — around the stadium parking lot, I realized why I was getting PE credit. In those days, we had to master marching in rows with precision...in high heels. I also wore my blue AF uniform to 'Principles of Air Power' and my other science preprofessional courses where women were in the minority. Like the women in my freshman class, the one or two other women in ROTC and I accepted our minority role as the norm.

"Although the Vietnam War was still ongoing and ROTC was not a 'popular' organization on campus, I do not recall any outright hostility as we marched in our uniforms. ROTC bound us together in so many ways, but it also helped to have others' encouragement — such as the outgoing junior in ROTC and an ND cheerleader, Charlie Morrison. Charlie was more comfortable interacting with women than the typical ND male, so having his support was key to me and my time in AFROTC.

By the end of sophomore year, I was reevaluating whether I should continue at Notre Dame and with ROTC. The timing seemed right to step back and focus on my courses. But my military story did not end at Notre Dame. In 1977, I returned to the US Air Force when I was commissioned as a second lieutenant as a member of the second class of the Uniformed Services University of the Health Sciences. Four years later, I earned my MD and served in the air force for eleven years as a military obstetrician–gynecologist."

◇ *Paul Cassani, ND 1976:* "Members of the class of 1976 who participated in ROTC saw a variety of firsts as the history of Notre Dame's relationship with the US Navy continued. In parallel with ND's decision to admit women in 1972, the navy opened NROTC [Naval Reserve Officers Training Corps] to women. This created an opportunity for the NROTC unit to commission a woman as a navy ensign in 1973 when Candace Kelly graduated. Three years later, it commissioned two women as ensigns: ND's Becky Banasiak became a specialist in meteorology, and SMC's Bernadette Baldy became one of the first women pilots when that field opened to women in 1978.

"The end of the draft in spring of 1973 saw a significant exodus of students from ROTC. In the first two years, we took mandatory courses required by the navy, even though [these classes] did not count toward the required credits for graduation; our courses [in junior and senior year] counted as elective credits. In addition, the NROTC program annually required its students to successfully complete weekly military training during the semester and for six weeks each summer prior to commissioning. The navy commissioned thirty-three Notre Dame and Saint Mary's men and women as ensigns and four men as second lieutenants in the United States Marine Corps on May 15, 1976, in the ACC.

"Most graduates incurred four years of obligatory service in exchange for financial support while attending ND. Those graduates who pursued specialty training such as Naval Flight School or Nuclear Power School incurred additional years of service. As is always the case, some gave more than others. At least one gave all he had: While flying as the bombardier navigator, Mike Ruflin lost his life when his A-6 Intruder crashed in Puerto Rico in 1978. A fun-loving and capable gent, Mike is deeply missed and remembered at each reunion.

"Notre Dame continues to commission officers. Despite the cost of a Notre Dame education, it is still cost-effective for the navy to retain its NROTC program. Current NROTC students are often children of ND NROTC graduates. You will also find children of senior navy admirals who, with no prior university connection except serving with ND graduates, entrusted their children to ND.

"The opportunities for women in all services have expanded. The navy modified its fleet to permit mixed-gender crews. ND women and men fly the same aircraft, drive the same ships, and command mixed-gender units, unlike restrictions in place in 1976. Today's US Navy has women serving in every rank as they compete successfully for merit-based promotions and assignments. ND women who serve today in the navy can trace their lineage back to Candy Kelly who, with the support of ND–NROTC leadership, completed four years of required training in one year to qualify for her commission. Candy, Becky, and Bernadette paved the way so many years ago."

The women in ND's ROTC program quickly made their mark. In February 1974, Notre Dame's Angel Flight, a service organization affiliated with ND's AFROTC detachment, and the Arnold Air Society took top honors in the Tri-Area Conclave. As Andie McGugan, Notre Dame's head commander, noted, "This award goes to the flight that best supports their university through services and promotes the interests of the United States, the Air Force and ROTC detachment."[17] The ND community-focused activities "included a Halloween party at Logan Center, work for the Muscular Dystrophy Drive, a bookfair for Wilkes-Barre College (victimized by flood), Christmas caroling at Memorial Hospital, and a monthly service project."[18]

The Arnold Air Society (AAS), "a professional, honorary service organization advocating the support of aerospace power," is affiliated with the Air Force Association (AFA). It is open to cadets in US Air Force officer candidate training programs, including university ROTCs and the Air Force Academy. AAS members help cadets develop leadership and organizational skills.[16]

Graduation weekend of 1974 also marked another landmark moment, when Kelly Levin (ND 1974) became the first woman commissioned as an officer from a Navy ROTC unit. Levin recalled reporting to her first Navy ROTC drill in jeans and tennis shoes because her uniform was not ready: "They tried to direct me to gym class, but I was their drilling petty officer and ordered them to 'Fall in!'"[19]

As Notre Dame students came to appreciate and, for many, embrace the link between God and country that existed on campus, they also united as part of the ND family. Just like in any family, the relationship was not always smooth; by graduation, however, most discovered not only themselves but also their place within this extended network.

◇ *Darlene Palma Connelly, ND 1977:* "My father's employer declared bankruptcy the summer before my senior year. With my dad out of a job, I was determined to take financial responsibility for my tuition. As all other student loan sources were maxed out for me, I went to the Notre Dame Credit Union before the fall semester and applied for a personal loan. I then went to see the bursar to have the hold [that had been] placed on my account released so I could register for classes. I explained the situation and the credit union loan. The bursar, a CSC priest, told me that the credit union interest rate was *outrageous*. He broke an awkward silence with, 'Will you pay it back?' Puzzled, I nodded yes. He then continued, 'Good. The university will give you the loan. The hold on your account has been removed.' I never saw him again. May that kind soul rest in peace."

◇ *Debbie McGraw-Block, ND 1977:* "I believe in the goodness of people whether I share their political views or not. I also marvel at the dedication to ND that families have developed over the generations. I'm a single-generation Domer — no one before and no one after — and that's OK with me. I delight in the love that families have for the place."

Often, the extended ND family offered solace in troubled times, condolences at losing loved ones, and support during health crises. The ND community also joined together in celebrating major milestones. As technology changed, face-to-face gatherings sometimes morphed into virtual events for occasions such as birthdays (e.g., the women of the class of 1977's "group hug" at age fifty). Even Zoom calls took these connections to new levels, especially during the 2020 COVID pandemic.

◇ *Pat Sarb, ND 1976:* "My grandson, Owen, was born in 2011 with nonketotic hyperglycinemia (NKH), a rare genetic disease, for which there is no cure...yet. Rare disease research takes time and money. My wife and I worked with Notre Dame's Department of Development and the Boler-Parseghian Center for Rare and Neglected Diseases (CRND) to establish the NHK Research Fund.

Our extended ND family continues to support this effort not just with donations but also with prayers."

◇ *Phil Potter, ND 1975:* "'God, Country, Notre Dame' is a statement so simple yet so profound. My first recollection of the epic statement was my wedding day, October 15, 1977. In those days, the groom's party waited just inside the basilica's engraved arch. I ducked out for air just before the ceremony to listen on my small transistor radio as the Irish football team played Army — how appropriate to read that inscription on the day we played Army.

"As years passed, the message gained significance as my faith, patriotism, and love for my university grew. Yet, as much as I love that simple inscription, if given the opportunity I would change it to 'God, Country, Family, Notre Dame'!"

◇◇◇

REARVIEW REFLECTION The principle of "God, Country, Notre Dame" played an important role in my life. Before Notre Dame announced its plans for coeducation, I briefly considered becoming a teaching nun. I saw a religious vocation as a way to give back that was similar to how the sisters had educated and mentored me. However, an eye-opening event caused me to reject this vocation — though not my faith.

When I was in the eighth grade, the nuns took my class on a Saturday retreat to their novitiate, Saint Joseph's College and Novitiate. As my best friend and I walked past the college's pool where several males were swimming, she playfully nudged me, and I didn't fight going into the water. I was quite the sight as my dress and heels floated to the surface, while the boys moved to help me. Other girls decided that this male attention was worth any punishment and followed me into the pool.

Because the nuns assumed that my friend had "pushed" me, they kindly took me to their quarters and dried my clothes. The other students wore their wet clothes home and suffered the nuns' wrath. This inconsistency set off an internal alarm, and I questioned whether my special treatment could have been due to an ulterior

In the mid-1960s, the Sisters of Saint Joseph admitted lay students to its Saint Joseph's College and Novitiate in Stuart, Florida. The nuns believed that Catholic institutions failed to meet the growing coeducational collegiate demand. In response, they opened admissions and built separate male and female dormitories. However, the nuns failed to provide adequate residential supervision, and the resulting disciplinary problems caused friction with the local community. This coed residential two-year college never overcame this negative image and closed in May 1972.

motive by the nuns to entice me as a novitiate candidate. After perceiving this as hypocritical, I decided that the religious life was not for me. Rebelling against the nuns' perception of me as a good girl, I stirred things up on the ride home. I encouraged my classmates to sing Tommy James and the Shondells' "I Think We're Alone Now" until the nuns shut us down!

Patriotism was inherent in the daily start to school with the Pledge of Allegiance each and every morning, but I never considered the armed services as a potential life path. While I did not serve in ROTC at ND or in the armed forces after graduation, I am personally beholden to the ROTC students who post twenty-four-hour watch of the Clarke Memorial Fountain every Veteran's Day. The memorial, dedicated ten years after our 1976 graduation (and known as "Stonehenge," given its similarities), honors times of peace, veterans, and five hundred members of the ND family who served and died in World War II, the Korean War, and the Vietnam War. It has become one of my favorite stops on campus where I can pause and give thanks while enjoying an Irish coffee.

Matthew M. Miceli, CSC, a theology professor and rector, guided the male residents of Cavanaugh Hall for more than twenty-seven years, stepping down in 1990. Despite his personal struggles with coeducation, he helped with this book by opening doors and sharing research materials.

During our collaboration, Miceli and I drank Bolla Bulla, his own white wine cultivated in his little vineyard off Bulla Road. He died in December 2012 and is missed by generations of residents, students, and friends.

With Father Miceli, Cavanaugh Hall (1977)

I also have given thanks for how the Notre Dame family assisted my own family over the years. Dean O'Meara arranged for us to continue living in Vetville while my father completed remedial courses after flunking out of law school. Eventually approving my father's readmittance, O'Meara also arranged tutoring for him to prevent history from repeating itself.

History did repeat itself, however, when I flunked out at the end of my sophomore year. I may not have been the first female to flunk out of ND, but I was definitely in the minority. My "Three Wise Men"—Hofman, Raymond, and Yeandel—supported my readmittance. They helped me to realize that, despite this significant misstep, I was still that driven, intelligent girl who joined the first class of Notre Dame women.

Shortly after my 1976 graduation, Matthew Miceli, CSC, arranged for my brother Doug's admittance into Holy Cross College. Doug had struggled during his freshman year at Loras College in Dubuque, Iowa, and my parents had pulled him out. In the fall of 1976, my other brother was living in Cavanaugh Hall when Miceli—his rector at the time—heard about the situation. Miceli agreed to allow Doug to live in my brother's room since the Holy Cross plans had gelled too late for other living arrangements. He monitored Doug's progress and, at the end of the year, offered to help Doug get into ND. Doug decided that the rigor of ND was not for him, and he eventually graduated from Loyola University of New Orleans.

O'Meara, Hofman, Raymond, Yeandel, and Miceli directly influenced my family's life direction; Hesburgh, other administrators, professors, rectors, classmates, and alumni went even further and helped me to achieve my dream of writing about the coeducation experience. All exemplified the ideology of this Catholic university. Whenever I pass under the basilica's "God, Country, Notre Dame" arch I reflect on how my Vetville and collegiate experiences encapsulated religion, patriotism, and family—immediate or extended—long before Hesburgh's 1990 biography of the same name. I am also reminded that the lore of Notre Dame extends far beyond its campus boundaries and is often tied to football...like the mythic story of Lou Holtz, Notre Dame's football coach, visiting Dan Henning, head football coach for Boston College, who claimed to have a phone line to Heaven. (After Denning balked at the difference in "charges" when using his phone in Boston and Holtz's version at ND, so the story goes, Holtz is said to have responded, "Because, from Notre Dame, it's a local call.")

Mile Markers

"A part of me lives here, the deepest part of me, always," says Bakul, India's ambassador to the United States in Anita Desai's novel, *Clear Light of Day*, when he is asked if he "might easily forget the Taj Mahal and the message of the Gita."[1] During the transitional years at Notre Dame, women became a part of the campus experience and Notre Dame became a part of them. Campus interests shifted greatly in those first five years of coeducation. As each class increased the number of women in its ranks, women became class officers and included Saint Mary's in activities. The quarterly *Notre Dame Magazine* and more than five hundred issues of *The Observer* (September 1972–May 1977) reported on these advancements as well as university policy decisions. These periodicals made capturing the tumultuous environment and milestones of coeducation possible.

◇◇◇

From the moment the class of 1976 arrived, these students heard about the unique nature of their situation: Undergraduate freshman women, alongside men, attending Notre Dame for the first time. University officials constantly stressed that they expected much from this group.

In October 1972, the class achieved one of the highest voter turnouts in ND class elections, with 965 students (about half of the total) electing Jim Bradley as president, Mary Dondanville as vice president, Sheila Elsner as secretary, and Pat Dore as treasurer.[2] As a class with many "firsts," these students would later elect Augusto "Augie" Grace as one of the first (if not the first) Black class presidents for their junior and senior years.[3]

Having graduated from a public coeducational high school outside Boston, Augie's interest in the role grew from recognizing ND's gender imbalance. He lived in Cavanaugh Hall, under the watchful eye of Father Miceli, with two roommates, also from public coeducational high schools. After quickly bonding with nine other freshmen, these students were members of a group of twelve freshmen who often discussed the challenges of that first year. All considered transferring,

358

but only one withdrew, and it was for reasons other than the unnatural social situation. The class officer election during junior year presented Augie with his chance to drive improvements in this challenging environment.

Just as Notre Dame needed Hesburgh as its change agent, Augie needed class officers who shared his dream of developing a unified platform of activities. He hoped that increasing class events would help to achieve a level of normalcy between the sexes—one individual at a time. Before the election, Augie approached several respected classmates to join his slate. In an unprecedented move, he actively recruited two women for his ticket: inviting Susan Caranci, an English major, and Betsy Kall, a business major, to run as vice president and secretary, respectively. Betsy then recruited Greg Marino as treasurer.

The group enlisted other sophomores in each residence hall to conduct meet and greets with classmates. Even during their spring campaign—two years into coeducation—more than one classmate asked, "Females are such a small percentage of our class, so why do you have two females running on your slate?" The answer was simple: Augie developed the team not based on percentages or quotas but based on who had the skills needed to achieve a shared vision.

> After graduation, classes elect officers at each five-year reunion. In the forty-five years since graduation, the following individuals—demonstrating commitment and spirit—have served as president of the ND class of 1976:
>
> - Augie Grace (1976–1981)
> - Tom Hogan (1981–1991)
> - Tom Paulius (1991–1996)
> - Ace Schroeder (1996–2005)
> - Debi Dell (2005–2016, 2021–   )

Following their election, these officers wasted no time creating social opportunities. Junior year started with charter buses to the Notre Dame–Northwestern football game in Evanston, Illinois. Except for bowl games, most classes only gathered for home games, so this was a unique start to the year. To keep the momentum going, the class hosted a happy hour at Kubiak's. Wanting to ensure inclusiveness, the organizers worked closely with their peers at Saint Mary's. Kubiak's offered inexpensive beer and a jukebox of Polish polkas as well as current hits. The extended team enjoyed seeing the crowded dance floor overflow into the parking lot—so dramatically different from the freshman tennis court mixer.

But even something as simple as the thank-you note from Kubiak's demonstrated inequities between ND and SMC. Augie had ensured that credit for the event was properly shared among the two colleges and stressed the importance of a better relationship with Saint Mary's:

> The Happy Hours have become a successful event through the efforts of the Junior Class officers at Notre Dame and St. Mary's. Unfortunately, the ad neglected to mention the excellent work

done by the girls....After [other misunderstandings that occurred on campus]...the girls are again faced with a growing separation between themselves and co-educational [*sic*] Notre Dame. The relationship that we have had with St. Mary's Junior Class has been one of the few healthy results of struggling coeducational plans. The class officers here at Notre Dame have always appreciated and respected the assistance we have received from Joan McDermott, Kathy McGuiness, Raquel Paez, and Michelle McGowan, the St. Mary's officers. Through the cooperation of the two classes, the Happy Hours have successfully provided a medium for both schools, both sexes, to meet in an informal atmosphere. Even though I would like to take the credit for an idea like the Happy Hours, it was actually a suggestion of the girls, and they worked equally as hard to insure [*sic*] its success.[4]

A thank-you ad from Kubiak's
The Observer, November 14, 1974

After this experience, SMC women became partners in planning joint events and, for many, lifelong friends with ND students.

The class officers also never forgot the impact of hall representatives in the election, and they asked many to remain as dorm representatives. In the 1970s, communications and networking meant face-to-face events, telephone calls, and printed posters. Some volunteers strictly hung posters and provided feedback; others, like Tom Spencer, Greg Sosnovich, and Wendy Duffey, served on committees and worked as event organizers.

In February of 1975 (the class of 1976's junior year), the officers hosted a booth designed by architectural student Williston Dye at the university's annual Mardi Gras celebration. Held at Stepan Center, this pseudo-casino gambling event helped students to fight off the winter doldrums while raising money for charity. Each dorm and some clubs built elaborate stalls for blackjack and poker. Live music brought in the crowds—which, in the first few years of coeducation, still included women bussed in from nearby colleges.

The class booth at this event replicated Sutter's Mill from the California gold rush. It took hundreds of volunteer hours to build and required a motor, procured by classmate Pat Dore, to run its twelve-foot-tall spinning waterwheel.

The committee made requests to "staff," not "man," the booth to acknowledge the progress of gender equality. In the spring of 1976, the class reused the wheel to rotate a large American flag, complete with a '76 logo, to support the Mardi Gras bicentennial theme.

The traditional Junior Parents Weekend, held in 1975 from February 28 to March 2, brought parents to campus for specially planned events. Starting on the Friday, each college invited the parents to attend classes. Jane Pitz worked tirelessly on Saturday's concelebrated Mass, with Hesburgh as the main celebrant and a slide show of images corresponding to the prayers and readings.[5] After Mass, more than one thousand classmates and parents attended the President's Dinner where Augie delivered a moving speech. The dinner ended on a lighthearted note, when Sue Caranci entertained the crowd with a scripted interview of a "priest" who still was not sure why women were at Notre Dame.

> ◇ *Augie Grace, ND 1976:* "Junior Parents Weekend was the first time my parents visited Notre Dame. As class president and the evening's student keynote, I sat with my parents at the head table for the dinner. I remember my mother was so impressed to share the table with Hesburgh and Joyce; she later confided, after talking to Joyce all evening, he was now her favorite priest. After dinner, my roommates and our parents went to The Library bar and played pool. Our parents asked each of us if this place was where we actually went whenever we told them that we were heading to 'the library.' Busted!"

At the end of the year, Patrick Dore joined Augie, Sue, and Betsy on the ticket as senior class officers. They had much to do before the first four-year coed class graduated in the year of the nation's bicentennial. The team had only a few months to increase class camaraderie before everyone became preoccupied with decisions about careers or postgraduation education. Returning in the fall of 1975, Augie

Thomas A. Spencer (ND 1976) passed away unexpectedly in February 2018. His planning of the Purdue tailgate was just one example of his selfless efforts. Tom and other deceased classmates left everlasting marks on the extended Notre Dame family. They are greatly missed and are commemorated annually with a butterfly release at Our Lady's Butterfly Garden, donated by the ND class of 1976 in 2016.

and the other officers planned a tailgate for the Notre Dame–Purdue University football game in West Lafayette, Indiana. Tom Spencer, recruited by Betsy Kall as a dorm representative, organized the party. He made arrangements for the location, beer trailers with spigots, grills, and food for the several hundred classmates who watched ND triumph over Purdue.

For years, senior classes also held an annual "Death March," a day spent going from bar to bar, to mark the final football weekend. Unfortunately, the administration squashed this tradition in response to Indiana's maniacal focus on underage drinking. Given the 8–3 football season that (while outstanding for most other schools) did not meet expectations at ND, students wanted to drown their sorrows. The class officers asked for and received approval to resurrect the march — minus the involvement of Senior Bar to limit the university's responsibility.[6]

Senior weekend during the ND–Georgia Tech game concluded with an "Armory Party" with forty-five kegs of beer, several pounds of pretzels, and live music. Crowded into the South Bend National Guard Armory, classmates spilled beer on each other and onto the floor, and the stickiness of the surface made dancing difficult — though hysterical! — to watch. Little did anyone know that they had just witnessed a part of ND football history with which many outside the ND community would eventually identify.

> ## SENIOR
> ## FOOTBALL WEEKEND
>
> **FRIDAY: DEATH MARCH**
> **CAMPUS VIEW 12:00-2:00**
> **MEET A&P PARKING LOT 2:00**
>
> Bridget's   2:00-3:00
> Corby's   3:00-4:00
> Nickie's   4:00-5:00
> Library   5:00-6:00
>
> **SATURDAY: LAST HURRAH**
> **ARMORY PARTY**
>
> Singles $3.00
> Couples $5.00
>
> Tickets: Student Union Ticket Office
> Dining Halls

That final game became infamous, and not because Notre Dame beat Georgia Tech. Traditionally, Notre Dame allowed its seniors to play in the last home game whenever the victory was not in jeopardy. Many seniors waited for this opportunity, but their participation was not guaranteed given NCAA restrictions on the number of players who could dress for a game. The story of this legendary game started when the game's dress list was posted. Missing from it was Rudy Ruettiger — a twenty-seven-year-old transfer student from Holy Cross College, US Navy veteran, and member of the class of 1976 — who was part of the practice team as a walk-on. The decision not to allow him to dress is at the core of the film Rudy, a story about pursuing one's dreams. What is not portrayed due to the film's creative license is how Ruettiger made the list.

> ◇ *Pat Sarb, ND 1976:* "I earned a varsity monogram as a second team defensive back on Ara Parseghian's 1973 national championship team. In 1974, I dressed for our six home games and for the 1975 Orange Bowl, Ara's final game as head coach. This was also the year that Rudy made the team as a walk-on. In 1975, the NCAA restricted the number of players who could dress for home games (60) and away games (48), making the dress squad more challenging.
>
> "During our senior season, I checked the dress squad list weekly since I had moved down on the depth chart. The Thursday

before Georgia Tech, my name appeared on the list for the only time that season; Rudy's name did not. Prior to Friday's practice, Cocaptain Ed Bauer asked me to give up my spot so Rudy could dress. I said yes, because I felt it would be an injustice if Rudy did not experience running through the stadium tunnel onto the field. I sat in the senior section with my wife, Lynda, and many Alumni Hall Dawgs as we watched the Rudy drama unfold in the game's final seconds. With minutes left, the senior section chanted, 'Rudy, Rudy.' Coach Dan Devine finally put in Rudy. He promptly sacked Georgia Tech's quarterback to end the game."

In March 1976, a committee chaired by Sister John delved into campus life far beyond "cattle drives," panty raids, and dining hall antics.[7] As the first undergraduate freshman class prepared to graduate, women comprised roughly 19 percent of the undergraduate population (1,318 women, 5,497 men).[8] *The Observer*, across several articles, reflected not only on such facts but also on highlights from a survey *Notre Dame Magazine*—in anticipation of coeducation—had conducted in the summer of 1972.[9] A quote from then-incoming freshman Janet Waltman (ND 1976) stood out:

> Don't call me a coed. I am a student. I'm at Notre Dame to acquire an education, not to serve the ego of Notre Dame. I am serving myself, not statisticians, or the [male–female] ratio, or socially deprived male students. I want to be taken seriously; I'm planning a career, not a wedding.[10]

The 1993 film *Rudy* fictionalized the life of Daniel "Rudy" Ruettiger, who briefly played football at Notre Dame. Although he didn't fit the stereotypical image of a football player and struggled (like many) to achieve the grades and the funding to attend the university, he eventually joined the ND class of 1976 and the football team as a walk-on. *Rudy* was the first film shot on Notre Dame's campus since 1940's *Knute Rockne, All American.*

Pat Sarb and Daniel "Rudy" Ruettiger

Two major social events remained during senior year, and the university's hypocrisy in handling them cannot be overlooked. Senior classes typically traveled to the last away football game together. Flying in the face of tradition, the class officers instead obtained university approval for a March 13–20, 1976, spring break trip to the Bahamas. Seniors filled two chartered planes to Freeport; two hundred eighty-five dollars covered airfare and hotel, with a seven-dinner meal package for an additional forty-two dollars. At the Saint Patrick's Day pool party, a Bahamian steel drum band played the "Victory March" to celebrate the gathering. After breaking with tradition for the senior trip, the officers also wanted to do something unique for the senior prom: a train ride to Chicago and overnight accommodations. After scoping out venues, the committee presented its plans to the university. Unfortunately, the administration, leaning heavily on its in loco parentis policy, felt that Chicago was a satellite of the campus and denied the request. The event was instead held in a suitable South Bend locale, and the limited number of attendees had an enjoyable time. However, no *Observer* articles mentioned the fact—nor discussed the irony—of the administration approving a week in the Bahamas but not a weekend in Chicago.

From the class of 1977 (L–R): Rob Tully, Darlene Palma, Carol Simmons, and John Donahue

Art by Father Michael Hinken

Through such class events, student-run organizations, and clubs, many students developed lifelong relationships as well as soft skills and the ability to work within diverse teams. In August 1972, males led most student organizations, except for rare instances involving Saint Mary's women. By the 1975–1976 academic year, women accounted for nearly one-fifth of ND's student population, and women led many organizations: Diana Merten in Student Government, Sally Stanton as editor of *Scholastic*, and Susan Darin, Dana Nahlen, and Lisa Moore (across three successive years) as editor in chief of *Dome*, the ND yearbook. Women also made their presence known in other areas:

- 4 women (17 percent) of the 23 members in Student Government
- 3 women (25 percent) of the 12 members of *The Observer*'s editorial staff
- 2 women (22 percent) of the 9 student union positions
- 3 women (33 percent) of the 9 Ombudsman Service executive positions[11]

Even more importantly, class officer elections were becoming truly coed tickets. The ND classes of 1976 and 1977 consistently achieved this balance from the start.

With graduation looming, Augie and Art Derse cochaired the university's Bicentennial Conference and Festival. Its theme, taken from Abraham Lincoln's speech "An Almost Chosen People," expressed the ambiguous nature of the nation's moral development. A concluding address by Hesburgh highlighted the fact that it took until 1920 for women and 1965 for African Americans (through the Voting Rights Act and reversal of Jim Crow laws) to vote in all states. The conference reinforced the class's own goal of being all-inclusive. By partnering with SMC, the class again demonstrated the value of women as equal partners.

◊ *Augie Grace, ND 1976:* "The addition of women brought dramatic changes to the character of Notre Dame's student body. The university was not as prepared for coeducation as it should have been, so its first women were appropriately called 'pioneers' because of the strength they displayed. I believe the men were also pioneers. Together, we confronted personal struggles and achieved accomplishments on a number of levels. I am grateful to the officers and many classmates who helped to mold coeducation at Notre Dame. We grew as individuals, and we grew as a class. We succeeded in making Our Lady's university a better place, paving the way for future classes of men and women."

◊ *Lionel Phillips, ND 1976:* "I attribute much of my success to the fact that I can rightfully claim to be a Notre Dame graduate and a member of the 'Greatest Class Ever, 1976.' Other alumni push back when I make this claim. However, I remind those detractors that our class was the first freshman class with female undergraduate students. I stress that few classes can claim that classmates are the university's president [John I. Jenkins], the athletic director [Jack Swarbrick], and officers in admissions and development. If that isn't convincing enough, I simply state, 'When they make a movie about one of your classmates [Daniel Ruettiger], come talk to me.'"

(For additional details on the major events of the first five years of coeducation, see "*The Observer*'s Top Ten Milestones" in the appendix.)

Notre Dame's first class of freshman females, 186 in number, graduated in May 1976. With this graduation ceremony and after four years of coeducation (during which time additional women transferred to Notre Dame as students), approximately six hundred women had received undergraduate degrees. The number increased to approximately sixteen hundred by the end of the 1970s. Sister John reflected that "this place brought women in without losing its traditions or greatness. It's enhanced. The first ones who came even resisted that sense of being pioneers. They didn't want to be different."[12]

The Committee to Evaluate Coeducation summarized the transformation and its effect on the women:

> From a set of rather negative experiences, a positive experience has emerged in the lives of many. In learning to handle some of the difficult situations...the women have gained an ability which they believe should serve them well in the future. They attest to a new self-sufficiency, a knack for handling discrimination, and a foundation for competitively entering a man's world of business and profession.[13]

These women entered a world where they would benefit from another key step in women's equality. Passed in 1974, the Equal Credit Opportunity Act granted women the right to financial freedom and to credit cards separate from their husbands. Lenders could no longer discriminate based on race, sex, age, nationality, or marital status. Whether single or married, working or staying at home, these women wanted—and could get—credit in their own names.

> ◇ *Ann Pytynia, ND 1976:* "I am grateful for having had this [ND] experience. Sometimes I look back at those years with regrets, sometimes in horror, but ultimately, I have a warm and nostalgic place reserved in my heart for Notre Dame. Even if some of us think that ND has no further place or importance in our lives, it surely does. The ups and downs and often confusing times we spent in those four years made us what we are today. I am a lucky person to have had this opportunity. There are only 125 of us [freshman women admitted in 1972] in the world who can say that."

> ◇ *Marianne O'Connor, ND 1974:* "The most lasting thing we take from Notre Dame is the set of values we developed here.... Today [graduation day] we both leave Notre Dame and take it with us."[14]

> ◇ *Bob Quakenbush, ND 1976:* "When we left Notre Dame after our commencement ceremony—seeing the Golden Dome in our rearview mirror—I know many classmates and I were emotional and, not knowing the road ahead, wondered when and if we would ever return to the campus. Honestly, I think some of us thought it might be the last time we would ever see Notre Dame! As it turned out, for many of us we couldn't have been more wrong.
>
> "We didn't know at the time we would be returning to South Bend regularly, as Notre Dame alumni, for football games, reunions, and even as university employees (including the

university's president!). As the years went by, classmates returned as residents of Saint Joseph County or as Notre Dame parents. Some engaged with the university through the Notre Dame Alumni Association, serving as volunteers and officers of local Notre Dame Clubs, or as class officers. We just didn't realize at the time that the gift of a Notre Dame education and diploma was the beginning of another incredibly special gift: a lifetime of connections with our alma mater, our classmates, and the lifelong friends made at Notre Dame."

◇◇◇

REARVIEW REFLECTION My graduation is but a faint memory. I remember spending the weekend with my family and a little time with my classmates. Most of my "cheerleaders" participated in that momentous event, including my maternal grandmother (I lost Grandma Ethel before sophomore year), my godmother, and a slew of cousins. Our family dinner included Father Miceli.

After dinner, the adults proceeded to the hotel bar for celebratory drinks and dancing. I was still surprised by the sight of women dancing together, as my mom, grandma, and aunt all hit the dance floor. Laughing at their antics, I celebrated my last four years, graduating with the first freshman class of women, and two viable career options: the Notre Dame JD–MBA program or working for Commonwealth Edison in Chicago. I had overcome self-doubt, objectification, poor decisions, a broken heart, and academic failure. I discovered my womanhood and recognized not only who I was when I arrived as a freshman but also who I became under the Golden Dome. I knew that my ND-inspired focus boded well for my suc-

Notre Dame's 131st commencement took place Sunday, May 16, 1976

cess in any professional role, the pursuit of a graduate education, and a lifelong connection to the university.

As I emptied my single room in Lyons, leaving my carpet and drapes for the next year's occupant, I thought about my journey until that moment. My time in Vetville had made me fall in love with the Lady on the Dome, and so I applied. I entered Notre Dame during a time of social revolution, leading to the admission of 365 undergraduate women. I met and spent time with Hesburgh, the first

Class of 1976 graduates (L–R): Sharon Zelinski, Ann Pytynia, Diana Wilson, and Jeanine Sterling

chaplain of Vetville and the man who changed the university in his lifetime and mine. The women who lived through those first five challenging years carved out spaces in Notre Dame's history; together, we ensured a future for its loyal daughters. (See the appendix for the names of the trailblazing women documented in the 1976 and 1977 commencement programs.)

Fortunately, I had more than just my memories of those transformative years. I also had my copies of each year's yearbook, the *Dome*. Since 1906, the *Dome* has chronicled the history of Notre Dame annually, except during the two World Wars. Its first editor, Charles O'Donnell, became a poet, priest, and Notre Dame president (1928–1934).[17] The *Dome*, as developed and delivered by its editor in chief and staff, presented those first years of coeducation in creative and varied ways. Reflections, quotes, and words from songs complemented the photos. The Indiana Collegiate Press Association rated the 1974 *Dome* first in photography and faculty presentation, while the 1975 yearbook ranked third nationally.[18]

Unfortunately, the tradition of signing yearbooks fell away in college. Since I did not have others' written comments, at the end of each year I marked the pictures in my copies of the *Dome* with asterisks—to help me recall those with whom I shared classes, residence halls, dates, or just fun. I cannot recall if I designed a scheme for the marks or based them on the available colored markers; I never anticipated the need for a key in the front of each yearbook.

During recent get-togethers with classmates, those asterisks often resulted in lots of probing about the color-coding and their number.

> ◇ *Tom Klein, ND 1976:* "The legend of the asterisk has grown over the years and has been the source of much laughter, debate, and conjecture (and some 'hurt' feelings). Were these would-be paramours? Why were both men and women 'asterisked?' If I weren't asterisked then, could I be now? Inquiring minds want to know!"

With (L–R) Mark Nishan, Ron Skrabacz*******, Tom Klein

◇ *Ron Skrabacz,******* ND 1976:* "I have nothing to say on this matter. I was non-asterisked back in 1976, and that is a hurt that never truly goes away. So, I will not bare my soul to the reading public about this blatant oversight of which I am still seeking therapy and counseling. And, might I add, any levity at the expense of those who did not rate back then would just add to the current dysfunction."

******* Asterisks added for emphasis and to correct a huge oversight from those earlier years.

Passing with Care

The Basilica of Sacred Heart
Art by Barbara O'Connell (2011)

"We aren't where we want to be, we aren't where we ought to be...but thank god we aren't where we used to be," Notre Dame football coach Lou Holtz has said about both football and the United States.[1] Because of coeducation, Notre Dame women shared their collegiate lives with a slowly increasing number of other females and members of minority groups—as undergraduate and graduate students, faculty, and administrators. These pioneers, first as students and later as alumnae, drove the administration to create a more inclusive environment, including improving gender-related courses and programs, instituting broader and more equitable policies, and launching activities for the university's increasingly diverse ND community. Still, after five years of coeducation, the question "Are we there yet?" remained a pressing concern.

Are We There Yet?

"Real change, enduring change," so said the late Ruth Bader Ginsburg, the second female justice to serve on the US Supreme Court, "happens one step at a time."[1] From the University of Notre Dame's inception, women continuously worked to strengthen its reputation, first as religious and graduate students, then as undergraduates, and later alumnae. By the end of its fifth year of admitting female undergraduates, the university had not only increased the number of women on campus but also benefited from their many accomplishments. These women's contributions are often acknowledged at the reunions and anniversaries of the September 1972 admittance of the first female undergraduates. Today, women can claim equal footing in many — but not all — aspects of this former male bastion.

◇◇◇

When Hesburgh became Notre Dame's president in 1952, the university primarily hired women to clean its residence halls and work in its kitchens. There were no female undergraduate students and no women on the faculty. Still, Hesburgh understood the cycle of progress better than most. Changing the complexion of Notre Dame — whether in admissions, faculty, administration, or the student body — took place slowly but inevitably. In his autobiography, he said that "it is really amazing what the very best people can do for a university. They attract...outstanding professors...outstanding students...more research and endowment money for more special faculty."[2]

The competition to enter Notre Dame was fierce in the 1970s. The candidate pool showed that both men and women were interested in a Notre Dame education. The qualities of those accepted improved the university's academic standing and reputation, as Hesburgh foretold.

What is lost in the growth and success of the past fifty years is the fact that the small number of women at Notre Dame initially had minimal impact on any one dimension of campus life. Without the transfer students from Saint Mary's, Notre Dame might have witnessed an even smaller female presence. Out of 365

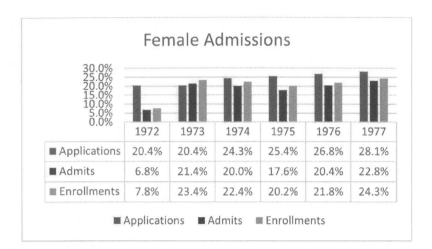

Female Admissions

	1972	1973	1974	1975	1976	1977
■ Applications	20.4%	20.4%	24.3%	25.4%	26.8%	28.1%
■ Admits	6.8%	21.4%	20.0%	17.6%	20.4%	22.8%
■ Enrollments	7.8%	23.4%	22.4%	20.2%	21.8%	24.3%

■ Applications ■ Admits ■ Enrollments

women who enrolled during the first year, 211 had transferred from Saint Mary's College.[3] Hesburgh gave a great deal of credit to the transfers: "Those women transfer students were our biggest break this year. We wanted kids who knew the place. It's a juggling act, but we'll have it under control in a few years."[4]

Two things affected the number of women on campus: the availability of women's dorms and the desire to have women undergraduates in all four classes beginning in year one of coeducation. Until 1981, Notre Dame only made room for women by converting men's dorms, a practice resulting in tension between the women and the men affected by the conversions. Even when Notre Dame did build two residence halls, slightly less than a decade after the women arrived, it still was not enough. Unfortunately, without funding for additional halls, the university continued its practice of converting male dorms (specifically Pangborn, Howard, and Cavanaugh) until the building explosion of new residence halls in the late 1990s.

In the second year of coeducation, the university admitted 417 freshman women, which dramatically improved the percentage of women admitted for the 1973–1974 academic year. Students experienced a slightly more balanced campus existence and an improved male-to-female ratio. Freshman female enrollment varied across the first five years of coeducation but averaged 22.4 percent after the first year's 7.8 percent enrollment. In less than ten years, the female undergraduate population grew from 365 to 2,100, a staggering 575 percent increase.[5]

That first decade was full of change and the impact inevitable. Still, except for surveys gauging the women's experiences and *Observer* articles documenting day-to-day student life, the "firsts" by the women were not captured to the same extent they are today. One little heralded fact was the addition of Notre Dame's first female trustee in 1971, just before the first female undergraduates arrived.

Rosemary Park, a leader in women's higher education, later received an honorary degree from ND in 1974. She served six years before her election as a life trustee.[6]

By the time of their commencements, the females in the classes of 1976 and 1977 had witnessed and celebrated significant firsts:

- **1972–1973:** Hesburgh appointed Susan Roberts as a consultant to the Office of the Provost, and Sister John Miriam Jones, SC, as assistant to the provost. Eight ND women, including Betsey Jaeger, Lucy Eberhart Cannata, Mary Beth Bruengardt, and Rosemary Crock, joined the 117-male members of the nation's oldest marching band. Two freshman women joined the Air Force Reserve Officer Training Corps (AFROTC): Mary Ann Palinski, a biology major, and Rosemary Tirinnanzi (now Lesser), a science major in the preprofessional program. The Navy ROTC unit commissioned Candace Kelly as a navy ensign in 1973. Walsh and Badin halls held their first powder-puff football game and participated in the Notre Dame Bookstore Basketball Tournament. Women joined the ranks of men on the fencing, skiing, sailing, crew, and diving teams. Women tennis players, led by Betsy Fallon, challenged the Saint Mary's women to a tennis match for the first time.

- **1973–1974:** WSND, the student radio station on the fifth and sixth floors of O'Shaughnessy Hall, added its first female commentator for ND football, Dede Lohle Simon, who broadcasted games to servicemen overseas. Eileen O'Grady and others began chronicling the emerging intercollegiate competitions in *The Observer.* Susan M. Darin became the first female editor for the 1975 *Dome* yearbook. Marianne O'Connor delivered the valedictory speech at the 1974 commencement. O'Connor's words still ring true: "Today we both leave Notre Dame and take it with us."[7]

- **1974–1975:** The university added its first female physical education teacher, Astrid Hotvedt, who wasted no time in volunteering to coach field hockey, golf, and track. Carole Moore, a history professor, took the helm of the women's first designated club team, tennis. The core interhall team from Farley, led by Mary Clemency, Patty Coogan, and Judy Shiely and coached by Jeanne Earley, formed the first intercollegiate club basketball team. Ellen Hughes and soon-to-be scratch golfer Barb Breesmen broke the Burke Memorial Golf Course's "men only" rule and established the golf team. Jane Lammers and Ellen Hughes-Cromwick founded Notre Dame's Women's Athletic Association (WAA) and, with team captains, gathered four hundred signatures on a petition supporting varsity sports for women at Notre Dame. The WAA met for the first time with the administration to petition for varsity sports teams.

- **1975–1976:** Hesburgh appointed Dr. Isabel Charles as dean of the College of Arts and Letters, the first woman dean in the university's then 134-year history. On May 17, 1976, tennis and fencing became the first women's teams elevated to varsity status. Kathy Cordes, the first woman to coach a varsity sport at Notre Dame, was hired that summer from a pool of more than two hundred applicants.[8]

- **1976–1977:** Five female athletes received ND athletic monograms for the first time: fencers Cathy Buzard Sazdanoff, Christina Marciniak, and Kathy Valdiserri and tennis players Jane Lammers, and Mary Shukis. Marti Hogan, a Saint Mary's alumna, became *The Observer*'s first female editor in chief. Bridget O'Donnell became ND's Ombudsman. In February 1977, Sister John chaired the Committee to Evaluate Coeducation and invited two students to assist with an exhaustive analysis of a twelve-page survey completed by six hundred ND women and, for the first time, men. SMC issued the same questionnaire to a subset of its population. Results reaffirmed the challenges of the transition, the ND–SMC relationship, male–female relationships, and changes in the classroom. Recommendations included dramatically increasing the enrollment of women each year for five years, building a new dorm for women, increasing the presence of female faculty members, adding varsity status for basketball and field hockey, and increasing funding for the varsity program, including scholarships. The report confirmed the existence of stereotyping, the need for better social centers and activities, and the overwhelming desire of the women of Notre Dame to change the words to the university's fight song, "Victory March."

- **1977–1978:** Sharon Petro was hired to coach varsity basketball, and women's field hockey, coached by Astrid Hotvedt, achieved varsity status. The first basketball and field hockey monograms were earned.

- **1979:** Margaret Lally became the first Academic All-American, with more than fifty-seven women athletes following in her footsteps by 2006. (For more details on women's athletics at Notre Dame, see "Athletic Replays" in the appendix.)

The firsts continued—albeit slowly—and in 1986, the first female freshmen returned for their tenth reunion.

- **1980–1981:** Toni Faini became the first ND woman to fill the role of student drum major along with Saint Mary's Linda Battista Lawson ten years after women joined the band. Women's lacrosse and volleyball were elevated to varsity status.

- **1982:** During the Mass celebrating the tenth anniversary of coeducation, Sister John offered:

[T]en years is really just a beginning. In a modern Church and in our society where change is the currency of life, we are anxious to learn quickly from our experiences so as to prepare for ever fuller living—all the while careful to treasure that which is changeless. What is it that we have learned from this decade and from its men and women?...In focusing [on] those questions and in daring some answers we are discovering today's Notre Dame man and woman—a rich discovery indeed for they are the heart of the place.[9]

- **1984:** Patricia Romano was elected first female class president.

- **1986:** Teresa Doering Lewis was Notre Dame's first female Rhodes Scholar. Others, such as Dana Nahlen, had achieved distinction as nominees and continue to do so:

  ◇ *Dana Nahlen, ND 1976:* "Like ND, opportunities to study at Oxford on a Rhodes Scholarship were originally limited to men. Following an act of Parliament in the [United Kingdom] to amend the Rhodes Trust, women were invited to apply for the first time in 1976. The scholarship would have allowed me to continue my studies at Oxford in the fall of 1977, following my 1976 ND graduation.

  "The application process was extensive and involved not only essays, documentation, and letters of recommendation but also three interviews. I was chosen as one of ninety-six US finalists in that first year of eligibility for women. Although not ultimately chosen for the award, having been chosen as a finalist remains one of my proudest achievements.

  "However, like many firsts at Notre Dame during those first five years of coeducation, this accomplishment was never acknowledged or recognized. I am glad, however, to have been one of the first female US finalists and to see members of the second generation of ND females actually achieve this recognition."

- **1997:** After initiating a gender-blind admissions policy in 1992, Notre Dame's male–female ratio nearly reached parity in 1997. Unlike Yale, which had achieved a 44.7 percent mark in 1979, just ten years after admitting women, it took Notre Dame twenty-five years after coeducation for women to comprise 45 percent of its approximately seventy-eight hundred undergraduates. Princeton's timeline was similar, achieving 47.5 percent in 1994, its twenty-fifth year of undergraduate coeducation.[10]

UNIVERSITY OF NOTRE DAME DU LAC

IN AUTUMN, 1972, THE UNDERGRADUATE STUDENT BODY OF THE UNIVERSITY OF NOTRE DAME NUMBERED 6722. 365 WOMEN WERE INCLUDED IN THAT NUMBER. THAT INCLUSION, THAT COMMITMENT ON THE PART OF THE UNIVERSITY TO EDUCATE WOMEN AS UNDERGRADUATES SHIFTED A 130 YEAR OLD TRADITION AND USHERED IN A NEW PHASE OF ITS HISTORY. IN THIS YEAR, THE 155TH IN ITS HISTORY, THE UNIVERSITY OF NOTRE DAME PROUDLY HONORS YOU,

Deborah Ann Dell '76

AS ONE OF THE WOMEN WHO PIONEERED THE POSITION OF WOMEN ON ITS CAMPUS, BECOMING ROOTED IN ITS STRONG TRADITION WHILE CONTRIBUTING UNIQUELY TO ITS HISTORY, BROADENING ITS HORIZONS AND ENHANCING THE QUALITY OF ITS ALUMNAE/I.

GIVEN AT THE
UNIVERSITY OF NOTRE DAME
NOTRE DAME, INDIANA
WOMEN'S 25TH REUNION
JUNE 6, 1997

Edward A. Malloy, csc
PRESIDENT

Carolyn Woo became dean of Notre Dame's business school. At the time, no female deans headed business schools at private universities in the United States and only eight women led public accredited business colleges. Occupying both the Martin J. Gillen Deanship of ND's College of Business Administration and the Raymond and Milann Siegfried Chair in Entrepreneurial Studies, she was only the second woman to serve as dean of a Notre Dame college. Woo's appointment filled a more than twenty-year gap between the 1973 appointment of Sister Isabel Charles, OP, as assistant dean in the College of Arts and Letters and her 1976 appointment as ND's first woman dean.

In 1997, Notre Dame's "eldest daughters" came home as a community to celebrate their twenty-fifth anniversary of entering ND. The idea of recognizing the pioneering classes of 1973–1976 came from Jamee Decio (ND 1975), who said: "Football teams routinely gather to reminisce about their athletic laurels, their championship seasons. Why not such a gathering for the first team of women?"[11]

Friday evening, the women convened for Mass in the Basilica of the Sacred Heart with Hesburgh as celebrant. With the lifting of the Catholic Church's ban on women serving as acolytes, readers, and ministers, more than twenty-five women participated in various roles, including as Eucharistic ministers. Afterward, they shared dinner and listened to speeches by President Edward Malloy, CSC, Hesburgh's successor, and Judge Ann Claire William (ND 1975, juris doctorate), recipient of that year's Notre Dame Women's Award of Achievement. Each "pioneer" woman received a personalized certificate honoring her contributions to ND's legendary traditions.

For many, the most memorable moment occurred on Saturday with the dedication of the "women's rock." Placed at the foot of the Grotto's granite lectern, Jane Pitz, once assistant director of Walsh Hall, read its inscription as Hesburgh blessed the stone.

Father Ted and Jane Pitz Blessing the Stone (1997)

◇ *Susan Newbould Andrews, ND 1976:* "I attended the first women's reunion in 1997. I left the reunion with a much better perspective on my time at Notre Dame. Since graduation, I have felt like a 'second-class citizen' because I transferred in as a junior. During the reunion, it dawned on me that most of the women from the early years (1972–1976) were also transfers. For the first time, I felt as though I really belonged....I had been part of history in the making."

◇ *Paul Hakel, ND 1976:* "I cannot pass the rock in the Grotto without always thinking of the women who blazed a path for all women who came after that first group of women. I can't fathom how difficult it must have been and the courage it took to get through those four years. Kudos to you brave women."

◇ *Pam McCormick, ND 1974:* "I am the young girl I was, the woman I am, and all that I will be. Time passes, paths intersect, and we find our way back, again and again."[12]

- **1999:** The university appointed Patricia O'Hara as dean of the Notre Dame Law School, where she served for ten years. During her tenure, she oversaw the $57.6 million design, funding, and construction of the Eck Hall of Law and the renovation of Biolchini Hall. Other women deans soon joined her: Sarah Mustillo in the College of Art and Letters, Patricia Culligan in the College of Engineering, and Laura Carlson in the Graduate School.

The new millennium brought an onslaught of notable firsts as well.

- **2000:** Students and alumni reveled in the addition of the first female Irish Guard Molly Kinder Smith.

- **2001:** The first class of freshman women celebrated their twenty-fifth anniversary of the class of 1976's graduation. However, even after a quarter of a century, a balanced perspective was sometimes lacking.

> ◊ *Anonymous, ND 1976:* "Our class will always be the first freshman coed class at Notre Dame. There was a great deal of tension during our four years on campus, some cruelty, and many wounds for both men and women. The women who were the pioneers in what others might depict as a hostile environment deserve accolades for their role in the development and growth of the university. However, let us not forget the silent majority — the anonymous men in that first coed class who were equally instrumental in the university's growth and development. Our twenty-fifth reunion featured a movie about our female classmates' lives at Notre Dame; a woman actually prepared the film. I doubt the slight was intentional, any more than some of the boneheaded things that the guys did over the years. I guess insensitivity applies to both sexes."

In the spring of this historic year, the press recognized significant changes within Notre Dame. *The Wall Street Journal* included ND on its list of the "new Ivy Leagues," with its incoming freshmen having SAT scores ranging from 1270–1425 and average GPAs of 3.85.[13] The university itself had a 34 percent acceptance rate. Under the leadership of University President Edward A. Malloy, CSC, the student body consisted of eight thousand undergraduates and two thousand graduate students with a one-to-twelve faculty–student ratio. For the first time, letters to prospective female students came not from the business school dean but from Muffett McGraw, coach of the university's 2001 NCAA number-one ranked women's basketball team. The ND family saw its first national championship victory by Notre Dame's women's basketball team and the addition of a female Black drum major Tambre Paster.

The class of 2001 experienced a Notre Dame now in the top tier of many rankings. During their four years, students from all fifty states and some eighty nations contributed to Notre Dame's increasingly diverse population. Roughly 94 percent of its 1,908 students received diplomas, a graduation rate exceeded only by Harvard and Princeton. Class members participated in volunteer and service-learning programs in the South Bend area and nationwide, and some continued their service by joining programs such as the Peace Corps, Teach for

America, the Jesuit Volunteer Corps, and Notre Dame's own Alliance for Catholic Education and Holy Cross Associates after graduation.

Other notable events improved campus diversity. Senior Reggie McKnight became ND's first African American athlete to become a Rhodes Scholar candidate; senior A. Stephen Smith became the first African American president of the Glee Club; and senior Michael Brown became the first African American to serve two years as the Irish leprechaun. For the first time in memory — and perhaps in the school's history — the valedictorian was a transfer student, Carolyn Weir, a liberal studies and theology double major.

This class also saw the election of junior Brooke Norton as the first female student body president. Unlike Georgetown — which elected its first female student government president, Deborah Canty, in 1977, eight years after going coed — Notre Dame took almost thirty years to achieve this milestone.[14] Three female student body presidents — Brooke Norton (2001–2002), Libby Bishop (2002–2003), and Lizzi Shappell (2006–2007) — were elected in the first decade of the millennium.[15]

Like student body presidents before them, these women acknowledged how each year brought its own set of problems. After taking on the role, Norton acknowledged in an interview with *Notre Dame Magazine*: "I've thought a lot about that first class of women here and how much pressure they faced. They had to prove that women could add something worthwhile to Notre Dame. I now feel a small amount of that pressure."[16] She also acknowledged in *The Observer* that she prioritized "servant leadership" and often relied on Hesburgh's well-known advice — "you don't make decisions because they are easy; you don't make them because they are cheap; you don't make them because they are popular; you make them because they are right."[17]

Bishop's election coincided with the administration's ban on hard alcohol, putting her in a difficult position as a mediator between students and the administration. She recalled that university decision-makers during her tenure were still all white males, noting that her "feet didn't even touch the ground" in the overstuffed chairs in which she sat during meetings with the administration. Shappell discussed dealing with controversial issues such as dorm evictions, staging *The Vagina Monologues*, and sexual assault on campus.[18] The year Shappell served as student body president (2006–2007) was also when Annie Envall (ND 2005) and Elizabeth Moriarty (ND 2000, ND 2007) cofounded a confidential support group, "Out of the Shadows," for college women who experienced unwanted sexual contact.[19]

During that summer's thirty-fifth celebration of coeducation, the Notre Dame Athletic Department presented a ten-minute documentary titled *Daughters of Notre Dame*. Meant to cover the early history of the women's athletic program, the video focused primarily on the 1980s. Several women attendees who participated in athletics in the 1970s were dismayed that their years were noticeably missing.

Afterward, a few discussed their concerns with the ND representatives and discovered that few records of those first teams existed — not in the University of Notre Dame Archives or in back issues of *The Observer* or *Dome* yearbooks.[20] The women realized that something needed to be done to ensure such memories would not suffer the same fate as Notre Dame's first bell-bottoms and halter tops.

The twenty-year delay in writing this story allowed for inclusion of even more achievements by ND women. In 2010, Katie Washington became the first Black female valedictorian, earning a 4.0 GPA as a biological sciences major with a minor in Catholic social teaching. Katie echoed one of Hesburgh's major teachings in her graduation speech, encouraging fellow students to move on "after the applause stops" and use their gifts to serve others.[21]

According to the US Bureau of Labor Statistics, the "educational attainment of women ages 25 to 64 in the labor force rose substantially from 1970 to 2016. In 2016, 42 percent of these women held a [b]achelor's degree and higher, compared with 11 percent in 1970. In 2016, 6 percent of women had less than a high school diploma — that is, did not graduate from high school or earn a GED — down from 34 percent in 1970."[22]

In 2012, at the fortieth anniversary of coeducation, Notre Dame's Cushwa Center for the Study of American Catholicism, the Department of American Studies, the Gender Studies Program, and Badin Hall came together to host "Paving the Way: Reflections on the Early Years of Coeducation at Notre Dame," a panel of five individuals who experienced the school's transition from one that was exclusively male to coeducational.[23] The panel included Thomas Blantz, CSC (ND 1957), a professor of history and the former vice president for Student Affairs; Kathleen Cekanski-Farrand (ND 1973), former rector of Badin and Breen-Phillips halls; Ann Therese Darin Palmer (ND 1973), the first female campus news editor for *The Observer* and editor of the book *Thanking Father Ted: Thirty-Five Years of Notre Dame Coeducation*; Susan Poulson, a professor of history at the University of Scranton and coeditor of *Going Coed: Women's Experiences in Formerly Men's Colleges and Universities, 1950–2000*; Dan Reagan (ND 1976), former associate vice president for University Relations; and Jeanine Sterling (ND 1976), a member of the ND Women Connect steering committee. As Hesburgh noted in 2000, while recalling those early years and the changes that he helped to usher in:

> I believe that one of the greatest things that happened in the history of Notre Dame was the admittance of women as students, as faculty members, and as trustees of the university. That may not sound like a big thing, but this was a great male bastion, and no one thought it could possibly assimilate women.... [W]e're a better university, a better Catholic university, a better modern

university today because we have women as well as men in the mix, and…in leadership positions.[24]

During this celebration, the work of capturing the athletic history of ND's women also continued. The Early Women Athletes Project, established in 2011 by Jane Lammers (ND 1977) and Anne Dilenschneider (ND 1977), collaborated with Irish Digital Media to record interviews with the pioneering athletes in attendance. Afterward, Hesburgh sent signed certificates to all female athletes identified by the project to that point. The Notre Dame Women's Initiative, which began in 2014, initially focused on raising money for the renovation of the north entrance to Hesburgh Memorial Library, and in 2016, the early female athletes of ND and SMC provided funding and photos for a new *Theodore M. Hesburgh* mural. (*The Word of Life* mural, aka *Touchdown Jesus*, adorns the building's south side.) Three years later, in 2019, Lynnette Wukie became the first female leprechaun, remarking that, though this "path" already existed, "[i]t just took someone to take it and to show other people that you can do anything you want, as long as you're willing to be brave enough to risk whatever it is you need to risk."[25]

Building on this momentum, the Hesburgh Women of Impact (HWOI) group — which grew out of the Notre Dame Women's Initiative and was officially launched in late 2017 — broadened the mission to "recognize and celebrate [all] female leaders of Notre Dame" and "empower, nurture, and develop future female leaders within the university."[26] In 2020, Notre Dame elected its first female provost, Marie Lynn Miranda, the former provost of Rice University and a dis-

tinguished scholar of children's environmental health. In anticipation of the fiftieth anniversary of co-education in 2022, HWOI focused on raising money specifically for financial aid for young women attending Our Lady's university. It met its goal by International Women's Day in March 2021 — during a pandemic and well ahead of schedule.

Besides administrators, deans, and involved students, Notre Dame women are doctors, lawyers, soldiers, scientists, journalists, commentators, and entrepreneurs. They

Notre Dame Magazine, Autumn 2003
Art courtesy of Jennifer Downey

are mothers and grandmothers. They are Olympic medalists. They are Rhodes scholars — including Teresa Doering-Lewis (ND 1986), Eva Rzepniewski (ND 1997), Emily Mediate (ND 2015), Christa Grace Watkins (ND 2017), and Alexis Doyle (ND 2017).[27] Many also have shaped law and politics: The Honorable Ann

Claire Williams, now retired, was the first woman of color to serve on a federal district court in the Seventh Circuit, "the third woman of color to serve on any federal circuit court," and "the first and only judge of color to sit on the US Court of Appeals for the Seventh Circuit";[28] Condoleezza Rice was the first female African American to serve as National Security Advisor and Secretary of State; and Amy Coney Barrett, who attended Notre Dame Law School on a full-tuition scholarship, served as an executive editor of its law review, and graduated first in her class in 1997, is the fifth woman appointed to the US Supreme Court.[29]

When Notre Dame opened its doors to the class of 2022, fifty years after the start of coeducation, it admitted 3,586 undergraduates out of a "record-breaking" 20,370 applications, with approximately "one third of the students considered to be at the very top" of their high school classes or in the top tenth of ACT and SAT scores. This equated with an "18 percent [increase] in what [admissions offices] would call 'highest-ability applicants.'"[30] While this class might not have encountered the same gender inequities as did ND students in 1972, they likely faced a more competitive academic environment. In 2021, the freshman class was approximately 48 percent women and 52 percent men, a ratio determined by the number of ND's residence halls.[31]

◇◇◇

REARVIEW REFLECTION Many of the female pioneers at Notre Dame celebrate the advancements of the past fifty years. Perhaps the biggest changes on campus are the visibility and confidence of the current women students and the increased resources and support of the institution. During a reunion visit to Notre Dame, my junior year roommate truly captured the university's progress in her contribution to this social history:

> ◇ *Janet Krier Breen, ND 1975:* "I traveled so many 'miles' before I ever returned to Notre Dame, a familiar, yet significantly different, destination. When looking in the rearview mirror, I found it both amusing and flattering that the fashion styles of the 1970s had come back into vogue again. The styles we favored while defining our self-images as feminine-though-serious students were again popular with our children's generation. The women once again wore hoop earrings, skirts, leather boots, hooded sweatshirts, clogs, peasant blouses, short-shorts, and thongs.
>
> "Sound familiar? Except that today, thongs go…you know, and flip-flops go on the feet.
>
> "While crossing North Quad, I viewed numerous female students walking to classes, playing sports, posing for pictures with male friends, and, for some, sharing the campus with their young families. They looked completely comfortable.

The Golden Dome looms over multiple generations at Notre Dame: Becky, Sarah, and Ron Skrabacz at Becky's graduation (2006)

Top: Ron Skrabacz, Tom Klein, Mark and Lindsay Nishan (ND 2014) Bottom: With Kelly (ND 2008) and Shelley Simon (2019)

"I also observed a lone female student lounging on the lawn with a blanket, books…and very little else! As my mouth dropped open in amazement, the view triggered this reflection. I never imagined wearing [or 'not wearing' such an] outfit as a student; however, it struck me that she felt completely comfortable. This 'feminine' female student was no longer seen as anything unusual at Notre Dame.

"When we attended Notre Dame, many of us chose between being feminine and being viewed seriously as students. A little too much makeup, hairstyling, or (gasp) perfume could get you labeled as seeking your 'Mrs. degree,' not an academic one! In our hearts, most of us wanted both. Unfortunately, the environment of our time made it awkward to express those desires.

"With today's generation of women at Notre Dame, it appears that women have finally arrived."

Eventually, many Notre Dame pioneer women added daughters and sons to the student body. According to the 2000–2001 surveys conducted for this book, which I verified with alumni directories, of the 186 women in the class of 1976, 124 had 319 children. Of those children, roughly 23 percent attended Notre Dame as undergraduates. Although the potential for a margin of error exists as the numbers fluctuate with new additions, the percentage demonstrates the continued commitment of those first alumnae families to the university. One anonymous student reflected on the differences between the Notre Dame of the past and the Notre Dame of the present:

> ◇ *Anonymous, ND 1977:* "As my son finished his freshman year, it surprised me how so many things were still the same — the importance of religion, the Grotto, the same-sex dorms, the competition, the pressure to succeed, the drinking, the conservative nature, the volunteerism, etc. Drinking is still a popular activity, but [today's students] don't have the big parties as we did. Formals are not as popular either. Although some ND males still hold the same opinion of the SMC chicks after all these years, in general the men are less chauvinistic — but aren't they everywhere? When you consider SMC, the women outnumber the men, and overall the students are smarter and more serious."

Dan Reagan attributed these changes in ND's culture to many of the advancements the pioneering women of 1972 initiated:

> ◇ *Dan Reagan, ND 1976:* "We could look at a lot of those women as role models for our future daughters, who were hopefully going to have an opportunity to come here and have even greater advantages because of the women entering in the fall of 1972."

In a 2013 *Notre Dame Magazine* article, Reagan also said:

> Those early women changed the place and its people — but maybe in ways they are not aware — that oblivious, listless, immature group of boys eventually did grow up and grow deep — and they graduated, and they married, and they became fathers and they became fathers of daughters, and I guarantee you that as we raised our daughters we had those early women, our classmates, in mind as role models. Strong. Faithful. Smart. Loyal. Because as Sister Jean also used to say, "People get you ready for other people." And they did just that; they prepared us to be fathers of the future women of Notre Dame.[32]

The Wheels Keep Turning

Inspirational writer Rusty Berkus acknowledges that individual and institutional progress can be unpredictable but real: "There comes that mysterious meeting in Life, when someone acknowledges who we are and what we can be, igniting the circuits of our highest potential."[1] In the pre-coeducation era, alumni of private higher education institutions often threatened to stop supporting their alma maters where admitting women seemed to jeopardize institutional traditions. The University of Notre Dame, however, asked its 157 alumni clubs to encourage women to apply in order to achieve the initial five-year goal of fifteen hundred female undergraduates. As the number of alumnae increased, the Notre Dame Alumni Association (NDAA) placed women in significant roles and acknowledged their contributions to the university's history.

◇◇◇

In 1868, when University President William Corby approved Auguste Lemonnier's request to form "the Associated Alumni of the University of Notre Dame," women were not part of the equation. More than a century later, when the university decided to admit women, many male alumni, faculty, and students questioned the decision. At a September 1972 alumni board meeting, Sister John asked its members for "dynamic patience that nourishes, suggests, prods, challenges the evolution of the ND woman; a new tradition—and the consequent evolution of the new ND—more excellent, more mature, more complete."[2] Interestingly, the first of three alumni meetings during the 1972–1973 academic year invited rectors only from the male residence halls to the event dinners.

For some male alumni who opposed ND going coed, their attitudes changed when their daughters were accepted.

> ◇ *Patricia Stead Spencer, ND 1976:* "The one thing about going to Notre Dame that I will never forget is my father's reaction. As an alumnus, he opposed ND going coed. Once I was accepted, he

was as proud as could be. He did not have any sons, so this was the only way that his children could go to Notre Dame — and we both lived in Farley Hall."

Many students who had only ever known a Notre Dame that was coed weren't sure how to respond to the negative reactions of alumni.

> ◇ *James A. "Mickey" Rowley, ND 1976:* "Some years after graduation, the early 1980s or so, I attended an alumni chapter social event in Washington DC, where I lived at the time. An older gentleman in his seventies, upon discovering I was in the class of '76, promptly inquired as to my thoughts about Notre Dame admitting women. I was momentarily flummoxed. I had never known Notre Dame without women so had never given it much thought. I thought his inquiry was so quaint."

An extensive alumni survey conducted in 1976 indicated that 63 percent supported coeducation.[3] By the tenth anniversary of coeducation, as alumni recognized that women improved academics, athletics, and campus life, the acceptance rating increased significantly. The admission of daughters and granddaughters has since squelched further debate on the merits of coeducation.

> ◇ *Matt Cavanaugh, ND 1974:* "We needed the change to normalize things. My daughter graduated about the time that the ratio reached fifty-fifty. Her experience could not have been better. What started in our time has really worked."

In addition to concerns over the impact of women on Notre Dame's long-standing traditions, the administration was also anxious about the impact on future alumni giving. In the fall of 1971, incoming Harvard University President Derek C. Bok voiced his trepidation about the effect of female graduates on the university's financial support from alumni. In a statement on the admission of undergraduates to the prestigious institution, Bok deemed equal access between the genders "too radical a step" and underscored that "Harvard alumni supported annual giving at a per capita rate over four times that of Radcliffe alumnae."[4] This concern was prevalent at Notre Dame even thirty years into coeducation.

The question of alumnae giving arose in 2000, during interviews with Edmund P. Joyce, CSC, executive vice president emeritus and Hesburgh's chief financial officer, and William Sexton, vice president of development. Despite a successful fundraising campaign, Joyce affirmed:

> As far as gifts are concerned, we have not come through with any huge gift from any alumna yet, but I am sure that day will come. I would say that those alumni who have been major benefactors had wives who went along with them. I have never heard

of any opposition on their part [regarding giving] to ND. So, the women are usually partners in this giving process, as indeed they should be.[5]

Sexton discussed the increasing contributions of alumnae, both financially and through service to their alma mater. He presented the university's plans based on the Generations campaign. We debated the reactions to and value of tying alumni contributions and donation levels to access to administrators, athletic and invitation-only events, and legacy admissions. Sexton concluded the meeting with this positive view:

> As women grow in the professional ranks and have their own disposable income, our concern is dissipating. Even those women who stay at home are increasing in the numbers who give some portion of the household disposable income in their own names.[6]

On December 31, 2000, "Notre Dame became the first Catholic institution to raise [one] billion dollars" in a single campaign—making it the twelfth private university to reach this achievement and the eighteenth overall. Notre Dame again joined Princeton in breaking tradition, this time as the only universities without medical schools to attain this level of fundraising.[7]

The Generations campaign demonstrated alumni commitment to provide for both undergraduate and graduate women. As Father Joyce noted about spouses as partners in giving, Meg and John P. Brogan made a substantial commitment to establish the Brogan Family Fellowship for the MBA program. Based on students' GPAs from the first year of study, the fund recognizes the top five MBA women in their second year.[8] Male and female alumni have established scholarships to assist female undergraduates in a variety of colleges and majors.

Concerns about alumnae giving continued to dissipate as the twenty-first century advanced. Using data provided by Tom Molnar, Noelle Stohler, and Ellen Roof of the Office of Development, a mid-2020 review of contributions by the class of 1976 indicated near-equal levels of participation. With a potential population of 1,295 (183 females and 1,112 males), 150 (82 percent) of alumnae contributed versus 1,023 (92 percent) of alumni. For Giving Societies that require significant contributions, 54 (36 percent) of the 150 women participated at this level versus 248 (24 percent) of the 1,023 men. Nine classmates—two females and seven males—gave at either the President's Circle level (a minimum of $25,000) or the Cavanaugh Council level (a minimum of $50,000).[9]

Ongoing involvement for the classes of 1976 and 1977 extends beyond monetary contributions. At the time of the review, three men and two women were members of the Notre Dame Board of Trustees, with even more serving on numerous advisory councils.

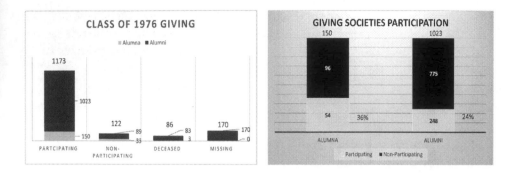

CLASS OF 1976 GIVING

Alumna   Alumni

1173 | 1023 | 122 | 89 | 150 | 33 | 86 | 83 | 3 | 170 | 170 | 0

PARTICIPATING | NON-PARTICIPATING | DECEASED | MISSING

GIVING SOCIETIES PARTICIPATION

150 | 1023 | 96 | 775 | 54 | 36% | 248 | 24%

ALUMNA | ALUMNI

Participating   Non-Participating

Today's Notre Dame Alumni Association is under the auspices of the Office of Development and spearheads activities intended to strengthen the bonds — both to the university and to each other — of the more than 103,600 alumni with undergraduate degrees and 30,000 with graduate degrees. Yet the male–female ratio in ND's alumni population remains lopsided at almost four to one, similar to the student ratio in 1976. This does improve each year, however, with roughly 50 percent of graduating classes comprised of women and a diminishing number of alumni from the all-male classes prior to 1972.

The NDAA's mission enables alumni to act as forces for good in their communities and the world through faith, service, learning, and work. Its structure includes clubs, affinity groups, and special interest groups that work to support the larger Notre Dame community.

> ◇ *Lionel Phillips, ND 1976:* "Since graduation, I worked for and retired from the IBM Corporation. During my professional career, I also served in many positions with local ND Alumni Clubs, such as the 2008 president of the ND Club of Saint Louis and on the Notre Dame Alumni Association Board from 2014 to 2017. During my time on the board, I actively recruited diversity students from nontraditional schools to Notre Dame. This process made me aware that some NDAA programming was stymied by tradition and failed to address the concerns faced today by people other than white straight males."

> ◇ *Jack Bergen, ND 1977:* "I love Notre Dame for the camaraderie it has afforded me over the years and for the alums I have met, especially once I became involved in various alumni board and officer positions."

Still, it took time for the first pioneer alumnae truly to be accepted within the NDAA structure. They often were forced to repeat the sometimes-grueling integration process in many professional roles and in some postgraduate environments. Even when they officially joined local NDAA clubs, few of these organizations initially made the necessary adjustments to address the increasing number of alumnae. Local ND clubs wondered why so few alumnae attended their traditional events such as golf tournaments, smokers, and prostate screenings.

Over time, the clubs and the NDAA as a whole did elect women as officers and directors, even as president. The first alumna joined the association's board of directors for the 1976–1977 academic year. The roughly sixteen hundred women from the first five years of coeducation are now part of ND's Senior Alumni affinity group, becoming eligible at age sixty.

Alumni of all ages get involved not only in their local clubs but also in service projects and organizations. Under the leadership of Chuck Lennon, the NDAA established various awards to recognize alumni who support the ND family and their communities. Members of the ND classes of 1976 and 1977 continue to demonstrate their love of "God, Country, [and] Notre Dame." Through 2020, several have received recognition by the university's NDAA award program, including:

- The James E. Armstrong Award, established in 1978, "is conferred on an alumnus [or alumna] who is a current or former employee of Notre Dame and has rendered distinguished service" to the university.[10]
  - 1996: Barbara M. Turpin (ND 1977)
  - 2020: Robert M. Mundy (ND 1976)
  - 2002: Daniel G. Reagan (ND 1976)

- The Dr. Thomas A. Dooley Award, established in 1984, "is conferred on an alumnus or alumna (living or deceased) who has exhibited outstanding service to humankind."[11]
  - 1985: Michael B. Bowler (ND 1977)
  - 1988: Cecilia H. Prinster (ND 1976)
  - 2007: Daniel Towle, MD (ND 1977)

- The Reverend John J. Cavanaugh, CSC, Award, established in 1985, "is conferred on an alum (living or deceased) who…has performed outstanding service in the field of government, patriotism, public service, [or] local, state, and national politics."[12]
  - 2000: The Honorable Kathleen Ann Blatz (ND 1976)

- The Reverend Anthony J. Lauck, CSC, Award, established in 2000, honors "fine arts and visual arts, [and] recognizes an alum, living or deceased, for…outstanding accomplishments or achievements as practicing artists."[13]
  - 2010: Reverend Austin Collins, CSC (ND 1977)

- The Reverend Edward Frederick Sorin, CSC, Award, established in 1965, "is conferred on an alumnus or alumna (living or deceased), not a current employee of Notre Dame, who has rendered distinguished service" to the university.[14]
  - 2007: The Honorable Hon. Sheila O'Brien (ND 1977)
  - 2017: Cindy Parseghian (ND 1977)
- The Distinguished Alumnus Award recognizes "exemplary service" to ND or the community.[15]
  - 2005: Dr. Michael A. Parseghian (ND 1977) and Cindy K. Parseghian (ND 1977)
  - 2009: Major General Frederick Roggero (ND 1976)
- The Volunteer of the Year Award, established in 2012, recognizes the "unsung heroes" who "continually go beyond expectations to ensure success for their club, class, or group and the Notre Dame Alumni Association."[16]
  - 2019: Jeanine Sterling (ND 1976)

(For a list of Notre Dame women who contributed in service to others through 2020, see "Women of Impact" in the appendix.)

To ensure that more women found value in the NDAA and alumni activities, a small group of alumnae from four clubs—those in Chicago, Detroit, Denver, and Washington, DC—discussed the importance of alumnae outreach. Started in 2005, this grassroots effort coalesced over the next four years into the Notre Dame Women Connect (NDWC) steering committee in 2009. The four pilot chapters, which advocated that ND women share special bonds that extend well beyond their years on campus, grew to fifty-five by 2014, and NDWC became an official Notre Dame affinity group.

Elizabeth "Dolly" Duffy, a 1984 ND graduate, is the executive director of the Notre Dame Alumni Association (NDAA) and the associate vice president for University Relations. Appointed in 2011, almost thirty years after the admission of undergraduate women, Duffy succeeded Charles F. "Chuck" Lennon in July 2011.[17]

Today, more than one hundred chapters offer an array of activities: book clubs, happy hours, service activities, and retreats. The NDWC's national board presents lectures and panels at reunions, a biannual shared reading project, an on-campus celebration of new female undergraduates called "Cheering Her Name," and a "Campus 2 Career" mentoring and professional development event for female students that occurs each fall. Board members stay connected with Notre Dame's more than 53,400 undergraduate and graduate alumnae via a quarterly newsletter and social media.

With class officers (L–R): Bob Quakenbush, John Carrico, and Ed Byrne at the University Club (2006)

NDWC group leaders also join forces with other affinity group leaders, regional directors, and club and class officers at the NDAA's annual Leadership Conference—an opportunity for networking, connecting with university administrators, and attending sessions on leadership best practices. Under Dolly Duffy, the NDAA's first female executive director, programming has expanded to include free online "digital neighborhoods" in which alumni "gather" to pray, learn, and share interests. In addition, conference participants attend the annual Blue–Gold football scrimmage, a tradition since 1929 that concludes the Fighting Irish's spring practice and often includes former ND football greats as honorary coaches.

Every five years after graduation, ND classes also gather at NDAA-sponsored reunions. Returning alumni and alumnae walk familiar paths and revisit any remaining haunts, both on and off campus. They connect with "old" roommates and friends, and some make "new" connections with those they did not know "back in the day." For many years, the early female pioneers were sometimes uncomfortable at the events as they struggled to put names with male faces; typically, the men more easily remembered the women, given the few women in their classes.

The NDAA granted Patrick "Murf" Murphy with honorary alumni status for his more than fifty years working at the Morris Inn. Murphy came to know generations of ND families. According to Murf, "I have known so many people over the years that kids will come in and say, 'My dad told me I had to come in and get my first drink with you because he got his first drink with you when he was here.'"[18]

During these weekends—or on any visit back to campus—many stop to see Patrick Murphy, the legendary bartender at the Morris Inn. Hospitality suites and tents also function as casual places to keep the party going— with no dorm hours and no parietals! Gathering late into the night (and sometimes until early in the morning), classmates share reflections on personal transformations, career achievements, and those inevitable bumps along life's road. Nights often end with classmates toasting Father Ted with his favorite drink, a Manhattan, followed by a late-night stroll around the lakes.

Father Hesburgh Manhattan

Ingredients:

1 ½ parts Canadian Club® whiskey

⅓ part sweet vermouth

Dash of Angostura® bitters

1 Maraschino cherry

Dash of Maraschino cherry juice

◇◇◇

REARVIEW REFLECTION I connected with Steve Klug (ND 1976) for the 2006 Leadership Conference. We planned to attend the Blue–Gold game together, the seventy-sixth such scrimmage. The day started sunny and in the low seventies—perfect for football—and we dressed for spring weather. Unfortunately, before the game started, the temperature dropped dramatically, and soon snow fell. Unlike fall football weekends, retail venues were limited, so I bought everything in sight at the bookstore. I donned size XXX sweatpants and two sweatshirts, pulling up the hoods over my scarfed head, and put socks over my shoes to cut the cold. I also picked up several copies of *The Observer* and scavenged plastic bags to cover the metal stadium benches. During college, I had a reputation for wearing skirts and dresses, never pants—and certainly not sweats!—so somewhere out there is a picture I hope never surfaces.

Steve and I entered the stadium, and I gave it my best effort, hoping I could stick it out for the entire game. Luckily, Steve was as cold and uncomfortable as I was, and we soon left to take the shuttle back to the hotel. As we approached the door of the bus, Steve went ahead of me—I could hardly see through my cover-ups—and asked the driver if he minded giving this "bag lady" a ride downtown. Given my cold, damp state, I didn't appreciate his poor attempt at humor at the time; however, recalling it today does make me smile.

Sometimes, female and male perspectives do align, as evidenced by numerous reflections in this social history and Steve Klug's own recollection of that day:

◇ *Steve Klug, ND 1976:* "In April 2006, I attended the ND Leadership Conference, arriving in seventy-degree weather. As I attended various meetings, I ran into seven '76 alums—including our class president, Debi Dell, stylishly dressed as always. The Saturday meeting ended at noon so that we could attend the annual Blue–Gold game. Before the game started, the weather began to cool off, and we expected rain. The NDAA provided ND plastic ponchos but nothing to keep us warm. I suggested we buy some warmer clothes at the bookstore. Debi reminded me that, in four years of college, she seldom wore pants. I told her that there was a first time for everything. Not finding anything that fit, she grudgingly agreed to buy larger-sized sweats and the annual ND shirt. The look coming out of the women's room in the oversized sweats was an interesting sight. As a light mist started falling, we grabbed *Observers* to sit on at the stadium; Debi eventually used some to insulate her flannel sweatpants.

"Well, the temperature dropped, and we ended up in a blizzard. As the announcer jokingly referred to this exhibition as the annual 'spring' game, snowball fights broke out in the stands. Drenched and frozen, we left before the end of the game. As we boarded the bus back to our hotel, I remarked to the driver that this 'bag lady' needed a lift downtown.

"Epilogue: My flight home was canceled, forcing me to stay until Sunday. Feeling a sense of community service, I took that 'bag lady' to dinner."

The ND Shirt Project started in 1990 to fund student activities. Traditionally announced at the NDAA conference, this annual shirt quickly became a unifying thread for students and alumni. Its unique design and availability in a single color add another dimension to ND's "twelfth man" at home football games.

In its first year, more than nine thousand shirts were sold, with profits near seventeen thousand dollars.[19] In 2018, more than 155,000 shirts were sold.[20] As the Shirt Project's popularity increased, revenue exceeded the needs of the ND Student Union Board, and the Shirt Project became its own student organization, with profits distributed to other clubs and organizations. Given these funds, the university has not raised student activity fees since 2004.

In 2022, the shirt included in its design a woman for the first time—a cheerleader—to celebrate fifty years of coeducation.[21]

On Sunday mornings of reunion weekends and other trips back to campus, I generally headed to Corby Hall for Mass and breakfast with Father Miceli. Corby Hall houses members of the Congregation of Holy Cross not assigned to student residence halls, and this group traditionally gathers at tables according to generation. When there, I always enjoyed strong

With Father Miceli (2006)   With Jo Lund Chamberlain

coffee and a waffle with an interlocked "ND" or a leprechaun in the center. To this day, I regret the time I turned down Miceli's wonderful offer to take a waffle iron home.

During one such breakfast while I was researching this book, Hesburgh joined us for coffee. Miceli had arranged many meetings with Father Ted but also interviews with Father Joyce, Father Blantz, Sister Jean Lenz, Sister John Miriam Jones, and so many others. Over the years of my project's lengthy development cycle, I saw Miceli mellow on the subject of women's presence on campus. Father Ted just shook his head when Miceli told him that I was the only female he trusted to stay in his dorm after parietals. I still do not know whether to be insulted or complimented by his comment.

After my traditional mornings with Miceli, I usually rejoined friends to picnic by the lake on a Notre Dame blanket with wine, French bread, cheese, and chocolate. We played music on our phones while gazing across the lake at the Dome and its nineteen-foot-tall statue of Our Lady. We marveled at the solitary female runners and the difference in their attire from our days as students. As we often did when we were in school, we stopped to feed leftover bread to the swans and ducks on

The Observer, June 12, 1975

Saint Mary's Lake. In more recent years, we added visits to Holy Cross Cemetery to pay our respects at the graves of Hesburgh, Miceli, Hoffman, and Joyce.

Such visits are not just one-way conversations. Darlene Palma Connelly recalled a memorable experience when paying respects at the graves of her mentors, Fathers Chambers, Mulcahy, and Tallarida.

> ◇ *Darlene Palma Connelly, ND 1977:* "I had never been to Holy Cross Cemetery until the fall of 2021. A friend with on-campus driving privileges drove me to the cemetery so I could pay my

respects. It did not take long to figure out that the identical headstones are arranged chronologically by date of death, so I started with Father Chambers, who was the last of the three to die. After visiting my other two mentors and friends buried there, I was overcome with unexpected grief. Recalling the phrase 'pushing up daisies' as I composed myself, I decided to return the next day with potted daisies for each of them. As I put the first one down on Father Chamber's grave, a shiny dime on the horizontal crossbeam of his tombstone caught my eye. It had not been there the day before. I still get goose bumps and an overwhelming sense of relief to know my mentors are still looking out for me today."

Janet Krier Breen has perhaps best summarized these return trips to our ND home when she likened them to her own family reunions:

◇ *Janet Krier Breen, ND 1975:* "Our family road trip frequently led to a summer family reunion. My father grew up in a small farming town near Lake Michigan. I possessed no sense of direction, so Dad always told me to watch for the lake shimmering on the horizon. When the air became pungent with the distinct nasal clue of nearby cows, we turned left at the overpass. Grandma's house was just a few more miles. My grandparents' property was at the edge of town, near a small village on one side and acres of farmland on the other. A welcoming gladiolus garden and a long gravel driveway along the edge of a bean field marked 'home.'

"We wore name tags at our family reunions, but the unofficial whispered labels proved more interesting! Descriptors included

Holy Cross Cemetery at Notre Dame is the last home for members of the Congregation of Holy Cross and "is one of the Congregation's most important landmarks" because it includes the graves of Father Sorin, the four Holy Cross brothers, and founder Basil Moreau.[22] Stone crosses dot the grounds, commemorating those whose lives and works have left indelible marks on Notre Dame. Except for Cardinal John O'Hara, CSC, whose tomb is inside the Basilica of the Sacred Heart, the deceased presidents of Notre Dame are buried in this cemetery.[23]

397

the rich one,' the 'broke one,' the 'three-times married one,' the 'spinster,' the 'handsome one,' the 'homely one,' the 'happy one,' the 'lonely one,' the 'creepy one,' and the 'one with too many kids.' However, none of it mattered. When the many small tables were lined up to look like one continuous setting, everyone had a place at the table. We all belonged. We all prayed. We all shared a meal together. We all knew that we were family.

"Every June, the Notre Dame Alumni Association holds class reunions. At the thirty-fifth women's reunion in May 2007, we welcomed one another, met younger alumnae, applauded our successes, and consoled our pains. Inside the main reunion tent, we watched the pouring rain as we drank beer and toasted with champagne into the wee hours.

Notre Dame class of 1976 flag

Continuing education courses, even a seminar for divorced Catholics, enlightened us. We prayed at the Grotto and Sacred Heart Basilica for our deceased.

"When the reunion concluded, we checked the rearview mirror and promised to return. We all belonged. We all prayed. We nurtured and enjoyed one another. We are members of the ND family."

Applying the Brakes

"From here, there's only once place to go...up!," comedian Eddie Cantor recalls his Grandma Esther saying of the basement apartment where the family lived when he was young. "And [she'd say] you had to be patient and go slowly. Everyone was trying to move too fast. 'People who go too fast don't see the scenery.'"[1] This advice from a Jewish *bubbe* may apply to institutions as well as to people. Notre Dame graduates returning to campus bring their own emotions and memories of a place they once knew well. Unfortunately, where Notre Dame is concerned, many return to find a campus barely recognizable as the place they attended in the 1970s. Gone are some of the "hallowed halls" and spaces where their memories were made. Increased investment in research, modernized residence halls, and first-class athletic facilities have changed the physical layout of campus and helped to improve the stature of the university. Notre Dame's faculty is world class, and the credentials of the student body are superlative. Members of 1970s cohorts often remark that they would not be admitted into Notre Dame today; many of their children have not. Even given the positives of the past fifty years, some wonder if the cumulative effects of change will eventually erode the character of the university.

◇◇◇

Notre Dame provided generations of students with strong academic programming, an idyllic campus, a broad range of developmental and social activities, and numerous ways to connect with classmates and alumni. While remaining steeped in its Catholic heritage, the university has long sought to address the changing times to ensure its continued relevancy in higher education and research.

Since the 1950s, three presidents have guided the University of Notre Dame during its transition to and through the growth of coeducation:

- 1952–1987: Reverend Theodore M. "Father Ted" Hesburgh, CSC

- 1987–2005: Reverend Edward A. "Monk" Malloy, CSC
- 2005–present: Reverend John I. Jenkins, CSC (ND 1976)

Father Ted served as president for thirty-five years during what Andrew Greeley called a "dramatic transformation."[2] This included transitioning to a lay board, enrolling the first female undergraduates in 1972, and increasing minority enrollments. His administration increased the university's resources, academic programs, and reputation. Under the leadership of Monk and Father John — who graduated with the ND class of 1976 with a bachelor's degree in philosophy, earned a master's degree in 1978, and was ordained in 1983 — the university completed numerous infrastructure and research expansions. Notre Dame's growth continued into the twenty-first century; its approximately thirteen-billion-dollar endowment is one of the largest of any American university.[3]

Endowments, academic standing, and stature are not the only elements that have increased in the past fifty years; tuition costs have made major leaps to stay abreast of the Ivy League schools.[4] Hesburgh realized that college costs, even in the 1970s, often required immense sacrifice by families. His May 20, 1975, letter informing students and families of the 1975–1976 tuition and room and board increases to $2,982 and $1,300, respectively, caused some angst. In his correspondence to parents, Hesburgh addressed the most frequently asked question when it came to cost: value. Comparing ND's tuition fees to those of peer institutions, Hesburgh noted that a Notre Dame education was a "comparative bargain" versus Ivy League tuition.[5] More importantly, he acknowledged the impact of the change: "The necessity of notifying you of these increased costs provides another opportunity for me to thank you for the confidence which you express in Notre Dame by entrusting the education of your sons and daughters to us."[6]

Yale	$4,050	Cornell	$3,775
Princeton, Dartmouth, Brown	$3,900	Harvard	$3,740
Stanford	$3,810	MIT	$3,700
Pennsylvania	$3,790	Columbia	$3,680

Average tuition costs at Ivy League institutions in 1975[7]

The 1975 North Central Association of Colleges and Secondary Schools agreed with Hesburgh, citing Notre Dame "as an institution with a clear and strong sense of purpose, outstanding leadership, academic and financial strength, high morale, and a strong sense of community."[8]

That sense of community has intensified with improved social centers and cultural opportunities not available on campus in the 1970s. During Hesburgh's tenure, Notre Dame's endowment increased by a factor of forty "from $9 million to $350 million," and research funding expanded by a factor of twenty "from $735,000 to $15 million." Enrollment nearly doubled (from 4,979 to 9,600), as did degrees awarded annually (from 1,212 to 2,500). The faculty also grew from 389 to 950, with compensation increasing tenfold. The annual operating budget rose by a factor of eighteen, from $9.7 million to $176.6 million, and the number of buildings went from forty-eight to eighty-eight.[9]

From 1987 when Hesburgh stepped down to the present day, the total student population has climbed from 9,851 to 13,139, a 33 percent growth, while the number of buildings has more than doubled from roughly ninety-five to two hundred.[10]

The alumni find a different Notre Dame each time they return to campus. Some alumni appreciate the new or renovated buildings that address safety issues and compliance with the Americans with Disabilities Act of 1990, and few object to the necessary upgrades, especially when the names of buildings remain unchanged — as in the case of Corby Hall. Others are concerned by the loss of green spaces. Visitors find it difficult to find campus parking, and to make matters worse, some parking is no longer free. What was once a mostly walkable campus is now populated with golf carts, bicycles, and campus shuttles.

In 1978, the National Register of Historic Places designated part of the Notre Dame campus a historic district. ND's Main and South Quadrangles, the university noted in its application, "contain[] twenty-one buildings of historic significance, nine additional buildings that positively support the general ambience of the district although constructed at a later date, [and] three buildings whose placement is important in defining the district....All of the buildings are currently in use."[11] These buildings were — and still are — all part of the 1970s Notre Dame experience.

◇ *Tom Young, ND 1976:* "I returned to ND several times after graduation, including attendance at the Notre Dame Alumni Association Leadership Conference (formerly Alumni Senate) as president of the ND Club of Boston. Each time that I have visited, I have still found my old haunts and the same feel of the old campus despite an ever-growing number of new buildings. In 2014, as a new member of the ND Senior Alumni (NDSA) Board, I attended its meeting at the Morris Inn, the only on-campus hotel. I knew that the inn had been renovated, although I could not detail the changes, having spent little time there. Exiting the building at the end of the day, I was completely disoriented. Gone was the University Club! Gone was the post office! Gone was the bus stop! It felt like a whole new quad had emerged.

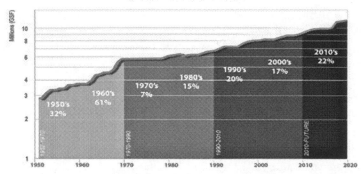

CAMPUS GROWTH BY DECADE

The gross square footage (GSF) of buildings continued to grow over the decades

In fact, several new quads and buildings had appeared where I never would have imagined. For the next three years on the NDSA Board, I was never quite sure of my direction. Another NDSA member drove me around the 'new campus' and the stadium Campus Crossroads Project and its outlying facilities. He also told me that, at the time, at least thirty-five donors waited for ND to purchase more land so they could endow buildings in their names. I was in awe but also wondered how much is too much and what was the purpose for all of it. Now when I watch a football game, and the *Goodyear Blimp* takes a shot from above the Dome, I pause the picture to recall the campus I once knew."

◇ *Ann Pytynia, ND 1976:* "Given it is more than ten years since I've been at ND, I would most likely not recognize it. So often college administrations now emphasize running schools like businesses, and I feel that emphasis is sometimes misplaced. Throughout this story, I noticed a pattern of ND not doing something because it was 'too expensive' (easy fixes like security lighting, etc.) during our time on campus. Yet, today, it spends so much on buildings and things donors want that might not be needed by the students. As the liaison to the Historic Preservation Committee as a public sector manager, I became increasingly impressed at [this group's] dedication to maintaining the city's character. Just think if the Romans would have thought to destroy the Forum, Colosseum, and Pantheon."

Excerpts from a letter from Dr. Philip E. Coyne Jr. to classmate and University President John Jenkins, CSC, reflect the feelings of those alumni concerned about the frenetic pace of physical changes on campus in the past decade:

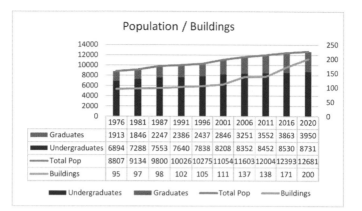

Population / Buildings	1976	1981	1987	1991	1996	2001	2006	2011	2016	2020
Graduates	1913	1846	2247	2386	2437	2846	3251	3552	3863	3950
Undergraduates	6894	7288	7553	7640	7838	8208	8352	8452	8530	8731
Total Pop	8807	9134	9800	10026	10275	11054	11603	12004	12393	12681
Buildings	95	97	98	102	105	111	137	138	171	200

■ Undergraduates ■ Graduates ——Total Pop ——Buildings

Population–building comparison compiled by examining enrollments and campus maps

◇ *Dr. Philip E. Coyne Jr., ND 1976:* "The historic core of our university should be a sacred space that is at all costs preserved from the wrecking ball....When I heard that the university planned to demolish Corby Hall, I was very troubled but somewhat comforted by the plans that the bricks would be salvaged and the footprint of the building would be essentially the same....

"[T]he same mentality that seems to pervade your administration, which does not seem to fundamentally value historic structures on campus, has plans to tear down Riley Hall, known during our days on campus as the Chemical Engineering building. This *should* be a designated National Historic Landmark, given that Father Nieuwland did his research on synthetic rubber in this building. That important scientific breakthrough was not only a huge scientific achievement but a fundamentally important part of Notre Dame's contribution to WWII, as important as the training of future US Navy officers....Historic preservation of buildings should be ingrained in our DNA."

◇◇◇

REARVIEW REFLECTION I still marvel at how my parents were able to simultaneously fund three children's private college educations, never requiring us to contribute. If anything, my father was angry whenever I took a part-time job, quickly reminding me that my only "job" was earning my degree. As I approached my senior year, my father discussed the Notre Dame tuition increases with me. He wanted me to understand that this was a significant investment, especially when coupled with my brother's junior year at ND and Doug's freshman year at Loras College.

403

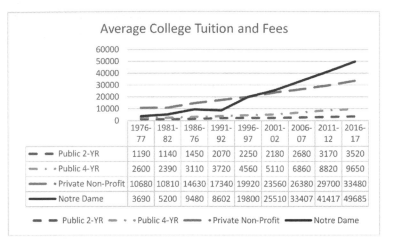

Average College Tuition and Fees

	1976-77	1981-82	1986-76	1991-92	1996-97	2001-02	2006-07	2011-12	2016-17
Public 2-YR	1190	1140	1450	2070	2250	2180	2680	3170	3520
Public 4-YR	2600	2390	3110	3720	4560	5110	6860	8820	9650
Private Non-Profit	10680	10810	14630	17340	19920	23560	26380	29700	33480
Notre Dame	3690	5200	9480	8602	19800	25510	33407	41417	49685

As my father noted upon my acceptance, my ND education, both academically and developmentally, provided a great start. However, according to the Consumer Price Index Inflation Calculator, our collegiate costs of four thousand dollars in the 1970s equate to roughly twenty thousand dollars in 2021. Looking at the price tag of a Notre Dame education today, I am relieved that I do not have to do any cost-benefit analysis myself. Of course, with the relationships I have built from my ND association, I guess the term "priceless" truly applies.

Notre Dame and its physical campus are part of me; I am convinced that the spirits of past students and faculty linger within every building. Even if a building or open space no longer exists, I remember what I learned and experienced there. Today, some of my favorite spots live on only in photographs and memories: Vetville; the old bookstore, with Gilbert's Campus Shop inside and the basketball courts outside; The Alumni Club, known in the 1970s as Senior Bar; Saint Michael's Laundry; and the old Fieldhouse with its basketball games, commencement exercises, pep rallies, track events, and the Bengal Bouts. In the intervening years, the university reduced its eighteen-hole golf course where I took my golf rotation to a nine-hole course, expanded nearby Cedar Grove Cemetery with new mausoleums, and constructed new residence halls.

My father always said that, as we age, some changes are harder to accept than others. Visiting campus, I am not alone in finding it increasingly challenging to recognize and relate to my former "home." My concern deepened after attending the 2005 NDAA Leadership Conference as president of the ND class of 1976, along with John Carrico, our class secretary. During the event's first dinner, we sat next to the university officer who had just presented additional campus expansion plans. At one point, this administrator asked my opinion of the brick columns and wrought iron arch proposed for the main entrance. Based on the drawings, the arch appeared to block the view of the Golden Dome when driving up Notre

Dame Avenue. I asked him why anyone would want to block that iconic view. He responded that "the important people" — trustees, officers, major donors — had not voiced such concerns. After that, he picked up his chair and turned his back to me. Even John commented that the snub was palpable. Others must have eventually provided similar feedback, as there is no arch (yet!), though columns with the university seal now appear through the windshields of those driving toward the Dome.

To accommodate a law school expansion and a new engineering building, we also lost the main circle bus stop, the post office, and the University Club. Dedicated in 1968, the University Club became one of my favorite places postgraduation. Donations at a certain level provided University Club membership, and in 1970, its board approved associate club membership for ND and SMC graduates and members of the local community. For me, nothing on campus today has replaced the experience of sitting next to the club's stone fireplace, with a view of its extensive stein collection, and sharing great conversations and affordable, tasty meals with the people who have supported this social history — administrators, professors, classmates, and friends. Given the additional loss in 2019 of Sorin's Restaurant and its vintage murals due to Morris Inn renovations, the last venue where I shared meals with Hesburgh and Miceli no longer exists. Only photos and saved Sorin menus help me to recall preconcert dinner dates and reunion breakfasts.

Today's ND women take for granted some of the resulting changes from all the construction and renovations. The LaFortune Student Center now has a beauty salon, and athletic facilities are built with locker rooms for both sexes. When an employee was asked during the first women's reunion how long the salon had been there, the young woman responded, "There's always been a beauty salon."

Oh really?

A View through the Windshield

"Travel isn't always pretty. It isn't always comfortable. Sometimes it hurts, it even breaks your heart," said celebrity chef Anthony Bourdain, who traveled much of the world in his well-documented television and writing career. "But that's okay. The journey changes you; it should change you. It leaves marks on your memory, on your consciousness, on your heart, and on your body. You take something with you. Hopefully, you leave something good behind."[1]

◇◇◇

FINAL REFLECTION My undergraduate experience at Notre Dame was just one stop on my life's journey, but it was absolutely the most consequential. I have returned to the stop known as Notre Dame numerous times—during my childhood, my adolescence, my professional life, and my senior years. Even as I changed relationships and career directions, I had three constants: my family, my faith, and Notre Dame. My parents supported me through all the starts and stops in my life and encouraged me to keep going when I got stuck. They instilled core values and nurtured a strength of character. My time at ND tested those values and challenged me academically, socially, and emotionally. By graduation, I had developed an inner strength that emboldened me to forge my own path—one that did not follow my father's dream of practicing law or my mother's traditional role within a family.

Many of my fellow graduates feel a similar connection to Notre Dame:

> ◇ *Bill Seetch, ND 1974:* "We are fortunate to be attached to such a place. The traditional four-year stay etches the paths and places that hold special meaning for us into our memories."

> ◇ *Dan Reagan, ND 1976:* "Wherever I go, whatever situation I find myself in, I will remain permanently connected to this maddening, beautiful place."[2]

As this social history evolved, so did my understanding of the impact of those four years at Notre Dame. I came to understand the many similarities — and differences — among our ND experiences, thanks to the light shone on them by the surveys and interviews.

> ◇ *Anonymous, ND 1976:* "At first, it [the survey] seemed daunting. Finally, when I took some time to reflect on [the] questions, I was glad that I had done so. By having to think about the questions, I came to some new insights on my past experiences."

> ◇ *Matt Cavanaugh, ND 1974:* "After [the] survey was sent to the past [male] residents of Badin, we kept the group email going. Two years later, in September 2019, we had a reunion for the 'Last Men of Badin.' Approximately twenty-five came back to campus for dinner, tailgating, a football game, and a tour of the newly remodeled Badin Hall."

Unfortunately, I could not include every quote or story I received. Some experiences were better left to the imagination and some questions better left unanswered. However, collectively, the more than one hundred fifty surveys, interviews, and stories I gathered influenced the content and arrangement of this book. Similar experiences, expressed with the same phraseology, validated the dimensions and challenges of our journey. Many confirmed that, while we were living the experience, we were not absorbing the magnitude of the change.

> ◇ *Shayla Keough Rumely, ND 1976:* "At 18 or 19, I did not have a clue about the magnitude of what we were doing."[3]

Early on, under the shadow of the Dome, the coeducation transformation seemed like "the worst of times."[4] In the haze of those years, I did not realize that some people had worse experiences than me. Reviewing their reflections over the years — in survey responses and during interviews — made me think, "Wow! I'm glad that didn't happen to me!" or "You think that was bad? I remember when…" or "Gee, I never knew *that* happened." Some expressed the bittersweet pain of those early days, but most acknowledged that the experience allowed them to learn things about themselves that might not have surfaced in a different environment or college campus.

I, too, was often unhappy with my collegiate life, as the negative voices both in- and outside my head focused on the failures, mistakes, and botched relationships. After much reflection, I attribute many of my negative feelings and missteps to youthful confusion. I did not initially excel in the classroom nor think through the impact of my decisions outside it. I struggled to handle the intense objectification of women and the resulting inner turmoil that I felt. Frequent stops at Sacred Heart and the Grotto provided some comfort during my times of doubt and despair, but I hated never having a definitive answer to the incessant question I asked myself just about every day: "What now?"

Others—ND's administrators, faculty, and male students—also wanted answers to that question. They were not prepared for women and did not understand how our needs differed from those of our male counterparts. Despite the university's best efforts, the first 365 undergraduate women and those who joined in the fall of 1973 experienced a hostile, sexist environment. However, I genuinely believe these attitudes reflected the norms of the time and, for the most part, not ill-will toward women. Coeducation has instead brought notable changes to the college classroom in the ensuing decades.

> ◇ *Paul Aspan, ND 1974:* "I've been a university creature for more than thirty-five years, of which two were spent in a full-time, nontenure-track ('visiting') position at Notre Dame.
>
> "As an undergraduate in that first semester of coeducation, I sat in a classroom with a profane, highly accomplished, often humorous theological ethicist as my professor. Most days, I wondered about the comfort level of the lone woman student who always sat in the front of the room while he regularly dropped f-bombs and used other colorful language. To be clear, the professor did not treat her any differently than the rest of us. Even still, I cringed for what she had to endure, both the language and the isolation.
>
> "When I taught classes from 1985–1987, the difference in classroom dynamics was palpable. It felt so much healthier to teach a room of thirty students in which a significant number were women—not to mention how rich classroom discussions had become. The women helped me to become a better teacher than if I had taught in an all-male environment.
>
> "The high caliber of today's student body can be traced directly to the decision to become coed at the undergraduate level. By any objective measure, the university was better off then and is far better off now. Admitting women served as the final catalyst in launching ND into the highest tier of US universities."

Like those who preceded us in the fight for women's equality, we accepted the challenges of our environment, often excusing the difficult situations we encountered as "just the way things are." We came to accept—but never liked—the foolishness of antics such as the dining hall rating system and panty raids. The time spent at bars and parties helped us to understand differences in human nature and to learn how to interact with different individuals—not to mention the opposite sex.

These experiences prepared us for careers where men and women worked together—and when, at times, we worked at cross-purposes. In these situations, we often found ourselves applying insights and lessons learned at ND.

> ◇ *Diana Wilson Ostermann, ND 1976:* "I majored in business and found [that] my courses barely scratched the surface of what I needed to be effective in my field; I really learned about business in my first year of working after graduation. What I did get at ND was four years of practice at fighting my way upstream, so it felt normal when I started my career in a male-dominated field. My male classmates learned to accept females, however grudgingly, as capable individuals. Had ND not become coed when it did, the male graduates would have been deprived of that lesson and taken much longer to appreciate women in the workforce as valuable team members.
>
> "Now that ND has been coed for…fifty years, issues of gender bias have somewhat lessened—at ND and in the workplace. Today's female students likely take for granted that they are the equals of their male classmates. Only because of the intense scrutiny experienced by those first classes of women are the current women free to better enjoy their time at ND."

Over time, both the diminishing number of male students coming from primarily all-male secondary schools and the graduation of the "old guard" slowly changed many attitudes and behaviors. After five years of coeducation, the darkness of objectification was lifting, and we started to feel that women truly belonged under the Dome. Now, with a half century of coeducation in the rearview mirror, tensions continue to abate, as women represent half the undergraduate population and serve in more visible roles. Today's female students will never understand what it meant to "rob" their male classmates of their residence halls or be the lone woman in a class of all males. Many do not even comprehend that there was an all-male Notre Dame.

According to Jay Newton-Small, author of *Broad Influence: How Women Are Changing the Way America Works* and a correspondent for *Time* magazine, "When women reach critical mass, somewhere between 20 to 30 percent of any institution, they change fundamentally the way that institution functions."[5] At Notre Dame, this occurred within the first ten years of coeducation. By 1997, twenty-five years after undergraduate women first enrolled, the ratio reached nearly one to one, with women making up 45 percent of ND's undergraduate population. The class of 2021 was 48 percent women and 52 percent men, due in part to residential hall capacity.[6]

◇ *Tom Young, ND 1976:* "Without coeducation, Notre Dame may have survived, but it would not have continued as the preeminent Catholic university. No institution can be as strong, as productive if it only addresses half of the eligible, capable pool of candidates. ND women have strengthened both the student and alumni bodies and made marks in academics, service, athletics, and a variety of professional fields."

The number of women in key administrative positions and within the faculty has increased and now contributes to a new "normal." Female role models are no longer rare, providing students with someone to emulate and from whom to learn about work–life balance.

◇ *Rosemary Schwendler, ND 1981:* "The women of Notre Dame, even back in 1977, were always thinking about more than being good wives and mothers....What's different is everyone else on campus — professors, [advisers], administrators, the male student population — thinks that way now, too."[7]

Still, those of us from that first decade remain grateful to the insightful males — priests, administrators, and professors — who understood that times were changing and believed in our ability to hasten change, not only at ND but also in our postgraduate worlds. Such caring individuals helped many of us to understand ourselves. Through their guidance, I eventually integrated the social "Debi" with the serious "Deborah." This came midway through my undergraduate years yet early enough to influence a positive outcome. When I entered the professional world, this integrated self was better prepared to interact with others who thought and acted differently. I was not the only one who benefited from those early, difficult days.

◇ *Beverly Cesen Winterscheid, ND 1976:* "It is definitely true that my experiences at Notre Dame, taken in their totality, shaped the person who I am today. I discovered new values, built upon old ones, met my eventual husband (a double Domer) of more than forty years, and received an excellent education that has served me well in my professional and personal life. Getting an undergraduate degree in Notre Dame's first coed class provided me with a competitive professional edge. It prepared me for the male-dominated corporate environment, where I ensured my presence and perspective were heard and integrated, working collaboratively on corporate teams.

"I was somewhat of a novelty in those days — a woman from ND with the ability to talk sports, especially football, with my male colleagues. I know that I obtained a high-level corporate job in a privately held company because the CEO attributed some of [ND football's] hard-charging, 'play like a champion' stereotypes and behaviors (and my achievements) to my job candidacy. Those behaviors were, and still are, my professional guiding principles, and they have served me well in all aspects of my life."

Despite women's increasing presence at Notre Dame, those who are female or nonbinary still face limitations. The university will always have a strong male persona, due primarily to the founders of the university, the Congregation of Holy Cross. We will most likely never see a female president at Notre Dame, even though peer institutions that admitted women around the same time as ND have taken this step. Shirley Tilghman, a scientist, became the first (and, so far, the only) female president of Princeton University in 2001 after it had been a coeducational institution for almost thirty-two years.[8] In a 2011 presentation to the Centennial Conference of the Headmistress Association of the East, Tilghman reflected on the differences between Princeton's early generation of coeducation pioneers and the women of Princeton today, words also applicable to the women of Notre Dame:

> In February 2022, Tania Tetlow, a former law professor and the president of Loyola University New Orleans at the time, was named the thirty-third president of Fordham University in New York City. She is "the first layperson and first woman to lead [this Jesuit] university in its 181-year history."[9]

> In a real sense, the female students of today stand on the shoulders of giants — those hardy few who braved the skepticism of faculty and the scarcity of women's bathrooms. What is the legacy that these remarkable women have created for this generation?

> And they were remarkable... excelling inside and outside the classroom and rising to positions of leadership that men had held and shaped since their inception. Initially outnumbered 20 to 1 and lacking all but a handful of female faculty role models, they made their presence felt in ways that were wholly disproportionate to their numbers, partly, it is true, because of their novelty, but chiefly because of their confidence in their own abilities — which were impressive.[10]

Even today's ND campus iconography remains predominately male — although the Melissa Cook Softball Stadium, named after an early female athlete and opened in 2008, is a notable exception. Most buildings and statues are named after clergy who have held prominent university positions, male alumni with the resources to fund buildings and memorials, or successful male coaches. Women

411

are reflected through the image of Our Lady, a virgin, on the Dome and at the Grotto; in the stained glass windows of the Basilica of the Sacred Heart and in various campus chapels; and in sculptures such as Ivan Mestrovic's *Christ and the Good Samaritan Woman* (outside O'Shaughnessy Hall) and Anthony Lauck's *The Visitation* that portrays two expectant women (near the entrances to the Eck Visitors Center and the Hammes Notre Dame Bookstore). Recent national events remind us that monuments capture moments in time and have lasting, and some-

times unfavorable, impacts on individuals. At the university's June 2022 celebration of coeducation, an announcement indicated that a "reimagining" of the main entrance to campus was in the works as a more visible landmark honoring ND women, thus joining the women's rock that was dedicated in 1997 at the twenty-fifth anniversary.[11] Speakers in June also reminded us how *The Visitation* is a concrete example of the embraces often shared by Notre Dame's women.

Change is inevitable and is continuing to occur, as evidenced by the 2021 announcement that a statue of Muffett McGraw, the women's basketball coach from 1987 to 2020, will be erected outside of the Purcell Pavilion. Returning and future generations of ND daughters will be able to pose for pictures with McGraw, while singing the re-

The Visitation by Anthony Lauck

cently updated closing lyrics of the Victory March: "While her loyal sons and daughters / March on to victory."

Despite these noteworthy pronouncements, gender inequality remains an issue within and beyond campus boundaries. In athletics, the university has settled on thirteen varsity teams for men and women. While the rate of approval for women's varsity sports was slow at first, women's teams rapidly soared to great heights, with budgets expanding exponentially. The women's basketball team, starting in 1973 from humble beginnings such as ND's Bookstore Basketball Tournament, has captured two national championship titles and made multiple visits to the Final Four. The university funds the maximum number of student-athlete scholarships permitted, and the salaries of female coaches have burgeoned (although they sometimes still lag behind those of the men). On the other hand, the same bookstore that offered the court to these women fifty years ago has only recently expanded its merchandising in the past decade to recognize Notre Dame's female athletes and the "Irish women [who] have won 14 national championships in fencing, soccer and basketball."[12] Even these talented women have faced significant salary inequities as professionals. In 2019, the starting salary in the NBA

($582,180) far outpaced the highest salary in the WNBA ($117,500).[13] However, both the fight for equality and some progress continue: In February 2022, the US Women's National Soccer team, after six years of legal action, won a settlement against the US Soccer Federation for discrimination and unequal pay.[14]

Today's female athletes will never feel the incredulity we did over the lack of university-supported women's sports teams. Although Title IX unlocked opportunities in athletics, it took committed young women — and individuals such as Astrid Hostevdt and Carole Moore — to ensure those doors opened to ND women. These women, and the many talented female athletes who followed, added to ND's overall championship sports legacy.

> ◇ *Mary Ryan, ND 1980:* "[R]epresenting ND athletics as some of the first women students was a privilege. We represented something. We were the women smart enough to be admitted — good enough — to attend Notre Dame....We were Notre Dame women."[15]

> ◇ *Jane Lammers, ND 1977:* "While working on the athletics project, Anne [Dilenschneider] and I returned to campus in 2012. When I walked into the South Dining Hall, I noticed the deep impressions that had been made on the stone stairs by the students going in and out of the dining hall one step at a time, one day at a time, one student at a time, year in and year out. It made me think [about how] everyone who attends ND makes some kind of impression on the place, and together we have all made the Notre Dame we know. I knew that the women who played sports in those early years had done just that, too. I kept thinking about those South Dining Hall steps during the project. Anne with her brilliant mind turned that observation into a thought that she and Ovid share. 'Water wears through stone one drop at a time.'[16] I like that, too. It's true."

Following the June 2022 coeducation celebration, the university announced:

> In recognition of the 50th anniversary of Title IX of the Education Amendments of 1972, the University of Notre Dame, its Athletics Department and the Notre Dame Monogram Club will celebrate the passionate group of women who paved the way for the success of the University's current women's varsity programs by awarding more than 250 honorary monograms.

> Given that their contributions represent the product of a true pioneering effort, the honorees, including both the founders of the Women's Athletic Association and the women who competed for

Notre Dame during the first five years of coeducation (1972–77), will receive honorary monograms in a ceremony this fall.[17]

Since I was never interested in athletics, the challenges facing our women athletes escaped me until I began working in this book. I came to better understand not only their experiences but also, through the patchwork of male and female messages and stories that I received, my lifelong connection to the university. My connection, as it turns out, was never to the school but to its people — the extended ND family.

Even though my desire to attend Notre Dame started in the heart of Vetville, what draws me back and keeps me close is the mystique emanating from the souls who have lived and worked under the Dome light. Just as the Dome's shadow sometimes caused us to suffer "the worst of times," its light allowed us to live in what perhaps was "the best of times."[18] Many of us left with our lives intertwined with those of lifelong friends and the family that we are privileged to call Notre Dame.

> ◇ *Beverly Cesen Winterscheid, ND 1976:* "The most important and valued gift of my time at ND was that of a deep, lifetime friendship with my roomie. We shared so many life-shaping experiences at ND (even though we sometimes drew vastly different lessons from them) and during our adult lives. The many years since we met that July of our freshman year has deepened our friendship and brought us closer together, seeking and sharing advice during the ups and downs in the separate journeys of our lives."

Before graduation, I seldom thought about life as an alumna or my future connection to the institution; I only cared about staying in touch with friends. As I worked on this book, staying connected to the institution also became important. The unquestioning support and candor of individuals such as Father Ted, Father Miceli, and Chuck Lennon made me want to make a difference beyond chronicling this story. I pursued opportunities to give back and to broaden my ND network: as president of the class of 1976, as a Notre Dame Alumni Association regional director for Florida, and through a brief stint on the NDAA Florida Senior Alumni Board. In these roles, I found others who, like me, reconnected with ND not to recreate our undergraduate days but to contribute more than we did as students. For me, these roles also provided a chance to correct some missteps I'd made along the way, and I reconnected with and met others who had also embarked on this journey.

> ◇ *Shelley Muller Simon, ND 1976:* "Debi and I worked together many times during the twenty years it has taken to complete this book. After one memorable work session, she thanked me for

helping to bring her dream to life after veering off course several times due to the challenges of life. She then looked at me with tears in her eyes and asked, 'Do you ever wonder what people thought of you in college? My mom says I have not changed, but I like to think I have.' My reply was that I only care what people think of me now, because I am so different than I was then.

"We had taken divergent paths starting from quite different backgrounds. She was the Southern belle, striking out on her own, somewhat of a loner, looking back at college. I was the Midwest pragmatist, used to crowds, looking forward, and putting the past in its place. Yet we were drawn together by this story that was so much bigger than the two of us.

"By working on this book, I learned about my female classmates—the special individuals who struggled in those first years of coeducation. And now, a generation later, we continue to celebrate the Notre Dame traditions but with the richness of the tapestry woven by both daughters and sons of Our Lady."

Through such university-related roles and in creating this social history, I also met older and younger generations of the Notre Dame family. Some, such as Emily Weisbecker Farley (ND 2007) and other second-generation ND alumnae, helped me to understand the things about ND that remain unchanged since those first five years of coeducation:

- The benefits of residential life and the building of lifelong relationships.
- The challenging academics.
- Support from faculty and the administration.
- The existence of stereotypes.
- The focus on God, Country, and Notre Dame.

These younger alumnae also shared their perceptions of what elements still required additional and increased focus:

- The lack of diversity and broader gender-related policies.
- Adequate recognition of women's athletics, athletes, and coaches.
- Medical, counseling, and career services that meet *all* needs of women and nonbinary students.
- The need for more relevant residential guidelines and choices.
- Increased protection from sexual harassment and assault.
- The disproportionately low numbers of female professors and administrators.

From 1996 to 2006, women faculty grew from 18 percent to 24 percent of Notre Dame's faculty, supporting University President Jenkins' view that "hiring female faculty is consistent with the vision of Catholic institutions as embracing diverse people and cultures in order to 'enrich our dialogue and test our ideas.'"[19] In 2008, a report by the University Committee on Women Faculty and Students concluded that, though Notre Dame

> excels at recruiting female assistant professors, the number of female faculty in the ranks of associate and full professors lags behind its institutional peers. Most alarmingly, for every one hundred full professors who are female at the [Association of American Universities private schools], there are only sixty-eight at Notre Dame, and this ratio has not changed in ten years.[20]

The committee found that women in 2006 comprised 28 percent of Notre Dame's associate professors and 13 percent of its full professors, with assistant professor levels reaching 41 percent.[21] In 2018–2019, even after nearly fifty years of coeducation, the Office of the Provost indicated that only 27 percent of the university's tenured or tenure-track faculty were women. The number of such female faculty from underrepresented minorities has remained even lower.[22]

W is for women, first admitted in 1972. These daughters of du Lac proudly wear the gold and blue.

September 5, 1972 was a historic day at Notre Dame. After 130 years, the all-male school admitted 365 undergraduate women and the era of coeducation began. Walsh and Badin were the first dorms to be home to women. In the early years, there were only a few females in each classroom but today the women's population is equal to the men's. Women have adapted well to the Notre Dame traditions. There have been female valedictorians, student body presidents, drum majors and even members of the Irish Guard.

These were not the first women to receive degrees from Notre Dame, however. During the summers in the 1950s and '60s, religious sisters in their long habits filled the classrooms and dorms earning graduate degrees. Because of President Hesburgh's decision, young women from around the world can attend Our Lady's University

Campus Stop:

Look for the rock near the entrance to the cave at the Grotto inscribed with words of thanksgiving from the first women's class.

Reprinted from L is for Leprechaun, courtesy of Barbara Gowan and Jane Pitz

Most importantly, through Emily's candor and extensive contributions to this social history, I found that college remains a time for self-discovery. Her family ties to Vetville, her casual interest in football and varsity sports, and her struggles to find herself at Notre Dame mirrored my own experiences, albeit thirty years later. I am relieved to know that our time in college — at Notre Dame, specifically — should, and did, change each and every one of us.

> ◇ *Lionel Phillips, ND 1976*: "Today, women appear more outwardly confident earlier in life than the great ladies with whom I attended ND. But the actions of my female classmates and those in the early years of coeducation laid the foundation for women to compete earlier and in broader circumstances than in the 1970s. I do not think Notre Dame would exist today had it not leaned into the wind and accepted women as undergraduates. Of all the groups considered in the diversity columns, women are the most significant: 'the hand that rocks the cradle...rules the world.'"[23]

Surviving our time at Notre Dame made many of us believe we could make things happen and change the world. As we shattered glass ceilings at work, we realized that Notre Dame, for all its early shortcomings, had not crushed our core strengths and values; rather, it had strengthened them. We suffered trials and tribulations as we blazed new trails. We broke records, and we broke new ground; sometimes we smashed old molds. Future ND generations will learn about the contributions of women to the university through this and other social histories but also through creative works like Barbara Gowan's (ND 1976) *L Is for Leprechaun: An ABC Book of Notre Dame* (illustrated by Jane Pitz).

Notre Dame deserves credit for its progress in accepting and promoting women as members of its student body, faculty, administration, and alumni communities. Some might argue it could have been done better; others feel it was always done with the best of intentions. The common ground is the recognition that adding women made the school more competitive and more relevant than it ever could or would have been had it continued as an all-male institution. No one realized this more than Reverend Theodore M. Hesburgh, CSC. Because of his vision and leadership, there will forever be daughters of Notre Dame. In my final interview with Father Ted, his comments summarized our story:

> I hope the atmosphere around here is such that, when [the women] return for a visit, they recognize the light that sparkles within each of them. I hope that coming back would not be just a revival of the spirit or a revival of faith from a wonderful college experience, but something that emerges as a warm feeling, a coming out of the cold, a sheltered feeling. I hope each looks upon this place as a second home, a place where they grew up, a

place of fairly considerable importance to them, a place where, given their druthers, they would like their kids to have the same experience.

A good institution puts its mark on its students. My hope is that the things you learned here have deepened your life. You did not come out of Notre Dame as a finished product, but you came out with enough skills to keep finishing the product.[24]

Postscript

Milestones in our life's journey come in many flavors. Birthdays, for example, are marked by individuals, while anniversaries are often observed by groups — whether an intimate acknowledgment of a significant date or a nation recognizing a landmark achievement.

This book celebrates the women and men who experienced the impact of the University of Notre Dame's decision to accept undergraduate women.

I am fortunate that many of my own milestones were part of the social history captured in *Objects in the Rearview Mirror.*

In June 2022, the University invited its graduates to return to campus to celebrate fifty years of coeducation. As I sat at this golden anniversary dinner, it brought back memories of the spring of 1982, when the campus commemorated ten years of women living and learning together. That was also a very personal milestone for me — the last spring I lived on campus with undergraduate women and worked alongside my Campus Ministry team.

To mark that occasion, I was invited to preach at the celebration's special liturgy on the Sunday evening following Easter. Even in the 1980s, it was so unusual for a woman to be invited to the pulpit in Sacred Heart Basilica that I kept my notes all these years! That homily captured the essence of our time together then and — more importantly — now:

> We sit side by side in the presence of this lighted candle to hear the Word and to break Bread.... [E]ach of us and all of us are meant to be the sign [of the Resurrection] by the quality of our lives, the choices made in our living by hope, love, and faith.

> The spring prior to this one, at the commencement ceremonies, Nancy Haegel, the co-valedictorian, said: "We have studied and lived at a special place, a place where people are not afraid to dream and to commit themselves to making those dreams come true.... [T]he vision is ours to keep, and it has been entrusted to

our keeping. Our theme is not merely live and let live — but live and share life fully."

Nancy's words still echo, don't they? As you finish sharing in the experiences of Notre Dame's women and men in this memoir, let me leave you with one more thought from that homily:

It is time to do the crazy, to splurge, to ask the embarrassing and believe the absurd. To offer the word of hope, lifting fractured and despairing spirits. We are summoned to make poetry of the darkness, to rouse stumbling hopes and become each other's patience.

For the grand experience of living with women fifty years ago, of working alongside a creative team of campus ministers and our student aides, of meeting men and women of the extended Notre Dame family who changed my life on this small spot of earth, gratitude. Great gratitude.

With peace and blessings,

Jane Pitz, MFA
ND 1972
August 2022

Appendix: Notre Dame Pioneers

University reports from 1999 and 2000 officially listed 186 undergraduate women as graduating in 1976. The *May 1976 Commencement Program*, the 1976 *Dome* yearbook, and the *2015 Alumni Directory* confirmed these names. In 2000–2001, 87 (46.7 percent) of these women responded to a lengthy survey. Their responses provided the background and quotations on the coeducational experience for this book. A special thank-you to all who responded or assisted with this story.

Key US Female Firsts

1869 — Susan B. Anthony and Elizabeth Cady Stanton found the National Woman Suffrage Association

1872 — Victoria Claflin Woodhull: first female US presidential candidate Susan B. Anthony cast her first vote to test if the 14th Amendment guaranteed women the right to vote and was convicted of "unlawful voting"

1918 — Margaret Sanger, two years after opening a birth control clinic, won her suit to allow doctors to advise married patients about birth control for health purposes; the clinic, along with others, became Planned Parenthood in 1942

1933 — Frances Perkins: first female cabinet member as Secretary of Labor

1966 — Betty Friedan, author of 1963's *The Feminine Mystique*, helped to found the National Organization for Women (NOW)

1971 — Gloria Steinem, Bella Abzug, and Betty Friedan formed the National Women's Political Caucus

1977 — Janet Guthrie: first woman to drive in the Indy 500

1981 — Sandra Day O'Connor: first woman to serve on the Supreme Court

1983 — Sally Ride: first American woman in space

1993 — Janet Reno: first female US attorney general

1995 — Shannon Faulkner: first woman admitted under court order to attend The Citadel in its 152-year history

1997 — Madeleine Albright: first female Secretary of State

2002 — Halle Berry: first African American woman to win Oscar for Best Actress.

2007 — Nancy Pelosi: first female Speaker of the House

2010 — Kathryn Bigelow: first woman to win an Oscar for Best Director

2020 — Katie Sowers: first woman and first openly gay coach in Super Bowl history Kamala Harris: first female, Black vice president-elect

Key Events in the Women's Movement
(through the 1970s)

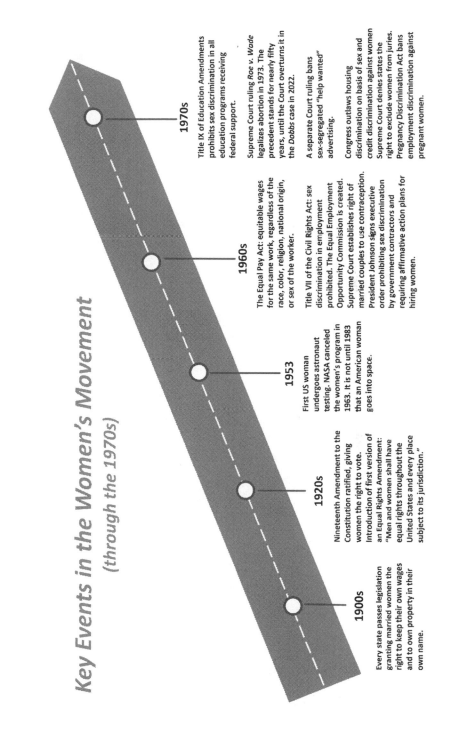

1900s

Every state passes legislation granting married women the right to keep their own wages and to own property in their own name.

1920s

Nineteenth Amendment to the Constitution ratified, giving women the right to vote. Introduction of first version of an Equal Rights Amendment: "Men and women shall have equal rights throughout the United States and every place subject to its jurisdiction."

1953

First US woman undergoes astronaut testing. NASA canceled the women's program in 1963. It is not until 1983 that an American woman goes into space.

1960s

The Equal Pay Act: equitable wages for the same work, regardless of the race, color, religion, national origin, or sex of the worker.

Title VII of the Civil Rights Act: sex discrimination in employment prohibited. The Equal Employment Opportunity Commission is created. Supreme Court establishes right of married couples to use contraception. President Johnson signs executive order prohibiting sex discrimination by government contractors and requiring affirmative action plans for hiring women.

1970s

Title IX of Education Amendments prohibits sex discrimination in all education programs receiving federal support.

Supreme Court ruling *Roe v. Wade* legalizes abortion in 1973. The precedent stands for nearly fifty years, until the Court overturns it in the *Dobbs* case in 2022.

A separate Court ruling bans sex-segregated "help wanted" advertising.

Congress outlaws housing discrimination on basis of sex and credit discrimination against women. Supreme Court denies states the right to exclude women from juries. Pregnancy Discrimination Act bans employment discrimination against pregnant women.

ND Path to Coeducation

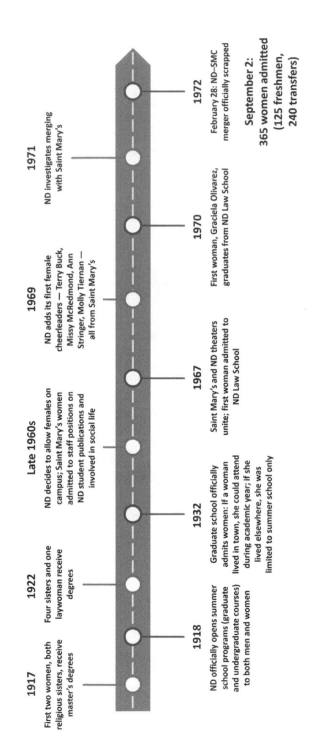

1917

First two women, both religious sisters, receive master's degrees

1918

ND officially opens summer school programs (graduate and undergraduate courses) to both men and women

1922

Four sisters and one laywoman receive degrees

1932

Graduate school officially admits women: If a woman lived in town, she could attend during academic year; if she lived elsewhere, she was limited to summer school only

Late 1960s

ND decides to allow females on campus; Saint Mary's women admitted to staff positions on ND student publications and involved in social life

1967

Saint Mary's and ND theaters unite; first woman admitted to ND Law School

1969

ND adds its first female cheerleaders — Terry Buck, Missy McRedmond, Ann Stringer, Molly Tiernan — all from Saint Mary's

1970

First woman, Graciela Olivarez, graduates from ND Law School

1971

ND investigates merging with Saint Mary's

1972

February 28: ND–SMC merger officially scrapped

September 2: 365 women admitted (125 freshmen, 240 transfers)

Top Ten Milestones

THE OBSERVER (1972–1973)	WORLD EVENTS
Coeducation	1972
Student Affairs revamped	• Equal Employment Opportunity Act for women and minorities
Academic manual adopted	• Equal Rights Amendment (ERA) ratification failed
Lewis Hall security incident	
Hesburgh resigns as Civil Rights Commission Chair	• *Ms.* magazine begins publishing • June Berenice Gera, first female pro baseball umpire
Student chairs Student Life Council	• XI Winter Olympics in Sapporo, Japan, had record 217 women
Kennedy, Shriver visits	• Warhol produces comedy *Women in Revolt*
Student body president election	• Boston Marathon allows women for first time
Farley, Breen Philips, Lewis selection; off campus guidelines	• Women recruited by the FBI for first time in its forty-eight-year history
Irish teams earn laurels	• Sally J. Pries ordained in Cincinnati as first woman rabbi in the United States, second in the history of Judaism
	• *Sports Illustrated* selects cowinners for Sportsman of the Year: John Wooden, coach of UCLA, and Billie Jean King
	1973
	• New Jersey is first state to allow girls into Little League
	• Supreme Court legalizes abortion with *Roe v. Wade*
	• Supreme Court upholds a lower court ruling allowing a New York hotel to refuse service to women in an all-male bar

THE OBSERVER (1973–1974)	WORLD EVENTS
National football championship	1974
Academic Council votes for pre-Labor Day start	• AP poll named Billie Jean King as Athlete of the Year
Pat McLaughlin elected student body president	• Princeton University trustees vote to abolish the quota system that limited the number of undergraduate women per class; the new policy admits women equally with men
Dillon Hall parietals violation challenges Judicial Board decision	• Supreme Court rules 7–2 that a school system cannot force a pregnant teacher to leave her position before her due date
Drug raids	• Supreme Court rules that women are entitled to equal pay for the same work performed by males in a major glass company
LaFortune renovations	
Student manual guidelines revised	
UCLA winning streak demolished	• Dr. Douglas Bevis tells of three babies conceived in test tubes
SMC president resigns	• String bikini is introduced — a long way from the 1900s sailor dress with hose

THE OBSERVER (1974–1975)	WORLD EVENTS
President Gerald Ford's visit*	1975
Ara's retirement*	• Pennsylvania is the first state to allow girls to complete with boys in high school sports
Football suspensions	
Academic calendar*	• United Nations proclaims 1975 International Women's Year
Lewis Hall	• Television favorites include *Laverne and Shirley, The Bionic Woman*
Basketball ticket compromise*	• •Susie M. Sharp becomes first woman chief justice of the North Carolina Supreme Court
Duggan appointment to SMC presidency	
COUL formed (Committee on Undergraduate Life)	• Italy passes a law that gives husbands and wives equal rights to make decisions
Alcohol regulations	• Karren Stead becomes first girl to win the All-American Soap Box Derby in Akron, Ohio
SLC's sexuality rule (Student Leadership Council)	• Government issues final regulations on barring discriminatory credit practices against women
* key events to the ND class of 1977	

THE OBSERVER (1975–1976)	WORLD EVENTS
Academic calendar	1976
Mock political convention	• Nadia Comăneci scores a perfect 10 on the uneven bars, an Olympic gymnast first
Duggan to SMC	• India announces plans to penalize parents who have more than two children
Not so Devine rumors	• Sarah Caldwell leads the Metropolitan Opera orchestra, becoming first woman to do so
Drug bust	
Collective bargaining	
CIA on campus	• Marian S. Heiskell becomes first woman elected to Ford Motor Car Company Board of Directors
Drinking bill no go	• First women students are admitted to the US service academies: West Point, Annapolis, and the Air Force
Affirmative action	
50 + 12 (alcoholism conference)	• Pope Paul VI calls the recent Anglican acceptance of women as priests an "element of serious difficulty" that might jeopardize the relationship between the two churches
Other top news: • ND–SMC politics • Difficulty enrolling in business electives • Emil T. Hofman resigned as dean of Freshman Year of Studies	• For the first time since 1902, women become Rhodes Scholars, with thirteen out of twenty-four awarded the Rhodes Scholarship
THE OBSERVER (1976–1977)	WORLD EVENTS
Other events include: • Overcrowding in the business school • Trojan signs before USC games • Sit-ins by Black students • ND's campaign to achieve $130 million in its endowment fund	• The world's first personal computer, the Commodore PET, demonstrated at Consumer Electronics Show in Chicago • Jimmy Carter is sworn in as thirty-ninth US president • *Star Wars*, directed by George Lucas, is released • Women Marines disbanded; women are integrated into the Marine Corps

For top ten lists from *The Observer*, see:
- "*Observer* Picks Top Ten of Year," *The Observer*, May 1, 1973, 3
- "The Top Ten of 73–74," *The Observer*, May 1, 1974, 13
- "Top Ten Stories of 1974–75," *The Observer*, April 30, 1975, 15
- "Our Top Ten Stories from This Year," *The Observer*, April 30, 1976, 8

Women of Impact

Impact is about so much more than money. Since 1978, the Notre Dame Alumni Association has presented more than 444 awards. Through 2019, 65 women have received such formal recognition, a mere 14.6 percent. Congratulations to these outstanding women, especially the first pioneers from the class of 1973–1977.

The Rev. Edward F. Sorin, CSC, Award
- 1998 Eleanor M. Walker, MD, '84
- 2004 Kathleen W. Andrews '63 MS, '03 Hon
- 2007 Hon. Sheila O'Brien, '77, '80 JD
- 2012 Hon. Ann Claire Williams '75 JD
- 2017 Cindy Parseghian '77
- 2019 Anne Thompson '79

The James E. Armstrong Award
- 1987 Sr. John Miriam Jones SC '61, '70
- 1995 Isabel Charles '60, '65 PhD
- 1996 Barbara M. Turpin '77
- 2009 Missy Conboy '82
- 2010 Patricia A. O'Hara '74 JD
- 2015 Jean T. Collier '83
- 2016 Catherine F. Pieronek '84, '95 JD
- 2018 Sarah Craig '98 MNA
- 2019 Ann (Stockmann) Firth '81, '84 JD

The Rev. John J. Cavanaugh, CSC, Award
- 2000 Hon. Kathleen Ann Blatz '76
- 2001 Christine Cervenak '82
- 2017 Stephanie Miley '82

The Rev. William Corby, CSC, Award
- 2010 Capt. Wendy Sue Kosek '04, '07 JD
- 1998 Lt. Col. Karen Daneu, USAF '77

The Dr. Thomas A. Dooley Award
- 1986 Ann C. Titus '80
- 1988 Cecilia H. Prinster '76
- 1993 Julie K. O'Brien '86
- 1997 Kathleen M. Osberger '75
- 2002 Mary Brosnahan Sullivan '83
- 2005 Sr. Joan Chittister, OSB, '68 MA
- 2006 Mary McCann Sanchez '79 MA
- 2018 Sr. Katherine Seibert, MD, '67 MS, '73 PhD
- 2020 Mary Meg McCarthy, JD, '80

The Harvey G. Foster Award
- 2011 Haley Scott DeMaria '95
- 2014 Lauran '06 and Justin Tuck '05

The Rev. Robert F. Griffin, CSC, Award
- 2014 Beth Ann Fennelly '93
- 2020 Christina Gorman Telesca '91

The Rev. Arthur S. Harvey, CSC, Award
- 2006 Christine Swanson '94
- 2007 Hannah Storm '83

The Rev. Anthony J. Lauck, CSC, Award
- 2015 Gita Pullapilly '99

The John Cardinal O'Hara Award
- 2004 Sr. Elaine V. Desrosiers, OP, '66 MS

The Rev. Louis J. Putz, CSC, Award
- 2004 Mary Lou '56 SMC *and* Richard Yeager '56
- 2005 James R. Kennedy '57 *and* Elizabeth "Betsy" Finneran Kennedy '59 SMC
- 2018 Gail Thomas McKenna '71 MA

The William D. Reynolds Award
- 1991 Sr. M. Jean Lenz, OSF, '67 MTh
- 2001 Elizabeth Bird '91
- 2002 Hon. Jeanne M. Jourdan '75 JD
- 2012 Hon. Kathleen A. Kearney '77 SMC, '80 JD
- 2015 Karen Gunter '79 MSA
- 2020 Patricia Emmanuel '82, MD

Outstanding Educator of the Year Award*
- 2002 Marianne Powers '74 MS
- 2008 Joy Michnowicz Anderson '96
- 2012 Julie Bernhardt '89
- 2017 Beth Burau '00, '02 MEd

Volunteer of the Year
- 2013 Mary Ellen Woods '80
- 2019 Jeanine Sterling '76

Distinguished Alumnus
- 2005 Ruth Riley '01

Honorary Alumnus
- 1986 Marie S. Gerencher
- 1995 Sr. Marietta Murphy, IHM
- 1996 Barbara (Bobbie) McGlinn
- 1997 Muffet McGraw
- 1998 Karen L. Anthony
- 1999 Jill Ann Fischer
- 2001 Pamela S. Spence
- 2005 Mary Ann Remick
- 2008 Joan Lennon
- 2011 Carolyn Y. Woo
- 2015 Wilma Veldman

* No longer given

The Rosenthal Award* and The Dr. William P. Sexton Award have no female recipients

The Class of 1976

College of Arts and Letters
Bachelor of Arts

Joanna Krystyna Bartosik *Highest Honors*
Elizabeth Holmes Bernard
Kathleen Ann Blatz *Highest Honors*
Nancy Anne Brenner *Honors*
Mary Theresa Brown
Geraldine Anne Burke *Honors*
Patricia Ann Burke
Susan Caranci
Beverly Jo Cesen *Honors*
Stephanie Leland Crotty
Denise Hazel Crowley
Donna Marie Crowley
Mary Patricia Culler *High Honors*
Virginia Reed Curlee
Rebecca Jean Curtis *Honors*
Susan Marie Darin
Susan Patricia Davis *Honors*
Laura Lane Dodge
Margaret Marie Doherty
Cathy Lee Donahue
Mary Susan Dondanville *Honors*
Wendy F. Duffey
Sheila Ann Elsner *High Honors*
Sheila Maureen Fahey
Elizabeth Beatrice Fallon *Highest Honors*
Ellen Marie Flanigan *Honors*
Margaret Mary Foran *High Honors*
Mary Patricia Frailey *Honors*
Ellen Margaret Freeman *Honors*
Theresa Gayle Fritz *High Honors*
Kathleen Mary Gallogly
Mary Elizabeth Anne Gillespie
Laureen Frances Goers *High Honors*
Mary Ann Grabavoy *Honors*

Karla Jeanne Grazier
Kathleen Marie Gwynn *High Honors*
Constance Lynn Hanahan
Patricia Louise Harper
Catherine Lu Hauersperger
Maryrose Hawkins
Mary Fran Hayes
Mari Adele Horak
Margaret Ellen Humphreys *Highest Honors*
Mary Elizabeth Iden
Barbara Ann Jakubowski
Linda Anne Johnson
Margaret Anne Kaiser *Honors*
Mary Patricia Kelleher
Mary Shayla Keough
Kim Sarahjane Kittrell *Highest Honors*
Angela Catherine Lamm
Michelle Louise Lapointe
Donna Losurdo
Jo Lynn Lund *Honors*
Mary Julia Lyon *Honors*
Catherine Matthews
Kathleen Susan McAllister
Kathleen Alice McCarthy
Nancy Susan Meier
Diana Renee Merten *Highest Honors*
Margaret Rose Miller
Mary Elizabeth Miracky
Lisa Anne Molidor
Laurie Jean Moore *Honors*
Susan Nash *Highest Honors*
Susan Alison Newbould
Kathleen Ryan O'Laughlin *Honors*
Maria Celeste O'Meara

College of Arts and Letters (cont.)
Bachelor of Arts

Joanne O'Rourke
A. Michelle Parnell
Mary Therese Philbin *Honors*
Eleanor Joan Popken
Cecilia Helen Prinster *Highest Honors*
Ann Marie Pytynia
Anne Kathleen Reilly *Highest Honors*
Mary Kathleen Riehle
Maryanne Ries *Honors*
Ellen Stacey Rocheleau *Honors*
Melissa Anne Roman
Ellen Marie Ross *High Honors*
Mary Elizabeth St. Ville *High Honors*
Kathleen Ann Salzer *High Honors*
Kathleen Anne Scarola
Lindsay P. Schneider *Honors*
Elizabeth Jane Short
Mary Ann Siegel

Jacqueline Ann Simmons *Honors*
Andrea Joanne Smith
Robyn Elizabeth Smith *Honors*
Kathleen Ann Smouse
Sally Agnes Stanton *High Honors*
Jeanine Marie Sterling
Tracy Strickland
Ellen Louise Syburg
Michele Lee Tate *Honors*
Mary Christine Teah
Jill Elayne Truitt
Ann Marie Waickman
Catherine Ann Walshe *High Honors*
Victoria Vach Walters
Margaret Mary Waltman
Patricia Ann Willing
Denise Wilt
Joan Wise

Bachelor of Fine Arts

Elizabeth Mary Jaeger
Mary Frances Lerner
Barbara Simonds Syburg

College of Science
Bachelor of Science

Rebecca Anne Banasiak *High Honors*
Michelle Marie Berberet *High Honors*
Kathleen Mary Buckley
Mary Virginia Clemency *Highest Honors*
Melanie Marian Connell
Marjorie Sue Duensing
Jean Marie Essling
Patricia Ann Gallagher
Jane Frances Garland
Claire Catherine Gordon *High Honors*
Marylu Iredale
Helen Kraus *Highest Honors*
Jeannette Carolyn Larkin
Eileen Marie Malko
Mary Josephine McGlew

Joan Elizabeth Miller
Kathleen Ann O'Connor *Honors*
Barbara Mary Ondercin
Barbara Anne Rapchak
Carol Marie Reimer
Margaret Anne Schuler
Mary A. Setlock *Honors*
Renee Marie Sittley
Patricia Lynn Stead
Rosemary Tirinnanzi
Cheryl Ann Todaro
Janet Judith Vokoun
Jule Elizabeth Wetherbee *Honors*
Mary Catherine Zwitt

College of Engineering
Bachelor of Science in Architecture

Susan Karen Funk
Ann Elizabeth Greenburg *Honors*
Roxanne Elizabeth Jabbra
Shelley Muller

Esther Catalina Rios
Susan Marie Schneider
Cynthia Stuermer

Bachelor of Science in Engineering

Margaret Curtin (Aerospace)
Sally Naxera (Civil)

Bachelor of Science in Metallurgical Engineering

Mary Elizabeth Resnik
Jessie Maria Verna

Bachelor of Science in Electrical Engineering

Kathryn M. Andersen
Jean Marie Dudek
Elizabeth Anne Raven

College of Business Administration
Bachelor of Business Administration

Mary Frances Barga
JoAnn Mary Barnes
Mary Katherine Baron
Sarah Louise Bartzen Christine Carroll
Loretta Beth Castaldi
Maureen Catherine Creighton *Highest Honors*
Deborah Ann Dell
Joan Idella Farmer
Monica Jean Flanagan
Mary Therese Foster
Jane Marie Frank
Carole Bridget Froling
Christie Ann Gallagher *Honors*
Ann Marie Hawkins *Honors*
Kathryn Mary Johnson *Honors*
Elizabeth Louise Kall
Deborah Sue Kanser
Mary Anne Kennedy *High Honors*
Judith Marie Kula

Patricia Ann Lane
Mary Bridget McCoy
Susan Elizabeth O'Brien
Susan Caroline Odmark *High Honors*
Margo Elizabeth Pallardy
Opal Ann Pinkerton *High Honors*
Judith Mary Ploszek
Marianne Geraldine Ridge *High Honors*
Mary Katherine Rochford *High Honors*
Debra Ann Schoeberleim
Susan Schoenherr
Linda Loretha Slaughter
Michelle Ann Smith
Judith Stepanek
Rebecca Lou Taiclet
Diana Marie Wilson
Sharon Patricia Zelinksi
Claudia Marie Zweber

The University of Notre Dame 1976 Commencement Weekend May 14–16
http://archives.nd.edu/Commencement/1976-05-16_Commencement.pdf

The Class of 1977

College of Arts and Letters
Bachelor of Arts

Karen Marie Abraham
Karen Sue Adams *Honors*
Patricia Kay Andrews *Honors*
Margaret Adeline Audette *Honors*
Sue Lynne Augustus,
Kathleen Anne Bailey
Leslie Patricia Barnes *High Honors*
Ann Marie Bebenek
Sheila Ann Bero
Leonie Maria Bertelt
Denise Marie Blanchard
Karen Frances Bledsoe *High Honors*
Betty Ann Boynton *Honors*
Rebecca Susan Bracken
Catherine Ann Brown *Highest Honors*
Ellen Maura Callahan *Honors*
Cathlynn Harrelson Cannon
Sheradi Daun Collins Cannon *High Honors*
Susan Capparell
Shirley Elizabeth Carey
Susan Mary Carey *High Honors*
Janet Elizabeth Carney *Honors*
Sharon Marie Carr *High Honors*
Candace Christopher Carson
Mary Christine Cella *Honors*
Elaine Marie Cerny
Barbara Ann Corcoran
*Maria Helen Costello *Honors*
Karen Marie Crowley
Nancy Gail Cueroni
Mary Barbara Curlee
Mary Therese Curtin *High Honors*
Josie B. Danini
Janet Estelle Deasy

Deborah Lynn de Lorenzo *Honors*
Marybeth Diamond
Anne Marie Dilenschneider *Honors*
Dorothy Tyrrell Dodson
Kathleen Maura Donohue *Honors*
Keiren Casey Donovan *High Honors*
Susan Ellen Doyle *Honors*
Sandra Anne Dryja
Florence Ellen Duff
Ellen Ann Duffy
Patricia Louise Dunn
Christine Marie Fahrenbach
Virginia Ann Faust *High Honors*
Nancy Jane Fehrenbacher
Mary Catherine Fineran *Honors*
*Mary Patricia Flack *Highest Honors*
Anne Smith Foley
Candice Christian Frankovelgia
Anne Therese Maura Frazel
*Joan Irene Gambee
Carol Hackett Garagiola, *Honors*
Diane Mary Gastineau *Honors*
Ann Sally Glaser
Kathleen Anne Gleeson
Judith Mary Gorske *High Honors*
Nora Mary Grace
Debra Jeanne Grady *High Honors*
Susan M. Gretkowski *Honors*
Maureen Griffin
Paula Annette Griffin
Carol Ann Guckert
Mary Josephine Gumble
Ann Therese Gwynn *Posthumous, High Honors*
Alisa Mary Hardiman

A mini-reunion of class of '77 Breen-Phillps residents, Chicago, November 2018

(L–R) Peg Hornback Culhane, Mary O'Meara Lee, Sharon Carr Winnike, Bridget O'Donnell Provenzano, Susan Allen Dalton, Kathy Walker Beenen, Louise Karas Hayden, Beth Lavins Fitzgerald, and Debra Grady

College of Arts and Letters (cont.)
Bachelor of Arts

Terri J. Harlan
Catherine Marie Harroun
Julianne Hartley
Christine JoAnn Hawley
Maryann Catherine Hayes *Honors*
Elizabeth Ann Heard
Barbara Ann Heck *Honors*
Terese Marie Herkes *Highest Honors*
Christie Ann Herlihy *Honors*
Peggy Anne Hester
Mary Beth Hines
Julia Ann Hofmann
Holly Elizabeth Holladay
Linda Marie Holleran *Highest Honors*
Margaret Elizabeth Hornback *Honors*
Mary-Louise Elizabeth Houghton
Ellen Lucy Hughes
Anne T. Hunckler
Deborah Katherine Jusczak
Ellen Blake Keane
Sheila Marie Keams *High Honors*
Mary Anne Keefe
Mary Ellen Baughman Keenan *Honors*
Mary Colleen Kelley
Ann Marguerite Kenney
Debra Ann Kenny
Deborah Klug *Honors*

Mary Colleen Koch
Ann Margaret Kopp
Karen Marie Kucharczuk
Kathleen Olga Kuryl
Lydia Rugile Labanauskas *Honors*
Jane Phyllis Lammers
Diane Marie Lampe *Honors*
Elizabeth Joan Lamping,
Patricia Mary Lasonde *Honors*
Carol Ann Latronica
Susan Irene Leonard *High Honors*
Martha Gordon Liebler *High Honors*
Barbara Ellen Lincer
Candace Lei Lopes
Kim Marie Lucas
Lisa Luccarell
Sarah J. Lynch
Eileen Frances Mackrell *High Honors*
Patricia Anne Maher
Susan Agnes Maino
Susan Elaine Manganiello *Honors*
Christina Maria Marciniak *Honors*
Joyce Elaine Marshall
Monica Ruth Marshall
Molly Martin *Highest Honors*
Sandra J. Martin *Highest Honors*
Marjorie Anne Matlak

Cathy Ann May
Colleen Christine McCarthy *High Honors*
Frances Carla McCollester
Mary Alice McGonigle
Virginia Anne McGowan
Sarah Louise McGrath
*Deborah Jean McGraw *Honors*
Cathleen Marie Mcinerny
Kathleen Ann McKeown *Honors*
Catherine Lynn McMurren
Jean Marie McQuillan
Jeanne Patricia Minahan *High Honors*
*Nancy Anne Mohr *Honors*
Theresa Marie Frances Molony
Ann Renee Montague
Gilda M. Montalvo *High Honors*
Ann Elisa Moore *High Honors*
Mary Elizabeth Mungovan *High Honors*
Maureen Ellen Murphy
Sheila Ann Murphy
Dana Gayle Nahlen *High Honors*
Jane Skahan Neff *Honors*
*Ernestine Cannichael Nickle
Regina Ann Norton
Mary Theresa O'Brien
Maureen Patricia O'Brien
Sheila Marie O'Brien
Bridget Ann O'Donnell
Eileen Mary O'Grady
Susan Ann O'Rourke
Jean Lee Ossenfor
Melody Sue Owens
Cynthia Elizabeth Paas
Sandra L. Pagna
Regina Pakalnis
Darlene Marie Palma
*Anne Michele Parnell
Mary Lynn Piha
Karen M. Pretzer
Phyllis Evelyn Provost
Jan Elizabeth Rackish
Kendall Joan Rafter *Highest Honors*
Bridget Ann Ragan *High Honors*
Donna Marie Rainone
Janette Marie Reedy
Mary Jane Reher

Lori Linn Richardson
Kathleen Ann Riley
Judith Ann Robb
Janet Marie Robert *Honors*
Judith Ann Robert
*Eileen Marie Robinson
Kathleen Agnes Rost
Renee Alyce Rozelle
Catherine Mary Russell
Lee Ann Russo *Honors*
Jennifer Anne Ryder
Harriet Ann Schroeder *Honors*
Iris Veronica Sejdina
Martha Ann Sexton *Honors*
Moira Shanahan
Patricia Ellen Sheehan
Patter Sheeran
Susan Jean Shellenbarger
Carolyn Patrice Short
Karen Marie Sikorski
Joanne Marie Skorich
Margaret Anne Smith *Honors*
Victoria Marie Smith
Marita Elizabeth Spadola
Mary Therese Stavinoha
Rosemary Steidle
Annemarie Sullivan *Honors*
Sharon Marie Sullivan *Honors*
Roxanna Mary Terz
Jean Marie Thornburgh *High Honors*
Rebecca Anne Thornton
Kristin Inger Thorson *Highest Honors*
Laura Jeanne Tolosko *High Honors*
Joan M. Tomassi
Maureen Francis Xavier Walsh *Highest Honors*
Sheila Elizabeth Walsh
*Bonnie Jane Watson *Honors*
Linda Jean Wilbert
*Nan Ellen Willard
Ellen Crowe Wilmes
Patricia Kay Wong *High Honors*
Elizabeth Ann Wood
Allison Anne Yuhl *Honors*
Donna Jo Zurawski
Valerie Mary Zurblis

Bachelor of Fine Arts

Joan Helen Bontempo
Bonita Louise Bradshaw
*Sharon Helena Garvey *Honors*
Louise Frances Karas

Susan Marie Micinski
Anne Sullivan Peeler *High Honors*
Eloise Michelle Tomei

College of Science
Bachelor of Science

Theresa Ann Adams *High Honors*
Cheryl Janet Baggen
Anne Marie Berges
Patrice Ann Biel
Karen Marie Breen
Barbara Lee Breesmen
Debra Anne Brodd
Laura Beth Campbell
Moira Elizabeth Carlson
Caren Eileen Conaway
Linda Marie Curigan
Karen Daneu
Marie Elizabeth Daugherty
Jean Ann Drury
Nancy Kathleen Farraher
Susan Mary Fitzpatrick
Mary Antoinette Fitzsimons *Highest Honors*
Susan Marie Fondi
Elizabeth Winifred Galloway
Lisa Marie Gambino *High Honors*
Ann Elizabeth Gardner *Highest Honors*
Isabella Marie Giannelli *Honors*
Joanne Marie Gormley
Jean Colette Gray
Patricia Anne Hinds
Jane E. Hogan
Susan Ann Hudak
Frances Anne Hudock *High Honors*
Diane Mary Jenis
Maureen Agatha Kelly *Honors*
Maria Antoinette Kimovec *High Honors*
Susan Antonina Kowal
Katherine Susan Krauss
Judith Anne Kseniak *Honors*
Pamela Sue Kuemin *Honors*
Cynthia Ann Labriola
Elizabeth Anne Lavins
Mary Fern Latourneau *High Honors*

Sharon Lorraine Lopez
Mary Alice Mack
Teresa Rose Maher
Donna Patricia Mangione
Mary Beth Mazanec *Highest Honors*
Mary Kay McGuinnis
Patricia Ann McHugh
Katherine Ann McRae
Sandra L. Meier
Dora Marie Menchaca
Carol Ann Miskell *Honors*
Ann T. Moriarty *High Honors*
Ellen Louise Myler
Barbara Ann Nanovic
Laura Jean Nymberg
Joanne Prusiecki
Robin Ann Raher *High Honors*
Susan Marie Reis *Honors*
Margaret Mary Rietman
Janet Elizabeth Scalon
Josephine Geraldine Schimizzi *High Honors*
Brenda Jeanne Sickle *Honors*
Janet Elaine Spillman
Judith Ann Temmerman
Sydney Brooks Thomas
Kristine Sue Thornton
Ann Therese Timm *High Honors*
Mary Anne Tomaselli
Marilyn Ann Tomasko *High Honors*
Marian Nancy Toth
Stephanie A. Urillo
Kathleen Mary VanEffen *Honors*
Cynthia Ann Weidner
Elizabeth Ann Whippo
Mary Katherine Wiegand
Florence Marie Wilczewski
Rosemarie Wrape
Ruth Irene Zurcher *High Honors*

College of Engineering
Bachelor of Architecture

Kathleen Melody Bauman
Melissa Hunt Erkins
Margaret Mary Fahrenbach
Elizabeth Hagan *Honors*

*Arlene Elizabeth Hunter *Honors*
Deborah Kay Mather
*Patricia Joy Weber

Bachelor of Science in Aerospace Engineering

*Margaret M. Curtin

Bachelor of Science in Chemical Engineering

Marguerite Marie Ferrero
Marie Cecilia McCarthy
Mary Elizabeth Spalding

Bachelor of Science in Engineering Science

Theresa Gayle Fritz *Highest Honors*

Bachelor of Science in Mechanical Engineering

Kathryn Louise Walker

Bachelor of Science in Metallurgical Engineering

Mary Katherine Anne Hanson
Mary Louise Heasly *High Honors*

College of Business Administration
Bachelor of Business Administration

Susan Marie Allen *High Honors*
Judith R. Arenson
Maria Terese Arminio
Beverly Elizabeth Baginski
Mary Elizabeth Bloom
Kathleen Ann Boron *High Honors*
Marian Elizabeth Borzelleca
EstelleRita Broussard
Cindy K. Buescher *High Honors*
Genevieve Lucy Burke
Ellen Mary Carnahan *Highest Honors*
Rosemarie Catalino
Mary Ellen Celeste *Highest Honors*
Mary Margaret Charchut

Kathleen Elizabeth Conklin
Mary Patricia Conley
Patricia Ann Coogan
Barbara Jean D'Aquila *High Honors*
Joya Cheryl DeFoor
Katherine Mary DePauw
Kathleen Dickinson
Julia Marie Dunn
Anne Elizabeth Eisele
Ann Fink
Barbara Faye Fisher
Sue Ellen Frisse
Kathleen Marie Grace *Honors*
Susan Jean Grant

Colleen Marie Harrington *High Honors*
Suzanne Mary Haug
Denise Marie Haylon
Donna Marie Hinton *Honors*
Deborah Ann Joggerst
Jill Ann Johnson
Nancy Jo Kirn
Karen Ann Kuenster
Diane Elizabeth Kuknyo *Honors*
Mary Janet Laughlin
Suzanne Marie Lefevre
Constance Ann Madden *Honors*
Catherine Ann Malkus *High Honors*
Carol Eileen Malone
Maureen Anne Maloney
Molly Ruth McGuire
Judith Ann McNitt
Kathleen Marie Mercer
Lynn Marie Mertensotto
Mariann Mihailidis
Joan Marie Miller
Gayla Ann Molinelli *High Honors*
Marianne Therese Morgan *Honors*
Phyllis Renee Mosley
Ann Maureen Murphy *High Honors*
Nancy Marie Murphy

Nona Mari Novak
Roxanne Mary O'Brien
Mary Beverly O'Connell
Candace Anne O'Conner
Susan Maureen O'Hearn
Julianne Faith Olech
Maryjane O'Meara
Jayne Elizabeth O'Reilly
Margaret Jean O'Rourke
Deborah Lynn Paul
Mary Margaret Reiner *Honors*
Kathleen Anne Riordan
Cheryl Lynn Schmidt
Judith Ann Shiely
Jean Therese Smetana *Honors*
Sally Jane Smith
Christine Louise Sordyl
Therese Suzanne Sullivan
Patricia Evalyn Tack
Mary Suzanne Thyen *Honors*
Joanne Marie Toeniskoetter *High Honors*
Mary Anne Tokarz *Highest Honors*
Helen Kit-Lan Tso
Mary Beth Ward
Diane Louise Wolf *Highest Honors*
Mary K. Zima

*January 15, 1977, graduates

University of Notre Dame 1977 Commencement Weekend May 20–22
http://archives.nd.edu/commencement/1977-05-22_Commencement.pdf

Athletic Replays

None of the stories of the early Notre Dame women's sports teams and programs would have been possible without the sweat, toil, and sacrifice of the athletes themselves. However, most of this history would have been lost if not for the arduous undertaking of the Early Women Athletes Project.[1] In 2011 and 2012, Anne Dilenschneider and Jane Lammers collaborated with more than one hundred athletes and coaches from the early era of coeducation at Notre Dame to recreate the schedules and rosters of the first sports teams. More than 230 women played intercollegiate sports for Notre Dame from 1972–1977. One early account, Jane Lammers' "The Early Women's Sports History," was used extensively in this book, while other accounts — such as Jody Gormley's "History of the Early Years of Women's Crew"; Mary Clemency's "Early Basketball History"; Patty Coogan's "Basketball Memories"; Donna Losurdo, Anne Dilenschneider, Becky Banasiak, and colleagues' "A History of Early Field Hockey"; Barb Breesmen's "History of Early Golf"; Judy Shiely and Mary Ryan's "History of Early Volleyball"; and Bonita Bradshaw's "Memories of the Early Days" — captured valuable insights shared in these replays. *The Observer* provided additional detailed replays.

As a web page honoring these pioneering women athletes explains:

> Notre Dame currently fields 26 varsity athletics programs, half of which are for women, beginning in 1976 with tennis and increasing through the years with fencing, field hockey, basketball, volleyball, swimming and diving, cross country, golf, soccer, softball, indoor and outdoor track and field, lacrosse and rowing. Irish women have won 14 national championships in fencing, soccer and basketball, as well as many individual national championships.[2]

BASKETBALL One of the most successful programs in Notre Dame's women's sports history grew from the humblest beginnings. In that first winter of

The First Coaches of University of Notre Dame Women's Teams 1972–1977

- **Basketball** Jeanne Earley, Sally Duffy
- **Crew** Clete Graham, Fred Heydrich, Jody Gormley
- **Fencing** Mike DeCicco (varsity head coach); Tom Coye, Rich Hosinski, Tim Taylor (assistant coaches)
- **Field Hockey** Astrid Hotvedt; Julianne Olech (assistant coach)
- **Golf** Astrid Hotvedt, Patrick Dore; J.J. Broderick (assistant coach)
- **Tennis** Kathleen Cordes (varsity head coach); Carole Moore (coach); John Donahue (technical coach); Tom Haywood, Dave Wheaton, Joel Goebel (assistant coaches)
- **Track and Cross-Country** Astrid Hotvedt; Joe Piane (assistant coach)
- **Sailing** Dr. D. Linge, Buzz Reynolds, Meme Hanson
- **Skiing** Peter Bartzen, Stan Ripcho

coeducation, several women discovered that an effective way to combat the sometimes polar blasts of South Bend air was with an indoor sports activity such as basketball. With only two women's dorms — Badin and Walsh — an interhall rivalry developed, with each dorm forming two basketball teams within a four-team division. Although the ND Athletic Department provided referees and scheduled the games, the women played in relative obscurity in the bowels of the ACC.

Invited to participate in the spring 1973 An Tostal Bookstore Basketball Tournament, the women's teams squared off to select the highest caliber team to face the Irish cagers in the tournament's final game. Dubbed the "Gentle Thursday" sports spectacular, the April 26 event pitted the ND men's varsity basketball team (somewhat neutralized with boxing gloves) against the best women's team available from the ND–SMC residence halls.

For the 1973–1974 season, Breen-Philips and Farley halls joined Badin and Walsh, expanding the women's interhall league to eight teams. From the outset, one Farley team dominated the program. The all-freshman (ND 1977) team — save for sophomore Mary Clemency (ND 1976) — included Susie Augustus, Cindy Buescher, Patty Coogan, Molly R. McGuire, Kathy McRae, Ellen Myler, Jayne O'Reilly, and Judy Shiely; ND students Mike LaVoie (ND 1975) and Steve Carroll (ND 1974) coached. After winning the interhall championship and the game against SMC, this team played the men's varsity squad at An Tostal '74.

Increasing interest in basketball drove Clemency and Sally Smith (ND 1975) to begin discussions with the Athletic Department about starting a women's club

Year	Athlete	Event	Medal
1980	Debbie Brown	Volleyball	
1988, 1992	Molly Sullivan	Fencing	
1996	Sara Walsh	Fencing	
1996	Jileen Siroky	Swimming	
2000, 2008	Kate (Sobrero) Markgraf	Soccer	Silver, Gold
2000, 2004	Christel Bouvron	Swimming	
2004, 2008, 2012, 2016, 2020	Mariel Zagunis	Fencing	Gold (2008)
2004	Jan Viviani	Fencing	
2008, 2012, 2016	Melissa Tancredi	Soccer	
2008, 2012, 2016,2020	Kelly Hurley	Fencing	Bronze (2012)
2008, 2012	Candace Chapman	Soccer	Bronze (2012)
2008, 2012	Shannon Boxx	Soccer	Gold (2012)
2012	Mary Saxer	Pole Vault	
2012	Amanda Polk	Rowing	
2012	Kelly Kiefer	Fencing	
2012, 2016, 2020	Courtney Hurley	Fencing	
2012	Molly Huddle	5,000 meter	
2012, 2020	Natalie Achonwa	Basketball	
2016	Margaret Bamgbose	400 meter	
2016	Molly Huddle	10,000 meter	
2016, 2020	Lee Kiefer	Fencing	Gold (2020)
2020	Molly Seidel	Marathon	Bronze (2020)
2020	Molly Bruggemann	Rowing	
2020	Jewell Loyd	Basketball	Gold (2020)
2020	Skylae Diggins-Smith	Basketball	Gold (2020)
2020	Francesca Russo	Fencing	
2020	Ewa Nelip	Fencing	
2020	Sabrina Massialas	Fencing	
2020	Amita Berthier	Fencing	
2020	Kaylin Hsieh	Fencing	
2020	Angie Akers	Beach Volleyball	Gold (2020)
2020	Jackie Young	Basketball	Gold (2020)
2020	Adriana Leon	Soccer	Gold (2020)

ND Women at the Olympics (1980–2020)

basketball team. Non-Varsity Sports Director Dominick "'Nappy" Napolitano and Assistant Director Richard O'Leary supported the women's request. In the fall of 1974, women's basketball achieved club status. Jeanne Early, a graduate student with a physical education degree from Indiana University, became the coach. This first team wore blue mesh jerseys and shorts with gold lettering, donated by Earley's father, Tony Earley (ND 1947). On January 30, 1975, the team, cocaptained by Clemency and Coogan, awoke to *The Observer* heralding its 1975 season opener "against the Michigan State Spartans in East Lansing."[3] The Spartans, ranked number two, showed little mercy to the Irish women in their intercollegiate debut, handing them an 84–23 defeat. Although a tough year, fifteen ND women had shared the ACC's hardwood floor with the men, and a new tradition had emerged.

The following year, Sally Duffy, the newly hired rector of Lewis Hall who had seven years of high school coaching experience and had been invited to try out for the US Olympic team, joined the coaching staff. Eleven players joined the club team, including junior Bonita Bradshaw. Bradshaw, a multisport athlete benched due to injuries in previous years, excelled in basketball, field hockey, and track. Her athletic prowess led ND's men's basketball coach, Digger Phelps, to call her "the best female athlete at Notre Dame" at the time.[4] The admiration was mutual:

◇ *Bonita Bradshaw, ND 1977:* "As a freshman and sophomore, I worked for Astrid Hotvedt in the athletic office. As a junior and senior, I worked with Digger in the men's basketball office. Watching him interact with his athletes and watching his practices gave me a bird's-eye view of what being a real coach was. He was passionate to a fault and never held anything back."

Posting records of 3–4 and 6–7 in its first two years, the team finished its 1976–1977 season under Duffy with a mark of 8–5. Laurie Reising women's sports editor for *The Observer*, reported on September 29, 1977, that women's basketball had achieved varsity status.[5]

CREW (ROWING) If basketball became the face of the ND women's sports program, crew is considered its heart. It takes dedication to roll out of bed before dawn, take a twenty-minute bus ride to the Saint Joseph River practice site in Mishawaka, unload the boats, row for an hour, run for a while longer, reload the boats, jump back onto the bus, and return to campus, often just in time for an 8:00 a.m. class. To quote a song from the 1955 musical *Damn Yankees*, "You gotta have heart!"[6]

In the fall of 1973, rowing teams in the Midwest were scarce, with even fewer women's teams. Returning Notre Dame Rowing Club (NDRC) officers met and considered a proposal by Clete Graham (ND 1975) to start a women's team. Females were not foreign to the club — they had already stepped onto the gunnels when SMC student Diane Johnson joined as a coxswain. Graham, along with Fred Heydrich (ND 1975), convinced the officers that adding the women would not tax their limited funds and equipment.

The Student Activities Night on September 11, 1973, saw fifty-three ND and SMC women sign up for crew, none with rowing experience. Since no collegiate association governed women's rowing, ND and SMC women competed together. Jody Gormley (ND 1977), a four-year women's crew member and later coach, noted that this was an advantage.

Within a month, Graham scheduled a race against the University of Wisconsin in Madison. The "four" team consisted of 1977 class members Jane Lammers, Bev Baginski (O'Brien), Mary Spalding (Burns), coxswain Linda Sisson (Trifone), and Marilyn Crimmins (SMC). Before racing, Graham reminded the squad that it was the first time for ND women to row intercollegiately. The women finished second, sandwiched between the two Wisconsin entries, the sixth-ranked team in the nation. When the lightweight crew of eight won the championship later in the spring of 1974 with a spectacular first-place finish, the last *Observer* for the 1973–1974 academic year gave the championship crew its due with the sports headline "Women Row to Midwest."[7]

At the end of the 1974 spring season, Graham put together a small group to participate in one last competition. Five women—Boni Burton, Beth Corbin, Jody Gormley, Mari Gumble, and Beth Storey—stayed to race a four at the Wichita River Festival. The team, along with Coach Graham, left campus on May 16 in a Chevy Impala rental car. They stopped at Gumble's home in Springfield, Illinois, to grab a bite to eat, sing, and play the guitar before driving through the night to Wichita.

The next morning, about sixty-five miles northeast of Wichita, the team's automobile collided with a semitrailer, crushing the passenger side. Burton, nineteen, was killed on impact, and Storey, twenty-one, died at the hospital. The other four suffered injuries but survived.[8] When the crew teams returned for the 1974 fall semester, they gathered for Mass and a memorial service. The teams dedicated the season to their fallen teammates and christened two racing shells the *Boni B* and the *Elizabeth Storey*. In the 1975 spring season, the lightweight eights successfully defended their title in the Midwest Rowing Championships. In May, the lightweights won the Mid-Atlantic Regional Championship to finish the season undefeated.

As women's club sports grew and provided other options besides crew, replacing seasoned rowers with novices became standard practice. Mary Fitzsimons and Jody Gormley joined in 1973 as freshmen and never wavered in their commitment to the ND Rowing Club. Fitzsimons would become captain for three years and an outstanding stroke. It was fortunate for crew that, in her freshman year, Fitzsimons—a national caliber AAU swimmer in high school—was the fastest swimmer not to make the Notre Dame swim team, at that time comprised only of men. After graduation, Gormley stayed for the 1977–1978 and 1978–1979 seasons to successfully coach the women's team. Twenty-five years after becoming a club sport, women's rowing was awarded varsity status by the university for the 1998–1999 season, becoming the thirteenth women's varsity sport. Nearly forty years after that time, both Fitzsimons and Gormley, along with former ND coach and rower Jill Delucia, formed NDAMES, a group of former Notre Dame women rowers who compete in senior rowing events throughout the country.

FENCING The early years of the ND women's fencing team were closely tied to Saint Mary's College. In 1971, with the ND–SMC merger (supposedly) just around the corner, Mike DeCicco, ND's fencing coach, welcomed six SMC women to practice with his team. However, when the merger fell through, the SMC women temporarily lost access to both his coaching and the ACC facilities; the women continued to practice at SMC's Angela Hall. With outdated equipment, cast-off uniforms, and occasional help from the ND male fencing team, SMC's six fencers endured a 2–4 season.[9]

The following year, which was coeducation's first, the fencing staff welcomed ND women into the fencing fold, including Cindy Rebholz along with the SMC players. The ND–SMC fencers showcased remarkable individual achievements when Kathy Valdiserri, Christine Marciniak, Cathy Buzard, and others joined the team. Rapid progress occurred during the 1974 and 1975 seasons. On January 29, 1976, Kathy Valdiserri became the first female athlete at ND to be individually featured in an *Observer* sports article, with the headline "Kathy Fences Way to the Top."[10] She and the other players returned for the 1976–1977 academic year to the news that women's fencing, along with women's tennis, had achieved varsity status.[11] Since 1972, more than 230 women have participated in the fencing program, and more than 220 have received monograms.

FIELD HOCKEY Of all the early women's sports teams, the ND field hockey team, formed in the fall of 1974, benefited from some good old "luck of the Irish." The core players included 1976 classmates Donna Losurdo and Becky Banasiak; 1977 class members Anne Dilenschneider, Bonita Bradshaw, Kim Manzi, and Maureen Maloney; and 1978 class member Maria Losurdo. This group caught wind that Hotvedt, already coach of the women's golf team, had played field hockey for Eastern Michigan. They immediately recruited her not only to coach but also to help with obstacles that stood in their way: time and numbers.

The organizers worried about the interest and availability of enough women to field a team, much less to create a deep roster. However, when twenty-two women committed to the sport, Hotvedt arranged five games for the inaugural season. Since the ND women had no field hockey field of their own, they played the games at Eastern Michigan, Purdue, Goshen, Valparaiso, and Central Michigan.

As an interest group, the team received only one hundred fifty dollars in university funding, so players had to cover their own expenses. But Irish eyes smiled once again: Linda O'Leary, a high school field hockey coach and wife of ND lacrosse coach Rich O'Leary, heard of the women's hustle putting together a team and their fall schedule and donated her school's used uniforms and equipment.

Records from that first season have yet to be discovered, but the memory of the team's first game is alive and well. The Irish women took on Eastern Michigan, a powerhouse team from the Mid-American Conference. Clad in secondhand uniforms, using hand-me-down equipment, and having had only a handful of practices, they played to a hard-fought tie. Granted, "Old Notre Dame" does not *tie* overall, but this band of women had vied with one of the best teams in the Midwest. Hotvedt claimed the contest as one of the best field hockey games she had ever seen.

That first season led to club status for the 1975 fall season. Twenty of the original twenty-two players returned and four more joined, growing the roster by two players. Yet not until the fall of 1978 did the women's field hockey team achieve varsity status. Regardless, the sacrifices of those early players laid the groundwork for future players. As a member of the first field hockey team, Anne Dilenschneider recalls how her father, John "Jack" Dilenschneider (ND 1953), enjoyed telling his friends that his daughter played fullback for ND, and she still gets emotional when thinking about how the work of the early women athletes has since paid off.

> The gray, rainy day our ragtag team tied Eastern Michigan on their muddy home field is one I will never forget. Three decades later, when I had the opportunity to host the Notre Dame women's soccer team on behalf of the San Francisco Bay Area Notre Dame Club, I burst into tears when the women and their coaches arrived in a large touring bus. I was seeing, right in front of me, what our small group of women had only dreamed about as we practiced through the dark, frosty nights so many years before.[12]

Team spirit was seriously damaged when an article in the January 29, 1988, issue of *The Observer* announced the dropping of Irish field hockey from varsity.[13] Today, however, field hockey is a competitive club sports team that accepts students of all skill levels from both ND and SMC; it even allows males to join.

GOLF Golf is not usually one of the first things that comes to mind when one thinks of Notre Dame. However, some students preferred golf to release their competitive urges. That was certainly true for Barbara Breesmen and Ellen Hughes when they arrived in the fall of 1973 as members of the class of 1977. The pull of the links was so strong that both tried out for the all-male varsity golf team. For the first time, women played golf on the Burke Memorial Golf Course.

As fate would have it, an errant golf ball found Breesman's head that day, and she could not finish her round. Undaunted, the freshman golfer took matters into her own hands and, in the spring of 1974, made plans with Hughes to organize a women's team. In the April 18, 1974, issue of *The Observer*, they invited interested women to an organizational meeting for the women's golf club.[14]

Breesmen and Hughes, who served as team captains for three years, received one hundred fifty dollars in seed money from the Women's Western Golf Association. They assembled a team that included ND '77 classmates Leslie Barnes, Sue Fitzpatrick, Louise Karas, Molly Martin, Joan Porter, and Kathleen Riordan. On April 10, 1975, the women's golf club hosted the first ND Women's Open event for all women students. Liz Adamson shot a ninety-three to pace all golfers, while Breesmen shot a ninety-four to finish second. Two days later, they hosted the ND Women's Invitational and, on April 18, received their first competition coverage in *The Observer*.[15]

The captains and Coach Hotvedt negotiated university funding, locker rooms at the Rock, and tee times at the formerly men-only golf course. Despite the club's record, the athletic board denied varsity status until the 1988–1989 academic year, more than a dozen years after its 1975 inception. On January 20, 1988, *The Observer* reported that three women's clubs had reached varsity level: softball, soccer, and golf.[16]

SAILING Ironically, one of the first sports to welcome women was one of the least known — sailing. On September 28, 1973, *The Observer* referred to sailing as "Notre Dame's unknown collegiate sport" and featured the boathouse, a historic landmark on Saint Joseph's Lake, as part of a pictorial entitled "The Notre Dame You Never Knew."[17] When women arrived on campus, the sailing team had existed for almost a quarter of a century. Notre Dame's oldest minor sport allowed participation by both ND and SMC women. Its dual options of club and team met the needs of both competitive and novice sailors, with members providing lessons.

While the sailing team toiled in relative obscurity at home, it established a name for itself nationally in the years leading to coeducation. In 1972, the Irish sailors narrowly missed a shot at the nationals in the spring and then competed for the Douglas Cup in the fall. ND's least known sport looked like a champion just before taking on a new group of sailors. In the spring of 1973, Christie Gallagher joined sailing, and Notre Dame competed in the Women's Midwest Championship. *The Observer* rhetorically noted: "They weren't first, but what other sport at Notre Dame lets girls compete inter-collegiately both on the regular team and as a women's team?"[18]

The answer was none. Sailing was ahead of its time, but the sport lent itself to coed competition. As with any athletic endeavor, physical fitness was a plus, but mental acuity and agility were equally important to navigational tactics. The women entering the sailing team's domain did not have the start-up issues facing other women athletes; they only needed to sail. With both ND and SMC women allowed to participate, nearly two dozen women sailed in the first four years.

The women sailors further solidified their presence on the ND sports scene in April 1974 when they hosted the inaugural Women's Regatta on Saint Joseph's Lake. Nine schools participated, with the Irish finishing third behind Purdue in second place and Michigan State in first. That month, *The Observer* recognized the individuals paving the way in this landmark event: Mary Anne Zdinak, Kathy Hughes, Camille Doan, Nancy Cueroni, Carole Froling, Jan Robert, Judy Robert, Sharon Dillion, and Fidele Galey.[19] Today, the ND sailing team is a coed club sport and a competitive member of the Midwest Collegiate Sailing Association.

SKIING Intercollegiate skiing returned to Notre Dame after a six-year hiatus when junior Bob Hellmuth revived a team for the 1973 winter season and allowed women to join. As with sailing, the skiing team's first three women — juniors Kristin Meyer and Coletta Miller of the class of '74, along with freshman Ann Hawkins of the class of '76 — did not face the pains of a new club or team. What they did endure that first season were limited practice facilities and an unusual scarcity of snow.

Yet the Irish, never known to shy away from challenges, competed against some of the best scholarship athletes from collegiate teams such as Wisconsin, Michigan, and Michigan State. The three women also competed in the February 1973 Ohio Governor's Cup. After turning in a strong showing, Hellmuth, the team's coordinator, hoped this initial experience would inspire more Notre Dame women to join the ski program. It did.

At the same Ohio meet in 1974, an expanded ND–SMC women's contingent made headlines and served notice that the women athletes on the ski team, in only their second season, were determined to add to the winning traditions at Notre Dame and ensure opportunities for future women skiers.

> The girls of the Notre Dame ski team, who have put on solid showings all year, struck gold last Saturday in Mansfield, Ohio. Notre Dame sophomore Anne Hawkins [ND 1976] took top honors with a second place finish in the long slalom course at Snow Trails Ski Resort. Right behind was St. Mary's soph, Janel Schliesman [SMC 1976]. These finishes plus the efforts of ND frosh Nora Grace [ND 1977], ND senior Kristan Meyer [ND 1974], and ND senior captain Coletta Miller [ND 1974], gave the female Irish enough points to capture the Ohio Governor's Cup. Second-run heroics by Hawkins enabled the Irish to overcome the strong challenge by Ohio State and Akron University.[20]

> ◇ *Ann Hawkins, ND 1976:* "I was on the National Ski Patrol and enjoyed helping others and noted this spirit at ND. In 1972, as an athlete, I could only pick tennis or skiing. I played some tennis and skied for four years. The ND setting during those first few years prepared me for the culture I would encounter in business.
>
> "The men's ski team was supportive of the women's team, both financially and showing us racing techniques. At one point, Moose Krause called me into his office to discuss making the women's ski team a varsity sport. Given our athletic success (we had won all our meets both junior and senior years), he asked what I thought. I inquired whether the men's ski team would be a varsity sport, to which he responded no, only the women's. I

explained how the men's team supported the women's team, so it didn't seem fair. Alas, neither women's nor men's skiing became varsity sports."

TENNIS When ND's male tennis team played its first match in 1923, Knute Rockne was in his sixth season as head coach of the Irish football team. Yet for Betsy Fallon (ND 1976), a skilled and competitive player since primary school who had participated in Junior Wightman Cup tennis, no women's team was available in the fall of 1972. As a member of ND's first freshman class of women, she was surprised that no structured women's sports program existed that first year. Yet Fallon was eager to play competitive tennis and tried out for the men's team. As one of two female athletes among more than one hundred male hopefuls, she was not intimidated by the competition. She had played on the boys' team in high school, as no girls' team existed there either. Despite her best efforts, she did not make the cut.

Desiring to keep playing, Fallon recruited interested women from Badin and Walsh halls. She attempted to meet with the athletic director about starting a tennis team but was redirected to Student Affairs, which suggested a social group for women players. The group became the Notre Dame Women's Tennis Group, where members played among themselves and challenged Saint Mary's College to a match. *The Observer* recognized the historic significance of the stage set by these pioneers:

> On Friday, November 17, 1972, Saint Mary's College tennis team and the women of the University of Notre Dame participated in a tennis match, the first of its kind for the two schools.[21]

Saint Mary's ended up winning 5–3, but this match served as a springboard for both programs against the backdrop of coeducation at Notre Dame.

In the fall of 1973, Fallon, then a sophomore, Carol Simmons, and two other women tried out for the male tennis team. The outcome was the same, but this time *The Observer* captured the results.[22] Fallon's second tryout was merely a minor detour on her quest for competitive tennis play. Another Junior Wightman Cup player, Jane Lammers, arrived at Notre Dame that fall, bringing her tennis aspirations to play in more than a social group. When she learned that there was no team for women, she immediately made an appointment to see Moose Krause — her father's former basketball coach at Notre Dame — to rectify the situation. Sympathetic with her desire to establish a formal tennis team for women, he referred her to Rich O'Leary and Tom Kelly in the Non-Varsity Sports Office, where the men explained the necessary steps for a women's team to become varsity, which involved registering as an interest group and then progressing to club status and finally varsity. This was the first time this critical information

was shared with any women students. O'Leary and Kelly also told her of a powerhouse player named Betsy, and soon the two women's shared enthusiasm for
tennis established an instant bond and a three-year association to expedite the
sport's promotion. Joined by Carol Simmons, Ellen Callahan, Sharon Sullivan,
Carolyn Schiffels, and Carol Guckert as well as sophomore Andrea "Andi" Smith
as manager, they quickly registered women's tennis as an interest group and advertised tryouts for October 23.

The tennis interest group distributed flyers to all the dorms announcing practices and weekly meetings. With the help of Smith, Fallon and Lammers served as
team captains for the interest group and occupied the first and second positions;
freshmen Callahan, Guckert, Simmons, Sullivan, Ann Colbert, Ann Gardner,
Linda Wilbert, and Janet Krier fleshed out the roster. The women worked together to raise funds, identify recruits, and secure competitions with schools in
the Midwest. From her dorm room, Lammers called coaches in Indiana, Ohio,
Michigan, and Illinois and invited teams to travel to Notre Dame for competitions. She said her mother wasn't too happy about her long-distance phone bill
that fall. Soon Smith retyped the schedule, and Fallon and Lammers met with
the men's coach to reserve courts for these matches. The team was relegated to
courts seven through twelve, which were open to all students and could not be
reserved, so the women recruited friends to save the courts to ensure their availability. Coach Janet Parks of Bowling Green State University still remembers with
a chuckle her amazement when she learned that it was the women students of
Notre Dame inviting teams to travel to competitions.[23]

After several competitions, the women petitioned for club status. Acknowledging
that teams normally waited at least a year for such a change, the captains argued
that the group established by Fallon in 1972 should count for at least one semester of play since it had engaged in intercollegiate competition against SMC in
the spring of 1973. The arguments worked, and by the spring of 1974, the team
achieved club status. During the 1973–1974 academic year, several ND men — John
Donahue (ND 1977), Tom Haywood (ND 1977), Dave Wheaton (ND 1976), and Joel
Goebel (ND 1976) — offered to coach and provide playing experience. In late fall,
Carole Moore, a former track star from the University of California Santa Barbara,
volunteered to serve as faculty adviser and coach for the club. She was eager to
establish women's athletics at Notre Dame, and for two and a half years, she took
over the team's scheduling, financing, paperwork and team building. She was as
passionate an advocate as any athlete and shared in their triumphs and heart-
aches. Coach John "J.D." Donahue served as the technical coach for three years;
he, too, was equally passionate and talented.

In the fall of 1974, thirty-three hopefuls vied for the club's thirteen spots. The
new roster consisted of Fallon and Lammers, along with sophomores Gardner,
Guckert, Simmons, Debbie Grady, and Pam Leary and freshmen Colbert, Schiffels,

Infrastructure changes were slow in coming, but progress with women's athletics was inevitable. Since the 1970s, the athletic venues and sports for both men and women have significantly expanded.

Italics = facilities available in the first decade of coeducation

- Alumni Stadium (2009): men's and women's soccer
- Arlotta Family Lacrosse Stadium (2009): men's and women's lacrosse
- Castellan Family Fencing Center (2012): men's and women's fencing
- Compton Family Ice Arena (2011): men's ice hockey
- *Courtney Tennis Center* (1967): men's and women's tennis
- Eck Tennis Pavilion (1987): men's and women's tennis
- *Edmund P. Joyce Center* (1968): men's and women's basketball, women's volleyball
- Frank Eck Stadium (1994): baseball
- *Knute Rockne Memorial Gymnasium* (1937)
- Loftus Sports Center (1988): men's and women's indoor track-and-field, lacrosse
- McConnell Family Boathouse (2015): women's rowing
- Melissa Cook Stadium (2008): softball
- *Notre Dame Golf Course*: men's and women's cross country
- *Notre Dame Stadium* (1930, renovations completed 1997, 2017): football
- Notre Dame Track and Field Stadium: men's and women's outdoor track-and-field
- Rolfs Aquatic Center (1985): men's and women's swimming and diving
- Warren Golf Course (1999): men's and women's golf

Mary Kay Baty, Sue Grace, Marianne Murphy, and Carmel Burke. Smith, then a junior, continued on as the team's student manager, while sophomores Donahue and Haywood served as assistant coaches.

The tennis program grew rapidly under Fallon, Lammers, and Moore. Unfortunately, before graduating in May 1976, Fallon never fulfilled her dream to play tennis as a varsity athlete, but she had prepared the team and propelled it forward in a significant way with her strong leadership. The Notre Dame Athletic Department granted the women varsity status in 1976–1977 under Kathy Cordes, newly hired as the first woman to coach a varsity sport at Notre Dame. With undergraduate women's enrollment approaching sixteen hundred, the talent and interest existed to field a first-class team. The women finished their first varsity season with a 7–3–1 record, as Lammers, a senior and the team's captain, and Mary Shukis, a sophomore, received two of the first five ND monograms awarded to women.

VOLLEYBALL The creation of a women's volleyball team was late to the coeducation party, yet its journey to varsity was more rapid than most. By the time

Mary Ryan arrived in the fall of 1976, Judy Shiely was in her senior year. Shiely, a member of her high school state championship volleyball team, had also helped to create the ND women's basketball team. Ryan and Shiely approached Hotvedt, the coordinator of women's club sports, for approval to start a women's volleyball team.

Hotvedt agreed to the request but left all arrangements — tryouts, selection, court reservations, practices, and transportation — to the team, and the women received no financial or staff support. Appropriately, the team elected Ryan and Shiely as cocaptains, and the women arranged matches — some official, some not — by calling other regional colleges. Their navy-blue PE shorts and T-shirts doubled as their volleyball uniforms.

On April 17, 1980, just before Ryan's graduation, the university announced the elevation of lacrosse and women's volleyball to varsity. According to Colonel John Stephens, associate athletic director, "This is part of Title IX and our efforts to give women more opportunities."[24]

Honorary Monogram Recipients

Only through the determination of numerous women was this part of Notre Dame's history — the efforts of its first female athletes — not lost. On June 23, 2022, Notre Dame announced that more than 230 pioneers of women's athletic teams will receive an honorary monogram for their efforts during the first five years of coeducation.

◇◇◇

The Pioneers of Notre Dame's Women's Athletic Teams
1972–1977

BB Basketball	S Sailing	## Academic Year
C Crew	SK Skiing	C (after the year) Captain
F Fencing	T Tennis	WAA Leadership Role
FH Field Hockey	TR Track	* Already a Monogram Recipient
G Golf	V Volleyball	† First Five Recipients 1976–1977

Adams Anne Marie BB75
Amato Kam T75
Anderson Kathryn BB74 BB75
Arenson Judy C74
Arminio Maria F73
Armstrong Lorainne SK75
Augustus Susie BB73
Baggen Cheryl FH74 FH75
Baginski Bev C73
Bailey Kathleen C73
Bailey Sue T75
Banasiak Becky BB7475C FH7475 G75 WAA
Barnes Leslie G73 G75 G76 PE Instr 73/74

Bartzen Sarah SK72 SK73 SK74 SK75
*Bathon Liz F76
Baty Mary K T74
*Behnke Sue F76
Benedett Jean S75
Berges Anne BB74, BB75, BB76
Bernard Betsy WAA Staff
Berry Liz BB75
Bitchakas Argery C74
Bledsoe Kim G75
Bond Ann BB75
Boylan Barb TR76

Bradshaw Bonita BB7576 FH747576 TR7475 WAA, WAA Staff

Brady Mary C74 C75 C76

Breesmen Barb G73C G74C G75C G76C WAA

Brenner Nancy G75

Buckley Kathy BB7475 Scorekeeper

Buescher Cindy BB73 C73

Burke Mary C. T74 SK75 SK76

Burke Pat C73

Burns Erin BB76 TR76

Burton Boni C73

*†Buzard Cathy F74 F75 F76

Calabrese Maria FH76

Callahan Ellen T73 T75 T76 WAA

*Carini Donna FH76

Champion Mary FH75

Clemency Mary BB73C74C75C WAA

Colbert Ann T74 T73

Conley Mary S75

Conlisk Beth BB76

Coogan Patty BB73C-76C WAA, WAA Staff

Corbin Elizabeth C73 C74

Cordes Kathleen Varsity Tennis Coach

Cueroni Nancy C73 S73 S74 S75C

*Cummings Carola BB76 FH76

Curtin Peggy TR76

Cushing MaryJo T75 T76

Dean Debbie C74 C75 C76

*DeCoste Patty FH75 FH76

Delucia Jill C75 C76 Coach80-84

Dilenschneider Anne FH74, FH75 Instr

Dilworth Kathy C75 C76

Doan Camille S75

Dodge Laura BB75 FH74 FH75

*Dooley Mary Anne FH74 FH75 FH76

Downs Kathy C76

Duffy Sally Basketball Coach

Early Jeanne Basketball Coach

Eresman Robin FH74 FH75

Essling Jeanne C74

Fallon Betsy T72 T73C T74C T75C WAA

Farhart Kathy C74

*Fischer Sally F73 F74

Fitzpatrick Sue G73 G74 G75 G76

Fitzsimons Mary C73 C74 C75C C76C WAA

Flaherty Laura C76

Flanigan Sue T75 T76

Flynn Maureen C74

*Foley Terri F76

Fondi Sue BB75 BB76

Fremeau Joan FH74 FH75

Frey Barb BB74 BB75 WAA Staff

Froling Carole S74 S75

Gallagher Christie S72

Gallogly Kathy D 72-74

Galloway Libby C74

Gardner Anne T73 T74 T76

Garland Jane C74

Gormley Jody C737475SEC76 WAA Coach

Grace Nora SK747576 TR7475

Grace Sue T74

Grady Debbie T74 T75

Guckert Carol T73 T74 T75

Gumble Mary C73 C74 C75

Hanson Mary Kay S74

Hanson Meme S75C

Hawkins Anne Marie SK727374C75C

Hayes Mary C76

Hester Peggy TR75 TR76

Hines Mary Beth C74

Hotvedt Astrid FH/G/TR Coach

Hughes Ellen FH7475 G73C-76C SEC WAA

*Hums Mary BB76 Mgr FH7576 TR7576 Staff

Jaeger Mary C74

James Mary FH74 FH75 FH76

Jones Kathleen C73

Juba Kathy T76

Kane Kathy FH74 FH75 FH76

Karas Louise G73 G74 G75 G76

Kelly Ann T75

Kilpatrick Roberta T76Mgr

Koch Mary F73

Krier Janet T73

Kseniak Judy C74 C75

Kunkel Sue BB76

Labriola Cindy FH76

*Lacity Karen F75 F76

*Lally Carol BB75 BB76C

*†Lammers Jane C73 T73C-T76C, Pres WAA

Lammers Mary D72-73

Latronica Carol C74 C75 C76

Leary Pam T74
Leonard MaryBeth T76
Lopez Geri C73
Losurdo Donna C73 FH74 FH75C WAA
Losurdo Maria FH74 FH75
Maloney Maureen BB747576C FH7475C76 VP
Malvezzi Adella TR76
Manzi Kim FH74C FH76 WAA
*†Marciniak Christina F75 F76
Marshall Melanie C73
Marten Mary C75 C76 FH75
Martin Molly G73 G74 G75 G76
Martin Rita FH75MGR
Mazanec Mary Beth BB74
McCann Kathy TR76
McCarthy Marie G75
*McGlinn Sue FH76
McGuire Molly (Ohio '78) BB75
McGuire Molly (Iowa '77) BB73 C73
McQuillan Jean C75
McRae Kathy BB73 BB74 BB75 BB76
*Meagher Marge BB76
Mertensotto Lynn V77 BB76 Scorekeeper
Meyer Kristin SK72 SK73
*Meyer Pat BB76
Miller Coletta SK72 SK73
Miller Nikki TR74C WAA
Molony Terry C74 FH74 FH75 TR74
Mooney JoAnn BB74
Moore Carole Tennis Coach
Morgan Meg FH74 FH75 FH76
*Mullen Paddy T76
Mulvihill Mary Lou BB74
Murphy Byrne BB74 BB75
Murphy Marianne T74
Myler Ellen BB73 BB74
Nahlan Dana S76
North Mairin C73
O'Brien WAA Staff
O'Connell Kathy C75
O'Grady Eileen WAA Staff
O'Haren Michele TR76
O'Donnell Trish F74 F75
Offerle Judith F73

Olech Julianne Rockne Staff 73/74 WAA
    Staff, FH Coach
Orbeson Sharon C74
O'Reilly Jayne BB73 BB75 BB76
Ortega Charmaine C75 C76
Ott Ginny (Virginia) C76
Pallone Brenda F75
*Politiski Jane BB76
Porter Joan G73 G74
Prestine Laure C75
Provost Phyllis V77 PE Instr 73
Prusiecki Joanne F75
Rebholz Cindy F73 F74C WAA
Reis Susan C74 C75 C76
Reising Laura T74
Rickhoff Nancy BB74 FH74
Rietman Maggy C73
Riordan Kathleen G73 G74 G75 G76
Robert Janet S74 S75
Robert Judy S74 S75
Robillard Gina TR76
Rohrbach Laura C76
Roman Melissa T75MG
Rortvedt Diane C73 C74 C75
Ryan Mary V77C WAA
Scanlon Janet S73 S74 S75
Schuler Margaret S74
Setlock Mary C74
Shanahan Kathy C76
Shiely Judy BB737475 BB76 V77C WAA
Schiffels Carolyn T74 C75
*Shillingburg Diane T75 T76
Short Elizabeth C73
*†Shukis Mary T75 T76
Siefring Ginger T76
Simmons Carol T73 T74 T75
Singer Mary T76
Sisson Linda C73 F73 T76 G75
Smith Andrea T73MG T74MG T75Mgr
Smith Sally BB7X
Spalding Mary C73 BoardG75 WAA Staff
    Mgr 74-76
Stoltz Nancy C73
Storey Elizabeth C73
Stupke Monica T76
Sullivan Eunice BB75 (red shirt)

Sullivan Kathy C76
Sullivan Sharon SK75 T73 T75 T76 WAA
Thornton Amy S74
Thornton Becky TR74
Tirinnanzi Rosemary C73
Towne Beth C76
*†Valdiserri Kathy F73 F74 F75C F76C WAA
Vogel Monica C74
Walsh Mary FH74 FH75 FH76
Warren Vicki C74
Weber Helen TR76
Weidner Cindy S75
Wetherbee Jule C73
White Mary FH74 FH75
Wilbert Linda T73
Wood Lauren C76 FH74 FH75 FH76
Zurcher Ruth C73 C74

Saint Mary's College Honorary Monogram Recipients

Ahoy S. S74
Banbury Kathy SK76
Bonifert J F73
Bottino Lenore C75
Boyle Martha S76
Caine Shotsie C73
Caroll Maura SK76
Christie Gallagher S72
Comerford Cathy C73 C74
Crehan Peg C75
Crimmins Marilyn C73 C74C WAA
D'Aquila Margaret SK76
Deighen Anne C75 C76
Dorzweiler Betsy SK76
Dressler D F75
Duffy Nora SK74 SK75 SK76
Dziwura Chris F75
Farhart Kathy C74
Farro Pat F73 F74 F76

Farro Pat S74
Flood Liz S75
Galey Fidele S74
Gallagher Erin C76
Johnson Diane C72
Keefe Veronica C75 C76
Kellow Jennifer C73
Kelso Regina C73 C74
Kerger Lory S76
Kiley Jay S76
Krakora Sue F73 F74
Longfellow Janet C73 C74 C75
Mannion Mary C73
Mattimore Anne C73
McAllister Laurie SK75
McGinley Pam C76
McKeon Karen C75
Noonan Margaret SK76
Norcross Barb C74
Parnell Sandy SK75
Prestine Laure C75
Richtsmeier Joan F73 F75 F76 F72?
Riley Barb C74 C75
Rockey Ann C75 C76
Rose Gill (ND/JD) C75
Rupprucht Judy S75
Schahade Gail SK75
Schliesman Janel SK72 SK73 SK74 SK75
Schoendienst C F73
Simony Chris F75 F76
Smiggen Sue S76
St. Hilaire Camille C74
Stasse Brooks C75
Temple Judy C76
Tressler Nina C75
Valentino Debbie F75 F76
Walsh Ellen C74 C75
Winkelman Lisa C75
Zablotny Cathy C76

Information provided by Jane Lammers, July 21, 2022

A Brief History of Sexual Assault
(Cases, Legislation, Media Coverage)

1957

One of the first published studies about campus sexual assault, "Male Sex Aggression on a University Campus," appears in the *American Sociological Review* (22, no. 1, 52–58)

1972

Title IX, a federal civil rights law in the United States, passes as part of the Education Amendments of 1972

1976

"Date rape," a term coined by Susan Brownmiller, describes a dating situation in which "an aggressor may press his advantage to the point where pleasantness quickly turns to unpleasantness and more than the woman bargained for" (*Women's Studies Encyclopedia*, 1989, vol. 1, 337, Greenwood Publishing Group)

1985

Ms. magazine and Mary R. Koss, then a psychology professor at Kent State University, surveys more than 6,100 undergraduates and reveals that one in four female college students had an experience of rape or attempted rape; *I Never Called It Rape* (1994) by Robin Warshaw is based on the study

1990

The Jeanne Clery Disclosure of Campus Security Policy and Campus Crime Statistics Act requires all colleges and universities participating in federal student financial aid programs to disclose and report crimes committed on campuses as well as policies and procedures in place for investigation and prosecution of sex offenses

2011

CBS' *60 Minutes* features Beckett Brennan, a woman attending the University of the Pacific on a full basketball scholarship, who was raped in May 2008 by three male basketball players

Yale University suspends Delta Kappa Epsilon fraternity after its pledges march through campus chanting, "No means yes, yes means anal," with a sign "We love Yale sluts"

2014

Twenty-three Columbia University students file complaints with the federal government charging systemic mishandling of sexual assault claims and mistreatment of victims by the university

The White House Task Force to Protect Students from Sexual Assault releases its first report, *Not Alone*, which defines the problem of campus sexual assault and offers its first action steps and recommendations

2015

Two Vanderbilt University football players are convicted of raping an unconscious woman in June 2013; after a 2015 mistrial, Corey Batey, is found guilty in April 2016 and three former Vanderbilt players are also charged with rape

The Hunting Ground documentary about rape on American campuses is released

Erica Kinsman, a former Florida State student, files a lawsuit alleging she was raped in 2012 by FSU quarterback and 2013–2014 Heisman Trophy winner Jameis Winston; Tallahassee Police Department never question Winston; in January 2015, Kinsman sues FSU, which clears Winston

2016

Baylor University fires its football coach, Art Briles, and removes Kenneth W. Starr as president after finding the university mishandled accusations of sexual assault against its players

Former Stanford University student and swimmer Brock Allen Turner is convicted of sexually assaulting an unconscious woman in 2015 and sentenced to six months in county jail, three years of probation, and registration as a sex offender; the sentence is decried by many, including the victim, as too lenient

ND Programs to Prevent Sexual Assault

Notre Dame proactively improved its programs in this important area, especially after the release of the 2015 film *The Hunting Ground.*[1] This documentary referenced Lizzy Seeberg, a Saint Mary's student who took her own life after filing a sexual assault report against a ND football player.[2]

- The Committee on Sexual Assault Prevention (CSAP), appointed annually by the vice president for Student Affairs, offers "guidance... on how to support victims of sexual assault." This committee, comprised of faculty, staff, and students, "facilitate[s] collaboration among departments and student groups."[3]

- Faculty and administration training, campus lectures, and publications.

- Annual performances of *Loyal Daughters and Sons* broaches the subjects of sexual assault, harassment, and intimidation on campus. A vignette-based meditation that focuses on relationships, values, sex, and the soul, each year new teams of students produce this educational tool with current stories.

- Green Dot (greeNDot) "is a violence prevention strategy" that prioritizes individual safety as a "community responsibility." As part of ND's Title IX effort, it aims to attract a proactive volunteer force "to communicate that violence will not be tolerated" within the community and that everyone has a role to play.[4]

- Gender Relations Center (GRC) "offers student programs that foster dialogue on issues of sexuality, gender, inclusivity, respect, and healthy relationships" as well as and violence prevention.[5]

• Men Against Sexual Violence (MAV) purports that "men must be role models in society," hold each other "accountable for their behavior," and communicate this message to other men.[6]

• Climate surveys in the fall of 2016 assessed "the knowledge, perceptions, and experience of Notre Dame students in relation to sexual assault, other sexual misconduct, dating or domestic violence, stalking, and other conduct that creates a sexually hostile environment."[7] Of the 12,227 students invited to participate in the survey, 5,493 (45 percent) completed it. Response rates were higher for females, first-year students, sophomores, and those students living on campus. Responding students indicated that common issues on campus included sexist remarks about women (67 percent), about men (45 percent), and about one's body or appearance (58 percent). Nonconsensual sexual intercourse (defined as penetration of any type) was reported by 5 percent of female students and 1 percent of male students, with other kinds of nonconsensual sexual contact experienced by 21 percent of women and 4 percent of men. Stalking behaviors affected 3 percent of women and 1 percent of men. Overall, findings indicted that 14 percent of students had experienced nonconsensual sexual contact and 1 percent had experienced dating or domestic violence.[8]

The Open Road
The Evolution of LGBTQ+ Rights on Campus

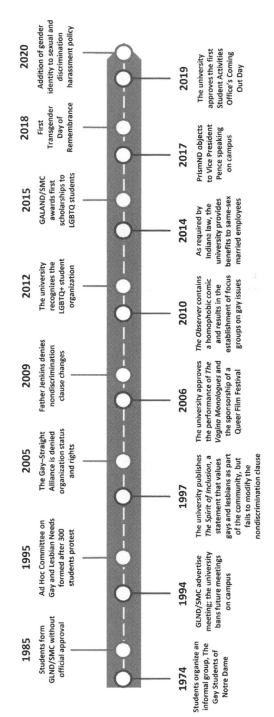

1974 — Students organize an informal group, The Gay Students of Notre Dame

1985 — Students form GLND/SMC without official approval

1994 — GLND/SMC advertise meeting; the university bans future meetings on campus

1995 — Ad Hoc Committee on Gay and Lesbian Needs formed after 300 students protest

1997 — The university publishes *The Spirit of Inclusion*, a statement that values gays and lesbians as part of the community, but fails to modify the nondiscrimination clause

2005 — The Gay–Straight Alliance is denied organization status and rights

2006 — The university approves the performance of *The Vagina Monologues* and the sponsorship of a Queer Film Festival

2009 — Father Jenkins denies nondiscrimination clause changes

2010 — *The Observer* contains a homophobic comic and results in the establishment of focus groups on gay issues

2012 — The university recognizes the LGBTQ+ student organization

2014 — As required by Indiana law, the university provides benefits to same-sex married employees

2015 — GALAND/SMC awards first scholarships to LGBTQ students

2017 — PrismND objects to Vice President Pence speaking on campus

2018 — First Transgender Day of Remembrance

2019 — The university approves the first Student Activities Office's Coming Out Day

2020 — Addition of gender identity to sexual and discrimination harassment policy

The Survey

A. PERSONAL INFORMATION

(If you wish to remain anonymous, please omit name and contact information)

1) Name   First _____ Maiden _____ Last _____
   - Home Address
   - City, State, Zip
   - Home Phone
   - Personal Email

2) Ethnic Background: _ Caucasian _ Native American _ African American _ Hispanic _ Asian _ Other _____

3) Are you a member of any organized religion? _ No _ Yes
   If yes, please indicate what religion: _____
   - If Catholic, are you a Eucharistic minister? _ No _ Yes
   - Is this the same religion as when you attended Notre Dame? _ No _ Yes
   - Do you practice: _ Faithfully _ Occasionally _ In times of crisis

4) Relationship Status: _ Always Single _ Married (length of time) _____
   _ Committed Relationship _ Married and Divorced
   _ Married, Divorced, Remarried _ Widowed
   - Is your spouse/significant other a Notre Dame graduate? _ No _ Yes
     Class year: _____

5) Do you have children? _ No _ Yes (how many) _____
   - Attending Notre Dame: __ Males __ Females Class year(s): _____
   - Notre Dame Graduates: __ Males __ Females Class year(s): _____

6) Degree(s)   #   Date(s)   Institution(s)   Area(s) of Specialty
- Bachelor's   _____
- Master's   _____
- PhD/Doctoral   _____
- Other   _____
- Professional Licenses   _____

7) Employer   _____
- Job Title   _____
- Sector   _ Education _ Government _ Medicine _ Law _ Corporate
  _ Other _____
- Salary Range _ < 50K _ 50–99K _ 100–150K _ >150K

B. THE ROADMAP: Your Youth, Family, and First Encounter with ND

1) What type of high school did you attend?
- Coeducational _ Catholic _ Public _ Private _ Other _____
- Single Sex   _ Catholic _ Public _ Private _ Other _____

2) Who most affected your decisions/actions before your ND experiences?
_ Mother   _ Father   _ Sibling   _ Grandmother   _ Grandfather
_ Other Relative(s) _____   _ Teacher   _ Priest   _ Nun
_ Friend   _ Boyfriend   _ Girlfriend   _ Other(s) _____

3) What is your first memory of Notre Dame? Your first encounter?
- Is it related to a family member who attended? If so, who and when?
- Is it related to your grade school or high school experiences? If so, how?
- Is it related to your religious education/background? If so, how?

4) What factors led to your decision to apply to ND? (check all that apply)
_ ND Family History   _ ND Traditions   _ Choice of Major/Career
_ Scholarship   _ Geographical Location   _ High School Guidance
_ Participate in the First Class of Women   _ Sports Affiliations
_ Religious Affiliations   _ Other _____

- Did you apply to both Notre Dame and Saint Mary's? _ No _ Yes
- If you made a conscious decision not to apply to Saint Mary's, why?
- Were you accepted at: _ Notre Dame _ Saint Mary's _ Both
- If accepted to both, why did you choose Notre Dame?
- To what other universities/colleges were you accepted?

5) Were you the first woman in your family to attend and/or graduate from college? _ No _ Yes What was her relationship to you? _____

6) Please describe any event in your pre-Notre Dame days that provided a life lesson or direction that contributed to:

- Your decision to attend Notre Dame.
- Your life decisions during the past twenty-five years.

7) What personal value/trait (e.g., loyalty, honesty, humor, strength, friendship, love, intelligence, etc.) was most important to you:

- During your ND experience?
- After your ND experience?

8) Is there a quote, prayer, book, etc., that prepared you for or helped you through Notre Dame?

C. THE JOURNEY: Your ND Experience(s) and Reflections

1) How would you describe yourself when you entered Notre Dame in 1972? (check all that apply)

_ Feminist _ Traditionalist _ Religious _ Athletic _ Career-Minded
_ Intelligent _ Shy _ Introvert _ Aloof _ Extrovert _ Friendly
_ Self-Confident _ Virginal _ Sexually Experienced _ Attractive

If you described yourself as a feminist, traditionalist, academic, career-minded, athletic, or religious, what did that mean to you in 1972? Does this still apply?

2) What advice did you receive upon entering Notre Dame or about life in general you still remember/cherish today?

- From whom did you receive this advice?
- Does it still apply today?

3) Was Notre Dame prepared for females? _ No _ Yes (if no, please explain)

4) What dorm(s) did you live in at ND? _ Walsh _ Badin _ Breen-Phillips
_ Farley _ Lyons _ Other _____

- Did you live in single / double / triple room(s)? _____
- What technology was part of your dorm life? _ B&W TV _ Color TV
_ Clock Radio _ Alarm Clock _ Radio _ Phonograph _ Stereo/Tape Deck
_ Popcorn Popper _ Refrigerator _ Typewriter _ Other _____
- Did changing dorms/moving off campus have any effect — on friendships, future life choices, personal habits (e.g., rising early for biology class, exercising), etc.?
- Have you remained friends/in contact with any of your roommates?
- What is it about the relationship that has survived the years?

5) What stands out in your memory about courses, professors, or the academic learning experiences at ND?

6) What stands out in your memory on your nonacademic life (e.g., social, emotional, religious, etc.) at ND?
- Did sports play a role in your experience (individual, hall, and varsity)?
- List clubs and organizations significant during your ND experience.

7) Did the ND code of ethics affect your decisions? After-class activities?

8) While at Notre Dame, did you experience any of the trends of the 1970s? (check all that apply)
_ Abortion _ Addiction _ Alcohol _ Anorexia _ Bulimia
_ Date Rape _ Drugs _ Peaceful Protests _ Riots _ Smoking
_ Same-Sex Partners _ Sexual Freedom _ Sexually Transmitted Disease
_ Other(s) _____

9) During your ND experience, did you ever use or have a need for:
- On-site psychological services? _ No _ Yes
- Private psychological services? _ No _ Yes
- If yes, can you share the impact on later life decisions?

10) Please describe a ND experience that stands out in your mind. What values or characteristics in life does it demonstrate and/or supports?

D. CROSSROADS: Post-ND Life Choices

1) Describe your life partnership (if any) re: job sharing, parenting, etc.

2) Is spirituality/religion a part of your life today? How does this affect your life choices? Your discussions with your children? Your approach at work?

3) What sports, hobbies, volunteer activities, personal interests, etc., give (or have given) meaning to your life?

4) Describe your working environment and its impact on your personal life.
- Did you feel like a token/trendsetter in your early career? _ No _ Yes
- Have you mentored younger women in recent years? _ No _ Yes

5) How often have you moved in the past twenty-five years?
  _ Domestic US _____ _ International _____
- For what reasons (family, education, personal career advancement, spousal career advancement, other)?

6) Has a significant event (e.g., parental loss, loss of a child, betrayal, unemployment/downsizing, illness, etc.) affected your:

- Decisions? Approach to life? Relationships?
- Did your ND experience help you through this?   _ No _ Yes (How?)
- Did your religious beliefs help you through this? _ No _ Yes (How?)

7) What ND experience affected the decisions/life choices described above?

8) Was there someone at ND:

- Who acted as a role model for your life choices? _ No _ Yes
- If yes, do you stay in contact with that person?   _ No _ Yes
- If so, through what means and how frequently?

9) Is there a quote, prayer, book, etc., that helps you through your daily life?

E. TELEPHONE INTERVIEW

1) Of all of your decisions/actions in the past twenty-five years, which makes you the proudest? The least proud?

2) Are you currently spending your time in a way that supports your personal values?

3) Do you believe there is a mystique at ND? If so, please describe it and its effect on you.

4) What advice would you like to give to others (current, past, future alumnae) based on your ND experience?

5) What was not asked but you would like to share?

Please indicate yes to at least one of the following:

- _ I agree to the use of this information in the book with my name.
- _ I agree to the use of this information but prefer to remain anonymous.
- _ I would like to be interviewed in person for this book.
- _ I would like to speak with you before I decide.
  - Preferred Method of Contact _____
  - Contact Information   _____
  - Day(s)/Time(s)   _____

Notes

Preface

1. Robert Burtt and Bill Main, *Time Passages 1972: Commemorative Yearbook* (Niagara-on-the-Lake, Ontario: Stewart House, 1999), 1.

2. Meat Loaf, "Objects in the Rear View Mirror May Appear Closer Than They Are," by Jim Steinman, recorded August 1991–June 1993, track 6 on *Bat out of Hell II: Back into Hell*, MCA and Virgin Records, vinyl LP, lines 16 and 18.

3. James S. O'Rourke, IV, ed., *Reflections in the Dome: Sixty Years of Life at Notre Dame* (Notre Dame, IN: Breffny Books, 1988), 8.

Choosing the Destination

1. Robert F. Griffin, *The Pocket-Size God: Essays from* Notre Dame Magazine, ed. J. Robert Baker and Dennis Wm. Moran (Notre Dame, IN: University of Notre Dame Press, 2016), ¶10 in "Part of the Myth."

In the Rearview

1. Ralph McInerny, *A Loss of Patients: A Father Dowling Mystery* (New York: Vanguard Press, 1982), 200.

2. See also The University of Notre Dame Archives, "Vetville," *Notre Dame Archives News and Notes*, 2022, https://archives.nd.edu/about/news/index.php/2011/vetville/.

3. Theodore M. Hesburgh with Jerry Reedy, *God, Country, Notre Dame: The Autobiography of Theodore M. Hesburgh* (New York: Doubleday, 1990), 49.

4. Dennis Brown, "In Memoriam: Notre Dame Law School Dean Emeritus Rev. David T. Link," *Notre Dame News*, October 29, 2021, https://news.nd.edu/news/in-memoriam-notre-dame-law-school-dean-emeritus-rev-david-t-link/.

5. Though the language used in this column is antiquated to modern ears, the content highlights that of a priest whose views of women changed. Cited in Dan Reagan, "Vetville: A City within a Campus," *The Observer*, February 12, 1975, 5, https://archives.nd.edu/Observer/1975-02-12_v09_079.pdf, 5. See also Brendan O'Shaughnessy, "A Temporary Tribe: Vetville Memories Reveal How Communities Thrive," University of Notre Dame, 2017, https://www.nd.edu/stories/a-temporary-tribe/.

6. Cited in Tom Shaffer, "The Dean," *Notre Dame Magazine*, Spring 1992, editorial page.

7. Cited in John Kryk, *Natural Enemies: Major College Football's Oldest, Fiercest Rivalry—Michigan vs. Notre Dame*, updated ed. (Lanham, MD: Taylor Trade Publishing, 2007), 247.

Studying the Map

1. Lao-tzu, *Tao Te Ching*, trans. Stephen Addiss and Stanley Lombardo (Indianapolis: Hackett Publishing Company, 1993), 64.

2. Edward Frederic Sorin to Basil Moreau, December 5, 1842. Cited in Arthur J. Hope, *Notre Dame—100 Years* (Notre Dame, IN: University of Notre Dame Press, 1999), chapter 3, http://archives.nd.edu/hope/hope03.htm, ¶13. This letter written by Sorin is frequently published.

3. Arthur J. Hope, *Notre Dame: One Hundred Years* (Notre Dame, IN: University of Notre Dame Press, 1948), 35.

4. Cited in O'Rourke, *Reflections in the Dome*, 8.

5. Hope, *Notre Dame—100 Years*, chapter 6, http://archives.nd.edu/hope/hope06.htm.

6. Hope, *Notre Dame—100 Years*, chapter 8, https://archives.nd.edu/hope/hope08.htm.

7. Cited in Hope, *Notre Dame—100 Years*, http://archives.nd.edu/hope/hope17.htm, ¶19.

8. Cited in Hope, *Notre Dame: One Hundred Years*, 145.

9. Cited in University of Notre Dame Alumni Association, "Father Edward Sorin, C.S.C.: Founder of Notre Dame," Faith ND, 2022, http://faith.nd.edu/s/1210/faith/interior.aspx-?sid=1210&gid=609&pgid=15963, ¶13 under "Narrated Text."

10. Cited in Hope, *Notre Dame—100 Years*, chapter 15, http://archives.nd.edu/hope/hope15.htm, ¶68.

11. Margaret Fosmoe, "Yesterday and Today Exhibit: A Portal to Student Life at ND," *South Bend Tribune*, October 14, 2001, E2.

12. University of Notre Dame, "Stamp Dedication," University of Notre Dame, 2022, https://hesburgh.nd.edu/remembering-fr-ted/stamp-unveiling/.

13. O'Rourke, *Reflections in the Dome*.

14. Bob Dylan, "The Times They Are a-Changin'," by Bob Dylan, recorded October 24, 1963, track 1 on *The Times They Are a-Changin'*, Columbia, studio album, line 10.

Paving the Way

1. Gloria Steinem, *My Life on the Road* (New York: Random House, 2016), xxii.

2. From Justice Hugo Black's dissent in *United States v. Yazell*, 382 U.S. 341, 361 (1966), criticizing this "now largely abandoned...old common law fiction." Cited in Patricia J. Gorence, "Women's Name Rights," *Marquette Law Review* 59, no. 4 (1976): 876–899, 883.

3. Oberlin College and Conservatory, "Oberlin History," Oberlin College and Conservatory, 2022, https://www.oberlin.edu/about-oberlin/oberlin-history, under "A Town of Firsts."

4. Shira Birnbaum, "Making Southern Belles in Progressive Era Florida: Gender in the Formal and Hidden Curriculum of the Florida Female College," in "Gender, Nations, and Nationalisms," ed. Jane Slaughter and Shane Phelan, special issue, *Frontiers: A Journal of Women Studies* 16, no. 2/3 (1996): 218–246. See also Alice Wallace, "Wilson, Supporter of Education, Dies at 89," *The Gainesville Sun*, July 21, 2006, https://www.gainesville.com/story/news/2006/07/21/wilson-supporter-of-education-dies-at-89/31490481007/, ¶5.

5. Woodrow Wilson, "Equal Suffrage: Address of the President of the United States" (speech, United States Senate, September 30, 1918), https://www.senate.gov/artandhistory/history/resources/pdf/WilsonSpeech1918.pdf, 3.

6. Janet Lever and Pepper Schwartz, *Women at Yale: Liberating a College Campus* (Indianapolis: The Bobbs-Merrill Company, 1971), 274.

7. Rachel Siegel, "Yale's Classrooms Were Full of Men. Then the First Female Undergraduates Enrolled," *The Washington Post*, November 14, 2018, https://www.washingtonpost.com/history/2018/11/14/yales-classrooms-were-full-men-then-first-female-undergrads-enrolled/.

8. 50 Women at Yale 150, "A Timeline of Women at Yale," Yale University, 2022, https://celebratewomen.yale.edu/history/timeline-women-yale and https://celebratewomen.yale.edu/sites/default/files/files/Timeline-of-Women-at-Yale.pdf.

9. Steven R. Antonoff, *College Finder: Choose the School That's Right for You*, 4th ed. (Westford, MA: Wintergreen Orchard House, 2017).

10. Title IX of the Education Amendments of 1972, Pub. L. No. 92-318, 86 Stat. 373 (1972), https://www.govinfo.gov/content/pkg/STATUTE-86/pdf/STATUTE-86-Pg235.pdf. See also Title IX of the Education Amendments of 1972, 20 U.S.C. § 1681(a) (1972), cited in Legal Information Institute, "20 U.S. Code § 1681 — Sex," Cornell Law School, n.d., https://www.law.cornell.edu/uscode/text/20/1681.

11. Ira Berkow, "Sports of *The Times*: Touchdown for Father Ted," *The New York Times*, May 14, 1987, Late Edition (East Coast), D.28.

12. Theodore Hesburgh, *God, Country, Notre Dame*, 70.

13. Andrew M. Greeley, *The Changing Catholic College* (Chicago: Aldine Transaction, 2013), 91.

Merging Lanes

1. Johann Wolfgang Von Goethe, *Conversations of Goethe in the Last Years of His Life, Translated from the German of Eckermann*, trans. S. M. Fuller (Boston: Hilliard, Gray, and Company, 1839), 43. Originally published as Johann Peter Eckermann, *Gespräche mit Goethe in den letzten Jahren seines Lebens* (Leipzig: F. A. Brockhaus, 1838).

2. Kristen Durbin, "Graduate Students Paved Way for Women on Campus," *The Observer*, February 25, 2013, 1, 6, https://archives.nd.edu/Observer/v46/2013-02-25_v46-097.pdf, 6.

3. Don Ruana, "Co-Exchange Program Increases Participation," *The Observer*, September 25, 1970, 1, https://archives.nd.edu/observer/v05/1970-09-25_v05_013.pdf.

4. Jennifer Barton, "First Women's College in Region Observes 175th Anniversary," *Today's Catholic*, December 10, 2019, https://todayscatholic.org/first-womens-college-in-region-observes-175th-anniversary/.

5. Michael O'Brien, *Hesburgh: A Biography* (Washington, DC: The Catholic University of America Press, 1998), 139

6. Richard Conklin, "Coeducation at Notre Dame — How Are the Girls Getting Along?" *South Bend Tribune*, January 21, 1973, 4.

7. *The Observer*, "Poll Shows Co-Education Favored," *The Observer*, January 15, 1969, 1, https://archives.nd.edu/Observer/v04/1970-01-15_v04_065.pdf.

8. Office of the President, "How Notre Dame Admitted Undergraduate Women 50 Years Ago," University of Notre Dame, March 1, 2022, https://50goldenyears.nd.edu/news-and-features/almost-mary-ed-near-merger-ended-with-notre-dame-welcoming-women-50-years-ago/, ¶3. See also Tom Blantz, "Going Co-Ed," *Notre Dame Magazine*, January 22, 2013, https://magazine.nd.edu/stories/going-co-ed/, and Thomas E. Blantz, *The University of Notre Dame: A History* (Notre Dame, IN: University of Notre Dame Press, 2022).

9. Cited in Fred Schaeffer, "Call Co-Education Inevitable," *The Observer*, September 23, 1970, 1, http://52.0.44.235/Observer/v05/1970-09-23_v05_011.pdf, 1.

10. Glen Sorge, "Students Voice Opinions on Co-Education," *The Observer*, December 8, 1970, 2, http://archives.nd.edu/Observer/v05/1970-12-08_v05_057.pdf.

11. Jerry Lutkus, "The Era of Coeducation: The First Women at Notre Dame: A Look at Coeducation," *The Observer*, September 8, 1972, 5, 8–9, 11, http://archives.nd.edu/observer/1972-09-08_v07_003.pdf.

12. Joe DeLong, "Congratulations Mary, Mary Ann and ND!" *The Observer*, November 5, 1971, 9, https://archives.nd.edu/Observer/v06/1971-11-05_v06_041.pdf.

13. Theodore M. Hesburgh, interview with author, October 5, 2000.

14. Cited in Jillian Barwick and Kaitlyn Rabach, "Alums Recall Effects of Proposed Merger in '71," *The Observer*, February 25, 2013, 1, 7, https://archives.nd.edu/Observer/v46/2013-02-25_v46-097.pdf, 7.

15. Elisabeth Peralta, "Across the Highway," *Notre Dame Magazine*, Summer 1992, 4.

16. Hesburgh, interview.

17. Hesburgh, interview.

18. Thomas E. Blantz, interview with author, October 5, 2000.

19. Conklin, "Coeducation at Notre Dame," 6.

20. Cited in Anthony Abowd, "A First Look at the New Rectors," *The Observer*, September 8, 1972, 6–7, http://archives.nd.edu/observer/1972-09-08_v07_003.pdf, 6.

21. Sister John Miriam Jones, interview with author, May 18, 2001.

22. Cited in Betty Washington, "The Notre Dames," *Chicago Sun-Times*, June 7, 1983, 43.

23. University of Notre Dame advertisement reproduced in Valerie Zurblis, "How Women Have Become a Part of the ND Community," *The Observer*, March 10, 1976, 6–7, https://archives.nd.edu/Observer/v10/1976-03-10_v10_103.pdf, 7.

Seventies Model

1. This quote attributed to Avijeet Das is frequently used in relation to leadership and has been posted to crowdsourced sites such as Goodreads (https://www.goodreads.com/quotes/10094479-she-is-a-warrior-capable-of-slaying-the-demons-in) and What Should I Read Next? (https://www.whatshouldireadnext.com/quotes/authors/avijeet-das?page=2).

2. Claudia Goldin and Lawrence F. Katz, "Putting the 'Co' in Education: Timing, Reasons, and Consequences of College Coeducation from 1835 to the Present," *Journal of Human Capital* 5, no. 4 (Winter 2011): 377–417.

3. Nielsen Media Research cited in Jack Simmons and Leigh E. Rich, "Feminism Ain't Funny: Woman as 'Fun-Killer,' Mother as Monster in the American Sitcom." *Advances in Journalism and Communication* 1, no. 1 (2013): 1–12, https://www.scirp.org/journal/paperinformation.aspx?paperid=29539. See also Alex McNeil, *Total Television: The Comprehensive Guide to Programming from 1948 to the Present*, 4th ed. (New York: Penguin Books, 1996).

4. Cathy Donahue, interview with author, August 12, 2001.

5. Marisa Iati, "Men Recall 'Gradual' Shift," *The Observer*, February 28, 2013, 1, 6, https://archives.nd.edu/Observer/2013-02-28_v46-100.pdf, 6.

6. Conklin, "Coeducation at Notre Dame," 5.

7. Richard W. Conklin, "Alice in Irishland: Some Looking Glass Views of Coeducation," *Notre Dame Magazine*, August 1972, 28–31.

8. Kathy Cekanski, "In the Halls," *The Observer*, April 5, 1974, 6, https://archives.nd.edu/Observer/v08/1974-04-05_v08_106.pdf.

9. Emil T. Hofman, interview with author, October 5, 2000.

10. Jack Kelly, "Admissions Office: 1100 Coed Applications," *The Observer*, January 26, 1972, 1, http://archives.nd.edu/observer/v06/1972-01-26_v06_064.pdf.

11. Hofman, interview.

12. Conklin, "Alice in Irishland."

13. Conklin, "Alice in Irishland," 31.

14. Conklin, "Alice in Irishland," 29.

15. Cited in Jim Ferry, "Conklin Becomes Instant Co-Education Expert," *The Observer*, October 2, 1972, 2, https://archives.nd.edu/Observer/v07/1972-10-02_v07_017.pdf, 2.

16. Matt Storin, "Love/Hate Thee, Notre Dame," *Notre Dame Magazine*, Spring 2013, 14.

17. Hofman, interview.

18. Conklin, "Coeducation at Notre Dame."

19. Conklin, "Alice in Irishland," 30.

Caution: Road Work Ahead

1. John Heywood, *The Proverbs of John Heywood*, ed. Julian Sharman, (London: George Bell and Sons, 1874), 17. Originally published as *A dialogue conteinyng the number in effect of all the prouerbes in the englishe tongue compacte in a matter concernyng two maner of mariages, made and set foorth by Iohn Heywood* (London: Thomas Berthelet, 1546).

2. Theodore M. Hesburgh and the Thanking Father Ted Foundation, *Thanking Father Ted: Thirty-Five Years of Notre Dame Coeducation*, ed. Ann Therese Darin Palmer (Kansas City, MO: Andrews McMeel Publishing, 2007), 174.

3. The Badin Hall Council, "Badin Hall Reacts," *The Observer*, February 9, 1972, 1, http://archives.nd.edu/Observer/1972-02-09_v06_074.pdf, 1.

4. Cited in Maria Gallagher, "It's Badin and Walsh!," *The Observer*, February 9, 1972, 1–2, http://archives.nd.edu/Observer/1972-02-09_v06_074.pdf, 2. It is unclear where this entire phrase is a direct quote from Father Biallis or partially paraphrased by Gallagher. The original article contains an error where an opening quotation mark is missing.

5. Cited in Gallagher, "It's Badin and Walsh!," 1.

6. Cited in Iati, "Men Recall 'Gradual' Shift," 6.

7. Cited in Washington, "The Notre Dames," 45.

8. Mike O'Hare, "Freshmen Cramped," *The Observer*, September 2, 1972, 3, http://archives.nd.edu/observer/v07/1972-09-02_v07_001.pdf, 3.

9. Jean Lenz, *Loyal Sons and Daughters: A Notre Dame Memoir* (Lanham, MD: Roman and Littlefield Publishers, Inc., 2002), 71.

10. Jerry Lutkus, "Changes in New Women's Dorms," *The Observer*, September 2, 1972, 10, http://archives.nd.edu/observer/v07/1972-09-02_v07_001.pdf, 10.

Packing Our Gear

1. Meat Loaf, "Objects in the Rear View Mirror," lines 5–6.

2. Cited in Susan Ratcliffe, ed., *Oxford Essential Quotations*, 4th ed. (Oxford: Oxford University Press, 2016), https://www.oxfordreference.com/view/10.1093/acref/9780191826719.001.0001/q-oro-ed4-00003260, ¶6.

Reading the Signs

1. Hesburgh, interview.

Dangerous Curves Ahead

1. Margaret Mead, *Continuities in Cultural Evolution* (New Haven, CT, and London: Yale University Press, 1964), 258 and 234, respectively.

2. Used with permission from Betsy Kall Brosnan; see also Mary Pat Dowling, *Grotto Stories from the Heart of Notre Dame* (South Bend, IN: Mary Sunshine Press, 1996).

3. Lee E. Klosinski, "Loyal Sons (and Daughters) March Onward to Victory," *The Observer*, September 29, 1972, 3, https://archives.nd.edu/Observer/1972-09-29_v07_016.pdf.

4. Paul Harvey Jr., ed., *Paul Harvey's For What It's Worth* (New York: Bantam, 1991).

5. Nancy Armour, "Notre Dame Celebrates 25 Years of Coeducation," *Los Angeles Times*, August 31, 1997, https://www.latimes.com/archives/la-xpm-1997-aug-31-mn-27519-story.html.

6. Robert Ackerman, "Coed Process at ND," *The Observer*, September 8, 1972, 10, http://archives.nd.edu/observer/1972-09-08_v07_003.pdf, 10.

7. Iati, "Men Recall 'Gradual' Shift," 1 and 6.

8. Cited in Jim Commyn, "Looking Back: The First Year at Notre Dame," *The Observer*, March 10, 1976, 5, http://archives.nd.edu/observer/1976-03-10_v10_103.pdf, 5.

9. Commyn, "Looking Back," 5.

10. Becky Banasiak Code, interview with author, August 25, 2001.

11. Ackerman "Coed Process at ND," 10.

12. Charles L. Ponce de Leon, *That's the Way It Is: A History of Television News in America* (Chicago and London: The University of Chicago Press, 2015).

13. Ike Pappas, interviews with Notre Dame students, CBS News, September 7, 1972, as provided by Vanderbilt TV News Archive to Brian O'Herlihy (2012), 83.

14. Pappas, interviews with Notre Dame students.

Travel Guides

1. Paulo Coelho, *The Witch of Portobello*, trans. Margaret Jull Costa (New York: Harper Collins, 2007), 9.

2. Cited in Notre Dame Student Government, *Freshman Directory*, September 1971.

3. Don Ruane, "Observer Picks the Top Ten Stories," *The Observer*, May 4, 1972, 3, 16, http://archives.nd.edu/Observer/1972-05-04_v06_123.pdf.

4. Cited in Notre Dame Student Government, *Freshman Directory*, 1973–1974.

5. A welcome letter cited in Notre Dame Student Government, *Freshman Directory*, 1975–1976.

6. Matt Storin, "The Need for a Campus Conscience," *Notre Dame Magazine,* Winter 2016, 10.

7. Ronald R. Parent cited in Barbara Breitenstein, "*Notre Dame Magazine*," *The Observer*, April 23, 1976, 7, 10, http://archives.nd.edu/Observer/1976-04-23_v10_122.pdf, 7.

8. Breitenstein, "*Notre Dame Magazine*," 7.

9. Kerry Temple, "Speaking of Notre Dame," *Notre Dame Magazine*, Spring 1997, 44.

10. Kerry Temple, "One Friday in January," *Notre Dame Magazine*, Spring 2006, 43. See also https://magazine.nd.edu/stories/one-night-in-january/, ¶7 under "Notre Dame's Richness."

11. From the March 1944 edition of *Scholastic*, cited in Irish Legends, "Semper Victurus," *Irish Reveries*, n.d., http://www.irishlegends.com/pages/semper/semper62.html, ¶1.

12. Cited in Pat Hanifin, "Scholastic," *The Observer*, April 23, 1976, 9, http://archives.nd.edu/Observer/1976-04-23_v10_122.pdf, 9.

Filling Stations

1. Pearl Bailey, *Hurry Up, America, and Spit* (New York: Harcourt Brace Jovanovich, 1976), 52.

2. Richard Rodgers and Oscar Hammerstein II, "There Is Nothing Like a Dame," *South Pacific*, lines 61–63.

3. "University Food Service Program" cited in Mary Catherine Stevens, ed., *Notre Dame Report: '73–'74*, vol. 3, no. 5 (Notre Dame, IN: University of Notre Dame, Department of Information Services, November 16, 1973), 86, http://archives.nd.edu/ndr/NDR-03/NDR-1973-11-16.pdf.

4. Ginna Barreca, *Babes in Boyland: A Personal History of Co-Education in the Ivy League* (Lebanon, NH: University Press of New England, 2004), 4–5.

5. Tom Brogan and Drew Danik, "Dining Hall Joke…," *The Observer*, March 7, 1975, 6, https://archives.nd.edu/Observer/1975-03-07_v09_096.pdf.

6. Brian O'Herlihy, "Letters," *Notre Dame Magazine*, Winter 2011–2012, 5.

7. See the American Psychiatric Association Work Group on Eating Disorders, *Practice Guideline for the Treatment of Patients with Eating Disorders*, 3rd ed. (Washington, DC: American Psychiatric Association, 2006 and 2010), https://psychiatryonline.org/pb/assets/raw/sitewide/practice_guidelines/guidelines/eatingdisorders.pdf, and Daphne van Hoeken and Hans W. Hoek, "Review of the Burden of Eating Disorders: Mortality, Disability, Costs, Quality of Life, and Family Burden," *Current Opinion in Psychiatry* 33, no. 6 (2020): 521–527.

8. Emilio Gutiérrez and Olaia Carrera, "Severe and Enduring Anorexia Nervosa: Enduring Wrong Assumptions?," *Frontiers in Psychiatry* 11 (2020, updated February 2021), doi:10.3389/fpsyt.2020.538997. See also Lauren Muhlheim, "Perfectionism in People With Eating Disorders," *Very Well Mind*, March 24, 2022, https://www.verywellmind.com/perfectionism-in-anorexia-nervosa-1138391.

9. Molly Sinclair, "Coeds Cheer Notre Dame Life," *Miami Herald*, January 2, 1973, C-1. For more about this game, see Bob Kearney, "Johnny's TDs a Parting Gift to Teammates," *Miami Herald*, January 2, 1973, 3-D.

Watch Out for Falling Jocks

1. Cited in Stephen Davis, "Eye on Education: Exercise Improves Learning," *Daily Republic*, January 30, 2020, reprinted by Interactive Health Technologies, https://ihtusa.com/eye-on-education-exercise-improves-learning/, ¶1.

2. *USA Today* Sports, "The Best Arnold Palmer Quotes," *USA Today*, September 25, 2016, https://www.usatoday.com/story/sports/golf/2016/09/25/best-arnold-palmer-quotes/91101166/, ¶3.

3. Cited in Margaret Fosmoe, "Notre Dame Dropping Phys Ed Requirement for Freshmen," *South Bend Tribune*, May 27, 2014, https://www.southbendtribune.com/story/news/local/2014/05/27/otre-dame-dropping-phys-ed-requirement-for-freshme/46404481/, ¶32–¶34.

4. Fosmoe, "Notre Dame Dropping Phys Ed," ¶22–¶24 and ¶3.

5. *The Observer*, "Badin Hall Sets Weekend Activities," *The Observer*, September 22, 1972, 12, http://www.archives.nd.edu/Observer/1972-09-22_v07_011.pdf.

6. *The Observer*, "Interhall Swim Meet Slated," *The Observer*, October 3, 1972, 8, http://www.archives.nd.edu/Observer/1972-10-03_v07_018.pdf, 8.

7. Tim Neuville, "Action Heavy in Interhall Sports," *The Observer*, October 25, 1972, 8, http://www.archives.nd.edu/Observer/1972-10-25_v07_034.pdf, 8.

8. Title IX of the Education Amendments of 1972; see also Legal Information Institute, "20 U.S. Code § 1681 — Sex."

9. Christina Johnson, "The Evolution of Title IX: Prospects for Equality in Intercollegiate Athletics," *Golden Gate University Law Review* 11, no. 3 (1981): 759–800.

License to Drive

1. Oprah Winfrey, "*The Oprah Winfrey Show* Finale," Oprah, https://www.oprah.com/oprahshow/the-oprah-winfrey-show-finale_1/2, ¶4.

2. See Nina Kuscsik, "The History of Women's Participation in the Marathon," *Annals of the New York Academy of Sciences* 301, no. 1 (October 1977): 862–876, https://doi.org/10.1111/j.1749-6632.1977.tb38253.x; Jimmy Golen, "Boston Marathon Marks 50th Anniversary of Allowing Women to Enter Prestigious Race," Associated Press reprinted in WBUR, April 18, 2022, https://www.wbur.org/news/2022/04/18/boston-marathon-women-runners-anniversary; and Gordon Bakoulis, "NYRR's History of Women in Leadership," New York Road Runners, March 15, 2022, https://www.nyrr.org/run/photos-and-stories/2022/womens-history-month-leaders?sf254790691=1&fbclid=IwAR1QDBIPxCSJvBQcceUtXOd6kmi-8XrDvqPOtBfUSeY3zzVw5lIeerJ6R0w.

3. Valerie Zurblis, "Women Sports Prosper: Future Optimistic," *The Observer*, October 1, 1975, 1, 5, https://archives.nd.edu/Observer/v10/1975-10-01_v10_021.pdf.

4. Bengal Bouts, "History," University of Notre Dame, 2011, https://bengalbouts.nd.edu/about/, and Baraka Bouts, "Notre Dame Women's Boxing Club," University of Notre Dame, 2019, https://www3.nd.edu/~wboxing/.

5. Cited in Zurblis, "Women Sports Prosper," 5.

6. "Fall Semester Enrollment" cited in Stevens, *Notre Dame Report: '73–'74*, vol. 3, no. 5, 86.

7. Helen Reddy, "I Am Woman," by Ray Burton and Helen Reddy, recorded 1971 and April 23, 1972, released as a single May 22, 1972, track 2 on *I Am Woman*, Capitol, studio album, line 2.

8. Cited in Ellen Syburg, "Interhall Athletic Competition Is on the Upswing," *The Observer*, October 11, 1974, 8, http://archives.nd.edu/Observer/v09/1974-10-11_v09_032.pdf, 8.

9. Maureen Flynn, "Women's Club Sports Are Growing," *The Observer*, October 11, 1974, 8, http://archives.nd.edu/Observer/v09/1974-10-11_v09_032.pdf, 8.

10. Anne Gardiner Perkins, *Yale Needs Women: How the First Group of Girls Rewrote the Rules of an Ivy League Giant* (Naperville, IL: SourceBooks, 2019), and Office of the President, "Fifty Years of Excellence and Determination in Women's Athletics," Yale University, April 24, 2018, https://president.yale.edu/president/notes-woodbridge-hall/fifty-years-excellence-and-determination-womens-athletics.

11. Mary Fran Hayes, "Women Athletes Attaining Club Status in Three Sports," *The Observer*, September 11, 1974, 8, http://archives.nd.edu/observer/v09/1974-09-11_v09_010.pdf.

12. Pete LaFleur, "Notre Dame Women's Athletics Turned 40 in 2012," University of Notre Dame, September 6, 2012, https://und.com/notre-dame-womens-athletics-turned-40-in-2012/.

13. Chris Evert Lloyd, *Chrissie: My Own Story* (New York: Simon and Schuster, 1982).

14. Val Zurblis, "WAA Varsity Proposals Denied," *The Observer*, April 22, 1975 8, http://archives.nd.edu/observer/1975-04-22_v09_119.pdf.

15. Monogram Club, "Monogram Club Legacy," University of Notre Dame, 2022, https://und.com/monogram-club-legacy/.

16. Cited in Zurblis, "WAA Varsity Proposals Denied," 8.

17. Cited in Zurblis, "WAA Varsity Proposals Denied," 8.

18. Cited in Zurblis, "WAA Varsity Proposals Denied," 8.

19. Cited in Zurblis, "WAA Varsity Proposals Denied," 8.

20. Gary Warth, "PE Trailblazer Cordes Recognized with Hall of Fame Induction," *Chicago Tribune*, March 27, 2017, https://www.chicagotribune.com/sd-me-miramar-cordes-20170327-story.html.

21. LaFleur, "Notre Dame Women's Athletics."

22. From a letter Newton wrote to Robert Hooke in 1675–1676, cited in Robert K. Merton, *On the Shoulders of Giants: A Shandean Postscript* (Chicago and London: The University of Chicago Press, 1993), 31.

23. Benjamin Hochman, "The Competitor," *Notre Dame Magazine*, Winter 2018–2019, https://magazine.nd.edu/stories/the-competitor/.

24. Cited in Gerald Lutkus, "First of Women Graduate at ND," *South Bend Tribune*, May 16, 1976, 53.

25. Cited in Gregg Bangs, "Women Change the Image of the ND 'Jock,'" *The Observer*, March 10, 1976, 8, http://archives.nd.edu/observer/1976-03-10_v10_103.pdf, 8.

Shattered Glass

1. Cited in Ratcliffe, *Oxford Essential Quotations*, https://www.oxfordreference.com/view/10.1093/acref/9780191826719.001.0001/q-oro-ed4-00006224, ¶1 and ¶4. From Keller's *Let Us Have Faith* (1940) and *Optimism: An Essay* (1903).

2. Larry Weaver, "Don't Ask Me: Changes and Coeducation," *The Observer*, April 10, 1973, 4, https://archives.nd.edu/Observer/1973-04-10_v07_111.pdf, ¶4.

3. Cited in Ann Therese Darin, "Hesburgh Vows Co-Ed Increase," *The Observer*, October 26, 1972, 1–2, https://archives.nd.edu/Observer/1972-10-26_v07_035.pdf, 1.

4. Karen Sikorski, "Carole Moore Lectures on Feminism," *The Observer*, February 26, 1976, 4, http://archives.nd.edu/observer/v10/1976-02-26_v10_094.pdf.

5. Barreca, *Babes in Boyland*, 48, *italics original*.

6. Cited in Mary Kate Malone, "Coeducation Pioneers Reminisce," *The Observer*, March 17, 2005, 1, 6, https://archives.nd.edu/Observer/v39/2005-03-17_v39_107.pdf, 6.

7. "Report of the Committee to Evaluate Coeducation" cited in Valerie Zurblis, ed., *Notre Dame Report: '76–'77*, vol. 6, no. 16 (Notre Dame, IN: University of Notre Dame, Department of Information Services, May 6, 1977), 367–395, https://archives.nd.edu/ndr/NDR-06/NDR-1977-05-06.pdf, 370.

8. Ronald Weber, "So Right," *The Observer*, April 8, 1974, 7, http://archives.nd.edu/observer/1974-04-08_v08_107.pdf.

Moving Violations

1. Dick Francis, *A Jockey's Life: The Biography of Lester Piggot* (New York: G.P. Putnam's Sons, 1986), 2.

2. Director of Security Arthur Pears cited in Jeanne Murphy, "Women Officers Complement Security Force: Hired in 1973," *The Observer*, February 19, 1975, 5, http://archives.nd.edu/observer/1975-02-19_v09_084.pdf, 5.

3. Cited in Mary Janca, "Kovatch, Pears Direct Security Departments: At Notre Dame," *The Observer*, February 19, 1975, 5, http://archives.nd.edu/observer/1975-02-19_v09_084.pdf, 5.

4. Dewitt Latimer, "Text Messaging as Emergency Communication Superstar? Nt So gr8," *EDUCAUSE Review*, 43, no. 3 (May/June 2008): 84–85.

5. *The Observer*, "Notre Dame Limits Irish1Card Dorm Access," *The Observer*, August 27, 2019, 4, https://issuu.com/the-observer/docs/the_observer_8-27-2019; Andrew Hudson, "Notre Dame Alters Irish1Card Dorm Access Policy," *CampusIDNews*, August 30, 2019, https://www.campusidnews.com/notre-dame-alters-irish1card-dorm-access-policy/.

6. Barb Boylan, "Women's Dorms to Be Unlocked," *The Observer*, October 4, 1974, 8, https://archives.nd.edu/Observer/1974-10-04_v09_027.pdf.

7. Jim Eder, "Students Evaluate Security: Most Are Satisfied," *The Observer*, February 19, 1975, 7, http://archives.nd.edu/observer/1975-02-19_v09_084.pdf, 7.

8. Jim Eder, "Pears Explains Tight Security Measures to HPS," *The Observer*, February 7, 1973, 1, http://archives.nd.edu/observer/1973-02-07_v07_075.pdf.

9. Robert Ackerman, "Women at Yale: A Review," *The Observer*, April 10, 1972, 5, https://archives.nd.edu/Observer/1972-04-10_v06_106.pdf.

10. Russell Williams, "Pledging, Rushing, Parties Dominate Campus Living," *The Observer*, November 13, 1995, 3, http://archives.nd.edu/observer/v27/1995-11-13_v27_055.pdf.

11. Cited in Eder, "Pears Explains Tight Security Measures to HPS," 1.

12. Cited in Mary Egan, "Campus Roundup: Security Escort Now Available for Women," *The Observer*, February 6, 1973, 6, http://archives.nd.edu/observer/1973-02-08_v07_076.pdf.

13. Eder, "Students Evaluate Security."

14. Patty Cooney, "Kovatch, Pears Direct Security Departments: At St. Mary's," *The Observer*, February 19, 1975, 5, http://archives.nd.edu/observer/1975-02-19_v09_084.pdf.

15. Bill McGinn, "Burtchael [sic] Praises Barkett Letter," *The Observer*, March 6, 1972, 1, http://archives.nd.edu/observer/v06/1972-03-06_v06_093.pdf.

16. Margaret Fosmoe, "Former Notre Dame Provost Burtchaell Dies," *South Bend Tribune*, April 13, 2015, https://www.southbendtribune.com/story/news/local/2015/04/13/former-notre-dame-provost-burtchaell-dies/45861441/.

17. Cited in *The Observer*, "The Letter: Make Some Sense, Father Hesburgh," *The Observer*, October 14, 1971, 4, http://archives.nd.edu/observer/v06/1971-10-14_v06_025.pdf.

18. See, for example, Frank Lipo, "Students Need to Respond to Parietals Violation Punishments," *The Observer*, November 1–2, 1985, Weekend edition, 2, https://archives.nd.edu/Observer/1985-11-01_v20_044.pdf.

Deer in the Headlights

1. Cited in Bonnie Azab Powell, "Being Larry Ellison," *Business Life*, July/August 2001, reproduced at https://web.archive.org/web/20040203051718/http://www.bonniepowell.com/ellison.html, ¶2 under "All You Can Do Is All You Can Do."

2. Originally, the band's name was one word and was later changed to two.

3. Tim Truesdell, "Campus Hangup: Obscene Calls," *The Observer*, April 13 1973, 3, https://archives.nd.edu/Observer/1973-04-13_v07_114.pdf.

4. Cited in Patti Shea, "Lathers, Waltman and McDonnell Win SLC Primary," *The Observer*, October 25, 1972, 1, https://archives.nd.edu/Observer/1972-10-25_v07_034.pdf, 1.

5. Cited in Shea, "Lathers, Waltman and McDonnell Win SLC Primary," 1.

6. Cited in Patti Shea, "Maureen Lathers Elected to SLC," *The Observer*, October 27, 1972, 2, http://archives.nd.edu/observer/1972-10-27_v07_036.pdf, 2.

Sharing the Road

1. Shannon Roddel, "Alumni Interpret Notre Dame Mystique in New Book," review of *We Are ND: The Story of Notre Dame as Told by Her Alumni*, ed. Angela Sienko and Walt Collins, *Notre Dame News*, September 28, 2008, https://news.nd.edu/news/alumni-interpret-notre-dame-mystique-in-new-book/, ¶2.

No Vacancy

1. Adam Kirk Smith, *The Bravest You: Five Steps to Fight Your Biggest Fears, Find Your Passion, and Unlock Your Extraordinary Life* (New York: TarcherPerigee, 2017), 12–13.

2. Jim Eder, "Stay-Hall Procedure Debated by the SLC: Room Picks Dominate SLC meeting," *The Observer*, November 30, 1972, 6–7, http://archives.nd.edu/observer/1972-11-30_v07_054.pdf.

3. Cited in Eder, "Stay-Hall Procedure Debated by the SLC," 6.

4. Cited in Steve Magdzinski and Jenne Murphy, "Women Asked to Move to North Quad," *The Observer*, February 21, 1973, 2, http://archives.nd.edu/observer/1973-02-21_v07_085.pdf, 2.

5. Cited in Magdzinski and Murphy, "Women Asked to Move to North Quad," 2.

6. See the last paragraph on page 2 of the University of Notre Dame's "2020–2021 Undergraduate Housing Contract," available at https://residentiallife.nd.edu/assets/350692/2020_21_undergraduate_housing_contract.pdf.

7. Margaret Fosmoe, "The Professor Next Door," *Notre Dame Magazine*, Spring 2020, 6–8.

8. Gregg Bangs, "Bedmaking Service Terminated: University Costs Rise," *The Observer*, September 10, 1973, 6, http://archives.nd.edu/Observer/1973-09-10_v08_004.pdf.

9. Marlene Zloza, "Women Fight Discrimination: Work to Get Off-Campus," *The Observer*, February 7, 1973, 1, 6, https://archives.nd.edu/Observer/v07/1973-02-07_v07_075.pdf, 1.

10. Jim Donathen, "O-C Possibility for Women Brings Mixed Reactions," *The Observer*, November 29, 1973, 1, http://www.archives.nd.edu/observer/v08/1973-11-29_v08_052.pdf.

11. Zloza, "Women Fight Discrimination," 1 and 6.

12. Cited in Eder, "Stay-Hall Procedure Debated by the SLC," 6–7.

13. William Murphy, "Shilts Announces Ideas for O-C Housing," *The Observer*, February 5, 1974, 1, http://archives.nd.edu/observer/v08/1974-02-05_v08_072.pdf.

14. Paul Young, "ND Women Against Acquiring Sixth Dorm: Also Oppose Lottery," *The Observer*, December 6, 1974, 9, 20, http://archives.nd.edu/Observer/v09/1974-12-06_v09_057.pdf.

15. Don Reimer, "Housing Lottery Eliminated: Need 400 to Move Off," *The Observer*, February 26, 1975, 8, http://archives.nd.edu/observer/v09/1975-02-26_v09_089.pdf.

16. Angela Sienko, "A Hardcover Thank-You Card," *Notre Dame Magazine*, Autumn 2007, 17. See also https://magazine.nd.edu/stories/a-hardcover-thank-you-card/, ¶9.

17. Kevin Murphy and Dean Janke, letter to the editor, "The Dump," *The Observer*, February 10, 1975, 4, http://52.0.44.235/Observer/v09/1975-02-10_v09_077.pdf, 4.

18. *The Observer*, "ND to Build Townhouses: For Grad Women," *The Observer*, September 8, 1975, 3, http://archives.nd.edu/observer/1975-09-08_v10_004.pdf.

19. Terry Keeney, "Committee Fails to Reach Housing Shortage Decision," *The Observer*, January 22, 1975, 1, https://archives.nd.edu/Observer/v09/1975-01-22_v09_064.pdf.

20. Jean Lenz, "A Room with a View," *Notre Dame Magazine*, Autumn 2002, 18–19. See also https://magazine.nd.edu/stories/a-room-with-a-view/.

21. Sister Jean Lenz, interview with author, October 5, 2000.

10-4 Good Buddy

1. Aminatou Sow and Ann Friedman, *Big Friendship: How we Keep Each Other Close* (New York: Simon and Schuster, 2020), 17.

2. Shelley E. Taylor, Laura Cousino Klein, Brian P. Lewis, Tara L. Gruenewald, Regan A. R. Gurung, and John A. Updegraff, "Biobehavioral Responses to Stress in Females: Tend-and-Befriend, Not Fight-or-Flight," *Psychological Review* 107, no. 3 (July 2000): 411–429, https://doi.org/10.1037/0033-295X.107.3.411, 411.

3. National Film Registry, "About This Collection," Library of Congress, n.d., https://www.loc.gov/collections/selections-from-the-national-film-registry/about-this-collection/.

4. Lisa Moore, "Dames and Grottos: The Anima of Notre Dame," *Scholastic*, September 26, 2002, 32, https://archives.nd.edu/Scholastic/VOL_0144/VOL_0144_ISSUE_0003.pdf, 32.

5. Sara Kettler, "The Story Behind Farrah Fawcett's Iconic 1976 Swimsuit Poster," Biography, June 26, 2019, updated July 14, 2020, https://www.biography.com/news/farrah-fawcett-swimsuit-poster.

6. See the Online School Center, "50 Most Haunted Colleges and Campuses," 2022, https://www.onlineschoolscenter.com/50-haunted-colleges-campuses/, and Eric Owens, "America's Most Haunted College Campuses: The Definitive List," *Daily Caller*, October 30, 2012, https://dailycaller.com/2012/10/30/americas-most-haunted-college-campuses-the-definitive-list-slideshow/.

7. Courtney Sexton, "The Accidental Invention of the Slip 'N Slide," *Smithsonian Magazine*, July 2, 2020, https://www.smithsonianmag.com/innovation/accidental-invention-slip-n-slide-180975236/.

Mixed Signals

1. Susan B. Anthony, "The Status of Woman, Past, Present, and Future," *The Arena*, December 25, 1897. See https://www.raabcollection.com/american-history-autographs/susan-anthony-1897-xmas and https://srpubliclibrary.org/wp-content/uploads/sites/4/2017/02/SusanBAnthony.pdf.

2. Merriam-Webster, s.v. "battle of the sexes (n. phr.)," https://www.merriam-webster.com/dictionary/battle%20of%20the%20sexes.

3. Cited in Robert Ackerman, "Women at Yale: Part 2," *The Observer*, April 11, 1972, 8, http://archives.nd.edu/observer/1972-04-11_v06_107.pdf, 8.

4. Cited in Nancy Weiss Malkiel, *"Keep the Damned Women Out": The Struggle for Coeducation* (Princeton: Princeton University Press, 2018), 79.

5. J. Barry O'Neil, "Co-Ed No Go," *The Observer*, February 20, 1974, 5, http://52.0.44.235/Observer/1974-02-20_v08_083.pdf, 5.

6. See, for example, Zosia Bielski, "Studying the Case for a New Mrs. Degree in Marriage," *The Globe and Mail*, April 4, 2013, https://www.theglobeandmail.com/life/relationships/studying-the-case-for-a-new-mrs-degree-in-marriage/article10790026/.

7. Father Griffin, "The Prospect of Women Living Among Us," *The Observer*, May 4, 1972, 19, 15, http://archives.nd.edu/Observer/1972-05-04_v06_123.pdf, 19.

8. *The Observer*, "The Typical ND freshman: What Is He Like?," *The Observer*, March 1, 1974, 4, http://www.archives.nd.edu/observer/1974-03-01_v08_090.pdf.

9. See Griffin, *The Pocket-Size God*; Gary Caruso, "The Judge Judy Side of the ND Scholarship," *The Observer*, December 1, 2006, 10, https://archives.nd.edu/Observer/v41/2006-12-01_v41_060.pdf; and Kerry Temple, "The Words of Father Griff," *Notre Dame Magazine*, Spring 2016, https://magazine.nd.edu/stories/the-words-of-father-griff/.

10. Griffin, "The Prospect of Women Living Among Us," 19.

11. Theodore M. Hesburgh, "Musing on Going Coed," *The Observer*, May 3, 1972, 8, http://archives.nd.edu/observer/v06/1972-05-03_v06_122.pdf, 8.

12. Trish Moore, "For Real?," *The Observer*, April 5, 1974, 7, https://archives.nd.edu/Observer/v08/1974-04-05_v08_106.pdf, 7.

13. Kathy Cekanski, "In the Halls," *The Observerr*, April 5, 1974, 6, https://archives.nd.edu/Observer/v08/1974-04-05_v08_106.pdf, 5.

14. Joscph B. Treaster, "Unofficial Sex Booklet Draws Mixed Notices at Yale," *The New York Times*, September 17, 1970, 49, https://www.nytimes.com/1970/09/17/archives/unofficial-sex-booklet-draws-mixed-notices-at-yale.html.

15. Anonymous (signed Those at Home on the Range), letter to the editor, "Cattle for the Cows," *The Observer*, February 5, 1974, 4, http://archives.nd.edu/Observer/v08/1974-02-07_v08_074.pdf, 4.

16. O'Neil, "Co-Ed No Go," 5.

17. See, for example, the letters to the editor in *The Observer*, February 8, 1974, 5, https://archives.nd.edu/Observer/1974-02-08_v08_075.pdf, including: Anonymous, "Male Apparition"; Sam LoBosco, Dean Bears, Bill Mahoney, Bill Keller, John Masteller, Steve Kindrick, Paul DuCharme, Ray Gans, Nick Weis, Tom Harrison, Paul Brun, Javier Lazo, and Joe Corcoran, letter to the editor, "To Greener Pastures"; Anonymous, "Bus Stop Waiting"; Bill Jensen, "My Friend's No Cow"; Anonymous, "Normal Cow-panionship"; Dave Richter, "From 'Herd' to 'Flock'"; Mark R. Huffman, "Head 'em Up"; Kevin Britt and Bill Gaudreau, "Move 'em Out"; and Anonymous (signed Cattleman's Association), "Consumers First."

18. Cited in *Saint Mary's College Courier*, "Panty Raids," *Saint Mary's College Courier*, Commemorative 2019, Online Extras, https://www.saintmarys.edu/courier/panty-raids, under "Mary Sheeran — Class of 1976."

19. Sister Jean Lenz, interview with author, October 5, 2000.

20. Ken Girouard, "Students Streak Emil: 'Best Class Ever,'" *The Observer*, March 28, 1974, 6, https://archives.nd.edu/Observer/v08/1974-03-28_v08_100.pdf.

21. Kai S. Swanson, "'Help! Police! Isn't This Wonderful?' The Augustana Panty Raid," in *Reflecting on the Past: 150 Years of Augustana Stories*, ed. Stefanie R. Bluemle, Sarah M. Horowitz, and Jamie L. Nelson (Rock Island, IL: Thomas Tredway Library, 2011), 112–113, https://digital-commons.augustana.edu/cgi/viewcontent.cgi?article=1000&context=ahsreflecting.

22. *The Observer*, "Inside…," *The Observer*, April 20, 1967, 1, https://archives.nd.edu/Observer/1967-04-20_v01_011.pdf, 1.

23. See Terry O'Brien, "Senate Censures Use of K-9 Police to Stop Panty-Raids," *The Observer*, April 20, 1967, 1–2, https://archives.nd.edu/Observer/1967-04-20_v01_011.pdf, 1, and *The Observer*, "Women Disapprove of raid," *The Observer*, April 28, 1970, 1, https://archives.nd.edu/Observer/1970-04-28_v04_118.pdf.

24. Selena Roberts, *A Necessary Spectacle: Billie Jean King, Bobby Riggs, and the Tennis Match That Leveled the Game* (New York: Crown Publishing, 2005).

25. J. Napier, "Of Billie Jean, Libbers and Mike," *The Observer*, September 25, 1973, 1, https://archives.nd.edu/Observer/v08/1973-09-25_v08_015.pdf.

26. United Press International, "Campus Streaking Turns Political," *The Observer*, March 6, 1974, 4, http://www.archives.nd.edu/Observer/1974-03-06_v08_093.pdf, 4.

27. See, for example, Anonymous (signed The Emperor Wears No Clothes), letter to the editor, "Super Streak," *The Observer*, March 22, 1974, 8, https://archives.nd.edu/Observer/v08/1974-03-22_v08_096.pdf; Tristan da Cunha, "The Cruellest [sic] Mumford," The Observer, April 1, 1974, 5, https://archives.nd.edu/Observer/v08/1974-04-01_v08_102.pdf; and Pat Flynn, "Lally Predicts Crackdown Against Streakers," The Observer, April 2, 1974, 3, https://archives.nd.edu/Observer/v08/1974-04-02_v08_103.pdf.

28. The UT History Corner, "The Bare Facts of Streaking," University of Texas, April 11, 2013, https://jimnicar.com/2013/04/11/the-bare-facts-of-streaking/.

29. *Time*, "Music: Streaking, Streaking Everywhere," *Time*, March 18, 1974, http://content.time.com/time/subscriber/article/0,33009,911123-1,00.html.

30. Ray Stevens, "The Streak," by Ray Stevens, recorded 1973, track 1 on *Boogity Boogity*, Barnaby and Janus, studio album.

31. The Rolling Stones, "Under My Thumb," by Mick Jagger and Keith Richards, recorded March 6–9, 1966, track 4 on *Aftermath*, Decca, studio album.

32. Reddy, "I Am Woman."

33. Cited in Ana Monroy Yglesias, "GRAMMY Rewind: Watch Helen Reddy Accept a GRAMMY For 'I Am Woman' in 1973," Recording Academy, May 29, 2020, https://www.grammy.com/news/grammy-rewind-watch-helen-reddy-accept-grammy-i-am-woman-1973, ¶4, *italics original*.

34. Debi Dell, classified advertisement, *The Observer*, February 5, 1974, 7, https://archives.nd.edu/Observer/1974-02-07_v08_074.pdf.

Slippery When Wet

1. Cited in Admin, "Country Music Icon: Living Life to the Fullest," *Think*, October 1, 2015, https://thinkmagazines.com/stars/country-music-icon-living-life-to-the-fullest/, ¶11, and by Rowan Tinker in Jeff Jones, "Eastside Graduates Urged to Overcome Life's Obstacles," *The Butler Bulletin*, May 29, 2022, https://www.kpcnews.com/butlerbulletin/article_8c0c1cb8-bbd2-570c-a057-6f7a19871ef6.html, ¶27.

2. Cited in Jerry Lutkus, "Notre Dame Hails First Women as Undergrads," *The Observer*, September 2, 1972, 5, 12, http://archives.nd.edu/observer/v07/1972-09-02_v07_001.pdf, 5.

3. Lenz, *Loyal Sons and Daughters*, 115.

4. Cited in Kathy Martin, "ND's 'Male Bastion' Gives Way to Women in 1972," *The Observer*, Spring 1987, Special Issue, 20-23, http://www.archives.nd.edu/observer/1987-05-Sp_v21_Hesburgh-Years.pdf, 21.

5. The Rolling Stones, "You Can't Always Get What You Want," by Mick Jagger and Keith Richards, recorded November 16–17, 1968, track 9 on *Let It Bleed*, Decca, studio album, lines 28–30.

6. Tom Young, Paul Shay, Rick Supik, Augie Grace, Jim Augustine, Mike Disbro, and Brian Sontchim, letter to the editor, "Games People Play," *The Observer*, October 16, 1974, 6, https://archives.nd.edu/Observer/v09/1974-10-16_v09_035.pdf.

7. *The Observer*, "First Band Wedding," *The Observer*, October 19, 1972, 5, https://archives.nd.edu/Observer/1972-10-19_v07_030.pdf.

8. Ed Cohen, "ND–Saint Mary's Marriages Dwindling," *Notre Dame Magazine*, Spring 2001, https://magazine.nd.edu/stories/nd-saint-mary-s-marriages-dwindling/, ¶2–¶3.

9. Mark Gray, "Divorce (Still) Less Likely Among Catholics," *Nineteen Sixty-Four* (blog), Center for Applied Research in the Apostolate at Georgetown University, http://nineteensixty-four.blogspot.com/2013/09/divorce-still-less-likely-among.html, ¶7.

10. See Mateus, "Here's the amazing story of Mateus Rosé," Mateus, 2022, https://www.mateusrose.us/our-story/.

11. Elton John, "Social Disease," by Elton John and Bernie Taupin, recorded May 1973, track 15 on *Goodbye Yellow Brick Road*, MCA and DJM, studio album, line 8.

Divided Highway

1. Henry David Thoreau, *Walden; or, Life in the Woods* (Boston: Ticknor and Fields: Boston, 1854). See https://etc.usf.edu/lit2go/90/walden-or-life-in-the-woods/1535/economy/, ¶14.

2. Cited in Hope, *Notre Dame—100 Years*, http://archives.nd.edu/hope/hope30.htm, ¶16.

3. Susan L. Poulson and Leslie Miller-Bernal, "Two Unique Histories of Coeducation: Catholic and Historically Black Institutions," in *Going Coed: Women's Experiences in Formerly Men's Colleges and Universities, 1950–2000*, ed. Leslie Miller-Bernal and Susan L. Poulson (Nashville: Vanderbilt University Press, 2004), 22–53, 27.

4. Maria Gallagher, "Feminism at SMC," *The Observer*, September 8, 1972, 4, http://archives.nd.edu/observer/1972-09-08_v07_003.pdf, 4.

5. Cited in Barwick and Rabach, "Alums Recall Effects of Proposed Merger in '71," 7.

6. Hesburgh, "Musing on Going Coed," 8.

7. *The Observer*, editorial, "The State Road 933 Divide," *The Observer*, March 1, 2013, 8, https://issuu.com/the-observer/docs/usethisfinished_template_20_pages_03-01-2013, 8.

8. Maryanne Ries, "The Technologies of Belonging at Saint Mary's College" (sociology paper, University of Notre Dame, December 7, 1972).

9. *The Observer*, "Steve 'from Cleveland' Appointed ND Rep to SMC," *The Observer*, November 8, 1972, 2, http://archives.nd.edu/observer/1972-11-08_v07_044.pdf.

10. Maria Gallagher, "A Campus Cookbook," *The Observer*, April 4, 1973, 5, http://www.archives.nd.edu/Observer/1973-04-04_v07_107.pdf, 5.

11. Jill Truitt, "Co-Ex Committees Merge," *The Observer*, September 11, 1975, 6, https://archives.nd.edu/Observer/1975-09-11_v10_007.pdf.

12. Barbara McKiernan, "Co-Education at Notre Dame?...Across the Lake," *The Observer*, April 5, 1974, 7, https://archives.nd.edu/Observer/v08/1974-04-05_v08_106.pdf, 7.

13. Christie Herlihy, "Women's Sports Growing Apart: In ND–SCM's Teams," *The Observer*, March 11, 1975, 1, http://archives.nd.edu/observer/v09/1975-03-11_v09_098.pdf.

14. *The Observer*, "Committee to Study ND–SMC Relations," *The Observer*, April 28, 1975, 4, http://archives.nd.edu/observer/1975-04-28_v09_123.pdf.

15. "Report of the Committee to Evaluate Coeducation" cited in Zurblis, *Notre Dame Report: '76–'77*, vol. 6, no. 16.

16. *The Observer*, "Women to Represent ND," *The Observer*, April 5, 1973, 9, http://archives.nd.edu/observer/1973-04-05_v07_108.pdf.

17. *The Observer*, "The State Road 933 Divide," 8.

Gaining Speed

1. Muriel Strode, "Wind-Wafted Wild Flowers," *The Open Court* 17, no. 8 (August 1903): 505–506, https://www.google.com/books/edition/The_Open_Court/duMeAQAAIAAJ?gbpv=1, 505.

2. "Report of the Committee to Evaluate Coeducation" cited in Zurblis, *Notre Dame Report: '76–'77*, vol. 6, no. 16.

3. Don Ruane, "Krashna, Winings 'Reply,'" *The Observer*, March 10, 1970, 3, 6, https://archives.nd.edu/Observer/v04/1970-03-10_v04_091.pdf, and *The Observer*, "Voter Turnout Increases in Student Body Election," *The Observer*, February 12, 2016, 1, https://archives.nd.edu/Observer/2016-02-12_v50_090.pdf.

4. Cited in Ann Therese Darin, "Hesburgh Vows Co-Ed Increase," 1.

5. Darin, "Hesburgh Vows Co-Ed Increase," 1.

6. Cited in Alisha Haridasani Gupta, "A Teacher Held a Famous Racism Exercise in 1968: She's Still at It," *The New York Times*, July 4, 2020, ¶10, https://www.nytimes.com/2020/07/04/us/jane-elliott-anti-racism-blue-eyes-brown-eyes.html.

7. Dean Mayors, "Black Enrollment Drops in Freshman Class," *The Observer*, October 17, 1972, 3, https://archives.nd.edu/Observer/1972-10-17_v07_028.pdf.

8. Cited in Mayors, "Black Enrollment Drops in Freshman Class," 3.

9. Cited in Mayors, "Black Enrollment Drops in Freshman Class," 3.

10. Cited in David Krashna and Don Wycliff, eds., *Black Domers: African-American Students at Notre Dame in Their Own Words* (Notre Dame, IN: University of Notre Dame Press, 2017), under "Chapter 3. The 1970s."

11. Author compiled information from several sources available via Notre Dame.

12. Janet Longfellow, "SLC Looks at Proposals of Black Students," *The Observer*, February 13, 1932, 1–2, https://archives.nd.edu/Observer/v07/1973-02-13_v07_079.pdf.

13. Greg Aiello, "'Blacks and the University': New Frontier Society to Hold Forum," *The Observer*, October 23, 1972, 7, https://archives.nd.edu/Observer/v07/1972-10-23_v07_032.pdf.

14. David Rust, "Black Faculty Form to Protect Black Image," *The Observer*, February 22, 1973, 1, https://archives.nd.edu/Observer/v07/1973-02-22_v07_086.pdf.

15. Nielsen Media Research data file used by Simmons and Rich, ""Feminism Ain't Funny."

16. Jim Eder, "HPC Hears Grievances of ND Black Students," *The Observer*, February 14, 1973, 1, 7, http://archives.nd.edu/observer/1973-02-14_v07_080.pdf.

17. Kurt Heinz, "SLC Listens to Status of Blacks: Black Student Affairs Director Addresses Meeting," *The Observer*, October 30, 1973, 1, http://www.archives.nd.edu/observer/1973-10-30_v08_036.pdf.

18. Aiello, "'Blacks and the University.'"

19. Cited in James Maycock, "How James Brown Flipped Soul Music on Its Head to Create Funk," *American Masters*, October 29, 2003, https://www.pbs.org/wnet/americanmasters/james-brown-soul-survivor/532/, ¶1.

20. Christie Herlihy, "Labor Policy Problems Explained: Vagueness and Bad Figures Cited," *The Observer*, October 13, 1975, 1, 3, http://archives.nd.edu/Observer/v10/1975-10-13_v10_029.pdf.

21. "University of Notre Dame Affirmative Action Statement" cited in Teresa A. Porro, ed., *Notre Dame Report: '75–'76*, vol. 5, no. 1 (Notre Dame, IN: University of Notre Dame, Department of Information Services, September 12, 1975), 28–38, http://archives.nd.edu/ndr/NDR-05/NDR-1975-09-12.pdf, 30.

22. Dennis Brown, "In Memoriam: Adam Arnold, First African-American Faculty Member," *Notre Dame Magazine*, April 24, 2017, https://news.nd.edu/news/in-memoriam-adam-arnold-first-african-american-faculty-member/.

23. "Report of the Committee to Evaluate Coeducation" cited in Zurblis, *Notre Dame Report: '76–'77*, vol. 6, no. 16.

24. "Report of the Committee to Evaluate Coeducation" cited in Zurblis, *Notre Dame Report: '76–'77*, vol. 6, no. 16.

25. Jesse L. Jackson, letter to the editor, *Time*, "Sickeningly Biased," *Time*, May 3, 1976, https://content.time.com/time/subscriber/article/0,33009,914102-2,00.html, ¶6, and https://content.time.com/time/subscriber/article/0,33009,914102-3,00.html, ¶1–¶3.

26. Margaret Fosmoe, "Fresh Approaches," *Notre Dame Magazine*, Summer 2021, 7. See also https://magazine.nd.edu/stories/fresh-approaches/, ¶2 under "Shaping the Class of 2025."

27. "Commencement Address" cited in Teresa A. Castle, ed., *Notre Dame Report: '75–'76*, vol. 5, no. 18 (Notre Dame, IN: University of Notre Dame, Department of Information Services, May 28, 1976), 401–404, http://archives.nd.edu/ndr/NDR-05/NDR-1976-05-28.pdf, 401.

28. Dennis Brown, "Black Alumni of Notre Dame Expands Scope of Frazier Thompson Scholarship," *Notre Dame News*, April 8, 2021, https://news.nd.edu/news/black-alumni-of-notre-dame-expands-scope-of-frazier-thompson-scholarship/.

The Open Road

1. *Furious 7*, directed by James Wan, written by Chris Morgan (Universal Pictures, 2015), 137 minutes. For quote from the dialogue, see https://subslikescript.com/movie/Furious_7-2820852, ¶20–¶22.

2. Anonymous, letter to the editor, "Gay Rapping," *The Observer*, November 2, 1972, 9, https://archives.nd.edu/Observer/1972-11-02_v07_040.pdf.

3. See, for example, Anonymous (signed One Who Cares), letter to the editor, "For Gay Lib at ND," *The Observer*, February 1, 1972, 9, https://archives.nd.edu/Observer/1972-02-01_v06_068.pdf.

4. See, for example, Suzanna Danuta Walters, *All the Rage: The Story of Gay Visibility in America* (Chicago: The University of Chicago Press, 2001); Stephen Tropiano, *The Prime Time Closet: A History of Gays and Lesbians on TV* (New York: Applause Books, 2002); and Ron Becker, *Gay TV and Straight America* (New Brunswick, NJ: Rutgers University Press, 2006).

5. Cited in *The Observer*, "Homosexuality to Be Discussed: At Workshop This Weekend," *The Observer*, October 17, 1974, 7, http://archives.nd.edu/observer/1974-10-17_v09_036.pdf, 7.

6. GLAAD, "How is Sexual Orientation Different from Gender Identity?" GLADD, n.d., https://www.glaad.org/how-sexual-orientation-different-gender-identity, ¶2–¶4.

7. *The Observer*, "ND Gay Students Organize: Group Outlines Priorities," *The Observer*, November 11, 1974, 4, http://archives.nd.edu/observer/1974-11-11_v09_045.pdf, 4.

8. Andy Praschak, "Homosexuality—A Separate Community," *The Observer*, January 22, 1975, 7, http://archives.nd.edu/observer/1975-01-22_v09_064.pdf; Andy Praschak, "Homosexuality—A Separate Experience," *The Observer*, January 23, 1975, 5, https://archives.nd.edu/Observer/v09/1975-01-23_v09_065.pdf; Andy Praschak, Homosexuality—A Separate Reality," *The Observer*, January 24, 1975, 7, http://archives.nd.edu/observer/1975-01-24_v09_066.pdf.

9. Anonymous, letter to the editor, "Homosexuality," *The Observer*, June 12, 1975, 11, http://archives.nd.edu/observer/v10/1975-06-12_v10_001.pdf, 11.

10. Praschak, "Homosexuality—A Separate Community," 7.

11. Cited in Praschak, Homosexuality—A Separate Reality," 7.

12. Anonymous, "Prayer of a Homosexual," *The Observer*, March 12, 1975, 5, https://archives.nd.edu/Observer/1975-03-12_v09_099.pdf.

13. Cited in *The Observer*, "Kelsey Discusses Alterations in Attitude of Christianity Towards Homosexuality," *The Observer*, April 9, 1975, 2, http://archives.nd.edu/Observer/v09/1975-04-09_v09_110.pdf, 2.

14. Cited in Don Reimer, "Gay Students Respond to *Time* Cover-Story: Members' Reactions Vary," *The Observer*, September 10, 1975, 4, https://archives.nd.edu/Observer/1975-09-10_v10_006.pdf, 4.

15. Reimer, "Gay Students Respond to *Time* Cover-Story," 4.

16. Cited in *The Observer*, "Conversations with a Campus Homosexual," *The Observer*, March 4, 1976, 5, https://archives.nd.edu/Observer/1976-03-04_v10_099.pdf.

17. See, for example, Clifford de Aragon, letter to the editor, "Gay Clarifications," *The Observer*, March 9, 1976, 4, https://archives.nd.edu/Observer/v10/1976-03-09_v10_102.pdf, and Peter H. Korth, letter to the editor, "Unfounded Assumptions," *The Observer*, March 26, 1976, 6, https://archives.nd.edu/Observer/v10/1976-03-26_v10_107.pdf. An opinion piece also was written later that year by Peter Korth, "A Part of N.D.," *The Observer*, September 14, 1976, 4, https://archives.nd.edu/Observer/v11/1976-09-14_v11_011.pdf.

18. ARC ND, "About," ND Alumni and Friends, n.d., https://my.nd.edu/topics/6118/.

19. Cited in Deanna Csomo McCool, "Opening Doors to Women Made School Better: Hesburgh," *South Bend Tribune*, March 12, 1998, C-6.

Taking the Scenic Route

1. Lenz, *Loyal Sons and Daughters*, 4.

Sun in Our Eyes

1. Cited in Daniel E. Harmon, *Notre Dame Football* (New York: Rosen Publishing Group, 2013), 39.

2. Lenz, *Loyal Sons and Daughters*, 171, *italics original.*

3. Notre Dame Archives, "Senior Bar," *Notre Dame Archives News and Notes,* June 29, 2012, http://archives.nd.edu/about/news/index.php/2012/senior-bar/.

4. Cited in Gary Allietta, "Knaked Klunker Cancels Act Because of Pressures," *The Observer,* October 9, 1973, 2, https://archives.nd.edu/Observer/1973-10-09_v08_025.pdf, 2.

5. For the full story, see Ralph Keyes, *The Quote Verifier: Who Said What, Where, and When* (New York: St. Martin's Press, 2006), 78.

6. *Notre Dame,* "New Structure Costs $250,000," *Notre Dame* 8, no. 4 (Winter 1955): 5–7, http://archives.nd.edu/NDM/ND_08_4_1955_WIN.pdf.

7. Lee Klosinski, "Loyal Sons (and Daughters) March Onward to Victory," *The Observer,* September 29, 1972, 3, http://archives.nd.edu/observer/1972-09-29_v07_016.pdf.

8. Cited in Klosinski, "Loyal Sons (and Daughters)," 3.

9. Cited in Margaret Fosmoe, "Notre Dame's Changes to Irish Guard Stir Outcry," *South Bend Tribune,* May 19, 2014, updated Aug 31, 2014, https://www.southbendtribune.com/story/sports/college/2014/05/19/otre-dames-changes-to-irish-guard-stir-outcry/46208895/, ¶6.

10. Cited in Fosmoe, "Notre Dame's Changes to Irish Guard Stir Outcry," ¶9.

11. Fosmoe, "Notre Dame's Changes to Irish Guard Stir Outcry."

12. Liz Harter, "Band Holds Annual Plaiding Ceremony," *The Observer,* September 5, 2008, 1, 4, https://archives.nd.edu/Observer/2008-09-05_v43_008.pdf.

13. Cited in Paul Colgan, "Scalpers Enjoy Heyday," *The Observer,* October 25, 1973, 2, http://archives.nd.edu/observer/1973-10-25_v08_033.pdf, 2.

14. See The University of Notre Dame, "Notre Dame Stadium Has Legendary History," The University of Notre Dame, 2022, https://und.com/notre-dame-stadium-history/, and College Gridirons, "Notre Dame Stadium," College Gridirons, 2004–2020, https://www.collegegridirons.com/stadiums/notre-dame-stadium/.

15. The University of Notre Dame, "Simplicity Order of the Day at Notre Dame Stadium," The University of Notre Dame, September 27, 2018, https://und.com/football-simplicity-order-of-the-day-at-notre-dame-stadium/, and *Chicago Tribune,* "Notre Dame Reveals FieldTurf Design," *Chicago Tribune,* July 16, 2014, https://www.chicagotribune.com/sports/college/chi-notre-dame-reveals-fieldturf-design-20140716-story.html.

16. Kristy Katzmann, "May I Have Your Attention, Please," *Notre Dame Magazine,* Autumn 2000, https://magazine.nd.edu/stories/may-i-have-your-attention-please/, ¶5.

17. See Mike Collins and Tim McCarthy, *May I Have Your Attention Please… Wit and Wisdom from the Notre Dame Pressbox* (Notre Dame, IN: Corby Books, 2009).

Did You See That?

1. Emma Chase, *Tamed* (New York: Gallery Books, 2014), 2.

2. Cited in Greg Corgan, "Irish Team Effort Downs Trojans," *The Observer,* October 29, 1973, 8, http://archives.nd.edu/observer/1973-10-29_v08_035.pdf, 8.

3. Cited in Corgan, "Irish Team Effort Downs Trojans," 8.

4. Vic Dorr, "Irish 23, Trojans 14," *The Observer*, October 29, 1973, 1, http://archives.nd.edu/observer/1973-10-29_v08_035.pdf, 1.

5. See Tom Noie, "Notre Dame Coaching Legend Ara Parseghian Dies at 94," *South Bend Tribune*, August 2, 2017, https://www.ndinsider.com/story/sports/football/2017/08/02/otre-dame-coaching-legend-ara-parseghian-dies-at-94/116987522/, and David Stout, "Ara Parseghian, Coach Who Returned Notre Dame Football to Greatness, Dies at 94," *The New York Times*, August 2, 2017, https://www.nytimes.com/2017/08/02/sports/football/notre-dame-coach-ara-parseghian-dead-at-94.html.

6. Leonard Koppett, "U.S.C. Routs Irish, 55-24, with 49-0 Half," *The New York Times*, December 1, 1974, 253, https://www.nytimes.com/1974/12/01/archives/usc-routs-irish-5524-with-490-half-usc-routs-irish-5524-with-490.html, ¶2.

7. See Robert Markus and *Chicago Tribune*, "Digger Rises to the Top," *Chicago Tribune*, March 8, 1987, https://www.chicagotribune.com/news/ct-xpm-1987-03-08-8701180780-story.html, and Kaitee Daley, "Digger Phelps' Biggest Victory," ESPN, December 7, 2010, https://www.espn.com/mens-college-basketball/columns/story?id=5895188.

8. Cited in Jeré Longman, "Remembering U.C.L.A.'s Streak's End," *The New York Times*, December 11, 2010, https://www.nytimes.com/2010/12/12/sports/ncaabasketball/12streak.html, ¶20.

9. Digger Phelps, interview with author, October 5, 2000. See also Matt Randall, "Digger Phelps Reflects on Legacy of Dick Enberg," ABD57, December 23, 2017, https://www.abc57.com/news/digger-phelps-reflects-on-legacy-of-dick-enberg.

10. Cited in Mike DeCourcy, "45 Years Later, Notre Dame Upset of UCLA's 88-Game Win Streak Still Resonates," *The Sporting News*, January 18, 2019, https://www.sportingnews.com/us/ncaa-basketball/news/notre-dame-upset-ucla-88-game-winning-streak-anniversary-college-basketball/5ekvt3dod93s1en5l6o8t4io9, ¶23.

Pit Stops

1. Divya Trivedi, *Goodness Is Happiness* (Nagpur, India: SpotWrite Publications, 2021), 31.

See Indiana Alcohol and Tobacco Commission, "Alcoholic Beverage Act of 1935," Indiana State Government, 2022, https://www.in.gov/atc/isep/about-isep/history/alcoholic-beverage-act-of-1935/, and Chris Sikich, "Indiana, Once a Last Bastion of Blue Laws, Considers Alcohol Sales 'Essential,'" *Indianapolis Star*, April 3, 2020, https://www.indystar.com/story/news/politics/2020/04/03/indiana-considers-alcohol-essential-after-years-embracing-blue-laws/5112715002/.

2. Cited in Howard Wood, "'No Drinking in Public': Macheca Issues Statement," *The Observer*, September 21, 1973, 3, http://archives.nd.edu/observer/1973-09-21_v08_013.pdf, 3.

3. Terry Keeney, "Dry Spell Grips Notre Dame," *The Observer*, August 28, 1973, 1, 3, http://archives.nd.edu/Observer/v09/1974-08-28_v09_002.pdf.

4. Matt Yokom, "Senior Club to Be Opened," *The Observer*, September 11, 1974, 2, http://archives.nd.edu/observer/1974-09-18_v09_015.pdf.

5. Notre Dame Archives, "Senior Bar."

6. Art Ferrant, "Raid Surprises 26 ND-SMC 'Minors': Arrested at Nickie's," *The Observer*, April 2, 1973, 1, https://archives.nd.edu/Observer/v07/1973-04-02_v07_105.pdf; *The Observer*, "The Night They Raided Nickie's," *The Observer*, April 3, 1973, 8, https://archives.nd.edu/Observer/v07/1973-04-03_v07_106.pdf; and Bill Sohn, "18 students Are Convicted, Others

Given Continuances: Arrested at Nickie's," *The Observer*, April 4, 1973, 3, https://archives.nd.edu/Observer/v07/1973-04-04_v07_107.pdf.

7. Associated Press, "Brewer Spends Millions to Promote 'Responsible-Drinking' Programs," *Los Angeles Times*, March 19, 1989, https://www.latimes.com/archives/la-xpm-1989-03-19-fi-566-story.html.

8. Cited in Dan George, "'Pit Stops' Steer Students from Drinking and Driving," AP News, March 5, 1988, https://apnews.com/7590194f3d3d0a4fd849baae3f247486.

9. Cited in Joseph LaFlare, "Louie's Doing O.K.," *The Observer*, September 14, 1973, 6, http://archives.nd.edu/observer/1973-09-14_v08_008.pdf, 6.

10. Kerry Segrave, *Drive-In Theaters: A History from Their Inception in 1933* (Jefferson, NC: McFarland and Company, 2006), and Jeff Kamm, "At Your Leisure: At the Drive-In," Historic Indianapolis, July 10, 2015, https://historicindianapolis.com/at-your-leisure-at-the-drive-in/.

Turning the Dial

1. William Congreve, *The Mourning Bride: A Tragedy* (London: John Bell, 1791), 13. For a digitized version of the play, see https://www.google.com/books/edition/The_Mourning_Bride/NmMLAAAAIAAJ?hl=en&gbpv=1.

2. Randall B. Woods, *Prisoners of Hope: Lyndon B. Johnson, the Great Society, and the Limits of Liberalism* (New York: Basic Books, 2016), and Robert O. Self, *All in the Family: The Realignment of American Democracy Since the 1960s* (New York: Farrar, Straus and Giroux, 2012).

3. Robert Christgau, "Rock in the 1970s: Journey Through the Past," *The Village Voice*, December 17, 1979, https://www.villagevoice.com/2019/12/11/rock-in-the-1970s-journey-through-the-past/, ¶1.

4. A crowd of about fifty students asked Miller questions at the Bulla Shed on February 12, 1974. Chris O'Brien, "Miller Speaks on 'The Exorcist,'" *The Observer*, February 13, 1974, 3, https://archives.nd.edu/Observer/1974-02-13_v08_078.pdf.

Two-Way Street

1. Cited in Thea Ormerod, "What Kind of Difference Do You Want to Make? Responding to Jane Goodall's Call to Low-Carbon Living," ABC, May 13, 2019, https://www.abc.net.au/religion/responding-to-jane-goodalls-call-to-low-carbon-living/11109324, ¶2.

2. John I. Jenkins, "Notre Dame Is Not a Final Destination," *Notre Dame Magazine*, Winter 2008–2009, https://magazine.nd.edu/stories/notre-dame-is-not-a-final-destination/, ¶7.

3. "Volunteer Services: The Neighborhood Study Help Program" in University of Notre Dame Yearbook Staff, *Dome: 1976 Notre Dame Yearbook*, vol. 67 (Marceline, MO; Walsworth Publishing Company, 1976), 99. See http://www.e-yearbook.com/yearbooks/University_Notre_Dame_Dome_Yearbook/1976/Page_99.html.

4. Although this word is considered derogatory today, it was not considered inappropriate during the 1970s and often appeared in print.

5. Jane Pitz, interview with author, February 26, 2022.

6. Jody K. Olsen, "Peace Corps Announces Suspension of Volunteer Activities, Evacuations Due to COVID-19," Peace Corps, March 15, 2020, https://www.peacecorps.gov/news/library/peace-corps-announces-suspension-volunteer-activities-evacuations-due-covid-19/, ¶13.

7. Scott Neuman, "National Service Act Continues U.S. Tradition," NPR, April 21, 2009, https://www.npr.org/2009/04/21/103336035/national-service-act-continues-u-s-tradition, ¶15 under "The Peace Corps and the Great Society."

8. Cited in Ann McCarry, "Idealism Leads ND Grads into Peace Corps," *The Observer*, May 4, 1972, 17, http://archives.nd.edu/Observer/1972-05-04_v06_123.pdf, 17.

9. Gregg B. Bangs, "World Food Crisis Becomes Major Concern," *The Observer*, November 11, 1974, 1, http://archives.nd.edu/observer/1974-11-11_v09_045.pdf.

10. Cited in *The Observer*, "Sondej Collects Food Funds," *The Observer*, September 11, 1975, 6, http://archives.nd.edu/observer/1975-09-11_v10_007.pdf, 6.

11. Terrence Rogers, "Remembering Alan Sondej," *Notre Dame Magazine*, March 18, 2013, https://magazine.nd.edu/stories/remembering-alan-sondej/, ¶3.

12. Ken Girouard, "Sondej Continues Dining Hall Charity Collection for Needy," *The Observer*, October 18, 1974, 2, http://archives.nd.edu/observer/1974-10-18_v09_037.pdf.

13. National Fallen Firefighters Association, "Roll of Honor: Alan P. Sondej," National Fallen Firefighters Foundation, https://www.firehero.org/fallen-firefighter/alan-p-sondej/.

14. Alan P. Sondej "Reflections on a Bangladesh Trip," *The Observer*, September 18, 1975, 1, 4, http://archives.nd.edu/Observer/v10/1975-09-18_v10_011.pdf.

15. Sondej, "Reflections on a Bangladesh Trip," 1.

16. Sondej, "Reflections on a Bangladesh Trip," 4.

17. Peter Arndt, "Sondej to End Food Collection; Called 'Most Effective Teacher,'" *The Observer*, April 6, 1976, 1–2, http://archives.nd.edu/observer/v10/1976-04-06_v10_114.pdf, 1.

18. Cited in Arndt, "Sondej to End Food Collection," 1–2.

19. Terrence Rogers, "Remembering Alan Sondej," *Notre Dame Magazine*, March 18, 2013, https://magazine.nd.edu/stories/remembering-alan-sondej/.

20. National Fallen Firefighters Association, "Roll of Honor: Alan P. Sondej."

Emerging from the Fog

1. Michelle Obama, *Becoming: A Guided Journal for Discovering Your Voice* (New York: Crown, 2021), 421.

(No) Passing Zone

1. Albert Schweitzer, *Memoirs of Childhood and Youth*, trans. C. T. Campion (New York: The Macmillan Company, 1949), 67–68.

2. See Dorothy V. Corson, "Rev. Julius Nieuwland Famed Notre Dame Chemist and Botanist," University of Notre Dame, December 12, 2001, https://www3.nd.edu/~wcawley/corson/nieuwland.htm, as well as a March 11, 1974, article from *The Wall Street Journal* reprinted in *The Observer*: *The Wall Street Journal*, "Wall Street Journal Reports: More than Football Found at N.D.," *The Observer*, March 20, 1974, 4–5, http://archives.nd.edu/observer/1974-03-20_v08_094.pdf.

3. Cited in The Wall Street Journal, "Wall Street Journal Reports," 4.

4. "Report of the Committee to Evaluate Coeducation" cited in Zurblis, *Notre Dame Report: '76–'77*, 374.

5. *The Observer*, "ND Men Lose at GPA Game," September 1, 1973, *The Observer*, 14, http://archives.nd.edu/observer/1973-09-01_v08_001.pdf.

6. See "Spring Enrollment" in Teresa A. Porro, ed., *Notre Dame Report: '74–'75*, vol. 4, no. 12 (Notre Dame, IN: University of Notre Dame, Department of Information Services, February 28, 1975), 263.

7. Hofman, interview.

8. Hesburgh, interview.

9. Gregg Bangs, "ND Faculty Salaries Below Nat'l Average," *The Observer*, October 8, 1974, 1, http://archives.nd.edu/observer/1974-10-08_v09_029.pdf.

10. Cited in Jerry Lutkus, "Coeducation — Part 11: It Will Work," *The Observer*, April 8, 1974, 7, https://archives.nd.edu/Observer/1974-04-08_v08_107.pdf, 7.

11. Tom Streit, "The Legend Who Never Stopped," *Notre Dame Magazine*, Autumn 2015, https://magazine.nd.edu/stories/the-legend-who-never-stopped/, ¶6.

12. Three Psyched Frosh, "The Night Before Emil," *The Observer*, October 16, 1975, 5, http://archives.nd.edu/observer/1975-10-16_v10_032.pdf.

13. As Meat Loaf says, "life is just a highway" and "the soul is just a car." See "Objects in the Rear View Mirror," line 18.

14. Garvey, "Vincent Raymond, Former Associate Business Dean, Dies," ¶4.

15. Katie Peralta, "The Many Careers of Frank Yeandel," *Notre Dame Magazine*, Spring 2010, https://magazine.nd.edu/stories/the-many-careers-of-frank-yeandel/, ¶5.

16. Paraphrased in Michael O. Garvey, "Vincent Raymond, Former Associate Business Dean, Dies," *Notre Dame News*, March 5, 2006, https://news.nd.edu/news/vincent-raymond-former-associate-business-dean-dies/, ¶4.

Riding Shotgun

1. Elizabeth Blackwell, *Medicine as a Profession for Women* (New York: Trustees of the New York Infirmary for Women, 1860), 17. For a digitized copy, see https://archive.org/details/62630060R.nlm.nih.gov/mode/2up.

2. University of Notre Dame, "Father Hesburgh President Emeritus: Milestones," University of Notre Dame, 2022, https://hesburgh.nd.edu/fr-teds-life/an-extraordinary-life/milestones/.

3. Bill McGinn, "Burtchael [*sic*] Praises Barkett Letter," *The Observer*, March 6, 1972, 1, http://archives.nd.edu/observer/v06/1972-03-06_v06_093.pdf.

4. Cited in the "Report of the Committee to Evaluate Coeducation" reproduced Zurblis, *Notre Dame Report: '76–'77*, vol. 6, no. 16, 370.

5. McGinn, "Burtchael [*sic*] Praises Barkett Letter," 1.

6. Marcia Synnott, "A Friendly Rivalry: Yale and Princeton Pursue Parallel Paths to Coeducation," in *Going Coed: Women's Experiences in Formerly Men's Colleges and Universities, 1950–2000*, ed. Leslie Miller-Bernal and Susan L. Poulson (Nashville: Vanderbilt University Press, 2004), 111–150, 120.

7. Everett Carll Ladd, Seymour Martin Lipset, Martin A. Trow, and the Inter-University Consortium for Political and Social Research, *Carnegie Commission National Survey of Higher Education: Faculty Study Subsample, 1969* (Ann Arbor, MI: Inter-University Consortium for Political and Social Research, 1984), and Gerald Rosenblum and Barbara Rubin Rosenblum, "Segmented Labor Markets in Institutions of Higher Learning," *Sociology of Education* 63, no. 3 (July 1990): 151–164.

8. Cited in Jim Ferry, "Reactions Vary as Co-Ed Year Culminates," *The Observer*, April 30, 1973, 9, http://archives.nd.edu/observer/1973-04-30_v07_119.pdf, 9.

9. "University of Notre Dame Affirmative Action Statement" of the Affirmative Action Committee cited in Teresa A. Porro, ed., *Notre Dame Report: '75–'76*, vol. 5, no. 1 (Notre Dame, IN: University of Notre Dame, Department of Information Services, September 12, 1975), 28–38, https://archives.nd.edu/ndr/NDR-05/NDR-1975-09-12.pdf, 30.

10. See "Report of the Committee to Evaluate Coeducation" in Zurblis, *Notre Dame Report: '76–'77*, vol. 6, no. 16, 367–395.

11. Pam McCormick, "Eldest Daughters Come Home," *Notre Dame Magazine*, Autumn 1997, 3–5.

12. Valerie Zurblis, "Hesburgh Cites Universities' Role: At Faculty Address," The Observer, October 21, 1975, 1, 3, http://archives.nd.edu/observer/v10/1975-10-21_v10_035.pdf, 1.

13. Cited in Lutkus, "First of Women Graduate at ND," 53.

14. Conklin, "Coeducation at Notre Dame"

15. Cited in Lutkus, "First of Women Graduate at ND," 53.

16. Cited in Conklin, "Coeducation at Notre Dame," 6.

17. Valerie Zurblis, "Hesburgh Cites Universities' Role: At Faculty Address," *The Observer*, October 21, 1975, 1, 3, http://archives.nd.edu/observer/v10/1975-10-21_v10_035.pdf, 1.

18. Cited in Zurblis, "Hesburgh Cites Universities' Role," 1 and 3.

19. Anne Jane Dregalla, "ND Discrimination Suit Goes to Court on Tuesday," *The Observer*, February 13, 1981, 1, 4, http://archives.nd.edu/observer/v15/1981-02-13_v15_091.pdf.

20. "Academic Affirmative Action Committee Review of Recruitment Efforts and Results for Academic Year 1985-86" cited in Bernadette Zoss, ed., *Notre Dame Report: '85–'86*, vol. 15, no. 19 (Notre Dame, IN: University of Notre Dame, Department of Information Services, July 11, 1986), 376–383, https://archives.nd.edu/ndr/NDR-15/NDR-1986-07-11.pdf, 376.

21. *Notre Dame Magazine*, "For Those Keeping Score," *Notre Dame Magazine*, Summer 2021, 15, https://magazine.nd.edu/stories/for-those-keeping-score/.

22. As defined by Barry Bozeman and Mary K. Feeney, "Toward a Useful Theory of Mentoring: A Conceptual Analysis and Critique," *Administration and Society* 39, no. 6 (October 2007): 719–739, https://journals.sagepub.com/doi/10.1177/0095399707304119, 731.

23. Cited in Alice Slade, "Notre Dame Women are 'Special Breed,'" *South Bend Tribune*, October 17, 1976, 73.

24. "Academic Affirmative Action Committee Review of Recruitment Efforts and Results for Academic Year 1985-86" cited in Zoss, *Notre Dame Report: '85–'86*, vol. 15, no. 19.

25. Synnott, "A Friendly Rivalry," 126.

26. Kerry Temple, "A Change of Course," *Notre Dame Magazine*, Spring 2019, 10, https://magazine.nd.edu/stories/a-change-of-course/, ¶4 and ¶6.

27. David Rust, "'Images of Women' Course Planned," *The Observer*, April 11, 1973, 3, http://archives.nd.edu/observer/1973-04-11_v07_112.pdf.

28. Mary Lynn Broe cited in Rust, "'Images of Women' Course Planned," 3.

29. *The Observer*, "On Campus Today," *The Observer*, October 8, 1974, 2, https://archives.nd.edu/Observer/1974-10-08_v09_029.pdf.

30. Cited in Judy Rauenhorst, "ND Offers Women's Courses," *The Observer*, December 7, 1973, 5, 7, http://www.archives.nd.edu/observer/v08/1973-12-07_v08_058.pdf, 7.

31. College of Arts and Letters Gender Studies Program, "History," University of Notre Dame, 2022, https://genderstudies.nd.edu/about/history/.

32. Cited in Karen Sikorski, "Carole Moore Lectures on Feminism," *The Observer*, February 26, 1976, 4, http://archives.nd.edu/observer/v10/1976-02-26_v10_094.pdf, 4.

33. Carrie Gates, "'Ways of Seeing and Changing the World': Gender Studies Program Marks 30 Years of Rigorous, Interdisciplinary Study and a Commitment to Social Justice," University of Notre Dame, College of Arts and Letters, February 18, 2019, https://al.nd.edu/news/latest-news/ways-of-seeing-and-changing-the-world-gender-studies-program-marks-30-years-of-rigorous-interdisciplinary-study-and-a-commitment-to-social-justice/.

34. Cited in Rauenhorst, "ND Offers Women's Courses," 7.

35. Slade, "Notre Dame Women are 'Special Breed.'"

Potholes

1. Nora Roberts, *Vision in White* (New York: Berkley Books, 2009), 218.

2. Jen Wulf, "Bottoms Up," *Scholastic*, November 20, 2008, 14–19, https://archives.nd.edu/Scholastic/VOL_0150/VOL_0150_ISSUE_0005.pdf, 16. See also John F. Quinn, "'It's Fashionable Here to Be a Total Abstainer': Temperance Advocacy at the University of Notre Dame, 1870–1940," *American Catholic Studies* 100 (Spring–Winter 1999), 1–27, http://www.jstor.org/stable/44195578.

3. Ed Cohen, "Sobering Debate," *Notre Dame Magazine*, Summer 2002, 5.

4. Gary Sieber, "Sobering Notoriety," *Notre Dame Magazine*, Spring 1997, 3.

5. Henry Wechsler, Jae Eun Lee, Meichun Kuo, and Hang Lee, "College Binge Drinking in the 1990s: A Continuing Problem: Results of the Harvard School of Public Health 1999 College Alcohol Study," *Journal of American College Health* 48, no, 5 (March 2000): 199–210, https://www.tandfonline.com/doi/abs/10.1080/07448480009599305.

6. Christine M. Dietz, "Development of Binge Drinking Behavior in College Students: A Developmental Analysis," *Graduate Journal of Counseling Psychology* 1, no. 1 (Spring 2008): 86–96, https://www.marquette.edu/library/gjcp/86_96-dietz.pdf, 88 and 91–94.

7. Henry Wechsler, *Binge Drinking on America's College Campuses: Findings from the Harvard School of Public Health College Alcohol Study* (Boston: Harvard School of Public Health and Robert Wood Johnson Foundation, 2000), http://archive.sph.harvard.edu/cas/Documents/monograph_2000/cas_mono_2000.pdf, 4.

8. Sieber, "Sobering Notoriety," 3.

9. Thomas McNally "Alcoholism and Notre Dame," *The Observer*, October 3, 1973, 5, https://archives.nd.edu/Observer/v08/1973-10-03_v08_021.pdf.

10. Cited in McNally, "Alcoholism and Notre Dame," 5.

11. Hazelden Betty Ford Foundation, "Stages of Alcoholism," Hazelden Betty Ford Foundation, March 13, 2019, https://www.hazeldenbettyford.org/articles/stages-of-alcoholism, ¶1.

12. Mayo Clinic, "Alcohol Use Disorder," Mayo Clinic, https://www.mayoclinic.org/diseases-conditions/alcohol-use-disorder/symptoms-causes/syc-20369243.

13. Cited in McNally, "Alcoholism and Notre Dame," 5.

14. McNally, "Alcoholism and Notre Dame," 5

15. Harold M. Schmeck Jr., "U.S. Report Says Top Drug Problem Is Alcohol Abuse," *The New York Times*, February 19, 1972, https://www.nytimes.com/1972/02/19/archives/us-report-says-top-drug-problem-is-alcohol-abuse-lives-of-9-million.html.

16. Fred P. Graham, "National Commission to Propose Legal Private Use of Marijuana," *The New York Times*, February 13, 1972, https://www.nytimes.com/1972/02/13/archives/national-commission-to-propose-legal-private-use-of-marijuana.html.

17. *The New York Times*, "Gallup Finds Rise in Marijuana Use," *The New York Times*, February 6, 1972, 36, https://www.nytimes.com/1972/02/06/archives/gallup-finds-rise-in-marijuana-use-51-of-college-students-say-they.html.

18. Cited in McNally, "Alcoholism," 5.

19. Jerry Lutkus, "Macheca Clarifies Drug Policy," *The Observer*, October 17, 1973, 1, http://archives.nd.edu/observer/1973-10-17_v08_031.pdf.

20. Fred Graver and Tom Drape, "Drug Raids Hit Three Halls: In St. Eds, Dillon and Grace," *The Observer*, October 16, 1973, 1, http://archives.nd.edu/observer/1973-10-16_v08_030.pdf.

21. Patrick Hanfin, "SLC Considers Student Paranoia," *The Observer*, October 16, 1973, 1, http://archives.nd.edu/observer/1973-10-16_v08_030.pdf, 1.

22. David P. Kraft, "One Hundred Years of College Mental Health," *Journal of American College Health* 59, no. 6 (June 8, 2011): 477–481, https://www.tandfonline.com/doi/full/10.1080/07448481.2011.569964, 477.

23. Dana L. Farnsworth, *Mental Health in College and University* (Cambridge, MA: Harvard University Press, 1957), and Rob Danzman, "CAPS and Other Counseling Services for College Students: Insider's Guide to On-Campus Support," Motivate Counseling, August 28, 2019, https://motivatecounseling.com/caps-and-other-counseling-services-for-college-students-insiders-guide-to-on-campus-support/, ¶3.

24. "Report of the Committee to Evaluate Coeducation" cited in Zurblis, *Notre Dame Report: '76–'77*, vol. 6, no. 16, 367–395.

25. Cited in Sieber, "Sobering Notoriety," 3.

26. "Report of the Committee to Evaluate Coeducation" cited in Zurblis, *Notre Dame Report: '76–'77*, vol. 6, no. 16, 375.

27. Dorothy V. Corson, *A Cave of Candles: The Story Behind the Notre Dame Grotto* (Nappanee, IN: Evangel Author Services, 2006), https://www3.nd.edu/~wcawley/corson/cors019.htm, ¶36.

28. Danzman, "CAPS and Other Counseling Services for College Students," ¶6, citing the American College Health Association, *American College Health Association-National College Health Assessment II: Undergraduate Student Reference Group: Executive Summary* (Silver Spring, MD: American College Health Association, 2018), https://www.acha.org/documents/ncha/NCHA-II_Fall_2018_Undergraduate_Reference_Group_Executive_Summary.pdf, and María del C. Fernández Rodríguez and Ivonne Bayron Huertas, "Suicide Prevention in College Students: A Collaborative Approach," *Interamerican Journal of Psychology* 47, no. 1 (2013): 53–60, https://www.ncbi.nlm.nih.gov/pmc/articles/PMC3809451/.

29. *South Bend Tribune*, "Family Sues Notre Dame Over Student's 2015 Suicide," *South Bend Tribune*, January 24, 2017, https://www.southbendtribune.com/story/news/crime/2017/01/24/family-sues-notre-dame-over-students-2015-suicide/45810153/.

30. Stacy St. Clair and Todd Lighty, "Notre Dame Football Coach Responds to Allegation of Sex Attack by Player," *Chicago Tribune*, November 21, 2010, https://www.chicagotribune.com/news/ct-xpm-2010-11-21-ct-met-notre-dame-folo-1122-20101121-story.html.

31. Griffin, *The Pocket-Size God*, 58–61.

Driving Defensively

1. Brené Brown, *The Gifts of Imperfection* (Center City, MN: Hazelden Publishing, 2010), 6.

2. Dolores Liebeler, "N. D. Girls — A New Era," *South Bend Tribune*, September 3, 1972.

3. Cited in McGinn, "Burtchael [*sic*] Praises Barkett Letter," 1.

4. Darin, "Hesburgh Vows Co-Ed Increase."

5. For several articles about the issue in 1972 and 1972, see Bob Higgins, "On Bulls and Birth Control," *The Observer*, October 25, 1972, 1, https://archives.nd.edu/Observer/v07/1972-10-25_v07_034.pdf; Greg Rowinski, "University Accused of Pro-Abortion Stand," *The Observer*, October 12, 1973, 1, https://archives.nd.edu/Observer/v08/1973-10-12_v08_028.pdf; Theodore M. Hesburgh and Edmund A. Stephan, untitled editorial, *The Observer*, October 12, 1973, 1, https://archives.nd.edu/Observer/v08/1973-10-12_v08_028.pdf; and Charles R. Rice, "A Call to Condemn Abortion," *The Observer*, October 31, 1973, 7, https://archives.nd.edu/Observer/v08/1973-10-31_v08_037.pdf.

6. *Dobbs v. Jackson Women's Health Organization*, 597 U.S. ___ (2022), 2.
Maurizio Valsania, "Abortion Decision Cherry-Picks History — When the US Constitution Was Ratified, Women Had Much More Autonomy Over Abortion Decisions Than During 19th Century," *The Conversation*, July 6, 2022, https://theconversation.com/abortion-decision-cherry-picks-history-when-the-us-constitution-was-ratified-women-had-much-more-autonomy-over-abortion-decisions-than-during-19th-century-185947, ¶1–¶2 under "18th-Century Woman: Active and in Control." See also Joshua Zeitz, "The Supreme Court's Faux 'Originalism,'" *Politico*, June 26, 2022, https://www.politico.com/news/magazine/2022/06/26/conservative-supreme-court-gun-control-00042417?cid=apn.

7. Leslie J. Reagan, *When Abortion Was a Crime: Women, Medicine, and Law in the United States, 1867–1973* (Oakland: University of California Press, 1997, 2022); Mary Ziegler, *Abortion and the Law in America:* Roe v. Wade *to the Present* (Cambridge, UK, and New York: Cambridge University Press, 2020); and Mary Ziegler, *Dollars for Life: The Anti-Abortion Movement and the Fall of the Republican Establishment* (New Haven, CT: Yale University Press, 2022).

8. John Nagy, "Student Health Facilities, Image Catch up with Quality of Care," *Notre Dame Magazine*, Spring 2007, 11–12, https://magazine.nd.edu/stories/student-health-facilities-image-catch-up-with-quality-of-care/.

9. Michele Tate, "Calvin Named First Woman Doctor at Infirmary," *The Observer*, September 11, 1973, 7, http://www.archives.nd.edu/observer/1973-09-11_v08_005.pdf.

10. Shawn Scannell, "Flu Epidemic Hits ND–SMC: Infirmary Swamped," *The Observer*, January 29, 1975, 6, http://archives.nd.edu/observer/1975-01-29_v09_069.pdf.

11. "Report of the Committee to Evaluate Coeducation" cited in Zurblis, *Notre Dame Report: '76–'77*, vol. 6, no. 16, 386.

12. Cited in Maggie Waltman, "No Gynecologists Needed: Infirmary Little Changed Since Co-Education," *The Observer*, January 15, 1976, 1, 3, 9, https://archives.nd.edu/Observer/1976-01-15_v10_064.pdf, 9.

13. Hofman, interview.

14. Boston Women's Health Book Collective, *Our Bodies Ourselves: A Book by and for Women*, 2nd ed. (New York: Simon and Schuster, 1973), 3, *italics original*.

15. Ann Therese Darin, "Masters & Johnson Pack Washington Hall," *The Observer*, October 24, 1972, 1, http://archives.nd.edu/observer/1972-10-24_v07_033.pdf.

16. Christopher P. Krebs, Christine H. Lindquist, Tara D. Warner, Bonnie S. Fisher, and Sandra L. Martin, *The Campus Sexual Assault (CSA) Study* (Washington, DC: National Institute of Justice, 2007), https://www.ojp.gov/pdffiles1/nij/grants/221153.pdf, viii.

17. Kathy Mills, "Rapes Increase on College Campuses: Lone Female Most Attractive," *The Observer*, April 10, 1975, 7, http://archives.nd.edu/observer/1975-04-10_v09_111.pdf.

18. Krebs, et al., *The Campus Sexual Assault (CSA) Study*. See also Bonnie S. Fisher, Francis T. Cullen, and Michael G. Turner, *The Sexual Victimization of College Women* (Washington, DC: US Department of Justice, 2000), https://www.ojp.gov/pdffiles1/nij/182369.pdf, and Charlene L. Muehlenhard, Zoë D. Peterson, Terry P. Humphreys, and Kristen N. Jozkowski, "Evaluating the One-in-Five Statistic: Women's Risk of Sexual Assault While in College," *Journal of Sex Research* 54, no. 4 (May 16, 2017): 549–576, 565, https://doi.org/10.1080/00224499.2017.1295014.

19. See, for example, RAINN, "Women Ages 18-24 Are at an Elevated Risk of Sexual Violence," RAINN, 2022, https://www.rainn.org/statistics/campus-sexual-violence; Darrell J. Steffensmeier, Renee Hoffman Steffensmeier, and Alvin S. Rosenthal, "Trends in Female Violence, 1960–1977," *Sociological Focus* 12, no. 3 (August 1979): 217–227; Anya Kamenetz, "The History of Campus Sexual Assault," NPR, November 30, 2014, https://www.npr.org/sections/ed/2014/11/30/366348383/the-history-of-campus-sexual-assault; and Kyla Bishop., "A Reflection on the History of Sexual Assault Laws in the United States," *The Arkansas Journal of Social Change and Public Service*, April 15, 2018, https://ualr.edu/socialchange/2018/04/15/reflection-history-sexual-assault-laws-united-states/.

20. "Report of the Committee to Evaluate Coeducation" cited in Zurblis, *Notre Dame Report: '76–'77*, vol. 6, no. 16, 386.

21. Helen Tierney, ed., *Women's Studies Encyclopedia*, revised and expanded ed., vol. A–F (Westport, CT: Greenwood Publishing Group, 1999), 337.

22. Susan Brownmiller, *Against Our Will: Men, Women and Rape* (New York: Simon and Schuster, 1975), 257.

23. Chris Meehan, "Sexual Offenses Committee Meets in McCandless," *The Observer*, October 10, 1974, 2, https://archives.nd.edu/Observer/v09/1974-10-10_v09_031.pdf; Maureen Flynn, "ND Law Students Propose Change in Rape Law," *The Observer*, November 18, 1974, 3, https://archives.nd.edu/Observer/v09/1974-11-18_v09_050.pdf; Maureen Flynn, "Sex Offense Committee Seeking Volunteers: Program Offers Help to Victims," *The Observer*, March 18, 1975, 10, https://archives.nd.edu/Observer/v09/1974-11-18_v09_050.pdf.

24. Cited in Murphy, "Women Officers Complement Security Force," 5.

25. Val Zurblis," Assault Cases Examined: Occurred this semester," *The Observer*, April 10, 1975, 6, http://archives.nd.edu/observer/1975-04-10_v09_111.pdf.

26. Pat Cuneo, "Administration to Revamp Campus Lighting: For Benefit of Student Safety, Security," *The Observer*, April 10, 1975, 1, http://archives.nd.edu/observer/1975-04-10_v09_111.pdf.

27. University of Notre Dame, *2016 Sexual Conduct and Campus Climate Questionnaire Report* (Notre Dame, IN: University of Notre Dame, 2016), https://titleix.nd.edu/assets/231426/2016_sexual_conduct_and_climate_questionnaire_report_final.pdf.

28. Office for Civil Rights, *Questions and Answers on the Title IX Regulations on Sexual Harassment* (Washington, DC: United States Department of Education, July 2021, updated June 28, 2022), https://www2.ed.gov/about/offices/list/ocr/docs/202107-qa-titleix.pdf, 4.

29. *The Palm Beach Post*, "Air Force Fights Cadet Sex Flaps While Army, Navy Go Unscathed," *The Palm Beach Post*, March 30, 2003, 6A.

30. 50 Women at Yale 150, "A Timeline of Women at Yale."

31. Courtney Becker, "Student Performance Promotes Discussion: *Loyal Daughters and Sons* Show Encourages Conversations on Gender, Relationships and Identity," *The Observer*, 1, 5, April 7, 2006, http://archives.nd.edu/observer/v41/2006-11-17_v41_056.pdf, and Eileen Duffy, "Play Reveals Prevalence of Assault," *The Observer*, 1, 6, November 17, 2006, http://archives.nd.edu/observer/v41/2006-11-17_v41_056.pdf.

32. Emily Weisbecker, "*Loyal Daughters*: Sexuality and Sexual Assault" (Boehnen Award, Gender Studies Program with help from the Undergraduate Research Opportunities Program, Notre Dame, IN, November 2006).

Roadside Assistance

1. Maya Angelou, *Letter to My Daughter* (New York: Random House, 2009), xii.

2. Anthony Abowd, "Class of '76 Sets Full Quotas: Marks First Year for Female Domers," *The Observer*, September 2, 1972, 1, http://archives.nd.edu/observer/1972-09-02_v07_001.pdf.

3. Cited in Abowd, "Class of '76 Sets Full Quotas," 1.

4. Abowd, "Class of '76 Sets Full Quotas."

5. Cited in Joel Burian, "Freshman Year Office Offers Career Seminar for Women," *The Observer*, March 26, 1974, 3, http://archives.nd.edu/observer/1974-03-26_v08_098.pdf, 3.

6. Undergraduate Career Services Meruelo Family Center for Career Development, "About Us," University of Notre Dame, 2022, https://undergradcareers.nd.edu/about-us/.

7. *The Observer*, "Placement Bureau Begins Sessions," *The Observer*, September 20, 1972, 3, http://archives.nd.edu/observer/1972-09-20_v07_009.pdf.

Under the Dome Light

1. Ayn Rand, *The Fountainhead* (New York: New American Library and Berkley, 1943), 11.

2. Pat Flynn, "Varied Liturgies Prevail at ND," *The Observer*, October 2, 1974, 3, http://archives.nd.edu/observer/1974-10-02_v09_025.pdf.

3. John Nagy, "An Extraordinary Liturgy Returns to Campus," *Notre Dame Magazine*, Winter 2007–08, https://magazine.nd.edu/stories/an-extraordinary-liturgy-returns-to-campus/, and Wilson D. Miscamble, *American Priest: The Ambitious Life and Conflicted Legacy of Notre Dame's Father Ted Hesburgh* (New York: Image and Crown Publishing Group, 2019).

4. Thomas McNally and William G. Storey, eds., *Day by Day: The Notre Dame Prayerbook for Students* (Notre Dame, IN: Ave Maria Press, 1975).

5. Heidi Schlumpf, ed., *The Notre Dame Book of Prayer* (Notre Dame, IN: Ave Maria Press, 2010), and Michael O. Garvey, "A New Prayer Book for Notre Dame Pilgrims," *Notre Dame News*, October 22, 2010, https://news.nd.edu/news/a-new-prayer-book-for-notre-dame-pilgrims/.

6. John Monczunski, "God? Country? Notre Dame?," *Notre Dame Magazine*, Spring 2001, 42, and https://magazine.nd.edu/stories/rotc-at-notre-dame/, ¶3–¶5. See also Brendan O'Shaughnessy, "God, Country, Notre Dame: The University's Long, Close History with

Military Service," University of Notre Dame, 2016, https://www.nd.edu/stories/history-of-nd-and-military/.

7. J.P. Hickey, "1924: T.L Hickey Built Notre Dame's World War I Memorial—Sacred Heart Church's East Entry," Tom and Kate Hickey Family History, May 26, 2014, updated May 30, 2016, http://tomandkatehickeyfamilyhistory.blogspot.com/, ¶1 under "Sacred Heart Church East Entrance, 1912," and Notre Dame Archives, "World War I Memorial Door," *Notre Dame Archives News and Notes*, May 30, 2016, http://archives.nd.edu/about/news/index.php/2016/world-war-i-memorial-door/.

8. Cited in *Notre Dame Daily*, "Memorial to War Heroes Dedicated: Father Walsh Speaks Before Field Mass; Col. Hoynes Leads Parade," *Notre Dame Daily*, May 1, 1924, 1, 4, http://archives.nd.edu/Daily/ND_Daily_1924-05-31_V2-126.pdf, 1.

9. Monczunski, "God? Country? Notre Dame?"; O'Shaughnessy, "God, Country, Notre Dame"; Office of Military and Veterans Affairs, "The University of Notre Dame and the U.S. Military," University of Notre Dame, 2022, https://omva.nd.edu/about/history/.

10. Mike Chiari, "Navy to Host Notre Dame Football Game for 1st Time in 94 Years Due to COVID-19," *Bleacher Report*, June 2, 2020, https://bleacherreport.com/articles/2894474-navy-to-host-notre-dame-football-game-for-1st-time-in-94-years-due-to-covid-19.

11. Monczunski, "God? Country? Notre Dame?," and O'Shaughnessy, "God, Country, Notre Dame."

12. Brandon O' Connor, "Forty Years Have Passed Since the First Women Graduated from West Point in the Class of 1980," US Army, May 27, 2020, https://www.army.mil/article/235994/forty_years_have_passed_since_the_first_women_graduated_from_west_point_in_the_class_of_1980, and Jennifer Silva, "Women in the Military: Through the Decades: Women Have a Larger Presence in Our Military Today Than Ever Before," *The Huffington Post*, March 15, 2017, updated March 20, 2017, https://www.huffpost.com/entry/women-in-the-military-through-the-decades_b_58c9630fe4b05675ee9c5c55.

13. Guy De Sapio, "Hesburgh Returns to Face Problems Hears Campus Leaders Air Grievances Reveals His Standing with Trustees," *The Observer*, October 2, 1969, 1, 8, https://archives.nd.edu/Observer/v04/1969-10-02_v04_013.pdf; *The Observer*, "Arson Attempt Fails," *The Observer*, November 9, 1970, 3, https://archives.nd.edu/Observer/v05/1970-11-09_v05_043.pdf; University of Notre Dame, "Father Hesburgh President Emeritus: The 1960s and Student Activism," University of Notre Dame, 2022, https://hesburgh.nd.edu/fr-teds-life/the-notre-dame-president/the-60s-and-student-activism/; and Robert Schmuhl, "Seven Days in May," *Notre Dame Magazine*, Winter 1989–90, https://magazine.nd.edu/stories/seven-days-in-may/.

14. Iver Peterson, "R.O.T.C. Apparently Making Cautious Comeback at Many Colleges," *The New York Times*, October 25, 1973, 36, https://www.nytimes.com/1973/10/25/archives/rotc-apparently-making-cautious-comeback-at-many-colleges-talk-of.html, ¶3 under "Talk of Reconsideration."

15. *The Observer*, "Two Girls Join Air Force ROTC," *The Observer*, October 16, 1972, 7, http://archives.nd.edu/observer/1972-10-16_v07_027.pdf.

16. Arnold Air Society, "About Us," Arnold Air Society, n.d., https://aas-sw.org/aboutus/, ¶2.

17. Cited in Leanne Jacques, "ND's Angel Flight Takes Top Honors," *The Observer*, February 21, 1974, 5, http://archives.nd.edu/observer/1974-02-21_v08_084.pdf, 5.

18. Jacques, "ND's Angel Flight Takes Top Honors," 5.

19. Cited in McCormick, "Eldest Daughters Come Home."

Mile Markers

1. Anita Desai, *Clear Light of Day* (Boston and New York: Mariner Books, 2000), 36.

2. These students were elected individually, rather than as a slate of officers. Lee E. Klosinski, "Freshmen Officers Elected: Bradley Wins Presidency," *The Observer*, October 13, 1972, 3, http://archives.nd.edu/observer/1972-10-13_v07_026.pdf.

3. 50 Golden Years, "Panel Discussion: In Their Own Words," University of Notre Dame, https://50goldenyears.nd.edu/featured-events/panel-discussion-in-their-own-words/, ¶6.

4. Augusto Grace, letter to the editor, "What About the Girls?," *The Observer*, November 22, 1974, 10, http://archives.nd.edu/observer/1974-11-22_v09_054.pdf, 10.

5. Terry Keelan, "Junior Parents Weekend Outlined: Hesburgh dinner," *The Observer*, February 21, 1975, 5, https://archives.nd.edu/Observer/v09/1975-02-21_v09_086.pdf, and *The Observer*, "Junior Parents Weekend Includes Workshop Series," *The Observer*, February 25, 1975, 2, https://archives.nd.edu/Observer/v09/1975-02-25_v09_088.pdf.

6. Maggie Waltman, "Senior Death March Resurrected," *The Observer*, November 6, 1975, 3, http://archives.nd.edu/observer/1975-11-06_v10_047.pdf.

7. *The Observer*, "Four Years Later: Time to Set new Goals," *The Observer*, March 10, 1976, 5, http://archives.nd.edu/observer/1976-03-10_v10_103.pdf.

8. Valerie Zurblis, "How Women Have Become Part of the ND Community," *The Observer*, March 10, 1976, 6–7, http://archives.nd.edu/observer/1976-03-10_v10_103.pdf.

9. Jim Commyn, "Looking Back: The First Year at Notre Dame," *The Observer*, March 10, 1976, 5, http://archives.nd.edu/observer/1976-03-10_v10_103.pdf.

10. Cited in Commyn, "Looking Back: The First Year at Notre Dame," 5.

11. Zurblis, How Women Have Become Part of the ND Community," 6–7.

12. Cited in Slade, "Notre Dame Women are 'Special Breed,'" 73.

13. Cited in Notre Dame Report: '76–'77, vol. 6, no. 16, 393.

14. Marianne O'Connor, "Valedictorian's Address," cited in Mary Catherine Stevens, ed., *Notre Dame Report: '73–'74*, vol. 3, no. 18 (Notre Dame, IN: University of Notre Dame, Department of Information Services, June 7, 1974), https://archives.nd.edu/ndr/NDR-03/NDR-1974-06-07.pdf, 345.

15. Val Zurblis, "Dome," *The Observer*, April 23, 1976, 7, http://archives.nd.edu/observer/1976-04-23_v10_122.pdf.

16. Zurblis, "Dome," 7.

Passing with Care

1. Cited in Ian Schwartz, "Lou Holtz on U.S.: We Aren't Where We Ought to Be, 'But Thank God We Aren't Where We Used to Be,'" RealClear Politics, January 6, 2018, https://www.realclearpolitics.com/video/2018/01/06/lou_holtz_on_us_we_arent_where_we_ought_to_be_but_thank_god_we_arent_where_we_used_to_be.html, ¶2.

Are We There Yet?

1. Cited in Joshua Barajas, "After RBG's Death, This Poet Urges Us to Follow in Her Footsteps," *PBS Newshour*, September 24, 2020, https://www.pbs.org/newshour/arts/poetry/after-rbgs-death-this-poet-urges-us-to-follow-in-her-steps, ¶2.

2. Cited in University of Notre Dame Archives, "Father Hesburgh Life and Legacy: Teaching, Research, and Faculty Growth," University of Notre Dame, 2022, https://hesburgh-portal.nd.edu/story-academic-teaching.html, ¶2 under "Faculty Growth."

3. Lutkus, "The Era of Coeducation: The First Women at Notre Dame."

4. Darin, "Hesburgh Vows Co-Ed Increase."

5. Nancy Armour, "Notre Dame Celebrates 25 Years of Coeducation."

6. 50 Golden Years, "Selected Women's Firsts at Notre Dame," University of Notre Dame, 2022, https://50goldenyears.nd.edu/news-and-features/selected-womens-firsts-of-notre-dame/.

7. O'Connor's "Valedictorian's Address" cited in Stevens, *Notre Dame Report: '73–'74*, vol. 3, no. 18, 345.

8. Warth, "PE Trailblazer Cordes Recognized with Hall of Fame Induction."

9. "Introductory Address at Eucharistic Celebration on the Tenth Anniversary of Coeducation" cited in Marianne Murphy, ed., *Notre Dame Report: '81–'81*, vol. 11, no. 16 (Notre Dame, IN: University of Notre Dame, Department of Information Services, May 7, 1982), 427–428, https://archives.nd.edu/ndr/NDR-11/NDR-1982-05-07.pdf, 428.

10. Synnott, "A Friendly Rivalry," 124–125.

11. Cited in McCormick, "Eldest Daughters Come Home," 3.

12. McCormick, "Eldest Daughters Come Home," 5.

Daniel Saracino, then-assistant provost for enrollment at the University of Notre Dame, said in response to *The Wall Street Journal* article: "I read it. I thought about it. I don't think I've picked it up since....It doesn't change what we do....Part of me would say, 'big deal.'" Cited in Patrick Cooper, "A League of our own?," *The Daily Northwestern*, April 11, 2001, https://dailynorthwestern.com/2001/04/11/archive-manual/a-league-of-our-own/, ¶3. See also Elizabeth Bernstein, "Schools Once Considered Backups Become as Selective as Ivy League," *The Wall Street Journal*, March 30, 2001, https://www.wsj.com/articles/SB985901932212288573; Ronald Alsop, "Under the Radar: We Asked Recruiters to Tell Us Their 'Hidden Gems' — Less-Heralded Schools with Great Graduates. Here Are 10 of Them," *The Wall Street Journal*, April 30, 2001, https://www.wsj.com/articles/SB988144405553657026; *The Wall Street Journal*, "Top 10 Small Schools," *The Wall Street Journal*, April 30, 2001, https://www.wsj.com/articles/SB988146417263798447; and *The Wall Street Journal*, "Top 10 Private Schools," *The Wall Street Journal*, April 30, 2001, https://www.wsj.com/articles/SB988218397174322672.

13. Mark McAdams and Ken Hafertepe, "Canty Tops Graham in SG Election," *The Hoya*, February 17, 1977, 1, https://repository.library.georgetown.edu/bitstream/handle/10822/555001/1977-02-17.pdf?sequence=1&isAllowed=y.

14. Sonia Rao, "Three Female Presidents Discuss Leadership," *The Observer*, 1, 6, November 30, 2006, http://archives.nd.edu/observer/2006-11-30_v41_059.pdf.

15. Cited in Megan Strader, "First Female Student Body President Elected," *Notre Dame Magazine*, Spring 2001, https://magazine.nd.edu/stories/first-female-student-body-president-elected/, ¶16.

16. Norton cited in Rao, "Three Female Presidents Discuss Leadership," 6.

17. Bishop cited in Rao, "Three Female Presidents Discuss Leadership," 6.

18. See Kathleen McDonnell, "Play, Groups Examine Sexual Assault: Post-Performance Panel Searches for Solutions," *The Observer*, November 16, 2006, 1, 9, https://archives.nd.edu/Observer/v41/2006-11-15_v41_054.pdf; Maddie Hanna, "Play, Groups Examine Sexual Assault: New Committee Works to Extend Dialogue," *The Observer*, November 16, 2006, 1, 6, https://

archives.nd.edu/Observer/v41/2006-11-15_v41_054.pdf; and Kate Antonacci, "Sexual Assault Advisory Committee Aims to Increase Resources, Awareness," *The Observer*, November 16, 2006, 1, 8, https://archives.nd.edu/Observer/v41/2006-11-15_v41_054.pdf.

19. Personal observation while attending these events.

20. Katie O. Washington, "Katie Washington Valedictory Address," *Notre Dame News*, May 18, 2010, https://news.nd.edu/news/katie-washington-valedictory-address/, ¶2.

21. US Bureau of Labor Statistics, "A Look at Women's Education and Earnings Since the 1970s," *TED: The Economics Daily*, December 27, 2017, https://www.bls.gov/opub/ted/2017/a-look-at-womens-education-and-earnings-since-the-1970s.htm?view_full, ¶1.

22. Michael O. Garvey, "Discussion to Celebrate 40th Anniversary of Coeducation at Notre Dame," *Notre Dame News*, October 31, 2012, https://news.nd.edu/news/discussion-to-celebrate-40th-anniversary-of-coeducation-at-notre-dame/.

23. Hesburgh, interview.

24. Cited in Emma Ferdinandi, David Korzeniowski, Genevieve Redsten, and Daphne Saloomey, "Becoming the Leprechaun," *Scholastic*, September 19, 2019, https://scholastic.nd.edu/issues/becoming-the-leprechaun-2019-mascot-cast-reflects/, ¶9 under "Lynnette Wukie."

25. Giving to Notre Dame, "Hesburgh Women of Impact," University of Notre Dame, 2022, https://giving.nd.edu/priorities/womens-initiative/, ¶4–¶5.

26. William G. Gilroy, "Notre Dame's Grace Watkins and Alexis Doyle Named Rhodes Scholars," University of Notre Dame Office of Public Affairs and Communications, 2016, https://www.nd.edu/stories/rhodes-scholars-2017/.

27. American Bar Association, "Ann Claire Williams: 2018 Fellows Honoree," American Bar Association, 2018, https://www.americanbar.org/groups/young_lawyers/leadership/fellows/ann-claire-williams/, ¶2.

28. *Catholic Courier*, "Judge Barrett's Nomination Gives Spotlight to Notre Dame Law School," *Catholic Courier*, September 28, 2020, https://catholiccourier.com/articles/judge-barretts-nomination-gives-spotlight-to-notre-dame-law-school/. See also John Nagy, "The Education of Amy Coney Barrett," *Notre Dame Magazine*, Winter 2020–21, https://magazine.nd.edu/stories/the-education-of-amy-coney-barrett/.

29. Don Bishop, associate vice president of undergraduate enrollment, cited in *College Bound*, "The Talk About the Class of 2022: Inside Admissions Offices," *College Bound* 32, no. 9 (May 2018): 1–2 and 4, https://ftp.collegeboundnews.com/17-18issues/May18.pdf, 4.

30. Fosmoe, "Fresh Approaches," 7.

31. Dan Reagan, "Grow Up and Grow Deep," *Notre Dame Magazine*, January 23, 2013, https://magazine.nd.edu/stories/grow-up-and-grow-deep/, ¶9.

The Wheels Keep Turning

1. Rusty Berkus and Christa Wollan, *Life Is a Gift* (Encino, CA: Red Rose Press, 1982), 54.

2. Cited in Jim Ferry, "Alumni Told Patience Needed," *The Observer*, October 3, 1972, 1, 7, http://archives.nd.edu/observer/1972-10-03_v07_018.pdf, 1.

3. "Report of the Committee to Evaluate Coeducation" cited in Zurblis, *Notre Dame Report: '76–'77*, vol. 6, no. 16, 388.

4. Nancy Weiss Malkiel, *"Keep the Damned Women Out": The Struggle for Coeducation* (New Haven, CT: Princeton University Press, 2016), 246.

5. Edmund Joyce, interview with author, October 5, 2000.

6. William Sexton, interview with author, October 5, 2000.

7. Kerry Temple, "The Impact of the Generations Campaign," *Notre Dame Magazine*, Autumn 2001, https://magazine.nd.edu/stories/the-impact-of-the-generations-campaign/, ¶16.

8. Carol Elliott, "Brogan Awards Given to Top Five Women MBA students," University of Notre Dame Mendoza College of Business, May 3, 2019, https://mendoza.nd.edu/news/brogan-awards-given-to-five-women-mba-students/.

9. Tom Molnar, Noelle Stohler, Ellen Roof, and the Office of Development, unpublished data, September 2, 2020.

10. ND Alumni and Friends, "James E. Armstrong Award," University of Notre Dame, n.d., https://my.nd.edu/page/armstrong/, ¶1.

11. ND Alumni and Friends, "The Dr. Thomas A. Dooley Award," University of Notre Dame, n.d., https://my.nd.edu/page/dooley, ¶1.

12. ND Alumni and Friends, "The Rev. John J. Cavanaugh, C.S.C., Award," University of Notre Dame, n.d., https://my.nd.edu/page/cavanaugh, ¶1.

13. ND Alumni and Friends, "The Rev. Anthony J. Lauck, C.S.C., Award," University of Notre Dame, n.d., https://my.nd.edu/page/lauck, ¶1.

14. ND Alumni and Friends, "The Rev. Edward Frederick Sorin, C.S.C., Award," University of Notre Dame, n.d., https://my.nd.edu/page/sorin, ¶1.

15. ND Alumni and Friends, "Distinguished Alumnus Award," University of Notre Dame, n.d., https://my.nd.edu/page/distinguished-alumnus, ¶1. The gendered language of the title of this award, however, perhaps remains problematic.

16. ND Alumni and Friends, "Volunteer of the Year Award," University of Notre Dame, n.d., https://my.nd.edu/page/volunteer-of-the-year, ¶1.

17. Brendan O'Shaughnessy, "Dolly Duffy Appointed New Executive Director of Notre Dame Alumni Association," *Notre Dame News*, February 1, 2011, https://news.nd.edu/news/dolly-duffy-appointed-new-executive-director-of-notre-dame-alumni-association/.

18. Cited in Natalie Weber, "Alumni Association Honors Rohr's Bartender," *The Observer*, October 28, 2016, 3, https://issuu.com/the-observer/docs/finished_template_10-28-2016, 3.

19. University of Notre Dame, "The Shirt: History of the Shirt," University of Notre Dame, 2022, https://theshirt.nd.edu/, ¶1 under "The Beginning."

20. University of Notre Dame, "The Shirt: 2018," University of Notre Dame, 2022, https://theshirt.nd.edu/history/timeline/2018/, ¶1.

21. The Shirt 2022 Designers, "The Shirt 2022 Design Story," University of Notre Dame, April 25, 2022, https://theshirt.nd.edu/blog/the-shirt-2022-design-story/.

22. Martin Lam Nguyen, "Sign of Our Mission: On Holy Cross Cemetery," University of Notre Dame, 2022, http://faith.nd.edu/s/1210/faith/interior.aspx?sid=1210&gid=609&pgid=44556&cid=85974&ecid=85974&crid=0&calpgid=44242&calcid=85757, ¶4.

23. Austin I. Collins, "Tour of Holy Cross Cemetery," University of Notre Dame, June 2, 2022, https://50goldenyears.nd.edu/featured-events/tour-of-holy-cross-cemetery/.

Applying the Brakes

1. Eddie Cantor with Jane Kesner Ardmore, *Take My Life* (Garden City, NY: Doubleday and Company, 1957), 13.

2. Andrew M. Greeley, *The Changing Catholic College* (New Brunswick, NJ: Transaction Publishers, 2013), 91.

3. Josh Moody, "10 Universities with the Biggest Endowments," *U.S. News and World Report*, September 21, 2021, https://www.usnews.com/education/best-colleges/the-short-list-college/articles/10-universities-with-the-biggest-endowments.

4. George Eckes, "Tuition May Increase 'Hundreds': Inflation Cited as Major Cause," *The Observer*, February 18, 1975, 1, http://archives.nd.edu/observer/v09/1975-02-18_v09_083.pdf; Brendan O'Shaughnessy, "Notre Dame Tuition Increase Same as Previous Year's," *Notre Dame Magazine*, February 13, 2013, https://news.nd.edu/news/notre-dame-tuition-increase-same-as-previous-years-3/; and Brian Bingham, "The Economics of Higher Education: Increasing Tuition and Endowments," *Fresh Writing* 16 (2016), https://freshwriting.nd.edu/volumes/2016/essays/the-economics-of-higher-education-increasing-tuition-and-endowments.

5. Cited in Teresa A. Porro, ed., *Notre Dame Report: '74–'75*, vol. 4, no. 19 (Notre Dame, IN: University of Notre Dame, Department of Information Services, June 27, 1975), https://archives.nd.edu/ndr/NDR-04/NDR-1975-06-27.pdf, 409.

6. Theodore M. Hesburgh, "Letter to Parents Regarding Tuition Increases," May 20, 1975, from author's personal archive.

7. Hesburgh, "Letter to Parents Regarding Tuition Increases."

8. Cited in Teresa A. Porro, ed., *Notre Dame Report: '74–'75*, vol. 4, no. 5 (Notre Dame, IN: University of Notre Dame, Department of Information Services, November 15, 1974), https://archives.nd.edu/ndr/NDR-04/NDR-1975-06-27.pdf, 131.

9. Tom Coyne, "Notre Dame's Rev. Theodore Hesburgh Dies at 97," *Indy Star*, February 27, 2015, https://www.indystar.com/story/news/education/2015/02/27/notre-dames-rev-theodore-hesburgh-dies/24106659/, ¶18, and Dennis Brown, "Father Theodore Hesburgh of Notre Dame Dies at Age 97," *Notre Dame News*, February 27, 2015, https://news.nd.edu/news/rev-theodorem-hesburgh-c-s-c/, ¶11.

10. See Darlene Cutrona, ed., *Notre Dame Report: '87–'88*, vol. 16, no. 5 (Notre Dame, IN: University of Notre Dame, Department of Public Relations and Information, November 6, 1987), https://archives.nd.edu/ndr/NDR-17/NDR-1987-11-06.pdf, 159, and University of Notre Dame, "Common Data Set 2021–2022," University of Notre Dame, n.d., https://www3.nd.edu/~instres/CDS/2021-2022/CDS_2021-2022.pdf, 3-B1.

11. University of Notre Dame, "National Register of Historic Places Inventory–Nomination Form," National Park Service, May 23, 1978, https://npgallery.nps.gov/NRHP/GetAsset/NRHP/78000053_text, under "7-Description"; National Register of Historic Places, "Indiana: St. Joseph County," *Federal Register* 43, no. 55 (1978): 11762, https://www.govinfo.gov/content/pkg/FR-1978-03-21/pdf/FR-1978-03-21.pdf; and William G. Gilroy, "Golden Dome to Be Regilded for the Tenth Time," *Notre Dame News*, March 3, 2005, https://news.nd.edu/news/golden-dome-to-be-regilded-for-the-tenth-time/.

View through the Windshield

1. Cited in Caroline Hallemann, "Anthony Bourdain's Best Quotes About Life, Travel, and Adventure: The Celebrity Chef and Television Host Has Died. He Was 61-years-old," *Town and Country*, June 8, 2018, https://www.townandcountrymag.com/leisure/dining/a21233639/best-anthony-bourdain-quotes/, ¶4.

2. Dan Reagan, "Letter from Campus: Time to Move On," *Notre Dame Magazine*, Spring 2012, https://magazine.nd.edu/stories/letter-from-campus-time-to-move-on/, ¶11.

3. Cited in Marilyn Hughes, "Going Coed," *South Bend Tribune*, August 24, 1997, A1, A6.

4. Charles Dickens, *A Tale of Two Cities* (London: James Nisbet and Company, 1902), 3.

5. Cited in Catherine Maddux. "You've Come a Long Way, Baby. But It's Still a Man's Game," Voice of America, June 17, 2016, https://www.voanews.com/a/youve-come-along-way-baby-but-its-still-a-mans-game/3380920.html, ¶6.

6. Fosmoe, "Fresh Approaches," 7.

7. Cited in Sarah Cahalan, "A Sisterhood of Sorts," *Notre Dame Magazine*, Summer 2019, https://magazine.nd.edu/stories/a-sisterhood-of-sorts/, ¶12 under "When, Whether…"

8. Princeton University, "Shirley Marie Tilghman: 2001–2013," Princeton University, April 16, 2018, https://pr.princeton.edu/pub/presidents/tilghman/, and Princeton University, "The Presidents of Princeton University," Princeton University, July 18, 2013, https://pr.princeton.edu/pub/presidents/index.html.

9. Patrick Ryan, "Fordham Names First Woman and Layperson to Lead University," *Catholic New York*, February 10, 2022, https://www.cny.org/stories/fordham-names-first-woman-and-layperson-to-lead-university,23421, ¶1.

10. Cited in *U.S. 1* Staff, "Princeton's First Woman President Speaks Out," *U.S. 1*, April 24, 2018, updated January 11, 2022, https://www.communitynews.org/princetoninfo/business/survivalguide/princeton-s-first-woman-president-speaks-out/article_5036a8b8-a4b9-5588-b389-da411544497b.html, ¶6–¶7.

11. *Notre Dame News*, "Notre Dame Commemorates 50th Anniversary of Admission of Undergraduate Women with Redesigned Campus Entry Circle, Change to Lyrics in Renowned Fight Song," *Notre Dame News*, June 3, 2022, https://news.nd.edu/news/notre-dame-commemorates-50th-anniversary-of-admission-of-undergraduate-women-with-redesigned-campus-entry-circle-change-to-lyrics-in-renowned-fight-song/.

12. Dennis Brown, "Notre Dame to Honor Pioneers of Irish Women's Athletics," *Notre Dame News*, June 23, 2022, https://news.nd.edu/news/notre-dame-to-honor-pioneers-of-irish-womens-athletics/, ¶9.

13. Selena Hill, "Top WNBA Salaries vs. NBA Salaries [2019 Update]," *Black Enterprise*, April 12, 2019, https://www.blackenterprise.com/top-wnba-nba-salaries-2019/.

14. Rachel Treisman, "The U.S. National Women's Soccer Team Wins $24 Million in Equal Pay Settlement," NPR, February 22, 2022, https://www.npr.org/2022/02/22/1082272202/women-soccer-contracts-equal-pay-settlement-uswnt, ¶3.

15. Cited in Anne Dilenschneider and Jane Lammers, "The Early Women Athletes Project" (University of Notre Dame, Notre Dame, IN, 2011).

16. Ovid's Latin phrase, *Gutta cavat lapidem, consumitur anulus usu*, from book four of *Epistulae ex Ponto* has been translated as "Dripping water hollows out a stone, a ring is worn away by use." Cited in Ratcliffe, *Oxford Essential Quotations*, https://www.oxfordreference.com/view/10.1093/acref/9780191826719.001.0001/q-oro-ed4-00008060, ¶4.

17. Brown, "Notre Dame to Honor Pioneers of Irish Women's Athletics," ¶1–¶2.

18. Dickens, *A Tale of Two Cities*, 3. Many know the opening sentence of Charles Dickens' novel:

> It was the best of times, it was the worst of times, it was the age of wisdom, it was the age of foolishness, it was the epoch of belief, it was the epoch of incredulity, it was the season of light, it was the season

of darkness, it was the spring of hope, it was the winter of despair, we had everything before us, we had nothing before us, we were all going direct to Heaven, we were all going direct the other way — in short, the period was so far like the present period, that some of its noisiest authorities insisted on its being received, for good or for evil, in the superlative degree of comparison only.

19. Cited in the University Committee on Women Faculty and Students, *Enhancing the Recruitment and Retention of Female Faculty: A Comprehensive Report* (Notre Dame, IN: University of Notre Dame, 2008), https://president.nd.edu/assets/334044/university_committee_on_women_faculty_and_students_final_report.pdf, 12.

20. University Committee on Women Faculty and Students, *Enhancing the Recruitment and Retention of Female Faculty*, 17.

21. University Committee on Women Faculty and Students, *Enhancing the Recruitment and Retention of Female Faculty*, 8.

22. Office of the Provost, *Inclusive Excellence Report* (Notre Dame, IN: University of Notre Dame, 2019), https://provost.nd.edu/assets/394262/inclusive_excellence_report_.pdf, 4.

23. William Ross Wallace, "The Hand That Rocks the Cradle," *Loomis' Musical and Masonic Journal* 31, no. 11 (June 1898): 1.

24. Hesburgh, interview.

Athletic Replays

1. Dilenschneider and Lammers, "The Early Women Athletes Project."

2. University of Notre Dame, "Notre Dame to Honor the Pioneers of Women's Athletics," University of Notre Dame, July 8, 2022, https://und.com/notre-dame-to-honor-the-pioneers-of-womens-athletics/, ¶9 under "The Honoree List."

3. *The Observer*, "Women's B-Ball," *The Observer*, January 30, 1975, 8, https://archives.nd.edu/Observer/1975-01-30_v09_070.pdf, 8.

4. Digger Phelps, interview with author, February 26, 2021.

5. Laurie Reising, "Varsity Status Given to Women," *The Observer*, September 29, 1977, 12, https://archives.nd.edu/Observer/1977-09-29_v12_023.pdf.

6. Richard Adler and Jerry Ross, "Heart," song 6 in *Damn Yankees*, 1955, line 1.

7. *The Observer*, "Women Row to Midwest, *The Observer*, April 30, 1974, 11, https://archives.nd.edu/Observer/v08/1974-04-30_v08_117.pdf.

8. *The Observer*, "Summer Fatalities, *The Observer*, August 28, 1974, 19, https://archives.nd.edu/Observer/v09/1974-08-28_v09_002.pdf.

9. *The Observer*, "Sports at Saint Mary's," *The Observer*, April 12, 1973, 5, https://archives.nd.edu/Observer/1973-04-12_v07_113.pdf.

10. Eileen O'Grady, "Kathy Fences Way to the Top," *The Observer*, January 29, 1976, 8, https://archives.nd.edu/Observer/1976-01-29_v10_074.pdf.

11. *The Observer*, "Varsity Status Awarded to Women's Tennis and Fencing," *The Observer*, August 28, 1976, 22, https://archives.nd.edu/Observer/1976-08-28_v11_001.pdf.

12. Anne Dilenschneider, interview with Ron Skrabacz, October 30, 2020.

13. Pete Gegen, "Irish Field Hockey Dropped from Varsity: Three New Teams Leave No Room," *The Observer*, January 29, 1988, 16 and 13, https://archives.nd.edu/Observer/1988-01-29_v21_079.pdf.

14. *The Observer*, "Women's Golf," *The Observer*, April 18, 1974, 7, https://archives.nd.edu/Observer/1974-04-18_v08_109.pdf.

15. *The Observer*, "Womens [sic] Golf Club Competing," *The Observer*, April 18, 1975, 12, https://archives.nd.edu/Observer/v09/1975-04-18_v09_117.pdf.

16. Pete Gegen, "Three Women's Clubs Reach Varsity Level," *The Observer*, January 20, 1988, 16, 12, https://archives.nd.edu/Observer/1988-01-20_v21_072.pdf.

17. Bruce Marek, "In the Shadows Exists Sailing," *The Observer*, September 28, 1973, 3, 8, https://archives.nd.edu/Observer/1973-09-28_v08_018.pdf, 8.

18. See *The Observer*, "Sailors Host, Win Frosh Regatta," *The Observer*, March 6, 1973, 8, https://archives.nd.edu/Observer/1973-03-06_v07_094.pdf; *The Observer*, "Sailors Third in N.Y.," *The Observer*, March 22, 1973, 8, https://archives.nd.edu/Observer/1973-03-22_v07_098.pdf; *The Observer*, "Sailors Win B.G. Regatta, Take on Detroit This Week," *The Observer*, April 13, 1973, 12, https://archives.nd.edu/Observer/1973-04-13_v07_114.pdf; and *The Observer*, "ND Sailors Win," *The Observer*, May 1, 1973, 16, https://archives.nd.edu/Observer/1973-05-01_v07_120.pdf.

19. *The Observer*, "Sailors Second," *The Observer*, April 18, 1974, 7, https://archives.nd.edu/Observer/1974-04-18_v08_109.pdf.

20. *The Observer*, "Women Skiers Capture Ohio Cup: Bartzen's Return Keys Men's Showing," *The Observer*, February 21, 1974, 12, https://archives.nd.edu/Observer/1974-02-21_v08_084.pdf, 12.

21. *The Observer*, "SMC, ND Women Set Tennis Tilt," *The Observer*, November 17, 1972, 55, https://archives.nd.edu/Observer/1972-11-17_v07_051.pdf, 15.

22. *The Observer*, "Tennis Try-Outs," *The Observer*, September 12, 1973, 8, https://archives.nd.edu/Observer/1973-09-12_v08_006.pdf.

23. Dilenschneider and Lammers, "The Early Women Athletes Project."

24. Cited in Beth Huffman, "Varsity Status Granted to Lacrosse, Volleyball," *The Observer*, April 17, 1980, 12, 10, https://archives.nd.edu/Observer/1980-04-17_v14_121.pdf, 12.

A Brief History of Sexual Assault

1. University of Notre Dame, "Campus Initiatives," University of Notre Dame, 2022, https://titleix.nd.edu/campus-initiatives/.

2. Marisa Iati, "Students Raise Money for Suicide Prevention," *The Observer*, September 26, 2011, 1, 7, https://archives.nd.edu/Observer/2011-09-26_v45-025.pdf.

3. University of Notre Dame, "Campus Initiatives," ¶1 under "CSAP."

4. University of Notre Dame, "Campus Initiatives," ¶1 under "GreeNDot."

5. University of Notre Dame, "Campus Initiatives," ¶1 under "GRC."

6. University of Notre Dame, "Campus Initiatives," ¶1 under "MAV."

7. University of Notre Dame, *University of Notre Dame 2016: Sexual Conduct and Campus Climate Questionnaire Report* (Notre Dame, IN: University of Notre Dame, 2016), https://titleix.nd.edu/assets/231426/2016_sexual_conduct_and_climate_questionnaire_report_final.pdf, 1.

8. *University of Notre Dame, Sexual Conduct and Campus Climate Questionnaire Report*, 14.

Additional Sources

1. James E. Armstrong, *Onward to Victory: A Chronicle of the Alumni of the University of Notre Dame du Lac 1842–1973* (Notre Dane, IN: University of Notre Dame Alumni Association, 2011).

2. Nicholas Ayo, *Signs of Grace: Meditations on the Notre Dame Campus* (Lanham, MD: Rowman and Littlefield Publishers, 2001).

3. Carol Barkalow with Andrea Raab, *In the Men's House: An Inside Account of Life in the Army by One of West Point's First Female Graduates* (New York: Poseidon Press, 1990).

4. Nona J. Barnett and Hubert S. Felid, "Sex Differences in University Students' Attitudes Toward Rape," *Journal of College Student Personnel* 18, no. 2 (1977): 93–96.

5. Thomas Blantz, *The University of Notre Dame A History* (Notre Dame, IN: University of Notre Dame Press, 2020).

6. C. Bohmer and A. Parrot, *Sexual Assault on Campus: The Problem and the Solution* (New York: Lexington Books, 1993).

7. Susan Brownmiller, *Against Our Will: Men, Women, and Rape* (New York: Bantam Books, 1976).

8. Gary Campana, Bob Gibbons, John Hickey, and David Sim, *Notre Dame Class of 1969* (Milwaukee: Hickorystick Press, 2019).

9. Kevin Coyne, *Domers: A Year at Notre Dame* (New York: Penguin Books, 1995).

10. Carol Kelly Gangi, *A Woman's Book of Inspiration* (New York: Fall River Press, 2017).

11. Barbara Gowan, *L is for Leprechaun* (Notre Dame, IN: Ave Maria Press, 2008).

12. Theodore M. Hesburgh, *The Hesburgh Papers: Higher Values in Higher Education* (Kansas City: Andrews and McMeel, 1979).

13. Kimothy Joy, *That's What She Said: Wise Words from Influential Women* (New York: Harper Collins, 2018).

14. Jingting Hang and Ian Tembe, *A Letter to my Freshman Self: Domers Reflect on Their Undergraduate Experience* (Notre Dame, IN: Corby Publishing, 2016).

15. Mirra Komarrovsky, *Women in College: Shaping New Feminine Identities* (New York: Basic Books, 1985).

16. Lewis B. Mayhew and Rosemary Park, "Relationships between St. Mary's College and the University of Notre Dame," University of Notre Dame Archives, December 29, 1970, 1–14, PNDP 30-SA-02 UNDA.

17. Edward A. Malloy, *Monk's Notre Dame* (Notre Dame, IN: Corby Books, 2020).

18. Edward A. Malloy, *Monk's Reflections: A View from the Dome* (Kansas City: Andrews McMeel Publishing, 1999).

19. Michael Medved and David Wallechinsky, *What Really Happened to the Class of '65?* (New York: Random House, 1976).

20. Leslie Miller-Bernal, *Separate by Degree: Women Students' Experiences in Single-Sex and Coeducational Colleges* (New York: Peter Lang Publishing, 2000).

21. Leslie Miller-Bernal and Susan L. Poulson, eds., *Going Coed Women's Experiences in Formerly Men's Colleges and Universities, 1950–2000* (Nashville: Vanderbilt University Press, 2004).

22. Hugh R. Page Jr., *A Letter to My Freshman Self* (Notre Dame, IN: Corby Publishing, 2016).

23. Susan L. Poulson and Loretta P. Higgins, "Gender, Coeducation, and the Transformation of Catholic Identity in American Catholic Higher Education," *Catholic Historical Review* 89, no. 3 (2003): 489–510.

24. Project on the Status and Education of Women (Association of American Colleges), *The Problem of Rape on Campus* (Washington, DC: Project on the Status and Education of Women, Association of American Colleges, 1978).

25. Cornelius Riordan, *Boys and Girls in School: Together or Separate?* (New York: Teachers College Press, 1990).

26. Barbara Miller Solomon, *In the Company of Educated Women: A History of Women and Higher Education in America* (New Haven, CT: Yale University Press, 1985).

27. Kerry Temple, ed., *Family: A Twenty-Fifth Anniversary Collection of Essays about the Family from* Notre Dame Magazine (Notre Dame, IN: University of Notre Dame Press and *Notre Dame Magazine*, 1997).

28. David Tyack and Elisabeth Hansot, *Learning Together: A History of Coeducation in American Schools* (New Haven, CT: Yale University Press, 1990).

29. Alice Woods, ed., *Co-Education: A Series of Essays by Various Authors* (London: Longsman, Green, and Co. and Wentworth Press, 1903).

30. Weisbecker, "*Loyal Daughters*: Sexuality and Sexual Assault."

Index

Acknowledgments

More than one hundred fifty members of the Notre Dame family contributed to this social history, and I thank each for their contributions. Besides the ND administrators and teachers mentioned in the dedication, I am grateful to Thomas Blantz, CSC, Edward Malloy, CSC, Jane Pitz, William Sexton, Don Bishop, and Digger Phelps for their insights.

The surveys from alumnae offering their heartfelt reflections of the ND experience are core to this story. Many from the 1976 and 1977 cohorts responded whenever I needed topical input or clarification. Darlene Palma Connelly (ND 1977) brought a slightly different vantage point — entering in the fall of 1973 as the number of women and residence halls doubled — ensuring I balanced the good and the bad. I especially appreciate Emily Weisbecker Farley for helping me to grasp the similarities and differences at Notre Dame — just a generation apart.

I am grateful for the alumni who added the male perspective — something often lacking in discussions on coeducation. Ron Skrabacz surveyed male friends, classmates, and displaced residents of Badin and Walsh halls to obtain the male "yang" to the female "yin." He also wrote the chapters on athletics and interviewed some of ND's first female athletes. Jane Lammers and Anne Dilenschneider made sure that I had the latest information in this area so unfamiliar to me.

Many others participated in this twenty-year development process. At the outset, Maria Beuttenmuller and Patrick Gleason (ND 1976) helped me to develop the initial survey and overriding theme. Nora Lee Mosher, Shelley Muller Simon, and Janet Krier Breen never gave up on the project, despite the numerous iterations on the cutting room floor. The artwork of Ed Brower, Barbara O'Connell, Jennifer Downey, Gary Hovland, Tom Paulius, and Jane Pitz has made *Objects in the Rearview Mirror* multidimensional.

Initially, Marie St. Hillaire and Elisabeth Chretien helped to focus the book's structure. I cannot thank enough the publishing team of Leigh E. Rich, Carol Linskey, and Carol Andrews for bringing style and a non-ND perspective as they made my dream a reality on an extremely tight schedule. They are truly a dream team and understand how to "Play Like a Champion."

Finally, a special thanks to Nora Lee Mosher for staying the course and providing her insights and camaraderie on this journey. Arriving at the destination also would not have been possible without Joe Garbarino, Jimita Potter, and my sister, Gina Dell, for their support as I worked to complete this book by the fiftieth anniversary of coeducation at the University of Notre Dame du Lac (September 5, 2022). Without these individuals, contributors, and my extended project team, this story would be yet unwritten and sitting in storage bins filled with research materials.

Contributors

The Project Team

Darlene Palma Connelly

Darlene Palma Connelly graduated in 1977 and received her law degree in 1980 from Notre Dame. Tired of the Midwest snow, she joined the Navy Judge Advocate General's Corp to see the world. Instead, she saw the East Coast cities of Newport, Virginia Beach, and Washington, DC. Once out of uniform, Darlene practiced law with firms in Washington, DC, and Florida and, later, the federal government. Before retiring, she formed her own legal consulting business. After forty years, she and her husband still reside in Virginia, a place where the occasional few inches of snow are treated like a major snowstorm. She rarely returns to campus but carries love in her heart for three Notre Dame priests: Reverends Tom Chambers, "Moose" Mulcahy, and "Piase" (aka Paison) Tallarida. Without their influence on her life, she might still live in Ohio up to her ears in snowdrifts.

Emily Weisbecker Farley

Emily Farley graduated from Notre Dame in 2007 with a BA in anthropology and English and a concentration in gender studies. In 2006, Emily received an Undergraduate Research Opportunities Program grant to research and write *Loyal Daughters*, a play about sexuality and sexual assault as told by Notre Dame students. First staged in November 2006 at the DeBartolo Performing Arts Center at Notre Dame, it is performed annually with updated stories. Currently, she is on hiatus from professional endeavors to focus on raising her children with David Farley (ND 2007) in Minneapolis, Minnesota.

Nora Lee Mosher

Nora Lee Mosher graduated from the College of New Jersey, earning a BA in elementary education in 1972. She earned an MS in the management of technology from the University of Miami in 1995. During her thirty-six years with IBM, she was an account specialist, supporting a variety of customers, and a branch operations manager in Miami, Florida. Nora Lee developed and taught courses for IBM employees and managed the development teams that created online courses and IBM products for K–12 educational solutions. Nora's invaluable research on the impact of women in business and the world broadened the appeal of this book beyond Notre Dame.

Ray Pikna

Upon his acceptance to Notre Dame, Ray informed his parents that he would earn a varsity letter in college. This surprised them, as he had only earned a monogram in high school for managing the basketball team. A freshman with no experience, Ray was a walk-on for the fencing team, but he earned two varsity letters under legendary Coach Mike DeCicco and later became the first fencer to serve on the board of directors of the Notre Dame Monogram Club.

Following his graduation from Notre Dame in 1976, Ray attended Case Western Reserve University's School of Law and earned his JD in 1979. For more than four decades, Ray enjoyed a successful law career, with appearances in courts across the country — including an oral argument before the United States Supreme Court. He and his wife, Christine, have two daughters and three grandchildren.

Ann Pytynia

One of the first 125 freshman women admitted to Notre Dame in 1972, Ann Pytynia graduated with a BA in anthropology in 1976. Ann lived in Walsh, Badin, and Lyons halls and worked her last three years at (what was then called) the Social Science Training Laboratory. Like many of her classmates, Ann has both fond and not-so-fond memories of those first four years of coeducation.

Ann obtained an MA in applied urban anthropology from the University of South Florida and an MS in urban and regional planning from Florida State. She had a forty-year career in urban planning in Florida and Oregon, working at local, regional, and state levels. Ann is married to Robert Hillier, and they are parents to two daughters.

Shelley Muller Simon

Entering Notre Dame as one of the 125 freshman women in 1972, Shelley began her studies majoring in civil engineering and architecture before graduating in 1976 with a bachelor's degree in architecture — completing a five-year program in four years. During her sophomore and junior years, she was a varsity cheerleader for football and basketball, forgoing her senior season to complete her final forty-eight credit hours.

After earning her degree, Shelley became a licensed architect, designing corporate, commercial, and higher education projects for firms in the Midwest before cofounding Simon Oswald Architecture — a majority woman-owned design firm — in Columbia, Missouri, in 1987. In her nearly five-decade career, her professional roles included design firm president, women's leadership foundation executive director, and university planning and design manager in Missouri, Illinois, New York, and Nevada. She has served on numerous nonprofit and corporate boards, and her current volunteer work focuses on community planning, angel investing, women's issues, and sustainability. Shelley returned to Indiana after retirement and lives near the beach in the Indiana Dunes. She was married for forty-four years to an ND alumnus, and they have a son and a daughter (who is a member of Notre Dame's 2004 national championship women's soccer team).

Ron Skrabacz

Ron Skrabacz graduated from the University of Notre Dame in 1976 with a bachelor's degree of business administration in marketing. As a student, he worked in the Administration Building's mail room and copy center for four years and learned the campus by walking his mail routes. Ron's favorite campus spot is one he shares with his Alumni Hall roommates, Tom Klein and Mark Nishan — a plaque on a bench behind the southeast corner of the South Dining Hall bearing Abraham Lincoln's quote: "The better part of one's life consists of his friendships."

Upon graduation, Ron attended Western Illinois University, where he studied athletic administration and physical education. He spent more than thirty-three years at AT&T, primarily in the areas of building facilities, network budgets and finance, and records management, before retiring in 2013. Ron also worked as a freelance writer and columnist for Chicago's *Daily Herald* newspaper, covering sports and recreation activities. As an avid sports fan, Ron's contributions on Notre Dame sports and women's athletics enriched this book. He married Rebecca Kutsunis in 1979, and they have three children and eleven grandchildren.

Maggie Waltman Smith

Maggie Waltman Smith transferred to the University of Notre Dame in 1974 as a junior to take advantage of the university's multidisciplinary approach to journalism and communications through its American Studies Department. Required to find off-campus housing because the women's dorms did not have enough room to meet early coeducation enrollment goals, she had a slightly different perspective of residential life than her dorm-centric classmates.

After graduating with a BA in American studies, Maggie's professional career took her to two midsize business-to-business advertising and PR firms in Indiana. Mid-career, she switched to the client-side. She remained at Fiserv, Inc., a global provider of financial services technology, for fifteen years and retired in 2015 as director of product marketing for the company's Lending Solutions Division.

Maggie has been married to her (non-Domer) high school sweetheart for forty-three years. They enjoy visiting their son, daughter-in-law, and grandchildren in Southern California.

Tom Young

Tom Young graduated as an English major from the University of Notre Dame in 1976 and earned a masters' degree in public administration from Harvard Kennedy School in 1982. After graduation, he worked for the Dukakis administration as director of economic development in the Department of Commerce for two years. He then worked for thirty-five years as a registered representative and agent for New York Life.

He served as president of the ND Club of Boston from 1978–1980. From 2011–2015, he served as the club's Senior Alumni coordinator, leading to a term on the Notre Dame Senior Alumni Board (2014–2017). His extensive ND contacts broadened the male perspectives within this coeducation social history.

Major Contributors

Janet Krier Breen

Janet Krier Breen graduated from the University of Notre Dame in 1975 with a bachelor's degree of business administration in finance. She attended Saint Mary's College for two years until the merger effort failed, then transferred to ND as a junior. While at ND, she participated on ND's fledgling women's tennis team, ice-skated at the Athletic Convocation Center, and worked with the disabled at Logan Center.

After graduation, she was a broker's assistant at the Chicago Board of Trade. In the evenings, she attended DePaul University, where she obtained an MS in accounting in 1979 and passed the Illinois CPA exam in 1980. She then worked as an auditor with Arthur Anderson and Company in the Chicago office of its financial services division.

In 1985, Janet became a stay-at-home mom for her two children and volunteered for her parish, her children's schools, and the community. She returned to work in 1994 and pursued a career in postsecondary education. Janet resides in Valparaiso, Indiana, where she is an accounting professor and program chairperson for Ivy Tech Community College of Indiana.

Ed Byrne

Ed Byrne received a BA in economics from the University of Notre Dame in 1976 and a JD from the National Law Center at George Washington University in 1981. He has a private law practice specializing in land use-related approvals and real estate transactions.

He is also the founder of Regional Planning Services (RPS), a governmental and public relations firm established in 1994 to help clients in the private and public sectors secure neighborhood and community support for well-designed mixed-use or infill/redevelopment projects. Ed married Anne Newhouse, and they raised their three children in Boulder, Colorado.

Jacob Dell Sedesse

As a student at the University of Florida, Jacob Dell Sedesse is pursuing dual degrees in film and television production in the College of Journalism and Communications. In spring 2020, he graduated high school as salutatorian and earned an associate's degree from Santa Fe College in theatre. Jacob served on Microsoft's first-ever Council for Digital Good, working on policies to shape the future of life online for teens. In addition to his work producing short films for school and live news with WUFT, his local PBS branch, Jacob is an actor and has appeared in various projects and films. In editing this book, Jacob paid attention to its pacing, cadence, and voice to make the book more appealing to a wider audience, including the younger generation interested in women's history.

Wendy Duffey

Wendy Duffey joined the inaugural class of women attending Notre Dame in 1972. After graduating in 1976 with a degree in psychology, Wendy worked in human resources. She worked for and consulted with several firms, including The Anaconda Company and its parent, Atlantic Richfield (ARCO); General Electric; Fidelity Investments; Arthur D. Little; Dove Consulting; The McCormick Group; and, most recently, Flow Consulting. Wendy serves on Ivy Tech's Business and Logistics Advisory Board and leads an interest group for the Ladies of Notre Dame and Saint Mary's College. She is a member of the Notre Dame Club of St. Joseph Valley.

Augie Grace

Augie Grace received a BA in American studies from the University of Notre Dame in 1976 and a JD from Boston College Law School in 1984. At Notre Dame, he served as junior and senior class president, continuing his role through 1981. Since then, he has served in a variety of government and community relations positions, including two terms in the Massachusetts State Legislature. For twenty years, he was executive director of the National Guard Association of Massachusetts; in his last four years, he served as an officer of the National Guard Executive Directors Associations. With his wife, Janice, he retired and moved to Tampa, Florida, where he is now the Notre Dame Senior Alumni representative for the state.

Jane Lammers

Jane Lammers, a photographer and certified public accountant, received a BA in theology from Notre Dame in 1977. She spent two years at Saint Mary's College in Campus Ministry and Athletics. During her career with the United States Treasury, she focused on innovation. Jane coauthored *Millennium Trails: Pathways for the 21st Century*, an official project of the White House Millennium Council. Her photography is featured in *America's National Historic Trails*, *America's*

National Scenic Trails, and several textbooks. Jane spends her time in San Diego County, where she enjoys her garden and swims, and in Sedona, Arizona, where she enjoys hiking in the outdoors.

Diana Wilson Ostermann

When Diana Wilson Ostermann first saw the Notre Dame campus in 1969, it was love at first sight. She entered in 1972 as part of ND's first coed freshman class and graduated with a bachelors' degree in business in 1976. Diana had a twenty-two-year career at AT&T and its spin-off Lucent Technologies, working in a variety of sales and marketing positions, culminating in wireless internet data strategy. She took early retirement in 2001 and shortly after met her husband, Theo, a radiologist. Diana and Theo split their time between their farm in Hawaii and a residence in South Haven, Michigan. Living through ND's coed transition prepared Diana to overcome similar challenges as the business world grudgingly accepted women.

Lionel J. Phillips

Lionel J. Phillips graduated from the University of Notre Dame with a with a bachelor's degree in business administration. As an undergraduate, he discovered his passion for volunteerism and leadership as he became involved in student activities. He served as spokesman for the African American student organization and was a cofounder of the Black Cultural Arts Festival, a program still celebrated today. Lionel also founded the League of Black Business Students.

In January 1977, Lionel began his career with the IBM Corporation as a systems engineer. After retiring from IBM in 2014 as an executive systems architect manager, he served as CEO and president of Phillips Concrete Services.

Phillip Potter

Phillip Potter graduated from Notre Dame with a BBA in 1975 and an executive MBA in 1999. He spent forty-two years in the transportation industry, first with General Motors and then with AM General. Phil cofounded the local First Tee program in South Bend, Indiana, a national organization that teaches life skills to children through purposed golf lessons. He is on the board of directors of the Indiana Golf Association and spends his retirement officiating at amateur and collegiate golf tournaments. He and his wife of forty-four years, Jimita Baldoni Potter, raised two daughters, both scholarship collegiate golfers.

Bridget O'Donnell Provenzano

After graduating from Notre Dame with BA in American studies in 1977, Bridget went job hunting in Chicago. An ND alum hired her to underwrite commercial insurance. She spent twenty-eight of her thirty-five-year career with The Hartford Insurance Company in various underwriting and management positions. She met her husband, Tom, at work, and they were married in 1983 at ND's

Sacred Heart Church (now Basilica of the Sacred Heart.) ND's five-year reunions help her to stay connected with classmates, especially Breen-Phillips dorm mates. After retiring, Tom and Bridget moved to Valparaiso, Indiana. Bridget is active in several book clubs, facilitates a parish Bible study group, and keeps track of Auggie, a rambunctious basset hound.

Bob Quakenbush

Bob Quakenbush worked in public relations, media relations, and marketing communications in Chicago for nearly twenty-five years, most notably as chief communications officer for Joseph Cardinal Bernardin and the Archdiocese of Chicago. After relocating to Indiana, Bob worked at The Culver Academies, handling communications for, at that time, the most successful fundraising campaign in American secondary education. He later served as assistant director for development communications at Notre Dame.

Always active as a Notre Dame alumnus, Bob served on the board of governors of the Notre Dame Club of Chicago and chaired the club's sixty-second annual Universal Notre Dame Night celebration and its twenty-fifth annual Knute Rockne Awards Dinner. He also was the club's newsletter editor for many years. Bob has served Notre Dame's class of 1976 in various roles as a class officer since 2005, including as class president from 2016–2021. Today he lives in Cary, North Carolina.

Jeanine Sterling

Jeanine's ND roots go deep as a former Vetville baby during the late 1950s and then as one of the 125 first female freshmen admitted in 1972. After graduating in 1976 with an English degree, Jeanine earned an MBA in marketing. Today, she is an industry director with a global research and consulting firm.

Jeanine received the Notre Dame Alumni Association's Volunteer of the Year Award in 2019. She served twelve years on the board of the ND Club of Detroit in multiple capacities. Her work helped to inspire the creation of ND Women Connect (NDWC), a national alumni affinity group; she served on its national steering committee for seven years. After her NDWC term, Jeanine joined the university's Senior Alumni board and improved its communications during her three-year stint. Jeanine, a second-generation alum -- her father was in the class of '61 — is pleased her oldest son, class of 2009, gives her family a three-generation association with ND.

Beverly Cesen Winterscheid

Beverly was in the first class of freshman ND women, graduating in 1976 with a BA in English. She received a PhD in business strategy from Case Western Reserve and combined a corporate career with academia, teaching MBA-level strategy and leadership development courses in the United States and in Belgium.

Ten years ago, she founded the Center for Nature and Leadership, which has grown to include members from three continents and twenty-five states, and her professional interest focuses on the personal and professional development of multigenerational women leaders who work to make the world a better place. She also launched an ongoing scholarship program for deserving-yet-economically challenged high school girls in Malawi, Africa, providing them a high school education, many of whom have gone on to university.

Artwork and Photography

Edward J. Brower

Ed Brower, a member of Notre Dame's class of 1976, graduated with a bachelor's degree in electrical engineering. He exemplifies the attitude of never being afraid to make a change in life. Ed left a twenty-year career in engineering for a career as a certified financial planner.

As he heads into retirement, he has more time for family, travel, and hobbies. His retirement goals include learning new skills and sharing his knowledge with the next generation; another goal is to finish the books he starts. Contributing photos to and reading *Objects* invoked memories of Notre Dame. He treasures his friendships with the ND men and women who inspired him with their talents and contribute to the future sons and daughters of the university. He loves recalling his favorite collegiate experiences: standing on the sideline for the Rudy game, working with Bill Delaney on one of Ara's final interviews, getting wisdom and encouragement from Father Griffin, and singing Christmas carols for Father Hesburgh in his office late on a December weekend night.

Jennifer Downey

Jennifer Downey is a visual artist based in the San Francisco Bay area. She began her art career as an illustrator, creating whimsical gouache paintings for editorial clients, publishers, design firms, and agencies. Over time, she has shifted exclusively to fine art, with oil paintings that explore environmental topics. Beginning in 2009, this focus has centered on hydropower dams — specifically, the impacts that dams exert on riverine ecosystems and species. Her work has been included in more than thirty group and solo exhibits at venues nationwide and is held in numerous private and corporate collections. In 2019, her artwork debuted on the small screen, as part of the HBO series *Mrs. Fletcher.* Her website is www.jenniferdowney.com.

Gary Hovland

For more than twenty-five years, Gary Hovland's traditional pen-and-ink and watercolor illustrations have appeared in the nation's most acclaimed magazines and newspapers, including *The Wall Street Journal, The New York Times, The New Yorker, Vanity Fair, Time, Newsweek,* and *The Washington Post.* He is a graduate of

Art Center College of Design in Pasadena, California, where he later returned as an instructor for an undergraduate course in "Humorous Illustration." He lives in Louisville, Kentucky.

Barbara Montgomery O'Connell

Barbara Montgomery O'Connell brings a professional touch to each painting she completes. House portraits are her specialty, and she ensures the personal details required by her clients are included in the composition. Barbara created the artwork in this book for note cards and giclées that have been auctioned at the last three reunions of the ND class of 1976 (2006, 2011, 2016). Her love of Notre Dame is evident in every element.

Tom Paulius

T. D. "Tom" Paulius, who graduated from the University of the Notre Dame in 1976, retired from a successful practice of law. He has worked as a freelance editorial sports photographer since 2001 and a fine art photographer and printmaker, capturing unique sports events, sunrises and sunsets, and marine and coastal life. His work has appeared in Chicagoland newspapers, *The New York Times*, and national sport magazines.

Jane Pitz

Jane Pitz was recruited in 1972 to assist in opening one of the first women's residence halls at Notre Dame. She was instrumental in expanding the role of the Council on International Lay Apostolate at Notre Dame during the first five years of coeducation. She lived for almost twenty years with students on campus and in England in the Arts and Letters London Program, while simultaneously serving in the office of Campus Ministry. Jane resides in South Bend, where she remains in touch with the unfolding growth of the university. She earned a master's degree in fine arts from Notre Dame and continues to develop her love of art as an illustrator.

Deborah A. Dell

Deborah "Debi" A. Dell was a member of the first class of undergraduate women admitted to Notre Dame in 1972. Inspired by her father, attending Notre Dame was a personal goal from the age of eight. (And, yes, she was at ND during the *Rudy* years!) She graduated with a bachelor's degree in business administration, with a focus on management, in 1976.

Raised in South Florida, her parents encouraged her to pursue her career in the big city — Chicago. While working for Commonwealth Edison as a technical sales representative, she completed an MBA at Loyola University Chicago.

After the blizzard of 1979, Debi returned to Florida, where she joined IBM in 1980 and earned a master's degree in the management of technology from the University of Miami in 1995. During her thirty-eight years with IBM, she worked on the PC AT, the PCjr, and the IBM ThinkPad; served as the national principal for IBM Mobile and Wireless Solutions, overseeing a team of professionals who enabled IBM's participation in the then-emerging wireless services market; and, after earning her certification as a project management professional, became program director for IBM's Project Management Center of Excellence. She has been interviewed in publications such as Andy Seybold's *Outlook*, *Computer Reseller News*, *Washington Technology*, and *Wireless Week* and, before retiring, often spoke on the topics of brand management, project management, and telecommuting.

She was one of the first employees to work from home. She experienced the joys and tribulations associated with teleworking — but that's another story!

Her experiences with IBM inspired her first book, *ThinkPad: A Different Shade of Blue*.

Debi is actively involved in service to the University of Notre Dame and continues to support the Notre Dame class of 1976.

monte ceceri

Made in the USA
Las Vegas, NV
04 December 2022

61151641R00289